01 INTRODUCING EGYPT

Top: Wadi Huweyit, Sinai desert

Above: Sabil-Kutab of Abdel Katikuda, Cairo

In pharaonic times the people of Egypt believed the sun was daily born of the goddess Nut and travelled westwards across the heavens until swallowed by her at day's end, to be born once more the following dawn. And they believed the waters of the Nile rose from beneath the firmament, flowed through their country and out beyond the Delta where they sank to their source and then rose to run their course again.

The cycle and continuity of natural events was translated into the philosophical basis of ancient Egyptian politics and religion. In hieroglyphics the name of a pharaoh or god always appeared within a cartouche, an oval ring that represented the unbroken, unending, unchanging power of ruler or deity. The order of natural events in Egypt continues to impress a sense of timelessness upon the country.

Herodotus described Egypt as a gift of the river, and Egypt's gift, like a great river of time, has been to carry within it the presence of the pharaonic, Hellenistic, Christian and Islamic periods, all embraced by the cartouche of the *fellahin's* millennial toil. Egypt's endurance and stability in a region of conflict, flux and immense creativity has been its outstanding contribution to the world. Egypt itself has not been exceptionally innovative; it did not give mankind mathematics, philosophy, science, medicine, Judaism, Christianity or Islam. But Egypt was essential to each, offering an impetus or a home, sometimes stamping them with the shape by which we know them today.

Egypt's sense of permanence and duration makes it *par excellence* the land of the past, and it is for this that the traveller usually comes, too often ignoring its living present. But for all the spectacle over the

millennia of migrations and invasions, probably 90 per cent of its population are the descendants of its ancient inhabitants, and they will not be ignored.

I first came to Egypt to see the Pyramids, but what I met with greater force were the Egyptian people. It was because of them that I cared enough to explore as best I could the totality of their history and their experience. They are a warm, friendly and generous people; ambitious, intelligent and proud; naive, religious and fatalistic; and also the most indefatigable hustlers on earth. They are all these things in such an open and sometimes importunate way that the novice visitor is likely to find himself swinging from one extreme reaction to another within minutes. But it is only their vitality you are reacting to, for though their conditions can be extreme they are not an extreme people. If you enjoy people, you will enjoy the Egyptian people especially.

Top: The 'Blue Lagoon', off Dahab
Above: Aswan market

Opposite: Temple of Sobek and Haroeris, Kom Ombo

CADOGANguides

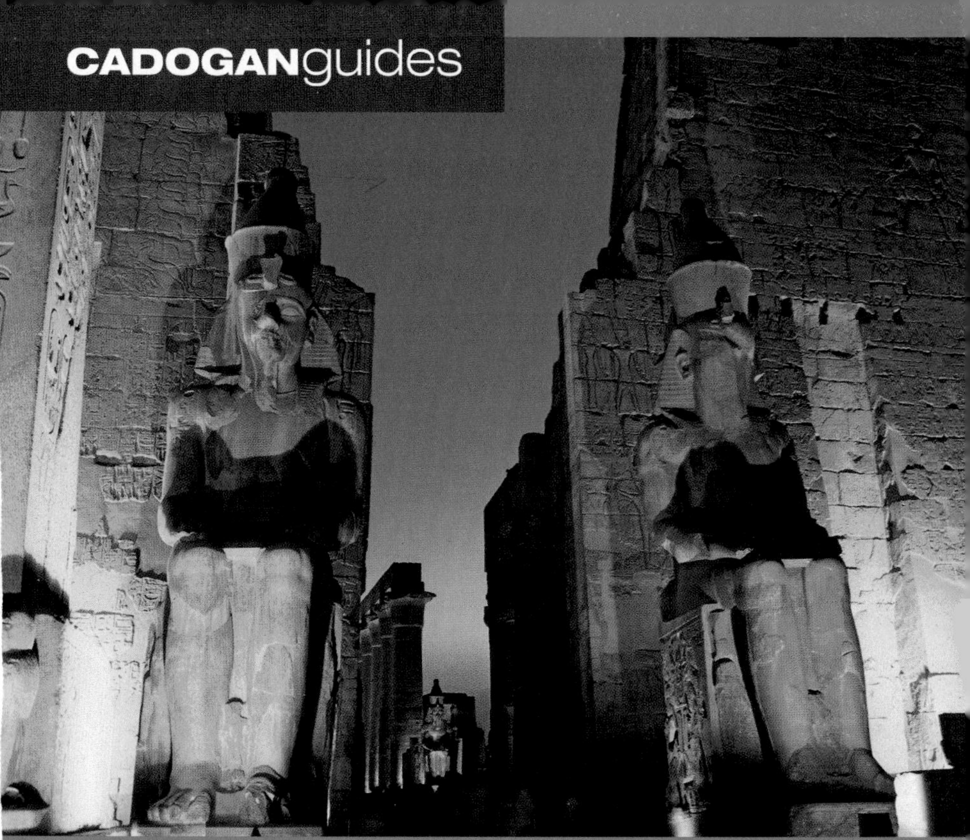

EGYPT

'The Nile is majestic, at sundown an implacable lava flow. By day, feluccas seem to stride upon its surface like pond insects, and distant palms rise from the level stillness, distinct and exactly outlined in the clear air and brilliant light.'

Michael Haag

About the Guide

The **full-colour introduction** gives the author's overview of the country, together with suggested **itineraries** and a regional **'where to go' map** and **feature** to help you plan your trip.

Illuminating and entertaining **cultural chapters** on Egypt's history, culture, religion and everyday life give you a rich flavour of the country.

Planning Your Trip starts with the basics of when to go, getting there and getting around, coupled with other useful information, including a section for disabled travellers. The **Practical A–Z** deals with all the **essential information** and **contact details** that you may need while you are away.

The **regional chapters** are arranged in a loose touring order, with plenty of public transport information. The author's top **'Don't Miss'** **sights** are highlighted at the start of each chapter.

A **language guide**, a **glossary** of cultural terms, ideas for **further reading** and a comprehensive **index** can be found at the end of the book.

Although everything listed in this guide is **personally recommended**, our author inevitably has his own favourite places to eat and stay. Whenever you see this **Author's Choice** icon beside a listing, you will know that it is a little bit out of the ordinary.

Hotel Price Guide (*see also* p.62)

luxury	$$$$$	over $200
expensive	$$$$	$100–200
moderate	$$$	$50–100
inexpensive	$$	LE110–275 ($20–50)
cheap	$	under LE110 (under $20)

Restaurant Price Guide (*see also* p.69)

expensive	$$$$	LE100 +
moderate	$$$	LE60–100
inexpensive	$$	LE30–60
cheap	$	under LE30

About the Author

Michael Haag, who lives in London, has written and photographed a number of books on Egypt and other countries of the Middle East and the Mediterranean. His journalism has appeared in major newspapers and magazines in Britain and America, and he has broadcast for the BBC. For further information, see Michael Haag's website: *www.michaelhaag.com*.

4th Edition published 2009

Where to Go

The guide begins at **Cairo**, an exploding metropolis which somehow preserves within it the finest medieval city in the world, and which since its founding by the Arabs over a thousand years ago has been Egypt's capital. Egypt's first pharaohs ruled from nearby Memphis; the grandest monuments of the Old Kingdom, the pyramids at **Giza** and **Saqqara**, still inspire awe today.

The guide then heads southwards, first to the **Fayyum**, then upriver into Upper Egypt, following the **Nile valley** to Amarna where the New Kingdom heretic Akhenaten built his capital; to **Abydos**, the spiritual centre of Egypt, sacred to Osiris; and to the temple of Hathor at **Dendera**.

Beyond these lies **Luxor**, site of ancient Thebes, the opulent cosmopolis of Egypt's New Kingdom pharaohs. It encompasses the grandiose temples of Luxor and **Karnak** on the east bank, and a vast necropolis on the west bank of the Nile, including the magnificent mortuary temple of Hatshepsut at Deir el Bahri, the tombs of the nobles and the queens, and the **Valley of the Kings**.

Farther upriver stand the Ptolemaic temples at Esna, Edfu and Kom Ombo, and then comes **Aswan**, one of the most beautiful places in Egypt, where the island temple of Isis at nearby Philae is also Ptolemaic. Farther south still, like a highwater mark of New Kingdom power, are the temples built by Ramses II at **Abu Simbel** near the Sudan border.

With Upper Egypt thoroughly explored, the guide then sweeps through the **Western Desert**, the antithesis both in mind and landscape to the yielding river valley. Calling first at the outer oasis of Siwa, it then follows the arc of the inner oases from south to north, Kharga, Dakhla, Farafra and Bahariya. Next come the monasteries, the world's oldest, in the Wadi Natrun between Cairo and Alexandria, and the Mediterranean coast.

More monasteries, reef diving, off-road adventures and the sight of ships sailing through the desert are further wonders to be found in the **Sinai, Red Sea coast** and **Suez Canal** chapters.

Finally, the guide reaches Lower Egypt where the Nile fans out to form the **Delta**, where, except at a few sites such as Tanis, the river's mud has swallowed almost all tangible traces of its past. The guide ends with **Alexandria**, the city's European heritage and its Mediterranean gaze giving it an atmosphere unlike any place else in Egypt.

Top: Colossus of Ramses II, Abu Simbel
Above: The Sinai
Right: The Red Sea at Dahab

Chapter Divisions

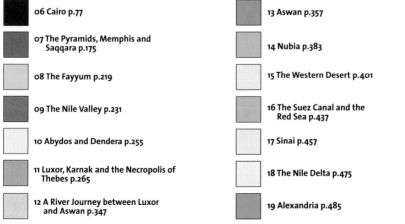

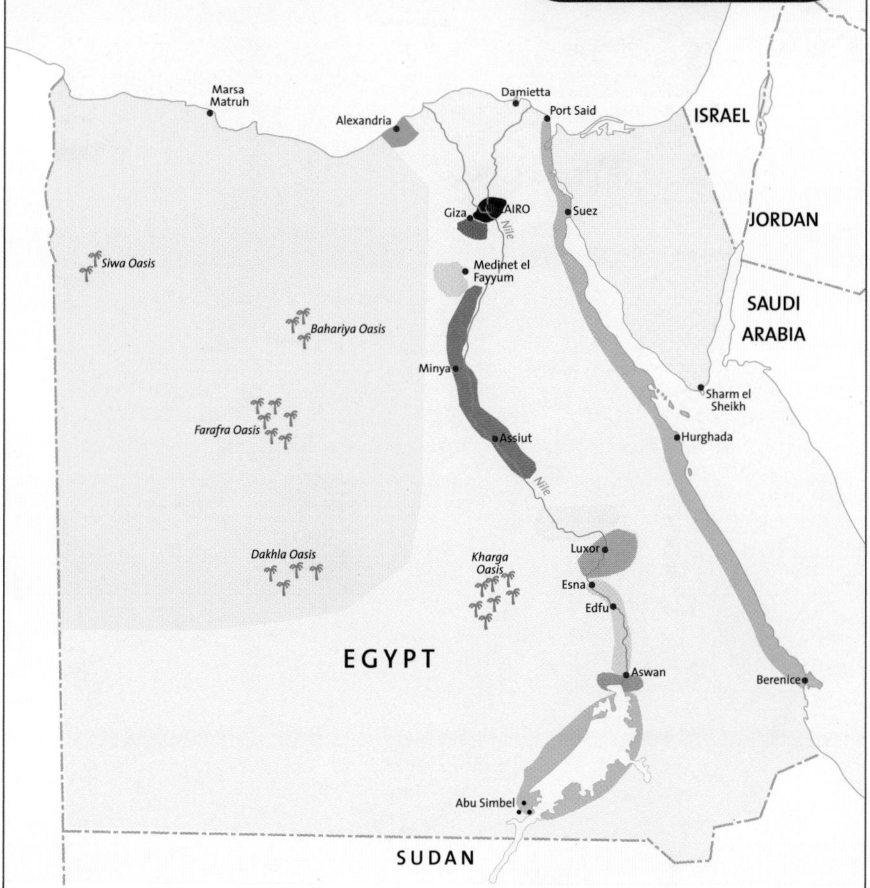

06 Cairo p.77

07 The Pyramids, Memphis and Saqqara p.175

08 The Fayyum p.219

09 The Nile Valley p.231

10 Abydos and Dendera p.255

11 Luxor, Karnak and the Necropolis of Thebes p.265

12 A River Journey between Luxor and Aswan p.347

13 Aswan p.357

14 Nubia p.383

15 The Western Desert p.401

16 The Suez Canal and the Red Sea p.437

17 Sinai p.457

18 The Nile Delta p.475

19 Alexandria p.485

Above: Tomb of Ramose

Opposite: Tomb of Sirenput II

The Joy of Life

The ancient Egyptians knew the joy of life, and there is nowhere that you can see this better than in their tombs. This may seem a contradiction, and even bizarre, but the ancient Egyptians were firm believers in an afterlife, and one that was an eternal recreation of the life they already knew and loved. But you will not see this in royal tombs such as those in the Valley of the Kings, where pharaohs would not be caught dead in the company of anyone less than the gods who endlessly enact the tedious ceremonies that adorn the walls, ceilings and pillars of their tombs.

For joyful scenes of everyday life, for the love of the world and the pleasure of being alive, you must visit the tombs of less exalted

people, for example those who inhabit the *mastabas* at Saqqara, or the noble tombs in the Theban necropolis or the tombs of the governors at Aswan. The following are well worth a visit:

- The mastaba of Ptah-Hotep, a V Dynasty priest of Maat, at Saqqara, is filled with beautifully carved painted reliefs of a man enjoying life to the full, including scenes of children running, wrestling and vaulting over one another, of a cow giving birth as a peasant guides its calf into the world, of grapes being cultivated and made into wine, and of fishing in the marshes. p.209.
- The mastaba of Ti, V Dynasty royal hairdresser, at Saqqara, is similar to that of Ptah-Hotep and even more varied; it is especially famous for its vivid hippopotamus hunt relief. p.211.
- Tomb 55 of Ramose, a XVIII Dynasty noble, at the Theban necropolis opposite Luxor, is filled with delicately carved reliefs of himself, his wife, their friends and family, all turned out at the height of New Kingdom fashion, the women elegantly dressed and exquisitely beautiful. p.329.
- Tomb 96 of Sennufer, a mayor of Thebes and chief vintner to Amenophis II, at the Theban necropolis, is entirely carved and decorated to look like an arbour of vines and grapes, its ceilings, walls and pillars seeming to wobble as though seen through the bottom of a glass of wine. p.328.
- Tomb 31 at Aswan of Sirenput II, a Middle Kingdom governor of the province, is brightly painted with pictures of his mother, wife and son on the walls, and of birds and animals, including a unique painting of an elephant. p.368.

Christian Egypt

Christianity took early root in Egypt and even after the Arab conquest in 641 it remained the faith of the majority of the population until the 11th century. It is still the religion of a significant minority. In a land familiar with the Osiris cult and its doctrine of resurrection and personal immortality, and familiar with images of Isis nursing the infant Horus, and also with the ubiquitous cross-like ankh, the ancient sign for life and rebirth, it is not surprising that Egyptians responded readily to the symbols and beliefs of Christianity. Pharaonic tombs became the homes of Christian hermits and temples became churches, while the first Christian monasteries were founded in remote parts of the country.

Top: El Muallaqa (The Hanging Church), Cairo
Above: Deir el Suriani

Some of the most ancient and intriguing monuments in Egypt are testimony to this long and remarkable heritage which the visitor can trace in the cities, the deserts and up and down the Nile. The most notable are:

- The church of Abu Sarga in old Cairo, which is thought to date from the 5th century and is built over the site of a cave traditionally associated with the Flight of the Holy Family. p.97.
- El Muallaqa, the so-called Hanging Church because it was built on the walls of the Byzantine fortress, probably dates from the 7th century; venerable icons fill its atmospheric interior which is

intricately decorated with cedar panelling and ivory screens. p.96.

- The Wadi Natrun, off the Cairo–Alexandria Desert Road, saw the first settlements of monks in the early 4th century and quickly developed into the flourishing centre of Christian monasticism. Four Coptic monasteries, surrounded by high walls against marauding Bedouins, survive to this day. pp.419–29.
- The Coptic monasteries of St Antony and St Paul in the mountains overlooking the Red Sea likewise date from the 4th century. pp.446–52.
- The City of St Menas, to the west of Alexandria, was a vast pilgrimage centre which was built up over the burial spot of a 3rd-century Christian martyr. Excavations are continuing to uncover and piece together the marble, granite and basalt remains of the original primitive 4th-century church, the 5th-century basilica and the sacred baths whose healing waters attracted pilgrims from as far off as Italy, France and England. p.429.
- The White Monastery on the edge of the desert beyond Sohag looks like a Ptolemaic temple and marks the transition between ancient Egyptian and Coptic architecture. Thousands of pilgrims come from all over Egypt during the week leading up to its saint's *moulid* on 14 July, their tents and market stalls creating the atmosphere of a vast medieval festival. p.251.
- Traces still remain of the churches that were once built inside the temples of Luxor (p.269) and Medinet Habu (p.337), in the temple of Isis at Philae (p.375), the temple of Osiris at Abousir (p.433), and elsewhere round Egypt. Ancient tombs served as Christian shrines or hermits' shelters, an example being the tomb of Ramses IV in the Valley of the Kings, its walls decorated with drawings of haloed saints (p.308).
- The Greek Orthodox monastery of St Catherine in Sinai dates from the 6th century and is special for its magnificent mosaics, among the finest anywhere in the world. p.464.

Right: Temple of Isis at Philae, Aswan

Above: Fishawi, Khan el Khalili

Café Culture

Egypt played a central role in the burgeoning 16th-century international trade in coffee, with dealers in Cairo importing coffee beans from Yemen and exporting them to Europe. Meanwhile in Egypt itself coffee became immensely popular, and a good century before even a single coffee house opened in Europe there were so many coffee houses in Cairo that they competed for customers by entertaining them with the best storytellers and poets. These cafés became gathering places where men could talk, write, read or entertain one another; they were centres of social interaction, but also over the centuries they developed into sources of cultural inspiration, attracting writers, artists and intellectuals. For locals and travellers alike, cafés still make enjoyable places to pass the time of day.

- Fishawi's in Cairo's Khan el Khalili has been open every day and night for over 200 years. pp.129, 172.
- Naguib Mahfouz Café, also in Khan el Khalili, makes use of the late Nobel prizewinning novelist's name, though he rarely came here; nevertheless its atmospheric location recommends it. p.170.
- Café Riche in downtown Cairo was genuinely one of Naguib Mahfouz's favourite haunts, and that of many other Egyptian writers, artists, actors and singers. p.172.

Top: Groppi, Midan Talaat Harb, Cairo
Above: Athineos, Alexandria

• Groppi in Midan Talaat Harb in Cairo is an Art Deco institution built by the Swiss chocolatier in 1925, but the famous gathering place of soldiers and writers during the Second World War, and which features frequently in Olivia Manning's *Levant Trilogy*, was Garden Groppi in Sharia Adli. p.171.

• In Alexandria, the Trianon, with its marvellous orientalist décor, was a favourite café of the poet Constantine Cavafy who worked upstairs in what was then the offices of the Third Circle of Irrigation. pp.497, 528. On the opposite side of the Ramleh tram terminus is Athineos, another ornate café-restaurant with beautiful views over the Eastern Harbour. pp.497, 528.

• Pastroudis, an Art Deco café and restaurant, was one of Lawrence Durrell's favourite watering holes during his years in Alexandria during the Second World War. pp.501, 528.

Above: *Bayt al-Suhaymi*
Below: *Mohammed Ali mosque*

Itinerary 1: A Week Exploring Cairo and its Surroundings

Cairo is one of the greatest storehouses of human achievement on earth, ranging from the pharaonic through the Christian and Islamic periods to the Belle Epoque. Cairo is also a huge metropolis with vast traffic jams at rush hours, and from May to October it gets very hot. And so it is best to take your time. The following are half-day excursions which you can easily expand into a full day or combine with something else. Relax and enjoy some lunch or refreshments along the way.

Day 1 Spend the morning in the Egyptian Museum, then take a walk downtown, heading for Midan Talaat Harb, enjoying some good examples of Belle Epoque and Art Deco architecture in passing. With the call to prayer booming from the loudspeakers of the nearby mosque, take a table beneath a tree at Garden Groppi at the eastern end of Sharia Adli and enjoy a beer or a cup of tea.

Day 2 Go into the Great Pyramid of Cheops, climb up through the Great Gallery and into the Cheops' burial chamber. Walk across to the pyramids of Chephren and Mycerinus, examining the lesser pyramids of queens and the mastabas of nobles. Then hire a camel and head out across the sands for the long view of the Pyramid ensemble. In the evening you can return for the sound and light show at the pavilion in front of the Sphinx.

Day 3 Hire a car with driver and visit the ruins of the former great city of Memphis and the vast metropolis of Saqqara. Explore Zoser's Step Pyramid and his Heb Sed court and look inside the Pyramid of Unas to see the famous Pyramid Texts, the oldest religious texts in the world. If you have time, strike off southwards to the Bent and Red pyramids and to the collapsed pyramid of Meidum.

Day 4 Discover a whole joyful gamut of Coptic art at the Coptic Museum at Old Cairo. Afterwards you can wander about the narrow alleyways within the ancient fortress walls, visiting the church of Abu Sarga and the recently restored synagogue of Ben Ezra. A short walk beyond is the wasteland that was Fustat, the city founded by the Arab conquerors of Egypt, and the much rebuilt mosque of Amr, the first mosque built by the invaders on Egyptian soil.

Day 5 The mosque of Ibn Tulun and the adjoining Gayer-Anderson House can mark the starting point of your tour of the southern quarters of the city. From there you can walk to the Sultan Hassan mosque. The Mohammed Ali mosque, the

Above: al-Nasr mosque
Below: Great Pyramid of Cheops

one with the dome and spindly minarets visible from all over the city, is impressive inside; but the truly magnificent structure atop the Citadel is the earlier Mameluke mosque of al-Nasr Mohammed. From the Citadel have a taxi take you along Sharia Salah-Salem to Al-Azhar Park and enjoy lunch with a wonderful view over the medieval city.

Day 6 Take a fascinating and atmospheric walk through the heart of the medieval city, starting from Bab Zuwayla, passing through the vast bazaar of Khan el Khalili, then continuing towards the Northern Walls. There are places to stop for refreshments or a meal along the way, for example by the madrasa of al-Ghuri or in the square in front of the mosque of Sayyidna al-Hussein. After you leave the magnificent complex of mosques, madrasas and mausoleums of the Mameluke sultans Qalaun, al-Nasr and Barquq, and before you reach the glimmering congregational mosque of the mad caliph al-Hakim, be sure to turn the corner into the narrow street to visit Bayt al-Suhaymi, the most beautiful example of traditional domestic architecture in Cairo.

Day 7 There is still so much more to see. Today you can revisit a favourite place and explore it more. Or you can go to the Islamic Museum, or the City of the Dead, or Manyal Palace on Roda Island, or stroll around the leafy streets of Zamalek.

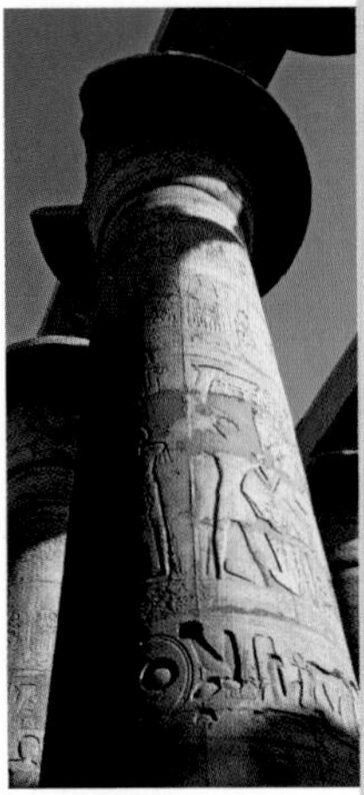

Above: Karnak, Luxor

Below: Bibliotheca Alexandrina, Alexandria

Itinerary 2: Egypt in Ten to Fourteen Days

Day 1 Cairo. The Pyramids and Saqqara.

Day 2 Cairo. The Egyptian Museum, the Coptic Museum and old Cairo.

Day 3 Cairo. Mosques of Ibn Tulun and Sultan Hassan. Walk from Bab Zuwayla to the Northern Walls, stopping at the mosque of al-Azhar, the mosque-mausoleum complex of Qalaun, al-Nasr and Barquq, the lovely Bayt al-Suhaymi and the mosque of al-Hakim. Take the overnight sleeper train to Luxor, or fly to Luxor tonight or in the morning.

Day 4 Luxor. On the East Bank visit the Temple of Luxor and Karnak. Either can be visited at night when the Temple of Luxor is beautifully illuminated and when they have the sound and light at Karnak.

Day 5 Luxor. Crossing to the West Bank, visit the Temple of Seti, the Valley of the Kings and Deir el Bahri. Visit the Luxor Museum in the evening.

Day 6 Luxor. Again crossing to the West Bank, visit the Tombs of the Nobles, the Ramesseum, Medinet Habu, the workmen's tombs at Deir el Medina, and the Colossi of Memnon. Take the evening train to Aswan.

Day 7 Aswan. Visit the Noble Tombs. From there ride a camel to St Simeon's monastery. Sail in a felucca to the Botanical Gardens. In the evening walk along Sharia el Souk, the street of the bazaar.

Day 8 Boat journey to the temple of Isis at Philae. Visit the Nubia Museum in the evening.

Day 9 Morning flight to Abu Simbel, back to Aswan in the afternoon. Take the overnight sleeper to Cairo.

Day 10 Take the train to Alexandria, see the Roman theatre and Villa of the Birds at Kom el Dikka, right next to the station; then visit the Catacombs at Kom el Shogafa. Take a taxi to Fort Qaytbey, the site of the ancient Pharos; walk or take a carriage along the Eastern Harbour corniche (stopping for lunch at the Tikka Grill or Fish Market), and look in at the new Bibliotheca Alexandrina. If you have a literary interest, visit the flat, now a museum, of the poet Constantine Cavafy. Stay overnight at Alexandria, or return to Cairo that night.

Days 11–14 If you have the extra days you can relax at a resort along the Red Sea or in Sinai, go coral diving there, or you can visit St Catherine's monastery in Sinai and do a bit of trekking.

CONTENTS

01 Introducing Egypt **1**
Where to Go 6

02 History **19**

03 Topics **41**
The Egyptian Condition 42
Problems and Changes 42
Homeless Childen 44
Islam 44
The Copts 45
Revolution in Egypt's Museums 47
Egypt's Grand Hotels 48

04 Planning Your Trip **51**
When to Go 52
Climate 52
Festivals 53
Tourist Information 54
Embassies and Consulates 54
Entry Formalities 55
Disabled Travellers 56
Money and Banks 57
Getting There 58
By Air 58
By Sea 58
Overland 58
Getting Around 59
By Air 59
By Rail 59
By Car and Taxi 60
By Bus 60
By Service Taxi 60
By Thumb 61
Nile Cruises 61
Where to Stay 62
Tour and Cruise Operators 63

05 Practical A–Z **65**
Conversion Tables 66
Baksheesh 67
Business Facilities 67
Children 67
Crime and Security 67
Electricity 68
Embassies in Egypt 68
Entertainment 68
Food and Drink 68
Health 70
Maps 71
Media 71
Opening Hours 72
Packing 72
Photography 73
Postal Services 73
Shopping 73
Sports and Activities 74
Students 75
Telephones 75
Toilets 76
Tourist Information in Egypt 76
Women 76

The Guide

06 Cairo **77**
History 79
Getting to and from Cairo 80
Orientation 85
Getting around Cairo 88
The Nile, Old Cairo and Fustat 91
Medieval Cairo 101
Around the Citadel 103
Al-Azhar Park 112
The Southern Cemetery 113
Darb el Ahmar 114
The Islamic Museum 119
Bab Zuwayla to Khan el Khalili 122
To the Northern Walls 129
The City of the Dead 140
The Egyptian Museum 144
Shopping 160
Where to Stay 164
Eating Out 169

07 The Pyramids, Memphis and Saqqara **175**
Some History: the Pyramid Age 177
The Great Pyramids of Giza 184
Memphis 196
Saqqara 199
Dahshur and Meidum 216

Maps and Plans

Egypt *inside front cover*
Central Cairo 78
Cairo Metro 89
Medieval Cairo 102
Ibn Tulun Mosque 104
Medieval Cairo: South 105
Sultan Hassan Mosque 109
Medieval Cairo: North 125
Khan el Khalili 130–1
Egyptian Museum 146
Pyramids, Memphis, Saqqara 176
Meidum Pyramid 179
The Pyramids of Giza 187
Great Pyramid of Cheops 188
Saqqara 201
Zoser's Funerary Complex 203
Zoser's Step Pyramid 204
Akhetaten 243
Abydos: Temple of Seti I 258
Dendera: Temple of Hathor 262
Luxor, Karnak and Thebes 266
Luxor 272
Temple of Luxor 273
Karnak 284–5
Valley of the Kings 307
Temple of Hatshepsut 323
Medinet Habu 341
Edfu: Temple of Horus 351
Temple at Kom Ombo 355
Aswan 358
Around Aswan 365
Philae 377
Nubia and Lake Nasser 384
The Western Desert 402
Wadi Natrun monasteries 421
The Suez Canal and the Red Sea 438
Sinai 458
The Nile Delta 476
Alexandria 486
Ancient Alexandria 501
Graeco-Roman Museum 503
Alexandria Corniche 522–3

Contents

08 The Fayyum **219**
The Fayyum: the Garden of Egypt 220
Entering the Oasis 223
Medinet el Fayyum 225
Excursions Around the Oasis 226
The Road towards the Nile 228

09 The Nile Valley **231**
Beni Suef to Minya 233
Minya and Surroundings 235
Amarna 240
South of Amarna: the Coptic Nile 247
Assiut 248
Sohag: Monasticism in Upper Egypt 250

10 Abydos and Dendera **255**
Abydos: Shrine of Osiris 256
Dendera 259
Beyond Qena 264

11 Luxor, Karnak and the Necropolis of Thebes **265**
The East Bank: Luxor and Karnak 269
The Temple of Luxor 269
The Mummification Museum 278
Museum of Ancient Egyptian Art 278
Karnak 279
The West Bank: the Necropolis of Thebes 299
The Valley of the Kings 306
Hatshepsut's Mortuary Temple at Deir el Bahri 320
The Ramesseum 331
The Valley of the Queens 334
Mortuary Temple of Ramses III at Medinet Habu 337
The Works of Amenophis III 342

12 River Journey between Luxor and Aswan **347**
Esna 348
Edfu 350
Kom Ombo: the Temple of Sobek and Haroeris 353

13 Aswan **357**
The Town 360
Elephantine Island 364
The Botanical Island 367
The Noble Tombs 367
The Mausoleum of the Aga Khan 369
St Simeon's Monastery 369
Philae: Island of Isis 375

14 Nubia **383**
Cruising Lake Nasser from Aswan 386
New Sebua 387
New Amada 389
Qasr Ibrim 391
Abu Simbel 392

15 The Western Desert **401**
Siwa Oasis 403
Kharga Oasis 414
Dakhla Oasis 415
Farafra Oasis 416
Bahariya Oasis 417
Monasteries of the Wadi Natrun 419
The City of St Menas 429
The Mediterranean Coast West of Alexandria 431
Alamein 434
Mersa Matruh 435

16 The Suez Canal and the Red Sea **437**
The Suez Canal 439
To Ismailia 441
Port Said 443
Suez 44
The Monastery of St Antony 446
The Monastery of St Paul 449
South to Hurghada and Beyond 452

17 Sinai **457**
Across Northern Sinai 459
El Arish 460
Into Southern Sinai 461
The Greek Orthodox Monastery of St Catherine 464
Gebel Musa 468
Gebel Katerin 470
Along the Gulf of Aqaba 471
Sharm el Sheikh, Na'ama Bay and Ras Mohammed 471
Dahab, Nuweiba and Taba 472

18 The Nile Delta **475**
Ancient Sites in the Eastern Delta 479
Damietta and the Crusades 481
The Western Delta 482

19 Alexandria **485**
History 487
Around Midan Saad Zaghloul 493
Literary Alexandria 497
The Roman Theatre and Baths at Kom el Dikka 500
The Graeco-Roman Museum 502
Alexandria National Museum 507
Around the Shallalat Gardens 507
Around Midan el Tahrir 510
The Turkish Town 512
On the Headland 514
The Pharos Lighthouse 515
Southwest Alexandria 516
Southeast Alexandria 519
The Bibliotheca Alexandrina 520
The Corniche to Montazah 521
East of Alexandria 523
Rosetta 524
Where to Stay 526
Eating Out 527

Reference

20 Language **530**
21 Glossary **531**
22 Further Reading **537**
23 Index **538**

History

The Pharaonic Period 20
The Graeco-Roman Period 23
The Arab and Turkish Period 24
The Modern Period 27
Chronology 30

02

The Pharaonic Period

5000–3000 BC: Predynastic Period

During this period, two kingdoms developed in Egypt, a northern one in the Delta, a southern one in the Nile valley. Though in frequent conflict with each other, they shared many features of a common culture. Hieroglyphic writing and monumental brick architecture were initiated.

3000–2647 BC: Early Dynastic Period (1st and 2nd Dynasties)

The king of the south, called **Menes**, known also as Narmer, triumphed over the north and established his capital at **Memphis**, near the juncture of the Nile valley and the Delta, from where he ruled over a united Egypt. The country's southern border was pushed southwards as far as Elephantine, in Nubia. Pharaohs and nobility alike were buried in substantial mudbrick mastabas.

2647–2124 BC: Old Kingdom (3rd to 8th Dynasties)

The Old Kingdom began with the widespread use of stone, not only in the burial mastabas of the nobility but also to realise a wholly new conception, the pyramid. The purpose of the pyramid was to provide an indestructible container for the ka, a vital force possessed by the king alone, but upon which the nobles and priests depended for their lives and afterlives. The pharaoh, in short, possessed absolute temporal and spiritual power and ruled over a highly centralized and rigidly hierarchical society.

The Step Pyramid of the 3rd Dynasty pharaoh **Zoser** (2628–2609 BC) was the first; the 4th Dynasty pyramids of **Cheops** (2549–2526 BC), **Chephren** (2518–2493 BC) and **Mycerinus** (2488–2460 BC) at Giza marked the apogee of the Pyramid Age and of Old Kingdom pharaonic authority.

Throughout the Old Kingdom, Egypt extended its spheres of trade, sending expeditions into Sinai, Libya and Nubia. But during the 5th Dynasty, pharaonic authority began to decline; the construction of sun temples such as those at **Abu Ghurab** indicate that the priesthood of **Re** was becoming more important than the pharaoh himself, while inscriptions in the Pyramid of Unas (2341–2311 BC) are early evidence of the rising cult of Osiris, with its message of universal redemption.

From the 6th Dynasty onwards, power increasingly passed out of royal hands and into that of the nobles, who often set up almost independent courts in their own localities.

2123–2040 BC: First Intermediate Period (9th to 11th Dynasties)

Low Niles, bad harvests, foreign incursions and a weakened royal authority led to the collapse of the central administration. Northern Egypt was ruled from Heracleopolis, near Beni Suef, while southern Egypt was ruled from Thebes. The Thebes-based 11th Dynasty pharaoh **Mentuhotep** II (2050–1999 BC) reunited the country in 2040 BC, inaugurating the Middle Kingdom.

2040–1648 BC: Middle Kingdom (11th to 13th Dynasties)

Following the reunification of Egypt by Mentuhotep II, the powerful kings of the 12th Dynasty established their capital at or near Memphis. Nevertheless, the supremacy enjoyed by Re, patron of the Old Kingdom pharaohs, was increasingly challenged by the worship of **Osiris** who could promise immortality not only to kings but to all believers who could demonstrate pious and worthy lives. This religious democratization was reflected in the architecture and distribution of tombs. Though pharaohs continued to build pyramids, such as those at Hawara and Lahun, these were of inferior quality, nor did nobles any longer feel obliged to build mastabas close by. Instead provincial nobles were interred in local rock-cut tombs, as at Beni Hasan.

Major building works and hydrological programmes were undertaken in the Fayyum by **Ammenemes I** (1980–1951 BC) and his successors. Trade flourished with the Aegean islands, Byblos (present-day Jubail in Lebanon), whence cedarwood was obtained, and Punt, probably corresponding to present-day Somalia, while Nubia was invaded and garrisoned to control its supplies of gold and hard stone. Egypt again prospered and became a great power. Central authority weakened, however, during the 13th Dynasty.

1648–1540 BC: Second Intermediate Period (14th to 17th Dynasties)

The collapse of central authority during the 14th Dynasty brought invasion from the northeast by the **Hyksos**, who comprised the 15th and 16th Dynasties. They gradually extended their rule over most of Egypt from Avaris, their Delta capital, and introduced the use of horses and chariots. Contemporaneous with Hyksos rule were the 17th Dynasty princes ruling at Thebes who eventually drove the Hyksos out of Egypt.

1540–1069 BC: New Kingdom (18th to 20th Dynasties)

In defeating the Hyksos and then pursuing them to extinction in western Asia, **Amosis I** (1540–1525 BC), founder of the 18th Dynasty, initiated the aggressive policy towards Palestine and Syria that characterized the New Kingdom, a period of power, luxury and cosmopolitanism. As royal residence and the religious and political capital of Egypt, Thebes and its necropolis were adorned with those monumental temples and magnificent tombs still seen today, as well as with palaces and homes which, because made of mud brick, have long since disappeared.

Tuthmosis I (1504–1492 BC) abandoned the pyramid and began the practice of royal burials in the Valley of the Kings, which owing to its constricted space required separate mortuary temples on the plain. His daughter **Hatshepsut** (1479–1457 BC) initiated Egypt's artistic revival; her mortuary temple at Deir el Bahri remains one of the finest architectural achievements of all time. Her co-ruler and then successor, **Tuthmosis III** (1479–1425 BC), conquered and then organized the petty states of western Asia into the world's first imperial system, so that Egypt prospered from their tribute and their trade, and gained their loyalty by educating and acculturating their young princes to Egyptian ways. Under **Amenophis III**

(1391–1353 BC), who built most of the **Temple of Luxor**, the New Kingdom reached its apogee of opulence.

A major beneficiary of imperial wealth was the priesthood of the god **Amun** at the great **Temple of Karnak**. Attempts to limit their power, which rivalled that of the pharaohs, came to a head during the reign of Amenophis IV, who, as **Akhenaten** (1353–1337 BC), established the worship of Aten and built a new capital at **Amarna**. Nothing so vividly portrays the break with past conventions than the sculpture and reliefs of the Amarna period, which are among the most striking artistic works of ancient Egypt. At the death of Akhenaten and his wife **Nefertiti**, however, the priesthood of Amun re-asserted its authority over the young pharaoh **Tutankhamun** (1336–1327 BC).

The 19th Dynasty began with the brief reign of **Ramses I**, an aged general whose son **Seti I** (1294–1279 BC) and grandson **Ramses II** (1279–1213 BC) restored royal prestige by means of their Asian campaigns whose booty ensured accommodation with the Amun priesthood. Seti reverted to Old Kingdom artistic canons and produced coloured reliefs of exquisite taste, most notably at Abydos. Ramses was a prodigious builder, adding to the temples at Luxor and Karnak, and constructing the Ramesseum, though his finest work is at Abu Simbel. Despite his bombast, Ramses II was not as successful a warrior as his father; he very nearly suffered defeat at Kadesh in Syria against the Hittites, whose capital was in central Anatolia. Iron weaponry was one reason why the Hittites were so formidable; the Egyptians had only bronze.

The Exodus under Moses may have taken place during the reign of Ramses II or that of his son **Merneptah** (1213–1203 BC). During the following century or so Egypt finally entered the **Iron Age**. But iron could only be obtained in western Asia, and partly because Egypt was short on iron weaponry, its hold on western Asia was slipping. Instead iron had to be bought with gold, which caused Egypt enormous economic difficulties. Indeed one reason why tomb robbing became so common during the 20th Dynasty and after was the rocketing value of gold which the country could no longer afford to leave buried with its dead. The outstanding pharaoh of the 20th Dynasty was **Ramses III** (1184–1153 BC), who recorded on the wall of his mortuary temple at Medinet Habu how he repelled an invasion by the Sea Peoples, marauders from across the Mediterranean who had already destroyed the Hittite empire. It was the last great Egyptian victory.

1069–332 BC: Late Dynastic Period (21st to 31st Dynasties)

This was a period of decline during which division and foreign rule were common. Native kings ruled as much of Egypt as they could from various capitals in the Delta, high priests of Amun often ruled Thebes and its surrounding area, and from time to time foreign dynasties, Libyans and 'Ethiopians' (in fact from the Sudan), controlled all or part of Egypt. Foreigner was sometimes compounded upon foreigner: during the 25th Dynasty (712–663 BC), when the massive First Pylon at Karnak was built, the Ethiopian king Taharka was defeated by the Assyrians who sacked both Memphis and Thebes, while the Assyrians in turn were ejected during the 26th Dynasty (663–525 BC) with the help of Greek mercenaries. This **Saite Dynasty**, as it is also known, after Sais, its Delta capital, was a period of prosperity and cultural revival, and also a time of large scale Greek settlement in the country. The Greek city of Naucratis in the Delta was granted the privilege of being the only port through which goods could be imported into Egypt.

The Persians invaded Egypt in 525 BC and were only removed in 399 BC, again with Greek help, though the Persians returned in 343 BC and remained until **Alexander the Great** entered Egypt in 332 BC.

The Graeco-Roman Period

332–30 BC: The Ptolemaic Period

In 331 BC, the year after he entered Egypt, Alexander founded Alexandria, though he did not stay long enough to see a single building rise. At his death in 323 BC, his new Hellenistic empire, which extended as far east as India, was divided between three of his Macedonian generals, Ptolemy taking Egypt. As **Ptolemy I Soter** (323–282 BC) , he established a dynasty which ruled the country for 300 years in the guise of pharaohs, albeit Greek-speaking ones. Egypt was colonized by the Greeks, who nevertheless respected and in some measure merged their own culture with the customs and religion of the Egyptians. Through the Ptolemies' control of trade – wheat, for example, was a royal monopoly – the dynasty became spectacularly wealthy and famous as great benefactors.

Ptolemy I Soter added Cyrene, Palestine, Cyprus and parts of the Asia Minor coast to his realm, and at Alexandria, its capital and geographical centre, he founded the Museion and Library. The Pharos, the lighthouse that was reckoned one of the seven wonders of the world, was built during the reign of **Ptolemy II Philadelphos** (282–246 BC), who also first invited the Jews to settle in the city. Within 100 years of her founding, Alexandria had reached the height of her splendour and was the greatest commercial, cultural and scientific centre of the age.

In Upper Egypt, **Ptolemy III Euergetes** (246–221 BC) built at Karnak and began the temple at Edfu. The temples at Dendera, Esna, Kom Ombo and Philae were also Ptolemaic works. Though these archaic temples were built to please the priests, the Ptolemies otherwise tied Egypt to the Mediterranean. Inevitably they encountered the rising power and rapacity of Rome, and through incompetence abroad and strife at home the later Ptolemies relied on the Romans for their very thrones. The last in the line was the great **Cleopatra** (51–30 BC), who with Mark Antony attempted to create a new Hellenistic empire in the east. Their defeat by a Roman fleet in the battle of Actium off Greece in 31 BC and Octavian's victory outside the walls of Alexandria the following year led to their suicides.

30 BC–AD 642: Roman and Byzantine Periods

After seizing Alexandria in 30 BC, **Octavian** (Augustus) incorporated Egypt into the **Roman Empire**. The Roman emperors followed the example of the Ptolemies in representing themselves to the Egyptian people as successors of the pharaohs and in maintaining the appearance of a national Egyptian state. They completed and added to many of the temples the Ptolemies had begun. The dominant culture of the country remained Greek, but whereas the colonizing Greeks had had a stake in the country and made it flourish through trade, the Roman administration increasingly ran Egypt as a command economy, milking it for taxes and grain entirely for the benefit of Rome. By the third century AD, living standards were falling and the infrastructure was in decline, and in places like the Fayyum, which the Ptolemies had raised to a level of prosperity that it has not regained even to this day, the sands washed in over once fertile fields and busy towns.

Alexandria, however, remained a great city, and to her eminence in science, mathematics and the arts she added philosophy and theology. Her mixed Greek, Jewish and Egyptian population provided the early cult of Jesus with much of its symbolism and intellectual underpinning, and during the first three centuries AD the new religion extended throughout the country, first among the Greeks themselves, but eventually among the native population. In AD 204 the Romans felt obliged to issue an edict prohibiting Roman subjects from embracing **Christianity**, and half a century later the Emperor Decius (AD 249–51) instituted a brief but severe persecution. During the reign of Diocletian (AD 284–305), persecution of Christians reached its peak, so many thousands dying that his accession marks the beginning of the 'Era of Martyrs' from which the Egyptian (that is Coptic) Church dates its calendar.

Christianity, which resonated so well with old symbols and beliefs, including the expectation of an afterlife, became the basis of a reawakened popular culture, expressed with an exuberance not found in the pharaonic or Graeco-Roman canons. Nor were native Egyptians content to follow the subtleties of Alexandrian theologians imbued with an alien Greek philosophy. Despite the **Edict of Milan** in AD 313, which granted toleration to Christianity, a gap in nationalist feeling opened up between native Egyptians and the Roman Empire.

In the West, that empire was in decline. In the East, the **Emperor Constantine** founded a new and Christian capital at Constantinople in AD 330, the beginnings of what historians now call the **Byzantine Empire**. Also at about AD 330 the first monasteries were founded in Egypt's deserts, and from them the imperial and religious authority of Constantinople and its representatives in Alexandria were opposed. In AD 451, at the **Council of Chalcedon**, the supposed Egyptian belief that Christ has only a single divine nature (monophysitism) was branded a heresy, and the Coptic Church was effectively expelled from the main body of Christianity. The bitterness felt at this decision, and grievances towards Roman and then Byzantine misrule, persuaded Egyptians to offer little resistance to the **Arab invasion** of AD 640–2.

The Arab and Turkish Period

AD 642–969: Umayyads, Abbassids, Tulunids and Ikhshidids

By the time Mohammed, the founder of Islam, died at Mecca in 632, the whole of Arabia had been united under his new religion. Within a further ten years, the Arabs had destroyed the Sassanian (Persian) Empire and had defeated the Byzantines in Syria, taking Damascus and Jerusalem. Under the leadership of **Amr**, 3,500 Arab horsemen invaded Egypt in 640 and in the following year founded

Fustat near the Byzantine fortress of **Babylon** (now in Old Cairo), which surrendered to them. In 642 Alexandria put the seal on the Arab conquest by opening its gates to them in welcome.

Though the rapidly expanding Arab empire was first ruled from Medina, from 661 it was governed by caliphs of the Umayyad dynasty at Damascus. After a violent transfer of dynasty in 750, the caliphate was moved to Baghdad. As far as Egypt was concerned, however, Arab policy always remained the same. There was little interest in making converts, for the poll tax could be imposed only on non-Muslims. During this first period of Arab rule, a succession of 80 governors was sent to milk the country, the level of taxation soon proving more oppressive than it had been under the Byzantines. The irrigation system further deteriorated, agriculture declined, prices rose and native Egyptians suffered growing impoverishment. Some converted to Islam, others rose in vain revolt during the 8th and 9th centuries.

In 870 the Abbassids sent **Ibn Tulun** to Egypt as governor. Instead he asserted his independence and soon restored the country's economy. His magnificent mosque, which owes an architectural debt to his native Mesopotamia, is the largest in Cairo and, apart from Amr's much rebuilt mosque at Fustat, the oldest. In 905 the Abbassids regained Egypt from Ibn Tulun's less able descendants, but Baghdad's authority was both nominal and brief as another governor, **Ikhshid**, had barely established his own dynasty when it was swept away by the Fatimid conquest.

969–1171: The Fatimids

In 909 an Arab dynasty claiming descent from Mohammed's daughter Fatima established its own Shi'a caliphate centred on Tunisia. Opposing themselves to the Abbassids' Sunni caliphate in Baghdad, in 969 the Fatimids under their caliph al-Muizz invaded Egypt where they founded **Cairo** and, to propagate their version of Islam, the great mosque of al-Azhar. During the reign of the second Cairo caliph, al-Aziz (975–6), the Fatimid empire reached its apogee, extending beyond North Africa and Egypt to Sicily, western Arabia and Syria. Egypt's foreign trade was expanded and its taxation reduced. The empire declined after the death of the third Cairo caliph, the mad al-Hakim (996–1021), though its tradition of architectural excellence continued unabated, not least in the late 11th century Fatimid city gates of Bab Zuwayla, Bab al-Nasr and Bab al-Futuh.

Two external events contributed to the extinction of the Fatimid empire. In 1055 the Seljuq Turks took Baghdad, their energy leading to a resurgence of Sunni Islam in Mesopotamia, Persia and Syria. Then in 1099 the First Crusade took Jerusalem.

1171–1250: The Ayyubids

When the Crusaders attacked Egypt in 1168, **Saladin**, a Kurd and son of Ayyub (from whom Saladin's dynasty took its name), successfully defended the country on behalf of the Sunni caliphate, overthrew the enfeebled Shi'a caliphate of the Fatimids and in 1171 made himself master of the country. Then after completing the Citadel in Cairo, he recaptured Jerusalem in 1187. Realising that Egypt was the key to their control of the Holy Land, the Crusaders twice more attacked the country after Saladin's death in 1193. In a remarkable incident on the occasion of Fifth Crusade's siege of Damietta in 1218, **St Francis of Assisi** crossed the Egyptian lines in a personal attempt to convert the Sultan al-Kamil. St Francis was kindly sent away with gifts and thereafter confined his preachings to birds. In 1249 the Seventh Crusade, led by the French king, St Louis, also landed at Damietta but was repulsed by an army of Turkish slaves, called Mamelukes, which had been built up by the Sultan al-Salih Ayyub. The campaign was in fact conducted by **Shagarat al-Durr**, Ayyub's wife, who kept it a secret that the sultan had meanwhile died in Cairo. She proclaimed herself sultan in 1250, but found she could rule only through the chief Mameluke, whom she married.

1250–1517: The Mamelukes

The Mamelukes discovered their power during the reigns of al-Salih Ayyub and in particular his wife Shagarat al-Durr. At her death in 1257, they raised sultans from their own ranks. Until 1382 it was the **Bahri Mamelukes**, named for their barracks on Roda island in the Nile (*bahr* means river), who ruled Egypt. They were mostly Kipchak Turks from the steppes north of the Black Sea. The most celebrated of these Mameluke sultans were **Baybars** (1260–77), **Qalaun** (1279–90) and **al-Nasr** (1309–40) – the beautiful mausolea of these last two are on Sharia Muizz in Cairo and also **al-Hassan** (1347–51, 1354–61), builder of the great madrasa bearing his name.

The Mamelukes were the most formidable fighting force of their time, and almost immediately, under Baybars in 1260, they won a stunning victory against the Mongols in Palestine, who until then had seemed unstoppable. Qalaun in turn reduced the Crusaders' holdings in the Holy Land to the port of Acre, from which they were driven in 1291, a year after his death.

The Bahri Mamelukes gave Egypt security and prosperity, at least until the end of al-Nasr's reign. Thereafter their rule descended into incompetence and vicious rivalries. From 1382 their place was taken by the **Burgi Mamelukes**, named for their barracks in the Citadel (*burg* means tower, referring to the towers of the Citadel), who were mostly Circassian Turks from the Caucasus.

The outstanding architectural works of the Burgi Mameluke sultans are owed to **Barquq** (1382–89, 1390–98), whose mosque is on Sharia Muizz, his mausoleum in the City of the Dead in Cairo; to **Baybars** (1422–38), whose mausoleum is in the City of the Dead; to **Qaytbey** (1468–95), known for his fortress on the site of the Pharos in Alexandria, and his mausoleum in the City of the Dead; and to **al-Ghuri** (1500–16) whose monuments stand near al-Azhar.

In the late 14th century, Barquq deflected **Timur** (Tamerlane) from Egypt by keeping him at bay in Syria, but the cost of the campaign ruined Egypt's finances. Famine, plague and Portugal's discovery of a sea route round Africa into the Indian Ocean combined to weaken Egypt's economic position during the 15th century.

Egypt's **Christians** paid the price. The Copts had remained in the majority at least until the Crusades, but the Latin capture of Jerusalem in 1099, the Mongol sack of Baghdad in 1258 and the internecine struggles of Egypt's Mameluke rulers from the mid-13th to the 16th century produced an atmosphere of insecurity and distrust which, combined with the growing impoverishment of the country, had sultans and mobs alike turning against the Christians. In the early 14th century, fanatical Muslims looted and destroyed all the principle churches of Egypt. In revenge the

Copts fired many mosques, palaces and private Muslim houses, whereupon Christians suffered wholesale massacre. Copts were expelled from official positions and subjected to a range of indignities, such as being forbidden to ride horses or asses unless they sat backwards, being forced to wear distinctive clothing, and even being required to have a bell tinkling round their necks when entering a public bath. Mass conversions to Islam followed.

1517–1798: The Ottomans

When **Selim**, the Ottoman sultan, entered Cairo in 1517, he had Tumanbay, the last Mameluke sultan, strung up at Bab Zuwayla. In fact the rope twice broke and Tumanbay had to be hanged three times before he was dead. It might have been an omen, for the Ottomans never controlled Egypt absolutely, and the Mamelukes were far from being a spent force. But officially, and usually so nominally that nobody noticed or cared, Egypt remained part of the Ottoman Empire until 1914.

At first the Ottoman Pasha (governor) was successful in the usual activity of drawing off Egyptian revenues, and indeed the Egyptian Bazaar in Istanbul was not so-called because it sold Egyptian goods but because it was maintained out of a small part of the heavy taxes imposed on Egypt. In return, the Ottomans allowed Egypt to rot. Cairo ceased to be an important cultural centre and Alexandria nearly disappeared altogether. As opposed to the bold forms and magnificent volumes of earlier Cairene architecture, the Ottomans contributed a few rather prissy minarets, several baroque public fountains and indulged their taste for tiles by slapping up some third-rate indigo and turquoise examples on the 14th-century **mosque of Aqsunqur**, accounting for its popular name of Blue Mosque.

But throughout the 17th and 18th centuries, the Ottoman Pashas were no more than straw men, and Egypt muddled along on shifting alliances between Mamelukes, merchants, guilds and religious functionaries. Indeed by the second half of the 18th century, certain Mamelukes had gathered up so much power that they became almost absolute masters of Egypt, and from that time all payments of revenue to Istanbul were stopped.

The Modern Period

1798–1914: Egypt's Encounter with the West

In 1798 **Napoleon** landed in Egypt with the aim of controlling the land and sea route between Europe and India. In the **Battle of the Nile**, fought that same year, Nelson met this threat to British interests by destroying the French fleet. Napoleon absconded to Paris in 1799; the British compelled his army to follow in 1801. But the brief expedition was to have profound effects. Egypt was exposed to the full impact of Western technology, while Western curiosity worked at turning Egypt's mysterious past into an open book. Napoleon's expedition had included a number of France's leading scholars, whose exhaustive survey of the country, *Description de l'Egypte*, was published in 20 volumes between 1809 and 1828. Their activities had included collecting antiquities and making detailed drawings of monuments and sites. Because their activities were well known to the army at large, the scholars were immediately notified when a soldier found an inscribed stone at **Rosetta**. The decipherment of its hieroglyphics by Champollion in 1822 opened up three millennia of ancient Egyptian history.

After the departure of the French, the Ottomans attempted to assert their authority. One of their Albanian commanders, **Mohammed Ali**, was made viceroy (khedive) in 1805; after massacring the Mamelukes in 1811 he became, effectively, the independent ruler of Egypt. Before his death in 1849, he placed his mark on the Cairo skyline with his Ottoman imperial-style mosque atop the Citadel. During his decades of power he began the modernization of Egypt. An improved strain of cotton, new industries and a massive public works programme laid the basis for a rise in population and prosperity which, by the end of the century, reached levels unknown to Egypt for 2,000 years. In 1821 he completed the **Mahmoudiya Canal** which linked Alexandria to the Nile and brought the city back to life. With a powerful fleet and a highly trained army under the brilliant command of his son Ibrahim, Mohammed Ali held sway over the Eastern Mediterranean and the Middle East, and nearly overturned the Ottoman Empire itself. Checked only by the superior power of the British, and in return for recognition of his dynastic claims, Mohammed Ali confined his ambitions to Egypt.

The opening of the **Suez Canal** in 1869, during the reign of **Ismail**, returned Egypt to the crossroads of international trade, a position it had lost in the 15th century when the Portuguese opened up the route around southern Africa to the Indian Ocean. The venture was more than Ismail could afford, however, and in selling his shares to the British in 1875 he not only gave them a controlling interest in the canal but a considerable stake in Egypt's security. Therefore in 1882, when **Colonel Ahmed Arabi** led a nationalist uprising against his own government in protest at its susceptibility to British, French and Turkish influence, and when hundreds of Europeans in Alexandria were massacred in consequence, the **British** occupied the country. The final word in Egyptian affairs was now that of British consul-generals, men like Evelyn Baring, later **Lord Cromer**, who between 1883 and 1907 was typical in encouraging the development of the country's railways, public services, agriculture and irrigation system, including the **first dam at Aswan**, while at the same time failing to understand Egyptian resentment and desire for independence.

1914–present: Egypt into the 21st Century

In 1914, after Ottoman Turkey allied itself with Germany in the First World War, Egypt was declared a British Protectorate. At war's end Saad Zaghloul, leader of the **nationalist movement**, demanded British withdrawal but was sent into exile. Continued nationalist activity, however, forced Britain to recognize Egypt as a sovereign state in 1922. Nevertheless, Britain retained responsibility for Egyptian defence, its foreign community and the Suez Canal, and maintained an army in the country until 1936, when it was withdrawn to the Canal Zone. But the **Second World War** (1939–45) brought the British army back in force, and after initial reversals it won a great victory at **Alamein** in 1942 over an invading German army commanded by General Rommel. Relations in the Middle East became bitter, however, with the end of the British Mandate for Palestine in 1948. Egypt, together with other Arab countries, went to war against the new state of Israel but was defeated. Many Egyptians blamed corruption in the army, weak government, favouritism in high places and purchases of obsolete arms for the debacle, all of which implicated **King Farouk** and his ministers. **Gamal Abdel Nasser**, a young colonel who had been wounded in the fighting, gathered round him a group of dissident army officers who vowed to overthrow the monarchy. The coup came on 23 July 1952, and on 26 July Farouk abdicated and left the country. With a decade or so to run before the foreign-owned Suez Canal Company reverted to Egyptian ownership, the British were persuaded to evacuate their troops from the Canal Zone. But Nasser's plans to help Egyptian agriculture and industry by building the **High Dam at Aswan** became a new source of international friction when the Americans, angry at his nonaligned policy, refused to lend the money. In July 1956 Nasser nationalized the Suez Canal to use its revenues to pay for the dam's construction, but in October that year Israel invaded Sinai to provide a pretext for France and Britain to reoccupy the Canal, supposedly thereby to keep Egypt and Israel from fighting. America, which was playing its own long-term game in the Middle East, and did not want the boat rocked, obliged the invaders to withdraw. For Nasser, it was a great moral victory, and on the back of nationalist fervour he threw most foreigners and Jews out of the country, and from 1961 introduced sweeping socialist measures, limiting incomes, nationalizing banks and the cotton industry, and further redistributing land. Enormously popular and genuinely concerned for the welfare of his people, his policies nevertheless stifled enterprise, encouraged corruption and cynicism, and contributed to falling standards in education and services. In the 1967 '**Six Day War**' against Israel, Egypt suffered a defeat even more humiliating than under Farouk 20 years earlier. Though the Canal was blocked and Sinai occupied, Nasser's offer to resign was rejected by an outpouring of national sentiment. But three years later he was dead.

After 1970, when **Anwar Sadat** succeeded Nasser as president, Egypt edged away from its pro-Soviet policy and its economy was gradually liberalized. Egypt's attempt to regain Sinai during the 1973 war was repelled, yet it was a triumph. Israel had been taken by surprise and was no longer seen as invincible, while Egyptian pride had been restored. Sadat could make his dramatic visit to Jerusalem in 1977, which led to a peace treaty between the two countries.

Hosni Mubarak became president after Sadat's assassination by Islamic fundamentalists in 1981, since when the country's economy has continued to be liberalized, with controls and subsidies lifted and virtually all its nationalized industries returned to private ownership. Egyptian stability is being tested as the country endures the strains of this transition while attempting to make its economy grow faster than its rapidly rising population eats into it. Mubarak has attempted to bring Islamic fundamentalists into the peaceful political fold, and to some extent he has been successful; but at the same time Egypt has become conformist and conservative, with Egyptians increasingly fearful of any expression that could be interpreted as anti-Islamic, while the government has done next to nothing to encourage the development of a secular democracy.

Chronology

Pharaonic Dynasties

This section, in the pages following, includes a list of the royal dynasties ruling Egypt. The priests drew up long lists of monarchs, attaching to the years of a pharaoh's reign the events they wished to record. An example is the list of Seti I's predecessors in his mortuary temple at Abydos.

Working from such lists, Manetho, an Egyptian priest under the early Ptolemies, arranged all the rulers of Egypt from Menes to Alexander into 31 dynasties. Egyptologists have relied on Manetho's list, and have been able to confirm its essential correctness. Egyptologists have in turn divided pharaonic history into periods, such as Old Kingdom, Middle Kingdom and New Kingdom, though there are competing classifications.

Dates for the Late Period are regarded as certain; otherwise the margin of error should not exceed 15 years for the New Kingdom, 40 years for the Middle Kingdom, 60 years for the Old Kingdom and about 100 years for the first two dynasties.

This dynastic arrangement has historical validity, for Egypt's fortunes were closely linked to the rise and fall of the various royal houses.

Throughout this guide the dynasty of each pharaoh is mentioned after his name so that his place in the scheme of things can readily be ascertained. Only the most important pharaohs have been mentioned in the chronology below, within their dynasties.

Predynastic Period: 5000–3000 BC

Early Dynastic Period: 3000–2647 BC

1st Dynasty and 2nd Dynasty

Menes (Narmer) — Unification of Egypt; capital at Memphis.

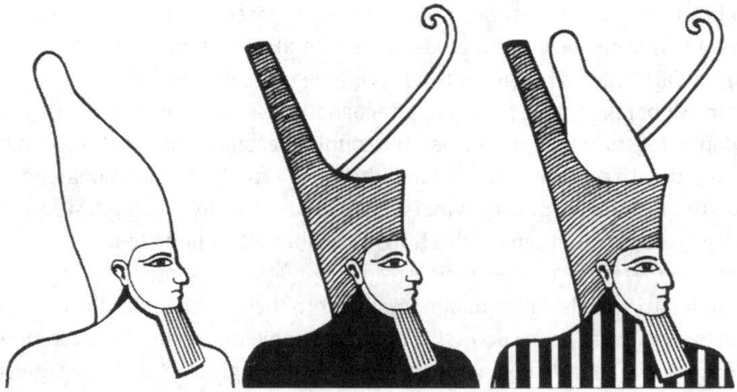

White (Upper Egypt) — Red (Lower Egypt) — Combined (Unified Kingdom)

Old Kingdom: 2647–2124 BC

	BC	
3rd Dynasty	**2647–2573**	Period of stability. Start of the Pyramid Age.
Zoser	2628–2609	
4th Dynasty	**2573–2454**	
Snofru	2573–2549	
Cheops	2549–2526	
Chephren	2518–2493	
Mycerinus	2488–2460	Effective end of the Pyramid Age.
5th Dynasty	**2454–2311**	
Userkaf	2454–2447	
Neferirkare	2435–2425	
Unas	2341–2311	Pyramid Texts.
6th Dynasty	**2311–2140**	Period of decline.
Pepi I	2280–2243	
7th and 8th Dynasties	**2140–2124**	

First Intermediate Period: 2123–2040 BC

	BC	
9th and 10th Dynasties	**2123–2040**	Collapse of central authority. Capital at Heracleopolis.
11th Dynasty (first part)	**2123–2040**	Capital at Thebes.
Mentuhotep II	2050–2040 (pre reunification)	

Middle Kingdom: 2040–1648 BC

	BC	
11th Dynasty (2nd part)	**2040–1980**	Conquest of Nubia.
Mentuhotep II	2040–1999	Reunites Egypt; capital at Thebes.
12th Dynasty	**1980–1801**	Royal residence moved to Memphis; major building works and hydrological programmes in the Fayyum.
Ammenemes I	1980–1951	
Sesostris I	1960–1916	
Ammenemes III	1859–1814	
13th Dynasty	**1801–1648**	

Second Intermediate Period: 1648–1540 BC

	Collapse of central authority.
14th Dynasty, and the (Hyksos) 15th and 16th Dynasties	All in Lower Egypt; introduction of the chariot by the Hyksos.

17th Dynasty		Contemporaneous with the Hyksos but ruling at Thebes.

New Kingdom: 1540–1069 BC

	BC	Period of power, luxury and cosmopolitanism.
18th Dynasty	**1540–1296**	Period of greatest contribution to the splendour of Thebes and Karnak.
Amosis I	1540–1525	Expels Hyksos; establishes royal residence and religious and political capital at Thebes.
Amenophis I	1525–1504	
Tuthmosis I	1504–1492	Burials begin at Valley of the Kings.
Tuthmosis II	1492–1479	
Hatshepsut	1479–1457	
Tuthmosis III	1479–1425	Struggle with Hatshepsut; after her passing, he lays foundation of Asian and African empire.
Amenophis II	1427–1401	
Tuthmosis IV	1401–1391	
Amenophis III	1391–1353	Apogee of New Kingdom opulence.
Amenophis IV (Akhenaten)	1353–1337	Assault on priesthood of Amun; establishes worship of the Aten.
Smenkhkere	1338–1336	
Tutankhamun	1336–1327	Return to orthodoxy.
Ay	1327–1323	
Horemheb	1323–1295	Military dictatorship.
19th Dynasty	**1295–1186**	Restoration of royal power.
Ramses I	1295–1294	
Seti I	1294–1279	New building work in Old Kingdom style.
Ramses II	1279–1213	Prodigious builder, e.g. Rammesseum and Abu Simbel.
Merneptah	1213-1203	Considered, along with Ramses II, possible pharaoh of the Exodus.
20th Dynasty	**1186–1069**	Dislocations as Egypt enters Iron Age.
Ramses III	1184–1153	Defeats Sea Peoples; succeeded by incompetent rulers.
Ramses VI	1143–1136	
Herihor	1098–1090	Priest-pharaoh at Thebes; rival ruler at Tanis.

Late Dynastic Period: 1069–332 BC

	BC	Period of decline; often foreign rule.
21st Dynasty	**1069–945**	Capital at Tanis.

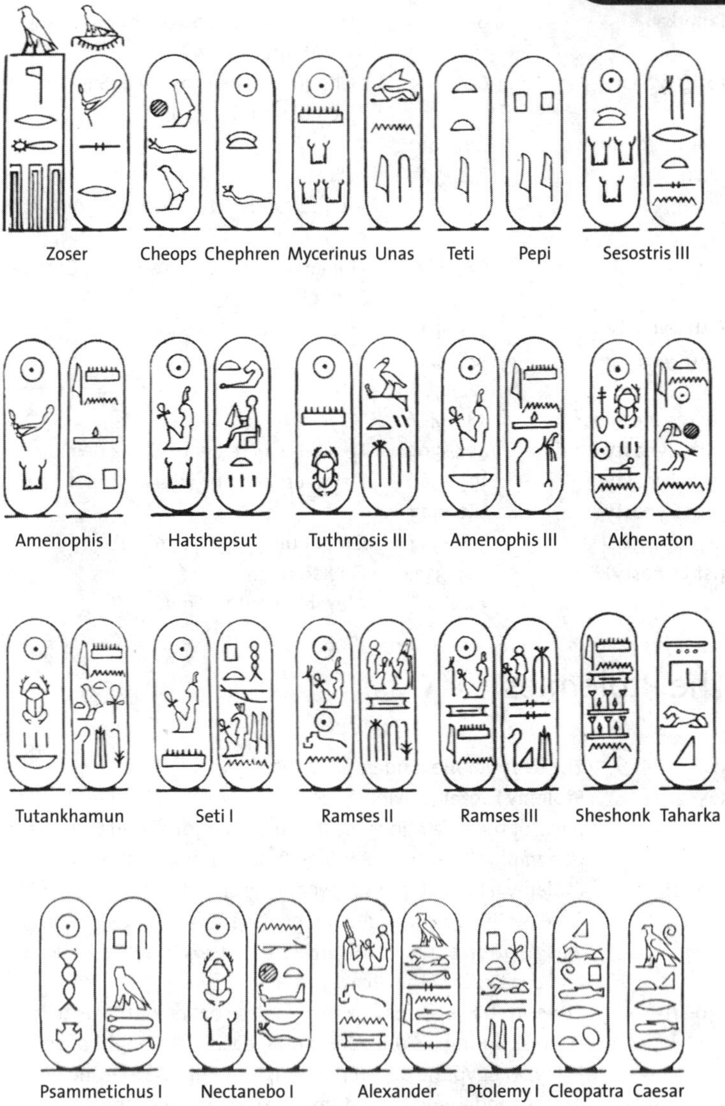

	BC	
22nd Dynasty	**945–745**	Warriors of Libyan origin; capital at Tanis.
Sheshonk I	945	Loots Jerusalem (I Kings 14, 25–26).
23rd Dynasty	**745–718**	Ethiopian kings control Upper Egypt.
24th Dynasty	**718–712**	Ethiopian kings control all Egypt.

	BC	
25th Dynasty	**712–663**	
Taharka	695–671	Ethiopian king defeated by Assyrians who sack Memphis and Thebes.
26th Dynasty	**663–525**	Delta rulers, their capital at Sais; Assyrians ejected with Greek help.
Psammetichus I	663–610	
Necho	610–595	Attempts to link Red Sea and the Mediterranean by canal; circumnavigation of Africa.
Psammetichus II	595–589	Nubian expedition recorded in Greek at Abu Simbel.
27th Dynasty	**525–404**	Persian rule.
Cambyses	525–522	
Darius I	522–486	
Xerxes the Great	486–466	
28th Dynasty	**404–399**	Persians ejected with Greek help.
29th Dynasty	**399–380**	Delta remains the vital centre of power.
30th Dynasty	**380–343**	
Nectanebos I	380–343	Great builder, e.g. at Philae.
31st Dynasty	**343–332**	Persian rule.
	332	Alexander enters Egypt.

The Ptolemies

BC	
323	The death of **Alexander**.
323–282	**Ptolemy I Soter** ('Saviour'). He added Cyrene, Palestine, Cyprus and parts of the Asia Minor coast to his realm, and at Alexandria, its geographical centre, he founded the Museion and Library.
282–46	**Ptolemy II Philadelphos** ('Lover of his Sister'). To the shock of the Greeks, though with Egyptian precedent, he married his sister. He was a patron of poets, first invited the Jews to settle in Alexandria, and constructed the Pharos.
246–21	**Ptolemy III Euergetes** ('Benefactor'). A soldier with a taste for science; during his rule Alexandria reached its height of splendour. In Upper Egypt he began the temple at Edfu. Abroad, he nearly reached India, and earned the title Conqueror of the World.
221–05	**Ptolemy IV Philopator** ('Lover of his Father'). Setback in Syria, revolt at Thebes; he began construction of the temples at Esna and Kom Ombo.
205–181	**Ptolemy V Epiphanes** ('God Manifest'). Child-king. Revolt at Alexandria, the interior in a state of anarchy, Epiphanes was placed under the protection of the Roman Senate, but by the time he came of age Egypt had lost most of her overseas possessions.

181–45 **Ptolemy VI Philometor** ('Lover of his Mother'). Seleucid invasion, Memphis captured, Egypt saved by Roman intervention.

145–4 **Ptolemy VII Neos Philopator**.

145–16 **Ptolemy VII Euergetes II**. Also known as Physcon ('Fatty'): when he came puffing along the quay to greet Scipio Africanus the Younger, the Roman sniggered, 'At least the Alexandrians have seen their king walk'. This Roman contempt applied to Egypt's sovereignty as well.

116–07, 88–80 **Ptolemy IX Soter II.** Competed with his brother, Ptolemy X Alexander I, for the throne, both borrowing money from the Romans to raise arms.

107–88 **Ptolemy X Alexander I**. To cover his debts he bequeathed Egypt to the Roman people, but as he had by then lost the throne his offer could not be accepted. But it was remembered.

80 **Ptolemy XI Alexander II**. Forced by Sulla to marry his (Ptolemy's) elderly stepmother, he then killed her and was killed in turn by an Alexandrian mob.

80–58, 55–51 **Ptolemy XII Neos Dionysos**. Also known as Nothos ('Bastard'), he rushed back from Syria so that the vacant throne should not attract Roman annexation, and bolstered his pedigree by adding Philopator (lover of his father) to his official names. He was the son of Ptolemy IX and father of Cleopatra VII. He built at Dendera, completed the temple at Edfu and left his mark on Philae. His reign was briefly interrupted by internal disruption.

51–49, 48–30 **Cleopatra VII**. Ruled jointly with her younger brother Ptolemy XIII who banished her (48 BC), but in the same year she received the support of Julius Caesar and Ptolemy was drowned in the Nile. Another brother, Ptolemy XIV, succeeded to the co-regency (47 BC), was assassinated (45 BC) at Cleopatra's instigation. Bore Caesar a son (47 BC), named Caesarion. He never ruled. Caesar assassinated (44 BC). Met Antony (41 BC). The battle of Actium (31 BC). Suicide of Antony and Cleopatra; Octavian (Augustus) makes Egypt a province of the Roman Empire (30 BC).

Roman and Byzantine Periods

BC

30 **Octavian (Augustus)** incorporates Egypt into the Roman Empire. The Roman emperors follow the example of the Ptolemies in representing themselves to the Egyptian people as successors of the pharaohs and in maintaining the appearance of a national Egyptian state.

AD

c. 30 Crucifixion of **Jesus of Nazareth** at Jerusalem.

45 Legend has **St Mark** make his first convert to Christianity in Egypt, a Jewish shoemaker of Alexandria.

AD	
98–117	**Trajan**. The canal connecting the Nile with the Red Sea reopened (AD 115).
117–38	**Hadrian**. Visits Egypt.
204	Edict prohibiting Roman subjects from embracing Christianity. The Delta is studded with Christian communities.
249–51	**Decius**. Severe persecutions.
c. 251–356	**St Antony** becomes the first hermit.
284–305	**Diocletian**. His accession marks the beginning of the 'Era of Martyrs' from which the Copts date their calendar. Persecution of the Christians.
312	**Constantine the Great** becomes emperor in the West.
313	**Edict of Milan**: Christianity tolerated throughout the Roman Empire.
324–37	Constantine the Great becomes sole ruler of the Roman Empire. Converts to Christianity on his death bed. Founds Constantinople (AD 330).
c. 330	Founding of the first monasteries at Wadi Natrun.
379–95	**Theodosius I**. Declares Christianity to be the religion of the Roman Empire (AD 392).
395	Partition of the Roman Empire into East (Constantinople) and West (Rome). Notional date for the beginning of the Byzantine Empire.
451	**Council of Chalcedon** declares monophysitism a heresy, effectively expelling the Egyptian (Coptic) Church from the main body of Christianity.
476	Fall of the Roman Empire in the West.
622	**Mohammed**'s flight from Mecca, the *hegira*, from which the Muslim calendar is reckoned. His death (AD 632).
636	Arabs defeat Byzantine army and take Damascus.
637	Arabs destroy the Sassanian (Persian) Empire.
638	Arabs take Jerusalem.
640–42	An Arab force under Amr enters Egypt. Fortress of Babylon taken (AD 641). Fustat founded; Alexandria surrenders and welcomes Arabs as liberators from Byzantine oppression (AD 642).

Arab and Turkish Periods

All dates are according to the Western calendar.

AD	
661	Murder of **Ali**, son-in-law of the Prophet; the caliphate passes to the Umayyads.
661–750	The **Umayyad caliphate**, with its capital at Damascus, rules over a united Arab empire stretching from the borders of China to the shores of the Atlantic, and up into France.

750–935	**Abbassids** and **Tulunids**. The Abbassids put a bloody end to the Umayyads in Syria and succeed to the caliphate, ruling the Arab world from Baghdad. Ibn Tulun, an Abbassid governor of Egypt, makes himself independent of Baghdad and establishes a dynasty (870–935).
c. 820	The Copts, resentful of their Arab conquerors, rise in revolt several times during the 8th and 9th centuries.
909	Establishment of **Fatimid caliphate** in North Africa.
935–69	A Turkish dynasty, the **Ikhshidids**, seizes power through the governorship.
969–1171	The **Fatimid caliphate** in Egypt, which now follows Shi'a rather than Sunni Islam. Cairo, its capital, founded (969). Al-Azhar founded (971). The Fatimid empire reaches its peak under Caliph Abu Mansur al-Aziz (975–96). He introduces the practice of importing slave troops, the forerunners of the Mamelukes. His successor, al-Hakim (996–1021), is an all-powerful psychotic; the decline of the Fatimid empire begins with his death.
1055	The **Seljuq Turks** take Baghdad, leading to a resurgence of Sunni Islam in Iraq, Syria and Iran.
1099	The **Crusaders** take Jerusalem.
1171–1250	The **Ayyubids**. The dynasty of Saladin, a Kurd from Iraq. He converts Egypt back to Sunni Islam. Drives the Crusaders from Jerusalem (1187). The Mamelukes rise to power during the rule of Shagarat al-Durr (1249–57).
1250–1382	The **Bahri Mamelukes**. The most celebrated of these Mameluke sultans are Baybars (1260–77); Qalaun (1279–90) and al-Nasr (1309–40), both of whose beautiful mausolea are on Sharia Muizz in Cairo; and al-Hassan (1347–51, 1354–61), builder of the great madrasa bearing his name. During early 14th century, severe persecution of Christians who until this time are still perhaps half the population; mass conversions to Islam follow.
1382–1517	The **Burgi Mamelukes**. The most celebrated of these Mameluke sultans are Barquq (1382–89, 1390–98), whose mosque is on Sharia Muizz, his mausoleum in the City of the Dead in Cairo; Baybars (1422–38), whose mausoleum is in the City of the Dead; Qaytbey (1468–95), known for his fortress on the site of the Pharos in Alexandria, and his mausoleum in the City of the Dead; and al-Ghuri (1500–16) whose monuments stand near Al-Azhar. Tumanbay (1515–17) was the last of the Burgi sultans; he was hanged three times by the Turks outside Bab Zuwayla in Cairo.
1517	The **Rule of the Ottoman Turks** begins in Egypt and continues, if only nominally, until 1914.

The Modern Period

1798–1801	**French occupation of Egypt**. Napoleon lands at Alexandria; Battle of the Pyramids; Battle of the Nile (1798). Napoleon departs from Egypt (1799). A British army compels the French to evacuate the country (1801).
1805	**Mohammed Ali** becomes viceroy of Egypt and after massacring the Mamelukes (1811) becomes, effectively, the independent ruler of Egypt, establishing a dynasty that was to end with Farouk.
1822	Champollion deciphers hieroglyphics.
1869	Opening of the **Suez Canal** during the reign of Ismail.
1882	Nationalist uprising led by Arabi. British occupation of Egypt begins.
1883–1907	Evelyn Baring (Lord Cromer) is British consul in Egypt and effective ruler of the country.
1902	British complete construction of dam at Aswan.
1914	Britain declares Egypt to be a **British Protectorate**.
1918	Saad Zaghloul, nationalist leader, demands British withdrawal.
1922	British recognize Egypt as a sovereign state, but maintain an army in Egypt.
1936	**Anglo-Egyptian Treaty**, formally ending British occupation. British army withdraws, except from the Canal Zone.
1939–45	Egypt nominally neutral during the Second World War, but British Army invited to return to fight the encroaching Germans. **Battle of el Alamein** (1942); Rommel repulsed.
1948	End of British Mandate for Palestine. Establishment of the state of Israel. Arab-Israeli war; Arab debacle. Resentful of political corruption, **Gamal Abdel Nasser** (1918–70) gathers round him a group of dissident army officers.
1952	25 January – British soldiers kill several Egyptian police in the Canal Zone. 26 January – **rioting** in Cairo at British action and Egyptian government's inaction. 23 July – Nasser's group stages a **coup** and parliamentary government is overthrown. 26 July – **King Farouk abdicates** and leaves the country.
1953	Egypt, now a military dictatorship, is declared a republic.
1954	**Nasser** becomes head of state.
1954–56	British evacuate the Canal Zone.
1956	United States cancels loan to Egypt for construction of the High Dam at Aswan. Nasser **nationalizes the Suez Canal** to use its revenues to pay for the High Dam's construction. Without the British in the Canal Zone to serve as a buffer, Israel fears an Egyptian attack and lays plans to invade **Sinai**, in which Britain and France join, their troops landing along the Suez Canal. American pressure forces Britain, France and Israel to withdraw, hugely boosting Nasser's standing in the Arab world.

1961	Nasser introduces sweeping socialist measures, limiting incomes, nationalizing banks and the cotton industry, further redistributing land.
1967	The June '**Six Day War**'. After threats from Egypt, which masses its army in Sinai and blocks the Straits of Tiran, Israel attacks and defeats Egypt, occupies all of Sinai. The Suez Canal is blocked.
1970	Nasser dies. **Anwar Sadat** becomes president.
1971	Egypt's official name becomes the Arab Republic of Egypt (ARE).
1973	October – Egyptian forces cross the Canal and briefly drive back the Israeli army, but the Israelis quickly recover, cross the Canal and march on Cairo, stopping only as a result of a ceasefire organized by the United States. Israeli forces continue to occupy the Gaza Strip and most of Sinai.
1975	Suez Canal reopened.
1977	**Sadat visits Jerusalem** in a dramatic peace bid.
1980	Egypt and Israel exchange ambassadors.
1981	6 October – **Sadat assassinated** by Islamic fundamentalists. **Hosni Mubarak** becomes president later that month.
1982	In accordance with its peace treaty with Egypt, Israel evacuates Sinai.
1988	Egyptian novelist **Naguib Mahfouz** wins the Nobel Prize for Literature.
1991	A start is made towards the liberalization and privatization of the Egyptian economy.
1993	September – Israel and the Palestine Liberation Organisation sign the Oslo Accords; they agree upon mutual recognition and begin the peace process in which Egypt plays an important part. But funded by oil money from the Gulf states, Hamas, an Islamist political and military organization dedicated to the destruction of Israel and the killing of all Jews, uses terror to undermine the Oslo accords.
1997	As Egypt's population reaches 65 million, Mubarak launches the **New Valley** scheme which is to draw water from Lake Nasser and bring huge areas of the Western Desert to life. In November Islamic terrorists murder 58 foreign tourists in Luxor.
2001	On **11 September** Al Qaeda suicide crews hijack American airliners and use them as flying bombs to destroy the World Trade Center in New York and attack the Pentagon in Washington DC, killing about 3,000 people. The head of Al Qaeda is Osama Bin Laden from Saudi Arabia, and his right-hand man is Ayman el Zawahari, a surgeon who had previously lived in the upper-class Cairo suburb of Maadi, and was leader of Egypt's fundamentalist terror group Islamic Jihad (which assassinated Anwar Sadat). The pilot of the first plane to hit the World Trade Center is Mohammed Atta, the son of a prosperous Cairo lawyer.

2002	Evoking the glories of Alexandria's ancient past and in an attempt to give the city a future, the **Bibliotheca Alexandrina**, the new Alexandria library, is opened with the idea that it should link Egypt with the wider Mediterranean world.
2004	Ayman Nour, a journalist, founds the liberal and secular **al-Ghad (Tomorrow) Party**. The funeral of **Yasser Arafat**, president of the Palestinian Authority, is held in Cairo before burial in the West Bank; he is succeeded by **Mahmoud Abbas**.
2005 May	Referendum vote backs a constitutional amendment allowing multiple candidates to stand in presidential elections.
2005 Sept	Hosni Mubarak wins a fifth consecutive term in Egypt's first contested **presidential race**. In an election plagued with low turnout and accusations of vote rigging, Mubarak takes 88 per cent of the vote. Ayman Nour, leader of the al-Ghad (Tomorrow) Party comes second with 7 per cent of the vote, though independent observers say his true figure is more like 13 per cent. Mubarak becomes the longest ruling leader of Egypt since Mohammed Ali.
2005 Dec	Ayman Nour is jailed for five years on spurious charges of having forged documents allowing him to establish the al-Ghad Party. In parliamentary elections Mubarak's National Democratic Party and its allies retain their large parliamentary majority, but **Muslim Brotherhood** supporters, elected as independents, win a record 20 per cent of seats.
2006 Aug	Death of novelist and Nobel Laureate Naguib Mahfouz.
2006 Nov	Egypt is developing a domestic **nuclear programme** to diversify energy sources, the International Atomic Energy Agency (IAEA) reports.
2007 April	**Amnesty International** criticizes Egypt's record on torture and illegal detention.
2007 Oct	Independent opposition newspapers protest against **government harassment** after seven journalists are imprisoned and an editor is put on trial.
2008 Mar	Al-Dustur newspaper editor Ibrahim Eissa is sentenced to six months in jail for reporting rumours about President Mubarak's health.
2008 April	Over 800 members of the Muslim Brotherhood are arrested in a crackdown on the organization's funding. Military courts sentence 25 leading Muslim Brotherhood members to jail terms.
2008 Nov	Egypt's **population** unofficially estimated at 76 million. With tight security measures in force throughout the country, **tourism** to Egypt reaches record levels.

Topics

The Egyptian Condition 42
Problems and Changes 42
Homeless Children 44
Islam 44
The Copts 45
Revolution in Egypt's Museums 47
Egypt's Grand Hotels 48

03

The Egyptian Condition

About 10,000 years ago a dramatic change in climate caused the once fertile lands of northern Africa and the Middle East to turn to dust. Rock drawings in the Sahara depict ancient man hunting herbivores where now there is only sand. The inhabitants of this great belt of arid land migrated towards the few remaining rivers.

The Nile provided water and its annual flood covered the fields with rich alluvial soil. The ancient Egyptians called their country 'The Black Land', and the Nile valley and the Delta is still today the most fertile land in the world. Were it not for the existence of the Nile, no part of Egypt would be capable of agriculture. But it was not entirely a gift. The river had to be regulated, swamps drained, canals dug, fields planted and irrigated, the entire complex system maintained. To this task the fellahin gave their unremitting labour, and the state provided direction.

During the Ptolemaic period Egypt reached a level of prosperity and population that it was not to enjoy again until the 19th century when the dynasty of Mohammed Ali reversed the country's long decline under Arab and Turkish rule. In 1882 Egypt's population stood at just under seven million – equivalent to the number of Cleopatra's subjects. But since then, the twelve-fold increase in population has worked against economic advance.

Though Egypt is larger than any European country except Russia, 93 per cent of its area is dry and barren desert where only a few oasis-dwellers and nomadic Bedouin can survive. In pharaonic times Egypt was likened to a lotus plant. The river was the stem, the Fayyum the bud, the Delta the flower. Within this figure of fertility today lives 95 per cent of the nation's population, its density one of the highest in the world.

Problems and Changes

Since completion of the Aswan High Dam in 1971 the Nile no longer floods. Instead the river flows evenly throughout the year, the harvests have multiplied, deserts have been brought to life. And Egypt gained the energy that would lead, it was hoped, to wholesale industrialization, releasing the fellahin from their drudgery, the nation from its poverty.

But as fast as the High Dam has helped bring new land under cultivation, other land has been swallowed by urban expansion. Fellahin seeking an improved existence have been abandoning their diminishing plots in the desperate hope of a better life in the cities, which now hold the majority of Egypt's population. In the 1970s Egypt was self-sufficient in food and even had a thriving export trade; now two-thirds of foodstuffs are imported.

Before Nasser's overthrow of the constitutional monarchy and Egypt's elected parliamentary government in 1952, foreign exchange reserves were $25 billion in today's terms. Now Egypt's national debt exceeds $30 billion. In consequence Egypt has become dependent on outside sources of finance. Of crucial importance are World Bank, International Monetary Fund and foreign government (principally

United States) loans, on the repayments of which Egypt routinely defaults. And then there is foreign aid; for example Egypt is the second largest recipient of United States foreign aid, receiving $2.2 billion a year as against the $3 billion a year given by the US to Israel.

Egypt's population numbers about 85 million, the largest in the Arab world, and is increasing by 1.5 million every year. Though the birth rate has been falling, it has not been falling fast enough: only 35 per cent of married women practise birth control, and the earning potential of additional children is seen as a way of augmenting family income and providing for parents in old age. Meanwhile, the death rate has fallen even faster, a reflection of improved health services. The strain that the rising population puts on Egypt's food supplies, housing, jobs and services – indeed on its political stability – is a part of the country's problem.

Whatever Nasser's nationalist ideals, his socialist and centralizing policies added to the problem. During the 1950s and 1960s land and wealth were redistributed, and industry and commerce were nationalized, but the creation of new wealth was neglected. Free education was given to all and every university graduate was guaranteed a government job by law. The result was a collapse in investment and a bloated, inefficient bureaucracy. The wait for a guaranteed job rose to six years, and the proportion of the population in employment fell. Military spending increased dramatically, while spending on education collapsed. The standard of teaching is now so low that in some places free education is not worth having. There is a grave housing crisis, illustrated by those millions Cairenes who live in the city's necropolises among the dead.

A quarter of a million foreigners, their families resident in Egypt for generations, were forced to leave the country in the decade or so following Nasser's 1952 coup d'état, most of them highly skilled. In recent years millions of Egyptians have followed in their footsteps, seeking opportunities in the Gulf and the West. Under the monarchy the 2,000 richest people owned as much land as the 1.5 million poorest fellahin. Now the fellahin are deserting the land if they can, and if they can find a factory job they will earn in a lifetime only as much as Egypt's top 100,000 people spend on a luxury car.

Agriculture remains a major pillar of the Egyptian economy, and its main crops are cotton, sugar cane, maize, rice and wheat, while the raising of cattle and poultry is increasing. Nowadays, however, the service sector employs the bulk of the working population. But the country's main foreign currency earners – tourism, oil, Suez Canal fees and remittances from Egyptians working abroad – are all peculiarly sensitive to political conditions in the Middle East.

Since the early 1980s, under pressure from foreign lenders, Egypt has moved towards abandoning all subsidies and privatized almost all industries and commercial organizations, while the government has encouraged massive investment in communications and physical infrastructure. The result has been a promising boom in economic growth. But the transition from traditional or state-guaranteed employment to a modern market economy has been a source of social anxiety, reflected in a growing conservatism, widely expressed in religious and often highly politicized fundamentalist terms, but also in the widespread use of drugs, amounting to about eight million addicts according to the Egyptian authorities.

Homeless Children

According to Egyptian experts reporting to the United Nations or writing in *Al Ahram*, over two million children are homeless and living in the streets, sleeping under bridges and in train stations, mostly in Cairo and Alexandria. Some have escaped parental abuse and others have been forced to leave home and do whatever it takes to survive. The average age is thirteen, and about one in ten are girls. The children fall prey to criminal gangs and drug dealers; some are killed, half the boys and nearly all the girls are raped, and the girls are forced to turn to prostitution. To cope with the hunger, pain and violence they experience on the streets, the children turn to drugs; sniffing glue is preferred because it is cheap and the effects are long lasting.

Interest in homeless children in Egypt only began in 1988 with the formation of two NGOs, one of them by a retired British teacher. They have proved more effective than anything the government has attempted. Until recently the government only took notice when children broke the law; then it sent them to penal institutions from which they often escaped or never appeared again. Now a change in the law means that children are no longer defined as deviants and criminals, rather as victims and at-risk. It is a small step in the right direction.

But as one Egyptian commentator wrote in *Al Ahram*: 'Homeless children are not the only problem in our streets. Traffic is a mess, bullying is common, and sexual harassment widespread. Meanwhile, our police are busy protecting the government, its officials and buildings. Our police should be maintaining the safety of citizens, but it is busy doing other things. This is why new forms of ill-behaviour emerge everyday.'

Islam

The principal belief of Islam is the existence of one God, the same God worshipped by Christians and Jews, whom the Muslims call Allah. 'Islam' means 'submission'. 'Muslim' means one who submits to monotheism as interpreted by the religion's founder, Mohammed (AD 570–632).

Muslims must hold six beliefs: that Allah exists, is unique and is omnipotent; that the Angels of Allah are his perfect servants, and intercede for man and are his guardians; that there is only one true religion and the Koran is the only tangible word of Allah; that there have been many prophets of Allah, among them Ibrahim (Abraham), Nuh (Noah), Musa (Moses), Isa (Jesus) and Mohammed who was the last, his message uncorrupted; that everyone will live in eternity and will be judged; and that whatever has been or will come has been predestined by Divine Will and it is forbidden to question or investigate this point.

There are five practical devotions, the five Pillars of Faith, that all Muslims must perform: pronounce publicly that 'I bear witness that there is no god but Allah and

Mohammed is His Prophet'; pray at five specific times of day (noon, afternoon, sunset, night and daybreak); pay a tithe, which is then dispersed to the poor, to needy debtors, for the ransom of captives, to travellers, and for the defence of Islam; fast during the month of Ramadan; and at least once in a lifetime make a pilgrimage to Mecca.

In addition, Islam is based on laws found in the Koran, in the Sunna (the actions of the Prophet), decided by the unanimous agreement of Muslim scholars (*Ijma*), and arrived at by reasoned analogy (*Qiyas*) – each of descending authority.

Mohammed was a merchant in Arabia. He often contemplated in the desert and at the age of 40 had a vision of the Angel Gabriel who commanded him to proclaim monotheism to the pagan Arabian tribes. In Arabic, 'to proclaim' is *Qur'an*, and so the Koran is the word of Allah as given to Mohammed. The merchants of Mecca, concerned by the unsettling effects of this new religion, drove Mohammed out of the city in 622. His flight (the hegira, though literally this means 'withdrawal of affection') from Mecca to Medina, where Islam first took root, is the event from which the Islamic calendar begins.

The Arab conquest of Egypt in ad 640–2 introduced Islam to the country, though until the 11th century the majority of the population remained Christian. Today nearly 90 per cent of the Egyptian population is Muslim, adherents of the Sunni sect.

The Copts

About 95 per cent of Christian Egyptians are Coptic Orthodox, and these represent about ten per cent of the Egyptian population as a whole.

Copt comes from the Greek word for Egypt, Aigyptos, and those who remain Copts today, having never intermarried with later peoples, can lay claim to being the pure successors of the ancient Egyptians. But it is also true that 90 per cent of Muslim Egyptians were once Copts, making it impossible to distinguish any physical difference between the two, though some Egyptians will say Copts have higher cheekbones or almond-shaped eyes.

Copts may choose to distinguish themselves by wearing a cross around their necks, for example. Some, usually fellahin or among the lower urban classes, have a cross tattooed on the inside of the right wrist – to ward off evil spirits or, in the past, to commit them to their faith during persecution. One possible identifier is choice of name: for example, George (Girgis), Antony (Antunius) and Ramses; though Gamal, Nasser and Anwar could be either Coptic or Muslim. And for both groups the mother tongue is Arabic. In fact the difference between Coptic and Muslim Egyptians is neither ethnic nor cultural, except that the Copts adhere to the old religion.

That Christianity was introduced to Egypt by St Mark is entirely legendary. Nevertheless it almost certainly was introduced during the 1st century AD and came from Jerusalem, appearing first among the Jewish population of Alexandria and then spreading among the Greeks of both the city and the country.

There is evidence that at the beginning of the 3rd century Christianity had taken root among native Egyptians, and by AD 300 most of the Bible had been translated from Greek into Coptic (antedating the translation of the Bible into Latin by a century). With the end of the Roman persecutions early in the 4th century there was a sudden flowering of Christianity in which, as a walk through the Coptic Museum in Cairo shows, was expressed in a vigorous folk art. Expressed in the form of monasticism, Egyptian Christianity also made a deeply spiritual impact on the wider world.

But political and theological disputes between Alexandria and Constantinople facilitated the Arab conquest of Egypt during 640–2. The Copts, that is the Egyptian people, several times rose in revolt against the Arab occupation during the 8th and 9th centuries, and though some converted to Islam, the majority of Egyptians remained Christians until the 11th century. During the following centuries Mameluke misrule combined with the accelerating impoverishment of the country turned sultans and mobs alike against the Copts, who suffered massacre, the widespread destruction of their churches and the loss of official positions. Under such conditions there was little opportunity to develop Christian thought; instead, the need was for unquestioning faith and social solidarity, even as the Copts slowly accepted a new culture.

As Arab civilization from Baghdad to Cordoba achieved its apogee in the 9th, 10th and 11th centuries, men of talent and ambition gravitated in its direction. Coptic artists began to serve the tastes of their Muslim patrons, and Arabic became the language of administration and learning. Sometime between the 11th and 13th centuries the Coptic language, repository of the demotic tongue of pharaonic times, ceased to be spoken and survives now only in church liturgy.

Egypt's contact with European influences in the 19th century improved the condition of the Copts, who went on to play an important role in and to benefit from the growing secular nationalist movement. Over the same period the Coptic Church has gradually reformed itself, initially to meet the challenge of foreign missionaries. Under the last two popes especially, Kirollos VI and Shenouda III, the Church has experienced a renaissance, attracting highly educated young men into the monasteries and the hierarchy, and reaching out into the community with schools and welfare programmes.

Today, Copts officially enjoy all civil, political and religious rights and occupy high posts in government, the military and in business. Boutros Boutros Ghali, recently Secretary General of the United Nations and formerly Egyptian foreign minister and deputy prime minister, is a Copt (and his wife, incidentally, is Jewish). Naguib Sawiris, the man behind much of Egypt's telecommunications industry, ranks sixty in Forbes' rich list where his fortune is valued at $12.7 billion.

It is not unusual when walking around Cairo or elsewhere in Egypt to come upon Christian celebrations, the streets festooned with decorations and lights, pictures and icons of Christ and Mary and the various saints. If you are in Egypt for the Coptic Christmas (7 January) or the Coptic Easter (moveable), it is worthwhile visiting a Coptic church for midnight mass (arrive no later than 11pm) on the eve.

Revolution in Egypt's Museums

Revolutionary changes are taking place among Egypt's museums, with new ones being built, old ones being refurbished, and collections being redistributed, as the country creates a variety of state of the art and accessible institutions for displaying its thousands of years of history. The aim is to make a fresh appeal to ordinary Egyptians and to foreign tourists alike, getting away from the idea of museums being dusty warehouses and presenting them as beautifully designed and engaging experiences. The plan involves five categories of museums, each fulfilling a special purpose.

First, there are the new site museums. Built near the entrances of specific archaeological sites, site museums will house artefacts found during local excavations, with a special focus on recent discoveries. The museums are designed so that upon entry, visitors are immediately provided with information about the history of the material they are about to see. The concept has been inaugurated by the new Imhotep Museum at Saqqara, which tells the story of the site throughout the pharaonic period. It also has a special room in honour of Jean-Philippe Lauer, the Egyptologist who dedicated his life to the restoration of the Zoser pyramid complex.

Second, there are the specialty museums, which will focus on the history and functions of specific aspects of Egyptian civilization. One of these is the new museum at Amarna, on the east bank of the Nile near Minya. Shaped like a pyramid, the museum concentrates on the history of the city of Akhenaten. Visitors learn about Akhenaten and Nefertiti and their role in the religious revolution that brought their god, the Aten, to prominence. The artefacts come mainly from Amarna and other sites where Akhenaten built temples for the worship of the Aten.

Third, there are the museums covering specific periods of Egyptian history, the Greek and Roman, the Coptic, and the Islamic – periods often overlooked by visitors to Egypt. To make them more appealing, the Coptic and Islamic museums in Cairo have recently been refurbished, their displays and their lighting much improved. The same is happening to the Graeco-Roman Museum in Alexandria. Libraries and educational facilities are being developed for each museum.

Fourth are the civilization museums which cover the entire span of Egyptian history, from the prehistoric to the modern day. Displaying regional artefacts, these museums highlight the history of the areas in which they are located: Aswan, Sohag, Hurghada, El-Arish, Suez, Alexandria, Qena and Sharm el-Sheikh. They focus on how ordinary Egyptians, not just the élite, participated in ancient society.

Fifth are the new or refurbished museums of the Cairo area. Collectively known as the Great Cairo Museums, they include the Grand Museum of Egypt, being built out by the Pyramids, the National Civilization Museum in Fustat, and the Egyptian Museum at Tahrir Square. Each museum will have something special. The centrepiece of the Grand Museum will be the 5,000 artefacts from the tomb of Tutankhamun, but its collections will go far beyond this, and will illustrate the historical, cultural and territorial evolution of pharaonic Egypt. The National Museum of Egyptian Civilization at Fustat illustrates the entire scope of Egyptian history, and it will also house the royal mummies. The hundred-year-old Egyptian Museum at Midan el Tahrir will be entirely refurbished and brought into the 21st century to tell the story of pharaonic art. A new wing on the west side will have two floors underground, where a cafeteria, bookshop and children's museum will be housed. Galleries devoted to the history of Egyptology will showcase major discoveries of pharaonic monuments.

The Egyptologist Zahi Hawass, secretary-general of the Supreme Council of Antiquities, explains the thinking that has gone into this museum programme. 'Tourists in general come to Egypt and stay for a short time and visit perhaps one museum. In this new era of museums, one of our principal goals will be to encourage tourists to visit many of these new museums, which will enhance their experience of Egypt enormously. We are reaching out to native Egyptians with new ways and opportunities to learn about their past, providing them with new hope and new skills for the future. By enhancing the aesthetic and informational value of our museums, we are offering unforgettable experiences to both foreign tourists and Egyptian visitors.'

Egypt's Grand Hotels

One of the glories of Egypt was its grand hotels, cavernous places with louvred doors and mosquito nets over the beds, offering an atmosphere of worn elegance. Too many of these have disappeared, replaced by modern nondescript hotels. Where grand hotels survive they have lost much of their old Egyptian charm, but they are worth knowing about all the same.

The Windsor in Cairo survives in its full decrepitude, the atmosphere literally peeling off the walls. The lift is more like one of those medieval iron cages in which bodies were hung from a gibbet to rot, and the most modern thing in the place is a calendar advertising BOAC. With an eye for a time warp, Michael Palin stayed here while making his own attempt at travelling *Around the World in 80 Days* (alas, his visit has spurred the Windsor to tart itself up a bit). British publishers, known for their parsimony, also take rooms here. They and other peculiar people gather in the comfortable old bar-cum-lounge, one of the friendliest in town.

In truth, the Windsor was never grand, rather solidly serviceable like a British railway station hotel, but it has bearing. In the 1920s Baedeker ranked it just after Shepheard's Hotel, which was burnt down during nationalist riots in 1952. The present-day Shepheard's carries the name but none of the character of the original.

But the Mena House, out by the Pyramids, has an authentic pedigree, built by the Khedive Ismail as a hunting lodge, then put into service as a rest house for the Empress Eugénie, wife of Napoleon III, when she came to Egypt to open the Suez Canal. Since then it has been a hotel, though only the wing directly facing the Pyramids is original. This is now taken up with 'honeymoon suites', where during nuptial interludes you can step out onto your balcony and ogle at more ancient wonders.

Churchill's meeting with Roosevelt at the Mena House late in 1943 to plan the D-Day landings at Normandy the following year is well known. Less celebrated is the time when King Farouk picked Churchill's pocket. It was August 1942, between the first and second battles of Alamein, and an anxious Churchill had come to give the campaign some zip by replacing General Auchinleck with General Montgomery. Farouk invited the British prime minister to the Mena House for dinner. While sitting next to one another, Churchill discovered that his pocket watch, a gift from Queen Anne to his ancestor the Duke of Marlborough for winning the Battle of Blenheim, was missing. It must have seemed an ill omen, but after much searching, Farouk 'found' it; he had, in fact, been taking pickpocketing lessons from a master thief.

In Luxor you should book into a Nile-facing room at the Winter Palace, preferably making sure that you have a balcony on which to breakfast or enjoy an evening drink. Built in 1886, care was taken with the restorations in 1993 not to spoil its atmosphere or its architectural details. A carriage drive sweeps up to the main entrance through which you enter a voluminous lobby from which ascends a grand staircase with Art Nouveau balusters. Curling up past towering windows through which you can already see the palms which fill the garden beyond, it is a staircase that invites an easy pace and elegance.

In the old days, the hotel closed for the summer; winter was the season, 'its portico heavily embowered with verdure, its terrace overhung by palms', as Olivia Manning described it during the war years in *The Levant Trilogy*. Now it is open throughout the year, and though you can still sit out front drinking tea, in summer you can pass through the garden filled with birds and monkeys and sit half immersed around a bar that rises like an island from the swimming pool.

Also in Luxor there is the clapped-out Luxor Hotel. It is the oldest hotel in Luxor, older than the Winter Palace. Owing to a legal dispute with the Egyptian government, nobody has spent a piastre on the upkeep of the hotel for decades and it has gone to wrack and ruin. Nor does it give any impression of being open for business. Roll up from the railway station at night and you are unlikely to find a single light burning in any of the rooms. Their shutters hang limply open. But there will be a dim light at the entrance as though to keep the snakes away. A phantom personage appears and leads you along silent and gloomy corridors to a big high-ceilinged room with a huge balcony overlooking the Temple of Luxor. This and the room next door are usually the only rooms prepared for visitors, and suddenly you realize that you are the only people staying at the Luxor Hotel. It is a spooky and absurd experience. Nothing works. There is no kitchen. Everything is impromptu and charming. For breakfast the phantom staff have to run out across the road and buy some eggs and coffee and bread and butter; in the afternoon you return from a gruelling tour of West Bank tombs to find your bed decorated with roses from the garden. The Luxor Hotel is broken down, but when they fix it up they will have spoilt it. So now is the time to savour a hotel as it was a century ago, give or take some dust and peeling paint and broken windows and threadbare carpets.

The finest of all hotels in Egypt is the Cataract at Aswan, mounted upon a granite outcrop opposite the southern tip of Elephantine Island. At the hotel's official opening in 1902, the *Daily Telegraph* described its dining room as 'unmatched even in Europe'. Beautifully restored, the splendour of the Cataract makes it one of the chief sights of Aswan. Nor is there a more magical place than its terrrace from which to fascinate yourself with the movement of feluccas and the shifting of colours on the Nile.

Planning Your Trip

When to Go 52
Climate 52
Festivals 53
Tourist Information 54
Embassies and Consulates 54
Entry Formalities 55
Disabled Travellers 56
Money and Banks 56
Getting There 58
Getting Around 59
Nile Cruises 61
Where to Stay 62
Tour and Cruise Operators 63

04

When to Go

Climate

In the days of leisurely travel it was often the custom to spend an entire winter, from November to May, in Egypt. This was 'the season', climatically, socially, and for those in search of dry mild conditions conducive to relief from asthma, chronic bronchitis, rheumatoid arthritis, gout, Bright's disease and other diseases of the kidneys. The modern visitor is unlikely to come to Egypt for medicinal reasons, nor to stay so long.

Late autumn through to early spring is still the most comfortable period within which to visit most of the country, particularly Cairo and southwards into Upper Egypt, though the reverse is true of the Mediterranean and Red Sea coasts (for those bent on swimming or diving, the best times are summer or early autumn when the sea is still warm and the crowds have gone). Only a thin strip of the northern coastline shares in a Mediterranean climate, giving Alexandria an annual rainfall of 180mm, most of this from December through to March when the city experiences cool, blustery and often stormy weather. This is true inland to Damanhur and Tanta in the Delta. But generally temperatures along the coast are moderated by the sea throughout the year, and are neither too cold nor too hot, except that Alexandria can become very humid in July and August. Farther inland Egypt is within the arid zone, with rainfall throughout most of the country well under 25mm a year.

Temperatures increase as you travel south, though in Cairo during December, January and February it can be chilly. Cairo can be very hot from June through to September, though the heat is often relieved by breezes from the north. It is hotter yet in Upper Egypt where summer can be reckoned from May through to October, but peak temperatures are to some extent compensated for by extremely

Average Temperatures (°C)

	Jan		Feb		Mar		April		May		June	
	min	max	min	max	min	max	min	max	min	max	min	max
Alexandria	9.3	18.3	9.7	19.2	11.2	21.0	13.5	23.6	16.7	26.5	20.2	28.2
Aswan	8.0	23.8	9.4	26.1	12.6	30.4	17.5	35.0	21.1	38.5	24.2	42.1
Cairo	8.6	19.1	9.3	20.7	11.2	23.7	13.9	28.2	17.4	32.4	17.9	34.5
Dakhla	4.6	21.5	6.1	23.9	9.7	27.9	14.4	33.0	19.6	37.4	22.4	38.8
Hurghada	9.6	20.6	9.9	20.9	12.3	23.0	16.1	26.0	20.7	29.6	23.5	31.4
Ismailia	8.2	20.4	9.1	21.7	11.0	23.9	13.6	27.6	17.3	32.1	20.2	34.8
Luxor	5.4	23.0	6.8	25.4	10.7	29.0	15.7	34.8	20.7	39.3	22.6	40.7
Mersa Matruh	8.1	18.1	8.4	18.9	9.7	20.3	11.8	22.7	14.5	25.5	18.2	27.8
Minya	3.9	20.6	5.4	22.5	7.8	25.4	11.7	30.2	16.7	35.4	18.8	36.3
Port Said	11.3	18.0	12.1	18.7	13.5	20.2	16.1	22.6	19.6	25.8	22.4	28.5
Siwa	4.1	19.7	5.7	21.8	8.2	25.0	12.1	39.9	16.8	34.3	19.2	37.1

	July		Aug		Sept		Oct		Nov		Dec	
	min	max	min	max	min	max	min	max	min	max	min	max
Alexandria	22.7	29.6	22.9	30.4	21.3	29.4	17.8	27.7	14.8	24.4	11.2	20.4
Aswan	24.5	41.2	24.7	41.3	22.2	39.6	19.3	36.6	14.5	20.2	9.9	25.5
Cairo	21.5	25.4	21.6	34.8	19.9	32.3	17.8	29.8	19.9	24.1	10.4	20.7
Dakhla	23.0	39.0	22.9	38.9	20.7	36.1	17.4	33.0	12.0	28.0	6.7	23.0
Hurghada	24.8	32.6	25.0	33.0	23.2	30.6	19.7	28.5	15.5	25.7	11.9	22.4
Ismalia	22.2	36.4	22.5	36.5	20.7	33.9	17.8	30.7	13.9	26.6	10.0	21.5
Luxor	23.6	40.8	23.5	41.0	21.5	38.5	17.8	35.1	12.3	29.6	7.7	24.8
Mersa Matruh	20.2	29.2	21.0	29.9	19.7	28.7	16.8	27.0	13.3	23.4	10.0	19.7
Minya	20.2	37.0	20.5	36.6	18.6	33.4	15.9	31.2	11.5	26.6	7.0	21.7
Port Said	24.1	30.4	24.9	30.9	23.9	29.2	21.8	27.4	18.4	24.0	12.7	19.9
Siwa	20.7	38.0	20.7	37.8	18.3	35.1	14.9	31.7	10.1	26.3	6.0	21.3

low humidity. From Cairo southwards at any time between March and May you may experience the *khamasin* ('fifty'), a hot dust- and sand-laden wind from the southwest which can be very unpleasant and can seem to last for 50 days. Everywhere in Egypt at any time of year, but mostly in the deserts, temperatures can fall off sharply at night.

But not too much emphasis should be laid on season, for a variety of reasons. Cairo and Upper Egypt are most visited from November to April and there is pressure on accommodation. From May to September prices are lower in Upper Egypt. Air conditioning is standard in all the better hotels. It can be very hot in Egypt, especially Upper Egypt, during summer, but seeing the sights early in the morning and late in the afternoon, and the extraordinary dryness of the air the farther south you go, can make your stay more agreeable. The proof is that Egypt has become a year-round destination.

Calendar of Events

National Holidays and Festivals

There are five secular holidays during the year, when banks, government offices, businesses and schools are closed.

25 April	Liberation of Sinai Day
1 May	Labour Day
23 July	Anniversary of the 1952 Revolution
6 October	Armed Forces Day
Monday after Coptic and Greek Orthodox Easter	Sham el Nessim, an ancient spring festival

Of more importance, however, are the various Muslim and Coptic holy days, and to understand these, something must be said about the Egyptian calendars.

Egyptian Calendars

Egypt uses three calendars: the Islamic, the Coptic and the Western. The Western calendar dates from the birth of Christ; the Coptic dates from AD 284, the accession of Diocletian, during whose reign the most ferocious Roman persecutions of the Christians, particularly in Egypt, occurred; while the Islamic calendar dates from the flight (*hegira*) of Mohammed from Mecca in AD 622. Both the Western and Coptic calendars are solar; the Islamic calendar is based on 12 lunar months and therefore rotates in relation to the other two, each Islamic year beginning 11 days sooner than the last.

If you want to know the equivalent Western date for an AH year (AH standing for Anno Hegirae, the number of years since Mohammed's flight from Mecca), you should use this simple formula:

1. Divide the Islamic year by 33 (the Islamic year is 11 days, or one thirty-third, shorter than a Western year).

2. Subtract the result of (1) from the Islamic year.

3. Add 622 to the result of (2) and this will give you the Western year.

For example:

1. AH 1431 divided by 33 = 43.

2. 1431 less 43 = 1388.

3. 1388 plus 622 = AD 2010.

In fact, AH 1426 begins in early December 2010.

Another point worth noting is that a day in the Islamic calendar begins at sundown. A consequence of this is that Islamic festivals start on the evening before you would expect if going by the Western calendar, that evening assuming as sacred a character as the following waking daylight period (compare Christmas Eve and Christmas Day in Western usage).

You will be relieved to learn, however, that in all official transactions in Egypt the Western calendar and method of reckoning the day are used. The Islamic and Coptic calendars only really come into their own at festivals.

The Islamic Calendar

Sequence of months		Duration (days)
1st	*Moharram*	30
2nd	*Safar*	29
3rd	*Rabei el Awal*	30
4th	*Rabei el Tani*	29
5th	*Gamad el Awal*	30
6th	*Gamad el Tani*	29
7th	*Ragab*	30

8th	*Shaaban*	29
9th	*Ramadan*	30
10th	*Shawal*	29
11th	*Zoul Qidah*	30
12th	*Zoul Hagga*	29 (30 in leap years)

Important Muslim Festivals

Ras el Sana el Hegira, the Islamic New Year, beginning on the first day of Moharram.

Moulid el Nabi, the Prophet's birthday, on the twelfth day of Rabei el Awal, marked in Cairo by a spectacular procession.

Ramadan, a month of fasting from dawn to sunset. As the last full meal is taken just before dawn, working hours are usually cut short to reduce afternoon effort to a minimum. Nothing is permitted to pass the lips during fasting hours nor is sexual intercourse allowed during sun up. Alcohol is not sold in Egypt during Ramadan, and while visitors are permitted to eat and smoke, you should not do so in the presence of fasting Muslims out of common courtesy. Interestingly, more food is consumed during Ramadan than at any other time of year, everyone making up at night for what they gave up during the day. Every Ramadan night, therefore, has the character of a festival. In 2010 the first day of Ramadan falls on 11 August.

Qurban Bairam, 10–13 Zoul Hagga, the month of the Pilgrimage. For days preceding the 10th, sheep, goats, cows and buffaloes fill the streets waiting to be slaughtered; on the 10th, throughout the residential areas of towns, they are killed and skinned – not for the squeamish.

Coptic festivals centring around Easter do not follow the Western (Gregorian) calendar. Other festivals fall on fixed dates: Christmas, 7 January; Epiphany, 19 January; the Annunciation, 21 March. A national holiday that is an important Coptic-pharaonic inheritance is Sham el Nessim ('sniffing the breeze'), which falls on the first Monday after Coptic Easter and during which the entire population of whatever religion takes a day off. This is a celebration of the advent of spring; families go out into their fields or gardens, or into the country, early in the morning and eat salted fish, onions and coloured eggs. The fish and onions are said to prevent disease, while the eggs symbolize life.

Tourist Information

In the UK: Egyptian State Tourist Office, 170 Piccadilly, London W1V 9EJ, **t** (020) 7493 5283, *www.egypt.travel*.

In the USA: **t** (877) 773-4978. Egyptian Tourist Authority, 630 Fifth Ave, New York, NY 10111, **t** (212) 332-2570; 645 N Michigan Ave, Chicago, IL 60611, **t** (312) 280-4666; 8383 Wilshire Blvd, Beverly Hills, CA 90211, **t** (310) 653-8815; *www.egypt.travel*.

In Egypt: the main Tourist Information Office, 5 Sharia Adli, Cairo, **t** (02) 2391 3454; at Ramses railway station, **t** (02) 2579 0767; and at the Pyramids, **t** (02) 3383 8823.

Misr Travel is the state-run tourist company. They are in business for themselves and so their advice is not necessarily impartial, but they can be helpful. **In the UK**: Old Inn House, First Floor, Suite D, 2 Carshalton Road, Sutton, SM1 4LE, **t** (020) 8643 2429, *info@misrtravel.co.uk*; **in the US**: 1270 Avenue of the Americas, Suite 604, New York, NY 10020, **t** (212) 332 2600 or **t** 800 223 4978, *info@misrtravel.org*; **Egypt head office**: 1 Sharia Talaat Harb, PO Box 1000, Cairo, **t** (02) 393 0010, *www.misrtravel.net*.

Otherwise, Egyptian embassies and consulates, and also offices of the national airline, Egyptair, may be able to provide basic information.

Information on the Internet

The **Egyptian Ministry of Tourism**, *www.touregypt.net*, and **The Egypt State Information Service**, *www.sis.gov.eg/En/Default.htm*, are good places to start.

Embassies and Consulates

For embassies in Egypt, *see* p.68.

Egyptian Embassies Abroad

USA

Embassy of Egypt: 3521 International Court, NW Washington, DC 20008, **t** (202) 895-5400

Consulate General of Egypt, Chicago: 500 N. Michigan Avenue, Suite 1900, Chicago, IL 60611, **t** (312) 828-9162

Consulate General of Egypt, Houston: 1990 Post Oak Boulevard, Suite 2180, Houston, TX 77056, **t** (713) 961-4915

Consulate General of Egypt, New York: 1110 Second Avenue, New York, NY 10022, **t** (212) 759-7120

Consulate General of Egypt, San Francisco: 3001 Pacific Avenue, San Francisco, CA 94115, **t** (415) 346-9700

United Kingdom

Egyptian Embassy: 26 South Street, London W1K 1DW, **t** (020) 7499 3304/2401

Egyptian Consulate, London: 2 Lowndes Street, London SW1X 9ET, **t** (020) 7235 9719

Australia

Egyptian Embassy: 1 Darwin Avenue, Yarralumla, Canberra, ACT 2600, **t** (61-2) 6273-4437/8

Egyptian Consulate, Sydney: Level 3, 241 Commonwealth Street, Surry Hills, Sydney 2010, **t** (61-2) 6273 4438

Canada

Egyptian Embassy: 454 Laurier Avenue East, Ottawa, Ontario K1N 6R3, **t** (613) 234-4931

Egyptian Consulate, Montreal: 1 Place Ville Marie, 2617 Montreal H3B 4S3, **t** (514) 866-8455

Ireland

Egyptian Embassy: 12 Clyde Road, Ballsbridge, Dublin 4, **t** (1) 660 6566

Entry Formalities

Passports and Visas

Note that the following information on passports, visas, customs and currency is subject to change and should be checked in advance.

Many visitors to Egypt can obtain a travel visa on arrival at Cairo, Alexandria, Luxor and Hurghada airports, among them travellers holding European Union, American, Canadian, Australian and New Zealand passports. No application form nor photograph is required; the cost is about $25. This visa is valid for one month.

Nationals of most other countries must obtain a visa in advance from an Egyptian consulate in their own country or en route. The process requires a photograph and application form, and can be done in person (usually within 24 hours) or by post (allow at least two weeks). This is a time-wasting activity for those who can obtain a visa on arrival, but it does have the advantage of giving you permission to remain in Egypt for three months and to make multiple entries and exits.

Passports must normally be valid for at least six months following the date of your arrival in Egypt.

Whether obtained before or on arrival in Egypt, visas can be extended for an additional month by visiting the Mugamaa in Cairo (*see* p.76) or at passport offices in Alexandria, Luxor, Aswan, Suez, Sharm el Sheikh, Mersa Matruh and Ismailia.

The exceptions to the above regulations apply to all foreigners arriving in Sinai, in which case you must obtain a visa in advance if you want to travel from there into the rest of Egypt. Or, if entering via St Catherine's airport, Sharm el Sheikh port or airport or Nuweiba port, you can obtain an on-the-spot free visa valid for 15 days (no extension permitted) but applicable only to the Gulf of Aqaba coast as far south as Sharm el Sheikh and inland only to St Catherine's. Note that you will not be allowed to enter the rest of Egypt with this visa, nor can you obtain an all-Egypt visa from Sinai. No visas are issued at Rafah. Those arriving overland at Taba from Israel must obtain a visa in advance. Those arriving at Nuweiba from Jordan can obtain a visa at Aqaba before boarding the ferry.

Most Arab countries except Egypt and Jordan will deny entry to anyone whose passport shows evidence of a visit to Israel. Though the Israelis are willing to give you an entry stamp on a separate piece of paper, the Egyptians always insist on stamping your passport with the consequence that an entry stamp for Rafah or Taba will give you away. Therefore if your Middle Eastern itinerary also includes Lebanon, Syria, etc., be sure to leave your visit to Israel till last.

Customs

Adults may bring in their luggage **without payment of duty** one litre of alcohol and 400 cigarettes (two cartons) or 250g of tobacco or 50 cigars, but if you bring in greater quantities you will be liable to customs duty and/or confiscation. However, in addition you may also then purchase at the duty-free shops at Cairo, Alexandria and Luxor airports a further four litres of alcohol and four cartons of cigarettes. These purchases are normally noted in your passport. If you do not take advantage of this (or even if you have, but airport customs have neglected to note the fact in your passport – usually next to your visa or on the inside back cover of your passport), you can go with your passport within 30 days of your arrival to one of the duty-free shops in Cairo or Alexandria and purchase four cartons of cigarettes but only three litres of alcohol. A carton of imported beer can be substituted for a litre of alcohol.

You may also bring into Egypt, exempt from duty and other taxes, all **personal effects,** used or new, including camera equipment, radios, recorders, word processors, jewellery, diving equipment. It is not mandatory but is probably a good idea to list these on the customs declaration form.

Genuine **antiquities**, including items from the Islamic period (indeed usually applying to anything over 100 years old), cannot be exported without the approval of the Supreme Council of Antiquities, 14 Sharia Fakhry Abd el Nour, Abbassia, Cairo, **t** (02) 685 9253, *www.sca.gov.eg*. The law also forbids the removal of coral from the sea and its export.

Currency

You may bring into and out of Egypt **unlimited amounts** of foreign and Egyptian currency, though you might be asked to declare the import of any very large sum. It makes little sense to buy Egyptian pounds abroad as you will get a better rate of exchange for your currency within Egypt; also you should change out of Egyptian currency before leaving the country, e.g. at the airport, as you are unlikely to find anyone interested in exchanging outside the country.

As large numbers of American $100 bills have been counterfeited in recent years (mostly in Lebanon), these will be closely examined when you try to exchange them.

There is no airport departure tax.

Disabled Travellers

Egypt is not conventionally geared up for disabled travellers, but given a sense of adventure and the helpfulness of its people, it is possible to achieve a great deal more than you might at first imagine, as this traveller's report received by the author conveys:

'We made our trip in somewhat unusual circumstances – my wife has a hip problem which limits her mobility for other than short distances and a few (low) steps and, consequently, we use a wheelchair for anything over a short walk to the shops. While planning the trip I contacted several tour operators, only to find they were unanimous in implying that our custom really would not be appreciated. Faced with this, and in view of our limited funds, I contacted Misr Travel and arranged a trip on our own. No guided tours, no coaches, we did it all ourselves and I doubt if we missed anything within our capabilities. Moreover, the total cost for the two of us for 16 days was less than the two-week tours offered by tour operators. We stayed at the Windsor in Cairo, the Etap [now the Mercure] in Luxor and the Old Cataract in Aswan, and we spent three nights on the MS Giza. The most valuable service, to us, was the attendant and transport at each change of location – stretched Mercedes, and knowledgeable representatives who, in each case, refused a tip. For anyone with a walking handicap, we strongly suggest, for visits such as to the Valley of the Kings, taking a taxi from the hotel onto the vehicle ferry [though now you can also cross by the bridge upstream]. We were able to take and use the wheelchair at every location, with not too much difficulty, since our time was our own. It would have been impossible to keep up with a group. At the tombs we were limited due to the large number of steps, but we were able to visit that of Ramses VI. Two possible items of interest, perhaps: Egyptair,

Disability Organizations

In the UK

Can Be Done, t (020) 8907 2400, *www.canbedone.co.uk*. Specialist holidays.

Holiday Care Service, The Hawkins Suite, Enham Place, Enham, Alamein, Andover SP11 6JS, **t** 0845 124 9974. *www.holidaycare.org.uk*. Publishes an information sheet on holidays for disabled and older people (£5).

RADAR (Royal Association for Disability and Rehabilitation), 12 City Forum, 250 City Rd, London EC1V 8AF, **t** (020) 725 3222 , *www.radar.org.uk*. Some travel information.

In the USA

Alternative Leisure Co., 165 Middlesex Turnpike, Suite 206, Bedford, MA 01730, **t** (718) 275 0023, *www.alctrips.com*. Organizes vacations abroad for disabled people.

Mobility International USA, 132 E. Broadway, Suite 343, Eugene, Oregon 97401, **t/TTY** (541) 343 1284, *www.miusa.org*. Information on international educational exchange programmes and volunteer service overseas for the disabled.

Other Useful Contacts

Access Ability, *www.access-ability.co.uk*. Info on travel agencies catering to disabled people.

Access-Able Travel Source, *www.access-able.com*. A database of information, travel operators, cruise liners, hotels, etc.

Emerging Horizons, *www.emerginghorizons.com*. An international subscription-based online (or mailed) quarterly travel newsletter.

for our flight from Cairo to Aswan, put us on the plane using one of those food vans with the lifting box, right to the rear entrance. The second item, a conversation with an Egyptian who spoke fluent English. When we told him how we felt completely secure on the streets, even at night, in every city, he said, "You must realize that to us Egyptians, you tourists are sacred! Five million Egyptians depend on tourism for a living". I doubt if we will visit Egypt again but we will never forget it. Particularly the people. We met with nothing but courtesy and smiles, not a single adverse memory.'

Money and Banks

The unit of currency is the Egyptian **pound** (LE, from *livre égyptienne*) which is divided into 100 **piastres** (PT, from *piastre tarifée*). Also, notionally, each piastre is divided into ten **millemes**, so that there are 1,000 millemes to the pound. But while there are coins for piastre denominations (though these are disappearing fast), and notes for both piastre and pound denominations, there are no milleme denomination coins. Nevertheless, prices may be expressed in pounds, piastres or millemes, which can add an alarming number of digits to a bill (all the more alarming as Egypt follows the continental European practice of using a comma instead of a decimal point). So a restaurant bill for 30,550 should not send you into the kitchen to start washing the dishes, it is simply LE30 and 55PT. Usually common sense will tell you what is meant.

Notes are in denominations of 25PT and 50PT, and LE1, LE5, LE10, LE20, LE50 and LE100. Note that the LE1 note is being replaced by the LE1 coin.

At the time of going to press the approximate **rate of exchange** was £1=LE8.5 and US$1=LE6; or, putting it the other way round, LE1 equals 12p or 17c.

There are **exchange banks** at the airports and other points of entry and at major hotels throughout Egypt. American Express and Thomas Cook also exchange money. You should hold on to your receipts to show when paying hotel bills and in the event you need to change money back out of Egyptian pounds on departure.

Cash and travellers' cheques can be exchanged at many banks. Credit cards are accepted at all major hotels, and also at some shops and restaurants, but generally you should count on being able to use them only in obvious tourist areas.

Egypt still largely runs on cash, so always carry a wad on you for your immediate needs. It is also a good idea when changing money to obtain a large number of LE1 notes to use for baksheesh and small purchases.

Cash machines (ATMs) are common in Cairo, Alexandria and other cities. Using a debit or credit card you can withdraw cash in Egyptian currency. But because of credit and debit card fraud, card companies and banks are wary when a card is suddenly used in another country, and they may block its use. So be sure to inform your bank or credit card company that you are travelling to Egypt. And if your card does get blocked, there is usually a telephone number on the back that you can call.

Getting There

By Air

Most flights, whether scheduled or charter, arrive at Cairo International Airport, though there are international flights also to Alexandria, Luxor, Sharm el Sheikh and Hurghada. You can save a great deal on the normal fare by booking ahead. Nonstop scheduled flights from Britain are operated by **Egyptair**, **British Airways** and **bmi** (London–Cairo 5 hours), and from the United States by Egyptair (New York–Cairo 11 hours). Egyptair offers an excellent service; the one drag is that it does not serve alcohol on its flights, but it does permit you to bring your own.

Even if you are an independent traveller, you should also see what **tour operators** (p.63) have to offer; they can have some very attractive deals. Tour operators sometimes offer flights only, or flights with a package at such a competitive price that you can afford to take as much or little of the package as you like and still come out ahead. Almost all travellers staying at five- and four-star hotels are on packages and probably paying no more, maybe less, than the independent traveller at three- and even two-star hotels.

By Sea

There are no regular shipping services between Europe and Egypt, nor even between any Mediterranean port and Egypt. Louis Cruises, *www.louiscruises.com*, and Salamis Cruise Lines, *http://salamis international.com*, sometimes operate cruises between Limassol in Cyprus and Port Said. From Aqaba in Jordan there are shipping services to Sinai and Hurghada on the Red Sea coast; *see* p.460 for details.

Overland

Travellers cross between Israel and Egypt at the Taba border point in Sinai, which is open 24 hours a day. Bus services linking the two countries are run by Misr Travel, Cairo, **t** (02) 335 5470, and Mazada Tours, 141 Ibn Gvirol Street, Tel Aviv, **t** +972 3 544 4454.

Airline Carriers

British Airways, *www.ba.com*; United Kingdom, **t** 0844 493 0787; USA, **t** 1 800 247 9297.

bmi, *www.flybmi.com*; United Kingdom, **t** 0870 6070 555; USA, **t** 1-800-788-0555.

Egyptair, *www.egyptair.com;* UK: 63 Conduit Street, London W1S 2GD, **t** (020) 7734 2343; USA: 19 W 44th Street, New York, **t** (212) 581 5600.

Discounted Fares

Sometimes the airlines themselves will offer discounted fares, especially when you deal with them through the Internet. In Britain and Ireland Trailfinders, *www.trailfinders.com*, is an excellent agent for discounted flights, with many offices in both countries.

Trailfinders, 194 Kensington High Street, London W8 7RG, **t** (020) 7938 3939; at Selfridges, 400 Oxford Street, W1A 1AB, **t** (020) 7408 9000; at Waterstone's, 203-205 Piccadilly, W1J 9HD, **t** (020) 7292 1888; in the City at 1 Threadneedle Street, EC2R 8JX, **t** (020) 7628 7628; at Canary Wharf at The South Colonnade (beneath the Reuters Building), E14 5EZ, **t** (020) 7147 5300.

Specialized Websites

UK and Ireland

www.trailfinders.com
www.opodo.co.uk
www.ebookers.com
www.expedia.co.uk
www.travelocity.co.uk
www.cheapflights.co.uk
www.statravel.co.uk
www.usit.ie

USA

www.expedia.com
www.travelocity.com
www.orbitz.com
www.cheapflights.com
www.statravel.com

www.mazada.co.il. You can also take a service taxi or local bus from Taba either into Israel or into Egypt.

Buses between Egypt and Jordan rely on the ferry service between Nuweiba in Sinai and Aqaba in Jordan. In Amman go to JETT in King Hussein Street, **t** (06) 569 6151. In Cairo go to the Cairo Gateway station.

The overland connection between Sudan and Egypt has now been restored, with trains from Khartoum to Wadi Halfa and ferries from Wadi Halfa across Lake Nasser to Aswan.

Getting Around

By Air

The principal carrier within the country is **Egyptair**, with flights from Cairo to Alexandria (about $50 one way), Mersa Matruh ($90), Assiut ($65), Luxor ($115), Aswan ($140), Abu Simbel ($220), Marsa Alam ($105), Hurghada ($90) and Sharm el Sheikh ($85).

Always try to make **advance reservations**. In winter it is advisable to make reservations as far in advance as possible for Upper Egypt, and especially to Abu Simbel; in summer ditto for flights to Alexandria.

By Rail

Air-conditioned rail travel is comfortable and fairly inexpensive. Students in possession of an International Student Identity Card get discounts of 30–50% (but not on sleepers).

All first-class and combined first- and second-class trains are air-conditioned; others are not. **Local trains** serving smaller stations are likely to be slow, crowded, uncomfortable and sometimes filthy, and they will not be air-conditioned – the experience can be interesting if it does not go on for too long. Travelling third class is to suffer an intimacy one would prefer to do without. No matter what class of train you are travelling on, bring **toilet paper**.

Almost all air-conditioned trains require **reservations** and you should book at least a day in advance; in winter try to book several days in advance for Upper Egypt if possible. You can try getting on a train at the last moment to see if there is any space (a bit of baksheesh to the carriage attendant would not go amiss); at worst you will wind up sitting on your luggage by the door (but you will still have to pay full fare). Note that when queuing for tickets, men approach the ticket window from the right, women from the left, taking turns. The women's queue is shorter and quicker. By way of example, from Cairo to Alexandria (208km, 3 hours) is LE48 first class; to Luxor (671km, 11 hours) LE140 first class; to Aswan (879km, 15 hours) LE175 first class. Second class fares are about two-thirds that of first class. **Snacks** and **meals** are served at your seat in first and second class for a few pounds.

There is a deluxe **sleeper** service between Cairo and Luxor/Aswan operated by Abela Egypt, *www.sleepingtrains.com*. Each compartment has a washbasin and two berths and is taken either as a single or a double. Meals are served in the compartments, and there is a club car for drinks and socializing – and this can sometimes be a lot of fun when a party atmosphere is got going by the exceptionally agile Nubian staff who dance across tables with stacks of drinks balanced on their heads. The one-way **fare**, either to Luxor or Aswan, is $60 per person on a double-berth basis (this is called second class); if one person takes the entire cabin for themselves (this is called first class), the cost is $80. **Reservations** are essential and should be made at least a week in advance if possible. There are daily departures, leaving in the early evening. Book through a good agent abroad or in Egypt, or go direct to the Abela office at Ramses Station, Cairo. In summer there is also an Abela sleeper service between Cairo and Mersa Matruh on the Mediterranean.

On all services, **children** under four travel free; those from four to ten obtain a 50% reduction and on sleepers are expected to share a berth with an adult.

Train timetables

Clerks at ticket windows and station masters can be helpful in telling you when the next train is to wherever, or how to get to some less-trafficked place. But it is nearly impossible to inform yourself comprehensively, and the few published timetables available to visitors assume that you want only to travel between Alexandria, Cairo, Luxor and Aswan, and then only on certain trains. More adventurous travellers should equip themselves in advance with a copy of the **Thomas Cook Overseas Timetable** (useful also for principal bus services, Nile cruises and shipping in the Mediterranean, the Red Sea and the Gulf of Aqaba), available from all Thomas Cook offices in Britain or by contacting Thomas Cook Publishing, PO Box 227, Peterborough PE3 8SB, England, **t** (01733) 416 477, *www.thomascookpublishing.com*, from whom you can order direct, for mailing worldwide.

By Car and Taxi

Car hire is not expensive in Egypt, and petrol is very cheap. To hire a car you should be not less than 25 and not more than 70 years of age, and you will need an **International Driving Licence**. This will be needed also if you are bringing your own vehicle, for which you will additionally need a *carnet de passage* (both obtainable from your motoring organization at home), special insurance (obtainable on arrival) and either a deposit or some form of guarantee against road tax and customs duties. The deposit is refundable on departure. For further details, contact the Egyptian State Tourist Office (*see* p.58) or your motoring organization.

Note that **diesel vehicles** are not allowed entry into Egypt. For more information on car hire, *see* **Cairo**, p.88.

But one problem is that Cairo is a madhouse on wheels, agricultural roads in the Delta and along the valley are often busy with trucks and donkeys and camels, at night oncoming car and truck lights are either beamed in the wrong direction or are not on at all, and Egyptians are in any case very odd drivers. With little appreciation of the virtue of keeping to a lane or even to the right-hand side of the road (they drive on the right), they meander and eddy about as though negotiating mudbanks in the Nile. The way to survive is to wander with them, which means needing eyes on the sides and the back of your head – or no eyes at all. But do not be put off: you soon get the hang of it, and having your own car gives you great freedom and flexibility, especially in discovering the less beaten paths and trodden sites of Egypt.

A word of **warning**, however. If you run somebody over outside a city, immediately get into your car and either await the police or drive off to find them. Do not hang about on a lonely country or desert road on your own, certainly not at night. The families of victims have been known to exact instant justice, especially if they are Bedouin.

You can still have the advantage of a car without any of the problems if you hire one with a driver from Misr Travel for example (not very expensive) or hire a taxi (*see* 'By Service Taxi', below) – among several people it can be quite reasonable to hire a taxi, say, from Cairo to Alexandria, stopping at the Wadi Natrun along the way.

By Bus

Long-distance buses can be fast, cheap and comfortable. From Cairo there are regular runs to Alexandria (also from Cairo Airport) and Upper Egypt. There are good services too from Alexandria to Siwa and Damietta, from Cairo and Assiut to the inner oases of the Western Desert, from Cairo and the Canal cities to Sinai and along the Red Sea coast, also from Luxor to Hurghada and from Aswan to Abu Simbel.

Except between Cairo and Alexandria, where the service is so frequent that you can almost always get a ticket for the same day, you should buy your ticket a day, preferably two days, in advance. Fares are significantly less than those by rail.

By Service Taxi

Service taxis run just about everywhere. They are like buses in that they follow regular routes from one city, town or village to another, and you pay a **fixed fare** for your seat. They are fast and cheap, and are good both for long-distance travel and for hopping from town to town, site to site. They operate on a first come first served basis and can usually carry seven passengers, setting off the moment they are full. You can buy the seat next to you for greater comfort (women especially often doing this to minimize groping; it is also advisable for women not to sit next to the driver). You can also hire the entire taxi for private use. Fares are a bit higher than most bus fares.

By Thumb

Hitchhiking is possible though uncommon and it can be difficult; a payment will in any case be expected.

Nile Cruises

Most likely, you will have arranged a cruise before coming to Egypt. It may form part of an overall package, or you may be arriving as an independent traveller but wanting to include a cruise somewhere in your plans. It is possible to do both from abroad.

But you can also, space permitting, book yourself onto a cruise once in Egypt. Agencies like **Cox and Kings, Misr Travel, Thomas Cook** and **American Express** can make the arrangements, either in Egypt or abroad. Also **Oberoi** operate Nile cruises, which can be booked through their hotels or reservations centres either in Egypt or abroad; they are the most luxurious, the best-run and have the best cuisine.

Prices are highest from October through May, falling by about 40% in summer, and include meals, sightseeing ashore, taxes and service charges. **Local operators** often offer cruises at substantially lower rates; among them are **Jolley's Travel and Tours,** 8 Sharia Talaat Harb, Cairo, **t** (02) 2579 4619, **f** (02) 771670; and **Seti First Travel**, 16 Sharia Ismail Mohammed, Zamalek, Cairo, **t** (02) 2736 9820, **f** 2735 2419.

The big boats – indeed 'floating hotels' as they are called – are the behemoths of the Nile. Equipped with boutiques, bars, hairdressers and discos, you are not certain that you have ever left dry land. They can provide luxury, though much of it may seem to you extraneous, and because of their size you may feel lost in the crowd. Often the fewer cabins a boat has, the better the ambience. The smallest boats have between 20 and 30 cabins.

An especially delightful way of travelling along the Nile is in a traditional ***dahabiya***, beautifully crafted wooden sailing vessels with half a dozen cabins. You can book with Bales Worldwide, Bales House, Junction Road, Dorking, Surrey RH4 3HL, **t** 0845 057 1819, *www.balesworldwide.com*.

There are now over 300 cruise boats on the river, plying **between Aswan and Luxor** and calling on Esna, Edfu and Kom Ombo along the way. Some of these loop a bit farther north to allow visits to Dendera and Abydos. Generally you spend 4–8 days on the boat, though for about half this time you will be tied up at Luxor and Aswan while you go off touring their local sights. When sailing along this upper part of the river, there is something to be said for heading south to Aswan for the sense of threading one's way more narrowly through the encroaching desert, but in whichever direction you sail, the Luxor–Aswan run certainly covers the greatest concentration of spectacular ancient sites.

Unfortunately the longer cruises between Aswan and Cairo, taking in Amarna and Beni Hasan, and lasting 11–13 days, were suspended in the 1990s for security reasons, and though the situation is now secure, the full-Nile cruises have not yet resumed. But should you get your chance to enjoy this most wonderful of voyages, there is the special cumulative impression that the Nile makes upon you.

Felucca Journeys

For the adventurous, sailing the Nile through Upper Egypt in a traditional small sailing boat, the **felucca**, is the thing. Sleeping bags may be necessary, though often blankets will be provided. Meals are usually included in the cost, which varies with the number of people aboard and your bargaining powers.

Arrangements can be made with agents, hotels or directly with boatmen at Luxor or (better) Aswan.

Lake Nasser cruises

Sailing across Lake Nasser is like voyaging over a Martian sea; instead of the fascinating scenes of life along the Nile there is an empty strangeness to it all, its fascination lying in the remoteness and the desolation, the fantastic quiet, the night sky exploding with stars.

Bales is one tour operator offering Lake Nasser cruises: Bales Worldwide, Bales House, Junction Road, Dorking, Surrey RH4 3HL, **t** 0845 057 1819, *www.balesworldwide.com*. In Egypt or through agents abroad, try Belle Époque Travel, with offices in Cairo, **t** (02) 2516 9649, *www.eugenie.com.eg* and *www.kasribrim.com.eg*. They operate the *MS Eugénie* and the *MS Belle Epoque*. Lake cruises are described on p.386.

Hotel Price Categories

Note: These are rates for double rooms. Remember to add 25% in Cairo and Alexandria and 30% in Upper Egypt and along the Red Sea for tax and services.

luxury	$$$$$	over $200
expensive	$$$$	$100–200
moderate	$$$	$50–100
inexpensive	$$	LE110–275 ($20–50)
cheap	$	under LE110 (under £20)

Where to Stay

Hotels in Egypt are officially **rated** from five-star (luxury) to one-star. (Some have not received any rating at all, in some cases but not always because they fall off the bottom of the scale.) The system is meant to indicate the level of amenities in each hotel, but its application can seem erratic and you may find that a three-star hotel is just as good as a four-star one, or that two four-star hotels charge markedly different rates. In this guide, hotels have been arranged according to price: luxury, expensive, moderate, inexpensive and cheap (*see* box, above). This system too has its faults, as price alone may not indicate quality, ambience or location. But taken together with the star-rating and the accompanying description, you should have enough information to help you form your own preliminary judgement.

As a rule of thumb, any three-star hotel will do; below that, you should have a look for yourself. Youth hostels are generally not worth bothering with; it is usually possible to find more congenial accommodation without damaging the most exiguous budget.

If possible you should make **reservations**, especially if you have your heart set on a particular hotel. Pressure on accommodation is most acute in Luxor and Aswan during winter, and in Alexandria during summer. Reservations can be made through an experienced travel agent, or you can contact the hotel directly. The international chain hotels can be booked by contacting one of their hotels in your own country.

The **rates** that follow are indicative only and are for double rooms. (Note that upper category hotels set their prices in US dollars, lower category ones in Egyptian pounds, and that this has been followed here.) To these must be added **service** and **tax** which put at least another 25% on top in Cairo and Alexandria, and 30% in Upper Egypt (e.g. Luxor and Aswan) and along the Red Sea (e.g. Hurghada).

Also, **breakfast** is often an obligatory extra. **Single rooms** or single occupancy of a double room costs about 20% less than the rate for a double.

Hotel bills must be paid either in foreign currency (the better ones will accept credit cards) or in Egyptian pounds accompanied by an exchange receipt from a bank.

Rates in Cairo are higher than elsewhere in Egypt and are the same year-round; in Alexandria and at the Red Sea and Sinai resorts they are about 10% lower in winter; in Upper Egypt about 10% lower in summer – except at some five-star hotels whose rates remain the same year-round. Some hotels will have rooms with and without bathroom, air conditioning, balcony, or whatever, and this can also affect the rate. If custom is slack, you may be able to bargain the rate down.

You can often get staggering **reductions** if you book your hotel through an agent/operator like Misr Travel as part of a ready-made or tailor-made package. However, the prices in the box above are what you can expect to pay at full whack.

Tour and Cruise Operators

A variety of package tours are offered to Cairo, Luxor and Aswan, allowing you to combine any or all of these destinations with a cruise on the Nile, a voyage on Lake Nasser or a flight to Abu Simbel. Some leave you to your own devices, others include guided tours and may also be accompanied by a guest lecturer. Prices vary accordingly and depend also on the quality of accommodation you require and your length of stay.

Bales Worldwide, Bales House, Junction Road, Dorking, Surrey RH4 3HL; **t** 0845 057 1819, *www.balesworldwide.com*. With a long and experienced track record in Egyptian travel, Bales offers a wide variety of affordable packages and tours, including tailor-made arrangements for as few as two people. Among their offerings are an intimate Nile cruise in a six-cabin *dahabiya*, a cruise across Lake Nasser, and tours to Siwa and Baharya oases combined with a stay at the Mena House across the road from the Pyramids.

Cox & Kings Travel, 6th floor, 30 Millbank, London SW1P 4EE, **t** (020) 7873 5000, *www.coxandkings.co.uk*; and in the US, **t** 1-800-999-1758, *www.coxandkingsusa.com*. They offer small group tours of 25 persons, tailored tours, private tours and short breaks to all the main places in Egypt. The premium is on quality and character, but they charge somewhat over the top, and if you shop around you can often do just as well for less money.

Explore Worldwide, Nelson House, 55 Victoria Road, Farnborough, Hampshire GU14 7PA, **t** 0845 013 1539, *www.explore.co.uk*. Inexpensive and adventurous tours to Sinai, Siwa, the inner oases, and all the major sites along the Nile; also cruises on Lake Nasser and the Nile in Upper Egypt.

On The Go Tours, 68 North End Road, West Kensington, London W14 9EP, **t** (020) 7371 1113, *www.onthegotours.com*. Runs exciting and adventurous group tours in Egypt, ranging from 6–13 days.

The Imaginative Traveller, 14 Barley Mow Passage, London W4 4PH, **t** (020) 8742 3049; USA, **t** 1-800 241 2137; all offices: *www.imaginative-traveller.com*. Offers a considerable variety of journeys, first class to camping, including Nile and Lake Nasser cruises, usually with small, youthful groups.

Kuoni, Kuoni House, Dorking RH5 4AZ, **t** (01306) 871 149, *www.kuoni.co.uk*. The emphasis is on pick and mix: starting from a basic price for a one-, two- or three-centre stay, you can then pretty much tailor-make your holiday by adding on tours and cruises, choosing your level of hotel and upgrading the service you receive, meaning that you can keep your costs down, though it is easy to let them rip.

Maupintour, USA, **t** 1-800-255-4266, *www.maupintour.com*. An established upmarket American operator offering a wide range of escorted tours and cruises, though somewhat lacking in imagination and style.

Misr Travel, in Britain: Old Inn House, First Floor, Suite D, 2 Carshalton Road, Sutton SM1 4LE, **t** (020) 8643 2429, *info@misrtravel.co.uk*; in the US: 1270 Avenue of the Americas, Suite 604, New York, NY 10020, **t** (212) 332 2600 or **t** 800 223 4978, *info@misrtravel.org*; Egypt head office: 1 Sharia Talaat Harb, PO Box 1000, Cairo, **t** (02) 393 0010, *www.misrtravel.net*. Egypt's national travel operator ('Misr' means Egypt); much of their business is wholesaling to operators worldwide, so that their offices may shun individual enquiries, but their Cairo and London offices have proved helpful. Apart from offering standard tours, their insider knowledge ensures that they can expertly tailor-make your arrangements for getting to and travelling around the country, and can fix up accommodation, often at a good price.

Thomas Cook Holidays, Coningsby Road, Peterborough PE3 8SB, **t** 0871 895 0055, *www.thomascook.com*. The inventors of the package holiday: Cook himself conducted his first tour of Egypt in 1869. Has a strong presence in the country, offering many tours and cruises.

The Traveller, 10 Bury Place, London WC1A 2JL, **t** (020) 7436 9343, *www.the-traveller.co.uk*. Formerly the travel arm of the British Museum and continuing with the same staff, The Traveller offers in-depth tours of Egypt accompanied by expert lecturers, usually from the British Museum, which not only cover the more familiar sites but get off the beaten track and visit many unusual and out of the way places. They are not cheap, however.

Voyages Jules Verne, 21 Dorset Square, London NW1 6QE, **t** 0845 166 7003, *www.vjv.co.uk*. Though an upmarket company, it has a tendency to dump holidays on the market using charter flights, so that often you can pick up a good and fairly cheap package such as Cairo or Luxor combined with a Nile or a Lake Nasser cruise.

Tours Booked in Egypt

You can always package yourself by deciding to take a tour on the spot. American Express offers a number of quickie tours from Cairo: Alexandria or the Suez Canal or the Fayyum or Luxor or St Catherine's, each in one day flat; or 2-, 3- and even 4-day tours of the Red Sea/Sinai resorts, Luxor, Aswan and Abu Simbel. Thomas Cook does the same sort of thing, but also offers more personalized tours for a few people at a time. Misr Travel offers the most varied and flexible packages of all.

Practical A–Z

Conversion Tables 66
Baksheesh 67
Business Facilities 67
Children 67
Crime and Security 67
Electricity 68
Embassies in Egypt 68
Entertainment 68
Food and Drink 68
Health 70
Maps 71
Media 71
Opening Hours 72
Packing 72
Photography 73
Postal Services 73
Shopping 73
Sports and Activities 74
Students 75
Telephones 75
Toilets 76
Tourist Information in Egypt 76
Women 76

05

Conversions: Imperial–Metric

Length (multiply by)
Inches to centimetres: 2.54
Centimetres to inches: 0.39
Feet to metres: 0.3
Metres to feet: 3.28
Yards to metres: 0.91
Metres to yards: 1.1
Miles to kilometres: 1.61
Kilometres to miles: 0.62

Area (multiply by)
Inches square to centimetres square: 6.45
Centimetres square to inches square: 0.15
Feet square to metres square: 0.09
Metres square to feet square: 10.76
Miles square to kilometres square: 2.59
Kilometres square to miles square: 0.39
1 acre = 1 feddan
4,200 sq m = 1 feddan

Weight (multiply by)
Ounces to grams: 28.35
Grammes to ounces: 0.035
Pounds to kilograms: 0.45
Kilograms to pounds: 2.2
Stones to kilograms: 6.35
Kilograms to stones: 0.16
Tons (UK) to kilograms: 1,016
Kilograms to tons (UK): 0.0009
1 UK ton (2,240lbs) = 1.12 US tonnes (2,000lbs)
0.45kg = 1 rotel
1lb = 1 rotel
100 rotels = 1 qantar

Volume (multiply by)
Pints (UK) to litres: 0.57
Litres to pints (UK): 1.76
Quarts (UK) to litres: 1.13
Litres to quarts (UK): 0.88
Gallons (UK) to litres: 4.55
Litres to gallons (UK): 0.22
1 UK pint/quart/gallon = 1.2 US pints/quarts/gallons

Temperature
Celsius to Fahrenheit: multiply by 1.8 then add 32

Fahrenheit to Celsius: subtract 32 then multiply by 0.55

Egypt Information

Time Differences
Country: + 2hrs GMT; + 7hrs EST
Daylight saving from late April to early October

Dialling Codes
Area codes are listed on p.75.
Egypt country code 20
To Egypt from: UK, Ireland, New Zealand 00 / USA, Canada 011 / Australia 0011 then dial 20, then the code without the initial zero, and finally the number
From Egypt to: UK 00 44; Ireland 00 353; USA, Canada 001; Australia 00 61; New Zealand 00 64 then the number without the initial zero
Telephone enquiries: 10 or 140

In an Emergency:
Contact the **Tourist Police**, *see* p.67.

Embassy Numbers in Egypt
UK: (02) 794 0850; **Ireland** (02) 735 8264; **USA**: (02) 797 3300; **Canada** (02) 794 3110; **Australia** (02) 575 0444

Shoe Sizes

Europe	UK	USA
35	2½ / 3	4
36	3 / 3½	4½ / 5
37	4	5½ / 6
38	5	6½
39	5½ / 6	7 / 7½
40	6 / 6½	8 / 8½
41	7	9 / 9½
42	8	9½ / 10
43	9	10½
44	9½ / 10	11
45	10½	12
46	11	12½ / 13

Women's Clothing

Europe	UK	USA
34	6	2
36	8	4
38	10	6
40	12	8
42	14	10
44	16	12

Baksheesh

Tipping is expected for all services, and often for no service at all. Too often tourists are absurdly ignorant or generous, which has led some Egyptians to believe, often rightly, that if they pull a sour face, even vociferously complain, they can milk you for more. The Egyptian term for a tip is baksheesh, which means literally 'share the wealth', and helps explain why sometimes an Egyptian is not at all abashed at wanting something for nothing: you have it, he does not but feels you should pass it round. Baksheesh can be a plague, and you may find yourself pestered for it in the streets. The rule is obvious: offer baksheesh only in return for a service, do not pay until the service has been performed, and do not pay too much.

Tip 10% on restaurant bills, LE2 to the porter who carries your bag to your hotel room (though LE3–5 at top hotels), and if you are staying at a hotel for a while, then LE15 per week or pro-rata is appropriate for the person who cleans your room and also to others, e.g. concierges and doormen, who have been of regular service to you.

Business Facilities

Five-star hotels in Cairo and elsewhere have business centres, usually for both guests and non-residents, which will do photocopying, send and receive faxes and email, and provide secretarial and translation services. Also their rooms are often wired, so that you can use your own laptop to send emails. Many other hotels throughout the country can at least provide you with a fax and Internet service.

Children

Egyptians are warmly indulgent towards children, and whether in hotels and restaurants or mosques and archaeological sites, you will find that they are welcomed everywhere. But this lack of fussiness about children can also expose a child to mishap. You should be alert to traffic and untended excavation sites (even around the Giza Pyramids there are some holes of terrific depth for the unwary to fall into). Be sure that your children observe careful hygiene, and protect them against the sun with sunglasses, hats and clothing. The better hotels can recommend a doctor if necessary, and if you want to leave your children for a few hours they can also provide child-minders.

Children will often more readily take to the strangeness of their environment than you do. Museums and tombs will probably seem not half so much fun to them as the dress, the scent and the bustle of the bazaar. They will enjoy carriage and camel rides, and sailing in a felucca; *son et lumière* shows will seem delightfully mysterious; and something as simple as dining outdoors can be novel.

Crime and Security

In terms of everyday crime, Egypt is a far safer place than Europe or North America. You can wander through any part of Cairo or Alexandria, for example, without the slightest concern that you might be mugged, though women should not walk in out of the way areas at night on their own. Egypt's strong sense of community works against all sorts of crime. Additionally, there is a particular regard for the welfare of visitors which is both traditional and based on the conscious awareness that tourism provides an income and employment, directly or indirectly, for millions of Egyptians.

Travellers in a strange country often feel apprehensive at first. But as you venture forth in Egypt, every experience will confirm that you are among an unusually kindly people, sometimes inquisitive, occasionally intrusive, almost never ill-intentioned or aggressive. Look after your things when in the company of fellow tourists: they are much more likely to steal from you than would any Egyptian.

If you need help or want to report a crime, you should contact the **Tourist Police**, whose uniform (black and white in winter, white in summer) is identical to that of the ordinary police except for an armband marked 'Tourist Police'. They will speak at least one language other than Arabic (usually English) and they are there specifically to look after you. They are posted at airports, ports, tourist sites, museums and at many hotels. The **Central**

Security Police, who guard embassies, government buildings and the like, wear a military uniform, which is black both winter and summer, and are armed with rifles bearing fixed bayonets or sometimes more powerful weapons. They are the people you do not point your camera at, nor do you point it at the place they stand in front of, if you want to keep your film in your camera and perhaps yourself out of jail.

Electricity

Electrical current throughout Egypt is 220 volts AC. Sockets take the standard continental European round 2-pronged plug. Plug adaptors and current converters, as well as dual voltage appliances, can be bought at home.

Embassies in Egypt

Your embassy can assist you by holding onto your mail, advising on emergency financial and medical problems and effecting emergency communications home. Embassies also encourage visitors, especially those not travelling in large groups, to register with them. It should be noted, however, that embassies cannot lend money to stranded travellers, though they can find ways of helping you.

Australia: World Trade Centre, 11th Floor, Corniche el Nil, Cairo, **t** (02) 575 0444, *www.egypt.embassy.gov.au*

Canada: Sharia 26 Kamel el Shenawy, Garden City, Cairo, **t** (02) 794 3110, *www.international.gc.ca/missions/egypt-egypte/*

Ireland: 3 Sharia Abu el Feda, 7th floor, Zamalek, Cairo, **t** (02) 735 8264, *www.embassyofireland-cairo.com*

UK: 7 Sharia Ahmed Raghab, Garden City, Cairo, **t** (02) 794 0850, *www.britishembassy.gov.uk/egypt*

USA: 8 Sharia Kamal el Din Salah, Garden City, Cairo, **t** (02) 797 3300, *http://cairo.usembassy.gov/*

Entertainment

The last 50 years or so have seen the complete disappearance of Egypt's cosmopolitan population and with it a marked reduction in the range, quantity and distribution of entertainment. Alexandria once had lively communities of Greeks, Jews, Italians and others; now it has virtually no cultural activity or nightlife that the passing visitor would notice apart from those at the Bibliotheca Alexandrina. The situation is even worse elsewhere, except in Cairo, and even there the oppressive mood of politically correct Islamic conservatism is making it harder for alcohol to be drunk and bellies to dance. It you are looking for a disco or nightclub, then in Cairo probably, and elsewhere in Egypt almost certainly, it will be at a hotel, though even those are sometimes dry. Many discos are restricted to hotel guests and members. Nightclubs combine a show with dinner.

Well-off Egyptians with Western tastes might go to Cairo's Opera House for ballet, opera and concerts, while foreign and cultural centres such as the British Council offer film, music and theatrical programmes, but these entertainments are unlikely to attract the visitor during a short stay. The self-conscious folkloric entertainments promoted during Nasser's time have long since succeeded in boring everyone stiff and are all but extinguished now, while television and DVDs are rapidly killing off what remains of popular culture. Among the few authentic entertainments still to be seen in Egypt are the *moulids* and other religious festivals.

In addition to referring to the listings in this guide, you can get a fairly good idea of what is going on by looking at the monthly magazine *Egypt Today*, the *Daily News Egypt* and the *Egyptian Gazette*, daily except Tuesday, and its sister paper the *Egyptian Mail*, published on Tuesday.

Food and Drink

Most hotels in Egypt, particularly the more expensive ones, cater to the tastes of foreign visitors by serving an international cuisine. In Cairo, as befits a large cosmopolitan city, there are also many restaurants specializing in one or other national cuisine: French, Italian, Lebanese, Greek, Chinese, Indian. Alexandrian cuisine is Levantine.

Though the classic Arab-Turkish cuisine of Egypt is best encountered in private houses, you should venture forth to Egyptian eating places, spanning the gamut in price and sophistication, for a taste of Egyptian cooking. Dishes are usually savoury, neither too oily nor too spicy, and as fresh ingredients are almost always used the menu varies with season. Except in the simplest eating places frequented exclusively by Egyptians, restaurant menus will be available in English and French as well as in Arabic, and the waiter will speak English. In the simple Egyptian places, as at a Greek taverna, you can go into the kitchen, have a look, a taste, and then point to what you want.

Egypt's **national dishes** are *foul* (pronounced 'fool'), cooked broad (fava) beans mashed with lemon juice and olive oil; *tamaiya*, the same beans pressed into a patty and deep-fried; *tahini*, a sesame paste; *baba ghanouj*, like *tahini* but made from aubergine (eggplant); and *koushari*, a mixture of rice, macaroni, lentils and chickpeas topped with a spicy sauce. Meat usually comes as kebabs and as *kofta*, a spicy ground meat patty.

At **cafés**, the preparation of mint tea and coffee is a ritual. Thick and black, Turkish-style, coffee is ordered according to the amount of sugar: sweet (*ziyada*), medium (*mazboota*), bitter (*saada*). While sitting there, ask for a waterpipe – a *shisha* or *narghile*. The tobacco is mild and sweet (*masil salom*) and the smoke is even milder by the time it has passed through the water. You do not inhale. Payment is a few piastres.

Beer long antedates wine as the regional drink of the Mediterranean, so it is not so strange to find it reintroduced and popular in Egypt. The commonest brand is Stella (nothing whatsoever to do with Stella Artois), in green bottles – unpredictable but usually very good. Stella Export, in brown bottles, is sweeter, more expensive and not as good. Both are lagers. Aswali is an excellent dark beer from Aswan, sometimes found elsewhere. Bock beer is available briefly in the spring and is referred to as Marzen (derived from *Marzenbier*, March beer).

Egyptian **wines** are from ex-Greek vineyards near Alexandria, 'mobilized' by the government. Omar Khayyam is a dry red, Cru des Ptolemées a dry white, and Rubis d'Egypte a rosé. A venture between Gianaclis and French wine cooperatives in the Gironde and Bordeaux has improved the quality of these traditional Egyptian labels and added a few others, notably a cabernet sauvignon bottled as 'Château Grand Marquis' and a Bordeaux bottled as 'Obelisk'. French wines are available at better hotels and restaurants, but are very expensive.

Restaurant Price Categories

The price of your meal will depend not only on the restaurant but also on what you have to eat. It is entirely possible, for example, to have a moderately priced meal in an expensive restaurant. And there can be surprises in less expensive restaurants, where certain meat and fish dishes can add greatly to your bill. Therefore you should take these price categories as approximate only. They represent the price of a three-course meal for one person including beverages and taxes but not alcohol. In addition, a 10% tip is normal.

expensive	$$$$	over LE100
moderate	$$$	LE60–100
Inexpensive	$$	LE30–60
cheap	$	under LE30

Imported **spirits** are extremely expensive. Egypt does make its own: the gin is undrinkable; the brandy compares with the Spanish variety; while *arak*, the Arab equivalent of Greek *ouzo*, Turkish *raki* or French *anisette* – often called *zibab* in Egypt – is excellent.

Beer, wines and, less readily, spirits can be purchased in shops, usually small places that are few and far between. When purchased at hotels and restaurants, the mark-up is considerable. If you are particularly fond of spirits, make sure you bring in several duty-free bottles.

Many middle-class Egyptians drink beer, wine or spirits, but the ever more vociferous Islamic fundamentalists, and also powerful fundamentalist business interests from Saudi Arabia and the Gulf, have ensured that even the international-style hotels do not always flourish their alcoholic drinks lists, but ask and you will receive – except in those hotels, run by powerful and intrusive Saudi and Gulf fundamentalist business interests, where alcohol is banned, full stop. Aboard trains (Abela sleepers excepted) only a rubbishy non-alcoholic beer is sold; on both domestic and international Egyptair flights, no alcohol is served, though you are permitted to bring your own. Some Egyptian governorates, such as Suez, are dry.

Western-style **soft drinks**, including Coca-Cola and 7-Up, are available everywhere and, unfortunately, are tending to drive out the far more delicious and wholesome local juices made from tropical fruits and sugar cane. Try also *karkodeh*, a local thirst-quencher made from hibiscus flowers.

Finally, it is said that if you drink from the **Nile** you will be sure to return to Egypt. You might think you would drop dead instead. But around Aswan the boatmen will assure you that it is better than the ice-cold drinks favoured by tourists, its temperature more agreeable to the stomach. The taste is fresh if somewhat organic. **Tap water** is heavily chlorinated; probably the best reason for drinking bottled spring water, which is universally available, is to avoid the chlorination rather than any disease. If Egyptian standards of bottled spring water are as low as in Europe, then it is no better than tap water anyway.

Health

Cholera and yellow fever **vaccination certificates** are required when entering Egypt from an infected area. In fact many doctors will now tell you that cholera shots are almost entirely ineffective, but they will recommend tetanus, polio, hepatitis and typhoid shots, and some might advise rabies shots and malaria tablets. **Bites** of all kinds need the immediate attention of a doctor. The bites of carnivores can be rabid, or at least can turn septic as can camel bites. If you have been bitten, get immediate attention; in Cairo contact the Hospital of the Rabies Institute in Embaba, **t** 3462042, called Maahad al Kilab in Arabic. To combat **AIDS**, Egypt has banned the importation of blood for transfusions unless it has an AIDS-free certificate. But you cannot be sure that gamma globulin, used against hepatitis, is AIDS-free, so avoid it. Otherwise, you should take the same personal precautions as you would at home.

Snakes may be encountered when you wander off the beaten path, and you should avoid turning over stones. Most Egyptian snakes are not poisonous (their bite is recognized by a double row of teeth), but some are, especially the cobra and the viper. The smaller Egyptian cobra (*Naja haje*), 120–200cm long, is normally a sandy-olive colour and is found throughout the country. The black-necked cobra (*Naja nigricollis*), 200cm long, is darker and is confined to southern Egypt. Both are capable of displaying the characteristic hood; the black-necked cobra has a dark band on the underside of the hood. Cobra bites display a single row of teeth plus fang-marks. It was *Naja haje* that appeared as the uraeus on the pharaonic crown, and was supposedly the viper that Cleopatra used to commit suicide. There are several kinds of viper, 34–150cm long, varying in colour from sandy to reddish, or sometimes grey. The most dangerous snake in Egypt is the carpet viper (*Echis carinatus*), 72cm long, with a light X on the head. Viper bite markings are simply the two fang punctures. It is helpful when seeing a doctor if you can describe the snake; better still, kill it and bring it along with you.

There are two diseases associated with Egypt, trachoma and bilharzia, though neither need unduly worry the visitor. **Trachoma** is a contagious infection of the eye, specifically the conjunctiva and cornea, and causes a cloudy scar and hence blindness. In the past, though less so now, many Egyptians have suffered from it. If you notice any inflammation of the eyes, you should at once consult an ophthalmologist. **Bilharzia** (or schistosomiasis) is caused by a worm which enters the body, causing disorders to the liver, bladder, lungs and nervous system. The worm lives only in stagnant water, so avoid irrigation channels and slow-moving parts of the Nile (such as in the shallows by the banks). The Nile is safe for swimming and drinking (or so the author has found) between the Aswan High Dam and Esna where, except possibly along its banks, it runs swiftly. If you have ventured or fallen into stagnant water, you should get a check-up when you return home. There is little risk of the visitor contracting either disease. Both can be successfully treated.

If you are unwell, you can first seek advice from your hotel. They will be able to refer you to a pharmacist, doctor, dentist or hospital, and may even have a doctor on call. Your embassy will also be able to recommend medical assistance. For minor complaints a visit to a pharmacy will suffice; pharmacists are usually very able at providing the appropriate remedy for basic ailments. Particularly in the major centres, the standards of medical care are high. Many doctors will have trained in Europe or North America and will speak English. Readers have reported on the excellent standard of **dental treatment** at a price that defrays much of the cost of their holiday in Egypt – and indeed have said that it would make financial sense for them to return to Egypt for major dental work.

Most likely the worst you will suffer will be a brief **upset stomach**. This is an entirely normal reaction to a change of diet and passes after a few days (Egyptians travelling to the West often experience the same problem). There is no need suddenly to stop eating Egyptian food; on the contrary, after a day's pause, you should continue. Your stomach will right itself in 24–48 hours; during this time, the only medical preparation worth taking is rehydration salts, available widely at home and in Egypt. Avoid diarrhoea treatments like Imodium, unless you simply must travel: aside from plugging you up (by paralysing your gut), all they do is get in the way of your body adjusting to a new diet. The one rule you should observe when eating in Egypt is to be sure your food has been washed; provided even the simplest eating place has running water, there should be no problem. Tap water is generally heavily chlorinated and safe to drink, though you can always have bottled water if you prefer.

The **sun** can be hot at any time of year, and the temperature can drop sharply at night. At both times it is wise to be appropriately covered. During the day you should wear a head covering and sunglasses. It is not advisable to drink spirits before sundown, nor to consume iced drinks during the heat of the day. A high-screen suntan lotion is advisable, factor 20 or more. Also insect repellent would be helpful.

And, of course, it can pay to be medically **insured**. At hospitals, patients will not be treated without a deposit of at least LE1,000. Be prepared to pay cash for treatment, though some hospitals will accept an American Express or Visa card. Medical insurance is not accepted, though you can claim costs back later.

Maps

The American University in Cairo Press publishes a map of Egypt, which also includes maps of Cairo, Alexandria, Luxor and Aswan. The AUC Press also publishes *Cairo Maps: The Practical Guide*, which is a booklet of 44 street maps with index. AUC Press publications are widely available at hotel kiosks and bookshops round the country.

Media

The *Daily News Egypt* is Egypt's only independent English-language newspaper. In addition to news and well-written features, it carries information on entertainments, museums, galleries, restaurants, etc. The rubbishy state-owned and propagandistic *Egyptian Gazette* is an English-language daily, except Tuesdays when its sister paper the *Egyptian Mail* is published instead, both containing agency reports and entertainments advertisements. Also in English is the *Al Ahram Weekly*, published on Thursdays, an offshoot of the government-owned daily Arabic newspaper. Its coverage, contaminated by propaganda, includes Egyptian and Arabic affairs, the economy, culture, lifestyle, sports, fashion, entertainment and travel. The independent monthly English-language magazine *Egypt Today* contains well-informed background features of interest to foreign residents and visitors. Additionally, most European newspapers are available the following day, and weekly European and American current affairs magazines are also quickly available.

On any radio with medium wave, you can tune in to the BBC World Service, which broadcasts 24 hours a day on 1323kHz and can be picked up in Alexandria, along the Mediterranean coast generally, in Cairo, and sometimes as far south as Luxor and Aswan. The World Service can also be picked up on the Internet, *www.bbc.co.uk/worldservice*.

Five- and four-star hotels usually pipe CNN, the BBC and other television news services straight into your room. Egyptian radio has

10-minute English-language news broadcasts on 94.5FM at 7.30am, 2.30pm and 8pm, while Egyptian television's Second Channel presents an English-language news programme from 8pm to 8.35pm.

Opening Hours

Museums, Monuments and Sites

Throughout this guide and unless otherwise noted, it is safe to assume that museums, monuments and archaeological sites are open daily; also that museums and monuments are open at least from 9am to 4pm, though on Fridays they may be closed from 11.30am to 1.30pm. During Ramadan these opening times may be curtailed. The hours of sunlight are usually the determining factor for the opening times of archaeological sites; that is, they tend to open earlier and close later in summer than in winter, but generally you can expect them to be open from at least 8am to 5pm.

Banks, Offices and Shops

Most **banks**, **post offices** and **government offices** are closed on Fridays, and banks are also closed on Saturdays. Banks are normally open from 8.30am to noon, and for currency exchange may also be open from 4pm to 8pm. Foreign banks are normally open from 8am to 3pm. Government offices are usually open from 9am to 2pm.

Private sector offices are usually open from 8.30am to 1.30pm and from 4.30pm to 7pm, though more Westernized businesses will be open from 9am to 5pm. They may be closed on Fridays or Sundays and occasionally on Saturdays.

Many **shops** are closed on Fridays, others on Sundays. Shop hours are usually from 9am to 1pm and from 5pm to 8pm, though many are open throughout the day.

During **Ramadan**, bank and government office opening hours are often reduced. Shops, however, often stay open as late as midnight.

Packing

The **clothing** you take will depend on where you go and the time of year. In winter you will need at least some light woollens and sweaters; in summer light cottons. In spring and autumn some combination of both is advisable against warm days and cool nights, and the possibility of changeable weather. Even in summer, however, at least one sweater or knit is likely to come in handy: at night the deserts can be cool, and Alexandria is freshened by strong sea breezes.

In summer especially the sun can be fierce; it is a good idea to have long-sleeved shirts or blouses with collars to protect your arms and neck. Clothes should be light in colour to reflect the sun and should be easily washable and drip-dry. In summer, anywhere in Egypt except Alexandria, you can wash a shirt at night and have it bone dry in the morning.

Although more liberal than many other Arab countries, and tolerant too of foreign habits even when not shared by the local population, Egypt is nevertheless conservative by Western standards and is becoming more conservative with each passing year. Your dress should allow for this. This is especially true if visiting mosques, churches and monasteries, where shorts or short skirts should not be worn, nor anything too revealing. At resort beaches and hotel swimming pools, however, the briefest swimwear is acceptable, not only on visitors but on Egyptians. There are now many designer store chains where you can get stylish clothing and shoes at very attractive prices. Also, Egyptian cotton is famous for its quality. Rather than overpack these things, it would be better to buy them once you are in the country.

There is too much dust and dirt for sandals to be generally useful; bring comfortable walking shoes. Sunglasses (preferably with polarized lenses) and a broad-brimmed hat will keep out the glare of the sun.

Egypt increasingly manufactures foreign-brand shampoos, soaps, toothpastes, razor blades and other **toiletries**, or otherwise imports them. All such things are readily available at the better hotels, but will be cheaper in local shops where you will also find less expensive Egyptian brands. The same applies to suntan lotions, tampons, insect repellents, batteries and film. But bring your own contraceptives. Think if you have any particular requirements which you would not want to find yourself without, and then bring those too – for example high-screen suntan lotion, a special contact lens solution, a certain size battery for your camera, and for those who have not yet gone digital bring high-speed film. Bring an initial supply of toilet paper and then keep yourself stocked with it as you travel: it is amazing how useful it can be and how often it is not available. A universal-size bath and basin plug may also come in handy.

A **flashlight** is invaluable for exploring tombs and other nooks and crannies. **Binoculars** are also useful, especially if you are cruising along the Nile, but also for examining the details of gargantuan ruins.

You may need a travel **plug-adaptor**; Egypt has continental-style double round-pin sockets, 220 volts AC.

Photography

If you haven't already moved onto digital photography, it is a good idea to bring with you a variety of both slow (low ASA) and fast (high ASA) films.

Taking photographs at museums and in tombs is forbidden more often than not, and when it is allowed you may have to pay a special fee. Usually a flash may not be used under any circumstances.

Therefore you will need very high speed film, not less than 1000 ASA (3200 ASA is the maximum normally available). You can get such films abroad, but almost certainly not in Egypt, where colour print or colour transparency 100 ASA film is common, 400 ASA is rare outside Cairo, Alexandria and Luxor, and anything faster is non-existent. So bring a supply of very fast film with you, or buy 400 ASA film in Egypt and uprate that by two stops to 1600 ASA. Note that you will almost certainly have to subject your film to airport x-ray or similar inspection, although it is claimed this is safe for films right up to 3200 ASA.

On the other hand the skies are blue, the sun is bright, and there is much reflected light off sand and water: for the best outdoor results use a 100 ASA or even slower film.

You are unlikely to experience any objection to taking photos in mosques or other Islamic monuments, nor in churches and monasteries, though you should be courteous and unobtrusive. During prayers, however, or at *moulids* when people are at their most fervent and conservative, you should be much more discreet and should not be surprised if you are told not to take photographs. By and large, **people** do not object to being photographed on the street; indeed, if you ask first, people often charmingly compose themselves – and then ask to be sent a copy. If someone objects, however, do not insist.

Occasionally you may meet with objections to photographing a street or village scene which seems attractive to you but which an Egyptian might think poor or dirty and thereby bringing shame on his country. Again, do not insist.

No doubt Egypt's enemies have more photographs of its airports, docks, bridges, dams and military installations than they know what to do with; nevertheless, photography of **military installations** certainly, and of the other locations possibly, can mean having your film confiscated at the very least. You may meet with the same reaction if you try to photograph government buildings or foreign embassies, etc.

Postal Services

The post between Egypt and abroad can be very efficient provided you use a letter box at a post office, or in a central location or in a major hotel. Elsewhere, some letter boxes appear to be visited by postal employees only rarely, if at all. Also, anything that is not a simple letter or postcard can attract the curiosity of the authorities and might therefore take a very long time to arrive.

Most hotels can provide you with stamps for postcards and letters, as can post offices.

Shopping

At smart shops in Cairo, Alexandria, Luxor and elsewhere you will discover that a new generation of craftsmen, designers and entrepreneurs is translating Egyptian themes into stylish and competitively priced clothing, jewellery, furnishings and so on, with an eye to international appeal. For **antiques** you should visit Alexandria's Rue Attarine which runs the gamut from Rococo to Art Deco. But the **traditional wares** and commodities of the bazaar – spices and perfumes, brass and copperware, gold and silver jewellery, ceramics, glass and precious stones, inlay work and *mashrabiyya*, cottons, carpets and leatherwork – are found in Cairo's Khan el Khalili and along Aswan's Sharia el Souq. Except where fixed prices are marked, **bargaining** is customary. Note that throughout Egypt if a customer is introduced to a shop, workshop or bazaar by a tour guide, the establishment normally pays the guide a 50% commission. As the cost of the commission will be passed on to you, this of course means that you will pay a much higher price than had you gone shopping on your own.

Further details on shopping are given within each relevant town account.

Bargaining

In the bazaars, price is usually what you agree on after a bout of bargaining. A stall-keeper will always ask more than he expects to get; the traditional response is to offer half as much. After several minutes, perhaps half an hour, a price midway between the extremes is agreed. That is the traditional way, but the visitor's impatience or foolishness can spoil the market, traders asking for and getting far more than their goods are worth. This is particularly true of hawkers at places like the Pyramids, and every now and again it is worth making a ridiculous counter-offer, perhaps only one-tenth of the asking price... and finding it immediately accepted.

Hawkers at tourist sights are taking advantage of their isolation and yours in demanding exorbitant amounts. The virtue of a bazaar is that there is plenty of competition. In Khan el Khalili you will find all the copperware, all the spices, all the wood and mother-of-pearl inlay in the same area, and you should browse around, examining the goods, asking the prices, getting a feel for the market. Try to be dispassionate; the more you want something the more you are likely to pay for it.

A good technique is to bargain first over something you do not want and then casually to start bargaining over what you do want – almost as though you did not want anything and just bargained for the sport. It *is* a sport and there are rules as well as tricks of the game. Your first extreme counter-offer will be laughed at and you may feel silly; do not worry, this is part of the game. After a few offers and counter-offers, walk out. If the shop or stall owner stops you, it means he thinks there is still a deal to be made; if he does not, you may have learnt you are aiming at too low a price – go back later, or go to another shop, with an adjusted view of the item's worth.

The essence of a bargain, of course, is not to arrive at some formula fraction of the original asking price, but to feel that you have paid the right price, a price you could not have bettered elsewhere, a price that makes the item worth it to you.

Sports and Activities

Apart from the Red Sea resorts with their almost exclusive concentration on **diving** activities, the main centre for sport is Cairo, with its tennis and golf facilities, keep-fit centres, cycling and running clubs, and spectator sports such as football, horse racing and rowing.

The luxury hotels are the places to look for **health clubs, tennis courts, golf courses** and the like. Staying at one gives you automatic membership, but some are open to non-residents as well, offering membership on a daily or weekly basis. There are also private non-hotel-based health clubs offering short-term membership, and free cycling and running groups.

For up-to-date information on spectator sports, get a copy of the English-language *Daily News Egypt* or *The Egyptian Gazette* (called *The Egyptian Mail* on Tuesdays). Egypt's most popular spectator sport is **football**, the two principal teams being Zamalek and Ahly. The season is from September to May, with games played on Fridays, Saturdays and Sundays at the Cairo Stadium in Heliopolis. The **horse racing** season is from

October to May at the **Gezira Sporting Club** on Gezira Island and at the Heliopolis Hippodrome, and at the Sporting Club in Alexandria. On Fridays year-round you can watch visiting American and British university **rowing** crews on the Nile being routinely thrashed by the Cairo police crew.

Felucca journeys, **camel trekking**, **off-road adventures** and **diving centres** are mentioned under place headings throughout the country.

Students

Egypt recognizes the International Student Identity Card (ISIC) and offers discounts at museums and archaeological sites (usually 50%) and on trains (30–50%, sleepers excepted).

In Cairo the ISIC can be obtained at the Egyptian Student Travel Services, 103 Sharia Mathaf el Manial, Roda Island, **t** (02) 531 0330 (open daily 8–6, Fri 9–4). A fee of about LE80 is payable, and you should bring your passport and a passport photograph. The ESTS is located opposite the Egyptian Tourist Authority office at Manyal Palace.

Telephones

For assistance dial **t** 10 or 140.

The Egyptian phone system has been opened up to private competition and is being upgraded. A consequence is that phone numbers are constantly changing: a digit altered, a new one added, or the entire number replaced by a new one – which, incidentally, explains why some phone numbers in this guide are almost bound to prove incorrect. Seek assistance by dialling **t** 10 or **t** 140, which respond in Arabic and English, though do not be surprised if those numbers too have been changed.

Both local and international phone services are available at better hotels throughout the country, but there will be a surcharge, sometimes as much as 100%. Local calls can also be made from public phones (when you can find them), and at some kiosks, shops and restaurants. International, long distance and local calls can be made from telephone exchanges ('*centrales*'); normally you pay first for a fixed number of minutes. There are 24-hour telephone exchanges, for example, in Cairo's Midan el Tahrir and in Alexandria's Midan Saad Zaghloul at the Ramleh tram terminus.

Phone cards are available at telephone exchanges in denominations of LE15, LE20, LE30 and LE50. These are used in the direct dial orange telephones found at many exchanges and at some airports and railway stations and occasionally elsewhere.

Mobile and satellite phones in Egypt usually start with 010 or 012, and these should be included when you phone the number. But in the case of area codes (*see*

Area Codes

Abu Simbel 097
Alamein 03
Alexandria 03
Assiut 088
Aswan 097
Benha 013
Beni Suef 082
Cairo 02
Dahab 062
Damanhur 045
Damietta 057
El Arish 068
Fayyum 084
Giza 02
Heliopolis 02
Hurghada 065
Ismailia 064
Luxor 095
Mallawi 086
Mersa Matruh 03
Minya 086
Nuweiba 062
Port Said 066
Pyramids 02
Qena 096
St Catherine's 062
Sharm el Sheikh 062
Siwa 03
Sohag 093
Suez 062
Taba 062
Tanta 040
Zagazig 055

box) do not include these in the number when phoning from within the area.

Toilets

In the best tradition of distant lands, and except in the better hotels and restaurants, Egypt's toilets are usually of the squat-over-a-hole variety and are generally disgusting. A bucket of water or a pipe for squirting water may or may not be provided. It is a good idea always to travel with toilet paper.

Tourist Information in Egypt

See p.54 for tourist offices outside Egypt.

Travel Permits

For travel in restricted areas, for example to outlying oases in the vicinity of Siwa and oases between Siwa and Bahariya, on certain minor roads in the Delta and Sinai, between Mersa Matruh and Libya, on roads to the Sudanese border, and off-road deep into the desert, you will need to go to the **Travel Permits Department** of the Ministry of the Interior, Sharia Sheikh Rihan, near Abdin Palace in Cairo, t (02) 355 6301 or 354 8661 (open 9am–2pm daily except Fri). Take two photographs, your passport and photocopies of the identifying pages of your passport and of your entry visa. You will also need to provide a justification for making your journey. Allow anything between 24 hours and seven days for processing.

Permission is no longer required for visiting Siwa, and to visit its outlying oases and those along the way between Siwa and Bahariya you can obtain permission from Military Intelligence at Mersa Matruh (*see* p.436). You can also ask Misr Travel for advice and help in obtaining permits.

Visa Extensions and Re-entry Visas

To extend your visa while in Cairo you must go to the Mugamaa, a huge government building (a gift of the Soviet Union in the 1960s) on the south side of Midan el Tahrir. It is open daily, 8am–3.30pm (closed Fri), but you should nevertheless go early if you hope to get anything done. Go to the first floor and to the section marked 'forms' to obtain a visa application form; you will also need a photograph and may be asked for pink bank exchange or ATM receipts showing that you have changed at least $200 into Egyptian currency within the last month. These you take with your LE15 fee to one of the appropriate windows, normally 23 to 29. Re-entry visas are dealt with at windows 16 and 17, while fines for overstaying your visa are paid at window 40 (a 15-day grace period is allowed, beyond which at least LE110 is payable). The whole process should take an hour. Visas can also be extended at passport offices in Alexandria, Luxor, Aswan, Mersa Matruh, Ismailia, El Tor and Suez.

Women

Westerners going to Egypt, whether men or women, are to some extent putting themselves in a position of contrast to the conventions of social life there. This is especially true of Western women. Family is extremely important in Egypt and an Egyptian woman's life is very much bound up with, indeed bounded by, her family relationships, whether as daughter, wife or mother. The entwined moral, religious and legal systems of the country enforce this. Even an educated woman would be most circumspect in her relationship with a man; both families would be involved and meetings would usually be limited to public situations.

Your Western view may be that that is their business and your business is your own. Some Egyptians will make an effort to see it that way, especially as you are only passing through. A great many more will not agree.

Therefore, dress and behave conservatively, but nevertheless be prepared for some hassle. Look confident and keep cool. It would be utterly unacceptable for an Egyptian woman to be molested, so there is no reason for you to put up with it. If, at worst, you are touched up, you can first say '*sibnee le waadee*', which means 'leave me alone'. If something stronger is called for, shout '*imshee*!', which means 'get lost!' By this time people should be coming to your assistance, and the man will be thoroughly ashamed and probably on the run.

Cairo

Cairo is an exploding metropolis at the head of the Nile Delta, its buildings dull brown as though camouflaged to blend with the impinging desert. The colour is of the local stone, but is also the result of sandstorms which sometimes dust the city. At sundown you can see a thin layer of sand clinging to the dome of the Mohammed Ali Mosque atop the Citadel, and as you walk along the cracked pavements the desert wells up from below.

Like a great lung the Nile breathes through the city, with its celebration of marvellous 19th- to 21st-century architecture, from Belle Epoque through Art Deco to soaring towers of glass. Farther east against the Moqattam Hills, minarets like blades of tall grass rise against the sky, marking the old medieval city of hidden beauty and palpitating energy which lends all Cairo its excitement.

06

Don't miss

1. Egypt's Christian past
   Coptic Museum p.94
2. Cairo's finest mosque
   Ibn Tulun p.103
3. Magnificent Mameluke mosque
   Sultan Hassan p.107
4. Beautiful old Cairene house
   Bayt al-Suhaymi p.137
5. Akhenaten and Tutankhamun collections
   Egyptian Museum p.144

See map overleaf

Central Cairo

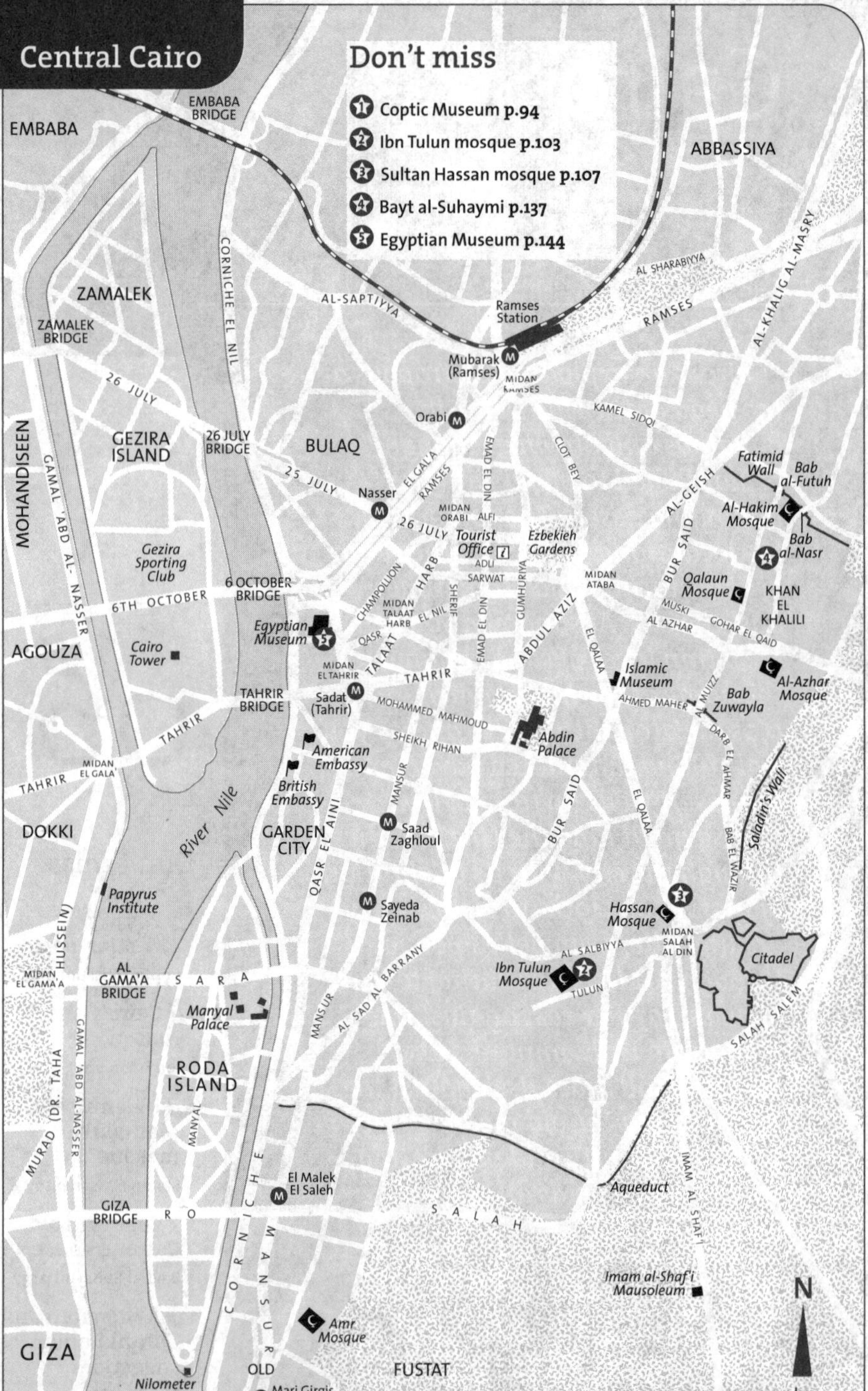

What one can imagine always surpasses what one sees, because of the scope of the imagination – except Cairo, because it surpasses anything one can imagine.
Ibn Khaldun, 14th century

In spirit Cairo remains as it began, an Arab encampment on the edge of the desert: hot, dry, the smell of glowing coals and musk, lively with throngs of people. To this sprawling caravanserai come visitors from all over the Arab, African and Asian world and beyond, fantastically varied in colour, dress, characteristics; yet easily talking, mingling, bargaining, like distant villagers meeting again in their market town.

For Cairo is the largest city in Africa and the political and cultural fulcrum of the Arab world. The treasures of three great civilizations, the Islamic, Coptic and pharaonic, await you at its musuems, while you can immerse your senses at Khan el Khalili, a vast bazaar as intricate as inlay work, sharp with spices, sweet with perfumes and dazzling with brass and gold and silver. You can ride in the desert, sail on the Nile, enjoy bellydancing or opera, smoke a hubble-bubble at a street corner café, and feed yourself on every cuisine from traditional to nouvelle.

The population of the metropolis is about 20 million, a seven-fold increase over the past 40 years or so, and owes its staggering growth to Egypt's unchecked birthrate, pressure on the land, and the desire of the fellahin to transform their lives in a city which, for all its seeming desperation, still offers at least the hope of opportunity. At rush hour Cairo threatens to burst or collapse with the pressure of Cairenes busily squeezing themselves into buses and the metro and noisily jamming the roads with cars.

But as the sun sets over the Nile the present slips away into timelessness, and from a high window over the river you can hear the call of the muezzins float across the darkening city, and you see the Pyramids at Giza glow gold against the Western Desert as they have done for one million, seven hundred thousand evenings past. The monuments of pharaohs and sultans lie within your compass, making Cairo and its environs one of the greatest storehouses of human achievement in the world.

History

Orientation about the city is aided by a knowledge of its history; and its history, as with so much else in Egypt, is linked to the Nile.

Antiquity

During the Old Kingdom the political capital of Egypt was at **Memphis** (20km to the south of present-day Cairo) so that it stood between the Delta to the north and the valley of the Nile to the south, thereby controlling the whole of the country. In this strategic sense Cairo, though founded 4,000 years later, is heir to Memphis.

Ancient **Heliopolis**, the city of the sun god (whose scant ruins are near the modern suburb of that name in northeast Cairo, en route

Getting to and from Cairo

By Air

Cairo Airport (**Matar al-Qahira**), 20km northeast of the city, has three terminals. Terminal 1 is used by several Middle Eastern airlines and by an increasing number of other foreign carriers, such as Air France and KLM. Terminal 2 serves primarily European and Far Eastern airlines, and airlines from the Gulf region and sub-Saharan Africa. Terminal 3, which opened in 2009, serves Egyptair flights, both domestic and international, and also other airlines which like Egyptair are part of the Star Alliance (e.g. Austrian Airlines, bmi, Lufthansa, Singapore Airlines, Swiss International Airlines and Turkish Airlines). Terminal 3 is adjacent to Terminal 2 and connected to it by a sky bridge; Terminal 1 is 3km away and is connected to the other two terminals by a free shuttle bus service that runs every 30 minutes 24 hours a day. An automated train service linking all three terminals is under construction. All three terminals are wired.

For speed, comfort and convenience, take a **limousine**. There are a score of limousine companies operating from the airport, there is a limo desk inside the arrivals halls, and there is always someone outside the terminals directing passengers to the limousines and collecting their fares in advance, about LE80 to central Cairo, more if going farther (you should also give some baksheesh to the driver on arrival). Official black and white Cairo **taxis** cost the same as limousines.

The **Cairo Airport Shuttle Bus** runs half-hourly from each of the three terminals to various destinations such as Heliopolis (LE30), Nasr City (LE35), downtown Cairo (LE40), Zamalek, Mohandiseen (LE45), Giza and along the Pyramids Road (LE50), and also to Maadi (LE50) and Helwan (LE120).

The inexpensive **Airport Bus Service**, publicly run, operates reliable air-conditioned buses into town (avoid the cheaper and less reliable non-air-conditioned public buses). The Airport Buses depart from Terminal 1 and cost LE3 to Midan el Tahrir and other central locations.

For Alexandria there are the Super-Jet and Western Delta buses, reliable and air-conditioned, which run every half hour and cost from about LE30 to LE35. You can also take a limousine or taxi to Alexandria.

The **metro** extension between Cairo and the airport is scheduled for completion in 2010.

Airline Offices

Most airline offices are either on Midan el Tahrir or downtown, with some in Zamalek.

Air France: 2 Midan Talaat Harb, downtown, **t** (02) 770 6262.
bmi: Its agent in Egypt is Travia, 19 Sharia al-Bustan, in front of the al-Bustan Mall, downtown, **t** (02) 2574 3300, **f** (02) 2574 4949.
British Airways: 1 Sharia al-Bustan, on the corner of Midan el Tahrir, **t** (02) 2578 0742/3/4/5/6.
Egyptair: downtown at 9 Sharia Talaat Harb, **t** (02) 2393 0381; national call centre: **t** 0900 70000.
KLM: 11 Sharia Qasr el Nil, downtown, **t** (02) 2580 5747.
Lufthansa: 6 Sharia al-Sheikh al-Marsafi, Zamalek, **t** (02) 2739 8339.
Olympic: 23 Sharia Qasr el Nil, downtown, **t** (02) 2393 1318.

By Train

Cairo's main train station is **Mahattat Ramses** (Ramses Station), at Midan Ramses (Ramses Square). All trains for Luxor and Aswan depart from here, as well as most trains for other destinations in Egypt. The station is about 2km north of Midan el Tahrir and plenty of taxis are always available; there is also a **metro** station here (named Mubarak), from which you can get to Midan el Tahrir (whose metro station is Sadat). First-class bookings should be made at least a day in advance.

Negotiating Ramses Station is simple. Entering from Midan Ramses, you will see platforms 1–7 for trains to Alexandria, the Delta and the Canal cities on your right; platforms 8–11 for trains to Upper Egypt (e.g. Luxor and Aswan) are straight on, beyond the main concourse.

There is a round **information booth** on the far side of the main concourse where helpful English-speaking staff can direct you to your platform or tell you where to buy tickets.

Buying **tickets** might require some patience. First you must go to the right place. On the left as you enter the station from Midan Ramses are the tourist information office, the tourist police and the ticket offices for the Abela Egypt sleeper services to Upper Egypt and Mersa Matruh. Straight on across the concourse are the ticket counters for trains to Alexandria, the Delta and the Canal cities. The ticket office for non-sleeper trains to Upper Egypt is beyond platform 11.

You may find that some windows will only sell tickets for reserved 1st- and 2nd-class air-conditioned services (which can be booked up to a week in advance), others only for 2nd- and 3rd-class non-air-conditioned services; ask first. When buying Abela sleeper tickets bring the passports of all those travelling. The tickets can also be bought at Abela Egypt's head office: 26 Sharia Mohamed Mazhar, Zamalek, Cairo, **t** (02) 2738 3682 or 2738 3684. At busy times of year, and for sleeper services especially, you should buy your tickets at the earliest possible moment, if possible at least a week in advance. Students with an ISIC are granted a discount of 30–50% on all services except sleepers. There is a good café to your right as you enter the station from Midan Ramses, and another facing platform 7.

By Long-distance Service Taxi

Long-distance service taxis have their different termini according to destination. Most departure points are near Ramses Station – ask and you will find.

Alexandria: al-Kulali terminal off Midan Ramses.
The Delta: Ahmed Helmi terminal immediately north of Ramses Station.
Ismailia, Suez & Sinai: al-Kulali terminal.
Red Sea: Ramses Station and Midan Giza (near the Cairo Sheraton).
Fayyum: Midan Giza.
Inner Oases: al-Kulali, Ahmed Helmi and Midan el Tahrir.
Upper Egypt: Ahmed Helmi (change at Assiut for points south).

By Long-distance Bus

Cairo's main bus station is Cairo Gateway (Mina el Qahira) at the Turgoman Garage, 300m northeast of the Orabi metro station (or 600m southwest from Ramses railway station and the Mubarak metro station). Long-distance bus services are operated by various companies and most have separate windows here, though some operate services from the Aboud bus station (for the Delta and Fayyum) in Shubra, 2km northeast of Ramses railway station, and the El Monib bus station (the Fayyum) in Giza, under a flyover 300m north from El Monib metro station.

All services (except the most frequent, to Alexandria, the Fayyum, the Canal) should be booked a day, preferably two days, in advance. You will need to go to the terminus to book, where you should also check the up-to-date departure times.

Alexandria: The Super Jet luxury service (about hourly from 6am to 1am) departs from the airport, from Midan Ismailia in Heliopolis, from Cairo Gateway and from Midan Giza (not far from the Cairo Sheraton).

Alexandria and Mersa Matruh: The West Delta Bus Company service departs from Cairo Gateway. Daily 7.30am departure to Mersa Matruh in winter, several morning departures to Mersa Matruh in summer. Hourly departures to Alexandria from 5.30am to 6.30pm (winter) and 9pm (summer).

Upper Egypt, the Suez Canal towns, the Red Sea and Sinai: The Upper Egyptian Bus Company, the East Delta Bus Company and Super Jet services all depart from Cairo Gateway.

Fayyum: Aboud and El Monib bus stations.

The Inner Oases: The Upper Egyptian Bus Company services to Bahariya, Farafra, Kharga and Dakhla all leave from Cairo Gateway.

Siwa: You will first have to go to Alexandria or to Mersa Matruh.

Overland Travel to Israel and Arab Countries

Buses from Cairo to Tel Aviv via Taba are operated by Misr Travel, contact their office at the Cairo Sheraton in Dokki, **t** (02) 335 5470. A service was formerly operated by Travco, 13 Sharia Mahmoud Azmi, Zamalek, near the Marriott Hotel, **t** (02) 2735 4493; you could check with them to see if it has resumed.

Coaches for Jordan, Syria, Saudi Arabia and Libya are operated by the Arab Union Bus Company, Cairo Gateway, **t** (02) 290 9017.

Additionally there are international service taxis on all these routes. For information and bookings, contact Hebton Misr Travel, between Midan Opera and Midan Ataba (in the block behind the multistorey car park), **t** (02) 591 9124.

Nile Cruises

The time-honoured way of making a progress through Egypt is to cruise along the Nile. Though for the time being there are no full-Nile voyages between Cairo and Upper Egypt, there are sailings between Luxor and Aswan, many of them taking in Dendera and Abydos too, and usually lasting four days and five nights.

Oberoi Hotels (who have the Mena House Hotel at Giza) run the best cruises; they can be booked abroad or in Egypt through Oberoi or Misr Travel.

There are also many **local operators**, good and generally less expensive, with whom bookings can be made through travel agents abroad or by contacting them directly in Cairo:

Jolley's Travel and Tours, 8 Sharia Talaat Harb, **t** (02) 2579 4619, **f** (02) 771670
Seti First Travel, 16 Sharia Ismail Mohammed, Zamalek, **t** (02) 2736 9820, **f** 2735 2419.

to the airport), was once the religious centre of Egypt. Travellers between Heliopolis and Memphis would have taken a ferry from the east bank of the Nile where Old Cairo stands today, opposite the southern tip of the island of Roda. In pharaonic times a settlement, perhaps even a town, sprang up on the spot which the Greeks were later to call **Babylon in Egypt**, probably a corruption of Roda's ancient name of Per-Hapi-en-Yun: House of the Nile of Heliopolis. The settlement's role was that of fortress rather than administrative centre, and Babylon never amounted to much. In the last centuries before Christ, Egypt was ruled by Alexander's successors, the Ptolemies, from their Mediterranean capital, Alexandria.

The Arab Conquest

It was the Arabs, for whom the desert and not the sea provided familiar lines of communication, who developed the logic of the site. In AD 641 Amr arrived in Egypt at the head of a small army, and both Alexandria and Babylon opened their gates to him. Amr was enchanted with Alexandria and wrote back to the caliph at Medina that this should be the Muslim capital of the conquered country, but Omar, referring to Alexandria's position on the far side of the Nile Delta, replied, 'Will there be water between me and the Muslim army?' Amr returned to Babylon where only sand separated him from Arabia; the tent (*fustat*) he had pitched there before marching on Alexandria was still standing and a dove had nested in it with her young. On this spot Amr built his mosque, the first in Egypt, and **Fustat**, the City of the Tent, grew up.

Fustat was the first of several planned developments which over the centuries contributed to the growth of the medieval city. The Nile in those days lay farther to the east along what is now Sharia el Gumhuriya, which runs up into Midan Ramses where the railway station is. All of what is now modern Cairo then lay on the west bank of the river, if not beneath it. And an ancient canal, once joining the Nile with the Red Sea, lay still further to the east, along the line of Sharia Bur Said (Port Said), built when the canal, called the Khalig by the Arabs, was filled in during the 19th century. So the city developed along the narrow corridor of land between the canal to the west and the Moqattam Hills to the east, and extended northwards as successive rulers were intent on catching the cool summer breezes blowing in from the Mediterranean.

When Ibn Tulun, Abbasid governor of Egypt, made himself virtually independent of the Baghdad caliph in AD 870, he built his palace, government buildings, a hippodrome and the famous mosque bearing his name to the north of Fustat. The **mosque of Ibn Tulun** apart, little survives of his city, and still less of Fustat. The heart of what grew into the Cairo of today was established by the Fatimids.

Cairo Founded by the Fatimids

On 5 August AD 969, with Mars in the ascendant, the first stone of the Fatimid capital was laid to the north of the Tulunid city. The city took its name, al-Qahira, the Triumphant, from the warrior planet. Our name for the city, Cairo, derives from this al-Qahira found on maps, though as often as not Egyptians call it **Misr**. Of vague and haunting meaning, far antedating Islam, Misr is emotionally the more important name of the two and refers to both city and the country as a whole. An Egyptian abroad who says 'I am going to Misr', means he is returning to Egypt. If he says the same thing in Luxor, he means he is returning to Cairo. In either case, 'going to Misr' carries the sense of going home. For the fellahin, Cairo is *Misr um al-dunya*: Misr, Mother of the World.

The Fatimids, of the persistent though minority Shia sect of Islam, invaded Egypt from Tunisia where their caliphate declared its legitimacy through descent from Ali, husband of the Prophet's daughter Fatima. They imposed their Shia doctrines (those same followed today in Iran and much of Iraq) on Egypt which, apart from the Fatimid interlude, has kept within the orthodox Sunni fold. The Azhar Mosque dates from this period and is still the centre of Koranic studies for the whole Muslim world.

The Medieval City

This walled city, centred on the popular market area known as **Khan el Khalili** and extending from the gate known as Bab Zuwayla in the south to Bab al-Futuh in the north, remains astonishingly intact both in structure and in atmosphere, the medieval city *nonpareil* in all the world. Its walls and area were extended by Saladin, a Kurdish general in the service of the Abbasid caliph in Baghdad. Foreign failures and the failure of the Nile itself led to the weakening of the Fatimid dynasty, which trembled in confusion before the onslaught of the First Crusade. In triumphing over the armies of the West, Saladin established his own empire in Egypt and Syria and his own Ayyubid dynasty, which ruled from 1171 to 1250. Orthodoxy was re-established and the **Citadel** begun, the redoubt of power and the centre of government throughout the troubled centuries of Mameluke and Ottoman rule.

Saladin's Ayyubid successors, however, relied increasingly on their slave militia, the **Bahri Mamelukes**. (*Mameluke* means white slave, while *bahri* means riverine and refers to their barracks on the island of Roda; these were mostly Turks and Mongols. The later **Burgi Mamelukes**, mostly Circassian, were quartered in the Citadel, hence *burg*.) The Mamelukes soon became an indispensable élite and successive sultans rose from their number, legitimizing their authority more by the blood on their hands than the blood in their veins. The Mamelukes ruled Egypt until the Ottoman domination in 1517. In spite of the violent and repressive character of Mameluke rule, they enriched the city with their architecture, their most outstanding monuments being the **mosque of Sultan Hassan** and the **mausoleum of Qaytbey**.

Around 1300 the island of **Gezira** was formed as the Nile shifted westwards, but the city remained largely within its old boundaries throughout the **Ottoman period**, its architecture following traditional styles with only a few Baroque exceptions inspired by the mosques of Istanbul. As a province of the Ottoman Empire, Egypt was ruled by a Turkish governor housed in the Citadel who delegated most of his authority. Though no longer providing sultans, the Mamelukes perpetuated their slave aristocracy by levees of Christian youths from the Caucasus. But their power now was chaotic and rapacious. What the Turks did not take, the Mamelukes did, and Cairo was further impoverished when Western merchants discovered how to bypass the troublous region altogether by sailing around the southern cape of Africa to India and the Far East. Egypt suffered from famine and disease, its population falling to two million compared to eight million in Roman times.

The Westernization of Cairo

The brief French occupation of Egypt, from 1798 to 1801, gave Cairo its first whiff of Western ways. **Napoleon** stayed in what was still then a country district, on the site where the old Shepheard's Hotel was later built, overlooking the Ezbekieh lake. He reorganized the government, introduced the first Arabic printing press, installed windmills on the Moqattam Hills and commissioned the twenty-four volume *Description de l'Egypte*, a complete cultural, social, political, economic and technological account of the country, a monumental census which filled a gap in human knowledge that had persisted since Roman times. But real change for Egypt and for Cairo only began with **Mohammed Ali**. After he secured his rule by massacring the Mamelukes in 1811, thereby founding a dynasty which ended only with the abdication of Farouk in 1952 and the proclamation of a republic the next year, he drove forward the Westernization of Cairo, which saw the canal filled in and the great swaths of **Sharia el Muski** and **Sharia el Qalaa** (formerly Sharia Mohammed Ali) mow down long rows of the medieval city. Fortunately, however, most of the modernization of Cairo, which began under the rule of Khedive Ismail and looked to Paris for its model, was undertaken on the virgin land

Highlights of Cairo

For those with very limited time in Cairo, an effort should be made to visit the **Egyptian Museum** and the **Coptic and Islamic museums**. But you should also see some of the great Islamic monuments of the city. The two outstanding mosques are those of **Sultan Hassan** and **Ibn Tulun**, which can both be combined with a visit of the **Citadel**. The new **Al-Azhar Park**, with its café and marvellous views over medieval Cairo, is a good place to pause and refresh yourself. Going to the famous bazaar of **Khan el Khalili** brings you to the heart of the medieval city, from where it can be especially evocative to walk south along Sharia Muizz to **Bab Zuwayla**, and north along the same street at least as far as **Bayt al-Suhaymi**, the finest old house in the city.

that the Nile provided after it shifted westwards and settled in its present bed.

Orientation

Midan el Tahrir

What now passes for the centre of town – for foreigners, anyway – is **Midan el Tahrir**, or Liberation Square, on the Nile's east bank. To its north is the **Egyptian Museum**, and beneath it is the **metro station** called Sadat. Hot, noisy, characterless and thick with exhaust fumes, Midan el Tahrir was created after Nasser's 1952 coup d'état on the site of a British barracks, the Qasr el Nil, and at the same time powers of compulsory purchase were used to cut the Corniche el Nil (the road running along the east bank of the Nile) through the many embassy and villa gardens to the south, the new roadway extending down to Maadi and Helwan.

South from Midan el Tahrir

Immediately to the south of Midan el Tahrir is the **Mugamaa**, the suitably massive headquarters of the state administration (which you will visit if you need to extend your visa), and near it the **National Assembly**, while some distance eastwards is **Abdin Palace**, formerly the royal residence and now the offices of the President of the Republic.

A short walk south from Midan el Tahrir, along the Corniche el Nil, are the **Semiramis Inter-Continental** and **Shepheard's** – although the famous Shepheard's Hotel of the past, where anyone who was anyone was seen on the terrace drinking four o'clock tea, was located near the Ezbekieh Gardens and was burnt down by a mob in 1952. Farther south along the river is the convoluted pattern of **Garden City**, a pleasant residential district of tree-lined streets and the home of the British and American embassies, but its ambience offended by the construction of the monstrous Four Seasons Hotel, while across the Corniche (which is impossible to cross without risk to your life) and over a bridge to the northern tip of Roda Island is the **Grand Hyatt Cairo Hotel**.

North from Midan el Tahrir

To the north of Midan el Tahrir, beyond the overpass leading to the **6 October Bridge** (named after the 1973 war), is the **Ramses Hilton**, and past that the one-time slum districts of **Bulaq** and **Shubra**, now redeveloped with skyscrapers along the river. On this stretch of the Corniche el Nil is the **Television Tower building**, housing radio and television studios and the press office, while the taller building beyond it is the new **Ministry of Foreign Affairs**. Continuing north along the Corniche, past the **26 July Bridge**, is the ultra-modern **World Trade Centre**, filled with trendy shops.

Sharia Ramses runs out from the top of Midan el Tahrir and turns northeast, leading to **Midan Ramses**. Here you will find **Mahattat Ramses**, the main Cairo railway station for trains north to Alexandria and south to Luxor and Aswan. Midan Ramses is named for Ramses II, whose colossal statue was brought here in 1955 from Memphis where its twin still resides. However, it suffered so much from traffic vibration and pollution that it was removed in 2006, and is being held in safekeeping until it can be erected outside the new Grand Egyptian Museum by the Pyramids, which is scheduled to open by 2012. A concrete clone has been erected on the way to the airport.

Downtown Cairo

Around Midan el Tahrir and along the streets radiating out from it are numerous **airline offices** and **travel agencies**, and extending into the northeast downtown area several less expensive **hotels**. This downtown area, the creation of Khedive Ismail and inspired by the elegant Paris of Napoleon III, is bordered by Sharia Ramses to the northwest, Sharia Tahrir to the south and Sharia el Gumhuriya to the east. Parallel to Sharia Ramses is Sharia Champollion; the **Thomas Cook** office is on the first street to intersect this, Sharia Mahmoud Basiony. Sharia Qasr el Nil heads eastwards in the direction of the Ezbekieh Gardens, though not quite reaching that far; soon after leaving Midan el Tahrir you will find **American Express** on the right-hand side. Farther on, this street intersects several others at Midan Talaat Harb. Along Sharia Talaat Harb, beginning at Midan el Tahrir and ending at Midan Orabi, are numerous **shops**, **cinemas** and **eating places** – also along Sharias Adli and 26 July running east–west. This is the liveliest area of modern Cairo, particularly on a Thursday night.

Until the creation of Midan el Tahrir in the 1950s, the **Ezbekieh Gardens** were the focal point for foreign visitors. The old Shepheard's Hotel stood on the corner of Sharias el Gumhuriya and Alfi at the northwest corner of the gardens, while at the southwest corner stood the old Opera House. It had been built in

The Yacoubian Building

***The Yacoubian Building*, the title of the bestselling novel by Egyptian writer Alaa Al Aswany, is a real place, just a stone's throw from Midan Talaat Harb in downtown Cairo. Published in Arabic in 2002, then translated into English by The American University in Cairo Press in 2004 and made into a film in 2006, *The Yacoubian Building* is a scathing attack on what Egypt has become since Nasser's coup d'état in 1952 – a country where political corruption, ill-gotten wealth and religious hypocrisy are natural allies, where the arrogance and defensiveness of the powerful find expression in the exploitation of the weak, and where youthful idealism can turn quickly to extremism. The actual building, which in the novel serves as a metaphor for the state of modern Egyptian society, is located both in book and reality at 34 Sharia Talaat Harb, though the characters more usually use the old name for the street, Sharia Suleiman Pasha. But whereas Al Aswany describes its fictional counterpart as built 'in the high classical European style, the balconies decorated with Greek faces carved in stone, the columns, steps, and corridors all of natural marble', the real building is Art Deco.**

1869, and the Khedive Ismail commissioned Verdi to write *Aïda* to celebrate here the opening of the Suez Canal and Egypt's return to the crossroads of the world. In the event, *Aïda* was late and *Rigoletto* was performed instead, before a glittering international audience which included the Empress Eugénie, wife of Napoleon III. The old Opera House mysteriously burnt down in 1971, but has been replaced by a handsome new one on Gezira Island. This area around Ezbekieh, though not what it used to be, is along with the adjacent downtown area one of the best places to stay for anyone who is serious about exploring the city on foot. It enjoys the ambivalence of being on the edge of modern Cairo and within easy walking distance of the medieval city to the east.

Medieval Cairo

The development and layout of the medieval Islamic city has already been outlined (*see* pp.83–4), and the details of its sights are provided later. Suffice it to say, for the purpose of orientation, that if you walk through the Ezbekieh Gardens you will come to **Midan Ataba** with its central **post office**, open 24 hours a day. From here you can press on into the heart of the **bazaar area** along Sharias el Muski or al-Azhar; or if instead you leave the square along Sharia al Qalaa (formerly Sharia Mohammed Ali and still called that by many) running south you come to the **Islamic Museum** at the intersection with Sharia Port Said, and still farther down you reach the **Sultan Hassan Mosque** and the **Citadel**. West of the Citadel is the **mosque of Ibn Tulun**.

The Island of Gezira and Views from the Cairo Tower

Returning again to Midan el Tahrir for bearings, to the west is the **Tahrir Bridge**, which crosses the Nile to the island of **Gezira** (*gezira* is in fact Arabic for island).

The central part of the island is taken up with the **Gezira Sporting and Racing Club**, next to it rising in lotus motif the 180m

Getting around Cairo

Although there is an extensive bus system, buses are usually extremely crowded and it is better to head for the general area you want by **metro, riverbus** or **taxi**, and then to walk about. Useful information about how to reach a particular sight is given with its description, and this is so throughout the book.

By Metro

The great boon to visitors (not to mention Cairenes) is the city's metro (*see* opposite for map). It was the first underground railway in Africa or the Arab world, and it is excellent. At LE1, regardless of distance, you can travel quickly, cleanly and in comfort between important points like Midan Ramses (metro station Mubarak), Midan el Tahrir (Sadat) and Old Cairo (Mari Girgis). A further intersecting line is under construction. Services operate from about 5am to 11.30pm. Note that the front carriage is off-limits for men.

By Taxi

Taxis, which are usually black-and-white Fiats or Peugeots, and have meters, are in theory a cheap way of getting about within Cairo. But Cairo taxi drivers hold to an opposite theory when giving rides to foreigners. Occasionally you will get into a **metered taxi** and the driver will actually turn the meter on, in which case you will be amazed at how cheap it is, amazed at the man's innocence, and can leave it to your conscience whether you will pay him according to the metered reading. More often than not the driver will 'forget', or say his meter is broken, or simply refuse to turn it on. You have the right to insist, but in reality you will soon learn not to bother about arguing or even raising the matter, and will instead devise your own rule of thumb. If, say, from Midan el Tahrir you go to Zamalek, Khan el Khalili or Midan Ramses (2km to 2.5km), pay LE10; from Midan el Tahrir to Old Cairo (5km), pay LE15; and from Midan el Tahrir to the Pyramids (11km), LE20. You can feel generous in knowing you are paying well over the proper fare. Your driver of course will have a fit. You then make noises about calling the police. Your driver will calm down, but even if he does not, ignore him. Taking taxis in Cairo is like bargaining in Khan el Khalili; you will soon get a feel for arriving at a fare acceptable to both of you. Most taxi drivers have mobile phones; if you are satisfied with your driver, you can take his number and use him in future.

By Bus and Minibus

The cheapest way of getting about within and around Cairo is by public bus. There are the large red-and-white or black-and-white buses, which rarely cost more than 50pt a ride. Their major terminus is in **Midan Abdel Moneim Riad**, behind (north of) the Egyptian Museum. They are crowded, uncomfortable, difficult to get on, even more difficult to get off, and the main interest they hold for the visitor is watching Cairenes embark and disembark through the windows. Also from the same terminus there are the small orange-and-white minibuses, which cost about LE1 a ride.

By Limousine (Car with Driver)

Costing somewhat more than taxis are the unmetered limousines, which charge fixed fares. The drivers speak English, and their cars, usually Toyotas, Volvos and Mercedes, are clean and in good order and have air conditioning. They can be hired for a specific journey or by the hour or day, which can be a cost-efficient, convenient way of making the most of your time when visiting many places in and around Cairo. They are found at the airport and at major hotels, where their fares are posted. Try Limousine Misr, **t** (02) 2342 2582.

Car Hire

If you are planning to drive extensively in and around Cairo or farther afield, it could be worth hiring a car (though you should also consider hiring a limousine with driver; *see* above). It is often cheaper to arrange this from abroad. You need to be at least 25 and not more than 70, must have an International Driver's Licence, and should have a sense of adventure: Cairene drivers, you will observe, meander from one side of the road to the other as the fancy takes them, and the only way to survive is to meander with them.

Both international and local car hire firms are represented; most of the major hotels will have agency desks, and there are offices downtown and at the airport. It is worth checking that everything essential (like brakes) actually works and that a record is taken beforehand of any dents or scratches in the bodywork. It is advisable to book a day in advance.

By Riverbus

Riverbuses make frequent runs from **Maspero Station** (on the Corniche in front of the Television Tower Building, which is just north of the Ramses Hilton) down to Old Cairo, with stops at either side of the river along the way. There are also boats from Maspero Station north to the Nile barrages daily 7am–5pm.

Tours

The alternative to public transport or car hire are **tours** by car or bus with a guide. There are morning, afternoon and evening tours to the Egyptian Museum, the Pyramids and Sphinx, Memphis and Saqqara, medieval or Islamic Cairo, Old Cairo, and Cairo by night, incorporating a visit to a nightclub.

Thomas Cook has a comprehensive list of tours by car with driver/guide. The more passengers, the less expensive it is per person. **American Express** does coach tours which for one or two people will work out about 40% cheaper than Cook's tours. These companies also offer tours throughout Egypt by rail or air. Possibly cheaper and more comprehensive is Egypt's own tourist company: **Misr Travel**. They are efficient, and can arrange accommodation, cruises, tours, and air, sea, road and rail travel.

Thomas Cook, 17 Sharia Mahmoud Bassiouni, near Midan Talaat Harb, **t** (02) 2574 5191.
American Express, 15 Sharia Qasr el Nil, a short walk from Midan el Tahrir, **t** (02) 2418 2144/5.
Misr Travel, 1 Sharia Talaat Harb, **t** (02) 2393 0010; also at 43 Sharia Qasr el Nil; with branches at the Ramses Hilton, Marriott, Semiramis and Cairo Sheraton hotels.

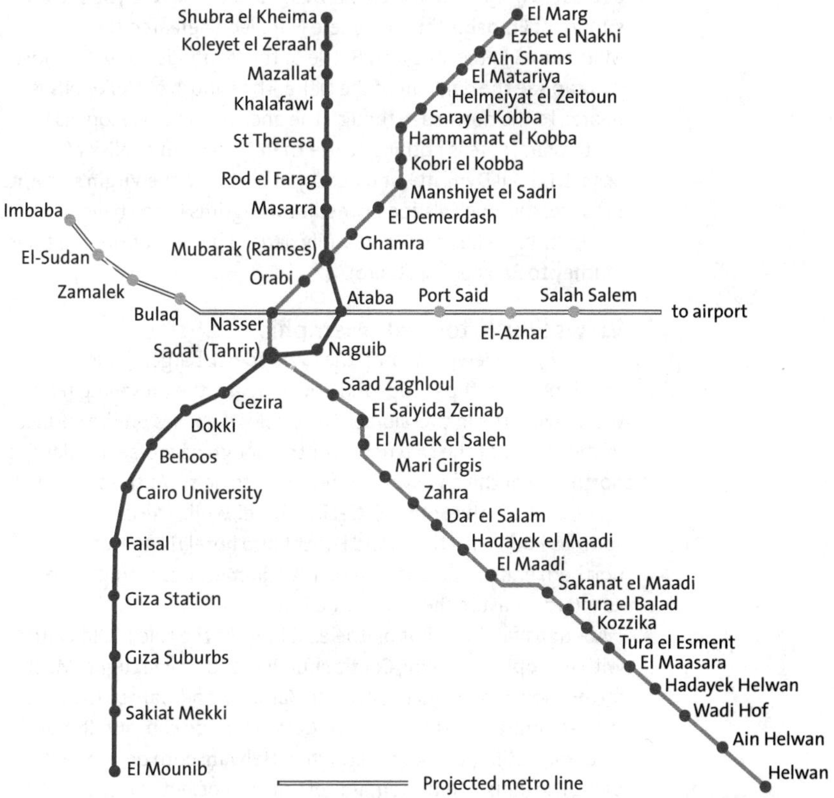

Cairo Metro

Cairo Tower
open daily 9am–midnight; steep fee for the ascent

Cairo Tower, completed in 1962. There is an open observation deck up top, and below it an enclosed coffee lounge and revolving restaurant. There are sweeping **views** of the city and beyond, and this is a good place (easy too on the feet) to establish the topography of Cairo's outlying areas in your mind. It is best to be up in the tower in the early evening as the sun sets over the Western Desert, the sharp outline of the Pyramids as ever marking the great divide between the distant haze of the void and the nearer ephemeral activity of the hive.

The north part of the island is called **Zamalek**, a cosmopolitan residential area of modern apartment buildings and fine old homes amid leafy streets. The **Marriott Hotel** is located here. This part of Gezira can be reached directly from Midan Orabi, along Sharia 26 July and across an old metal bridge.

Following Sharia 26 July (the date on which King Farouk abdicated in 1952) across to the west bank of the Nile you see the suburb of **Embaba**, the site where Napoleon defeated the Mamelukes in the so-called Battle of the Pyramids. Far to the north you can see the dark fan of the Delta. The suburb of **Heliopolis** is nearer, to the northeast, though the ancient site of Heliopolis is north of it. There is nothing to see there except an **obelisk of Sesostris I** (XII Dynasty), and nearby at Matariya the **Virgin's Tree**, its predecessor much visited by medieval pilgrims in the belief that under its branches the Holy Family paused before continuing their journey to Babylon (old Cairo).

Views South, towards Memphis

Below your viewpoint atop the Cairo Tower, barges, feluccas and small motor craft pass up- and downstream, the prevailing north wind giving the impression by the ripples it causes on the surface of the river that the Nile flows south, though of course it is flowing north, one of the few rivers in the world to do so. At the southern tip of Gezira is the **Sofitel El Gezirah hotel**, while the island to the south is **Roda** with the **Grand Hyatt Cairo hotel** rising from its northern end. At its southern tip is a **Nilometer**, constructed in AD 716 to measure the level of the Nile.

About as far down but on the east bank of the Nile is **Old Cairo** with its **Coptic Museum, Coptic churches** and a **synagogue**. Much farther south is **Maadi** (along with Zamalek and Garden City, one of the residential areas favoured by Cairo's foreign community), and farther on still the industrial town of **Helwan**, both on the east bank. The indiscernible remains of Egypt's ancient capital, **Memphis**, lie on the west bank opposite Helwan.

Views East and West

From the Cairo Tower you can sweep your gaze round to east and west and see how the city is bounded on either side by desert. The **Moqattam Hills** are to the east and beyond them the plateau of the Eastern or **Arabian Desert** where places like New Cairo are being developed amid the sands. On a spur of the hills is the **Citadel**, distinguished by the dome of the **Mohammed Ali Mosque**, and spread before it in dark sand-brown confusion is the **medieval city**, as though lurking in past centuries behind the higher, more lightly dusted buildings of the new. Away to the west is the plateau of the **Western Desert**.

Along the west bank of the Nile, opposite Gezira and south of Embaba, are the suburbs of **Agouza**, **Mohandiseen** and, around the Cairo Sheraton, **Dokki**. Mrs Sadat, who now divides her time between America and Egypt, continues to live in a villa here overlooking the Nile, just south of the hotel, once President Sadat's official residence.

Sharia el Giza runs southwards from the Sheraton to the **Zoological Gardens** and **Cairo University**. This is **Giza**, here long before the suburbs began their sprawl along the west bank to the north and out towards the desert escarpment, obliterating the once extensive fields of the fellahin.

The Nile, Old Cairo and Fustat

Old Cairo, and particularly the **Coptic Museum** there, should be high on your list of places to visit in Cairo – you should allow 2 to 3 hours. Otherwise, the circular tour immediately below is really a stroll of two or three hours, which the visitor short on time can skip. The highlights are the **Manyal Palace** on Roda Island and the **Cairo Tower** on Gezira Island – you could simply go direct to the Cairo Tower for its magnificent 360° view over Cairo.

The Nile

A Circular Tour

South along the Corniche el Nil from Midan el Tahrir is **Garden City**, a fashionable residential and diplomatic quarter (rivalled by Zamalek at the north end of Gezira). The British and the American embassies are at its northern end. The area, developed by British planners early in the 20th century, is a latticework of winding tree-shaded streets in contrast to the geometrical regularity of downtown Cairo, which was inspired by the French taste for

Getting to the Nile, Old Cairo and Fustat

Old Cairo and Fustat are about 5km south of Midan el Tahrir, from where you can take the **metro**, though you can also go by **bus**, **riverbus** or **taxi**. There are several places on either side of the Nile and on the islands of Roda and Gezira which can be visited as a circular tour or combined with a visit to Old Cairo.

---

geometry. Feluccas are tied up here and can be hired for sailing on the river.

The **Grand Hyatt Cairo hotel** at Roda's northern tip can be reached across its own bridge from Garden City: stop for refreshments and a commanding view of the Nile from its cascading lobby café, or go up to the revolving restaurant on the top floor. A quarter of the way down Roda, in a lush garden of semi-tropical trees overlooking the eastern branch of the Nile (its entrance on Sharia Sayala, facing the road to El Gama'a Bridge), is the oriental-rococo **Manyal Palace**. Built in 1903 by Prince Mohammed Ali, brother of Khedive Abbas II and uncle of King Farouk, it is now a museum worth visiting for its decorative opulence. On view is a reception palace, the palace proper, a private mosque and the prince's private hunting museum, magnificently and eclectically adorned with wall tiles, painted glass, oriental carpets, colossal Turkish chandeliers, and with architectural elements salvaged from crumbling Mameluke and Ottoman buildings. Continue south to the Nilometer at the southern tip of Roda, or you can cross to the east bank of the Nile to the Fumm el Khalig (in either case, *see* below). Or cross over El Gama'a Bridge to the west bank of the Nile, in which case ahead of you are the **Zoological Gardens** (*see* p.91), while heading north brings you to **Dokki**.

Manyal Palace
open daily 9–4; adm LE30

On a houseboat tied up along the west bank corniche road, Sharia el Nil, just south of the Cairo Sheraton, is the **Papyrus Institute**. Founded by Professor Hassan Ragab, this is a workshop, research centre and small museum demonstrating the manufacture and use of this first flexible writing material. Only *cyperus papyrus*, the same plant used by the ancients, is used here (the institute has several commercial imitators, but they use the modern *cyperus alopecuroides* of inferior quality). The institute grows at least some of its own papyrus, exhibits copies of ancient papyri and sells others. As you go down the quayside steps, notice on your left the plaque marking the highest level of the Nile during the flood of September 1887.

Papyrus Institute
open daily 10–7

At the west end of 6 October Bridge in Dokki, in gardens planted with specimen trees off Sharia Abdel Aziz Radwan, are the fascinating **Historical Museum**, with displays on agricultural life in pharaonic times, and the **Agricultural and Cotton Museum**, which concentrates on all aspects of present-day Egyptian rural life,

Historical Museum, Agricultural and Cotton Museum
open daily 9–3, closed Mon; adm cheap

especially on the country's single most important crop. The handsome new **Opera House** is also here, built in 1989 with Japanese assistance; in its grounds, also in a fine modern building, is the **Museum of Modern Egyptian Art**.

Museum of Modern Egyptian Art
open Tues–Sun 10–1 and 5–9.30; adm

Towards the lower end of the island of Gezira is the **Cairo Tower** (*see* p.90), which rises 180m and offers marvellous panoramas from its enclosed 14th-level restaurant, 15th-level cafeteria and its open 16th-level observation platform. You can now complete the circle by returning to Midan el Tahrir.

South along the East Bank of the Nile

Coming down the corniche from Midan el Tahrir towards Old Cairo, at a point two or three blocks south of your view across to the Manyal Palace on Roda, is a traffic roundabout called **Fumm el Khalig**. This is where the canal, now covered by Sharia Bur Said (Port Said Street) and its southern extension, left the river. There is a large octagonal tower of stone here, once housing great waterwheels which lifted water from the Nile to the level of the Mameluke **aqueduct**, which can still be followed almost all the way to the Citadel. At this end, the aqueduct dates only from 1505 and was an extension made necessary by the westward-shifting Nile; the main part of the aqueduct, farther east, was built by al-Nasr around 1311.

A few blocks farther south is the Malek el Saleh bridge crossing over to the southern end of Roda. At the lower tip of the island is the **Nilometer**, built in 716, though the superstructure with its Turkish-style conical roof dates from Mohammed Ali's time. The stone-lined pit goes down well below the level of the Nile, though the water entry tunnels have been blocked up and you can descend by steps. At the centre of the pit is a graduated column for determining whether the river would rise enough, not enough, or too much, so announcing the expected fertility of all Egypt over the coming year. A reading of 16 ells (8.6m) ensured the complete irrigation of the valley; the Nile crier would broadcast the Wafa el Nil, or superfluity of the Nile, and the dam to the Khalig would be cut amid great festivity. The Nile used to reach its flood in mid-August, but the High Dam at Aswan now regulates its flow and it keeps a steady level year-round.

Nilometer
open daily 9–4, closed Fri; adm cheap

Immediately north of the Nilometer is the former **Monasterly Palace**, built in 1851, noteworthy for its architectural detail and painted ceilings; it is now the **Centre for Art and Life**, a cultural institute devoted to Egyptian art from ancient to modern times, where students' work can be purchased. An annex to the palace is the new **Oum Kalsoum Museum**. Born around the turn of the 20th century into a poor Delta family, Oum Kalsoum first attracted notice as a Koranic chanter at country weddings. By the 1930s she

Centre for Art and Life
open daily 10–2, closed Fri

was earning a Hollywood-size fortune in Cairo singing love ballads specially written for her by Egypt's leading composers. For over 30 years, into the 1960s, her broadcasts on the first Thursday of every month over Cairo Radio brought all of Egypt to standstill and enthralled the entire Arab world.

At her death in 1975 two million people filled the streets of Cairo for her funeral, a greater crowd than even at the death of Nasser. Oum Kalsoum's music remains as popular as ever today.

Old Cairo

The angel of the Lord appeareth to Joseph in a dream, saying, Arise, and take the young child and his mother, and flee into Egypt, and be thou there until I bring thee word: for Herod will seek the young child to destroy him.

Matthew 2:13

Old Cairo's **Coptic Museum** is a must, and a delightful one at that. After spending an hour or two wandering around its rooms, you should look at the remains of the **Roman fortifications**, visit the **Hanging Church** which sits on top of them, and then visit the **church of Abu Sarga** and the **Synagogue**. Allow three hours in all.

Qasr el Shamah (Fortress of the Beacon)

The section of wall and two towers here formed part of the Roman fortress of Babylon, first built in the time of Augustus, added to by Trajan and remodelled by the Byzantines. The technique of dressed stone alternating with courses of brick is typically Roman. The portal between the towers was a water gate and excavation has revealed the original quay 6m below present street level, but the Nile has since shifted 400m to the west.

The Coptic Museum

⑪ Coptic Museum
open daily 9–5; adm LE40

Now the towers of the Qasr el Shamah fortress mark the entrance to the Coptic Museum, pleasantly set in gardens. It is a charming building, decorated with wooden *mashrabiyyas* from old Coptic houses, embracing green courtyards, airy and light within, its spirit in keeping with its collection. The exhibits cover Egypt's Christian era, from AD 300 to 1000, and are both religious and secular, linking the art of the pharaonic and Graeco-Roman periods with that of Islam. The museum is arranged in sections, covering stonework, manuscripts, textiles, icons and paintings as well as decorated ivories, woodwork, metalwork, and pottery and glass. Often, as in stone carving and painting, the work is crude, though agreeably naïve. High artistic achievement, however, is found in the textiles, and there are many fine chemises, tapis and clothes here

Getting to Old Cairo

If taking a **taxi** to the fortress of Babylon in Old Cairo, ask first for Misr (also pronounced Masr) el Qadima, Old Cairo, and then specify Mari Girgis (St George), and you will be brought right to the walls outside the Coptic Museum. By **metro**, get off at Mari Girgis station; by **riverbus** the landing stage is also called Mari Girgis. There is also a **bus** from the main city terminus behind the Egyptian Museum. Old Cairo describes the general area, but you want to arrive specifically at the Roman fortress (known in Arabic as Qasr el Shamah, Fortress of the Beacon) opposite the Mari Girgis metro station.

---

embroidered with motifs of St George, or graceful women and gazelles. Throughout, the museum has beautifully carved wood ceilings and beams.

New Wing: Ground Floor

Room 1. Pre-Christian reliefs and architectural fragments, 4th and 3rd century BC. The themes are pagan gods, such as Pan and Dionysus.

Room 2. Again, reliefs and fragments, but of the 4th to 6th centuries and so early Christian. The cross is incorporated at every opportunity, often surrounded by flowers or backed by a shell forming the half-dome of a niche – see exhibit 7065, a shell with dolphins on either side. Technically the work is similar to the pre-Christian, but there is a sense of excitement at working with the new imagery – Pan and other pagan motifs had become hackneyed.

Room 3. Reliefs and frescoes, 6th century AD. See 7118, showing Christ ascending to heaven in a flaming chariot. **Rooms 4–8** contain more of the same, including work from Abu Jeremias Monastery at Saqqara.

Room 9. Reliefs and frescoes, from the 6th to the 10th centuries AD. See 3962, 10th-century Fayyum frescoes, showing Adam and Eve before and after the Fall. On the right they are naked, enjoying the fruit; on the left they clasp fig leaves to their genitals and Adam points accusingly at Eve as if to say 'You made me do it'.

New Wing: First Floor

Rooms 10, 11 and 12 all contain textiles. Room 10 also displays manuscripts and ostraca; note especially Case 4, exhibit 7948, the tapestry showing a musician and dancers (3rd to 4th centuries AD), beautifully observed, fluid, rhythmic, happy. The Copts were at their best in textiles, which they developed from ancient Egyptian tradition, adding to it Graeco-Roman and Sassanid (Persian) influences. Plants, animals, birds and human beings blend in sumptuous decorative patterns that have a liveliness Byzantium itself could not rival.

Room 13 contains icons and ivories. **Rooms 14, 15 and 16** display metalwork (including armour and weapons). **Room 17** has objects and several striking frescoes from Nubia.

Courtyard

You step out from the main museum building into a courtyard like that of a grand Cairo house, planted and with *mashrabiyyas* round the walls. Across the court is part of the Roman wall and a gate of Babylon; you can descend to the level of the seeping Nile and step along concrete gangways beneath great arches and vaults, where once were prisons, stables and a grain mill.

Old Wing

Entered through the courtyard, the rooms here contain items of wood, pottery and glass. Most agreeable are the *mashrabiyyas*, fixed together without glue or nails, admitting a diffused light through their intricate Christian patterns.

Old Cairo's Churches and Synagogue

Old Cairo's churches and synagogues
the churches close at 4pm; the synagogue keeps irregular hours and usually Rabbi Cohen or Ahmed is there after 4pm to show you around; adm to buildings free, but all are in need of donations

Alexandria was the Coptic Rome. Old Cairo was never a city, never a place of monuments, and it is not a ghetto. Copts live throughout Cairo and all over Egypt, and are particularly numerous in Upper Egypt. But especially within these walls it is an old and holy place, to Jews as well as Copts, and although Muslims are in the majority in the environs of Old Cairo, there are tens of thousands of Copts as well as a number of Jewish families living in the area.

The oldest Coptic churches sought security within the fortress walls, and usually they avoid facing onto the street and so are indistinguishable from neighbouring houses. Their main entrances were long ago walled up against attack, entry being through a small side door. Their plan is basilical, with a narthex or porch admitting to an aisled nave with an iconostasis placed across the sanctuary. In seeking out the five churches within the fortress precincts, and also the synagogue, there is interest too in the winding little streets, glimpses within windows and doors, the decorations of the houses, the domes of some (as in Upper Egypt) and the atmosphere of remove, of an almost rural village.

The **church of El Muallaqa**, the **Hanging Church**, is so named because it rests on the bastions of the southwest gate into the fortress, its nave suspended above the passage. It is reached by going out from the museum grounds between the two great towers and turning left. Though the church claims origins in the 4th century AD, it is unlikely that the present structure, which in any case has been rebuilt, would have been built on the walls until the Arab conquest made them redundant. Certainly, it is known to have become the seat of the patriarchate when it was moved from

Alexandria to Cairo in the 11th century. The interior of El Muallaqa, with pointed arches, cedar panelling and translucent ivory screens, is intricately decorated – the carved white marble pulpit inlaid with marble of red and black is the finest in Egypt. Services are held in the dead Coptic language and in Arabic. On the right, as you come in, is a 10th-century icon of the Virgin and Child, Egyptian faces, Byzantine crowns. On the same wall is an ancient icon of St Mark, by tradition the founder of Christianity in Egypt. El Muallaqa is dedicated to the Virgin and is properly called Sitt Mariam, St Mary. Its central sanctuary is dedicated to Christ, its left sanctuary to St George, its right sanctuary to St John the Baptist, scenes from the saints' lives decorating their iconostases.

Now walk back out to the street and turn right so that you pass by the entrance to the Coptic Museum. Atop one of the Roman towers is the circular Greek Orthodox church of **St George** (Mari Girgis), rebuilt in 1909 after a fire; the adjoining monastery of St George is the seat of the Greek patriarch. Farther along, steps on your right lead down to a narrow street at the level of the early settlement. Walking along this, you will find the Coptic **convent of Mari Girgis** on your left. Still farther along, you are obliged to turn left or right. If you turn left into the narrow lane you pass (right) the Coptic **church of Mari Girgis**, built originally in the 7th century but burnt down in the 19th, only a 14th-century hall surviving. The modern church is of no interest. At the end of this lane you come to **al-Adra**, the **Coptic church of the Virgin**, first built in the 9th century but destroyed and rebuilt in the 18th century. It is known also as Kasriyat el Rihan, 'pot of basil', a favoured herb of the Greek Orthodox Church. Al-Hakim's mother had been of that faith and for the duration of his reign it was transferred to Orthodox use. (For more on Al-Hakim, *see* p.139.)

If where you turned left for al-Adra you had instead turned right, you would at once be at **Abu Sarga**, the **Coptic church of St Sergius** (which can also be reached by steps down from the ticket kiosk in front of the Coptic Museum). This is possibly the oldest church within the fortress, thought to date from the 5th century AD, though it was restored and partly rebuilt in the 12th century. European pilgrims are recorded as visiting the church from at least the 14th century because of its associations with the Flight into Egypt; steps to the right of the altar lead down to the crypt, supposedly once a cave (though in fact it stands upon the paved embankment of the Roman canal to the Red Sea), where according to tradition the Holy Family found refuge after fleeing from Herod.

Abu Sarga is typical of early Coptic churches, being a basilica with aisles separated from the nave by two rows of columns, which support a high timbered roof. One column is granite, the other 11 are marble, and some bear faded paintings of the apostles, probably dating from the 8th century AD. Paintings of saints, probably 11th- and 12th-century, can also be made out within the central apse. A usual feature of early Coptic churches was a basin set in the floor of the narthex, used for Epiphany blessings. It is now boarded over. The central altar screen, inset above with ebony and ivory panels, is 13th-century, but a century or so older are the carved wooden panels depicting (right) three warrior saints and (left) the Nativity and the Last Supper, probably once the leaves of a door. There is an icon in the south sanctuary of the Flight into Egypt. The marble pulpit is modern; the original rosewood pulpit and the canopied altar are now in the Coptic Museum.

Turning right out of Abu Sarga and then right at the corner, at the end of the street you see **Sitt Barbara** (St Barbara's) to the left, a synagogue to the right. The Coptic Church of Sitt Barbara was built in the 7th century AD to a similar pattern as Abu Sarga and like it was restored in Fatimid times. The central screen is 13th-century; the icons atop it are 18th-century. The marble pulpit is very fine. The relics of St Barbara are in the right-hand sanctuary; she had the misfortune to be born into the 3rd century AD, daughter of a pagan father who, discovering that she was a Christian, turned her over to the Roman authorities to be tortured and beheaded. Off to the left, as though an annexe, is the separate **Church of SS Cyrus and John**, also beheaded in the 3rd century.

The **synagogue of Ben Ezra** is a neighbourhood temple whose neighbourhood has gone away – almost all Egyptian Jews were driven from the country in the 1950s and 1960s. It is a forlorn place, a forgotten outpost, yet it claims a more ancient history than anything else in Old Cairo. The synagogue is the oldest in Egypt and resembles in its basilical arrangement an early Christian church. The Coptic church of St Michael did stand here from the 4th to 9th centuries AD, but the Copts had to sell it to the Jews to pay Ibn Tulun's tax towards the erection of his mosque. Sources differ as to whether the original church was destroyed or its fabric remains in what the Rabbi of Jerusalem, Abraham Ben Ezra, at least renewed in the 12th century. But the Jews say the site has far older associations than that: here in the 6th century BC Jeremiah preached after the destruction of Jerusalem under Nebuchadnezzar, and it was the presence of their community here, they say, that drew the Holy Family to Babylon. For the same reason, say the Copts, the apostles Peter and Mark came here; as proof of this they cite Peter 5:13: 'The church that is at Babylon elected together with you, saluteth you; and so doth Marcus my son.' The rest of Christendom argues that Babylon is here a metaphor for Rome; but there is the suspicion that this interpretation is ingenuous, serving to appropriate Peter to Rome in order there to crown him pope and martyr, legitimating the Vatican's claim to apostolic supremacy.

Ben Ezra's synagogue sits in a small shady garden, its exterior plain, a Star of David in wrought iron over the gate. Inside there is an arch of *ablaq* masonry and a small stained-glass window towards the far end above the sort of intricate stone inlay work you would expect to see around the mihrab of a mosque. The majestic proportions of the interior are a reminder that by the 12th century the Jews of this vicinity formed the most important Jewish community in Egypt, North Africa, Palestine and Syria. Thousands of their books and documents were amassed in a hiding place, or *genizah*, within the synagogue, which was only rediscovered in the 1890s, when its treasures were distributed among several of the greatest libraries in the world. They have since enabled scholars to piece together a remarkably detailed picture of religious, commercial and social life in medieval Egypt, the Middle East and throughout the Mediterranean. Ben Ezra has undergone extensive restoration, paid for by the Egyptian government and foreign donors.

Turning right out of the synagogue gate, a lane passes an abandoned Jewish school on the right and leads into a **Coptic cemetery**, a complete town of bungalows for the dead.

Fustat

A short walk north from the Mari Girgis metro station (that is north of the fortress with the railway line on your left) you will come to the **mosque of Amr**, so restored and expanded that nothing remains of the original built here in AD 642, the first mosque in Egypt and the point from which the country's conversion to Islam began. Except for its associations, the present mosque is without interest. Its dimensions date from AD 827 when it was doubled in size: it has several times since been restored, and has fairly recently been restored yet again. It is a pedestrian reminder of a cheaply won victory, and you pause to wonder what it would take to reverse the effect of Amr's 3,500 men.

Behind the mosque extends what appears to be a vast and smoking rubbish dump. The curious should wander into its midst and be amazed and rewarded with one of the most fascinating sights in Cairo. Among the smouldering heaps is a community of **earthenware manufacturers** whose seemingly rubbish houses (be careful not to fall through their ceilings as you walk over them) stand, or settle, amid a complete and complex process for the making of fine clay and the fashioning of narghile stems, drums, small pots, large amphoras and road-sized drainage pipes – indeed these people could equip a band, a kitchen or a city, and probably do meet the earthenware needs of a large part of Cairo. There are vats dug into the ground for mixing and refining clay, subterranean workshops where potters draw from shapeless lumps beautifully curved vessels with all the mastery and mystery of a fakir charming a thick brown snake, and there are enormous beehive kilns like Mycenaean tombs fired from below with mounds of wood shavings shovelled in by Beelzebub children. At evening these mud-covered people wash themselves off, the women appear from out of their hovels in bright dresses, flowers are arranged in soft-drink bottles, a television – wired up to a car battery – is switched on, tea is made, chairs set out, and if you are there then you will be invited to join them in watching the setting sun.

Beyond this potters' community – or, more easily, by returning towards the fortress of Babylon but turning left up the road running alongside the cemetery wall – lie the dismal remains of **Fustat**, the foundations and lower walls of the first Arab city in Egypt, the true beginnings of Cairo. Once famous for its glassware and ceramics, with water supply and sanitation facilities far more advanced than anything in Europe until the 18th century, the city was destroyed and abandoned in 1168 rather than allowed to fall into the hands of the Christian king of Jerusalem. Fustat's destruction fell most heavily on the Copts, who had been the majority here and lost everything. When the threat had passed, the Muslims turned their attention to their new city of Cairo, which you can see rising to the north, and filled it with some of the greatest monuments of medieval civilization.

The **Islamic Ceramic Centre** is at the Fustat site, opposite the cemetery. Built in 2001 in striking traditional style, it is designed for the study of the crafts of pottery and ceramics, and contains workshops, lecture areas, dormitories, exhibition galleries, glazing rooms, a specialized library, and guest rooms for artists, all of which are centred around a series of open air courtyards. With the exception of reinforced concrete, indigenous materials were used in the construction of the centre which has become an important teaching institution as well as a catalyst for the revitalization of the surrounding area. The centre also sells traditionally-crafted ceramics and pottery at competitive prices.

The **National Museum of the Egyptian Civilization** is being built in Fustat, but though scheduled to open in 2009 it has been several times delayed. This is not a museum dedicated to Fustat, rather it will illustrate the entire scope of Egyptian history. It will display artefacts according to themes such as writing, crafts, trades, arts, agriculture, government, society, beliefs, folklore and the Nile – and it will also house the royal mummies, transferred here from the Egyptian Museum in Tahrir Square.

Medieval Cairo

He who has not seen Cairo cannot know the grandeur of Islam.

Ibn Khaldun, 14th century

Islam in Egypt began at Fustat and flowered into a great civilization, many of whose most beautiful monuments survive throughout the medieval quarters of Cairo. The following ten sections tour this Islamic city, progressing generally from south to north.

In the 14th century the Arab historian Ibn Khaldun wrote of Cairo: 'It is the metropolis of the universe, the garden of the world, the nest of the human species, the gateway to Islam, the throne of royalty: it is a city embellished with castles and palaces and adorned with monasteries of dervishes and with colleges lit by the moons and the stars of erudition.' Along with Cordoba and Baghdad, it was one of the great centres of the Arab world, but while Cordoba fell to the Reconquista and Baghdad was destroyed by the Mongols, medieval Cairo survives. The erudition Ibn Khaldun refers to was more the Muslim version of how many angels could dance upon the head of a pin, but otherwise many of the marvels he describes still wait for you, often so unobtrusively that you could pass a façade a hundred times and never guess at the grandeur within.

The streets may be ancient, narrow and dusty, full of strange colour and smell. People may be curious, children occasionally a

Islamic Monuments Identification Numbers

The Islamic monuments of Cairo, and there are hundreds of them, are each marked with a **small green enamelled plaque** bearing an Arabic number. These numbers are given in brackets after the name of each monument covered in the following itineraries, to ensure identification. Although these are historical monuments, they are often places of current worship and when touring this most conservative part of the city you should **dress and act** with decorum. Women should not wear short dresses or too-revealing blouses. Inside mosques you must remove your shoes, or shoe coverings will be provided. For this, and if you accept the services of a guide, or sometimes if you ask to be shown the way up a minaret, **baksheesh** of no less than LE1 will be expected. Whenever local assistance is solicited, not only is it expected, it is usually demanded, but you should avoid paying until you have seen everything you want to, otherwise the demand for baksheesh will be made again and again, at each stage. It is a good idea to carry round a lot of small change to meet these expenditures. Also there is an **entry fee** of around LE40 to the more important monuments, which if not places of community prayer are likely to close at 4pm.

You may sometimes find yourself in a mosque at **prayer time**, and then, though visitors are otherwise welcome, you might be asked to retreat into an alcove or out onto the street. Normally though, the atmosphere is relaxed.

Comfortable **walking shoes** are recommended. Though you might rely on a taxi or other transport to get you to the beginning of the itinerary or to some of the major monuments along the route, walking is otherwise preferable for a sense of leisure and atmosphere, and also because some places are difficult to get at or to discover, even once you are in the vicinity. There are occasional *kahwehs* along the way: that is, places to sit – perhaps just a few chairs beneath the shade of a tree or awning – for a coffee or more likely a refreshing cup of mint tea. Then there is immediate tranquillity; you give your feet a rest and let the city parade by before you.

Medieval Cairo

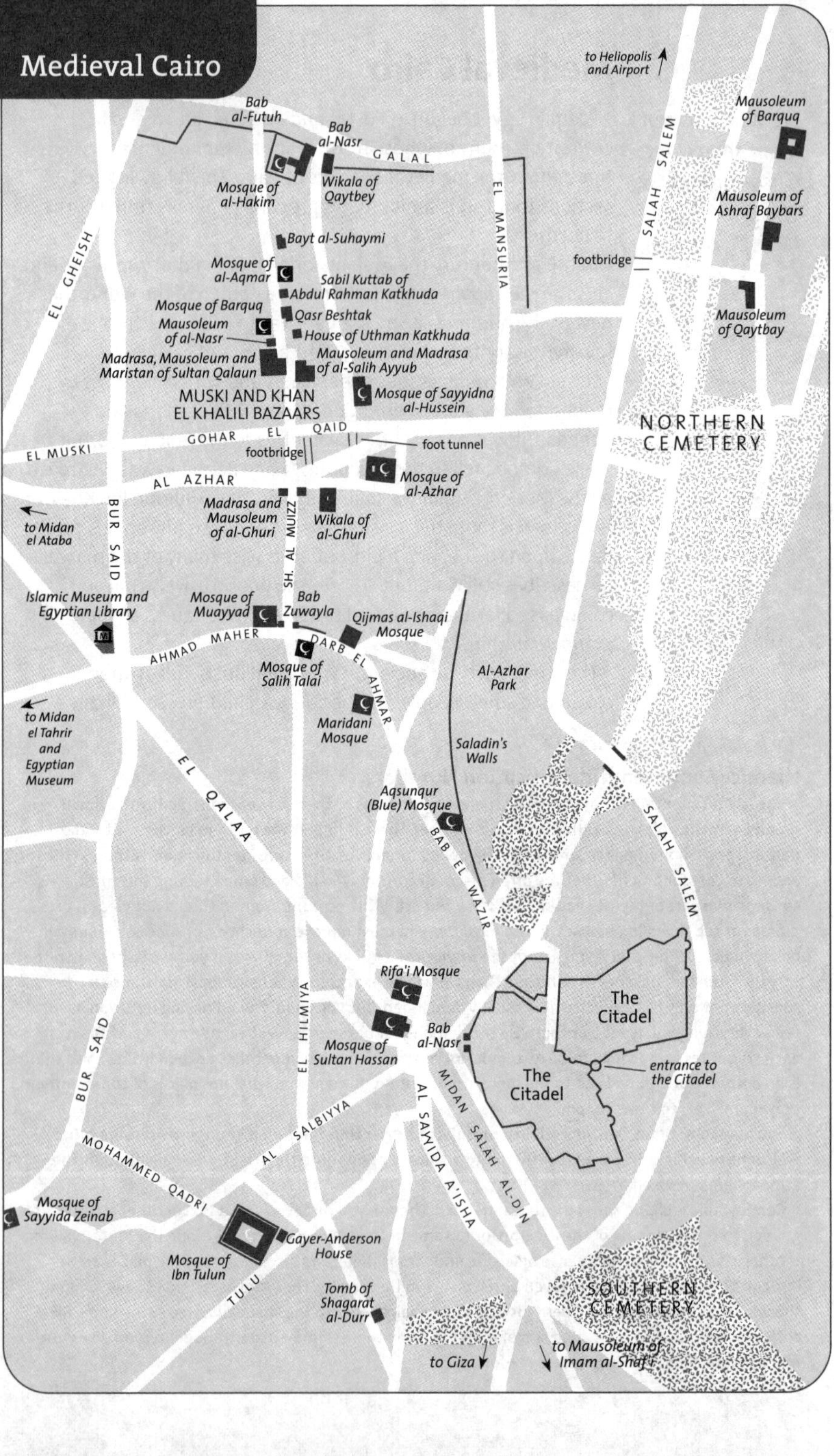

to Heliopolis and Airport
Bab al-Futuh
Bab al-Nasr
GALAL
Mosque of al-Hakim
Wikala of Qaytbey
Mausoleum of Barquq
Mausoleum of Ashraf Baybars
Mausoleum of Qaytbay
EL MANSURIA
SALAH SALEM
footbridge
EL GHEISH
Bayt al-Suhaymi
Mosque of al-Aqmar
Sabil Kuttab of Abdul Rahman Katkhuda
Mosque of Barquq
Qasr Beshtak
Mausoleum of al-Nasr
House of Uthman Katkhuda
Madrasa, Mausoleum and Maristan of Sultan Qalaun
Mausoleum and Madrasa of al-Salih Ayyub
Mosque of Sayyidna al-Hussein
MUSKI AND KHAN EL KHALILI BAZAARS
NORTHERN CEMETERY
GOHAR EL QAID
EL MUSKI
footbridge
foot tunnel
AL AZHAR
Mosque of al-Azhar
Madrasa and Mausoleum of al-Ghuri
Wikala of al-Ghuri
BUR SAID
SH. AL MUIZZ
to Midan el Ataba
Islamic Museum and Egyptian Library
Mosque of Muayyad
Bab Zuwayla
Qijmas al-Ishaqi Mosque
AHMAD MAHER
DARB EL AHMAR
Mosque of Salih Talai
Al-Azhar Park
Maridani Mosque
to Midan el Tahrir and Egyptian Museum
Saladin's Walls
EL QALAA
Aqsunqur (Blue) Mosque
BAB EL WAZIR
SALAH SALEM
Rifa'i Mosque
The Citadel
EL HILMIYA
Bab al-Nasr
Mosque of Sultan Hassan
The Citadel
entrance to the Citadel
BUR SAID
MIDAN SALAH AL-DIN
AL SAYYIDA A'ISHA
AL SALBIYYA
MOHAMMED QADRI
Mosque of Sayyida Zeinab
Gayer-Anderson House
Mosque of Ibn Tulun
TULU
Tomb of Shagarat al-Durr
SOUTHERN CEMETERY
to Giza
to Mausoleum of Imam al-Shafi'i

nuisance and merchants in the tourist bazaars importunate, but generally the inhabitants of these quarters, like Egyptians throughout the country, will be friendly and helpful. This is the heart of Cairo, a heart that anyone with the least sense of adventure will come to love.

After sometimes centuries of neglect there is a new Egyptian and international appreciation of Cairo's Islamic monuments, and a recent drive has been very ably restoring these treasures against the ravages of earthquakes, rising groundwater and the wear and tear of time.

Around the Citadel

The **Citadel** and its **mosque of Mohammed Ali**, sitting on the Cairo skyline, seem irresistibly attractive to tourists. But truly magnificent are the **mosques of Ibn Tulun** and **Sultan Hassan**; if you have time to see only two of Cairo's Islamic monuments, these should not be missed.

The Mosque of Ibn Tulun

Mosque of Ibn Tulun
no adm fee

If you have time to visit only one Islamic monument, the **mosque of Ibn Tulun** (220) should be your choice. The mosque is midway between Midan al-Sayyida Zeinab at the bottom of Sharia Bur Said (Port Said) to the west and Midan Salah al-Din below the Citadel to the east. The area is poor and rundown, but behind its outer courtyard or *ziyadah* the mosque achieves an isolation which heightens the dramatic effect of the inner courtyard's bold simplicity.

Ibn Tulun was sent to govern Cairo by the Abbasid caliph at Baghdad and the mosque, built in AD 876–9, displays strong Mesopotamian influence. A congregational mosque with an inner courtyard or *sahn* of parade-ground proportions, it strives to fulfil the ideal of accommodating all the troops and subjects of the fortress capital for Friday prayers. Arcades run round the *sahn* on four sides, deeper along the qibla wall facing Mecca. Brick piers support the pointed horseshoe arches which have a slight return (that is, they continue their curve inwards at the bottom) and the arches are decorated with carved stucco (restored on the outer arches but original on the others within the arcades), a technique Ibn Tulun introduced to Cairo. The windows along the qibla wall (to your left as you enter the mosque) have stucco grilles (the fifth and sixth from the left are original), permitting a faint light into this deeper arcade with its prayer niche or mihrab and beautifully carved pulpit or minbar, 13th-century restorations. The roof, like the repaired stucco work, is owed to the efforts of 20th-century

Getting to the Citadel

To reach the starting point of this tour you can take a **taxi** direct to the mosque of Ibn Tulun. Or, taking the **174 bus** or **54 minibus** which run from Midan el Tahrir through the Sayyida Zeinab quarter to Midan Salah al-Din (lying between the Citadel and the Sultan Hassan Mosque), you can get off within sight of the Mosque of Ibn Tulun. The **Sayyida Zeinab metro stop** is 500m west of Midan al-Sayyida Zeinab; the mosque is then 600m farther east.

All the monuments in this section are quite close together, with the exception of the **mausoleum of Imam al-Shaf'i** – to reach this take the **405 bus** south from Midan Salah al-Din; it turns left towards the Moqattam Hills and, just where it does so, there is a bus stop. You then walk down Sharia Imam al-Shaf'i a few hundred metres. Or take the **tram** from Midan Salah al-Din, following the same route except that instead of it turning left it continues straight on, terminating just short of the mausoleum.

restorers. Original, however, is the Koranic inscription carved in sycamore running at a height round the interior of the four arcades.

The effect as you enter the *sahn* is of severe simplicity, yet these details of carved stucco and sycamore and returning arches offer subtle relief. You should walk round the *sahn* under the arcades to

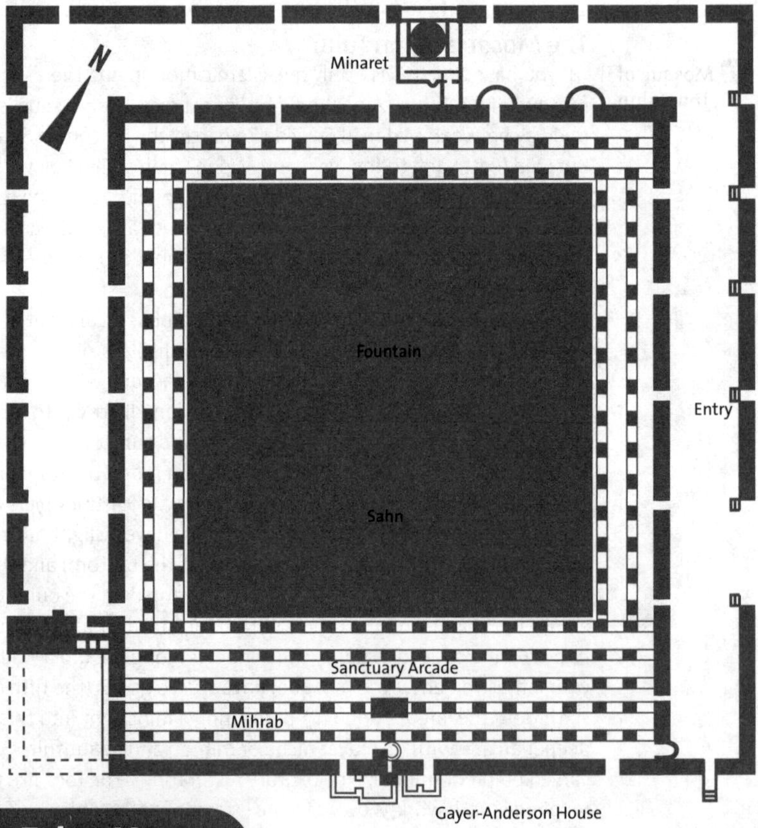

Ibn Tulun Mosque

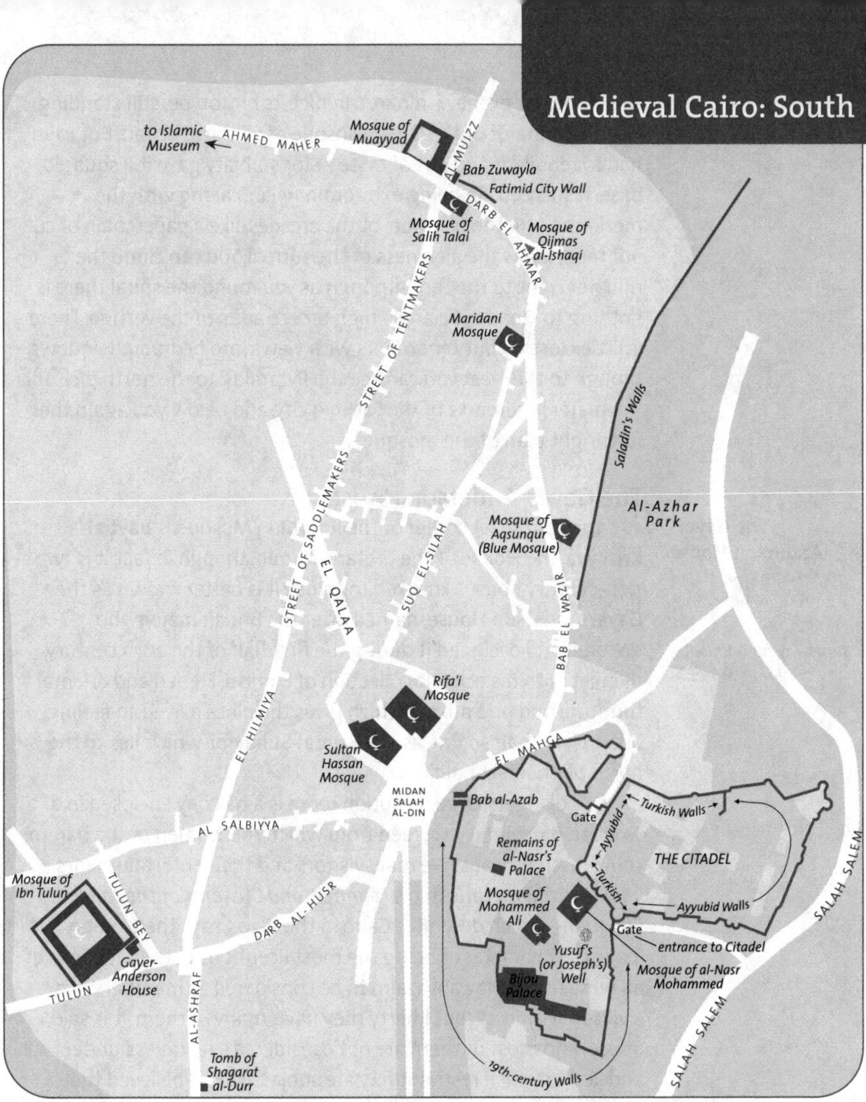

appreciate the play that is made with light and shadows, the rhythm of the arches, the harmony of the ensemble.

At the centre of the *sahn* is a 13th-century fountain. All these 13th-century restorations and additions were undertaken by Sultan Lajin, who had assassinated the incumbent sultan and hid in the then decrepit mosque. He vowed that if he survived to be raised to the sultanate he would restore his hideaway, and to him belongs an explanation also for the striking minaret opposite the qibla wall. The original was Tulun's, in the form of a spiral, and there is a story of Tulun, normally of grave demeanor, absentmindedly twiddling a strip of paper round his finger to the consternation of his audience, excusing himself with the explanation that it was the model for his new minaret. In fact its prototype, still standing, was the minaret of the Great Mosque of Samarra in Iraq. But Lajin had to rebuild it and out of taste or for stability gave it a squared base. It succeeds in being extraordinary and along with the merlons along the parapets of the arcades, like a paperchain of cut-out men, it has the alertness of the surreal. You can climb the minaret right to the top, although as you round the spiral there is nothing to steady you and a high breeze adds to the vertigo. There is little close by but tenements with views into bedroom windows, though to the west you can see the Pyramids, to the north pick out the major landmarks of the Fatimid city, and below you again the forthright plan of the mosque.

The Gayer-Anderson House

The Gayer-Anderson House
open daily 8–4, closed Fri 12–1; adm LE40; tickets are valid on the same day for admission to the Islamic Museum

At the southeast corner of the Ibn Tulun Mosque is **Bayt al-Kritliyya**, the House of the Cretan Woman, though in fact it is two 17th-century houses knocked together. It is better known as the **Gayer-Anderson House**, named after the British major who restored and occupied it during the first half of the 20th century, filling it with his eclectic collection of English, French and oriental furniture and bric-a-brac, which gives the place a lived-in feeling, but it is not half so fine as the Bayt al-Suhaymi, which lies to the north of Khan el Khalili.

Overlooking its large reception room is a balcony enclosed in a wooden *mashrabiyya* screen from which the women of the harem could discreetly observe male visitors and their entertainments. Edward William Lane in his *Manners and Customs of the Modern Egyptians*, which describes Cairo in the 1830s, says the women 'have the character of being the most licentious in their feelings of all females who lay any claim to be considered as members of a civilised nation... What liberty they have, many of them, it is said, abuse; and most of them are not considered safe unless under lock and key, to which restraint few are subjected. It is believed that they possess a degree of cunning in the management of their intrigues that the most prudent and careful husband cannot guard against.' Indeed, Lane believed that Egyptian women were under less restraint than those in any other country of the Turkish Empire, with those 'of the lower orders flirting and jesting with men in public, and men laying their hands upon them very freely.' As for those of the upper classes: 'They generally look upon restraint with a degree of pride, as evincing the husband's care for them and value themselves upon their being hidden as treasures.' The only man allowed into the harem, the female domestic quarters, was the husband – and so the strictures also worked against men, the only unveiled women they could see being their wives or female slaves.

Mausoleum of Shagarat al-Durr

Those interested in making a romantic pilgrimage to the **tomb of Shagarat al-Durr** (169) should walk southwards along the medieval city's main street, here called Sharia al-Ashraf, which passes just to the east of Ibn Tulun's mosque. The tomb is at the edge of the Southern Cemetery in one of Cairo's poorest areas; it stands within iron railings and is kept locked to prevent neighbourhood encroachment. Built in 1250, it is small and simple, though in allusion to her name ('Tree of Pearls'), the prayer niche inside bears fine Byzantine-style mosaics of the tree of life inlaid with mother-of-pearl. Until Pakistan's Benazir Bhutto and Turkey's Tansu Çiller each became prime minister of their countries, Shagarat al-Durr and a near-contemporary at Delhi were the only two Muslim women rulers in history. It can be a dangerous game and Shagarat al-Durr played it fast and loose, coming to a sticky end: only part of her body lies within her tomb – the rest was eaten by dogs. (Her story is told on p.134, in conjunction with a visit to the mausoleum and madrasa of al-Salih Ayyub.)

Midan Salah al-Din

Rifa'i Mosque
adm LE30

Walk to Midan Salah al-Din; to your left (north) are two large mosques pressed against each other like the walls of a canyon, Sharia el Qalaa cutting between them. The mosque on the right (east) is the **Rifa'i**, a modern imitation of Bahri Mameluke style, where members of the late royal family, including King Farouk, are buried, as is the ex-Shah of Iran. The best thing about the Rifa'i is its near-abutment with the mosque of Sultan Hassan on the left (west), the canyon enhancing the massiveness of the latter.

Both mosques are lit by orange lights at night, as though the light itself is old, not bright and white, and has been lingering on the façades for so long it has darkened with age. In the darkness comes the booming call to evening prayer, not mysterious but electrically amplified, saving the muezzin not only his voice but the long trudge up to the top of the minaret. It is a regrettable practice.

Sultan Hassan Mosque

3 Mosque of Sultan Hassan
adm LE30

The **mosque-madrasa of Sultan Hassan** (133) is genuinely of the Bahri Mameluke period and was built in 1356–63 of stone (reputedly from the Great Pyramid) – unlike the brick of Tulunid and some Fatimid mosques. Its short distance from the mosque of Ibn Tulun allows a ready comparison between these exemplars of the two principal forms of Cairo mosque. The purpose of the congregational is to gather in, and architecturally the emphasis is on the rectangular and the horizontal. But the Sultan Hassan served as a theological school, a madrasa. The madrasa was first introduced to Egypt by Saladin as part of his effort to combat and suppress the Fatimid Shia. Classrooms and dormitory space required a vertical structure, most functionally a cube. The central courtyard remains a feature, but opening onto each of its sides are four enormous vaulted halls or liwans, creating a cruciform plan. The doctrinal justification for four liwans was that each served as a place for teaching one of the four Sunni – that is, orthodox – Muslim rites (Shafite, Malikite, Hanefite and Hanbalite), though the origins of the liwan are found at Hatra in Iraq, an Arab city flourishing at least 400 years before Mohammed. But it was the Mamelukes who arranged them with magnificent effect in cruciform plan and who also added to their mosque-madrasas domed mausolea. Hassan's mausoleum is appended to the south end of the mosque but his tomb is empty; he was executed two years before its completion and his body disappeared.

There are many who regard the Sultan Hassan as the outstanding Islamic monument in Egypt, and certainly it vies with the Ibn Tulun. Though entirely different in type, the two mosques share a boldness of conception and clarity of execution, gathering still more strength in restraining decoration to the minimum necessary solely to underline architectural form. There is self-confidence, and at the Sultan Hassan even architectural insolence, but rarely indulgence.

The Sultan Hassan already impresses from the outside. Though it stands beneath the glare of the Citadel it holds its own, its great cornice and the strong verticals of its façade rising to the challenge. Notice how the broad surfaces along the east and west sides are relieved by blind recesses into which are set the paired arched windows of the dormitories. Height is especially emphasized as you enter on Sharia el Qalaa the towering portal with its stalactite decorations – a favourite Mameluke motif. The portal is at an angle to the main east flank of the mosque and the west flank too is bent, though at first sight the building had seemed more regular. Earlier periods had enjoyed more space, but as Cairo grew and became more dense the Mamelukes had to squeeze in their buildings where they could, though they had a fetish for achieving a cubistic effect no matter how irregular the plot. The liwans had also to be cruciform, regardless of the exterior and in the Sultan Hassan this has been neatly done, all hint inside of the irregularity of the outer walls suppressed except for the slight angle of the door in the west liwan.

The portal leads to a domed cruciform vestibule and you turn left into a dark angled passage. It empties suddenly into the north end of the brilliantly sun-filled *sahn*, certainly a deliberate effect and a preparation for the play of light and shadow, concrete and void, intended for the courtyard and its liwans. It is important that you

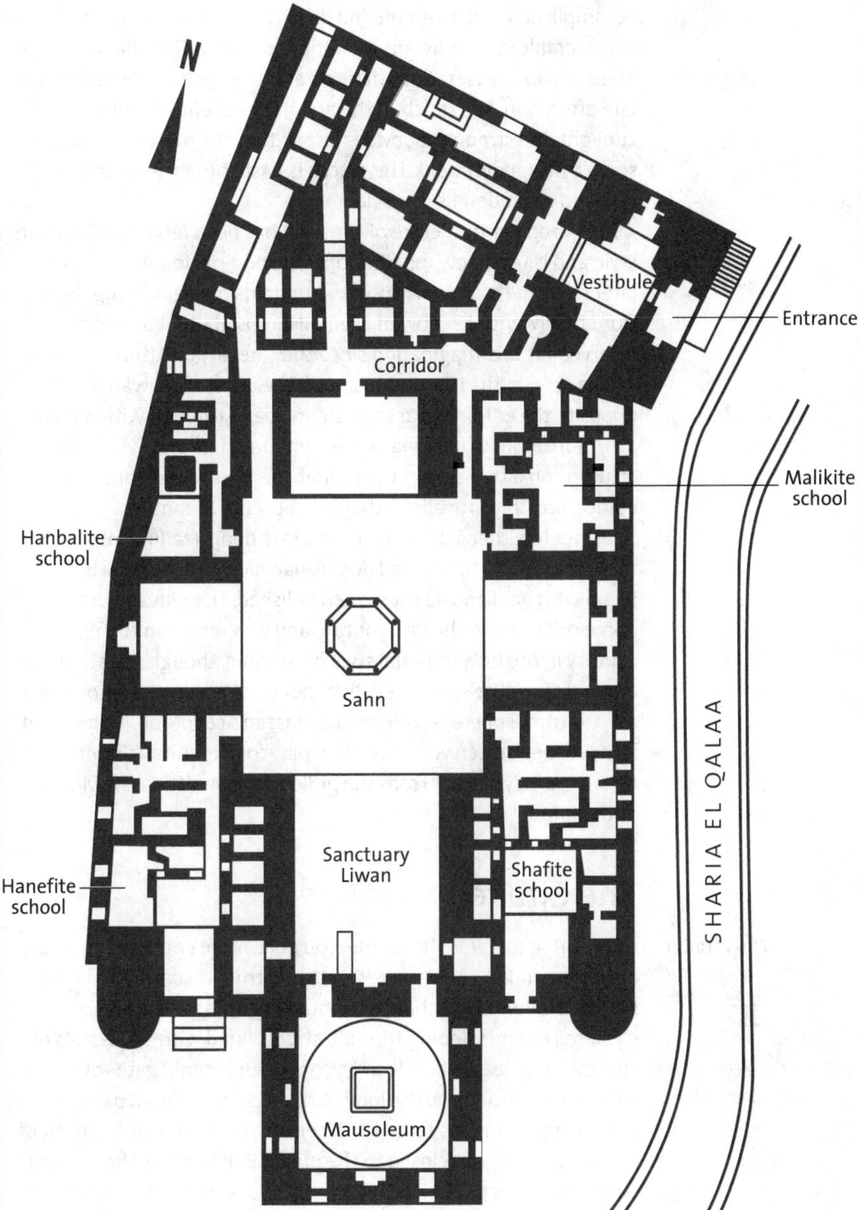
N
Vestibule
Entrance
Corridor
Malikite school
Hanbalite school
Sahn
SHARIA EL QALAA
Sanctuary Liwan
Shafite school
Hanefite school
Mausoleum

do not come too late in the day; indeed, it is best that you visit the Sultan Hassan in the morning when the sun lights up the mausoleum and west liwan and begins its long and rarely accomplished reach into the full depth of the *sahn*. Its depth is considerable, for the liwans lift about as high as the *sahn* is long. The sun soon passes, illuminating hardly more than the merlons by late afternoon, and much of the architectural effect of direct sunlight and strong shadows is lost so that the mosque can then seem a disappointment. The stucco is pasty brown with sand and dirt, and other details need cleaning.

The gazebo at the centre of the *sahn* has been rebuilt in Ottoman style and is used now for ablutions. The original fountain is met later on at the Maridani Mosque. Hundreds of chains hang down from the liwans, the glow of their oil lamps at night a delight reserved for the imagination since they are all gone (though some can be seen in the Islamic Museum). The sanctuary liwan is opposite the entrance passage, a Kufic band running within it and an unfortunately fussy marble decoration on its qibla wall. The columns on either side of the mihrab are from some Christian edifice, possibly Crusader – they do not seem Byzantine.

Farther to either side of the mihrab are doors leading into the mausoleum. The right-hand door is panelled with original bronze inlaid with gold and dazzles when polished. The mausoleum dome collapsed in the 17th century and was rebuilt in the 18th century in the lofty imperial style of Istanbul, though it rests on the original stalactite squinches. Rich though the restored decorations are, the atmosphere is sombre and Hassan's cenotaph, surrounded by a wooden screen where women pray for the sultan's intercession, is very simple. From the grilled windows there are views of the Citadel.

The Citadel

The Citadel
open daily in winter 8–5, in summer 8–6; museums close at 4.30; adm LE50; entrance on the east side, off Sharia Salah Salem

Returning towards the Citadel you once more enter **Midan Salah al-Din**, extended by clearances at the instruction of General Kitchener. It was here that the annual pilgrimage to Mecca gathered before winding through streets lined with thousands of spectators, to leave the city at the northern Fatimid gates of Bab al-Futuh and Bab al-Nasr. The long park to its south was a parade ground and polo field for the Mamelukes. Up a ramp at the front of the Citadel is a gate, closed to the public, **Bab al-Azab**. The crooked lane behind the gate, enclosed by high walls, was the scene of the massacre of nearly 500 Mamelukes by Mohammed Ali in 1811. Only one escaped, leaping on horseback through a gap in the wall into a moat. During the Ottoman occupation and even under Napoleon the Mamelukes survived and were a power to be reckoned with, though more in the nature of warlords and mafiosi who wreaked havoc on the country. Mohammed Ali invited them to dinner at the Citadel, bidding them homewards via this cul-de-sac and cutting them down with their bellies full, thus making himself undisputed master of Egypt and bringing order, security and progress to the country.

But the tourist entrance to the Citadel is on its east side, off Sharia Salah Salem, which means a long walk from the Bab al-Azab or the Hassan and Rifa'i mosques or a short taxi ride. The military still occupies part of the Citadel, an echo of its role as stronghold of the city from 1176, when Saladin built his fortress here, to the reign of Mohammed Ali. For almost 700 years nearly all Egypt's rulers lived in the Citadel, held court, dispensed justice and received ambassadors. A succession of palaces and elaborate buildings thrown up during the Mameluke period were mostly levelled by Mohammed Ali when he built his mosque and the **Qasr al-Gawharah** (the Jewel or Bijou Palace) in their place. The palace, to the south of the mosque, now serves as a museum, housing 19th-century royal portraits, costumes and furnishings in its French-style salons.

The **mosque of Mohammed Ali**, a Turkish delight on the Cairo skyline, proves disappointing close up – though perhaps not for those who have never visited an imperial Ottoman mosque in Istanbul. Half-domes rise as buttresses for the high central dome and the two thin minarets add an ethereal touch, possibly more in tune with our oriental dreams than the robust Arab minarets of Cairo. But the alabaster cladding, a gesture of Baroque luxe, has cheapened with time, while the pretty courtyard with its gingerbread clock (given by Louis Philippe in exchange for the obelisk in the Place de la Concorde in Paris) suggests a folly rigged up for fashion and amusement. That could explain why the mosque is so popular with tourists; also the interior is vast and agreeably cool, the dome huge and the decorations in opulent bad taste. Principally, though, the architecture is routine; there is no feeling of lift or weightlessness to the dome that you find in the better Istanbul mosques, nor an appeal to spiritual contemplation. Mohammed Ali, whose tomb is on the right as you enter, meant this more as a symbol of the Ottoman power he had snatched.

From the parapet to the southwest there is a good view of the mosques of Sultan Hassan and Ibn Tulun, and a panorama of the city (which will be more or less impressive depending on the cinereous haze in which Cairo is smothered by heat) and Helwan, the industrial area to the south.

Across from the entrance to the courtyard of the Mohammed Ali Mosque is the true jewel of the Citadel, the recently restored and magnificent **mosque of al-Nasr Mohammed** (143), dating from 1318–35. Once the principal mosque of the Citadel, it was built in the congregational style with an arcaded courtyard, many of the columns re-used from pharaonic, Roman and Byzantine buildings. The entrance to the al-Nasr mosque is decorated with a typically Mameluke stalactite motif, but the minaret rising above it shows Persion inspiration in its chevron patterns and its fluted cap, still partly covered in green faience tiles. The mosque is beautiful inside, all the more so as Turkish vandals stripped it of its marble panels, revealing its simple elegance and emphasizing the powerful march of its colonnades.

Just beyond the southeast corner of the mosque of al-Nasr is a tower which stands over **Bir Yusef** (305), Joseph's Well, also known as Bir al-Halazun, the Well of the Snail, for the spiral staircase leading 88m down the great central shaft to the level of the Nile. Yusuf was one of Saladin's names and the well was dug during his time by Crusader prisoners, providing a secure source of water in case of siege. The water reaches the well by natural rather than artificial channels, and was brought up by donkeys, the rock steps covered with earth to provide them with a foothold.

Passing through the Bab al-Qullah, which is northeast of al-Nasr's mosque, you enter the northern enclosure where the Burgi Mamelukes were quartered and where there are still military barracks. Here there is both the **Carriage Museum**, which includes a golden state carriage presented to Khedive Ismail by Napoleon III, and the **Military Museum**, its collection of weapons and costumes illustrating warfare in Egypt from ancient times to October 1973.

Al-Azhar Park

Al-Azhar Park
open daily 10am-12 midnight; adm; entrance from the east side off Sharia Salah Salem between the Citadel and Sharia al-Azhar

Al-Azhar Park stands on high ground and enjoys commanding views over the medieval quarters of Cairo and the City of the Dead. The play of sparkling fountains, waterfalls and pools set amid an undulating landscape of lawns, palms, sycamores, black thorns and acacias is reminiscent of the grandeur and mystery of the gardens of Andalusia. Inaugurated in 2005, the park is the creation of the **Aga Khan Trust for Culture**. As the spiritual leader of the world's Ismaili Muslims, whose faith is that of the Fatimid founders of Cairo, the Aga Khan intends the park to work as a catalyst for economic, social and cultural renewal, especially in the neighbouring Darb el Ahmar area. Al-Azhar Park is also meant as a step towards the **ecological rehabilitation** of Cairo generally, which has one of the lowest ratios of green space to urban population in the world, working out to about a footprint per inhabitant.

There was a park here in Fatimid times, but later the site became a rubbish dump. Five hundred years worth of rubble and debris, amounting to 80,000 truckloads, had to be removed. Three large reservoirs for providing Cairo with fresh water were sunk into the spot, and the entire area was landscaped and planted with hundreds of thousands of specially grown plants and trees. In the process a 1.5km section of all-but-buried **Ayyubid wall** was excavated, its towers, gates and battlements now revealed in all their splendour along the western boundary of the park.

From its Moorish-style hilltop restaurant to its charming lakeside pavilion, al-Azhar Park offers marvellous panoramas across Cairo's historic quarters and is bringing renewed life to this once-neglected area.

The Southern Cemetery

At this point you can interrupt your progress north with a visit to the **Southern Cemetery** (al-Qarafah al-Kubra, the Great Cemetery), a vast, confusing and dilapidated Muslim necropolis stretching as far as Maadi. The Eastern Cemetery (known as 'the City of the Dead'; *see* p.140) generally offers the more impressive monuments, but if you avail yourself of transport (or make the long walk there and back), the **mausoleum of Imam al-Shaf'i** (281) in the Southern Cemetery would more than repay an excursion.

The mausoleum is most easily reached by heading south from the Citadel along the street bearing the Imam's name, a distance of about 2km from Midan Salah al-Din.

A descendant of an uncle of the Prophet, al-Shaf'i was the founder of one of the four rites of Sunni Islam and died in AD 820. The cenotaph was put here by Saladin and the mausoleum built by his brother-successor's wife, who is also buried here. The mausoleum is covered by a large wooden dome sheathed in lead and is the largest Islamic mortuary chamber in Egypt. Inside, a couple of cats, some birds chirping, men lying about or reading the Koran, and above this the magnificent dome painted red and blue and gold, a pattern of flowers rising to the highest sound of birdsong. The original lighting system of lamps suspended from carved beams is intact – the only one to be seen in Cairo.

The spot itself is of significance: here Saladin founded the first madrasa in Egypt to counter the teachings of the Fatimid Shia, and it became a centre of Shafite missionary work, the orthodox rite predominant even today in southern Arabia, Bahrain, Malaysia and East Africa. The majority of Cairenes, too, are Shafites, and the

Imam is revered as one of the great Muslim saints (achieved by popular acclamation, as there is no formal notion of sainthood in Islam). Because of this, the mausoleum is annually the site of a great *moulid*, an anniversary birthday festival in honour of Shaf'i, which takes place in the eighth month of the Muslim calendar and lasts for a week from, usually, the first Wednesday. Atop the dome, like a weathervane, is a metal boat in which there used to be placed on the occasion of the *moulid* about 150 kilos of wheat and a camel-load of water for the birds. The boat is said to turn sometimes when there is no wind to move it, and according to the position it takes to foretoken various events, good or evil, such as plenty or scarcity, or the death of some great man.

Darb el Ahmar

The road issuing from the northeast end of Midan Salah al-Din and passing by the northern walls of the Citadel is Sharia el Mahga. Branching north off this road, between the midan and the Citadel and plunging downhill, is Sharia Bab el Wazir, the Street of the Gate of the Vizier; later as it runs up to Bab Zuwayla it becomes Darb el Ahmar, the Red Road. This entire district is also known as **Darb el Ahmar,** a name which throughout the 20th century epitomized a poorer, broken-down section of the city, though it was once a prosperous neighbourhood and included both Muslims and Jews, as the Star of David on the broken-down gates and doorways of some of the houses indicates. Nowadays Darb el Ahmar is being revived again thanks to an infusion of investment by the Aga Khan, the spiritual leader of the Nizari Ismailis, who has also created the adjacent al-Azhar Park. Not only is the Aga Khan's project restoring mosques and other historical buildings, but it is also providing loans for residents to buy their own homes, as this is most likely to promote their sense of responsibility towards their domestic and neighbourhood environment. At the Citadel end, which is entirely residential, the street is fairly quiet; it becomes livelier as you enter the bazaar area farther north. Apart from the ruins of many old houses and some fine intact monuments, you may also encounter the gaiety of a marriage procession – a great noise of motor scooters, car horns, tambourines, ululations, whistling, chanting and cries – an amazing public racket by no more than two dozen people escorting the bride and groom through the streets.

The pleasure of this itinerary is the slow **walk** and the occasional pause at the mosques along the way – enjoyment of atmosphere. At the end of it, in 1.5km, you will arrive at the square before the **mosque of Salih Talai** and **Bab Zuwayla**. From there, subsequent

Getting to Darb el Ahmar

To reach the starting point of this tour take a **taxi** to Midan Salah al-Din, which you can also reach by taking the **174 bus** or **54 minibus** from Midan el Tahrir.

itineraries take you to the Islamic Museum and continue your walk northwards, from Bab Zuwayla to the Northern Walls via Khan el Khalili. The mosques visited in this chapter are still very much places of worship rather than tourist sights and they are usually open throughout the day and into the evening. Nevertheless, tourists may sometimes have to pay an entrance fee, and baksheesh should be paid for services, such as shoe coverings or being taken up a minaret.

Along Sharia Bab el Wazir

Soon after setting off down Sharia Bab el Wazir you come on your right to the **mosque of Aqsunqur** (143), better known as the **Blue Mosque** and much beloved for the wrong reasons by tour guides. It was built in 1347 but usurped in 1652 by the Turkish governor Ibrahim Agha, who slapped up the tiles that give the mosque its popular name. The best Turkish tiles were from Iznik; however, these were made in Ottoman factories at Damascus and are poorly decorated, and often marred as well in the glazing. They are along the qibla wall and around the walls of Agha's tomb, which you enter through a door on the right side of the courtyard. The worst thing about the tiles is their incongruity, for the mosque is otherwise charmingly simple. A stand of palms and other trees makes the courtyard an agreeable place to linger after the hot, desolate *sahns* of other mosques. The pillars round the courtyard, and especially the octagonal ones of the sanctuary, are crude, but contribute to the rustic pleasantness. The finest work is the carved stone minbar, which is original. On the left before entering the courtyard is the **tomb of Sultan Kuchuk**, the Little One, a brother of Hassan who ruled for five months at the age of six, but was then deposed, imprisoned in the Citadel, and three years later strangled by another of his brothers.

From the street you can see behind the Aqsunqur a section of **Saladin's walls**, which extended from the Fatimid city in the north to Fustat in the south, the Mamelukes using a part of its southern section to carry their aqueduct. Across the street from the mosque is a Turkish apartment building from 1625.

Into Darb el Ahmar

Continuing north, Sharia Bab el Wazir becomes Darb el Ahmar and set at an angle to this street, on the left-hand side, is the **Maridani Mosque** (120). Built in 1339–40 in the early Mameluke period, it is one of the oldest buildings in the quarter which until the 14th century had been Fatimid and Ayyubid cemeteries.

Entering from the hurly-burly of the street you are soon absorbed into the restfulness of the Maridani; a monument, yes, but no museum, no entry fee, and no one to ask baksheesh for shoe covers, for there are none (you leave your shoes inside the door and walk about in your socks).

Isolation from the outside world is as much a matter of tranquil ambience as it is of ritual cleanliness. The atmosphere attracts many who come not only for prayer: here you may see men sleeping, boys doing their homework leaning up against the qibla screen, a dozen women talking and their children playing at the fountain (the one removed from the Sultan Hassan). Yet all these things are against the precepts of Mohammed. Lane reported eating, sewing and spinning as well 170 years ago, though these activities ceased during prayers; here you may see the hum of the everyday continue while men are on their palms and knees, submitting themselves to Allah.

If you stand in the open courtyard of the Maridani in the evening, you may see a crescent moon hanging from the approving sky. An easy rhythm of arches on slender antique columns with a variety of capitals – pharaonic, classical, Byzantine – runs round the courtyard, an inner and an outer series, a third and partial fourth (on either side of the mihrab) added to the qibla arcade. A wooden screen separates the qibla from the courtyard, a unique feature in Cairo, and, inside, the arcade is agreeably dark. The mihrab and the minbar wall have had their mosaic decorations restored well. The dome above the mihrab is supported by several red Aswan granite pharaonic columns. The merlons along the parapet of the courtyard are at intervals topped by curious pots. Try, if you can, to climb up the minaret for a more immediate view of the medieval city than you can get from the Citadel.

Another 150m up the street is the **mosque of Qijmas al-Ishaqi** (114), built in 1480–1 during the Burgi Mameluke period. It has been squeezed into a triangular plot where a street joins Darb el Ahmar from the right, yet, despite this the Mameluke fashion for rectangular illusion, succeeds, at least at first glance. Inside however, a sacrifice has been made in the cruciform plan: the north and south liwans are merely vestigial. So restricted was the space that the *kuttab*, the Koranic school usually part of the mosque, had to be sited across the street joining from the right; it is now derelict.

But the mosque itself has been very well restored and though around this period – only a few decades before the Ottoman domination – Mameluke architecture began to deteriorate, there

Rituals and Prayers

Not that you need worry about form, but as a matter of interest a Muslim will carry his shoes in his left hand, sole to sole (the left hand being for unclean uses), and he will put his right foot first over the threshold. If he has not already performed the ablution outside, he will at once go to the inner fountain. Before praying he will place his shoes on the matting, a little beyond the spot where his head will touch the ground, and again to avoid contaminating the mosque he will put his shoes one upon the other, sole to sole.

Prayers are performed five times a day, though mostly at home, with better-off people rarely visiting a mosque except for Friday prayers. But wherever they are performed, prayers follow the same procedure, which is quite involved. First the worshipper will stand facing Mecca and inaudibly propose a prayer of so many *rek'ahs*, or inclinations of the head. He then says '*Allahu Akbar*' ('God is great'), and recites the opening chapter of the Koran followed by three or more other verses; again says '*Allahu Akbar*', and makes an inclination of the head and body. Next he drops gently to his knees, places his palms upon the ground, his nose and forehead touching the ground between them, and during this prostration says 'I extol the perfection of my Lord, the Great', three times. Though still kneeling, he raises his head and body, again says 'God is great', and bends his head a second time to the ground and repeats what he has said before. This – and it is a simplification of the full litany – completes one *rek'ah* and will take about a minute, though several *rek'ahs* will be performed and there must be no wandering of the mind, no irregular movement and no interruptions, otherwise the procedure must be gone over from the beginning. 'Islam' means literally 'submission', and that is what the procedure achieves. The concentration required explains why mosques are often so austere: architecturally they should be conducive to prayer, but should not distract with decorations. That does not explain why nowadays, and in some mosques, women should be chattering in the corner and children splashing in the fountain – yet it does all fit together most agreeably.

was a last bravado of decorative artistry with fine marble inlays, beautifully carved stone and stucco. Within this covered mosque is a feast of detail, yet all of it harmonious and restful; nothing jitters, jumps or jars. The east and west liwans are supported by arches with a slight return, the stonework in alternating red and white, the vaults very fine and the stucco windows excellent.

The inlaid marble floor is covered with mats (the mosque is in daily use), but the keeper will lift these if you ask, the best section being the mosaic flooring of the east liwan. You can also ask to go up the minaret from which there is a clear view of Bab Zuwayla.

The **tomb chamber** by the entrance is plain and dignified beneath a lofty dome. But Qijmas, Master of the Sultan's Horse and officer in charge of the yearly pilgrimage to Mecca, died in Syria and is buried at Damascus; the chamber contains the more recent tomb of a 19th-century holy man. Mamelukes and Turks of Qijmas' rank built not only for Allah or themselves, but also for the community, and a *sabil* or public watering fountain was often provided. This was in keeping with Mohammed's reply when asked what was the most meritorious act: 'To give people water to drink.' You can see its grille outside at what was a convenient height for drawing water 500 years ago, though it is now well below street level.

Outside Bab Zuwayla

Darb el Ahmar now bends to the west, a surviving section of Fatimid wall concealed by the building on your right, and opens into a square dominated by **Bab Zuwayla** (*see* p.122), the massive southern gate into the Fatimid city. The place has long had a reputation for being unlucky, perhaps because it led out to the cemeteries now built over by the Darb el Ahmar quarter, though it was also the site of public executions. Tumanbay, the last independent Mameluke sultan, was hanged here by the Turks. Twice the rope broke, and the third time, his neck.

The street running directly south from Bab Zuwayla is the continuation of the principal Fatimid street to the north, and extends all the way down, past the mosque of Ibn Tulun and through Saladin's walls to the vicinity of the mausoleum of Imam al-Shaf'i. This was the longest thoroughfare of the medieval city and along here amid great festivity the Mecca pilgrims would begin their arduous journey. It changes its name several times and can be worth following for its own sake a little to the south, where it is first the Street of the Tentmakers, becoming less colourful as the Street of the Saddlemakers before crossing Sharia el Qalaa.

On the corner of this street and Darb el Ahmar, facing the square in front of Bab Zuwayla, is the **mosque of Salih Talai** (116), built in 1160 towards the close of the Fatimid period. Salih Talai was an Armenian and a governor of Upper Egypt from where he was summoned to put down disturbances in Cairo. Six years later he was poisoned by a conspiring princess, whom he had executed before him as he died. His congregational mosque, perfectly rectangular in the Fatimid pattern, is one of the most handsome in Cairo. A lower level of shops, again once at street level, was part of Salih Talai's *waqf*, or endowment, as other mosques might have had fields or adjacent apartment buildings, the rents contributing to the mosque's upkeep. The façade therefore would have been higher, its effect still more imposing. Its five keel-arches, supported by classical columns linked by wooden tie-beams, are flanked by sunken false arches or panels topped by stylized shell niches – a perfect expression of the Fatimid style. The arches, however, form a narthex unique in Cairo. Along its interior wall another set of panels, each one immediately behind an open keel-arch, runs in muted harmony. In its proportion and reserve the narthex is a fine composition in classical measure. The mosque interior is spacious, an agreeable rhythm of keel-arches and tie-beams running around the arcades.

The Islamic Museum

The Islamic Museum
open daily 9–4, Fri 9–11.30 and 1.30–4; adm LE40; tickets are valid on the same day for admission to the Gayer-Anderson House (see p.106)

The **Islamic Museum** lies to the west of the Bab Zuwayla, and is at the intersection of Sharia el Qalaa and Sharia Bur Said. Of course the museum could be visited before you explore any part of medieval Cairo, but for the neophyte a visit at this point, halfway through the tour, might be best: you will already have seen enough to make you conversant with form and curious about detail, and you will explore the Fatimid city with greater appreciation. The museum is not visited nearly as much as it deserves to be, so you often receive personal attention from the attendants.

Because of the Sunni Muslim prohibition on the depiction of humans and animals, this is a museum without statues or paintings, where nearly every object is beautifully worked design. A different sort of attention is required, and perhaps you wish sometimes – more here than at other museums – that the exhibits could have remained in situ, admired as parts of a whole. But then the collection began, in 1880, precisely because the monuments from which they mostly came had suffered a long period of neglect – it was only then, in part at European instigation, that the Egyptian government first seriously undertook preservation of Cairo's Islamic treasures.

The exhibits are well presented and lit and are arranged in 23 rooms which proceed chronologically for the most part, though some rooms specialize in examples of a single subject, such as textiles, from several periods. Though no guide book is available, the exhibits are numbered and labelled, often in English and French as well as in Arabic.

A satisfying tour can be accomplished in an hour and a half. With one exception, all the rooms are on one floor. A brief outline follows, but please note that the museum has recently been undergoing extensive renovation, meaning that the contents of a room may have been transferred to another, while some rooms may be closed and their contents inaccessible.

A Tour of the Museum

Room 1 contains recent acquisitions, though also some permanent exhibits, including a magnificent **14th-century lantern** of bronze chased with silver from the Sultan Hassan Mosque.

Room 2 deals with the Ummayad period (7th–8th centuries AD), whose art was representational and drew on Hellenistic and Sassanid (Persian) sources.

Room 3 is Abbasid (8th–10th centuries AD) and includes Tulunid works (9th–10th centuries AD). Here there is greater stylization, with the emphasis on decoration rather than representation, with

Getting to the Islamic Museum

The Islamic Museum is at Midan Ahmed Maher, where Sharia Bur Said (Port Said) and Sharia el Qalaa intersect. A **taxi** can take you here or to nearby Bab Zuwayla (the driver may know it better as Bab al-Mitwalli), or you can take the **66 bus** from Midan el Tahrir.

great use of stucco, characterized by its slant cut. There are stucco panels from Samarra in Iraq, and tombstones, of which 3904 (dating from AD 858) has fine Kufic inscriptions.

Room 4 displays works of the Fatimid period (10th–12th centuries) with examples of very fine woodwork, carved with human and animal figures and foliage. The Fatimids, who were Shia, did not observe the Sunni prohibition on representation of high living forms, and were much influenced by the Persians, whose craftsmen they imported.

Room 4B, off Room 4, has fine wood, marble and stucco carving of the Ayyubid period (12th–13th centuries).

Room 5. Before entering, note above the dividing arch the windows of openwork plaster filled with coloured glass (16th–18th centuries, Ottoman period). The attendant will turn off the main lights for you and illuminate the coloured windows for effect. The room contains works of the Mameluke period (13th–16th centuries). There is a beautiful 14th-century fountain sunk into the floor (the attendant will turn it on). Despite the bloody succession of Mameluke sultans, Egypt during much of this period enjoyed peace and the decorative arts flourished. A Chinese influence was felt in Mameluke ceramics and pottery. Soft woods were inlaid with ivory, bone, tin and ebony, usually in star-polygons, the Naskhi cursive supplanted the squat Kufic style of decorative inscription, and arabesque floral designs found favour. A 13th-century wooden door (602) at the far end of the room shows both square Kufic and cursive Naskhi calligraphy. It is from the mausoleum of al-Salih Ayyub.

Rooms 6–10 are devoted to woodwork, illustrating the development of the art. In Room 6 on the far wall is a carved frieze, originally from the western Fatimid palace (10th century), showing scenes of hunting, music and other courtly activities rarely found in Islamic art. In **Room 7** are *mashrabiyyas*, wooden screens which preserved the privacy of the house from the gaze of the street while still admitting refreshing breezes. They were also used to screen off interior harem rooms from courtyards and reception halls. The projecting niches were for placing porous water jars for cooling. **Room 8** has examples of inlaid wood, while **Room 9** displays wood and bronze work.

Room 10, off Room 9. Here you will be asked to sit down on a lattice-backed seat round a column fountain, which will be turned on for you and illuminated. This is a restful and eye-filling place to linger: gaze up at the exquisite woodwork ceiling, carved and coffered, with three dome recesses, the centre one with windows round it for ladies of the harem to see below. The period is 17th and 18th centuries.

Room 11 is hung with 14th-century bronze chandeliers, and in the cases are various metalwork objects, such as a perfume brazier (15111, Case 7).

Room 12 contains armour and weapons, many of them chased and inlaid. In Case 7 are swords belonging to Mehmet II (4264), who conquered Constantinople, and Suleiman the Magnificent (4263). In the same case, opposite the windows on the right, is the sword of Muradbey, commander of the Mamelukes, which has a remarkable history. It was taken by the French general Murat after he had chased the Mamelukes up the Nile, and was presented to Napoleon, who in turn wore it when calling on the Directory shortly before seizing power on 18 Brumaire 1799. He had it with him also at Waterloo and left it in his carriage, which he abandoned in haste after the battle; it then was presented to Wellington.

Rooms 13–16 contain pottery of various periods from Egypt, and from as far west as Spain and as far east as China.

Room 17 is up the stairs on your right as you enter from the garden. It displays textiles and carpets of various periods from Egypt and elsewhere in the Islamic world.

Room 18, off Room 19, is an outdoor court which contains principally Turkish headstones and tombs, but also other stonework objects, including a sundial and water-level measures.

Room 19 is devoted to the art of the book, its changing exhibits sometimes including illuminated Korans, at other times manuscripts such as those of Avicenna on anatomy and botany. Avicenna (which is the Westernized version of 'Ibn Sina') lived from AD 980 to 1037 and was one of the greatest physicians of the Middle Ages. Chaucer mentions him in *The Canterbury Tales*. He was an example of the way in which the Islamic world passed on the medical theory of the Greeks, enriching it by practical observation and clinical experience.

Room 20 exhibits Turkish art since the 15th century, including tapestries, china and jewellery. Between Rooms 20 and 21 are enamelled glass lamps which the attendant will illuminate.

Room 21 has more glass lamps in cases round the walls, and in the centre a fine Isfahan carpet that once belonged to King Farouk. The lamps are from mosques (and include some of those now entirely missing from the liwans of the Sultan Hassan) and are arranged chronologically from left to right, from the 12th to the 15th centuries.

Room 22 contains Persian objects, mostly pottery, some of which (Cases 1 and 2) have been copied from Chinese models.

Room 23 is for temporary exhibitions.

The **garden** can now be enjoyed on your way out; there are welcome refreshments for sale in a flower-planted setting with a shaded gazebo, a fountain, columns and other large stone pieces. Particularly fine are the large marble panels bearing Fatimid figurative reliefs of plants, birds, fish and animals. The fountain comes from the Monasterly Palace, now the Centre for Art and Life, on Roda Island. Its purpose was to run a stream of water through channels decorated with creatures of the Nile, the channels encircling a large dining table, the flowing water keeping the diners cool.

In the same building but on the upper floor is the **Egyptian Library**, with its entrance on Sharia el Qalaa. Containing over 750,000 volumes and a vast collection of manuscripts of the Koran dating back to the 8th century AD and, most outstanding visually, a collection of Persian manuscripts adorned with miniatures of imaginative conception and frequently employing living forms as distinct from the purely ornamental art of the Korans.

Bab Zuwayla to Khan el Khalili

Though the distance covered by this walk is less than 1km, you should allow at least an hour – and that does not include wandering about Khan el Khalili itself, for you are now entering the heart of the **medieval city**, where streetlife as much as monuments will hold you spellbound in fascination. The most impressive thing to do is to climb one of the minarets above Bab Zuwayla.

The City Gates

When you stand before **Bab Zuwayla** you are standing at the entrance to the Fatimid city of al-Qahira. Nothing remains of the luxurious palaces, the pleasure pavilions and the fabulous gardens that the Fatimids built within their walled royal enclosure. Only the massive gates stand testimony to the Fatimids' might. Though the street level has risen over the centuries and the foundations of the gate are now buried deep in the ground, Bab Zuwayla still overwhelms with its imposing walls of giant limestone blocks, some of them taken from pharaonic structures. The minarets belong to the adjacent mosque and are later Mameluke work.

Bab Zuwayla was built at the same time (11th century) as, and in a plan similar to, Bab al-Futuh and Bab al-Nasr to the north. These three are the last surviving of the 60 gates that once encircled medieval Cairo and which, well into the 19th century, were shut at

Getting to Bab Zuwayla and Khan el Khalili

From Midan el Tahrir, take the **66 bus** to the Islamic Museum at Midan Ahmed Maher, where Sharia Bur Said (Port Said) and Sharia el Qalaa intersect, then walk east along Sharia Ahmed Maher to Bab Zuwayla. The 66 bus also goes to Khan el Khalili, north of Bab Zuwayla. A **taxi** can take you direct to Bab Zuwayla (the driver may know it better as Bab al-Mitwalli).

---

night, enclosing the city's then 240,000 population. Except that Bab Zuwayla had long since found itself outflanked by the growth of the city to the south (where it was delimited by Saladin's walls), and in fact marked the city centre. The architects of all three were Armenians from Edessa (present-day Urfa, in what is now Turkey), and their work is contemporary with and resembles the fortifications of the former Armenian capital of Ani in eastern Turkey. Certainly here at Bab Zuwayla, the projecting round towers connected by a walkway and an arch, repeating the curve of the gateway below, show Armenian or Byzantine rather than Arab inspiration. Springing from the massive towers are the elegant minarets of the mosque of Muayyad, its serrated dome farther back seeming to rise between them.

The gate was named after the al-Zawila, a Berber tribe whose Fatimid soldiery were quartered nearby. But most inhabitants know it as the **al-Mitwalli**, after El Kutb al-Mitwalli (*see* box below).

Passing through the gate, you should enter the **mosque of Muayyad** (190) on your left, noting the magnificent doors, removed here from the mosque of Sultan Hassan. You enter less for any intrinsic interest, though the Muayyad is restful and has a garden, than for access to the top of Bab Zuwayla or even up one of the minarets.

This is a view of medieval Cairo from its heart, and it is splendid. The last of the great open courtyard congregational mosques, the Muayyad was built in 1416–20 by the Burgi Mameluke Muayyad Shaykh, who had been imprisoned on the spot before becoming sultan.

The Story of a Saint

El Kutb al-Mitwalli was the holiest man alive at any one time, who would assume a humble demeanour and simple dress, and station himself inconspicuously, even invisibly, at certain favourite places. Bab Zuwayla was the most famous of these in Egypt, though he could flit to Tanta in the Nile Delta or to Mecca and back in an instant. His service was to reprove the impious, expose the sanctimonious and to distribute evils and blessings, the awards of destiny. Into the 20th century passers-by would recite the opening of the Koran, while those with a headache would drive a nail into the door and sufferers from a recent toothache would fix their tooth to it as a charm against recurrence. Locks of hair and bits of clothing would also be attached by the sick in search of a miracle – indeed they still are, and it is said the saint still makes his presence known by a gleam of light appearing mysteriously behind the west door.

Along Sharia Muizz: Souks and Wikalas

The street running north from Bab Zuwayla is **Sharia Muizz** (named after the caliph of the Fatimid conquest), though over its distance between Bab Zuwayla and Bab al-Futuh it enjoys successive traditional names, each one demarcating a **souk** reserved to a particular trade or the sale of a particular type of merchandise – ensuring, subject to proper bargaining, price control by competition between neighbours. Hence alongside Muayyad's mosque the street is Shari'es-Sukkariya, the sugar bazaar.

A short distance farther north and on the right where the street makes a small wiggle is the ornate Ottoman-style **Sabil Kuttab of Mohammed Ali**, built in 1820 by Mohammed Ali, the new ruler of Egypt, in honour of his son Tusun who had led the early campaigns against the Wahhabis in Arabia and died there in 1816. The Wahhabis, led by Abdullah ibn Saud, had recently captured Mecca and Medina in the Hejaz where they were imposing their fundamentalist version of Islam. Responding to a request from the Ottoman sultan to rid him of the Wahhabis, Mohammed Ali sent an army under the command of his son Tulun. When that failed, he put another son, Ibrahim, in charge of the army, and in 1818 Ibrahim drove the Wahhabis out of Mecca and Medina and captured Abdullah ibn Saud, who was sent to Constantinople where the sultan struck off his head. A hundred or so years later and the Wahhabis, still under the leadership of the Saud family, again captured the Hejaz and made themselves rulers of what they now call Saudi Arabia.

Continuing up to the intersection with the modern Sharia al-Azhar, you find yourself between two Mameluke buildings, the **madrasa of Sultan al-Ghuri** (189) on the left and his **mausoleum** (67) on the right. **Al-Ghuri** was the penultimate Mameluke sultan and the last to reign for any duration (1500–16). A keen polo player into his 70s, a grandiose builder, an arbitrary despot, a torturer, murderer and thief – in short, no less than what you would expect a Mameluke sultan to be – he inaugurated his madrasa in May 1503 with a great banquet attended by the Abbasid caliph and all the principal civil, military and religious officials, the souks down to

Spot Checks and Punishments

In Mameluke times competition was not the only control on market prices: the *mohtesib*, an officer on horseback, would regularly ride through the souks, preceded by a man carrying a pair of scales and followed by the executioner. If spot checks revealed short weights, a butcher or a baker would have his nose pierced with a hook, a piece of meat, a loaf of bread, suspended from it as the poor man was himself tied to the grilled window of a mosque and left to endure the heat of the sun and the indifference of passers-by. One butcher who sold short was deprived of that much flesh from his own body, while a seller of *kunefeh*, a sweetmeat made from that vermicelli pasta (*atayif*) you still see prepared along the streets at night, was fried on his own copper tray for overcharging.

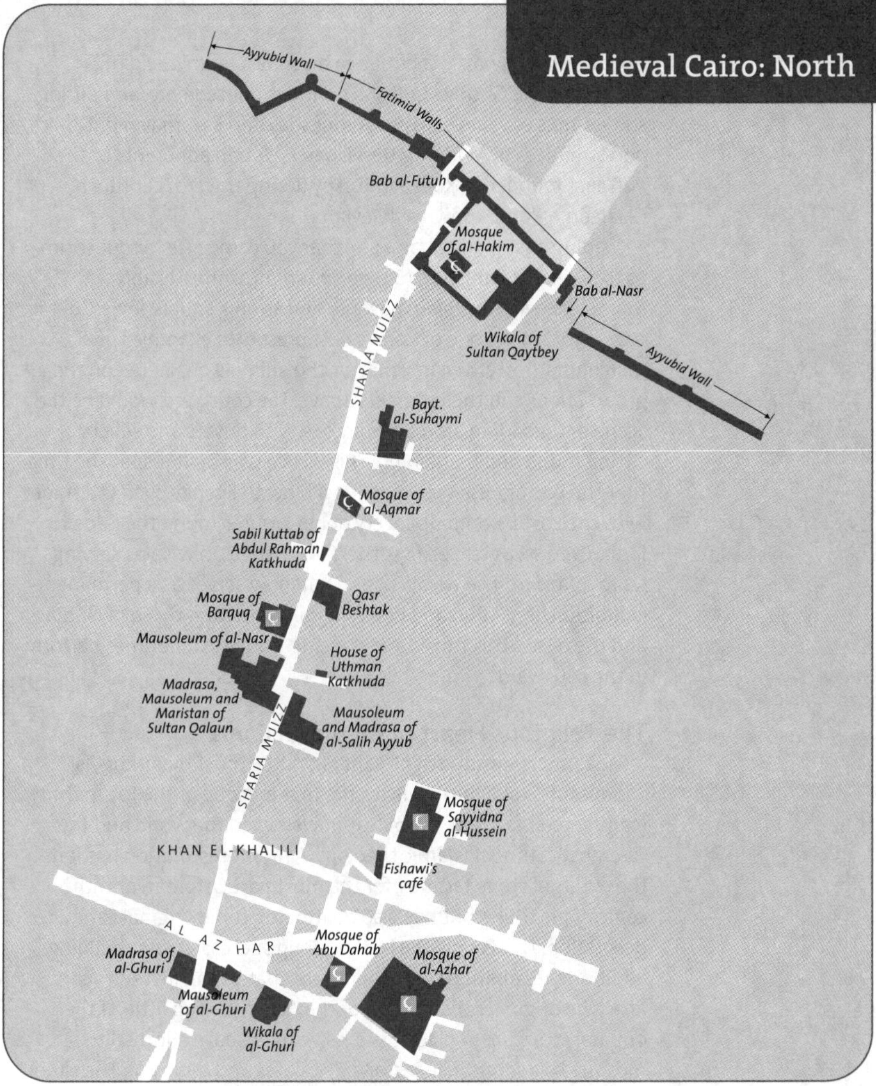

Medieval Cairo: North

Bab Zuwayla magnificently illuminated and decorated. But though agreeably exotic at first impression, with strong lines and bold *ablaq* (that red-and-white pattern of the minaret with its curious topping of five small bulbous domes), on closer inspection there is lack of elegance in the details, and in climbing up to the roof you see that the *ablaq* is not contrasting stone but crudely painted on.

Across the street, the mausoleum dome, now collapsed, had to be rebuilt three times during al-Ghuri's reign and, as though shrewdly realizing that this might be an unsafe place to be buried, he got himself killed outside Aleppo in a losing battle against the Turks. His luckless successor, that same Tumanbay who was hanged three times at Bab Zuwayla, is buried in his mausoleum (*see* p.118). Nowadays the Ghuriya Cultural Centre is housed here, and during some times of year there are Wednesday and Saturday night performances by **Whirling Dervishes**, Egyptian adherents of the Sufi sect founded in Konya in Turkey during the 13th century by Celâleddin Rumi, known as Mevlâna.

Heading east along Sharia al-Azhar you come after about 100m to the **wikala of al-Ghuri** (64) on your right, unmistakably Mameluke with its *ablaq* masonry and strong, square lines. Built in 1504–1505, this is one of Cairo's best preserved examples of a merchants' hostel or caravanserai, the animals quartered on the ground floor and their masters above. The courtyard would be the scene of unloading aromatic cargoes, with buyers and sellers sitting round and bargaining. This wikala was built just at the time that the Portuguese were dealing a blow to Egypt's overland trade with the East by their discovery of new routes round the Cape to India. Even so, as late as 1835 there were still 200 wikalas serving Cairo's bazaars. The wikala of al-Ghuri now serves as a permanent exhibition of fellahin and Bedouin **folk crafts**, and those of Nubia and the oases. Folk music and dancing troupes sometimes perform in the courtyard.

The Religious Heart of Medieval Cairo

The famous **mosque of al-Azhar** (97), 'the most blooming', is 100m east of al-Ghuri's wikala, the first mosque of the Fatimid city (completed in AD 971), the oldest university in the world and the foremost centre of Islamic theology. A recent restoration has left the external stone façades, for the most part Ottoman or 19th-century, gleaming but has also obliterated some original Fatimid decoration. This is only the last in a long succession of rebuilding, additions, restorations and alterations that began just ten years after the original construction of the Azhar, leaving little of the original structure in place. Successive rulers have adorned the mosque by adding colleges, arcades, gates and minarets. The varied minarets and domes added in Mameluke times have given the Azhar an almost fairy tale silhouette, but the sun-swept central court and its surrounding arcades retain the simple noble splendour of the Fatimid original. People still gather here, as they have done for over a thousand years, among them students and teachers at lessons, some pacing back and forth, mumbling to themselves, memorizing religious texts, others dozing.

Throughout the millennium of its existence, al-Azhar has offered free instruction and board to students from all over the Islamic world, from West Africa to the East Indies, its courses sometimes lasting 15 years. *Riwaqs* or apartments are set aside around three

Shia and Sunni

Mohammed was more than a prophet: he organized the Arab tribes into an enduring political and military force that within a hundred years or so of his death in AD 632 advanced as far west as Morocco and Spain, as far north as Poitiers and as far east as the Indus. But he died without naming a successor. His son-in-law Ali, husband of the Prophet's daughter Fatima, advanced his claim; but after some argument Abu Bakr, one of Mohammed's companions, won acceptance as Khalifat rasul-Allah, or Successor to the Apostle of God. Abu Bakr was succeeded by Omar, who was succeeded on his death by Othman, an old, weak and vacillating man but a member of the powerful Umayyad family of Mecca. Tribal tensions within the ever-expanding Arab Empire led to revolt and his murder in AD 656. Again, Ali put himself forward as the natural inheritor of the caliphate, for not only was he related to Mohammed through Fatima, but he was a man of considerable religious learning and sincerity, while his supporters claimed the Umayyads were no more than power-seeking opportunists – to some extent both sides cloaked political and economic aspirations in religious arguments. Ali however was opposed by Aisha (who had been Mohammed's favourite wife) and her Umayyad family, and many of Mohammed's surviving companions. Ali took to arms and won his first battle, but later saw his authority dissolve when rebels advanced on his army with copies of the Koran fixed to the points of their spears and his troops refused to fight. Ali was assassinated and the Umayyads were installed once again in the caliphate.

The real wound to Islam occurred however when Ali's son – no mere in-law of the Prophet but of his blood – led a revolt against the by now overwhelming forces of the Umayyads, and after a fanatical struggle was slain with all his men. In a sense the Prophet's own blood had been shed – excusable, said the Ummayads, for Hussein was no more than an outlaw; martyrdom, replied those who had supported Ali and Hussein.

It was on this matter of succession – divine right versus might – that Islam was riven, for the partisans, or *Shia*, of Ali refused to accept as caliph any but Ali's descendants; while the Sunni, followers of the *sunna*, the Way, barred the caliphate to the Prophet's descendants for all time. In fact, the Shia went on to win some notable victories, as when the Fatimids took Egypt, and to this day one-tenth of all Muslims (Iranians, most Iraqis and Bahrainis, and significant numbers in Yemen, Syria, Lebanon and eastern Arabia) still hold to the Shia conviction that with the deaths of Ali and Hussein the greater part of Islam was stained with betrayal.

sides of the court for specific nationalities or provinces of Egypt, and students have traditionally studied religious, moral, civil and criminal law, grammar, rhetoric, theology, logic, algebra and calculations on the Muslim calendar which is based on the moon, its festivals changeable but always advancing against the secular solar calendar. The **chapel of the Blind** at the eastern angle of al-Azhar accommodates blind students, once notorious for their outrageous behaviour. Fanatical in their belief and easily thinking themselves persecuted, they would rush out into the streets, snatching at turbans, beating people with their staves and groping about for infidels to kill.

Al-Azhar's religious curriculum has remained unchanged since the days of Saladin, who turned al-Azhar from a hotbed of Shi'ism to the home of orthodoxy, though Nasser obliged the university to include, too, schools of medicine, science and foreign languages, so that in many ways it is now in competition with other institutions of higher education in Egypt. The modern university buildings are behind the mosque.

You enter the mosque through the double-arched **Gate of the Barbers** (the only one open to visitors), where formerly students had their heads shaved, and for a bit of baksheesh you can ascend the minaret of Qaytbey. Passing into the courtyard, on the left is the library, worth a visit, and to the right a 14th-century madrasa with a fine mihrab. The sanctuary hall directly opposite the entry gate is very deep, though in Fatimid times it did not extend beyond the fifth row of columns (that is five rows beyond the two of the east arcade), and the original mihrab remains. These columns were taken mostly from early churches. The sanctuary was extended to eight rows in the 18th century and a new mihrab placed at its farthest qibla wall.

Leaving al-Azhar and walking north, you pass under the busy Sharia al-Azhar and stand before the **mosque of Sayyidna al-Hussein**, a modern structure with slender Turkish-style minarets built on a Fatimid site. This is the main congregational mosque of Cairo and the President of the Republic comes here on feast days for prayers, while the open square before it is the centre for popular nightly celebrations throughout the month of Ramadan – well worth seeing.

The Hussein, named for a grandson of the Prophet, is supposedly forbidden to non-Muslims, though if you show interest you may well be invited inside. The claim is that Hussein's head was brought to Cairo in 1153 in a green silk bag and was deposited in the mausoleum (it is also said to be in the Great Mosque in Damascus), a relic of one of the most critical events in Islamic history, the schism between the Sunni majority and the Shia. It is remarkable that it is here in the old Fatimid city, by the mausoleum supposedly containing the very head of the Shia martyr, that the president of thoroughly Sunni Egypt should come to pray.

Muski and Khan el Khalili

The terms 'Muski' and 'Khan el Khalili' are used interchangeably by both foreigners and Egyptians alike to describe what are historically two different **bazaars**. **Muski** lies astride Sharia el Muski, a street of Mohammed Ali's period running east from Midan Ataba, pots, pans, plastic bowls and other prosaic wares sold at its western end but blending with the oriental atmosphere of Khan el Khalili, which it joins to the east. Both are lively throughout the day and well into the night, especially on Thursdays and Fridays, but most shops are closed on Sundays.

Khan el Khalili (*see* map on pp.130–1) is the larger and older of the two, and grew round a khan or caravanserai built in 1382 by Sultan Barquq's Master of Horse, Garkas el Khalili. It became known as the Turkish bazaar during the Ottoman period and has always attracted foreign merchants – Jews, Armenians, Persians and Arabs

– and so it is not surprising that today, along with the Muski, it is Cairo's tourist bazaar, selling souvenirs, perfume oils, jewellery, leather goods and fabrics. Of course the sight of so many tourists invites relentless importuning, but there is adventure all the same. Escape down back alleyways where an artisan sitting in his hole in the wall may be patiently making beads one by one from rough bits of stone, turning them on a spindle by means of a bow. Or start in bargaining and then break off – an accepted, indeed the expert pattern – and instead sip a proffered glass of tea, idling for hours if you like upon a pile of carpets without there being any sense of the need for business. Or go into **Fishawi's**, the famous café just off Midan Sayyidna al-Hussein. Here you can have the chance of easy conversation and a gentle smoke of a hubble bubble water pipe ('Do not inhale, it is not hashish'), and open the pages of *Children of the Gebelawi* (banned in Egypt for being blasphemous) or *Midaq Alley* by Naguib Mahfouz, Egypt's Nobel Prize-winning novelist, who set these books around this area:

> *Many things combine to show that Midaq Alley is one of the gems of times gone by and that it once shone forth like a flashing star in the history of Cairo. Which Cairo do I mean? That of the Fatimids, the Mamelukes or the Sultans? Only God and the archaeologists know the answer to that, but in any case, the alley is certainly an ancient relic and a precious one... Although Midaq Alley lives in almost complete isolation from all surrounding activity, it clamours with a distinctive and personal life of its own. Fundamentally and basically, its roots connect with life as a whole and yet, at the same time, it retains a number of the secrets of a world now past.*

Khan el Khalili extends in part over the site of the now vanished Fatimid palaces, which covered an area of 400,000 square metres and housed 12,000 domestics. The palaces, al-Muizz on the east side of Sharia Muizz and al-Aziz on the west, loomed like mountains when seen from afar; near to, they could not be seen at all, so high were the surrounding walls.

To the Northern Walls

Allow two to three hours for this walk of about 1.5km, from Khan el Khalili to the northern gates of the Fatimid city, **Bab al-Futuh** and **Bab al-Nasr**. Along the way, you should not fail to visit **Qalaun's mausoleum** and **Bayt al-Suhaymi**, the finest of the old Cairene houses open to the public.

It is also good to walk here at night, when the stones still seem to breathe the tales of the beautiful Shagarat al-Durr and the crazed Caliph al-Hakim.

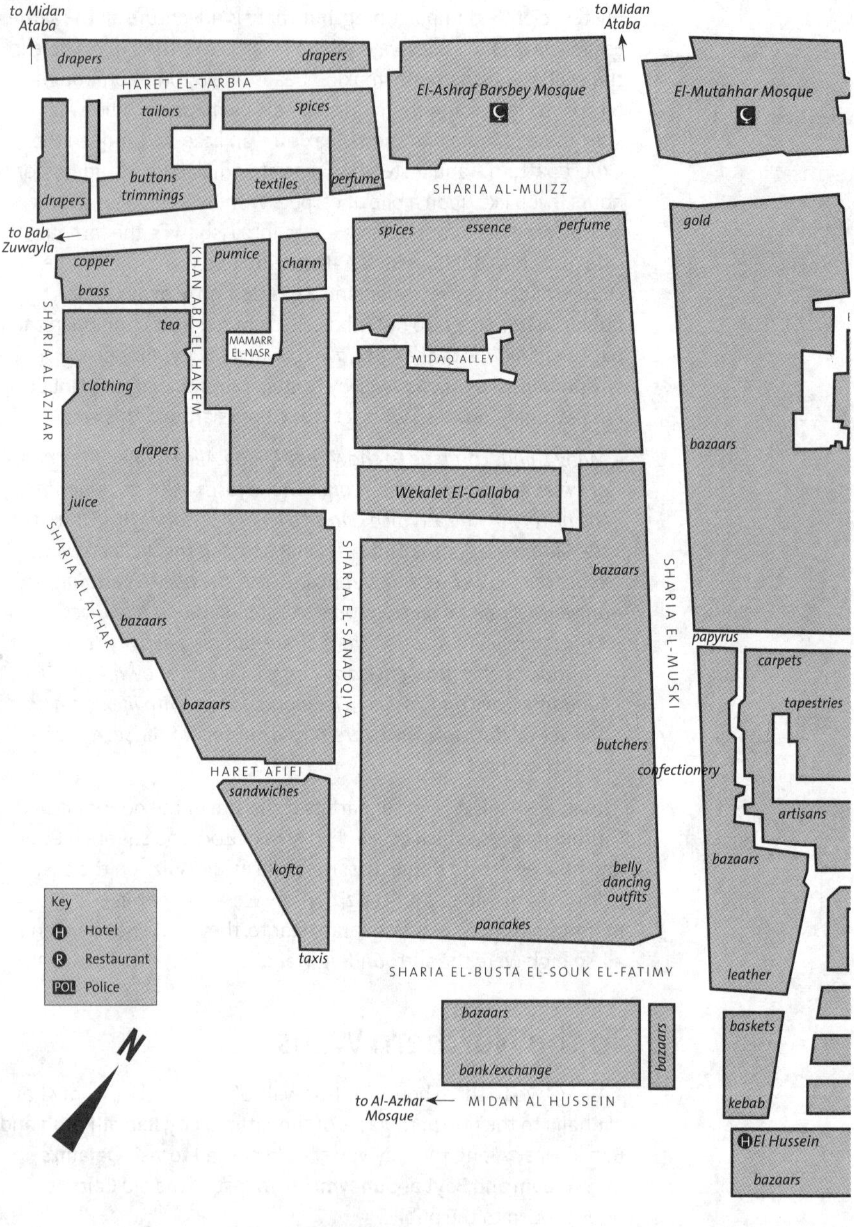
to Midan Ataba
drapers
drapers
HARET EL-TARBIA
tailors
spices
buttons trimmings
textiles
perfume
drapers
to Midan Ataba
El-Ashraf Barsbey Mosque
El-Mutahhar Mosque
SHARIA AL-MUIZZ
to Bab Zuwayla
copper
brass
pumice
charm
KHAN ABD-EL HAKEM
spices
essence
perfume
gold
tea
MAMARR EL-NASR
MIDAQ ALLEY
SHARIA AL AZHAR
clothing
drapers
bazaars
Wekalet El-Gallaba
juice
SHARIA AL AZHAR
SHARIA EL-SANADQIYA
bazaars
SHARIA EL-MUSKI
bazaars
papyrus
carpets
bazaars
tapestries
butchers
confectionery
HARET AFIFI
sandwiches
artisans
bazaars
kofta
belly dancing outfits
Key
Hotel
Restaurant
POL Police
pancakes
taxis
SHARIA EL-BUSTA EL-SOUK EL-FATIMY
leather
bazaars
bank/exchange
bazaars
baskets
kebab
N
to Al-Azhar Mosque
MIDAN AL HUSSEIN
El Hussein
bazaars

Khan el Khalili

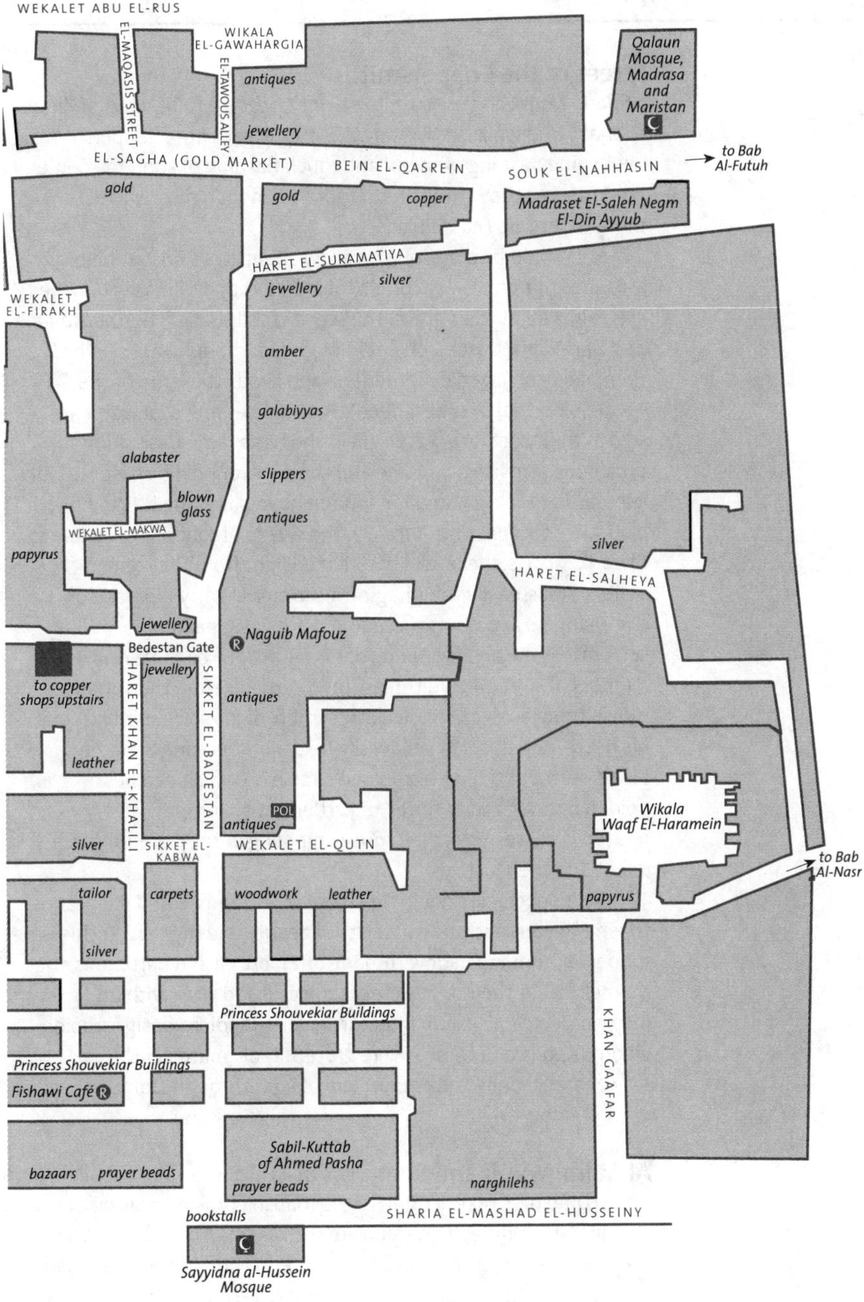
WEKALET ABU EL-RUS
EL-MAQASIS STREET
WIKALA EL-GAWAHARGIA
EL-TAWOUS ALLEY
antiques
jewellery
Qalaun Mosque, Madrasa and Maristan
EL-SAGHA (GOLD MARKET)
BEIN EL-QASREIN
SOUK EL-NAHHASIN
to Bab Al-Futuh
gold
gold
copper
Madraset El-Saleh Negm El-Din Ayyub
HARET EL-SURAMATIYA
jewellery
silver
WEKALET EL-FIRAKH
amber
galabiyyas
alabaster
slippers
blown glass
antiques
WEKALET EL-MAKWA
papyrus
silver
HARET EL-SALHEYA
jewellery
Naguib Mafouz
Bedestan Gate
jewellery
to copper shops upstairs
HARET KHAN EL-KHALILI
SIKKET EL-BADESTAN
antiques
leather
Wikala Waqf El-Haramein
POL
antiques
silver
SIKKET EL-KABWA
WEKALET EL-QUTN
to Bab Al-Nasr
tailor
carpets
woodwork
leather
papyrus
silver
Princess Shouvekiar Buildings
KHAN GAAFAR
Princess Shouvekiar Buildings
Fishawi Café
Sabil-Kuttab of Ahmed Pasha
bazaars
prayer beads
prayer beads
narghilehs
bookstalls
SHARIA EL-MASHAD EL-HUSSEINY
Sayyidna al-Hussein Mosque

Getting to the Northern Walls

To reach the beginning of this itinerary take a **taxi**, or from Midan el Tahrir take the **66 bus**. You could also **walk** east from downtown Cairo, across the Ezbekieh Gardens, and then along Sharia Muski.

Street of the Coppersmiths

Sharia Muizz, as you leave the awning-covered alleyways of Khan el Khalili and walk north along it, is the Street of the Coppersmiths, with some bashing of metal and much flashing of sunlight. Some reminders of the Fatimid period survive, though mostly the monuments are Mameluke.

There should be a mosque on every street, it is said, but here mosques fight for every corner, their domes and minarets bunched like palms in an oasis grove. The scene is still that of the *Thousand and One Nights*, ostensibly set in Baghdad (though Baghdad by then had been razed by Tamerlane and it was the Cairo of the Mamelukes that was described). Sweet juices and cool water are sold in the street by a waterseller, who has a large flask slung under one arm like a bagpipe and the cups round his waist. He will lean forward to pour and for a moment you imagine this to be an obeisance to a passing sultan: in the sweep of robes, the clattering of donkey carts, the bursts of reflected light from the coppersmiths' stalls, easily you imagine a triumphal entry, a parade of state, singers and poets preceding the royal appearance, celebrating the achievements of his reign. You see fluttering banners of silk and gold thread, then carried before the sultan himself the jewelled saddlecloth, symbol of his sovereignty; above his head is a parasol of yellow silk held aloft by a prince of the blood, surmounted with a golden cupola on which perches a golden bird. A band of flutes, of kettledrums, trumpets and hautboys passes now, their music mingling in the clamour of the street and then lost.

There is spectacle enough in Sharia Muizz and behind its façades to remind you that this was a city of beauty and mystery. Ruthless for power, cunning in government, often brutal and barbarous, the Mamelukes at their best were resourceful and vital, with an incomparable flair for architecture. Their grandiose designs, bold, vigorous and voluminous, were gracefully decorated with the play of arabesques, the embroidery of light through stained-glass windows.

Al-Salih Ayyub and Shagarat al-Durr

You come first, on the right, to the mausoleum and madrasa of al-Salih Ayyub, diagonally opposite the Maristan of Qalaun. Where the street now presses its way was once, in Fatimid times, a broad avenue, so broad it served as a parade ground, the great palaces looking down upon it from either side. Throughout the Fatimid and Mameluke periods, this was the very centre of Cairo.

The **mausoleum and madrasa of al-Salih Ayyub** need to be searched for. You turn right off Muizz into a lane – there is a tiny teashop on the corner with some round brass tables outside, an agreeable place to sit for a while. A short distance along the lane is an arch set into a façade with a Fatimid-style minaret rising from it. This is the madrasa, and you enter what remains of it by turning left into what is now used by neighbourhood youths as a playing field, liwans to east and west. The mausoleum is reached by returning to the Street of the Coppersmiths and turning right. You will see the dome on your right, and the door will be locked, but ask (or gesture to) anyone nearby for the key: they will find the keeper.

The interest of this place is historical, for it marks a political and architectural transition. **Al-Salih Ayyub** (38) was the last ruler of Saladin's dynasty. His wife, who completed his madrasa and mausoleum after he died in 1249, was Shagarat al-Durr, a beautiful Armenian or Turkish slave girl who ushered in Mameluke rule. While it has Fatimid elements, the madrasa was also the first to provide for all four schools of Sunni Islam, and was the first also to link madrasa and mausoleum – in short, it was the prototype for the Mameluke mosque-madrasa-mausolea to follow. Throughout the Mameluke period it was used as Cairo's central court (the schools teaching, among other things, law as at al-Azhar), and the street outside, Sharia Muizz, served as the place of execution.

Qalaun, al-Nasr and Barquq

Looking up and across Sharia Muizz you see on its west side the splendid cluster of domes and minarets that are the madrasa and **mausoleum of Qalaun** (43), the mausoleum of al-Nasr, his son and successor, and the mosque of Barquq. Qalaun – the name means duck and has an absurd ring in Arabic – was one of the ablest, most successful and long-lived (1220–90) of the notoriously short-lived Mameluke sultans, who moreover founded a dynasty lasting nearly 100 years. His name suggests Mongol origins, and he is known to have been brought from the lower Volga region, ruled at the time by the Golden Horde. It was al-Salih Ayyub, buried across the street, who first began importing slaves from the Volga, employing them as bodyguards. Qalaun served the country of his purchase well: Damascus and Baghdad had fallen to the Mongols, Egypt and Arabia being the sole remaining bulwarks of Islam; Baybars checked the threat, Qalaun eliminated it, and then marched against the Crusaders at Acre, their last stronghold in the Holy Land, but died en route. An outstanding builder, his tribute to his

The Story of Shagarat al-Durr

Shagarat al-Durr, whose name means 'Tree of Pearls', shares with Hatshepsut and Cleopatra that rare distinction of having been a female ruler of Egypt (1249–57). She rose to power at a critical moment, when St Louis at the head of the Sixth Crusade seized Damietta in the Delta. Ayyub, dying from cancer, was too weak to dislodge him, and St Louis was content to await the sultan's death and what he imagined would be the collapse of government and all resistance to Christian occupation of the country. But Shagarat al-Durr was of independent and possibly nomadic stock, whose women went unveiled and were the equals of their men. She hid her husband's corpse in the Mameluke barracks on Roda while pretending he was merely ailing, and for three months ruled Egypt by appearing to transmit orders from Ayyub to his generals.

Egypt played for time and offered the Crusaders Jerusalem if they would abandon Damietta. St Louis refused. Meanwhile, in the heat, and fed bad fish by the Delta people, the Crusaders became sick with scurvy and plague. St Louis then accepted the offer of Jerusalem, but now it was the Egyptians who refused, and the Mameluke general Baybars fell upon the Crusaders, capturing St Louis, who had to buy his freedom with a vast indemnity and the renunciation of all claim to Egypt.

Shagarat al-Durr now openly proclaimed herself sultana and for 80 days was the only female Muslim ruler in Middle Eastern history (until 1993 when the Turks elected a woman as prime minister), but the Abbasid caliph refused to recognize her, quoting the Prophet who had said, 'The people that make a woman their ruler are past saving.' So she married the leader of her Mameluke slave-warriors, Aybak, ruling through him; but when she heard he was considering another marriage, she hired assassins to murder him in his bath. Hearing his screams, seeing his body hacked at with swords, at the last moment she tried to save his life, but the assassins went on: 'If we stop halfway through, he will kill both you and us.'

When the murder was discovered, Shagarat al-Durr offered to marry the new Mameluke chief, but instead she was imprisoned and is said to have spent her last days grinding up all her jewels so that no other woman should wear them. The Mamelukes had discovered their power to make and unmake rulers; in future they ruled themselves. Shagarat al-Durr was turned over to the wife whom she had forced Aybak to divorce and who instructed her female slaves to beat Shagarat al-Durr to death with bath clogs. They tossed her naked body over the Citadel wall to be devoured by dogs. Her few remains were deposited in her tomb on the edge of the Southern Cemetery not too far from the mosque of Ibn Tulun.

Christian enemies was the adoption of Gothic elements in his complex here, the maristan, madrasa and mausoleum of Qalaun.

First you go through the gate and down a wide tree-shaded walk, the heat and noise of the Street of the Coppersmiths falling away behind you. At the end is a modern hospital, built within the vaster limits of **Qalaun's maristan** or hospital and insane asylum – a hospital has stood on this spot for 700 years. Three great liwans of the original remain, the windows of the east liwan still displaying their carved stucco surrounds.

Islam was a wonder of enlightened medical care at a time when the ill, especially the mad, were pariahs in Christian Europe. From Spain to Persia, hospitals flourished, were divided into clinics, surgery was perfected, such delicate operations as the removal of cataracts were performed, musicians and singers entertained the sick, and upon their discharge patients were given sums of money to enable them to live until they could again find employment.

Returning to the street and turning left, the wall on your left-hand side is that of **Qalaun's madrasa**. At the far corner the line of the building then retreats and you come to what was the original entrance to the maristan. This great marble Gothic arch is in fact a magnificent piece of booty, taken by Qalaun's son and successor al-Ashraf Khalil from the church of St Andrew at Acre after its capture in 1291 and placed facing the street for all to see, a reminder to the Mamelukes' subjects of the triumph of Islam over the Crusaders. The arch opens onto a corridor, blocked at the far end, which runs between the mausoleum on the right and the madrasa on the left. During recent reconstruction of the madrasa the opportunity was taken to excavate for clues to the Fatimids' western palace, which once stood here. The plan is a courtyard with a liwan at either end, the sanctuary or eastern liwan suggesting a north Syrian basilical church, with three aisles and classical columns. The stucco work farther in from the arch is original.

Qalaun's mausoleum is off the other side of the corridor. The plan has been influenced by the Dome of the Rock at Jerusalem, well known to the sultan: an octagon approaching the circular within a square, the arches supported by square piers and classical columns. The dome has been restored. The structure perhaps does not seem light enough, the decorations too rich, and the *mashrabiyya* screen obstructs a total view (the best is from the entrance) – though it also has the effect of making the relatively small interior seem endless. But there is splendour all the same, in carved stucco, the stone inlay, the wood ornamentation, slowly revealed as your eyes get used to the filtered coloured light from the stained-glass windows – those high, double round-arched windows with *oculi* above, framed (from both inside and out on the street) by deeply recessed pointed arches inspired once again by the architecture of the Crusaders.

On your way out through the corridor have a look at its beamed and coffered ceiling, which is marvellous. The street is just before you, yet in this complex all has been private, cool and quiet – birds chirping, trees and shade and shafts of sunlight. The buildings and their purpose reveal a dignity and humanity; they provide the peace by which you recognize an unexpected civilization.

The next building on the left, continuing north on Sharia Muizz is the newly-restored **mausoleum of al-Nasr Mohammed** (44), until fairly recently ruinous except for the façade with its Gothic doorway, removed from the Crusader church of St John at Acre. Al-Nasr's reign marked the zenith of Mameluke civilization; his principal monuments are the mosque on the Citadel and the aqueduct bringing water there from the Nile. He is in fact buried next door in Qalaun's mausoleum.

The third of this group is the **mosque of Barquq** (187), the first Burgi Mameluke sultan. It dates from 1386, about a century later than Qalaun's buildings, and the change in style is evident: the minaret is octagonal and, compared to the square blocks of Qalaun's, slender; the high monumental entrance is topped with stalactite decorations, seen also at the Sultan Hassan, which became typical of Mameluke architecture. This mosque-madrasa, in cruciform plan, was in use until the 20th century and has been well maintained and restored. The portal is of black-and-white marble, the doors of bronze inlaid with silver. The sanctuary liwan is flat-ceilinged, not vaulted like the others, and receives support from four pharaonic columns of porphyry quarried in the Eastern Desert. The exquisite domed tomb chamber with marbled floors and walls of varying colours, painted ceiling, latticed and stained-glass windows and ornate wooden stalactites in the corners, contains the grave of one of Barquq's daughters – he himself was removed to his mausoleum in the Eastern Cemetery, the City of the Dead. Go to the far end of the mosque and look back across the open court for a wonderful view of the gathered minarets and domes of the Qalaun, al-Nasr and Barquq monuments.

Some Grand Cairene Houses Along the Way

Nearby are two houses of the Bahri Mameluke period (there should be someone selling tickets outside each). The **house of Uthman Katkhuda** (50) is in the street running east from Sharia Muizz, opposite Qalaun's mausoleum. It is about halfway down on the left-hand side.

Katkhuda was an 18th-century lieutenant governor of the city who made what in fact was a mid 14th-century palace into his home. Only a part of the whole remains, but it is an impressive example of Mameluke domestic architecture. Suddenly you find yourself in a narrow hall of enormous height, its bare stone walls rising to support a wooden dome, distant sunlight streaming through the windows of its octagonal drum. This was the reception room, and guests sat in the raised area at the south end. The walls were once wainscotted with marble; the woodwork remains, though the consoles within the arches date from the 16th century. Ask to go up to the roof for a view of the quarter, and look at the *malqaf*, or ventilator, a rectangular scoop common to old Cairene houses and always facing north to catch the Mediterranean breeze. One of the best things about this place is that you will almost certainly be the only visitor; its fresh bareness invites pleasing, undisturbed thoughts of moving in and where to put the furniture.

The other house, even more so a palace, is the **Qasr Beshtak** (34). This is back on Sharia Muizz, just to the north of Barquq's mosque and on the right-hand side. The entrance is the second door along the little street of the north façade. The Emir Beshtak was married to the daughter of al-Nasr and was a man of great wealth. He built his palace on part of the foundations of the eastern Fatimid palace and it once rose to five storeys, with running water on all floors. You pass though a courtyard, up some stairs, and enter the harem reception room, even more vast than Katkhuda's, with *mashrabiyya* screens along the galleries. From these there is a perfectly medieval view of the streets below.

The **Sabil Kuttab of Abdul Katkhuda** (21) was built in 1744 by Uthman Katkhuda's son and is one of the most charming structures in Cairo. It stands on a triangular plot, causing a fork in the street, the kuttab's porches overhanging the roadways on either side, the great grille of what was the fountain at its base facing south towards you as you approach. The kuttab is still used as the neighbourhood Koranic school, while the rest of the block is taken up with a renovated 14th-century apartment building.

Continue along the left-hand fork and eventually at the next block, on the right-hand side, discover a rare surviving Fatimid structure in this Mameluke-dominated part of the city, the **mosque of al-Aqmar** (33). *Aqmar* means moonlit, and the mosque was so named for its pale stone – the Fatimids, who meant to stay, building in stone rather than the earlier brick and stucco. The mosque dates from 1125 and displays a typically Fatimid keel-arch portal. The niche ribbing, used here for the first time, was to become a favourite Cairene motif. The medallion set into the niche ribbing is very finely executed. The recesses on either side of the portal have stalactite decorations, also appearing here for the first time and later taken up by the Mamelukes. The interior is original, but the slapdash minaret is modern. The mosque is being restored by the Bohra sect of India (*see also* the mosque of al-Hakim, p.138), their work including modern damp-proofing against the rising groundwater.

(4) Bayt al-Suhaymi
adm LE30

The **Bayt al-Suhaymi** (339), a merchant's house of the Ottoman period, built in the 16th and 17th centuries, is the finest house in Cairo and achieves the ambition of Islamic secular architecture – the anticipation of paradise – wonderfully. You reach it by taking the first right a block after the mosque of al-Aqmar. The street is called Heret ed-Darb el Asfar and the house is at No.19 (in case you do not notice the little green-and-white plaque) on the left-hand side. There is a broad wooden door. If there is no guardian selling tickets outside, knock.

Nothing on the façade prepares you for what lies within. The house consists of numerous rooms on irregular levels, *mashrabiyya* screen windows looking out onto the streets at one side, screened and latticed windows and arched galleries giving onto a garden courtyard on the other. You will want to wander, to enjoy the perspectives across the court from every possible angle and elevation, though sometimes you are guided by well-informed students. They will take you to the women's bedroom which faces the street but is closely latticed, to the women's chapel outside it, a *malqaf*, air conditioner, above your head. You will then be deposited in the harem reception room overlooking the garden, its floors of marble, its walls covered with the most delicate green-and-blue plant-patterned enamel tiles, and carved and painted wooden decorations. Here you can rest and begin taking it all in – for it is not the plan, not the details, but the ambience of the place that seduces you, and you want time.

Though this house was built in later centuries, in ambience it cannot be different from Cairene houses of earlier times, and illustrates how throughout its history the East offered such a luxuriantly pleasurable life for those with the means. The only discomfort to contend with was the summer's heat, but here in this house they so easily defeated heat and burning sun, creating shadows and breezes, bringing plants and birds into their home, embracing a nature they had made kinder.

Behind the Bayt al-Suhaymi is a second court that links it with two other houses in the Heret ed-Darb el Asfar, towards Sharia Muizz. The nearest house is used for concerts, exhibitions and functions, while the farther one, on the corner of Sharia Muizz, serves as a computer school.

The Mosque of al-Hakim

Return once again to Sharia Muizz and turn right (north). It is wonderful to walk along this seemingly humble street, learning its secrets; the treasures offered in this guide are only a sample of the many more that would require a far longer exploration. You are heading towards Bab al-Futuh and the walls which limit the Fatimid city. But first, on your left, is the clean, pencil-like minaret of the **Silahdar Mosque,** a Turkish-style structure of Mohammed Ali's time. Though centuries out of place for this quarter, the minaret is a graceful landmark that never fails to draw your attention as you pass by.

After about two blocks, the street broadens into a **market** area where garlic and onions are transported into the city and sold. The trucks which rumble in and out of Bab al-Futuh are painted with eyes as talismans against the evil eye. It is an appropriate place for superstition: on your right and leading to the Fatimid wall is the **mosque of al-Hakim** (15), completed in 1010. For centuries this mosque had an aura avoided by Cairenes, who rarely used it for worship and let it crumble. It had been used as a prison for Crusader captives, as a stable by Saladin and as a warehouse by

The Legend of al-Hakim

Al-Hakim was the third of the Cairo Fatimid caliphs, who ruled with absolute political, military and religious authority. He was a paranoiac who declared himself God and answered objections by inciting mobs to burn half the city while he lopped off the heads of the well-to-do, claiming the assistance of Adam and Solomon in angel guise. Jews he made walk about Cairo wearing clogs round their necks, and Christians he made carry heavy crosses. In the company of only a mute slave, he would spend his wary nights riding a donkey into the Moqattam Hills to observe the stars for portents. Then, exchanging clothes with his slave, he would secretly descend into the city and mix with the people to learn their complaints, though assuming the role of a cadi to punish infractions with summary decapitations. One night, returning from the hills, he was assassinated – at the instigation, it is thought, of his sister Setalmulq, whom he had intended to marry.

Some say he survived the attack and retreated to the desert. The Copts claim that Christ appeared to him and that he begged for and was granted pardon. Others say he withdrew to the sanctuary of Ammon at the Siwa Oasis, deep in the Western Desert, where more than a thousand years earlier Alexander had heard himself declared the son of Zeus. There, it is said, al-Hakim formulated his doctrine of a tolerant religion similar to Islam, which was carried by Darazi, his disciple, to Lebanon – where the Druze, as they are now known, view al-Hakim's life as a kind of Passion, giving him his due as their messiah.

Napoleon. As recently as 1980 it was ruinous, its haunting roofless arcades dominated by massive brooding minarets, in keeping with the Fatimid wall. These minarets proved unsound soon after construction and needed buttressing by great trapezoid bases, which project out into the street so that they seem like ziggurats (especially when viewed from outside the walls) with pepperpot domes, the latter placed by Baybars II at the begining of the 14th century.

The mosque has been entirely restored – perhaps over-restored – by the Indian-based Bohra sect of Ismailis who claim spiritual descent from the Fatimid imams. They will tell you that al-Hakim was not mad, that these are the lies of his enemies. And here certainly they have erased the darkness: there is the bright glitter of white marble and gold leaf, and at night the once forbidding arcades are illuminated by the warm glow of suspended glass oil lamps. Even the minarets seem lighter when you hear the story that al-Hakim used them as great incense burners, their scent drifting across the city.

The Northern Gates: Bab al-Futuh and Bab al-Nasr

It was at **Bab al-Futuh**, the Gate of Conquests, that the great caravan of pilgrims returned each year from Mecca and then made its way along Sharia Muizz and Sharia Bab el Wazir to the Citadel. Nowadays the journey is made by jet. The gate is similar to Bab Zuwayla, with projecting oval towers – though the masonry is finer and the impression greater, for the space outside has been cleared and there is a magnificent view of the ensemble of Bab al-Futuh, **Bab al-Nasr** (the Gate of Victory, to the east), the linking **Fatimid wall** and al-Hakim's minarets. The Fatimid wall extends to the west; beyond that, where it retreats, and also to the east of Bab al-Nasr, the wall dates from Saladin. You can walk both within and along the top of the wall between the gates: to do this you should make yourself appear obviously interested at either gate and eventually someone will come along with the key.

Re-entering the medieval city through Bab al-Nasr, you find the immediate area is noisy with metal workshops. On the right (west) against the east façade of al-Hakim's mosque is the **wikala of Sultan Qaytbey** (11), built in 1481. Until recently inhabited by tinsmiths and their families – with women scrubbing, washing strung across the courtyard, children beating a kitten and throwing it into the air – the caravanserai has now been cleared and is, apparently, in line for renovation.

The City of the Dead

You may already have noticed the **City of the Dead** as you drove in on the Heliopolis road from the airport, and thought it did not seem inviting. It has the look of a *bidonville* – hot, dusty, dilapidated, and with a quantity of domes. It is in fact the burial ground of the Mameluke sultans and of others who aspired to their end, and some of its mausolea are as wonderful as anything in the city of the living.

Nor is the cemetery without life. There were monasteries and schools, part of the mausolea. The poor have always made their homes here, as have the keepers, and relatives visit the family plots on feast days for a picnic. This is reminiscent of the ancient Egyptian practice of feeding the dead, though it is practised elsewhere in the Mediterranean, as in Greece, where it is more a cheerful popping of the cork and celebration of life.

The Three Most Outstanding Mausolea

Follow the road that runs east outside Bab al-Nasr, and on reaching the cemetery you will see ahead of you a broad building with two domes and two minarets. This is the **mausoleum of Barquq** (149), completed in 1411. Its plan is similar to that of a cruciform madrasa, but the liwans are not vaulted: instead there are multi-domed arcades. You enter nowadays at the southwest corner and, stepping over a black granite threshold bearing the remains of pharaonic reliefs, pass through a corridor into the *sahn*, its vastness relieved by a tamarisk tree and by some palms planted round the fountain. On the eastern side is the sanctuary liwan with a beautifully carved marble minbar, dedicated by Qaytbey. At either end of the liwan are domed tomb chambers: Barquq (removed here from his mausoleum in Sharia Muizz) and his two

Getting to the City of the Dead

The Eastern Cemetery (Qarafat al-Sharqiyya), or City of the Dead, lies to the east of the Fatimid city. The mausoleum of Barquq is 1.5km from Bab al-Nasr, and Qaytbey's mausoleum is 1km from al-Azhar. So a **walk** from Bab al-Nasr, visiting these two mausolea as well as that of Ashraf Baybars – the three most outstanding buildings – and then back to al-Azhar, will cover about 3km. You may prefer to make a separate journey of it, hiring a **taxi**. From Midan el Tahrir you can take the **500 bus** to Midan Barquq, by the mausoleum of that name.

---

sons buried in the left chamber, women of the family in the right. These domes are the earliest stone domes in Cairo; the zigzag ribbing on their exteriors was to develop into the elaborate polygons of Qaytbey's domed mausoleum. From the outside, the domes are minimized by the surrounding structure, so once inside their marvellous shape and soaring height comes as a surprise.

Go back across the courtyard to the northwest corner and up the stairs. These lead you to the *khanqah*, or dervish monastery, its four storeys a warren of rooms, cells and corridors. For some extra baksheesh the keeper will usually let you go up the northern minaret for a sweeping view of the necropolis itself and all of Cairo, from Heliopolis to the Citadel.

The **mausoleum of Sultan Ashraf Baybars** (121) – he is also known as Barsbey – is south down the paved but dusty road that passes along the front of Barquq's mausoleum. This building is less visited than the other two, and finding the keeper may be more difficult than usual. Apprehend the first child or lounger you see and make it known you want the key; normally the keeper will appear quite quickly. Baksheesh will then of course be expected all round.

This mausoleum was originally planned solely as a *khanqah* and so is unusually elongated; also it is recognized by its ungainly minaret which comes to a point too soon. Baybars, whose mausoleum dates from 1432, was a Burgi or Circassian Mameluke,

The City of the Dead, from Napoleon's Description de l'Egypte, *1798*

The Return of Pilgrims from Mecca

As many as 30,000 people were about to swell the population of Cairo. I managed to make my way to Bab al-Futuh; the long street which leads there was crammed with spectators who were kept in place by soldiers. The procession advanced to the sound of trumpets, cymbals and drums; the various nations and sects were distinguished by their trophies and flags. The long files of harnessed dromedaries, which were mounted by Bedouins armed with long muskets, followed one another monotonously, but it was only when I reached the countryside that I was able to appreciate the full impact of a spectacle which is unique in all the world.

A whole nation on the march was merging into the huge population which adorned the flanks of the Moqattam on the right, and, on the left, the thousands of usually deserted edifices of the City of the Dead; streaked with red and yellow bands, the battlements on the walls and towers of Saladin were also swarming with onlookers. I had the impression that I was present at a scene during the Crusades. Farther ahead, in the plain where the Qalish meanders, stood thousands of chequered tents where the pilgrims halted to refresh themselves; there was no lack of dancers and singers; all the musicians of Cairo, in fact, competed with the hornblowers and kettledrummers of the procession, a monstrous orchestra perched upon camelback.

Late in the afternoon, the booming of the Citadel cannons and a sudden blast of trumpets proclaimed that the Mahmal, a holy ark which contains Mohammed's robe of cloth of gold, had arrived within sight of the city. From time to time the Mahmal came to a halt, and the entire population prostrated themselves in the dust, bending their foreheads low upon their hands. An escort of guards struggled to drive back the negroes who, more fanatical than the other Muslims, aspired to the honour of being trampled to death beneath the camels, though their only share of martyrdom was the volley of baton blows showered upon them. As for the santons, who are even more wildly devout than the dervishes and whose orthodoxy is more questionable, several of them pierced their cheeks with long sharp daggers and walked on, dripping with blood; others devoured live serpents, while a third group stuffed their mouths with burning coals.

Gérard de Nerval, *Journey to the Orient*, 1844

Nerval was a precursor of surrealism; he enjoyed going over the top. But in this case that sober chronicler Edward William Lane, author of *Manners and Customs of the Modern Egyptians*, who observed the arrival of the caravan ten years before, is hardly less fantastic in his description, though he says the swallowing of serpents went out with the Mamelukes. The journey from Mecca took 37 days across rocky desert, the caravan moving at night. Not everyone survived:

Many of the women who go forth to meet their husbands or sons receive the melancholy tidings of their having fallen victim to privation and fatigue. The piercing shrieks with which they rend the air as they retrace their steps to the city are often heard predominant over the noise of the drum and the shrill notes of the hautboy, which proclaim the joy of others.

Lane also mentions that the Mahmal was empty; its purpose was entirely symbolic, dating back to the reign of Shagarat al-Durr. She went on the pilgrimage one year, travelling in a magnificent *hodag*, or covered litter, borne by a camel, and for several successive years her empty *hodag* was sent with the caravan merely for the sake of state. The practice was continued by Egypt's rulers till 1927, when the puritanical Saudi king, on the pretext of objecting to the soldiers accompanying it, forbade passage of this 'object of vain pomp'. These days, alas, you wait in vain for pomp at Bab al-Futuh.

and is not to be confused with his namesake who held St Louis to ransom. He neither drank nor swore, though he was martial enough and took Cyprus from the Franks in 1426. The appeal of the place is in its few but well-chosen elaborations – the polygonally decorated dome rising above the simple façade, through which you pass by a doorway with trefoil arch. The tomb chamber is at the north end of the mosque, dimly illuminated by stained-glass windows subsequently introduced, though the mihrab of mother-of-pearl and marble mosaic is original. But really you have come for the interior view of the dome and its impression alone is sufficient: it ascends effortlessly upwards, almost losing itself to infinity.

It is a longer distance down this same dusty road to the **mausoleum of Qaytbey** (99), completed in 1474 and a jewel of Mameluke architecture. First, from across the square, look at the *ablaq* masonry of the façade, the intricate polygonal relief on the exquisitely proportioned dome, and the slender minaret of three tiers (the Mameluke fashion), each tier ornately decorated with columned recesses, raised arabesques or stalactite clusters. Along with the mosques of Ibn Tulun and Sultan Hassan, this rates as one of the great buildings of Cairo. Unlike them it is free with decoration, but like them it uses its decoration to great effect – the frequent play of filigree flowers upon star-shaped polygons, which has been described as 'a song for two voices', a geometrical base with floral melody.

The perfection of this mausoleum, however, like the splendour of Qaybey's reign, marked the final apogee of Mameluke vigour. Decadence ensued, but two decades later the Turks were in the city, Bab Zuwayla was ornamented by the last Mameluke sultan, a rope round his neck. Inside is a cruciform madrasa with vestigial liwans to east and west. The decoration of ceilings, pavings, arches and windows is breathtakingly variegated, yet overall it is measured and subdued.

There is deliberate though sensitive contrast with the scale of the courtyard and sanctuary in the immense height of the tomb chamber, its walls drawn into the ascending dome.

Finally, from the sanctuary, you should climb the roof to enjoy at closer hand the tracery of stone carving on the dome and minaret, as delicate as previous periods had managed in wood and stucco.

Qaytbey

He is an old man of about 80, but tall, handsome and as upright as a reed. Dressed in white, he was on horseback, accompanied by more than 2,000 Mameluke soldiers... Whoever wishes can have access to the sultan: there is in the town a great and splendid fortress at the entrance of which he sits publicly on Mondays and Thursdays, accompanied by the governor of the city; a guard of more than 3,000 Mamelukes surrounds him. Whoever has been manhandled or robbed by one of the Mameluke princes or emirs can there complain. Thus the nobles refrain from actions that might carry condemnation.

Meshullam ben Menahem

This description of Qaytbey by an Italian Jew portrays him in a sympathetic light. Along with al-Nasr, Qaytbey was the grandest of Mameluke builders, emblazoning his cartouche on buildings religious and secular throughout the Middle East, as well as in Cairo and Alexandria. He was also the last Mameluke ruler of strength. He came up through the ranks, having been bought by Ashraf Baybars, and apart from al-Nasr ruled longer than any other sultan.

The Museum of Egyptian Antiquities (The Egyptian Museum)

The Museum of Egyptian Antiquities
the museum is on the north side of Midan el Tahrir. This square is the main depot for Cairo's buses, and metro station Sadat is also here; open daily 9–4.45, closed Fri lunchtime (summer 12–2; winter 11.30–1.30); adm LE60, plus LE100 for the Mummy Room and LE20 for the basement exhibition; tickets used Fri morning are not valid that afternoon

The **Museum of Egyptian Antiquities**, more commonly known as the Egyptian Museum (though this may prove confusing when the new Grand Egyptian Museum opens at Giza), is housed in a rose-coloured neoclassical building in what was one of the quietest areas of Cairo when the museum was built in 1902; now it stands at Cairo's busiest traffic intersection. Within the ill-lit, leaking building, which relies on open windows for ventilation, 120,000 catalogued objects (of which 44,000 are on display at any one time) bathe in pollution levels reaching 80 per cent of those outside (as compared to 0.5 per cent in environmentally controlled museums).

Allowing one minute for each exhibit on display, you could see everything in about four months. The average guided tour lasts two hours. The selection offered here would take one hard-working day to cover, though it would be better to break that down into two or three half-day visits. The exhibits are numbered and some carry background notes in English, French and Arabic. The rooms are also numbered, as shown on the plans.

The collection is arranged more or less chronologically, so that starting at the entrance and walking clockwise round the ground floor you pass from Old Kingdom to Middle and New Kingdom exhibits, concluding with Ptolemaic and Roman exhibits. The first floor contains prehistoric and early dynastic exhibits and the contents of several tombs, including Tutankhamun's. Not every room is mentioned in the tour below.

Note that some objects may have been moved elsewhere, and that some rooms close early; note also that the museum's basement has now been opened to present special exhibitions. The entrance is round the left-hand side of the building, and a separate entry fee is payable.

The Ground Floor

Immediately upon entering (from the south), you walk into a rotunda that is **Room 48**. Apart from the monumental Sphinx at Giza, the colossal head to the left of Userkaf (V Dynasty) is the only large sculpture surviving from the Old Kingdom. The rotunda contains other giant works (out of chronological order), including three colossi (1, 2, 4) of Ramses II (XIX Dynasty) and a statue of Amenhotep son of Hapu (3), architect to Amenophis III (XVIII Dynasty).

Major Changes Affecting Cairo's Museum Collections

Note that major changes are taking place to this museum as part of the wider scheme of opening new museums at Fustat and Giza (*see* Topics, pp.47–8). The National Museum of the Egyptian Civilization at Fustat, its opening much delayed but possibly happening in 2009, will become the new home to the royal mummies. The Grand Egyptian Museum near the Pyramids on the Giza plateau, which is meant to open in 2012, will house the Tutankhamun collection. The Museum of Egyptian Antiquities here at Midan el Tahrir will undergo complete renovation and a new wing will be added on the west side to bring it up to date as a new showcase for pharaonic art. The current description is of the museum as it has been, but because of the changes in store you should approach a visit with a high degree of adventurousness.

The Old Kingdom

Room 47 contains IV, V and VI Dynasty items. The walls are lined with sarcophagi. Most interesting are the figures in the central aisle cases, including, in Case B, statuettes of the dwarf (160), the man with a deformed head (6310) and the hunchback (6311), but also, in Case D, those of people grinding corn, kneading dough and preparing food (a goose about to be gutted and plucked).

Room 41. The V Dynasty bas-relief (79) with scenes of country life is particularly worthy of close observation. Farm tasks and crafts are carried on through a series of registers. The women wear ankle-length chemises, but the men wear only a cloth or are sometimes entirely naked. They are circumcised as was the Egyptian custom. There is also one episode of a malefactor being held and brought before a court.

Room 42. The very fine statue of Chephren (138) in black diorite with white marbling was found in a shaft at his valley temple at Giza, where he built the second of the Great Pyramids. The falcon god Horus embraces Chephren's head with his wings, at once transferring the ka and protecting the pharaoh. The remarkably preserved wooden statue of **Ka-aper** (**140**) is vividly executed. You feel you would recognize the face in the original, and indeed when Mariette found it at Saqqara his workmen immediately dubbed it Sheikh el Beled because of its resemblance to their village headman. The living eyes are copper inlaid with quartz. It is said of some paintings that the eyes follow you; in this case it is uncanny how they fix you with their sure and level gaze when faced head on, but as soon as you shift even a centimetre they gaze off – not inert, but reflectively, into an internal dream world of their past.

Room 31. Outstanding here are the six wooden panels of the II Dynasty priest Hesire (88). This and the IV Dynasty were two unusual periods in ancient Egyptian history when moustaches were fashionable.

Room 32. One gets so used to the rigid frontality of Egyptian sculpture that it is a surprise to see the wooden statue in the far

First Floor

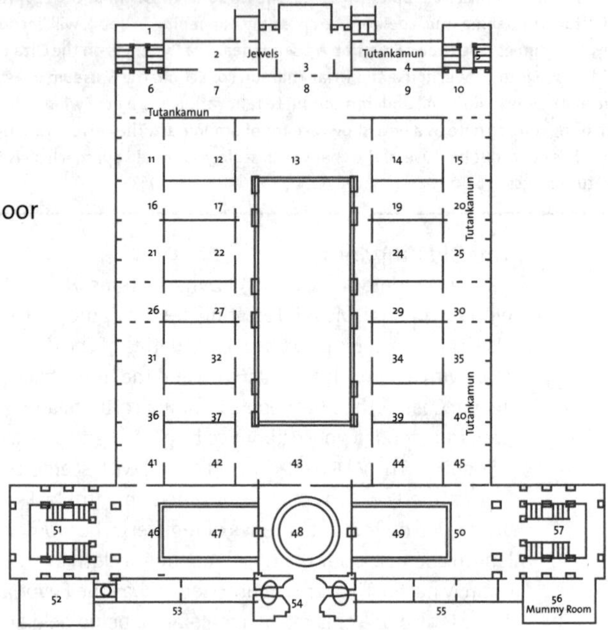

Ground Floor

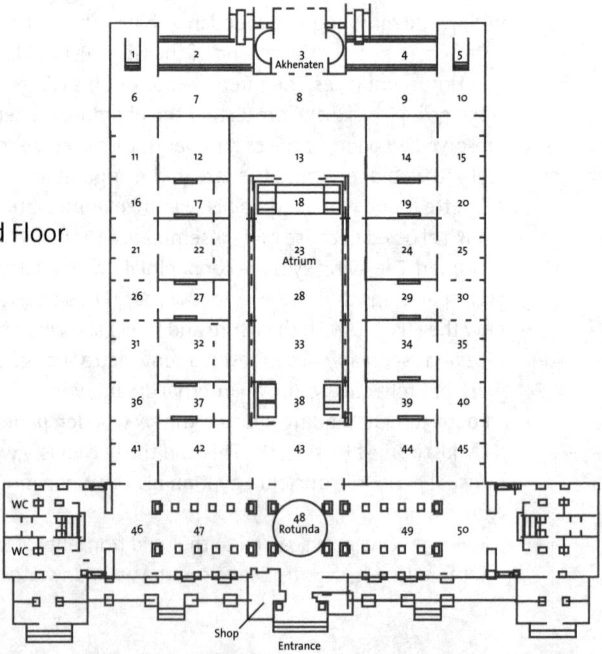

right corner with its slight twist. At the centre of the room are the IV Dynasty statues (223, 195) of Prince Rahotep and Princess Nafrit; her skin painted yellow, his ruddy brown. He has short back and sides and sports a natty moustache. In his white waist cloth he looks for all the world like an advertising executive taking a sauna. The group representing the dwarf Seneb, Chief of the Wardrobe, with his wife and two children (6055) deserves close attention. It is delightful, but also a puzzle. Despite his small size, Seneb is a man of importance; he looks pleased with himself, sure of his position, his family, his wife's proud affection. Notice his legs: they are too short to hang over the edge of the chair; instead his children stand where his legs would be – is this a mere compositional nicety or has it a symbolic intention? And look at the children, their right index fingers to their lips as though they were keeping a secret. The III/IV Dynasty '**Geese of Meidum**' (**136**) are vividly coloured. The copper statues (230, 231) of Pepi I and his son are the first metal statues known, and that of Pepi the largest of its kind. He is a great striding figure, reminiscent of an archaic Greek *kouros*.

The Middle Kingdom

With **Room 26** you pass into the Middle Kingdom. Here (or hereabouts, as he is unusually peripatetic) is a rare and astonishing wooden ka statue (280) of the Pharaoh Hor (XII Dynasty) stepping out from his naos. It actually stands on a sliding base to demonstrate the wanderings of Hor's double – and that it is his ka is clear from the ka hieroglyph of upraised arms on his head, and his nakedness.

Room 22. Generally sculpture and stone monuments of the Middle Kingdom. At the centre is the burial chamber of Horhotep (300). The walls are painted with oil jars and offerings are closely listed. The decorated doors, like patchwork curtains, were for the ka to flit in and out at will. Around the chamber are ten statues of Sesostris I (301). On the sides of each throne are reliefs of the gods of Upper and Lower Egypt entwining the lotus and papyrus, symbolizing the unity of the country.

The New Kingdom

Room 11. Here you pass into the New Kingdom, with a fine statue of Tuthmosis III (XVII Dyn) in grey schist (400).

Room 12. XVIII Dynasty sculpture. The brightly decorated chapel built for Amenophis II or his predecessor Tuthmosis III once contained Hathor as cow (445, 446) – she now stands before it in a glass case. To the right is a pink granite statue (952) of Hatshepsut. Look also for the case containing a small statuette (6257), delicately carved out of Sudanese ebony, of Thay, a royal equerry.

Room 8. It is unusual for mud-brick houses, even palaces, to survive, and so our impression of ancient Egypt is largely determined, often distorted, by rock tombs and stone mortuary temples. But the Egyptians did concern themselves with this world and at the centre of this room is a model of a typical house as excavated at Amarna, Akhenaten's brief capital on the Nile near Minya.

The Akhenaten Room

Room 3 contains perhaps the most astonishing works in the museum, from the reign of Akhenaten. Some find the Amarna style – particularly when applied in its most exaggerated form to Akhenaten himself – grotesque. Others think it powerful and often beautiful. Staring down at you are four colossi of the pharaoh: the glare of revolution, elongated face, narrow eyes, long thin nose with flaring nostrils and full, perhaps sardonic lips. The belly and thighs protrude like some primitive female fertility figure. These are from the temple he built, at Karnak, later destroyed, its blocks serving as foundations and pylon filler for others' works. In its own glass case there is a magnificent head, probably of Nefertiti, and this is not distorted at all – though examples of Amarnan distortion applied to Nefertiti are seen on the stele in Case F, and the centre stele in Case H. This distortion is sometimes called realism; there is a theory that Akhenaten was indeed deformed and that some of his family may have been also – hence the Amarna style was a mass acquiescence to this misfortune. But you might prefer to think that this style was deliberately experimental, calculated for effect, indeed to illustrate opposition, and as readily dispensed with (as with the bust of Nefertiti, above) when sheer beauty rather than shock value was desired. There is a note of realism, if not intimacy, in the centre stele in Case F. Instead of showing the royal family in formal adoration of the sun disc Aten, Akhenaten is seen playing with his eldest daughter Meritaten, while Nefertiti holds their other two daughters on her lap. This expression of family joy, or any personal feelings whatsoever, was never before and never again seen in depictions of the pharaohs.

Here too are those cuneiform tablets, the famous **Amarna Letters** (Case A), found in 1887 on the site of the Foreign Office in Akhetaten. Writing upon them in Babylonian, the diplomatic language of the day, Egypt's Syrian vassals complain to the pharaoh of military encroachments in their region by some great power to the north – a clue which helped the late 19th-century scholar A.H. Sayce to infer the existence of a previously unsuspected civilization, the Hittites of Anatolia. Sayce was able to identify them, too, as the adversaries who, a hundred years after these letters were written, checked the ambitions of Ramses II at

Kadesh (*see* pp.271–2 and p.397). Note as well the representational **masks**, either models or perhaps death masks, in Case D.

Coins

Room 4 contains a collection of Greek, Roman, Byzantine and Arab coins. Quite a few bear the head of Alexander, and on the left side of the first case on the right are several coins bearing the head of Cleopatra VII.

The Ramessids

Room 15. Items from the reign of Ramses II, including a painted limestone statue of a XIX Dynasty queen from the Ramesseum (Case A).

Room 14. On the right is a statue (743) of Ramses VI (XX Dynasty), unusual for its attempt at movement, dragging a doubled-up Libyan by the hair. A painted sunk relief (769) in the left near corner shows Ramses II similarly apprehending three prisoners, one black, one red, one brown. At the centre (unnumbered, but catalogued as 765) is a unique freestanding coronation group sculpture, Ramses III at the centre, Horus on the left, Seth on the right. Though it has been greatly restored, enough was found to determine that the figures stood on their own legs without supports.

The Late Period

The New Kingdom, in any case tottering since the end of the XX Dynasty, ended with the XXI Dynasty. Objects from the Late Period begin with **Room 25**. One ruler of the XXV Dynasty, Taharka, left his mark at several sites in Upper Egypt, for example the remains of his kiosk in the Great Court at Karnak. Here you see his sculpted head (1185) with curled hair – he was from the Sudan (which the Greeks called Ethiopia). He enjoys the distinction of being mentioned in the Bible (II Kings 19:9).

Room 24 contains a green schist statue of the goddess Tweri (791) – finely finished, though an utterly ridiculous image of a pregnant anthropomorphic hippopotamus. Otherwise, the most interesting items are the Osiris, Isis and Hathor group (855, 856, 857) at the centre, and to the left 1184, an attempt at portraiture of the Mayor of Thebes.

Room 30. At Medinet Habu are the mortuary chapels of the Divine Adorers of Amun. Amenardis, in white stone (930), was one of these princesses, of the XXV Dynasty.

The Graeco-Roman Period

Room 34. Note the colossal bust (1003) of Serapis. This god, an invention of Ptolemy Soter, combined Osiris with Apis, the bull god of Memphis, but with Greek features and dress.

Room 44. The contents of royal tombs of a Nubian people, the Blemmyes, who lived just south of Abu Simbel during the Byzantine period and were under the dominion of Meroë in the Sudan. Their aristocracy was strongly negroid. Long after Christianity came to Egypt, they worshipped Isis, Horus and Bes. The burial of kings and queens was accompanied by strangled slaves and servants, and gaily caparisoned horses which were led into the tombs and axed to death. Crowns, the skeleton of a horse, the models of two others, complete with trappings, along with spearheads, jewellery, pottery and other artefacts form this fascinating exhibit. The artefacts of the Blemmyes have a strong, handsome look, similar to Celtic work – a fine brutality. (At least some of the exhibits in this room are being transferred to the new Nubian Museum in Aswan.)

Room 49. An exceptional piece is the coffin of Petosiris (6036), a high priest of Thoth at Hermopolis (*c*. 300 BC). The hieroglyphics are beautifully inlaid with stone and enamel. From Saqqara during the Persian period is the stone sarcophagus (on the right, near the rotunda) of a dwarf dancer at the Serapeum Apis ceremony. He has been well rewarded: his true-to-life figure is cut on the outside of the adjacent lid, while on the inside of the lid and at the bottom of the sarcophagus is carved a sex-bomb (the goddess Nut) for him to lie on and stare up at for eternity.

The Atrium. On the ground floor there now remains only the atrium to visit. At the centre of **Room 43** is the Palette of Narmer (3055), possibly the oldest record of a political event, the unification of Egypt, *c*. 3000 BC. Narmer was probably one of the names of Menes, the founder of the I Dynasty, from which Egypt's historical period is dated. Writing was not yet able to convey complex sentences and this slate palette tells its story by means of pictures which are easily translated into words. On the obverse, Narmer is shown braining an enemy, and to the right is a complex symbol relating the significance of this action. The falcon is Narmer, holding a rope attached to the head of a bearded man. The head protrudes from a bed of papyri, representing Lower Egypt. Therefore the symbol reads, 'The falcon god Horus (Narmer) leads captive the inhabitants of the papyrus country.' Narmer came from Upper Egypt, as the crown he wears on this side shows. On the reverse, Narmer wears the crown of Lower Egypt as he reviews the spoils of his victory, which include the decapitated bodies of his foes. The centre panel shows two fantastic beasts, their necks entwined but restrained from fighting by bearded men on either side: Upper and Lower Egypt joined, if not yet altogether at ease. On either side of the room are two large wooden boats, for solar sailing from the pyramid of Sesostris III at Dahshur.

Room 38 is really a stairway leading down into the well of the atrium and contains the rectangular stone sarcophagus (624) of Ay, at first an adviser to Akhenaten, then to Tutankhamun, and later his successor. Four goddesses at each corner extend their wings protectively: Isis, Nephthys, Neith and Selket.

Room 33 displays various pyramidions from Dahshur, the capstones to pyramids. Under 6175 you can see the stone peg which slotted into the pyramid top. The sarcophagus (6337A) of Psusennes I, a XXI Dynasty pharaoh ruling from Tanis in the Delta after Egypt had split in two, has its lid (6337B) raised over a mirror so that you can see the lovely raised relief of the goddess Nut suspended from its underside. Stone sarcophagi in fact represented the goddess, for just as the sun god Re entered her mouth at sunset to be reborn at dawn, so the deceased was symbolically engorged within his sarcophagus and awaited his own rebirth. Indeed the symbolism goes further, for Nut was mother to Osiris with whom the deceased was also identified. Stone sarcophagi, therefore, which first came into use with Cheops (IV Dyn), combined ancient Egypt's two greatest cults, of the sun and of Osiris. To the left, from the XVIII Dynasty, are the stone sarcophagi of Tuthmosis I (619), that of his daughter Hatshepsut made before she came to the throne (6024) and her final sarcophagus (620).

Room 28, at the centre of the atrium, has a painted floor with a river scene (627) from the palace of Akhenaten at Tell el Amarna.

Room 23 contains two interesting lintels, the one on the left (6189) showing the Heb-Sed of Senusret III (XII Dyn) very finely cut in sunk relief, while the one on the right is a tenth-rate copy by a later pharaoh.

Room 18 (the stairway leading out of the atrium well) has the colossal group (610) of Amenophis III and his wife Tiy with three of their daughters (XVII Dynasty). They are serene, almost a portrait of Victorian contentment but for the play of a smile on their lips and the physicality of their bodies. Despite the formality of the work and its size, there is a great sensuality to it. The reign of Amenophis was marked by luxury and a sudden eruption (or at least recording) of fashion consciousness: note particularly Tiy's full wig, the hair falling down to her breasts, a style associated almost exclusively with this reign.

Room 13. On the right is a fascinating document, a stele (599) inscribed on the reverse during the reign of Amenophis III with all that the pharaoh had done for Amun, but later inscribed on the obverse by Merneptah, pharaoh at about the time of the Exodus, with the sole known reference in Egyptian texts to the Israelites: 'Israel is crushed, it has no more seed.'

Corridors on each side of the atrium (allowing communication between Rooms 43 and 8 but not with the atrium itself) are lined with pottery, wall paintings and inscription fragments.

The First Floor

To see the first-floor rooms in approximate chronological order you should start at Room 43, overlooking the atrium from the south, and follow the corridors in a clockwise direction.

Old and Middle Kingdom Tomb Contents

Room 37 is full of wooden coffins and sarcophagi of the Middle Kingdom. The coffin of Sepi (3101 in Case C), a XII Dynasty general, is particularly well-painted. This is the oldest anthropoid coffin in the museum. See also the dismantled panels of his sarcophagus (3104 in Cases A and L), finely painted and extensively inscribed. Artefacts from the tomb of General Mesah at Assiut are displayed in several cases and include his sandals, mirror and neck pillow, and models of Egyptian soldiers (3345), black soldiers (3346) and a pleasure barge (3347).

Room 32 contains models (Case E: 3246, 4347) of solar boats. The solar boats are unmanned, operating on autopilot. They are the abstraction of the other boats displayed: funerary boats for carrying the dead man on a canopied bier, or for transport of the living. There is a delightful model of a boat (3244 in Case F) with its mast down, its rowers pulling at full strength, one rower taking a quick sidelong glance at you as the boat shoots by.

Room 27 contains marvellous models (6077–86) from the XI Dynasty tomb of Meketre at Thebes, including a plantation owner reviewing a parade of his cattle and workers (6080); a carpenter's workshop (6083); a pleasure garden with pool, lined with sycamore-figs, at one end a columned verandah (6084); and two boats dragging a net between them, taking fish from the Nile (6085).

New Kingdom Tomb Contents

Room 22 contains many interesting small figures, including XII–XXX Dynasty *ushabtis* (Cases I and J: 6062–72), and women, perhaps concubines of the dead man, lying on beds (Case C: 9435, 9437). Cases O, P and R contain New Kingdom funerary gear: painted linen or woven cloth for covering the chest, body and feet, beautifully designed and all the more fine for being highly perishable materials that have survived.

Room 17 is especially interesting for the papyri on its walls from the Book of the Dead.

Room 12 contains artefacts from royal tombs: a chariot of Tuthmosis IV (3000), the mummies of a child and a gazelle (Case I:

3776, 3780), and a collection of priestly wigs and wig boxes (Case L: 3779).

Room 13, at the north end of the atrium, displays furnishings from the intact Theban tomb of Yuya and Tuyu, parents-in-law of Amenophis III, with beds, chairs, whippet-like chariots, mummified food and time-serving *ushabtis*.

Gold, Dung and Jewels

Most of the north end of the first floor and all the outer rooms along its east side are devoted to Tutankhamun's treasures, but it is not easy to include them in the middle of this tour. Their profusion is described separately, on pp.156–7.

Room 2 has material from the Late Period royal burials at Tanis, including gold masks and a falcon-headed sarcophagus of silver, a treasure as exquisite as Tutankhamun's.

Room 6, nearby, contains a collection of scarabs. This black dung beetle, running everywhere about the desert sands pushing a ball of dung before it, symbolized the self-creator, the morning sun.

Room 4 closes a quarter of an hour before the rest of the museum and is specially guarded: it contains jewellery from the I Dynasty to the Byzantine period: necklaces, pectorals, diadems, daggers and much else in gold, silver and precious stones. The most splendid sizeable object is the VI Dynasty gold falcon head (case 3: 4010). The best workmanship is found in the jewellery of the XII Dynasty, and the stones are real (carnelian for red and orange, amethyst for purple and violet, lapis lazuli for blue, feldspar for green) – in Tutankhamun's time, as you will see in the nearby rooms containing objects from his tomb, paste and glass were used instead and though the settings are gold it is mere costume jewellery.

Graeco-Roman Burials

Room 14 holds portraits – among the most affecting exhibits in the museum. These people, Greeks from the Fayyum, continued the Egyptian practice of mummification, yet from their portraits, so lifelike and modern, you cannot imagine they would have accepted the ancient belief. The encaustic portraits (colours mixed into molten wax) were bound onto the mummies – there are shelves of these. A collection of panels is against the south wall (4310): the technique is superb, with shading, highlighting and perspective, two or three of them qualifying as masterpieces in their own right. Those garbage bodies, yet these living faces in which you can read whole lives: all are marked by a seriousness, rarely pompous, occasionally sad, a faint smile on one man's lips. They have steadfastly faced the passing millennia and now look at you as you look at them as though suddenly we might recognize one another.

Room 19 displays the main gods of the Egyptian pantheon; from various periods.

Sketches, Papyri, and Fixtures and Fittings

Room 24 is full of painted ostraka, limestone fragments. Case 18 contains interesting representations of animals: a monkey eating, a man leading a bull and a lion devouring a prisoner. People too: an intriguing picture of a woman relaxing and playing a stringed instrument. There is also, in the east doorway, a plan of a Theban tomb (4371), with what appear to be doorways shown in elevation. **Room 29** contains further ostraka, but written on, and papyri – 6335 especially worthwhile: a Ptolemaic Book of the Dead in finest detail, showing the 'Weighing of the Heart' ceremony.

The **corridor outside Room 34** has an Amarna toilet seat. Is this the loo on which Akhenaten sat?

Room 44 displays decorative details, most interesting the faïence from palaces of Ramses II and III.

Room 57 is around the southeast staircase. The square red and green leather tent (3848) belonged to a XXI Dynasty queen and was used at her funeral.

Room 48, at the centre of the south wings, contains a model of a funerary complex, showing how a river temple linked with the pyramid on the desert's edge. There is also a cross-sectioned pyramid showing the internal buttressing. A case to the north contains beautifully worked statuettes from various periods.

Prehistoric and Pre-dynastic Periods

Rooms 54, 55 and 53 are devoted to prehistoric and pre-dynastic artefacts such as pottery and tools, and are generally dull, except that in Room 53 are mummified animals: baboons, a dog, a crocodile and the skeleton of a mare – and these are disgusting! You can understand that the Egyptians, having convinced themselves of the efficacy of preservation, would wrap each other up. But to impose this on animals (look at their little linen-wrapped legs) seems perverse.

This is perhaps an unfair view, for human beings are at the centre of our cosmology, animals only soulless lookers-on, whereas Egyptian religion grew out of animal worship, totemism, an admiration of their qualities (strength, swiftness, beauty) or a desire to appease: wild dogs, the 'Egyptian wolf', prowled the cemeteries by night in search of bones and bodies that the Egyptians hoped would remain unmolested, and so this predator of their eternal life was transformed into their funerary deity, Anubis. Animal cults proliferated towards the end of the pagan period and were extremely popular, religious societies collecting the sacred animals (from shrew mice to hippopotami) that died in the district, mummifying them and burying them in special cemeteries (*see* 'Saqqara', pp.212–3 and pp.215–6).

The Mummy Room

The more I walk along, the more I listen, the more I move around the columns, the more do I experience the feeling of a dark world which fastens on to ours and which will not loosen the suckers through which it takes its life. Whatever it may cost, they find it necessary to confirm their existence, to perpetuate themselves, to incarnate, to reincarnate, to hypnotise nothingness and to vanquish it... They did not hide themselves in order to disappear, but in order to await the cue for their entry on the stage. They have not been dragged from the tomb. They have been brought from the limbo of the wings with masks and gloves of gold... Seti the First! How beautiful he is, with his little nose, his pointed teeth showing, his little face which belongs to death, reduced to one requirement alone – not to die. 'I! I! I!' This is the word which the rafters throw back.

Jean Cocteau, *Maalesh, A Theatrical Tour of the Middle East*

Room 56 (*closes 15mins early*) is the Mummy Room where some of the mightiest men in ancient history lie half-naked and bird-boned in glass cases. Jean Cocteau believed that the pharaohs did not intend to hide away, but Sadat decided in 1981 that visitors should be forbidden entry. It was meant as a gesture to fundamentalist Islamic sensibilities, but to no avail: the same year they made a mummy of him.

The mummies had been kept in Room 52 under indifferent conditions, though the poor state of preservation of some was not so much due to that, nor to any failure of the embalming process (*see* box, p.156), as to early exposure by grave robbers (*see* p.308). Various initiatives to rebury the royal bodies either in their original tombs or in a chamber built for the purpose were overcome by inertia. Then, after some sprucing up, which in the case of Ramses II meant a trip to Paris where he was received with the full honours due to a visiting head of state in need of urgent medical treatment, it was announced in 1993 that some of them at least would again be presented to the public gaze. Here in Room 56 eleven royal mummies, not all those previously on display (some were quite gruesome, while some of the women were perhaps too fetching), lie like cigars in sealed humidity-controlled cases under a dim sepulchral light where, under strict injunction neither to take photographs nor chatter (thankfully no guides are permitted), you circle round them along a ramp in chronological order.

Making Mummies

Not only were royalty and the nobility mummified but all classes of ancient Egyptian society according to their ability to pay, the practice continuing well beyond the pharaonic age, as demonstrated by a mummified Christian in the Graeco-Roman Museum at Alexandria. Herodotus, who visited Egypt in the mid-5th century BC, noted the varieties of mummification in his day:

The embalmers, when a body is brought to them, produce three specimen models in wood, painted to resemble nature, and graded in quality. After pointing out the differences in quality, they ask which of the three is required, and the kinsmen of the dead man, having agreed upon a price, go away and leave the embalmers to their work.

The most perfect process is as follows: as much as possible of the brain is extracted through the nostrils with an iron hook, and what the hook cannot reach is rinsed out with drugs. Next the flank is laid open with a flint knife and the whole contents of the abdomen is removed. The cavity is then throughly cleansed and washed out, first with palm wine and again with an infusion of pounded spices. After that it is filled with pure bruised myrrh, cassia and every other aromatic substance with the exception of frankincense and sewn up again, after which the body is placed in natron for seventy days. When this period, which must not be exceeded, is over, the body is washed and then wrapped from head to foot in linen cut into strips and smeared on the underside with gum. In this condition the body is given back to the family, who have a wooden case made, shaped like the human figure, into which it is put.

When, for reasons of expense, the second quality is called for, no incision is made and the intestines are not removed, but oil of cedar is injected into the body through the anus which is afterwards stopped up. The body is then pickled in natron for the prescribed number of days, on the last of which the oil is drained off. The effect is so powerful that as it leaves the body it brings with it the stomach and intestines in a liquid state, and as the flesh, too, is dissolved by the natrun, nothing of the body is left but the bones and skin. After this treatment it is returned to the family without further fuss.

The third method, used for embalming the bodies of the poor, is simply to clear out the intestines with a purge and keep the body seventy days in natron. It is then given back to the family to be taken away.

When the wife of a distinguished man dies, or any woman who happens to be beautiful or well known, her body is not given to the embalmers immediately, but only after the lapse of three or four days. This is a precautionary measure to prevent the embalmers from violating the corpse, a thing which is said actually to have happened in the case of a woman who had just died. The culprit was given away by one of his fellow workmen.

Among those permitted out for an airing you see Sequenenreta'a, otherwise known as Sekenenre (XVII Dynasty), who died of an axe wound in the forehead (clearly visible) received in the heat of battle. He was probably mummified on the spot – his lips scream with agony, his legs are contracted with pain. Tuthmosis II and IV (XVIII Dynasty) seem to lie sleeping, though the latter as if forever weeping silently at his death. There is Seti I (XIX Dynasty), serene and majestic, his profile exactly as you see it on the reliefs at Abydos. His son Ramses II (XIX Dynasty) looks as though he is straining to awaken, his arms rising from his chest, his hands opening, his fingers uncurling – this happened as he was unbandaged. Nor, whatever uncertainty there may be that Merneptah (XIX Dynasty) was the pharaoh of the Exodus, can there be any doubt that he was his father's son, bearing as he does Ramses II's unmistakable conk.

The Tutankhamun Exhibition

You can now walk back to the north end of the first floor of the museum to see the plenitude of objects found buried with **Tutankhamun** in the Valley of the Kings. Yet this king was a minor figure who died young and was stuffed into a small tomb; imagine the impedimenta that Seti I tried to take with him. Rooms 3, 7, 8, 9, 10, 15, 25, 30, 35, 40 and 45, and also part of Room 13, contain 1,700 items in all. The eyes jadedly search for the highlights of the highlights, or otherwise fix on curiosities.

Tutankhamun's mummy, his outermost coffin of gilded wood and his granite sarcophagus are all in his tomb in the Valley of the Kings, but the second **coffin** of gilded wood and the third of solid gold are in **Room 3**, along with the **gold mask**. Each of these, placed one within the other like Russian dolls, were in turn placed within a gilded wood shrine – which again fitted within three more (**Rooms 7 and 8**). The ancient Egyptians employed these gold casings in part because gold was thought to be the flesh of the gods, but also because they believed it warded off all outside contamination.

Among the finer or more curious items in the east gallery (Rooms 15 to 45) are a jewellery casket of gilded wood (**Room 45**, Case 54, 447) in the form of a naos, with the figure of Anubis on top; a chest for the pharaoh's clothes (**Room 35**, Case 20, 324), decorated with a desert hunt on the lid, on the large panels with Tutankhamun waging war, and on the small panels with the royal sphinx trampling on his enemies; and the famous **small throne** (**Room 1**), its back richly decorated with a scene of Tutankhamun's queen placing her right hand on his left shoulder. This is often interpreted as a relaxed domestic scene, though probably the gesture confirms the young pharaoh's position, as she was after all the daughter of both Akhenaten and his wife Nefertiti, and though Akhenaten may also have fathered Tutankhamun (though by a different wife), the royal ka was transferred through the female line (explaining the frequent sister and daughter marriages of pharaohs). The armrests too are beautiful, the lovely shape of falcons' wings extending in protection, the birds' heads wearing the crown of Upper and Lower Egypt. As you leave the gallery, on either side of the doorway are **statues of the two guards** in the form of Tutankhamun who were found standing in the boy-king's tomb. It was a job they quietly performed for well over 3,000 years until Howard Carter caught them napping. In penance they must stand here in the museum for a few more years yet.

Also in the Tutankhamun rooms you may have noticed a curiosity resembling one of those cookie-cutters used for making gingerbread men, but life-size. It is in fact a vegetating Osiris: a wooden silhouette of the god, his image again carved out within this and the depression once filled with earth, from which grass would sprout with symbolic effect.

ⓘ **Cairo >**
Cairo Airport,
t *(02) 291 4255*

Ramses railway station,
t *(02) 2579 0767*

downtown *(head office)*
5 Sharia Adli, at the Ezbekieh end,
t *(02) 2391 3454*

Pyramids,
Sharia al-Ahram,
t *(02) 3383 8823*

Tourist Information in Cairo

Tourist Information Offices

All Tourist Offices can provide brochures and a good free **map** of Cairo with practical information on the reverse. The people working at their offices are charming and helpful (most helpful is the head office), but they are used to tourists going to the obvious places by the slickest means, and so have to be pressed for alternative information. If you do not want a tour and do not want to take taxis everywhere, then make it clear that you do not mind taking the local bus or train to Memphis, Saqqara, Meidum or wherever, and they will come up with the information you require.

Tourist Police

The **Tourist Police, t** (02) 2391 9144, or **t** 126, are found browsing about the airport, the railway station, in the bazaars and at tourist sights, and are recognized by a small blue strip on their left chest and an armband marked 'Tourist Police' in Arabic and English. Otherwise they wear the normal police uniform, which is black in winter and white in summer. They usually speak at least two foreign languages and are helpful with information while doing their best to ensure that tourists are not excessively importuned. They are based at the airport, at the Midan Ramses railway station, at the Pyramids near the Mena House, in Midan el-Hussein on the edge of Khan el Khalili, and downtown at 5 Sharia Adli, towards Ezbekieh Gardens, as well as in all tourist areas in the rest of the country.

Communications

Telephones

Note that Telecom Egypt is adding numbers to Cairo's telephone numbers, and therefore some of the numbers in this guide might be incomplete. Usually adding 2 or 3 before the last seven numbers will do the trick. For information, telephone Telecom Egypt on **t** *111.*

For local phone calls, some shops, restaurants and hotels will have **payphones** for public use, or you may encounter a public phonebox at a public place or in the street. For long-distance and international calls you can phone from most hotels (at the better hotels it does not matter whether you are a guest or not), but you will pay a hefty premium, as much as 100%. You can make reverse charge (collect) calls from some of the luxury hotels, e.g. the Marriott and Semiramis Inter-continental, or British Airways in Midan el Tahrir (to the UK only).

Or you can phone at the normal rate from a **telephone exchange** (PTT). Known as Centrales, these are on Midan el Tahrir (north side), Sharia Alfi by the Windsor Hotel and on Sharia Adli. The one at Midan el Tahrir is open 24 hours. You can buy phonecards here and use them in the orange direct-dial phones located at the exchanges (and sometimes elsewhere, e.g. airports and railway stations).

For more information on telephone services and area codes within Egypt, *see* p.75.

Email and Fax

Internet centres come and go; most are used by game-playing adolescents rather than for sending emails. Some hotels will have email facilities for use by their guests.

All the better hotels have **fax** services, which can be used by guests and others. Faxes can also be sent and received at the telephone exchanges at Midan el Tahrir, Sharia Alfi and Sharia Adli.

Post and Telegrams

The **Central Post Office** is at Midan el Ataba, near the Ezbekieh Gardens (open Sat–Thurs 7–7, Fri 7–noon). The **Poste Restante** is here, down the side street to the right of the main entrance (open Sat–Thurs 8–6, Fri 10–noon). Other post offices are open 9–4, closed Fri. Most hotels have letterboxes and can supply you with stamps for cards and letters. Do not use street letterboxes unless you want to arrive home before your postcards. EMS Mail is an express service offered at all post offices. It is faster and safer than the usual postal service, while slower than, but a quarter of the price of, a courier service.

To send a **parcel** out of Egypt requires an export licence. You must obtain this at the Post Traffic Centre, Midan Ramses (open 8.30–3, closed Fri). The building is to the right of the main entrance to Ramses railway station. Go there with your parcel unwrapped; here it will be inspected and, for a small fee, wrapped for you; for a further small fee you will be guided through the remaining formalities and paperwork. Your parcel must not weigh more than 20kg if going to Europe or Africa, 30kg if going to North America. Its dimensions must not exceed 1m x 1m x 50cm. If sending home fabrics or souvenirs you have bought, ask first at the shop whether they will do it for you. Most shops catering to tourists have export licences and are reliable.

You can **receive post** at your hotel, or care of American Express (if you have their traveller's cheques or card), or care of your embassy (the envelope should be marked 'Visitors' Mail'). American Express will forward mail arriving after your departure for about LE3.

Telegrams in English or French can be sent from the PTT offices on the north side of Midan el Tahrir (open 24 hours), or in Sharia Alfi or Sharia Adli – or from major hotels.

Courier Services

Federal Express, **t** (02) 357 1304, **t** (02) 351 6070, and **t** (02) 268 7888

DHL, **t** (02) 3302 9801

TNT, **t** (02) 3749 9850

Emergencies

Police **t** 122

Tourist Police **t** 126

Ambulance **t** 123

Fire Service **t** 180

Telephone Enquiries **t** 140

Hospitals and Medical Care

In an emergency you can phone the **Tourist Police, t** 126, or the **police ambulance service, t** 123, which will take you to the nearest hospital, but if you need urgent treatment the best thing is to get yourself (by taxi or whatever means) to the nearest hospital as quickly as possible. Only two (private) hospitals send ambulances with on-board professional paramedics or life-support equipment; they are **As Salam International Hospital** and **Nil Badrawi Hospital**. In addition the following two centrally located private hospitals are often recommended: the **Anglo-American Hospital** and the **Italian Hospital**.

All of these hospitals are modern and fully equipped. But note that private hospitals may not accept you if you do not have medical insurance; even if you do have insurance, not only should you be prepared to pay cash, but a substantial deposit will be required before you are admitted, though in some cases payment can be made by credit card.

For medical care, ask at your hotel. Most will be able to refer you to a **doctor** or **dentist**, while some of the major hotels will have a doctor on call. Most Egyptian doctors have been trained in Europe or North America and speak English. Your embassy can also recommend doctors and dentists.

There are several **pharmacies** around Midan el Tahrir and downtown with a wide range of medications not requiring prescriptions – describe your symptoms and, if the ailment is minor, the pharmacist will prescribe on the spot. Both imported medicines and those locally licensed are heavily subsidized by the government. You will probably be able to obtain your favourite medicine at a fraction of its usual price. Cosmetics, perfumes and toiletries are also stocked.

Anglo-American Hospital, al-Burg (which means the Cairo Tower; it is just west of it), Zamalek, **t** (02) 2735 6162/3/4/5.

As Salam International Hospital, Corniche el Nil, Maadi, **t** (02) 2524 0250, emergency **t** (02) 2524 0077; also at Sharia Syria, Mohandiseen, **t** (02) 3303 0502.

Maps

Tourist Information Offices can provide you with a good free map of

Cairo. A far better map is *Cairo Maps: The Practical Guide*, which has over 40 pages of street maps and a street index; it is published by The American University in Cairo (AUC) Press, and is sold at bookshops and newsstands.

Money

To **change money**, go to Thomas Cook, American Express, or to the banks in the major hotels – all the 5-star hotels have 24-hour banks. For a full-scale commercial banking service, there is **Barclays Bank International** (7 Sharia El Gergawy, Dokki, Cairo, **t** (02) 16222). If you have Egyptian pounds which you want to convert back into foreign currency before your departure, you can go to any bank (including the one at the airport) and show them a receipt indicating that you had previously converted at least such an amount from foreign currency into Egyptian pounds. They will then subtract what they reckon you should have spent per day, with the result that you will probably be stuck with a load of unwanted Egyptian currency. Moral: never change too much at any one time, and what you do change, spend. This is made easier by the regulation allowing you to spend up to LE1,000 at the airport duty-free shops on departure.

If stranded, you can go to Thomas Cook, American Express or Barclays International and have them send a telegram or fax requesting your bank or persons at home to arrange the **transfer of money** to you in Egypt. This can be accomplished in 2–3 days. Western Union offers its faster Money Transfer service ('in minutes'). Or you can go to an airline office and ask for a pre-paid ticket, the airline faxing or cabling whomever you suggest to pay for the ticket home. Authorization to issue you with a ticket can be received back in Cairo within 2 days.

Western Union, t 0 800 88 000 88 (toll free).

ATMs

Cash machines, or ATMs, are located on every main street in Cairo, at banks and in hotels.

Shopping in Cairo

While shopping at the bazaar stalls is a matter of haggling over **prices** (*see also* **Practical A–Z**, pp.73–4), shops and department stores in the modern part of Cairo sell at fixed prices. Except in those shops occupying the arcades of major hotels, prices are usually marked in Arabic numerals. Sometimes prices are stated in piastres (100pt=LE1). So an item priced at 1,000 is likely to be 1,000pt – that is, LE10. Usually, common sense will tell you whether piastres or pounds are intended.

Department stores and shops are generally open 9am–1pm and 5–8pm or later, though some may remain open continuously throughout the day, particularly in Khan el Khalili. Some shops will close on Fridays, others on Sundays. During Ramadan, shop hours are likely to be 9.30am–3.30pm and 8–10pm or even later.

Antiquities

Antiquities offered to you on the street are bound to be fake. Which is not to say there are not any genuine pharaonic, Coptic and Islamic artefacts around, but they will cost a lot of money and your only guarantee of their authenticity is to buy them from a shop displaying a licence from the Department of Antiquities. The shop will also give you a certificate of authenticity. You will also need a **permit** from the Department of Antiquities to export your purchase.

Try Ahmed Dahba at 5 Sikket el Bedestan, and Old Shoppe, opposite at 7 Haret Khan el Khalili, in the heart of Khan el Khalili; they both also sell reproductions.

Antiques

Note that anything over 100 years old requires an export permit.

Zamalek is the main hunting-ground in Cairo both for genuine antiques and reproductions, but prowling downtown and in Khan el Khalili is also worthwhile.

Atrium, 4 Sharia Mohammed Mazhar, Zamalek; and **Nostalgia**, 6 Sharia Zakaria Rizk, Zamalek. Both very smart, the former mainly for furniture, the latter good for accessories.

Old Shoppe, 7 Sharia Khan el Khalili. Like a great dusty warehouse and fun to rummage about in.

Osiris Auction House, 15 Sharia Sherif, downtown. If you are an expert, try your luck here.

Books and Prints

Books on Egypt and Egyptology, and light holiday reading in paperback, are found in the major hotel bookstalls, which also sell magazines and newspapers.

For a more extensive selection, the following bookshops are recommended:

The American University in Cairo (AUC) Bookshop, first floor, Hill House, AUC downtown campus, 113 Sharia Qasr el Aini, just off Midan el Tahrir. The best bookshop in Egypt, with a very wide range of books including all titles published by The American University in Cairo Press.

Diwan, 159 Sharia 26 July, Zamalek. Stocks a wide and interesting range of books; this is an agreeable place to browse, have a coffee and meet friends.

Lehnert and Landrock, 44 Sharia Sherif, downtown near Sharia Adli. A good general bookshop, with also a superb collection of vintage photographs for sale. They also run the bookshop at the Egyptian Museum.

L'Orientaliste, 15 Sharia Qasr el Nil, downtown. Specializes in old and rare books, maps, lithographs and postcards.

Anglo-Egyptian Bookshop, 165 Sharia Mohammed Farid, downtown. One of the oldest bookshops in Cairo.

Brass and Copper

Brass and copper work has long been a Cairo tradition, and the standards are still high today. The best place for it is in **Khan el Khalili** along or just off Sharia Muizz, south of the mosque complex of Qalaun. Small plates intended as ornaments and candlesticks, gongs, lamps, mugs and pitchers are the easiest to carry off – though be sure that anything you intend to drink out of is coated on the inside with another metal, like silver, as brass or copper in contact with some substances can be highly poisonous. The finest items are the big brass trays which can serve as table tops; wooden stands are available.

Camels

The camel market (Souk el Gimaal) has moved from Embaba to the village of Birqash, 30km northwest of Cairo, where it is open Monday and Friday mornings from dawn, LE25 admission fee. It is a smelly business, and not for sentimentalists. The camels have been brought in from Sudan via Aswan and Daraw, a journey done on foot in the recent past but now more often done by boat and train or truck. You should be there no later than around 7 or 8am; it is pretty much over by late morning. A taxi will cost about LE100 round trip, or you can take a bus from the terminus behind the Egyptian Museum to Manashi by the Nile Barrage at Qanatir, from there taking a service taxi. On your return you ought to be able to find a service taxi to bring you back to Cairo – unless you have bought a camel: docile females make the best mounts; expect to pay LE5,000. Less expensive are the camels chopped up for consumption. A great deal of camel meat is eaten in Egypt where it is a specialty; not only is it delicious but it is also virtually cholesterol-free.

Carpets, Tents, Tapestries and Weaving

Weavings, carpets, tents and tapestries require further adventures if you want the best. In fact, Egypt is not particularly well known for **carpets**, and if you are going to Aswan you should look there first, rather than Cairo, for small rugs and weavings. Old rugs are auctioned off from time to time; look in the *Egyptian Gazette* for announcements.

Carpets and rugs are found in Khan el Khalili and elsewhere around town, including at Sednoui, a department store just north of Midan Ataba, which is worth visiting for its own sake (*see* Sednoui under 'Clothes and Shoes', below).

Tent-making, on the other hand, is a Cairene speciality, and for these you should go to the Street of the Tentmakers (Sharia Khayyamiya), south of Bab Zuwayla. There are six or seven workshops along this covered section of medieval Cairo's major north–south street, creating beautiful appliqué tents used at mosques or street festivals (and funerals). Some are decorated with scenes of pharaonic or Islamic themes, but the best have abstract arabesque designs or intricate calligraphy. Not that you don't have to buy a tent; they are made in sections and you can buy a piece about big enough to serve as a pillow cover.

Two villages outside Cairo are centres of the best **tapestry-weaving** in Egypt. Harraniyya, about 3km along the canal road from Giza to Saqqara, was developed by the late Ramses Wissa Wassef; he taught the children how to card, dye and spin their own wool and weave it into tapestries of their own design, usually village scenes, primitive and boldly coloured. His tapestries are now world-famous, and the workshop, on the right of the road, continues to be run by Wassef's daughter. The other village is Kardassa (*see* p.195).

Clothes and Shoes

Clothes (in continental sizes) will be found in the hotel shops, shops downtown (for example in Sharia Talaat Harb and Sharia 26 July), boutiques in Zamalek, Heliopolis and downtown at the World Trade Centre on Corniche el Nil, north of the 26 July Bridge and in the big department stores:

Chemla, 11 Sharia 26 July; where low prices are more important than quality.

Cicurel, 3 Sharia 26 July; for quality and higher prices.

Omar Effendi, a good department store with several branches: on Sharia Talaat Harb just off Midan el Tahrir, on Sharia Adli near Sharia Talaat Harb, and also at Heliopolis and Dokki.

Sednoui, just north of Midan Ataba, worth visiting for the building itself, modelled after the Galeries Lafayette on Boulevard Haussmann in Paris and one of the most spectacular sights in Cairo; a vast atrium encircled by rising balconies. Nationalized in 1961 along with Egypt's other department stores (mostly Jewish-owned, but Sednoui was owned by Syrian Christians), it has since become a complete stranger to enterprise, but it makes a marvellous mausoleum, and apart from the possibility that it might actually attempt to sell some clothes and shoes, it does have a good range of carpets.

Cairo also has **designer fashion** shops with international appeal – stylish clothes that cost a fraction of what they would at home:

On Safari, 10 Sharia Lutfalla, Zamalek; also found at the World Trade Centre, 1191 Corniche el Nil, Boulaq, and branches throughout town.

Nomad at the Marriott Hotel, Zamalek; and at their nearby shop, 14 Serai el Gezira. They have adapted Bedouin designs to Western styles.

Mobaco at the Marriott Hotel, Zamalek, also at the Semiramis Hotel on the Corniche el Nil, and branches throughout the city; using Egyptian cotton and taking care with their tailoring, they make superior shirts and other garments, men's and women's, and they have expanded into France. New Man is part of Mobaco, in a trendy youthful guise.

Concrete, at the Ramses Hilton, and at 27 Sharia Adly, downtown, also 11 Sharia Lebanon, Mohandiseen, and branches throughout Cairo. Style, elegance and quality at very affordable prices, often combining Egyptian cotton with tailoring in Italy.

The **galabiyya**, the full-length traditional garment of Egyptian men, is popular with both male and female visitors as comfortable casual wear. Fancier versions can also serve as evening wear for women. There are three basic styles: the *baladi* or peasant style, with wide sleeves and a low rounded neckline; the *saudi* style, more form-fitting, with a high-buttoned neck and cuffed sleeves; and the *efrangi* or foreign style, looking like a shirt with collar and cuffs but reaching all the way down to the floor. Several shops sell galabiyyas along Sharia Talaat Harb between Midan Talaat Harb and Sharia 26 July, and also the department stores (and *see* 'Fabrics', below). Fancier ones (both fixed price) are:

Ammar, 26 Sharia Qasr el Nil.

Atlas, Sikket el Bedestan, the main east–west street through Khan el Khalili, and at the Semiramis Inter-continental.

Shoes are found in many of the shops mentioned above; also there is a plethora of shoe shops downtown along Sharia Qasr el Nil, Talaat Harb and 26 July.

Fabrics

Fabric is found in variety and quality at Omar Effendi (*see* 'Clothes and Shoes', above); Salon Vert, Sharia Qasr el Nil; or Ouf in el Mashhad el Hussein: heading south along Sharia Muizz and approaching Sharia al-Azhar, take the first right after Sharia el Muski/Sharia Gohar el Qaid and the first left; Ouf is on the right down this alley. Each of these stores also sell off-the-peg galabiyyas.

Glass and Narghilehs

Muski glass, usually turquoise or dark brown and recognizable by its numerous air bubbles, has been handblown in Cairo since the Middle Ages and is now turned out as ashtrays, candlesticks and glasses. It is inexpensive, but also very fragile.

The best **nargilehs** (hubble-bubbles) will have glass, rather than brass, bottoms. For these, try around the Street of Coppersmiths, south of the mosque complex of Qalaun.

Sayed Abd al Raouf, 8 Haret Khan el Khalili. Try this shop for Muski glass.

Jewellery

There are numerous **jewellery** shops in Sharia Abdel Khalek Sarwat (near Garden Groppi) and in the small street leading off it, Sikket el Manakh. And of course, there are numerous jewellers in Muski and Khan el Khalili. Too often, Egyptian jewellery is disappointing, much of it mimicking the more obvious pharaonic motifs (cartouche, ankh, Eye of Horus), and those of Islamic motif showing little popular imagination – hands and eyes for warding off evil, or as pieces inscribed with 'Allah'. At first it may seem exotic, but it is limited and grows tiresome, while much outside these two motifs is usually conceived in bad taste. Nor is there much, if any, genuine Bedouin jewellery around anymore; almost all traditional old pieces have been sold and taken out of the country, while the Bedouin themselves come to Cairo and Alexandria and other towns and buy glittering junk. However, for a selection of handsome pieces, often based on Bedouin designs, go to Nomad at the Marriott Hotel, Zamalek, or their shop nearby at 14 Serai el Gezira.

Musical Instruments

Sharia Qalaa, between Midan Ataba and the Islamic Art Museum, has several shops selling traditional **musical instruments**. These include the *oud* (lute), the *rabab* (viol), the *nai* (flute), the *kanoon* (dulcimer), the *mismare baladi* (oboe), the *tabla* (drum), and the *riq* and *duf* (forms of tambourine).

Scents and Spices

One of the most enjoyable excursions, whether you intend to buy or not, is to wander through the **spice market** which lies off Sharia Muizz, between Sharia el Muski (Sharia Gohar el Qaid) and Sharia al-Azhar. There are bottles of perfume essences, boxes of incense and bags of herbs and spices. Also there is kohl, a black eye cosmetic. The fragrances, and the quality of the light in awninged alleyways, awaken sensation.

Woodwork and Leatherwork

Inlay of **wood** and **mother-of-pearl**, and also **leatherwork**, are plentiful in the bazaar. Egyptian leather is not the best, however. The most common items are handbags, suitcases and hassocks; more interesting than useful or comfortable are camel saddles. Wooden trays, boards (including backgammon and chess boards) and boxes inlaid with mother-of-pearl and coloured bits of wood are not quite as good as those made in Syria, but are intricate and beautiful enough. *Mashrabiyyas*, those intricate screens found in old Cairene houses, made from bits of wood fitted together without nails or glue, occasionally come on sale in the bazaars.

Sports and Activities in Cairo

One of the most effortless and pleasurable things to do is to sail up and down the Nile in a **felucca**, especially in the evening. These can be hired along the Corniche el Nil by Shepheard's Hotel and near the Grand Hyatt.

For skiing and golf, *see* p.195.

Archaeology

The **Egyptian Exploration Society** holds lectures and organizes field trips to watch British archaeologists at work. Its office is at the British Council, 192 Sharia el-Nil, Agouza, Cairo, **t** (02) 3300 1886.

The **American Research Centre in Egypt** likewise holds lectures and conducts educational visits to American-run excavations. ARCE is at 2 Midan Simón Bolívar, Garden City, Cairo, **t** (02) 2794 8239.

Cycling and Running

Cycling, running and similar activities are organized by groups composed of both foreigners and Egyptian residents. Contact telephone numbers are usually home numbers; check the back pages of *Egypt Today* where the most up-to-date announcements appear, complete with meeting places. The **Cairo Cyclists** meet Fridays and Saturdays at 7am at the front gate of the Cairo American College, Midan Digla. The route, distance and pace is decided by those joining the ride. A second group, devoted to fast-paced training rides, meets at 7am on Saturdays.

The **Hash House Harriers** meet every Friday afternoon at about two hours before sunset for non-competitive fun runs, jogs and walks at the Pyramids, in the desert and through the more traffic-free parts of Cairo. Members include people of all abilities, nationalities, sexes and ages.

Health Clubs

For greater exertion, all the luxury hotels have health clubs; staying at the hotel gives you automatic membership, but many are also open to non-residents on a daily or weekly basis. Typical facilities at these places include a gym with rowing and cycling machines, tennis courts, pool, sauna, jacuzzi and health food bar.

Spectator Sports

For sports like football, horse-racing and rowing, check the daily *Egyptian Gazette* (on Saturdays called the *Egyptian Mail*). The national craze is **football**, and the standard of play is very high: the Egyptian national team is one of the best in Africa. The season is from September to May, with the two main club sides, Ahly and Zamalek, playing at the Cairo Stadium in Heliopolis on Fridays, Saturdays and Sundays. There is **horse-racing** from October to May at the Gezira Sporting Club and the Heliopolis Hippodrome. On Fridays year-round you can watch **rowing** on the Nile, the premier crew being the Cairo police, who routinely thrash visiting Oxford, Cambridge and other foreign crews.

Where to Stay in Cairo

If you have not already made a reservation, then on arrival at Cairo Airport you can go to the **Tourist Information Office** or **Misr Travel** and see if they can help. Alternatively, do your own hotel hunting, probably running no greater risk than having to visit a couple of hotels before finding something suitable. Often a hotel will volunteer or can be prevailed upon to telephone ahead on your behalf, saving legwork and fares.

All hotels in the luxury and expensive categories (*see* p.62) will have air conditioning and a TV, normally with satellite stations, and usually the moderate-category hotels will too. Many of the hotels in the moderate and inexpensive categories are survivors from an earlier age; while some of these have been modernized, and others at least maintained in good order, yet others have sunk into decrepitude. Some of these hotels may have style, but they may not have air conditioning or heating or hot water, and rooms and bathrooms should be checked for cleanliness and comfort. If you are not satisfied with the first room you are shown, ask to see another; in these categories, rooms can vary greatly within the same hotel.

The following is a selective list of hotels in and around Cairo itself. For rates, *see* p.62; for tipping, *see* p.67. For **hotels in the area of the Pyramids**, *see* pp.195–6. These are ideal when visiting the Pyramids themselves, but note that it can be difficult to return the 11km to Cairo: the bus service is infrequent, and you find yourself relying on taxis.

The famous **Nile Hilton Hotel** is no more. Located at Midan el Tahrir, right next to the Egyptian Museum and overlooking the Nile, it was the first international hotel built in Egypt (opening ceremonies in 1959 were attended by Nasser and Tito) and was the first Hilton in the Middle East. Over the course of half a century it become something of an institution. Its annexes and malls, added later, housed a concentration of travel agencies, airline offices, banks, shops and business facilities. But the property itself is owned by an Egyptian government holding company, and the new lease has gone to Ritz-Carlton, who are entirely renovating the hotel and its extensions. It will reopen as the Nile Ritz-Carlton in 2011. To keep track of developments, *see*: *www.ritzcarlton.com/en/Properties/Cairo/Default.htm*.

Luxury ($$$$$)

Near Midan el Tahrir and along the Corniche el Nil

Conrad >

*******Conrad**, 1191 Corniche el Nil, Bulaq, **t** (02) 2580 8000, *www.conradhotels.com*. A Hilton hotel with exceptionally comfortable rooms and a pleasingly relaxing atmosphere with palm trees planted in the foyer. The place makes a point of being somewhat sedate, with no nightclub or other noisy entertainments, but it has a pool, a health club and good continental cuisine.

*******Four Seasons at Nile Plaza**, 1089 Corniche El Nil, Garden City, **t** (02) 2791 7000, *www.fourseasons.com/caironp/*. A complete disaster for Garden City, this hotel has been imposed on a lovely residential area over which it now looms like some monster from another planet. If there were such a thing as planning in Egypt, this hotel would not have been allowed. The more expensive rooms have Nile views; cheaper rooms look towards the Citadel, which is not saying much. The service is good, the rooms comfortable and spacious, and the hotel offers a pool, spa, fitness facilities and 10 restaurants and bars.

*******Grand Hyatt Cairo**, Roda Island, **t** (02) 2365 1234, *www.cairo.grand.hyatt.com*. Travellers should beware: the Grand Hyatt has recently been taken over by a Saudi who is a strict Wahabbi Muslim fundamentalist and has banned alcohol throughout the hotel, though legal pressure by the Hyatt group has forced him to allow alcoholic drinks to be served, if only grudgingly and under highly restrictive and inconvenient conditions, at the Revolving Restaurant on the 40th floor, and through room service in the privacy of your room, but it is not served in any of the other restaurants, cafés and lounges in the hotel. If you object to having fundamentalist values imposed on you at a supposedly international hotel, the Grand Hyatt is not the place to stay. Otherwise the hotel offers all the usual facilities expected of a luxury hotel, including spa, fitness centre and pool. Dining choices include the Baccarat, a Nile yacht with oriental cuisine and belly dancer; the Nubian Village restaurant with Lebanese and Egyptian cuisine in an ethnic Nubian setting; the Lobby Lounge with a magnificent view of the Nile towards Gezira; and the Revolving Restaurant on the 40th floor which provides a 300-degree view of the city (the other 60 degrees being of the hotel itself), its suburbs and the Pyramids, though the rotation is tediously slow and the French cuisine is frankly indifferent.

*******Ramses Hilton**, 1115 Corniche el Nil, **t** (02) 2577 7444, *www.hilton.co.uk/*

ramses. A 1981 tower, all rooms with balconies, many with a Nile view, a short walk north of the Egyptian Museum. The rooms are a bit small. The best thing about the hotel, which guests and non-guests alike can enjoy, is its top-floor cocktail lounge with sweeping night-time panorama. Facilities include a British-style pub, an Indian restaurant, an outdoor pool, health club, casino, business centre, shops, Hertz and travel agent.

*****Semiramis Inter-Continental**, Corniche el Nil, **t** (02) 355 7171, *www.InterContinental.com*. Overlooking the Nile, a short walk from Midan el Tahrir. Its jumble of tiered reception area-cum-bar-cum-café-cum-ballrooms-and-meeting-rooms is a good example of how not to design a hotel, but it has a high reputation for service and is favoured by businessmen. Pool, health club, business centre, shops, travel agent and car hire desk are among the usual facilities.

On Gezira Island and the West Bank of the Nile

*****Cairo Marriott**, Serai el Gezira, Zamalek, **t** (02) 2728 3000, *www.cairo marriotthotel.com*. On Gezira Island overlooking the Nile. The public areas of the Marriott inhabit with effortless vulgarity an 1869 royal palace (which was purchased soon after by the Lebanese magnate 'Prince' Lutfallah, and its parkland sold off to make the Gezira Club), while the rooms are in new, purpose-built towers. The garden is very pleasant, however, and makes an enjoyable place to have drinks or dine. Facilities include a swimming pool, tennis courts, health club, casino, business centre, shops, car hire and travel agent. Unless you like long walks, it is a taxi-ride to almost anywhere of interest in the city.

*****Cairo Sheraton**, Midan el Galaa, Dokki, **t** (02) 3336 9800, *www.star woodhotels.com/sheraton/cairo*. Located on the west bank of the Nile across the Tahrir bridge and within walking distance of the Egyptian Museum, this was the first Sheraton in Egypt; it opened in 1970, with a second tower added in 1990. Today the hotel is tired-looking, though the service is very good. Insist on an upper-storey room with a Nile view. Several restaurants and dining lounges, including oriental, Japanese, Italian, and a 24-hour Tea Garden; also pool, health club, beauty parlour, casino, business centre, many shops and an Avis desk.

*****Sofitel El Gezirah**, Gezira Island, **t** (02) 2737 3737, *www.sofitel.com*. Newly renovated in French-oriental décor, this landmark circular tower at the southern tip of the island offers wonderful Nile views from every room. A short walk from the Opera, the museums and downtown Cairo, the El Gezirah offers all the usual luxury-class facilities. Service is poor, however, due to poorly trained staff.

*****Four Seasons at First Residence**, 35 Sharia Giza, **t** (02) 3573 1212, *www. fourseasons.com/ cairofr/*. Located on the west bank of the Nile facing the Zoological Gardens with distant views of the Pyramids, an over-the-top luxury hotel, more flash than taste. It has all possible facilities, good service, and its eateries make it a popular meeting place.

Expensive ($$$$)

****Novotel Cairo Airport**, Heliopolis, **t** (02) 2291 8520, *www.novotel.com*. One of several hotels in the vicinity of the airport, which is not where anyone in their right mind would want to stay unless they had to catch an early flight. If you do, this is a good choice. Frequent courtesy buses deliver you within minutes to the airport; the rooms are soundproofed, air-conditioned and provided with satellite TV; there are tennis courts, a garden and an outdoor pool.

****Om Kolthoom**, Sharia Abu El Feda Street, Zamalek, **t** (02) 2736 8444, *www.omkolthoomhotel.com*. This elegant 16-storey hotel stands on the site of the villa of Um Kalthoum (the name can be spelt in a variety of ways), Egypt's great singer of the mid-20th century, and overlooks the Nile. Rooms have balconies, bathrooms, satellite television, minibars and sofabeds. Restaurant with informal atmosphere and a coffee shop which extends outdoors during the evenings.

***Safir Hotel Cairo**, Dokki, **t** (02) 3748 2424, *www.safirhotels.com*. Fairly conveniently located across the Tahrir bridge from downtown Cairo, completely renovated in 2008. Spacious rooms, excellent breakfast, good service, pool, various eateries including a sushi restaurant and a pub.

****Shepheard, Corniche el Nil, Garden City, t (02) 2792 1000, *www.shepheard-hotel.com*. Not the famous Shepheard's; that was near Ezbekieh Gardens and was burnt down in the nationalist riots of 1952. This Shepheard's, south of Midan el Tahrir, was built in 1956. The atmosphere is sedate, the 24-hour café is comfortable and the top-floor bar and restaurant have good views of the river. Some rooms can be small and gloomy, but the preferred Nile-side rooms are spacious, have ceiling-to-floor picture windows and balconies, and are equipped with satellite TV, hairdryer and minibar. Shops, casino, beauty parlour, banks, travel agent, car hire, but no pool.

Moderate ($$$)

Downtown

***Cosmopolitan, 1 Sharia Ibn Taalab, off Sharia Qasr el Nil, t (02) 2392 3956, f 2393 3531. Old, traditional hotel, tucked away in a quiet side street at the centre of town. Full of character but badly in need of refurbishment. It has a restaurant, bar, coffee shop and bank. Most rooms are air-conditioned with bath.

***Fontana, Midan Ramses, t (02) 2592 2321. A good hotel despite its grim location near Ramses Station, and conveniently welcome if you have arrived by rail at some unearthly hour. Surprisingly, it has a pool, and a lovely one at that, and there is a enjoyable café on the rooftop. The rooms are clean and spacious, and have baths, air conditioning and TV.

***Grand Hotel, 17 Sharia 26 July, t (02) 2575 7700, *www.grandhotel cairo.com*. An Art Deco survival at the intersection with Sharia Talaat Harb. Its rooms, with parquet floors, are clean and comfortable, some with shower.

Luna >

***Luna, 27 Sharia Talaat Harb, t (02) 2396 1020, *www.hotellunacairo.com*. Large, clean rooms, some with en-suite bathrooms and air conditioning, others with fans. This is a welcoming and well-run place, and excellent value for money.

***Victoria, 66 Sharia el Gumhuriya, t (02) 2589 2290, *www.victoria.com.eg*. 1930s-vintage but renovated downtown hotel towards Midan Ramses. There is a bar and good food in the restaurant, and a hairdresser and bank on the premises. The rooms are spacious, often furnished in mahogany, and air-conditioned.

Windsor >>

***Windsor, 19 Sharia Alfi, t (02) 2591 5810, *www.windsorcairo.com*. Ranked by Baedeker early in the 1920s as just below the old Shepheard's, since when it has hardly changed, though it was renovated in 2002. High-ceilinged rooms for ventilation, much old wooden furnishing, a delightful bar/lounge/dining room hung with weird curios, beers served by berobed and elderly waiters – this is the place to come for Cairo as it once was, if you are prepared to enjoy class in tatters and atmosphere in abundance. It is situated towards Ezbekieh Gardens. Rooms with either shower or bath. Reservations advised.

On Gezira Island

****Golden Tulip Flamenco, 2 Sharia El Gezira el Wasta, Zamalek, t (02) 2735 0815, *www.goldentulipflamenco.com*. At the northwest end of Gezira Island in a peaceful residential area, this is a popular business hotel known for its good service and business facilities. The hotel is Spanish-run, reflected in its café and restaurant cuisine. Facilities include shops, business centre and travel agent. Some rooms have Nile views.

***Horus House, 21 Sharia Ismail Mohammed, Zamalek, t (02) 2735 3634, *www.horushousehotel.4t.com*. Small, friendly and very pleasant hotel with a restaurant, bar and café; set in a residential area north of Sharia 26 July near the President Hotel.

Longchamps >>

***Longchamps, 21 Sharia Ismail Mohammed, Zamalek, t/f (02) 2735 2311, *www.hotellongchamps.com*. One of the best moderately-priced hotels in Cairo, this shares the same building with the Horus. It is run with a personal touch by Hebba Bakri, daughter of an Egyptian actress. Rooms are spotless, have very comfortable beds, and come with bath, air conditioning and satellite TV. Its restaurant is excellent.

***President**, 22 Sharia Taha Hussein, Zamalek, **t** (02) 2735 0718, *www.presidenthotelcairo.com*. In a quiet residential area of many embassies and diplomatic residences north of Sharia 26 July. Rooms are large and clean; all have private baths and satellite television. There is a business centre, a rooftop bar and a restaurant with Nile views, and the lively Cellar Pub in the basement.

Pensione Roma >>

Inexpensive ($$)

Downtown

Dahab, 26 Sharia Mahmoud Bassiony, Midan Talaat Harb, **t** (02) 2579 9104, *www.dahabhostel.com*. This 7th-floor rooftop encampment seemingly transferred from Sinai to the heart of Cairo offers single, double and triple rooms, also dorm accommodation, with shared bathrooms and hot showers, in whitewashed huts set among potted trees.

***Garden City House**, 23 Sharia Kamal al-Din Dalah, **t** (02) 2794 8400, *www.gardencityhouse.com*. Centrally located behind the Semiramis Inter-Continental on the edge of Garden City. From outside there is a small sign three storeys up: the rooms are here and on the floor above; take the lift. Long a favourite with visiting Egyptologists, it is clean, respectable and friendly, and the food is good. Some rooms have baths, some face the river, most have balconies. There are not many single rooms. Half-board is compulsory; booking essential.

El Malky >>

***Ismailia House**, 1–3 Midan el Tahrir, **t** (02) 2796 3122, *www.ismailiahousehotel.com*. Central at the cost of being noisy if your room is in the Tahrir side, but otherwise this is a clean, safe and relaxing place on the 7th floor, with good views. The prices are good too, with single, double and triple rooms with or without bath, also dorms.

****Lotus**, 12 Sharia Talaat Harb, **t** (02) 2575 0966, *www.lotushotel.com*. Occupies the top three floors in the Art Deco building opposite the Felfela restaurant in downtown Cairo. The hardwood floors and spacious rooms with baths (those with showers are smaller) lend an extra touch of calm to this clean and well-run place, which is a sister hotel of the Windsor.

***Pensione Roma**, 169 Sharia Mohammed Farid, **t** (02) 2391 1088, *www.pensionroma.com.eg*. Two blocks south of Sharia 26 July and just east of Sharia Talaat Harb. An Italian-run 4th-floor pension decorated in style and taste with an eclectic mix of antique furniture, white window curtains and polished parquet flooring. The service is low-key and extremely friendly. Its clean, airy rooms, its grand lounge and dining room, and the good service make it a popular place, so book ahead.

In Medieval Cairo

****El Hussein**, Midan el Hussein, **t** (02) 2591 8089. In the heart of Khan el Khalili, with Fishawi's tea house next door and with views out over the Sayyidna al-Hussein and the Azhar mosques. This is the best hotel for those wanting to be amid the sights and atmosphere of medieval Cairo. The restaurant on the roof looks out over the medieval city. Rooms are large, simply furnished, of variable cleanliness and have balconies; all are air-conditioned, but insist on one with a bathroom.

El Malky, 4 Sharia el Mashad el Husseiny, the street running along the side of the Hussein mosque, **t** (02) 2589 6700, *www.server2002.net/malky*. The hotel is opposite the northwest corner of Sayyidna al-Hussein mosque and near the main entrance to Khan el Khalili. Superior to the nearby Hussein Hotel, if less 'atmospheric', this is a good clean place, up to international standards, with marvellous views over the medieval city, comfortable air-conditioned rooms with international phone lines, a restaurant and a coffee shop.

On Gezira Island

***Mayfair**, 9 Sharia Aziz Osman, Zamalek, **t** (02) 2735 7315, *www.mayfaircairo.com*. On Gezira Island in the leafy residential and diplomatic Zamalek area. Newly renovated and under Canadian management, this is a clean, simple and comfortable place, with a verandah and garden as well as plenty of peace and quiet.

*Zamalek Pension, 6 Sharia Salah ad-Din, Zamalek, t (02) 2735 9318. Set in leafy environs, this is a small and cosy place (only half a dozen rooms) with an air of quiet and privacy. Air conditioning available as an extra.

Eating Out in Cairo

You can spend a fortune or a few piastres on a meal in Cairo, and choose between the world's cuisines. Cairo's hotels each have a number of restaurants offering a variety of cuisines, though only a few are worth going out of your way to dine at and are included among the pick of the best below. Not only restaurants, but coffee shops, tea rooms and snack bars are included here. You should also look at 'Nightlife', below.

Expensive ($$$$)

Asia House, Shepheard's Hotel, Corniche el Nil, **t** (02) 2792 1000. Excellent Chinese and Indian cuisine served in opulent surroundings, though the service is not as good as the food.

La Bodega, 157 Sharia 26th July, Zamalek, **t** (02) 2736 2188. Despite the name, faintly Asian. Best at lunchtime when not too crowded.

Casablanca, at the Cairo Sheraton, Dokki, **t** (02) 3336 9800. Moroccan restaurant on the 26th floor; oriental show starts at 11pm.

Chin Chin, at the Four Corners complex, 4 Sharia Hassan Sabri, **t** (02) 2736 2961. Chinese cuisine beneath a mirrored ceiling, which makes it no less suitable for business, family or intimate dinners.

Fish Market, aboard the American boat, 26 Sharia el Nil, Dokki, **t** (02) 3570 9694. A good range of seafood with Nile view, good service, relaxed atmosphere.

Garden Promenade Café, in the garden courtyard of the Marriott in Zamalek. A pleasant place for lunch, tea, drinks, a light meal, at any time of day or evening.

La Gourmandise, Four Seasons Hotel, Giza, **t** (02) 3569 2557. Excellent French menu and exquisite desserts.

Justine, 4 Sharia Hassan Sabri, Zamalek, **t** (02) 2736 2961. French cuisine in an intimate setting with discreet service.

The Moghul Room, at the Mena House Oberoi, out at the Pyramids, **t** (02) 3383 3222. Offers both Western and Indian dishes in an incense-fragranced atmosphere and a background of live sitar music.

Hilltop Restaurant, al-Azhar Park, Sharia Saleh Salem. In fact this is a two-storey building featuring a full restaurant, an outdoor terrace, and on the upper floor a tea room and café. Beautiful setting with views over medieval Cairo and towards the Citadel, this is one of the newest yet most atmospheric places to dine in the city, with excellent Egyptian cuisine.

Le Pacha, a Nile cruiser converted into numerous restaurants (which they change at the drop of a hat, to catch the latest fashion), tied up at Saray el-Gezira near Zamalek, **t** (02) 2735 6730. The restaurants include: *l'Asiatique*, Thai, Japanese and Chinese cuisines; *Piccolo Mondo*, Italian; Le Steak, French; *Carlo's*, open-air café and restaurant; *Le Tarbouche*, Egyptian cuisine, oriental entertainment; The *Tycoons*, bar and restaurant, international cuisine with live Western entertainment, good Nile view; *l'Oasis*, dine and dance restaurant with live Western entertainment, upper deck Nile views; *River Boat*, oriental restaurant strong on fish, oriental entertainment; *Maharani*, Indian setting and cuisine; *Greek Taverna*, on the quay, decorations give it a very Greek feeling as does the excellent Greek chef.

La Piazza, at the Four Corners, 4 Sharia Hassan Sabri, **t** (02) 2736 2961. Italian cuisine, the atmosphere brightened by white latticework hung with plants.

Taboula, 1 Sharia Latin America, Garden City, **t** 2792 5261. Traditional Lebanese food in a softly-lit and cosy

★ Justine >>

★ The Moghul Room >>

★ Hilltop Restaurant >>

★ Garden Promenade Café >

setting with bench seating at giant round wooden tables.

Moderate ($$$)

L'Aubergine, 5 Sharia el Sayed el Bakry, Zamalek, **t** (02) 2738 0080. Sophisticated cuisine, extensive menu, ranging through Tunisian, Greek and Ethiopian, with a vegetarian emphasis.

★ Naguib Mahfouz Café >>

The Cellar, at the President Hotel, 22 Sharia Taha Hussein, Zamalek, **t** (02) 2735 3752. Restaurant-cum-bar open till 2am, frequented by regulars and cosy, though sometimes noisy. Its changing menu, written up on blackboards, ranges from mezze and omelettes through pasta, seafood and steaks.

La Chesa, 21 Sharia Adli, downtown, **t** (02) 2393 9360. A haven of Swiss cleanliness, excellent food and a very good cake and pastry section.

Christo's, also known as **Vue des Pyramides**, 10 Sharia al-Ahram, Giza, **t** (02) 3376 3582. Specializes in Mediterranean seafood, Red Sea lobster and Egyptian mezze. The kitchen is on the ground floor and you either eat outdoors or upstairs from where there is a, yes, *vue des pyramides*.

★ Estoril >

Estoril, 12 Sharia Talaat Harb, downtown, **t** (02) 2547 3102. Quiet and agreeable haven in the centre of town, good for seafood, mezze and drinks. *Open until 2am*.

Florencia, on the 10th floor of the Golden Tulip Flamenco Hotel, 2 Sharia el Gezira el Wasta, Zamalek, **t** (02) 2735 0815. At the northwest end of Gezira island, a charming and little known culinary treasure with an ambitious Spanish and continental menu, live guitar music and pleasant views over houseboats moored in the Nile.

Longchamps, at the Longchamps Hotel, 21 Sharia Ismail Mohammed, Zamalek, **t** (02) 2735 2311. All but unknown to Cairenes, yet this is one of the best restaurants in Cairo, small and intimate with hospitable service; oriental and continental menu; the food is fresh and the meals are excellent.

El Mashrabia, 4 Sharia Ahmed Nessim, near the Zoo and El Gama'a Bridge, Giza, **t** (02) 3748 2801. An intimate restaurant with dark wooden décor, a good choice for a romantic evening, with excellent but unobtrusive service. The menu is overwhelmingly aimed at carnivores, however.

Naguib Mahfouz Café, 5 Sikket el Bedestan, **t** (02) 2590 3788. In the heart of Khan el Khalili, a classy place to which the Nobel Prize-winning novelist seems to have sold his name (it is run by Oberoi Hotels) rather than the sort of place he would hang out, but all the same its location makes it interesting and the traditional Egyptian dishes are excellent; also it stays open until 2am, well after the souk has gone quiet and dark, making it a good starting point for an atmospheric night walk.

Papillon, Sharia 26 July, Tirsana Shopping Centre (a few blocks west of the Zamalek Bridge and Midan Sphinx) in Mohandiseen, **t** (02) 3303 5045. A favourite with vegetarians for its wide variety of Lebanese mezze that make a meal in themselves. There is also tender and savoury lamb, beef and chicken entrées for carnivores.

Peking, Sharia Saraya el Ezbekia, off Sharia Emad El Din and behind the Cinema Diana, downtown, **t** (02) 2591 2381. Chinese restaurant popular for its sophistication and flair, its menu varied and imaginative.

Sometimes you just want to rest your feet, cool off and have a drink and a bite to eat. The **cafés** in the major hotels have the advantage of being open 24 hours; even better, they are air-conditioned. There is a small minimum charge.

The Cairo Tower, Gezira Island. Offers coffee, tea, beer, and snacks – all at a slight premium for having been carried up to the top, where the atmosphere is pleasant, the views wonderful.

Inexpensive ($$)

In wandering around the streets, either in modern or medieval Cairo, you will encounter numerous **simple establishments** for having a snack, even a meal, and certainly a refreshing mint tea. There are also peripatetic **street vendors**, good for drinks though perhaps less so for food, which may not be particularly clean.

In buying anything to eat, always be sure the place has running water – if so, a modicum of hygiene can be counted upon. Forget the Cokes and 7-Ups for a change; instead pause for fresh guava, mango, orange, sugar cane or strawberry juice, and after you have drunk it, scoop the strawberries from the glass with a spoon.

A cheap but nutritious way to stuff yourself in Cairo is to dine on ***koushari***, a plateful of lentils, onions, noodles and macaroni topped with a hot tomato sauce. One of the best places to get it is at **Lux**, Sharia 26 July, near the intersection with Sharia Sherif, in the downtown area, or **Abou Tarek**, 40 Sharia Champollion at the corner of Sharia Maarouf.

★ 'Garden Groppi' >>

Andrea, 59–60 Marioutiya Canal, near the Pyramids, **t** (02) 3383 1133. A marvellous place to eat out in the open air after dark, the menu traditional Egyptian. *Open until midnight*.

Cilantro coffee shops, an excellent chain found throughout Cairo and its surburbs, e.g. 31 Sharia Mohamed Mahmoud, opposite the American University in Cairo downtown campus, **t** (02) 2792 4572, and 157 26th July Street, Zamalek, **t** (02) 2736 1115, towards its eastern end. Sandwiches, salads, pastries and speciality coffees. Their places are wired. *Open 24 hours*.

El Hatti, 3 Sharia Halim, off Sharia 26 July, behind the Windsor Hotel. A decrepit survivor from the 1930s, full of cracked and faded style, but excellent cuisine. Unusual for an Egyptian restaurant in that it sparkles (when the lights are on) – mirrors cover the walls and brilliant chandeliers hang from the high ceiling. The food (roast lamb is the speciality) and atmosphere all make this a worthwhile place to search for. There is another branch nearby, not so interesting but also good, on the other side of Sharia 26 July in the passage off 8 Midan Halim.

Felfela, 15 Sharia Hoda Sharawi, downtown, **t** (02) 2392 2833. Just off Sharia Talaat Harb near Sharia el Bustan, popular with tourists and foreign residents, but also a favourite of Egyptians. The food is certainly good and inexpensive. Tree trunks serve as tables. The speciality is *fool*, in all its varieties of preparation, but the menu extends to meat dishes and ice creams.

The Greek Club, above Groppi's (*see below*) at Midan Talaat Harb, entrance on Sharia Bassiouni, **t** (02) 2575 0822. Serves decent food (hardly Greek, but then the Greeks of Cairo were hardly Zorbas) and passable alcohol from 6pm to 1.30am, and in summer you can dine out on its terrace. You pay a nominal subscription of LE5 or so to join the club.

The downtown area also has a number of good **cafés**. **Groppi** is a famous Cairo institution with three branches, one at Midan Talaat Harb, another on Sharia Adli and a third in Heliopolis. It is '**Garden Groppi**' (as the one at the Midan el Opera end of Sharia Adli is called) that was so famous among British servicemen during the Second World War, and its outdoor café remains a pleasant place to sit by day or by night. There is a delicatessen here too, selling cold cuts, pastas, jams and bottles of wine.

Abu Shakra, 69 Qasr el Aini, at the south end of the street, about 3km from Midan el Tahrir, near the bridge crossing over to Roda at the Manyal Palace, **t** (02) 2531 6111. The epitome of a good, simple Egyptian restaurant, this is a strict Muslim establishment, serving no alcoholic beverages and closed Fridays and daytime during Ramadan. The interior is all alabaster and marble, and the specialities are kofta and kebab, though sometimes pigeon or grilled chicken is available. Usually (though not always) the food is excellent. *Open until 2am*.

Ataturk, 20 Sharia Riyadh, off Sharia Shahab, Mohandiseen, **t** (02) 3347 5135. Cosy and relaxing Turkish restaurant serving delicious hot bread and good mixed grills.

Deals, 2 Sharia el Sayed el Bakry, off Sharia 26 July, Zamalek, **t** (02) 2736 0502. Restaurant and bar, open till 3am, with film-poster décor, a young clientele and blasting rock and roll music. The food ranges from hamburgers and chicken drumsticks to salads and seafood, with French wine served by the glass.

Fishawi Café, in a small alley just behind the El Hussein Hotel, Midan Sayyidna el-Hussein. This is famous: sit on cane chairs at marble-topped tables, in a narrow passage lined with mirrors. As coffees pass by on brass trays you are propositioned with any number of offers, including perhaps a shoeshine, a device for making catcalls, a woman's song accompanied by a tambourine, or necklaces of jasmine flowers, their scent thick on the night air.

Nightlife in Cairo

It can be difficult to find a place that **sells beer, wines and spirits**; you have to hunt around. But one well-known place in Zamalek is the aptly-named **Drinkies**, Sharia 26 July at its eastern end, near the Diwan bookshop, Cilantro, and not far from the Marriott. They also deliver throughout Cairo; dial **t** 19330 from anywhere.

Bars

Café Riche, 17 Sharia Talaat Harb, downtown. Once the centre for writers, artists, actors, singers, intellectuals, etc., and also a meeting point of conspirators during the 1919 revolution (their printing press is still in the cellar), it is now pretty daring to sit here and have a beer.

The Cellar, at the President Hotel, 22 Sharia Taha Hussein in Zamalek, **t** (02) 2735 3752. Popular meeting place for young Cairenes.

Gemayka, Sharia el Bank el Ahly, a small street off Sharia Sharia Sherif, downtown. Named for the Caribbean island of Jamaica. In the face of growing official persecution of drinkers, the place has a speakeasy feel, with men drinking and trading jokes behind windowless, nondescript façades meant to avoid scrutiny from the street outside.

Matchpoint, in the Four Corners complex, 4 Sharia Hassan Sabry, Zamalek, **t** (02) 2737 2119. Live music and darts.

Windows on the World, on the top floor of the Ramses Hilton Hotel, Corniche el Nil, **t** (02) 2577 7444. For fantastic night views over Cairo.

Casinos

Casinos (admission to non-Egyptians only) are found at **Shepheard's**, the **Marriott**, the **Mena House**, the **Conrad**, the **Ramses Hilton**, the **Sheraton** and the **Heliopolis Mövenpick** hotel. Play is in US dollars, with free drinks for punters; doors close no earlier than dawn, and some will take your money 24 hours a day.

Nightclubs

Nightclubs in the big **international hotels** usually offer a programme of both oriental and Western acts, such as a first-class **Egyptian belly dancer** followed by some unemployed London showgirls pretending to be from Las Vegas or Paris. The comparison between the two can be embarrassing. The Western conception of dancing, at least as expressed in the pseudo-Folies Bergères variety, is to throw oneself about as though somehow velocity has any meaning other than to disguise a lack of sensuality. The Egyptian dancer, on the other hand, knows how to stand still, to flick and ripple her body like some night plant licking up the moonlight and starlight, curling and uncurling to the faint brush of cosmic rays so that she and all the dark sky pulse as one.

Some other nightclubs, like those along the Pyramids Road (Sharia al-Ahram) and a few downtown will stage a more purely Egyptian programme, and these, even if sometimes second-rate, can be delightful.

Scheherazade on Sharia Alfi, near Midan Orabi, is a recently restored belly-dance club under 30-foot-high ceilings, with velvet curtains, part of an attempt by Al Ahram Beverages, Egypt's largest alcohol drinks company, to restore downtown establishments to their former glory. The audience is predominantly Arab, almost all men, though a few women and even children may be present. A few Westerners go there and take their women – a great mistake, as the latter sit prune-faced throughout the performance, which is indoors during winter, but on the roof (and more enjoyable for that) in summer.

For further adventures among human contortionists and laid-back finger-cymbal players, with the additional incentive of incredibly fat and ugly belly dancers of ill repute, and if you do not mind joining an audience even less respectable than the performers, go to **Arizona** (the sign is in Arabic only, but you will know it by the photographs outside), across the road from the Scheherazade and a bit to the east.

Entertainment in Cairo

It is the popular mysteries – the man staging a backstreet show with a snake and a guinea pig, or a marriage procession of loud cries and ribald song making its way down the middle of a road – that are most entertaining in Cairo. For some help in locating more conventional amusements, get a copy of *Egypt Today*, the monthly English-language magazine.

Cinemas

Cinemas are mostly located around Midan Talaat Harb and Midan Orabi, and several are likely to be showing English-language films subtitled in Arabic. The *Egyptian Gazette* carries listings. The problem is that the Egyptians, being able to read the subtitles, do not have to listen to the dialogue. Instead the audience chatters throughout the film, which often has its sound turned down anyway, so that you will be lucky to hear much of it – which is, however, perhaps not so important when you consider the entertainment potential of the audience. Tickets are cheap, and all seats are reserved. You should buy your tickets several hours in advance of the performance you intend seeing, as seats go very quickly. Women never go to cinemas singly.

Cultural Events

Many events with a Western content in the performing arts are arranged by foreign **cultural organizations** such as the British Council, the Goethe Institute and the French Cultural Centre. These can tell you about films, theatre and dance productions, and concerts in which they are involved or which they know something about.

The American University in Cairo's **Wallace Theater** presents English-language plays, musicals and concerts during the academic year (Oct–May). The Japanese-designed **Opera House** on Gezira Island hosts foreign productions, as well as the **Cairo Opera** (from Mar), the **Cairo Ballet** (from Jan) and the **Cairo Symphony Orchestra** (throughout the year except July and Aug).

The **National Troupe** and the **Reda Troupe**, both dreadfully boring folk dance leftovers from Nasser's cultural socialism years, perform regularly at the Balloon Theatre. The **Oum Kalsoum Arabic Music Troupe** performs twice-monthly in winter at Sayed Darwish Concert Hall. The **Folkloric Orchestra of Egypt**, which performs with ancient Egyptian instruments, may be found at various venues.

Balloon Theatre, Sharia 26 July at Sharia el Nil, Agouza, **t** (02) 3347 1718.

British Council, 192 Sharia el Nil, Agouza, **t** (02) 19789.

French Cultural Centre, 1 Sharia Madraset el Huquq el Fransia, **t** (02) 355 3725.

Goethe Institute, 5 Sharia Abdel Salam Aref, **t** (02) 2575 9877.

Opera House, Gezira Island (near the Tahrir Bridge), **t** (02) 342 0603.

Sayed Darwish Concert Hall, Sharia Gamal al-Din al-Afghani (near the City of Art), south of Sharia al-Ahram, **t** (02) 560 2473.

Wallace Theater, Sharia Qasr el Aini, **t** (02) 354 2964.

For Children

Two fixtures appealing at the level of popular mysteries are the **Egyptian National Circus**, a good one-ring affair next to the Balloon Theatre, Agouza, by the Zamalek Bridge, **t** (02) 347 0612 (daily performances except Wed, 8–10.30pm; in summer the circus moves to Alexandria); and the **Cairo Puppet Theatre** in Midan Ataba, at the southeast end of Ezbekieh Gardens, **t** (02) 910 954 (Oct–May, performances at 11.30am, Thurs–Sun). The repertoire includes Ali Baba and

Sindbad the Sailor, and shows are performed in Arabic, which hardly matters as it is easy to follow the action, and anyway adds to the enchantment of the productions, appealing to adults and children alike.

There is also the ersatz **Dr Ragab's Pharaonic Village** on Jacob Island, 2km south from the Giza Bridge, reached by half-hourly boats from the Corniche el Nil (open daily in winter 9–5, in summer 9–9; tickets are LE40 per person, LE20 for children under 6). A two-hour tour takes you round a replica temple and a nobleman's villa, and floats you down the Canal of Mythology where you encounter the ancient gods, while perfectly silly-looking Egyptians dressed in bedsheets perform various domestic and priestly duties. It is probably best to approach the **son et lumière** at the Pyramids on this level too (*see* pp.194–5).

Over 400 species of animal, from free-flying parakeets to wallowing hippopotami, inhabit the extensive and well-stocked **Cairo Zoo**, Sharia el Giza, on the west bank of the Nile (open daily 8.30–4.30, last entry 3.30). Next to it are the **El Urman Botanical Gardens**, formerly belonging to the khedives of Egypt, a good place for picnics except on Fridays when everyone else has the same idea. (A small fee is charged at both places.)

Muslim Celebrations and Whirling Dervishes

Moulid el Nabi, which is a nationwide Muslim celebration of the Prophet Mohammed's birthday on the 12th day of Rabei el Awal, is marked in Cairo by a spectacular procession. As at **Ramadan**, the place to be is the square in front of the Sayyidna al-Hussein Mosque in Khan el Khalili (*see* p.128).

Mevlâna, the 13th-century Sufi master who founded his sect of **whirling dervishes** at Konya in Turkey, has his followers in Egypt. Almost entirely suppressed in Turkey and suspect in most other Muslim countries, their intention is to achieve mystical union with God through ecstatic whirling. They whirl for ecstasy and tourists alike at the cultural centre inside the al-Ghuri Mausoleum on Sharia Muizz in medieval Cairo (Wed and Sat, 8–9pm). *See* p.126.

The Pyramids, Memphis and Saqqara

Founded 5,000 years ago, Memphis was the first capital of a united Egypt. Built of mud brick for the living, little of it remains, and it lies mostly swallowed by the mud on the west bank of the Nile, 20km south of Cairo. But overlooking Memphis, on the edge of the desert plateau at Saqqara, the ancient Egyptians buried their noble and royal dead in imperishable tombs of stone. Here at Saqqara is the world's first pyramid, the Step Pyramid built by King Zoser and his great architect Imhotep. Within decades of this achievement, yet vaster and more perfect pyramids were constructed to the north at Giza, among them the Great Pyramid of Cheops, which even today is the most massive monument in the world.

07

Don't miss

1. **Older than time**
   Great Pyramid of Cheops **p.187**
2. **Enduring mystery**
   Sphinx **p.191**
3. **The world's first pyramid**
   Zoser's Step Pyramid **p.204**
4. **Pleasures of eternity**
   Mastaba of Akhti-Hotep and Ptah-Hotep **p.209**
5. **Burials of the sacred bulls**
   Serapeum **p.213**

See map overleaf

The Pyramids, Memphis and Saqqara

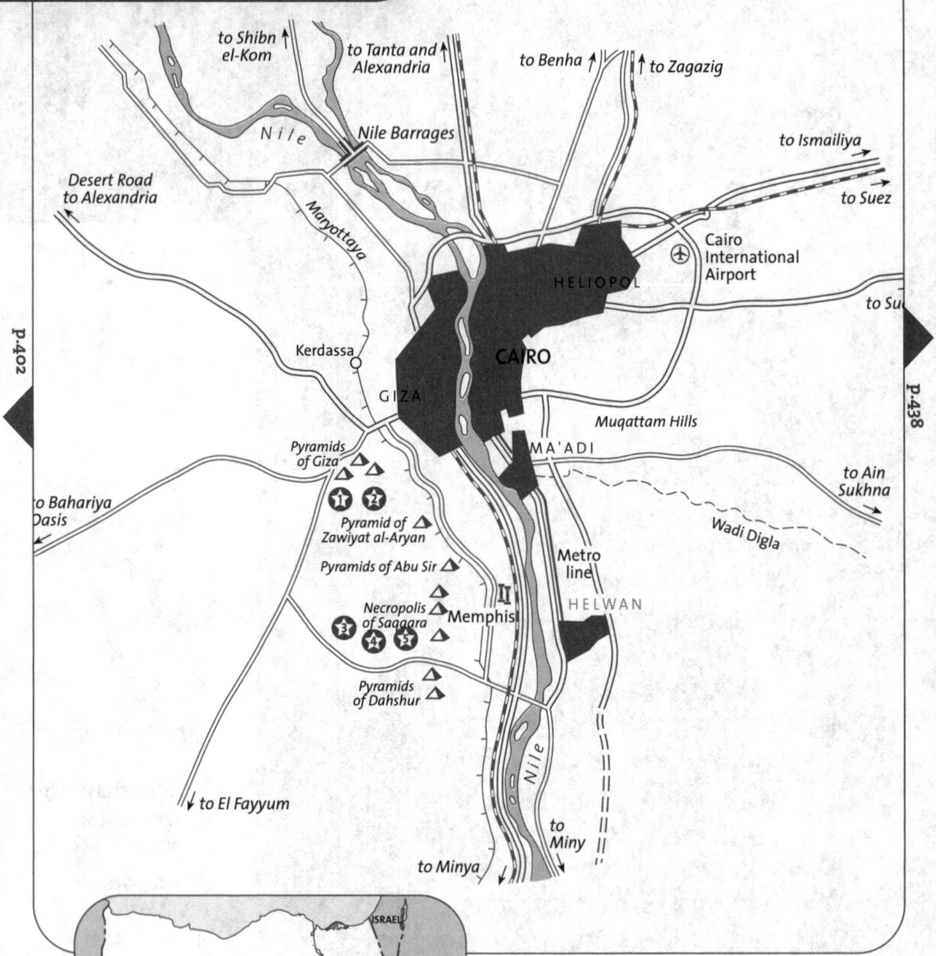

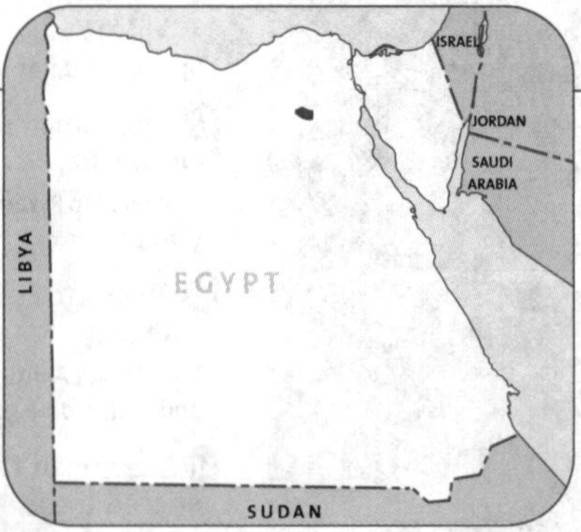

Don't miss

1. Great Pyramid of Cheops **p.187**
2. Sphinx **p.191**
3. Zoser's Step Pyramid **p.204**
4. Mastaba of Akhti-Hotep and Ptah-Hotep **p.209**
5. Serapeum **p.213**

Everything fears time, but time fears the Pyramids.
12th-century Arab physician

Before taking the Giza road out to that desert escarpment where the famous Pyramids of Cheops, Chephren and Mycerinus stand, it is worth knowing something of the period in which they were built, and to know too something of that entire line of Old Kingdom pyramids which extends from Abu Roash north of Giza to Meidum near the Fayyum, a line that is 70km long and numbers over 80 pyramids. This introduction will refer to the main pyramid clusters, and will explain why and how, at the very beginning of recorded history, these most prodigious and enduring monuments in stone were built.

Some History: the Pyramid Age

The First Pyramid

Around 3000 BC, Upper and Lower Egypt were united under Menes and the I Dynasty established. It is not certain that **Menes** was an individual; he may represent a conflation of early warrior-princes, and the conquest of the Delta may not have been a single campaign but a struggle lasting over generations. There is evidence of fighting and rebellion during the I and II Dynasties, and the energies of this period would have been devoted to consolidation. Building was in mud brick and reed, though during the II Dynasty some stone was used underground in tombs.

Below ground these tombs were built like houses: rectangular and divided into chambers. Above ground they had a low, flat-topped form with sloping walls. This mud brick superstructure was sometimes faced with mud plaster and covered with white gypsum stucco. Mariette called them *mastabas*, the Arabic for those stone benches outside the shops and coffee houses of medieval Cairo.

About 350 years after unification, that is around 2650 BC, Egypt entered into a long period of security and order known to us as the **Old Kingdom**, which begins with the III Dynasty. Awareness of the two Egypts, Upper and Lower, remained acute, as can be read from the ritual of Zoser's Heb-Sed festival at Saqqara, and the village and tribal units up and down the Nile continued to worship their local gods, that prolific pantheon that never disappeared but which eventually was overlaid by a few powerful national cults.

During the reign of **Zoser** (III Dyn) there was a sudden use and mastery of stone at Saqqara. His mortuary complex of courts and chapels, 544m long and 277m wide, surrounded by a wall 10m high, was all of stone, beautifully detailed and architectured. And dominating the whole was the first pyramid, over 62m high, built in steps. Stone had risen from the darkness of the tomb into the confident light of the sun.

The explanation is not found in technology; stone was not new and tools and construction methods remained as simple as they had been in the past – the lever was used but the wheel and pulley were unknown. Rather there was peace and stability; there was a developing theocratic doctrine that invited the use of stone; and there was a man of genius who knew how to build with it.

That man was **Imhotep**, Zoser's grand vizier, chief judge, minister of agriculture and supervisor of building works. He was also high priest at Heliopolis, centre of the increasingly important sun cult. His range of accomplishment typified the opportunities and needs of a new civilization, where everything was still to be invented and then organized. He was revered throughout pharaonic history, though recalled as a healer rather than as an organizer, statesman or architect, and he became a mythical figure, a demi-god, and was eventually raised to unqualified divinity – but his contemporary existence is certain from inscriptions found at Zoser's complex.

The doctrine that begged the use of stone was that of the pharaoh's sole possession of the **ka**, the vital force emanating from the god to his son, the king, who could then dispense it to his subjects. The ka was eternal so long as it was linked to the pharaoh, and so it was essential that ka and king be given an indestructible container of stone.

A stone mastaba was built for Zoser which was twice enlarged. Then in three further stages, Imhotep made a qualitative leap, a sudden vertical thrust, and created the world's first skyscraper, the **Step Pyramid**. Political and cultural revolution in Egypt has always swept down through the valley, nomadic in inspiration. The mastaba belonged to the earthbound world of the Delta farmers; the pyramid and generally Egyptian architecture thereafter eschewed the enclosure of space and instead posed itself against the sun and the stars. Stone permitted it; Imhotep mastered the physics required; and yearning for the vast and timeless cosmos was its inspiration.

It is interesting and important, though, that Zoser's complex remains human in feeling. Zoser was the son of the god, and even if he was the god himself, he at least relished the life of man, for in the house-like arrangement of chambers beneath his pyramid, with their faïence decorations imitating domestic reeding, there is the desire to project his present life into the hereafter. This sense never again appears inside a pyramid, and rarely at any mortuary structure of a pharaoh throughout Egypt's history. Instead the savouring of the everyday was excluded, divinity insisted upon, and ritual became obsessive.

So there was a first revolution, an eruption, in stone. But the second revolution was an adventure even more astonishing and led to the perfection of the pyramid form at Giza. We think of the vastness of Egyptian history and how slowly it must have unfolded, yet from Zoser's complex to Cheops' Pyramid no more time passed than our fast-moving age took to travel from the beginnings of iron construction to the Eiffel Tower – around 75 years in fact. What is more, the age of the great pyramids was over within 200 years. What explains its sudden coming and going, and the intensity, the phenomenal labour, with which it was pursued?

At Giza you confront the apogee, but you do not find the answer. That lies to the south of Saqqara, at Dahshur and at Meidum.

The Pyramid Production Line

The pyramid at **Meidum** is about 90km by road south of Cairo and even without visiting it you can see it, if you are alert, from the left side of the overnight train back from Luxor soon after it passes El Wasta in the morning. Like all the pyramids, it stands beyond the belt of cultivation on the edge of the desert. It is an amazing sight: a steeply inclined tower rising from a low hill – and that is exactly what it was thought to be by early travellers. In fact it is a pyramid that collapsed. It did not slowly crumble over time; near the moment of its completion there was some catastrophe. Then or after further collapses only a part of the core remained clear of the mound of debris all around.

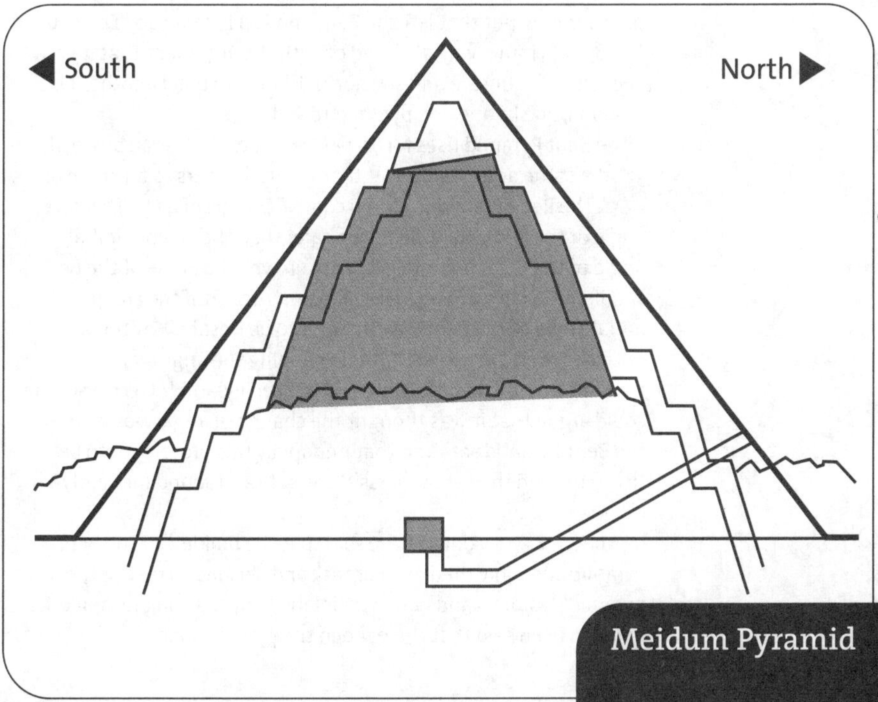

Meidum Pyramid

This was the first pyramid after Zoser's and it was conceived at first as a step pyramid. A second, larger stepped structure was soon superimposed and finally a true pyramidal shell was added, its smooth sides rising at an angle of about 52°. But there were serious design faults, including the badly squared stones of the outer casing which stood on horizontal limestone blocks embedded in compacted sand instead of on a bedrock foundation given an inward slope. The weight of the pyramid, instead of being directed downwards and inwards, was directed outwards; it was destroyed by its own lateral forces.

Pyramid Puzzles

This disaster leads to an explanation of the pyramid craze that marks the succeeding dynasty to Zoser's. An inscription at Meidum says it was built by **Snofru** (IV Dyn). But this has disturbed Egyptologists because Snofru was known to have built two pyramids at Dahshur. If the purpose of a pyramid was to provide an indestructible container for the pharaoh and his ka, why did Snofru need three? Snofru's inscription was explained away as a usurpation of his predecessor's pyramid: 'It cannot but seem extraordinary that one and the same king should have built for himself two pyramids of vast dimensions at no great distance from one another ... and since it is hard to imagine that he erected three pyramids, the one at Meidum is now tentatively ascribed to Huny,' wrote Sir Alan Gardiner, the noted Egyptologist, in *Egypt of the Pharaohs*. But that left the Bent and Red Pyramids at Dahshur. The Bent Pyramid was disposed of with the argument that it had been deemed unsafe and so Snofru decided to build another. One pharaoh, one ka and one pyramid to suit.

The **Bent Pyramid** rises for 70 per cent of its bulk at an angle of 52°, the same as at Meidum. It then abruptly alters to an angle of 43.5°. The **Red Pyramid** rises at a constant angle of 43.5°. The lower angle of the Red would clearly be safer than the steeper initial angle of the Bent, but it fails to explain why the angle of the Bent should have been changed in mid-construction. If the steep initial angle of the Bent was thought to be unsafe, why not at once abandon the project? But if changing the angle was thought to make it safe, why build the Red Pyramid? Of course, one could argue that it was thought the change of angle would make the Bent Pyramid safe and that unhappily this proved not to be true – though the pyramid has stood safe and sound for nearly 5,000 years.

Eminent Egyptologists have said that the builders of the Bent Pyramid suddenly tired of their task and decided to reduce the pyramid's volume, and hence their labour, by reducing its angle. It has also been said that the bend in the pyramid was predetermined and meant to express a 'double pyramid', that is two pyramids of different angles superimposed, and that this symbolized some unexplained duality. It has also been said that the architect lost his nerve, but one reason for this tantalizing possibility – the collapse of the Meidum pyramid at a point when the Bent Pyramid was 70 per cent of the way towards completion – has not been countenanced by Egyptologists because, as Sir Alan Gardiner pointed out, it would reintroduce the 'unpalatable conclusion that Snofru did possess three pyramids'. The key word is possess, for it signals the insistence that pyramids were built for the sole reason of providing a container for the pharaoh's ka, so that Snofru had no business building what he believed at that point to be two perfectly good pyramids.

The Egyptologists' evasions could have gone on indefinitely as long as they could have believed that the pyramid at Meidum had belonged to Snofru's predecessor and had merely crumbled with time. But in *The Riddle of the Pyramids* and the *Journal of Egyptian Archaeology*, Kurt Mendelssohn, Professor of Physics at Oxford, has argued that Meidum, while nearing completion, came down with a bang when Snofru was already well advanced on his second pyramid – which only then, and for that reason, was continued at a bent angle. (Mendelssohn's opponents in the *Journal of Egyptian Archaeology* argued well against a single bang, but some initial partial disaster seems likely.)

So why should several pyramids be built in overlapping succession during the reign of a single pharaoh? It is a fact that more large pyramids were built during the IV Dynasty than there were pharaohs to fill them. The answer is in the scale of the task. Herodotus says it took 20 years to build Cheops' Pyramid with 100,000 men working a three-month shift. Modern calculation of the workforce required does not vary substantially from Herodotus' figure, though it is likely that several thousand men, highly skilled as stone-cutters, masons and surveyors, would have been employed year-round, while the larger requirement for unskilled labour would have been drawn from the fields between July and November, the period of the inundation. All these people needed training and organization, as well as feeding, clothing and housing, and the logistics of the operation must have been formidable. It is not the sort of operation that is easily or efficiently mounted on the uncertain occasion of a pharaoh's accession, nor is the size of a pyramid – and so the time it will take to build – readily geared to the uncertain duration of a pharaoh's reign. The suggestion is rather that pyramid construction was continuous and independent of whether or not there would be enough pharaohs to fill them. And this is what the evidence of Meidum and the Bent Pyramid suggests did happen, the overlap accounted for by the fact that as the first pyramid tapered towards completion, the surplus workforce was immediately engaged on starting a second pyramid.

Unification and Authority

Whether by intention or as a consequence, this pyramid production line must have had two important effects. The first was that the vast levy of men required would have cut across the division of Upper and Lower Egypt and the parochialism of villages and tribes throughout the length of the valley and the breadth of the Delta. Pyramid building would complete, down to the fibres of society, the unification of the country begun by Menes by force of arms. The second effect was that whoever was responsible for pyramid building would see their power enhanced. But production of pyramids surplus to the requirements of any one pharaoh, surplus even to the requirements of an entire dynasty, demanded a transcending organizing authority. Imhotep's own career suggests the composition of that authority: in part the power of the pharaoh, but also that of the bureaucracy and the priesthood. Pyramids created the apparatus of the state.

Symbolism of the Pyramids

There is then the pyramidal form. One can see how constructionally the pyramids began with the mastaba; Zoser's pyramid is in fact a stepped mastaba. The achievement in architecture of the pure abstract pyramidal form came, briefly, at Meidum, when before it collapsed its steps were being sheathed in planes. If anything, the disaster was a spur to the technical perfection of the pyramidal symbol. That symbol preceded construction rather than technology dictated symbol seems likely.

In Egyptian creation myths there is a primal hill which rises from the chaos of the waters. And until the High Dam at Aswan finally put an end to the annual inundation, that was very much the scene in Egypt: villages huddled on mounds to avoid the flood, then its subsidence and the sun drawing the harvest from the mud. This myth is referred to at Medinet Habu and Hermopolis. Heliopolis, centre of the sun cult where Imhotep was high priest, also claimed a primal hill, the *benben*, a tapering megalith, a word whose root, *bn*, is bound up with the notion of shining, brilliant, ascending. It is depicted in II Dynasty inscriptions, that is before the pyramid age.

Variations on the pyramidal form continued to be popular throughout Egyptian history, as for example the **obelisks** whose points or pyramidions were sheathed in electrum, a mixture of silver and gold. Pliny the Elder described obelisks as petrified rays

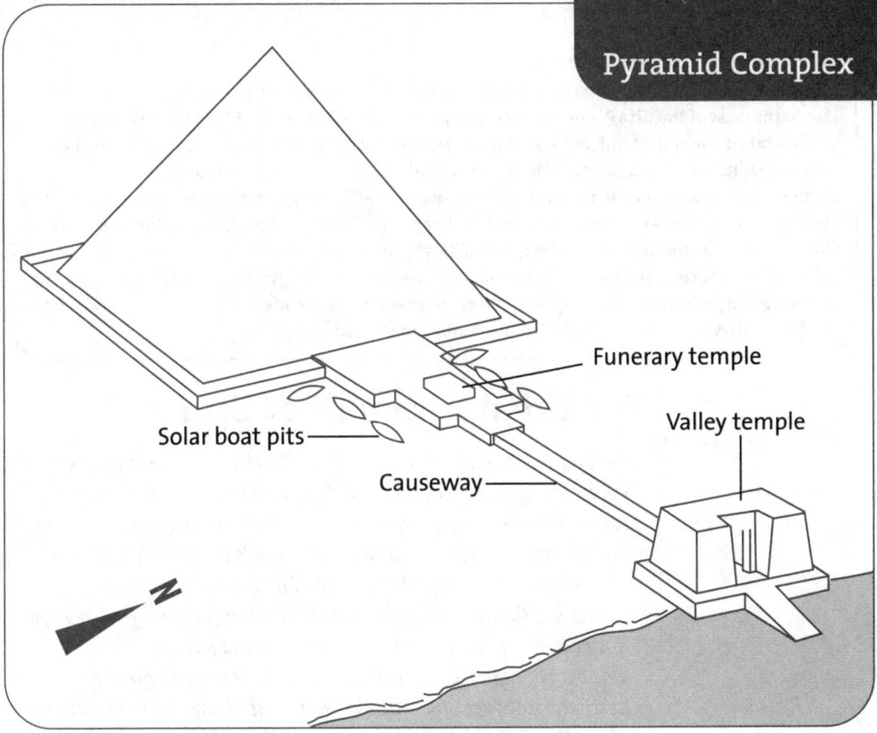

of sunlight, and more than one modern writer has remarked on the pyramid-like form of a burst of sunlight through the clouds after a rare Egyptian rain.

The building of pyramids would have been no mere drudgery inflicted on the population by some megalomaniac pharaoh. The symbolism would have been appreciated throughout all levels of society, and it is quite likely that far from being built by slave-labour, as Herodotus claims, they were built willingly and with a shared sense of exalted purpose which at the time would have seemed far more important, and certainly would have been more conscious, than creating new political forms.

But here the gods died sooner than the works of men. And those works included not only the pyramids, but the creation for the first time in human history of an organizational principle, the state, that was to serve Egypt until her absorption into the Roman Empire, and is the basis of human organization to this day. Once the pyramid production line had achieved this, their symbolism could be carried on in lesser forms, such as obelisks; in any case, it was no longer politically necessary to build pyramids, and apart from some inferior examples in later dynasties, by 2450 BC the age of the pyramids was over.

The Grand Egyptian Museum

The new Grand Egyptian Museum, many times delayed, is now expected to open in 2012 on a site 2km to the west of the Giza Pyramids. The centerpiece of this state-of-the-art museum will be the 5,000 artefacts from the tomb of Tutankhamun, removed here from the century-old Egyptian Museum in town, but its collections will go far beyond that and will illustrate the historical, cultural and territorial evolution of pharaonic Egypt. The new museum will be organized in five themes. The Land of Egypt gallery will look at the geography and landscape of the country; the gallery of Kingship and the State will focus on the activities and responsibilities of the king, his family and his highest officials. The gallery of Man, Society and Work will illuminate the lives of ancient Egyptians of varying stations. The Religion gallery will deal with the gods and their state and popular cults, along with mortuary beliefs. The fifth gallery will be dedicated to Culture, Scribes and Knowledge.

The Great Pyramids of Giza

Familiarity (though at second-hand) had led me, not to despise the Pyramids, but to discount them. They had become international commonplaces, degraded to the level of the tourist souvenir. They had passed through so many million minds as one of the 'Wonders of the World' that their sharp edge of real wonder had been blunted. ... But in actuality, they make an overpowering impression. It is not one of beauty, but on the other hand not one of mere bigness, though size enters into it, and there is an element of aesthetic satisfaction in the elemental simplicity of their triangular silhouette. But this combined with an element of vicarious pride in the magnitude of the human achievement involved, and with a sense of their bold novelty and their historical uniqueness, to produce an effect different from that of any other work of man.

Sir Julian Huxley, *From an Antique Land*, 1954

Approaching the Pyramids

There they rose up enormous under our eyes, and the most absurd, trivial things were going on under their shadow.

William Makepeace Thackeray, *Notes of a Journey from Cornhill to Grand Cairo*, 1846

Half a day should be allowed for the visit to the Giza Pyramids, though you should return again at night. They are approached along a broad straight road, originally built for Empress Eugénie, so that she could cover the 11km from Cairo in her carriage. This Sharia al-Ahram or Road of the Pyramids once passed across fellahin's fields which would flood with the rising of the Nile, but nowadays the entire route has been built up. There is therefore, at first, something ordinary about the approach, as though you were off to a funfair on the edge of town, expecting at any moment the distant screams of roller coaster passengers as they plunge down papier-mâché mountains. But even the Pyramids themselves initially conspire to deflate anticipation.

The Egyptian authorities have recently erected a 12km fence, complete with infra-red sensors, security cameras and alarms, entirely surrounding the Pyramids site, for the express purpose of

Getting to the Great Pyramids

Apart from taking a **taxi** or **limousine**, you could take the **355 bus**, an air-conditioned service which runs every 20mins from just outside the Egyptian Museum in Midan el Tahrir and costs LE2.

For the ***son et lumière*** show, hop off the bus 1km before the Mena House Hotel where you see the Sound and Light sign on your left and then walk. Almost any taxi driver will know what you mean if you say Sound and Light. Agree a per-hour or all-in rate if you want him to wait (thus avoiding any difficulty in getting a ride back, though you can walk over to the Mena House and get a taxi there); the limousines have a set rate for this.

Another alternative is to take a **tour**, which will include admission and the ride out and back. This works out at about as much as it would cost one person to take a taxi and keep it waiting; for two or more people it is better to take the taxi.

keeping out touts. Until then visitors had to contend with hordes of touts urging them to ride their horse or camel, numberless 'guides' and 'watchmen' who gathered about them like mosquitoes, endlessly trying to lure them into ruined little temples with the promise of an undiscovered mummy or reliefs of pharaonic pornography. In the old days, visitors would come with a dragoman who wielded a big stick. Mark Twain, who led a party of tourists here in the 1860s, attempted escape by climbing to the top of Cheops' Pyramid, but he was pursued by an Arab to whom he offered $1 if he could race to the top of Chephren's Pyramid and back to the top of Cheops' within nine minutes, in the hope that the man would break his neck. Three dollars later an exasperated Twain, now joined by the man's mother, offered them each $100 if they would jump off the Pyramid head first.

The best times to visit the Pyramids are at dawn, at sunset and at night when they form as much a part of the natural order as the sun, the moon and the stars. Flaubert recalled the view from the top of Cheops' Pyramid: 'The sun was rising just opposite; the whole valley of the Nile, bathed in mist, seemed to be a still white sea; and the desert behind us, with its hillocks of sand, another ocean, deep purple, its waves all petrified.' Or you might visit them after the *son et lumière*, when the lights go out and the sky is black, and the great stones rise on either side, picked out by the moon and stars. Then especially you get the feeling, as Napoleon said to his army, of 'forty centuries of history looking down upon us', and feel it in the most awesome way.

Access and Fees

Access to the Pyramids site is 6.30am–midnight daily in summer, and 7am–8pm daily in winter; adm LE60. Tickets for entry to the interior of the pyramids of Chephren (adm LE40) and Mycerinus (adm LE60) must be purchased at the site entrance: the kiosk is at the top of the road coming up from the Mena House Hotel towards the north side of the Pyramid of Cheops. Access to the interior of Cheops' Pyramid (adm LE120) is limited: only 300 tickets are sold each day, 150 at 7.30am and another 150 at 1.30pm. These are sold at a special kiosk behind the Pyramid of Cheops. Tickets for the Solar Boat Museum (open daily 9–5 summer, 9–4 winter) are purchased at the museum; adm LE50.

The road arrives at the Mena House Hotel and then curves sharply to the left, mounting a gentle slope and finishing at the north end of the plateau, almost directly opposite the **Great Pyramid**, that of **Cheops**. This is the oldest of the group and the largest, and the others, **Chephren** and **Mycerinus**, stand in descending order of age and size along a southwest axis, each identically oriented 8.5° west of magnetic north; when built they were probably aligned precisely with the North Star, their entrance corridors aiming straight at it. At first the second pyramid, that of Chephren, seems largest, but that is because it stands on higher ground and retains its casing towards its peak. Its present height is 136.4m (originally 143m) and its volume is 2,200,000 cubic metres; this compares with a height of 137.2m (originally 146.6m) for the Great Pyramid of Cheops, which has a volume of 2,550,000 cubic metres. This pyramid was built of over 2,500,000 enormous blocks of limestone cut from the Moqattam and locally, though about 170,000 have been removed by Arabs and Turks since the founding of Cairo. Mycerinus is much smaller, rising only to a height of 65.5m, though it is still imposing, and it contributes to the satisfying arrangement of the group. Napoleon astonished his officers with the calculation that the stones from these three pyramids would be sufficient to build a wall 3m high and 0.3m thick around the whole of France.

But the Pyramids do not have this rocky ledge entirely to themselves. There are smaller **attendant pyramids**, some at least for royal wives, and suburban rows of **mastabas** for nobles and princes of the blood. There are the remains of **temples** and **causeways**; there are **solar boat pits**; and there is the **Sphinx**. A pyramid was never merely a self-sufficient geometrically shaped tumulus of masonry raised above a royal burial; it was the culminating point of a vast funerary area comprising a valley temple, a funerary temple and a causeway linking the two. Near the desert edge and overlooking the cultivation so as to be accessible by boat in the inundation season was a modest valley chapel. From it led a walled-in causeway, as long as 500m, upwards to the funerary temple proper, this abutting the east side of the pyramid, where a false door permitted the deceased pharaoh to emerge in order to partake of the offered feasts. Also, on several sides of a pyramid, set in pits, wooden boats have been found. Whether these were only symbolic or actually used is not known; some have supposed they enabled the pharaoh to follow the sun god across the skies, but as they have been found facing all four points of the compass they could as easily have been intended to enable the pharaoh to go wherever he desired. For convenience, however, they will be referred to here as solar boats.

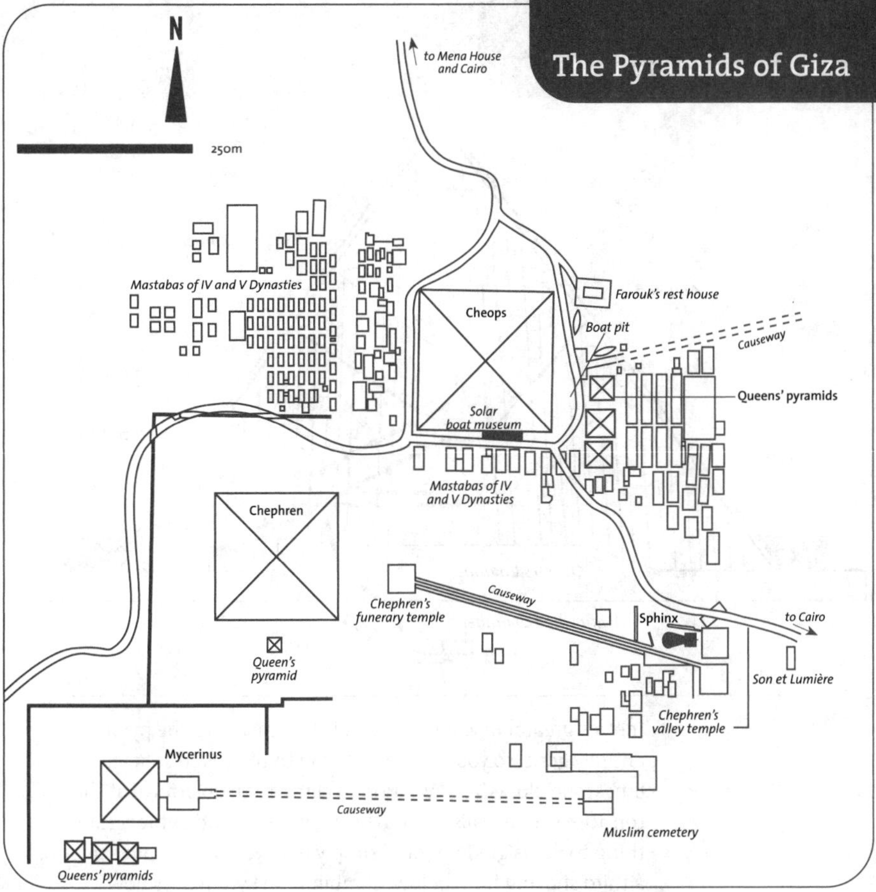

The Great Pyramid of Cheops

What are the hopes of man? Old Egypt's King
Cheops erected the first pyramid,
And largest, thinking it was just the thing
To keep his memory whole and mummy hid;
But somebody or other rummaging,
Burglariously broke his coffin's lid.
Let not a monument give you or me hopes,
Since not a pinch of dust remains of Cheops.

Byron, *Don Juan, Canto I, 219*

1 Great Pyramid of Cheops

The **Great Pyramid of Cheops** (or Khufu), later regarded by the Greeks as one of the seven wonders of the ancient world – and the only one to have survived intact – has a volume of 2,550,000 cubic metres, making it the second most massive structure ever built by man; the pyramid at Cholula in Mexico, built nearly 4,000 years later and largely destroyed by the Spaniards, was 500,000 cubic

Great Pyramid of Cheops

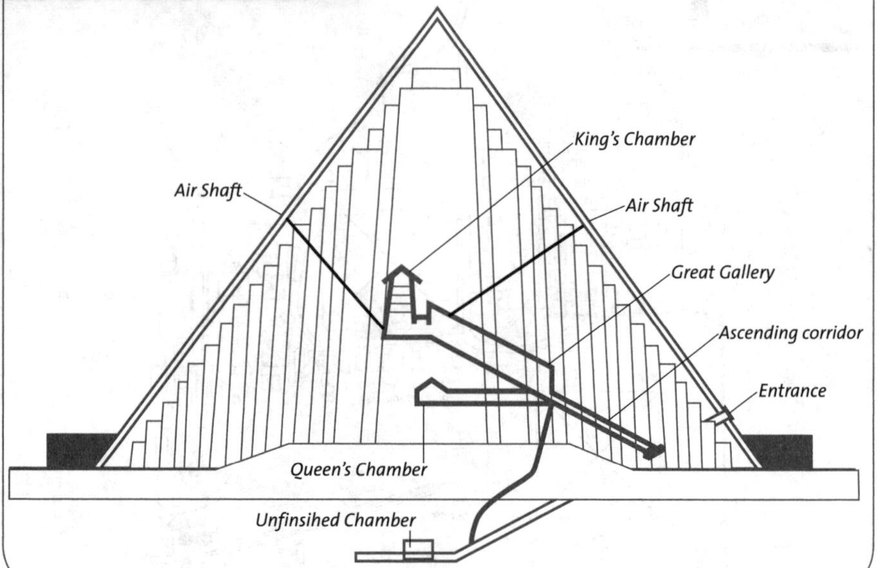

metres greater in volume. The polished casing to the pyramid is entirely gone, so you are presented with the tiered courses of limestone blocks, an invitation to climb to the platform at the top, 10m square. This used to be a fairly easy and entirely safe thing to do, as guides would simply haul you up, one at each arm, a third shoving from below. Climbing the Pyramids is now forbidden, however, which leaves the field open to the more adventurous or the more foolhardy to make the attempt unassisted. The ascent is best made at the northeast corner, each 'step' a metre-high block, and will take 15 to 20 minutes. The footing is more difficult on the way down; also you are more prone to tiredness and vertigo (you must not look down). Some time ago a young man who slept on top while awaiting the dawn fell out of bed, so to speak. There is no stopping a fall; he bounced only twice before obliteration.

Inside the Pyramid

The squeamish might content themselves with going inside. Here the only thing to fear is fear itself, in the form of claustrophobia, and difficulty for some in breathing due to inadequate oxygen. You enter at the north face through an opening made by the 9th-century caliph al-Mamun, son of Haroun el Rashid of *A Thousand and One Nights* fame; coming from Baghdad to suppress an Egyptian uprising in the Delta against the Arab occupation, he took the opportunity to search for treasure (though it is probable that this pyramid had been robbed as early as the First Intermediate Period).

Soon you come to the original corridor which descends for 100m to a depth of 30m beneath the surface of the bedrock. It reaches an unfinished chamber and, as this corridor is constricted (1.3m high, 1m wide) and slippery, it is not usually open to the public. Instead, about 20m from the entrance along the descending corridor you come to a block of granite designed to prevent access to the ascending corridor, though al-Mamun merely hollowed out the rock to the left, and you find yourself crouching your way upwards (height again 1.3m, width 1m) for 40m. The gradient is 1 in 2 and so can be quite tiring, but arrival at the Great Gallery at least permits a stretch. Here there is a shaft (right) which winds down to the descending corridor – purpose unknown. There is also a horizontal corridor, again only 1.3m high for most of its length, which leads to the so-called Queen's Chamber (the name given it by the Arabs), nearly square with a pointed roof of gigantic blocks. But best by far is the ascending **Great Gallery**, 8.5m high, 47m long, a marvel of precision masonry, of which it has been said that neither a needle nor a hair can be inserted into the joints of the stones. This leads on to the principal tomb chamber, commonly called the King's Chamber.

Why there are three burial chambers has been one of the enduring riddles of the Great Pyramid. In 1993 an answer was proposed by Dr I.E.S. Edwards, formerly Keeper of Egyptian Antiquities at the British Museum, who noted that the subterranean chamber 'resembles a quarry in which work had come to an abrupt end owing to some unexpected development'. That development, he argued, was the new belief that the pharaoh must be buried not in a wooden coffin as before, but in a **stone sarcophagus**. The pyramid shape, a stairway to the sun, had already been adopted in support of the doctrine that at death the pharaoh would be assimilated into the sun god Re. But now there was a further requirement: just as the setting sun was swallowed by the goddess Nut to be born again the following dawn, so too the dead pharaoh should be enclosed within a stone sarcophagus symbolic of the goddess, thereby ensuring his rebirth (for more, visit Room 33, Ground Floor, of the Egyptian Museum).

But this new idea came after a corridor, too narrow for the huge sarcophagus now proposed for Cheops, had already been cut through the bedrock, and so the subterranean chamber was abandoned. Instead, it was intended that the sarcophagus should be placed in a new chamber – the so-called **Queen's Chamber** – which was scheduled into the building programme 'at as low a level as would be compatible with the estimated delivery date of the sarcophagus'. But for some reason, according to Dr Edwards, delivery was delayed and, so that work on the Pyramid could continue, the Queen's Chamber was roofed over but never used, and yet another chamber, the King's Chamber, had to be built higher up. Mystery dissolves into familiarity as you imagine the unfortunate architects pulling their hair out each time they had to redesign their building in mid-construction to suit the unpredictable desires of their clients.

The **King's Chamber** is 42.5m above the surface of the bedrock and is 5.22m wide and 10.44m long, that is a double square, aligned east–west. On the north and south walls, a metre above the floor, are the rectangular mouths of the two ventilation shafts (or perhaps they had a religious significance) which extend to the surfaces of the pyramid. The chamber is built entirely in pink Aswan granite and roofed over with nine huge granite slabs laid horizontally. Above these (seen by means of a ladder leading to a passage in the upper south wall of the Great Gallery) four more granite layers, their purpose to create five relieving chambers, one on top of the other, which were meant to distribute the full weight of the pyramid away from the King's Chamber, though in fact this job is accomplished by the topmost pointed roof of limestone blocks. It was in these relieving chambers that the only inscriptions in the Great Pyramid were found – the cartouche, traced several times in red, of Khufu, Cheops. His mummy, if it found its way to this pyramid at all, would have been placed in this King's Chamber. But, as Byron observed, the sarcophagus is empty.

Though Byron was wrong about it being the first pyramid, he was right about it being the biggest, and it is here that you might think about the great weight upon you. Over your head is 95m of solid pyramid, more than enough to squash you very thin for a very long time. Unlike the Meidum pyramid, however, the Pyramid of Cheops has been shown by engineering studies to be exceptionally stable. The building blocks are far larger than those used for earlier pyramids and they are precisely fitted together, while the casing blocks overlaying the basic step structure rest upon foundations slotted into the bedrock. The weight of the pyramid itself contributes to its stability, but not simply its dead weight; the stepped inclined buttresses throw much of this weight towards the centre. At every level the pyramid's horizontal thrusts are directed towards the central core, while 35 per cent of the vertical thrusts are transmitted to the inner core (that is the line running from the top of the pyramid through you to the base), only the remaining thrusts being carried down into the bedrock. In fact the bigger the pyramid the more stable it becomes.

Around the Pyramids

Coming out of the pyramid you can see on the north side, also on the east, the remains of the original **enclosure wall**, about 10m from the base. Backing against this wall on the east side is the basalt paving of Cheops' **funerary temple**, about all that remains of it, and only occasional traces too of the **causeway** that came up from the valley temple, which was discovered in 1990, 4m below street level in the village lying at the foot of the plateau. The three **small pyramids**, 15–20m high, probably belonged to Cheops' queens or sisters.

Three empty **boat pits** have been found near Cheops' Pyramid, but in 1954 a fourth pit revealed a dismantled **solar boat** of Syrian cedar. This magnificent craft has been reassembled and housed in its own specially constructed **Solar Boat Museum** on the south side of the pyramid. Some evidence of wear suggests that the boat was not just intended for burial with the king but actually served Cheops in life. Video cameras lowered through drill holes into a fifth pit in 1987 discovered another boat perfectly preserved in 4,500-year-old air beneath the hermetic seal of 1.5m-thick limestone slabs.

The Sphinx

2 Sphinx

An outcrop of hard grey and soft yellow limestone, useless as building material, was left standing in the quarry from which Cheops cut many of the blocks for his pyramid. His son Chephren had the happy idea of shaping it into a figure – lion's body, god's face, though perhaps Chephren's own, and wearing the royal headdress with uraeus (sacred serpent). The Egyptians would have regarded it as a symbol of strength and wisdom combined, but the Greeks applied their word 'sphinx' to it, recalling a lion's body but the breasts and head of a woman given to putting riddles to passersby, and so this most famous **Sphinx** has acquired an air of mystery quite foreign to its intention.

Nevertheless, some mysteries are associated with it. Neither Herodotus nor any other classical writer until Pliny the Elder mentioned the Sphinx, presumably because it was buried in sand. Prints and photographs of recent times show its features looming from an engulfing sea of sand, but this is all too assiduously cleared today, some mystery swept away with it. The future Tuthmosis IV (XVIII Dyn) dreamt here that if he was to become pharaoh he must clear away the sands: his stelae between the Sphinx's paws commemorate this first known restoration. During the Turkish period the Sphinx was used for target practice and its nose, which originally had been cemented on, fell off; 18th-century

The Pyramid of Cheops and the Sphinx, from Napoleon's Description de l'Egypte, *1798*

drawings show that it was missing long before Napoleon was supposed to have done the damage. The uraeus has also gone, but the beard is being pieced together and should soon be stuck back on.

In the Sound and Light programmes, the Sphinx is given the role of narrator which it performs much better in Arabic when you cannot understand a word. This is in fact one of the best times for viewing it or, after the programme, having a drink on the terrace of the Pavilion of Cheops, for then it gains in perspective against the more distant Pyramids. It may not otherwise seem as large as you had imagined: it is 20m high and 48.5m long, much of its bulk crouched within the quarry so that only its head overtops the horizon.

Chephren's Pyramid Complex

Immediately in front of the Sphinx and associated with it is a IV Dynasty **temple**, one reason for believing the face on the Sphinx is a god's and not Chephren's, for the Egyptians did not build temples to their kings. Adjacent and to the south is **Chephren's valley temple**, facing east. This is the only IV Dynasty sanctuary to retain its grandeur. It owes its exceptional state of preservation to the fact that it was buried in the sands until it was discovered in 1853 by Mariette (though it may prove to be rivalled by Cheops' valley temple, now being excavated). The material is pink Aswan granite, majestically and simply assembled in strong verticals and horizontals, square monolithic pillars supporting massive granite architraves. It was here that Mariette discovered the magnificent diorite statue of Chephren (Room 42, Ground Floor, Egyptian Museum). The purpose of this temple is uncertain, or rather certain for some and contradicted by others. One view is that valley temples were used for mummification; others think the site too exposed and that embalming would have been done either at the pharaoh's Memphis palace or at the base of the pyramid, in the funerary temple. There is at least more general agreement that here was performed the 'Opening of the Mouth' ceremony at which the ka entered the deceased's body. The ka always required a secure residence, hence pyramids and immutable bodies, though it would also inhabit the mortuary statue of the pharaoh, such as the one in the Egyptian Museum, one of 23 that sat round the main T-shaped chamber.

You should now follow, if you can, the traces of Chephren's causeway up to his **funerary temple** at the base of his pyramid. More of this temple survives than of Cheops', the walls formed of possibly the largest blocks ever used in building, one of them 13.4m long and weighing 163 tonnes. To the south of the pyramid is a ruined small pyramid, probably of a queen.

The **Pyramid of Chephren** (or Khafre) compares to Cheops' in size, seemingly exceeds it in height and is also capped with its original casing. Its interior is less interesting, and the outside ascent is much more difficult, requiring an hour to get to the casing. Progress then becomes very dangerous because the smooth surface offers no hold. One of the earlier explorers and snatchers of antiquities was Belzoni, born in Italy but first achieving fame for his 'human pyramid' act on the stage of the Sadlers Wells in London. He was the first European to enter this pyramid, in 1818, and promptly emblazoned his name on the south wall of the burial chamber. When Flaubert entered the chamber 33 years later he recorded: 'Under Belzoni's name, and no less large, is that of a M. Just de Chasseloup-Laubat. One is irritated by the number of imbeciles' names written everywhere: on the top of the Great Pyramid there is a certain Buffard, 79 Rue Saint-Martin, wallpaper manufacturer, in black letters; an English fan of Jenny Lind's has written her name; there is also a pear, representing Louis-Phillipe.'

When the Egyptians built their pyramids it was with a feeling for the sublime power of the plane, without reliefs, inscriptions or any detailing whatsoever. Once the polished limestone casings were set in place, the pyramids both literally and symbolically repulsed the touch of mortals – well, that was the idea, anyway. One of the high points of a visit to the Pyramids in Roman times was the spectacle of men from a nearby village shinning up from the ground to their very tips; one Roman woman scribbled on a casing stone, 'I saw the Pyramids without you; sadly I shed tears here', a lament copied down by a 15th-century pilgrim, when the casing was more extensive than now.

The Pyramid of Mycerinus

The **Pyramid of Mycerinus** (or Menkaure) has only one-tenth of the volume of the other two pyramids and effectively marks the end of the pyramid age. The last pharaoh of the IV Dynasty built a quite different sort of tomb at Saqqara, while the pyramids of the next dynasty were small and shoddy. Though last of the great pyramids, Mycerinus' was built well, with granite used for the lower courses and a casing that remained almost entirely intact until the 16th century. An attempt was made by the sultan in 1215 to destroy all the Pyramids and his workmen started with Mycerinus'. After eight months they gave up. 'Considering the vast masses that have been taken away, it might be supposed that the building would have been completely destroyed, but so immense is the pile that the stones are scarcely missed. Only on one of its sides can be noticed any trace of the impression which it was attempted to be made,' wrote the 13th-century historian Abd el Latif. Though you can enter, the interior is not interesting. The sarcophagus was removed early in the 19th century and put aboard ship for England, but ship and sarcophagus sank off the Spanish coast. Opposite the south face are three small pyramids, while against the east are the remains of Mycerinus' funerary temple.

ⓘ **Pyramids >** *opposite the Mena House Hotel, on the approach road to the Pyramids*

Tourist Information at the Pyramids

At the Tourist Office you can confirm opening hours and entry charges and learn the going rate for hiring camels, horses and horse-drawn buggies.

Tours and Activities at the Pyramids

Various agencies offer tours of the Pyramids, some including Memphis and Saqqara. **Misr Travel**'s Cairo office is at 7 Sharia Talaat Harb, downtown, **t** (02) 2393 0010, **f** (02) 2392 4440, and they also have an office at the Mena House Hotel, **t** (02) 2383 5315.

Son et Lumière Show at the Pyramids

There are four *son et lumière* ('sound and light') shows nightly (6.30pm, 7.30pm, 8.30pm and 9.30pm in winter; 8.30pm, 9.30pm, 10.30pm and 11.30pm in summer; hours may be different during the month of Ramadan; adm LE75). Seating is on a terrace facing the valley temple of the Pyramid of Chephren, by the Sphinx. Bring a sweater; it can get cool on the edge of the desert, even in summer. The language in which the programmes are presented (English, French, Italian, German, Spanish, Russian, Japanese and Arabic) varies from evening to evening: for information call **t** (02) 3386 3469. The English programme is the first each night except on Thursdays when it is the second, and

Sundays when it is the fourth. If you do not understand Arabic, then the Arabic programme (fourth programme on Thursdays) is definitely recommended; it saves you from having to listen to the drivel while giving you all the benefit of the coloured lights and booming sounds.

Riding at the Pyramids

The classic view of the Pyramids is from the south across the sands. It is easy enough to walk and indeed to go further, past the Christian and Muslim cemeteries you see in the distance and to climb the rocky outcrop beyond them. But for the fun of it you might like to ride a camel or horse (*see* also p.197), and as you walk round the Giza plateau there will be plenty of Bedouins importuning you to do so. The Tourist Office opposite the Mena House Hotel will tell you the official rates, about LE60 an hour for a camel, LE70 for a horse.

Mena House Oberoi >>

In fact you will be asked for about LE100 for the ride as from experience the Bedouins know there are enough takers at that price, though you can certainly get it down from that, especially when business is slow. Probably you will be asked to ride two on a beast, but refuse; and no doubt you will be asked for baksheesh in addition to whatever is agreed, to which you should reply with silence and a smile, paying nothing until you have completed your ride and then only the price you originally agreed.

Golf and Skiing at the Pyramids

The best nine-hole **golf course** in the Cairo area is at the Mena House Hotel, a well-watered oasis beneath the brow of the Pyramids, **t** (02) 3377 3222. Before and during the Second World War the British would go **skiing** at Giza. 'You can eat your cake and still have it!', went a local magazine article in the autumn of 1939. 'Under the sunniest of blue skies, you will find sand dunes where you can both ski and bronze yourself to your heart's desire' – an accompanying photograph showing a tent set up just south of the Pyramids, a sort of portable chalet, with men and women wearing swimsuits and strapped into skis slipping down the desert slopes.

Shopping at the Pyramids

For excellent **tapestry-weaving** go to the village of Kardassa, about 3km off Sharia al-Ahram (turn right several hundred metres before the Mena House at the Pyramids, at the sign for Andrea's Restaurant). Here you can buy tapestries, and also bedspreads, rugs, shirts, dresses and black Bedouin dresses with bright cross-stitching – usually old, with a patchwork look after repairs, and becoming quite expensive and rare.

Where to Stay at the Pyramids

For accommodation in Cairo, *see* pp.164–9.

Luxury ($$$$$)

*******Mena House Oberoi**, Sharia al-Ahram, Giza, **t** (02) 3377 3222, *www.oberoimenahouse.com*. A historic hotel, originally a khedivial hunting lodge (converted to a hotel in 1869), where Churchill and Roosevelt initiated the D-Day plan during the Second World War. This is one of the great hotels of Egypt; the Pyramids are just across the road. The old wing is magnificently decorated, and its balconied suites overlook the Pyramids. The garden wing was added in 1976; it is pleasant, but lacks the old style and the dramatic Pyramid views. The hotel has the reasonably priced Khan el Khalili café, with views to the Pyramids, as well as a bar, a drinks lounge and several excellent restaurants, including Indian, Egyptian and continental, and a delightful garden restaurant that is perfect for summer dining. Pool, tennis, golf, casino, nightclub, business centre, car hire and Misr Travel office make the Mena House a self-sufficient resort on the desert's edge. The hotel is 11km from Cairo's central Midan el Tahrir.

*****Movenpick Resort Cairo Pyramids**, Alexandria Desert Road, 2km from the Pyramids, **t** (02) 3377 2555, *www.movenpick-pyramids.com*. All rooms have their own private balcony or terrace, some with distant views of the Pyramids, and they have interactive TV and Internet access. Several restaurants, cafés and bars; a swimming pool (heated in winter), four floodlit tennis courts, a fitness centre, sauna and massage, jogging track, football court and children's playground. Farther from the Pyramids and from Cairo than the Mena House and inferior to it in every way, the question is why stay here at all? The same question applies to any other hotel in the vicinity.

Camping at the Pyramids

Camping Salma, **t** (02) 384 9152, **f** (02) 385 1010, at Harraniyya, 3km along the canal road from Giza to Saqqara. A long way from anywhere and only for people with a vehicle; it is mostly used by overland tour groups. Harraniyya is the village where the late Ramses Wissa Wassef established his famous tapestry-weaving school, so the way is known and easily found: turn left off the Pyramids Road towards Saqqara and then look for the signposted turning to Harraniyya. There are toilets, showers, meals and a delightful garden; pitching a tent costs about $3, renting a cabin about $20.

Eating Out at the Pyramids

★ Khan el Khalili café >>

★ Moghul Room >>

In the Mena House Oberoi Hotel at the base of the plateau there is the reasonably priced Khan el Khalili café, with views to the Pyramids; also the hotel has a bar, a drinks lounge and several expensive restaurants, including the Moghul Room, which offers the best Indian cuisine in Egypt.

For eating places in Cairo, *see* pp.169–72.

Memphis and Saqqara

Saqqara is 32km by road from Cairo and 21km south of the Giza Pyramids. The necropolis extends about 7km north to south along the desert plateau and looks down over the palm groves that cover the site of **Memphis**, about 6km to the southeast in the valley of the Nile. Memphis was the capital of the Old Kingdom, its palaces and shrines of that period built of mud brick for the span of the living and now vanished; Saqqara, built of stone to endure eternity, survives.

Memphis, the Old Kingdom Capital

On the land which had been drained by the diversion of the river, King Menes built his city.
Herodotus

Memphis probably began as a fortress by which Menes controlled the land and water routes between Upper and Lower Egypt and kept the conquered inhabitants of the Delta in subjection. By the III Dynasty it must have become a sizeable capital, as the Saqqara necropolis suggests, but it may not have been fixed. The IV Dynasty pharaohs built their pyramids to the north at Giza and might well have had their palaces near there too. One can imagine Memphis developing in stages like Arab Fustat and its successors, decamping northwards. Whether it was the

Getting to Memphis and Saqqara

You can reach Saqqara by **horse** or **camel** from the Giza Pyramids, though as the journey takes 3 hours in each direction you will not be left with much time to explore the site, and a visit to Memphis would probably be out of the question. You can, however, ride to Saqqara and return by **taxi**, taking in Memphis en route, or you can hire a camel at Saqqara for a little trot round the site. There is also a **bus** from the Giza Pyramids to Badrashein, a village near Memphis; ask about it at the Mena House Hotel or the Tourist Police at the Pyramids. Also there are **tours** or a **taxi** from Cairo. Tours do not include Meidum with Memphis and Saqqara, but ask the travel agent if it can be included at an extra cost, or go to Misr Travel, whose Cairo office is at 7 Sharia Talaat Harb, downtown, **t** (02) 2393 0010, **f** (02) 2392 4440, and they also have an office across the road from the Pyramids at the Mena House Hotel, **t** (02) 2383 5315.

If journeying **by road**, you turn left off the Pyramids Road (Sharia al-Ahram) at the traffic lights immediately after a canal about 1.5km before the Mena House Hotel. It is a pleasant country road with glimpses to the right of the Western Desert and the V Dynasty pyramids of Abusir. You come first to the turning, on your right, for Saqqara; or you can carry straight on for the left-hand turning to the Memphis site.

Riding to Saqqara

You can ride on horseback or camelback across the desert from the Pyramids to Saqqara, negotiating the hire of an animal with one of the many importuning Bedouins or visiting the stables near the Sphinx. First you should check at the **Tourist Office** opposite the Mena House to learn the official rates (though these are ignored in practice, it is nevertheless good to know them, as it will strengthen your resolve to bargain hard) and perhaps also enquire at **Misr Travel**, **t** (02) 383 5315, inside the Mena House, who can organize a journey for you.

The journey will take at least 3 hours in each direction, and spending just a little time at Saqqara means an 8-hour expedition in all. For this reason you should resist offers of hire by the hour and negotiate a price for the entire journey – though many will be happy to ride only one way and take a taxi back. Expect to pay LE200 per beast for a one-way journey (remembering that you will have to pay for a taxi back, about LE30) or LE400 for the return journey plus LE50 for waiting time at Saqqara.

Out of summer take a sweater as the desert can be cold, especially in the morning and towards sundown. Some stables near the Sphinx also offer a return journey with overnight camping at a palm grove near Saqqara, and will provide Bedouin-style tents and Egyptian food.

Camels can carry two people, but this is not advisable. There is some dispute as to which animal is better; most people prefer horses over longer distances. Either way, all but the most hardened rider can expect to end the day feeling pretty sore.

Mediterranean breezes that attracted, or the growing dominance of the sun cult at Heliopolis, so closely associated with pyramid development, is not known. By the VI Dynasty, however, the old site of Memphis had been reoccupied, its attraction the venerable sanctuary of Ptah. From the court of Pepi and its associated monuments came the name Men-nefru-Mire, the Beauty of King Mire (Pepi), later abbreviated to Menfe, in Greek Memphis.

Although no longer capital, in the New Kingdom Memphis rivalled Thebes in grandeur, embellished in particular by Ramses II's

Access and Fees at Memphis and Saqqara

The almost entirely buried site of Memphis is being excavated and is off-limits, but it can be glimpsed from the nearby statuary garden with its building sheltering the colossal statue of Ramses II, which is open 7.30–4 in winter, 7.30–5 in summer; adm LE40. The Saqqara site is open 7–5; adm LE60, which includes the Imhotep Museum, Zoser's Step Pyramid enclosure and a number of mastabas, but an additional fee of LE40 is payable to visit further mastabas – you should ask at the booking office which mastabas and other sites are open before trudging off across the sands. In summer it is best to visit Saqqara early in the morning to avoid the heat, and so to call on Memphis afterwards, but for context Memphis is mentioned here first. Refreshments are available at both Memphis and Saqqara.

mania for building. During the 5th century BC when the Persians ruled Egypt from here and Herodotus visited the city, it was a great cosmopolitan centre, a foreshadowing of Alexandria, with many Greeks and Jews, Phoenicians and Libyans among its population, as full of oriental spectacle as Cairo is today. Herodotus, in his hydrology of Egypt, which fascinated him, wrote that 'when the Nile overflows, the whole country is converted into a sea, and the towns, which alone remain above water, look like islands in the Aegean. At these times water transport is used all over the country, instead of merely along the course of the river and anyone going from Naucratis to Memphis would pass right by the Pyramids... The priests told me that it was Menes, the first king of Egypt, who raised the dam which protects Memphis from the floods... On the land which had been drained by the diversion of the river, King Menes built his city and afterwards on the north and west sides of the town excavated a lake, communicating with the river.'

The decline of Memphis began with the founding of Alexandria, and the final blow was struck when the Arabs founded Fustat as their capital. Even so, as late as the 12th century Abd el Latif could write that 'the ruins still offer, to those who contemplate them, a collection of such marvellous beauty that the intelligence is confounded, and the most eloquent man would be unable to describe them adequately'. But towards the end of the Mameluke period the dikes around Memphis fell into disrepair and at every inundation the level of the ground was raised.

The Site of Memphis

Today the centuries of Nile mud have swallowed Memphis entirely, so much so that it is impossible to soliloquize on how the once mighty has fallen – there is, simply, so little to stir reflection. And even had the dikes been maintained, the more ancient stratas of Memphis would have been lost. Herodotus exactly describes those conditions, persisting until the building of the High Dam at Aswan, which annually drowned the valley and the Delta and gradually covered the past with mud, so that settlements built upon themselves, one strata upon another, to form what in Arabic are known as *tells*. The earliest mud brick houses, palaces and sanctuaries have long since disintegrated beneath the wash of the annual flood, explaining why so much is known of the Egyptian dead, who dwelt in stone on high desert ground, while so little is known of the living.

At Memphis there is a modern building erected for the sole purpose of roofing over a supine **colossus of Ramses II**. The statue is the victim of monumental indifference: the Egyptian government gave him to the British Museum – which failed to collect. He lies here with his right fist clenched, like a cataleptic

Gulliver, bound down by brain seizure rather than ropes. Several smaller statues stand or lie in the grass beneath palms near the covered colossus. Otherwise the immediate area has been turned into a garden, and set up along the central pathway like a plaster gnome is a friendly **alabaster sphinx** dating from the New Kingdom.

If you walk a bit beyond this, no more than 100m eastwards, you can survey the shapeless mounds that cloak the ancient city. The faint remains of the vast **Temple of Ptah** lie waterlogged beside the village of Mit Rahinah. Or from the garden with its sphinx follow the road to Saqqara for 100m; off its north side are the alabaster mummification beds where the **Apis bulls** (*see* pp.212–3) were prepared for burial.

The Egypt Exploration Society is now excavating at Memphis; perhaps in a decade or so there will be more to see.

Saqqara

The Saqqara site has a far more desert feel than Giza; the sands wash about your feet nearly everywhere. Also it is dotted with untended holes left by excavators, some of great depth and not

A Desert Ride from Giza to Saqqara

One way of reaching Saqqara is by **horse** or **camel** from the Giza Pyramids (*see* p.197). The 3-hour journey in each direction takes you along the edge of the cultivation and often strikes across the desert, allowing you to see several rarely visited pyramids and sun temples along the way. There are stables behind the *son et lumière* pavilion. A camel costs more than a horse to hire and is more exhilarating to ride, but be sure there is plenty of padding round the pommel. You will be accompanied by a guide, so finding your way is not a problem.

As you leave the Giza Pyramids you pass adjoining Christian and Muslim cemeteries on the left; you then head south into the desert, though you will always be in sight of the cultivation of the Nile valley. After about an hour and a quarter you come to the **Zawiyat el Aryan pyramids**, both awash in sand. The northerly **Unfinished Pyramid**, abandoned during the IV Dynasty, is surrounded by unused blocks of limestone and granite. About 15 minutes to the southeast and nearer the cultivation is the III Dynasty **Layer Pyramid**, older than the Giza group, built of small blocks and probably meant to be a step pyramid. Another half-hour farther south and near the cultivation (where roses are a speciality) you come to the two V Dynasty **sun temples of Abu Ghurab**. In the courtyard of the northernmost sun temple, that of Neuserre, stands an altar and the base of a solar obelisk. The obelisk has vanished, but you can climb up within the base for the view. The southerly sun temple of Userkaf is utterly ruinous and not worth stopping at.

At the edge of the cultivation 400m southeast and taking their name from a nearby village are the V Dynasty **Abusir pyramids.** The northernmost pyramid of Sahure is badly damaged, though you can crawl through a narrow passage into its tomb chamber. Climbing to the summit, you can gain a fine panorama of the other pyramids in this cluster, together with their attendant mortuary temples. These are the pyramids of Neuserre, Neferikare and Neferefre, neither the first nor last of which was ever finished, perhaps owing to the early deaths of their pharaohs. Work on the pyramid of Neferikare continued, though he too died early; but what had begun with red granite and limestone was completed in mud brick.

From Abusir you can clearly see the Step Pyramid and other structures at Saqqara, less than 30 minutes' ride farther south.

Sun Temples and the Supremacy of Re

Before ascending the throne, Userkaf, the first king of the V Dynasty, had most likely been high priest at Heliopolis, and it was from this time that the cult of Re was raised to the official state religion. Userkaf together with the five kings who succeeded him, though they all built pyramids, diverted considerable resources to building sun temples.

In effect a measure of royal power and wealth was being transferred to the priesthood of Re, and by comparing the dimensions of pyramids to sun temples we can see how far this process went. For example, the pyramid that Neuserre built for himself at Abusir had a base 81 metres square and rose to a height of 52m, but the sun temple he built nearby at Abu Gharab enclosed an area 87m square and within it rose a masonry-built obelisk, symbolizing Re, 53m high. The pharaoh was quite literally overtopped by the god.

always enclosed. It would be dangerous for children on the loose, and adults should mind their step. Many tombs, once discovered and examined, have been closed again and some even sanded over. The most comfortable way to explore the site is to go first to Zoser's funerary complex, visiting also the Pyramid of Unas nearby, and then to drive round to the refreshment tent (or walk across the sands to it) where you can visit the mastaba of Akhti-hotep and Ptah-hotep, the mastaba of Ti and the Serapeum.

History

Saqqara – from Sokkar, the Memphite god of the dead – was a necropolis from the unification of Egypt throughout the Ptolemaic period, and it is the site also of a Coptic monastery destroyed by the Arabs *c.* 960, so that discoveries here span 4,000 years. In historical range and the quantity and value of what has been found here – monuments, works of art, texts and vases – there can be few archaeological sites in all the world, let alone Egypt, to compare with Saqqara. Even so, serious examination of the site only began in the mid-19th century and what remains to be discovered is incalculable.

Except for Zoser's Step Pyramid, Saqqara was ignored, its revelations unsuspected, until 1851 when Auguste Mariette discovered the Serapeum. Even the funerary complex immediately surrounding the Step Pyramid went undiscovered until 1924, and its restoration, to which Jean-Philippe Lauer (1902–2001) gave a lifetime, continues to this day. Cecil M. Firth's campaign of 1924–7 overturned accepted notions about the origins of Egyptian architecture in stone which, because of the gigantic blocks used at Giza, was thought to have developed from megalithic monuments. Instead, at Zoser's complex, one sees a stone architecture which replicates the use of brick in its size and courses, and which is full of imitative references to rush matting, reed and wood forms. One of the greatest achievements of Egyptian civilization was to sever stone from the rock and on a large scale to make of it a building

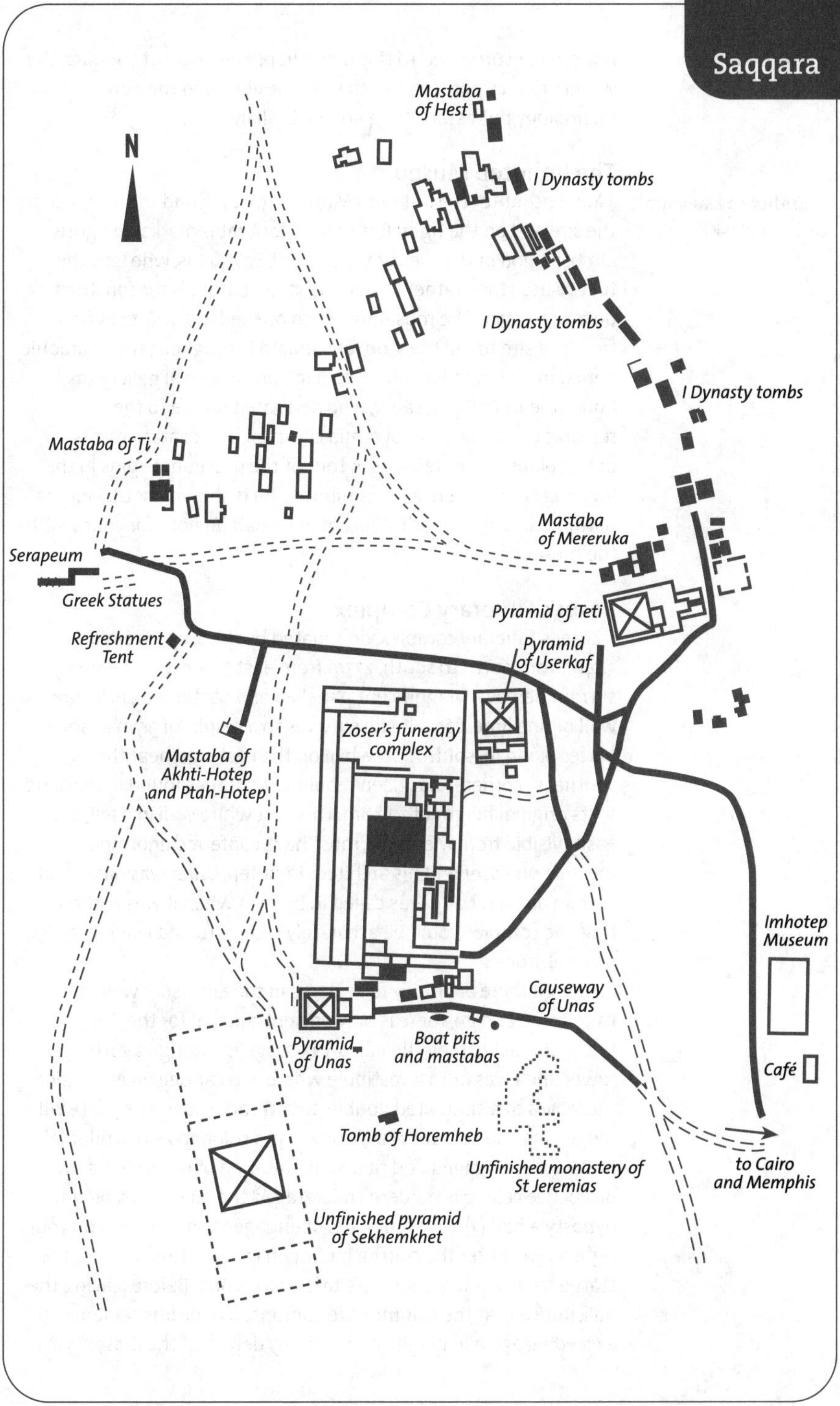
N
Mastaba of Hest
I Dynasty tombs
I Dynasty tombs
I Dynasty tombs
Mastaba of Ti
Mastaba of Mereruka
Serapeum
Greek Statues
Pyramid of Teti
Refreshment Tent
Pyramid of Userkaf
Zoser's funerary complex
Mastaba of Akhti-Hotep and Ptah-Hotep
Imhotep Museum
Causeway of Unas
Pyramid of Unas
Boat pits and mastabas
Café
Tomb of Horemheb
Unfinished monastery of St Jeremias
to Cairo and Memphis
Unfinished pyramid of Sekhemkhet

material unsurpassed to this day. It happened here at Saqqara, the world's first city of stone, with some hesitancy in the new technology but astonishing artistic brilliance.

The Imhotep Museum

Imhotep Museum
open daily 9–4pm

You encounter the Imhotep Museum just beyond the entrance to the site and on the right. It is named for that remarkable figure, almost a god in the eyes of the ancient Egyptians, who was the first to use stone rather than perishable materials for construction on a large scale. The museum, which opened in 2006, uses finds from the site to tell the story of Saqqara throughout the pharaonic period in five themed halls, which include a special gallery to honour Jean-Philippe Lauer, who dedicated his life to the restoration of the Zoser pyramid complex, and containing his books, plans and notebooks. A tour of the museum begins in the Viewing Room where a nine-minute film is shown about Saqqara, narrated by Omar Sharif. Allow at least half an hour for your visit to the museum.

Zoser's Funerary Complex

Zoser's funerary complex, dominated by the **Step Pyramid**, is 544m from north to south, 277m from east to west, and entirely surrounded by a magnificent panelled and bastioned **enclosure wall** of fine limestone. It still survives to a height of 3.7m at some places along its south side, while on the east side, near the southeast corner, it has been rebuilt with stones found in the sand to its original height of 10.48m. This vast white wall in itself, once easily visible from Memphis, must have conferred enormous prestige on Zoser and his architect Imhotep. Lauer was himself at first an architect and was called in by Firth when it was realized that the complex could be accurately reconstructed using the original stones.

Though there are many false doors in the enclosure wall for the ka to come and go, there is only one **entrance (1)** for the living, at the southeast corner. The narrow passage is through a fortress-like tower and gives onto a vestibule where you can see on either side the leaves of a simulated double door thrown open, complete with hinge pins and sockets. Ahead of you is a **colonnaded corridor (2)**, its columns engaged and ribbed in imitation of palm stems (the protective ceiling is modern concrete). At the far end is a broad **hypostyle hall (3)** with four pairs of engaged columns, and on your right as you enter the court a half-open ka door. This is where the statue base bearing Imhotep's titles was found. Before leaving the hall, notice that the columns are comprised of drums seldom exceeding 25cm in height, one of many details of the masonry

Zoser's Funerary Complex

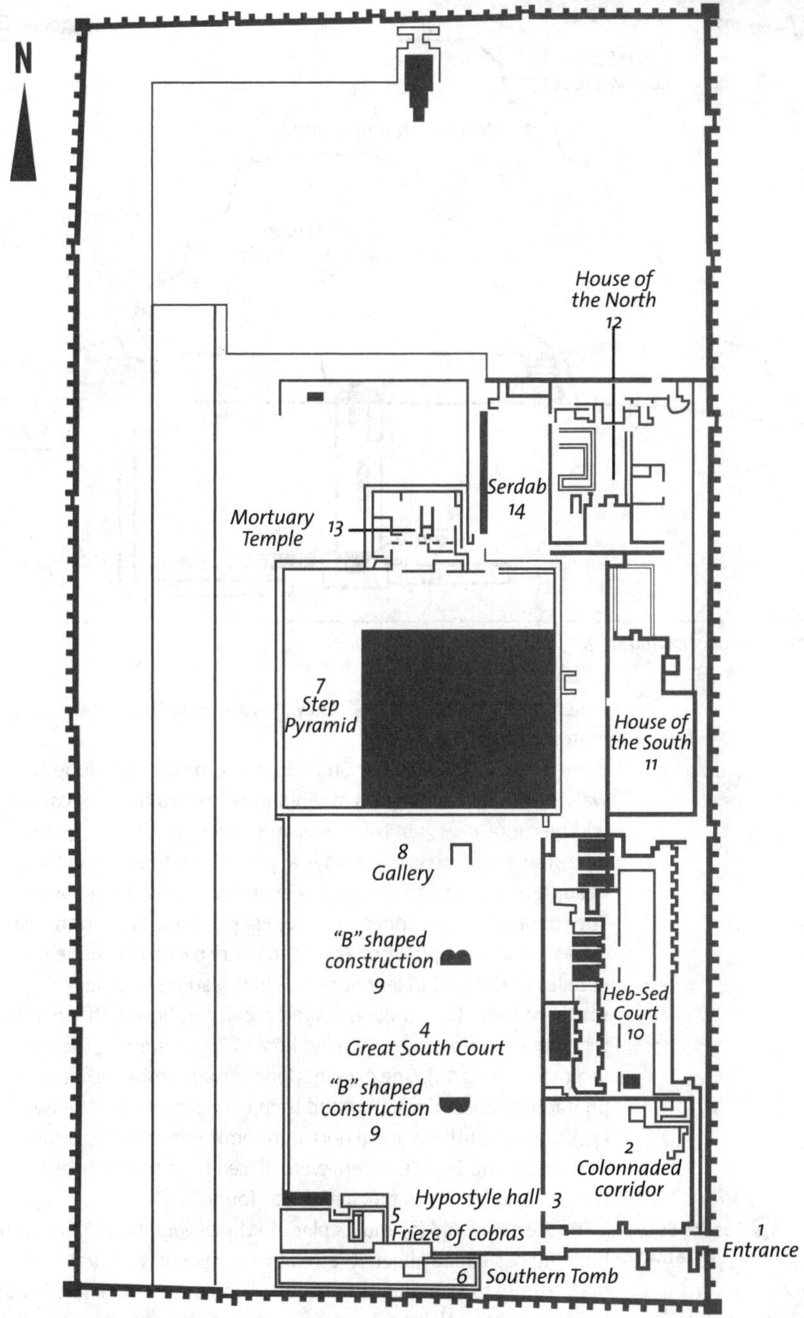
N
House of the North 12
Serdab 14
Mortuary Temple 13
7 Step Pyramid
House of the South 11
8 Gallery
"B" shaped construction 9
Heb-Sed Court 10
4 Great South Court
"B" shaped construction 9
2 Colonnaded corridor
Hypostyle hall 3
5 Frieze of cobras
1 Entrance
6 Southern Tomb

Zoser's Step Pyramid

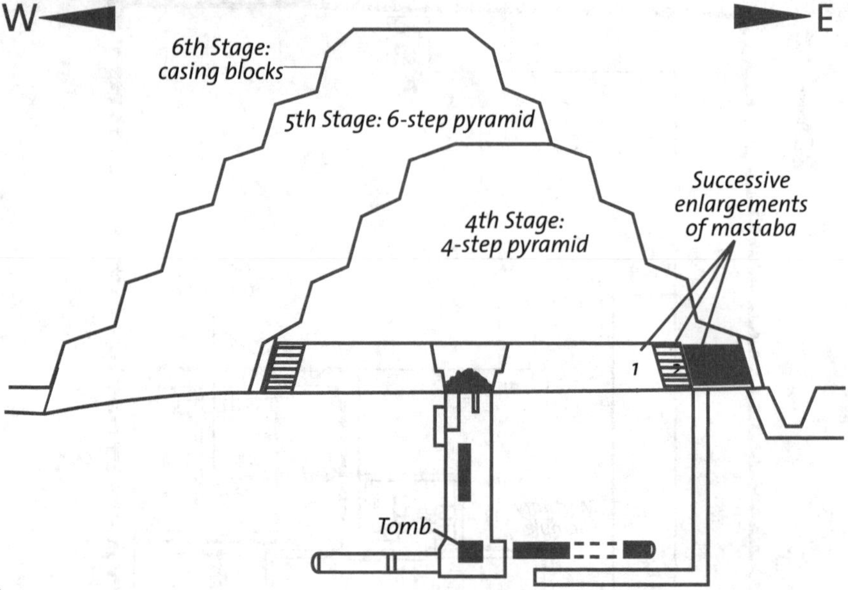

Cross-section showing stages from mastaba to skyscraper

which betray Imhotep's hesitancy in working with this new material, stone.

You now emerge into the **Great South Court (4)**, and along the wall to your left is a section of rebuilt wall with a **frieze of cobras (5)**. The cobra, *uraeus* in Latin, was an emblem of royalty and an instrument of protection, always appearing on the pharaoh's headdress and able to destroy his enemies by breathing flames. The cobra was worshipped in Lower Egypt, and so here in this early dynasty it also emphasizes Zoser's mastery over the conquered peoples of the Delta. Near here is a shaft leading to Zoser's **southern tomb (6)**, similar in its faïence decoration to that beneath the Step Pyramid. There is a relief here of Zoser running the Heb-Sed race (*see* p.206). One explanation for two tombs is that early pharaohs thereby demonstrated their connection with the two Egypts, so a southern and a northern tomb. Possibly the canopic jars containing Zoser's viscera were placed here, the body beneath the pyramid (where in fact a foot was found).

Zoser's Step Pyramid

The **Step Pyramid (7)** and its place in the development of pyramid building has already been referred to. Now you have a first-hand opportunity to examine its features. Despite its 62m height, it was built of fairly small limestone blocks, far smaller than those enormous blocks at Giza. Though working with stone, Imhotep was still thinking in terms of mud brick. But even in the enlargement of his monument from mastaba to pyramid (*see* illustration left), you can detect signs of Imhotep's growing confidence in the new medium: at the southeast corner where the casing has come away you can see the smaller stonework of the mastaba, as you can if you walk along the east face of the pyramid. Also note how regularly the courses are laid, both of the mastaba and the pyramid as a whole, and how well shaped and fitted the stones are. In technique, Imhotep was without fault. The last enlarged mastaba measured 63m each way and a little over 8m high. Recall that the first pyramid erected over this mastaba rose four steps; the further pyramid of two additional steps increased the total volume by more than four fold. The entire monument was then sheathed in fine limestone from Tura, just to the south of modern Cairo, as were the Giza Pyramids.

The original entrance to the Step Pyramid was at the north face, but in the XXVI Dynasty, known as the Saite period for its dynasty's origins at Sais in the Delta, a **gallery (8)** was dug from the Great South Court to the chambers beneath the pyramid. Permission and keys will have to be asked for at the office of the Inspector of Antiquities to the northeast of the Pyramid of Teti. The Saites admired the works of the Old Kingdom and it is quite possible they tunnelled their way into the pyramid out of sheer archaeological curiosity. After 60m you come to the main central shaft from where there are impressive views up into the pyramid and down towards the burial chamber which is sealed with a huge granite plug.

Emerging once again into the Great South Court, you see two **B-shaped constructions (9)** near the centre. These marked the limits of Upper and Lower Egypt, the gap between them symbolically spanned by Zoser in the Heb-Sed race. (A relief in the southern tomb shows Zoser in full stride, the two B-shaped constructions to the rear and fore.) The Heb-Sed race was one of the ceremonies during the 5-day jubilee which occurred in the thirtieth year – that is at the interval of one generation – of the pharaoh's reign. It is possible that at some earlier period power was granted for only 30 years, the chieftain then deposed, perhaps killed, to spare the land from decline because of his failing strength. This jubilee, therefore, was a renewal of the vital forces of the pharaoh and his ka, and so of all Egypt.

Also at his jubilee the pharaoh re-enacted his coronation, sitting first on the throne of Upper Egypt, then on the throne of Lower Egypt, each time presenting gifts to the various priesthoods before they returned to their provinces. Participation in the festival obliged the priests to recognize the supremacy of the pharaoh over their own local deities. These ceremonies, however, including the ritual race, would not have taken place here but at Memphis. The funerary complex was meant as a cosmic 'stand-in' for the actual jubilee site – it perpetuated the regenerating Heb-Sed in eternal stone. This explains the extraordinary film set quality of the Heb-Sed Court.

The **Heb-Sed Court (10)** in the southeast part of the complex is rectangular and flanked to east and west by shrines, each one representing a province. They are hardly more than façades, as in a Hollywood western. Access to the offering niches is by circumventing a screen wall, disguising the lack of depth, for the tall buildings are mere dummies, filled with rubble. Half-open doors with hinges, imitations of the wooden originals, receive immortality in stone. In actuality, these shrines would have been tents with wooden poles and cross-supports. The chapels are not uniform; some have a curved cornice, as though the underlying frame represented flexed wood; other roofs are horizontal with the outward curve of the cavetto cornice that was to become so familiar a feature of Egyptian architecture, and torus moulding. Drawing on earlier building materials, Imhotep here invented the language of stone architecture. Cornices, torus mouldings, stone corner posts and columns and a variety of capitals appear for the first time in history at Saqqara. All the more astonishing that the effect is so delicate and beautifully proportioned. A stone platform at the south end of the court is probably where the two thrones of Egypt stood for the re-enactment of the coronation, while at the north end of the court, to the left, is a base with four pairs of feet, most likely those of statues of Zoser, his wife and two daughters.

North of the Heb-Sed Court is another spacious court and the **House of the South (11)** with engaged proto-Doric columns. These Doric-style columns were never popular in Egypt where planes and hence smoothly rounded columns were preferred to the Aegean play of light and shadow. There is the peculiarity of the door being placed asymmetrically, owing to the prototype façade being no more than a curtain, the door therefore needing to abut a column for support. As with the shrines in the Heb-Sed Court, the House of the South and the House of the North would actually have had wooden frames. They may have been sanctuaries, or possibly they represent government buildings of Upper and Lower Egypt.

Inside the corridor are the first known examples of tourist graffiti, written in a cursive form of hieroglyphics and dating from the New Kingdom. The visitors, scribes from Thebes, express their admiration for Zoser's achievement, though here and elsewhere some settle for the ancient equivalent of 'Kilroy was here', while one pedantic crackpot, taking exception to some illiterate graffiti he must have seen, scribbled: 'The scribe of clever fingers came, a clever scribe without his equal among any men of Memphis, the scribe Amenemhet. I say: Explain to me these words. My heart is sick when I see the work of their hands. It is like the work of a woman who has no mind.'

The **House of the North (12)** is similar to that of the South except that the columns have the form of a papyrus plant, the shaft the triangular stem, the capital the fanning head.

The **mortuary temple (13)** at the north face of the pyramid is largely in ruins. The original entrance to the burial chamber beneath the pyramid led from this temple. To the east of the temple is the **serdab (14)**, as startling now as it was to Firth when he uncovered it. It is a masonry box, tilted slightly back and with two small holes drilled through its north face. A window at the side, put there by the excavators, allows you to peer in. And there is Zoser! A life-size painted limestone statue, as you realize after the initial surprise, but for all the world like a strapped-in astronaut in his space capsule, his eyes fixed through the holes on the North Star, awaiting blast-off and immortality. The circumpolar stars and the North Star itself were 'those that know no destruction' or 'those that know no weariness', for they never set and so never died; this was the place of eternal blessedness for which Egyptians longed. And there is Zoser. It is absolutely convincing. It is this which impresses about the ancient Egyptians again and again, how they gave as well as they could mechanical effect to their illusions. They put California body-freezers to shame. Alas for poor Zoser, the unbelieving Mr Firth removed the original statue to the Antiquities Museum in Cairo; this is a copy. But then again, the substitution probably does not bother Zoser's ka, and it lives here still, and at dark of night it rockets starwards and mingles with the universe.

The Pyramid of Unas

Unas was the last pharaoh of the V Dynasty. About 300 years mark the distance between Zoser's Step Pyramid, the Great Pyramids at Giza, and this heap of rubble that is Unas' pyramid. These monuments graphically portray the rise and decline of the Old Kingdom sun cult.

The Pyramid of Unas was approached by a 1km causeway, part of which has been reconstructed, including a very short section of its walls and roof, for it was entirely enclosed. A slit in the roof allowed the sunlight to illuminate the inscribed walls which were lively with everyday scenes. On the north side several mastabas are arranged like village houses on either side of narrow lanes. The best is of Princess Idut (V Dyn) with 10 rooms. On the south side of the causeway there are impressive boat pits. Also, about 150m to the south are the sanded over ruins of the **monastery of**

St Jeremias, founded in the second half of the 5th century AD and destroyed by the Arabs around AD 960. Practically all of its paintings and carvings have been removed to the Coptic Museum in Old Cairo.

The Pyramid of Unas looks like a pile of dirt, certainly when approached from the east. On the west side its stones are more evident, but are disarrayed. Even originally it rose only about 18.5m; its core was loose blocks and rubble, its casing alone in hewn limestone. Nevertheless, the pyramid has proved of immense historical importance, for when Gaston Maspero entered the tomb chamber in 1881 he found the walls covered with inscriptions, the **Pyramid Texts**, which are the earliest mortuary literature of Egypt and the first known religious texts in the world. These are hymns and rituals that preceded and accompanied the interment of the body; prayers for the release of the ba or soul; another section listing offerings of food, drink and clothing for use in the afterlife. Until this time, pyramids had gone unadorned. Thereafter, funerary literature underwent considerable elaboration and embroidery, culminating in that collection – or rather genre, for no such definitive compilation existed – of New Kingdom literature known to us as the Book of the Dead.

Despite its exterior, the pyramid of Unas remains internally sound and you can creep down the 1.4m-high corridor, entered from the north face, past three enormous slabs of granite meant to block the way. Unlike the New Kingdom texts which were full of advice on how to steer a course clear of the forces of evil, which in effect emphasized the dangers that preceded safe arrival in the afterlife and were the tools of the trade of a blackmailing priesthood, the Pyramid Texts celebrate eternal life and identify the deceased pharaoh with Osiris. Nevertheless, there is anxiety in the prayers. The confident era of the sun cult was waning; a personal god and a note of redemption marked the rising cult of Osiris. The state was weakening; the troubled times of the First Intermediate Period were approaching.

The Pyramid Texts and Osiris

The only complete account of the Osiris myth was given by the Greek writer Plutarch more than 2,000 years after the passing of the Old Kingdom, by when it represented a compendium of evolved belief. Nevertheless, aspects of the story are preserved in various Egyptian literary sources, including the Pyramid Texts. These show that already by the end of the V Dynasty Osiris was described as born of the sky goddess Nut after her union with the earth god Geb, whose other children included Isis and Seth. Osiris and Isis, in turn, were the parents of Horus, who became associated with the sun cult and with whom the living pharaoh was identified, while at death he was identified with Osiris. The king therefore was linked to cults of both sky and earth, life and afterlife, and existed simultaneously and undyingly in all spheres and realms. In time the cult of Osiris would extend far beyond the royal sphere, and its message would become one of universal redemption.

Visiting the Outstanding Mastabas

You can now trudge across the sands or drive to the refreshment tent which stands near the site of Mariette's house, where he stayed during those first serious explorations of Saqqara. The beer is cold and in the heat goes straight to your head. You can walk around the rest of the necropolis in a state of intoxication. When visiting the Serapeum, you may be grateful for that.

Viziers and Priests

But first you can visit some mastabas. The **mastaba of Mereruka**, with 32 rooms, is the largest at Saqqara. He enjoyed in death not only elbow room, but the prestigious company to which he had become accustomed in life. For Mereruka was vizier to the pharaoh Teti (VI Dyn), whose pyramid is next door, and he married and was buried with the boss's daughter. The entry passage shows Mereruka painting a picture of the seasons and playing a board game to pass away the time, while the first three chambers are decorated with scenes of hunting, furniture making and goldsmiths at work. At the far end of the mastaba is a chapel with six pillars, containing a statue of the vizier himself. The scenes to the left of this are interesting: they show the domestication of gazelles, goats and hyenas.

4 mastaba of Akhti-Hotep and Ptah-Hotep

The double **mastaba of Akhti-Hotep and Ptah-Hotep** is to the southeast of the refreshment tent, along your way if you are walking between the complexes of Zoser or Unas or Mereruka's mastaba and a beer. Ptah-Hotep describes himself as a priest of Maat and he may have held other positions too. At any rate, he seems to have been a very important official during the reign of Djedkare (V Dyn), predecessor of Unas. In later generations he would be celebrated for his wisdom text, a set of instructions addressed to his son. 'If you are a wise man', Ptah-Hotep said, 'establish a home and love your wife. Fill her belly, clothe her back. Ointment is a good remedy for her limbs. Make her happy as long as you live. She is a good field to her master.' Akhti-Hotep, who may have been Ptah-Hotep's father, was vizier, judge and chief of the granary and treasury. Their mastaba is smaller than Ti's, which we come to next, but is more developed and is particularly interesting for the reliefs which are in various stages of completion.

You enter from the north and come into a corridor. On its left wall are preliminary drawings in red with corrections by the master artist in black. On the right wall are various stages of low relief. The background is cut away first to yield a silhouette and then the details are pencilled in and cut. In the lower registers, servants carry fowl in their arms towards Ptah-Hotep who stands at the far end of this right-hand wall. Though somewhat stylized, with his shoulders squared but with head and limbs in profile, the detailed musculature shows the artist's sound sense of anatomy.

At the top end of the corridor you turn right into a pillared hall and then left, passing through a vestibule, into **Ptah-Hotep's tomb chamber**. The ceiling imitates the trunks of palm trees while the mural reliefs, still retaining some colour, are the finest preserved of the Old Kingdom, surpassing even those in the more famous mastaba of Ti.

Food and Entertainment for the Ka

On the right wall are two door-shaped stelae, representing the entrance to the tomb. Between them is Ptah-Hotep, depicted in the panther-skin of a high priest, seated at a cornucopian table of offerings, a goblet raised to his lips. In the upper register, priests make offerings; in the lower three rows, servants bear gifts. They are lucky to get off so lightly; during the I Dynasty they were sacrificed and interred around their master's mastaba. On the far wall Ptah-Hotep is again at table, this time with a stylized loaf of bread before him and copper basins and ewers alongside so that he may cleanse himself before eating. In the upper register women representing various estates bring him the products of his farms, while in the second register animals are being thrown and slaughtered. The reliefs on the left wall are the finest and most interesting, a catalogue of events in the life of the deceased. On the right, according to the text, Ptah-Hotep is inspecting the 'gifts and tribute that are brought by the estates of the North and South'; boys are wrestling and running, caged animals (lions, gazelles, hares and hedgehogs) are drawn up, and a cow is giving birth, a peasant guiding the calf into the world. The bottom register shows domestic poultry and the text claims that Ptah-Hotep possessed '121,000 geese of one variety, 11,210 of another variety, 120,000 small geese, 111,200 goslings and 1,225 swans'. On the left of this wall Ptah-Hotep 'witnesses all the pleasant activities that take place in the whole country'. In the top registers, boys and girls are playing; there is one episode of two boys seated and facing each other as their friends vault over them. This game, called Khaki la wizza, is still played today by Nubians. The third register is devoted to aspects of viticulture; the fourth shows animal life (note the hare emerging from its hole with a cricket in its mouth); the fifth is a hunting scene, the cow tied as bait for the lion; the fifth and sixth registers show marsh and boating scenes.

Above the entrance is a faded mural, but you can make out Ptah-Hotep preparing for his day, a manicurist at his hands, a pedicurist at his feet, musicians entertaining him, greyhounds beneath his chair and a pet monkey held by his valet. The sophistication of this scene is all the more striking when you recall that it depicts daily Egyptian life, albeit at the very top of the social ladder, nearly 4,500 years ago, at a time when Europe and most of Asia were still in the Stone Age. The purpose of these reliefs was to provide food, indeed a complete experience of life, for the ka. They began during the IV Dynasty as it was realized that relatives and descendants did not always provide fresh offerings; the reliefs were imitative magic against default. But one can also imagine the great pleasure they must have given the tomb owner, an assurance that he was going to take it all with him, and to his relatives when they did gather in his tomb. Think of some of the more elaborate marble tombs in Greek cemeteries today; they are like small shrines with an inner chamber for the deceased and an outer chamber with seats for the living, and they are the cheeriest places, often attracting bountiful picnics. Unas, a generation later, was already worried about his relationship with Osiris; but here there is not a single god, no judgement, no doubt – afterlife follows on from life as assuredly as day follows day, and without even an intervening night.

Now, returning to the pillared hall you turn left for the **chamber of Akhti-Hotep**, similarly though less finely decorated. A passageway leads out of the side of this and opening off it, on your left, is a chamber containing an anonymous mummy. The passageway leads back to the pillared hall and the entrance corridor.

Hairdresser and Estate Manager

The **mastaba of Ti** is to the north of the refreshment tent and you can follow the road that leads to the Serapeum part of the way there. The mastaba was discovered by Mariette in 1865 and has been well restored by the Egyptian Department of Antiquities. It originally stood above ground but is now entirely sunk in the sand. Its reliefs rival those in Ptah-Hotep's tomb chamber and exceed them in variety. Ti was a parvenu and royal hairdresser during the early V Dynasty; he was also overseer of several royal mortuary temples and pyramids and controller of royal ponds, farms and stock from which he evidently enriched himself. His wife was related to the royal family and his children bore the title 'royal descendant', to which Ti himself was not entitled. Ti's wife and eldest son were also entombed here, but some later would-be arriviste made off with the goods and disposed of the bodies.

In plan, the entrance is from the north, a two-pillared vestibule leading to a spacious open-pillared court at the centre of which a flight of stairs descends to a subterranean passage ending in an antechamber and the tomb chamber. Otherwise, a corridor leads out from the rear of the open court and passes a chamber on the right, arriving at the funerary chamber and the serdab.

Once through the open court, whose reliefs have been badly damaged by exposure, the walls of corridors and rooms are finely decorated with familiar scenes. The most interesting room, with the most beautiful reliefs, is Ti's **funerary chamber**. Through the slot in the far (south) wall you can see Ti (this is a cast of the original statue now in the Cairo Museum) staring vacantly northwards from his serdab, though lacking Zoser's look of adventure. Needless to say his hair, or rather his wig, is well done. Most enjoyable are the reliefs on the near (north) wall, all concerned with life in the marshes of the Delta. Look particularly at the central relief of Ti sailing through the marshes. This is a classic representation of a **hippopotamus hunt**; the hippopotamus, to the lower right, has seized a crocodile which, meanwhile, is desperately trying to bite the hippo's leg. Ti is shown larger than his huntsmen who, from another boat, are harpooning the hippo. Below the boats are fine Nile fish of different species, identifiable as favoured catches in the river today. On the right, in a small boat with a curiously truncated stern, a fisherman is about to club a large schal fish over the head. Above Ti, among the papyrus clusters, birds are being attacked in their nests by carnivorous animals, the reeds bending with their weight. In the register below is a line of elegant female bearers, their transparent coloured dresses surrendered to time, their nakedness and varied poses freshly pleasing.

This relief is unusual for having two layers of meaning. Literally it is a hunt in the marshes; but symbolically it is Ti against the forces of evil and chaos. The hippopotamus was particularly feared and hated in ancient Egypt, but Ti together with a helpful crocodile is killing it. Fish and birds represented chaos, but here again man and animals are subduing them.

Tombs of the Apis Bulls

When I first penetrated into the sepulchre of the Apis, I was so overcome with astonishment that, though it is now five years ago, the feeling is still vivid in my mind. By some inexplicable accident one chamber of the Apis tombs, walled up in the thirtieth year of Ramses II, had escaped the general plunder of the monuments, and I was so fortunate as to find it untouched. Three thousand seven hundred years had had no effect in altering its primitive state. The finger mark of the Egyptian who set the last stone in the wall built up to cover the door was still visible in the mortar. Bare feet had left their traces on the sand strewn in a corner of this chamber of the dead; nothing had been disturbed in this burying-place where an embalmed ox had been resting for nearly forty centuries.

Auguste Mariette

Sacred Bulls and Egyptian Nationalism

Sacred bull cults go back into the prehistory of Egypt, and during the I and II Dynasties a bull would wander across the field of the Heb-Sed race, symbolically fertilizing the two lands. But animal cults enjoyed an astonishing popularity during the Late Egyptian Period as the old beliefs degenerated. Herodotus, attempting to demonstrate the madness of Cambyses, the Persian ruler of Egypt, records that 'the priests brought Apis and Cambyses, half mad as he was, drew his dagger, aimed a blow at its belly, but missed and struck its thigh. Then he laughed, and said to the priests: "Do you call that a god, you poor creatures? Are your gods flesh and blood? Do they feel the prick of steel? No doubt a god like that is good enough for the Egyptians; but you won't get away with trying to make a fool of me", and he had the priests whipped and forbade the cult, but when finally Apis died of his wounds he was buried by the priests without the knowledge of Cambyses.' In this instance, at least, Cambyses sounds quite sane, but it is understandable that the once mighty priesthood should cling to some tangible shred of belief as the old order was being attacked by foreign rulers. The Ptolemies were more shrewd and flattered the priesthood, encouraged their cults, built temples and ruled Egypt for 300 years, the Serapeum in particular surviving as a weird testimony to their policy.

Serapeum

The **Serapeum** is the strangest place at Saqqara. A temple once stood here amid the sands but what remain are the long underground galleries cut through the rock where the Apis bulls were buried. This was Mariette's great discovery in 1851 which began the serious excavation of Saqqara that has continued ever since.

Entry is to the west of the refreshment tent; you follow the road which first bends right towards Ti's mastaba and then turns left. At this second bend was Mariette's house, and immediately by the roadside, on your left and under the protective roof, is the surprising sight of several Greek statues arranged in a semicircle. These and their unlikely connection with bull burial requires some explanation.

The Legends

The huge tombs of these Apis bulls were previously known only from references to them by various writers of antiquity. For instance, Herodotus wrote: 'The Apis is the calf of a cow which is never afterwards able to have another. The Egyptian belief is that a flash of light descends upon the cow from heaven, and this causes her to receive Apis. The Apis-calf has distinctive marks; it is black, with a white diamond on its forehead, the image of an eagle on its back, the hairs on its tail double, and a scarab under its tongue.'

Apis thus miraculously conceived was considered to be an incarnation of Ptah, the god of Memphis. Worshipped as such during his lifetime within a special sanctuary in the Temple of Ptah, he was mummified after his death on those alabaster beds you can still see among the few surviving stones of Memphis. Then, identified with Osiris under the name Osiris-Apis, he was taken with great pomp to these underground galleries at the Serapeum and placed within a gigantic sarcophagus.

Mariette's Discoveries

The **galleries** of the Serapeum date from three periods, the earliest to the reign of Ramses II (XIX Dyn), enlarged by his son Khaemwas; a second to the reign of Psammetichus I (XXVI Dyn); and a main gallery to the Ptolemies. It was the Greek Ptolemies who encouraged an identity between Osiris and Dionysos, and Plutarch comments that 'as for what the priests openly do in the burial of the Apis when they transport its carcass on a raft, this in no way falls short of Bacchic revelry, for they wear fawn-skins and carry thyrsus-rods' – a staff tipped with a pine cone, in short a phallus – 'and produce shouts and movements as do the ecstatic celebrants of the Dionysiac orgies'. (Recall the sarcophagus of the dwarf in Room 49 on the ground floor of the Cairo Museum.) It is from the Ptolemaic period that the semicircle of **Greek statues** of poets and philosophers dates. Homer is at the centre, Pindar plays the lyre at the far right, and at the far left is a base inscribed with the name of Plato. They must be turning over in their graves.

Mariette was led to the Serapeum by recalling a quotation from Strabo (24 BC): 'One finds at Memphis a temple to Serapis in such a sandy place that the wind heaps up sand dunes beneath which we saw sphinxes, some half-buried, some buried up to the head, from which one can suppose that the way to the temple could not be without danger if one were caught in a sudden wind-storm.' Mariette had found one such head at Saqqara, and removing the sand in the area found an entire avenue of sphinxes leading to the Greek statues and to the Serapeum galleries. The avenue has since sanded up again.

Saqqara can seem strange enough today. When Mariette was excavating here, he described the conditions in his house: 'Snakes slithered along the floor, tarantulas or scorpions swarmed in the wall crevices, large spider webs waved from the ceiling like flags. As soon as night fell, bats, attracted by the light, entered my cell through the cracks in the door and kept me awake with their spectral flights. Before going to sleep, I tucked the edges of my mosquito net beneath my mattress and put my trust in God and all the saints, while outside jackals, hyenas and wolves howled around the house.'

Today's Experience

Your own impression might be of a terrifying moronic force at work. You descend a ramp slipping under the formless desert surface and reach a corridor leading off to left and right. Down to the left it meets a transverse gallery and left into that, on the left, within a vault, is a massive pink granite **sarcophagus** with panels and across the top edge hieroglyphics – on the right an Apis bull is depicted with the characteristic black markings. The rest of this gallery is blocked off by a grate.

You now reverse direction, heading down a 150m gallery. On either side, in alternating succession, are more vaults, in all but one of which squats a monstrous black sarcophagus – bull-size. The finest sarcophagus of all is at the very end of this gallery, on the right, with carved decoration and polished to a glassy lustre. You can climb down into its pit and stand on a step at the back to peer inside. Until a few years ago the Serapeum was lit only at lengthy intervals by dim yellow lights which in the murky darkness cast a greenish glow. At some places, the lights would have gone out and you had to walk through velvety blackness. In the silence and the dim light, the repetition of vaults and sarcophagi became like a bad dream you could not awake from, and you just walked on, with literally no light at the end of the tunnel. It was macabre, and with your capillaries shot full with beer you achieved enough perspective to find it utterly incredible that the Ptolemies, whose gallery this is, could have perpetuated anything so repulsive. The lighting has now been greatly 'improved', diluting the atmosphere of what was once the weirdest place in Egypt.

It was not here, but in the Rammessid gallery, now inaccessible, that Mariette found the one untouched Apis tomb, a mummified bull inside, and also the mummy of Khaemwas, who had been appointed by his father Ramses II High Priest of Ptah. And there he found those ancient **footprints**. You notice footprints in the sand in this Ptolemaic gallery too, of more recent visitors, and they bring to mind, as so often encounters with Egypt's pharaonic past do, our own voyages into the cosmos, those footprints left in the dust on the surface of the windless moon which may remain for millions of years undisturbed.

Retracing your steps from the end of the main gallery, turn to the left and then to the right. An empty sarcophagus almost blocks the route. A little farther on is its lid. It seems to have been abandoned before the interment of the sacred bull, suggesting the cult was abruptly ended.

Other Animal Cults at Saqqara

This account of Saqqara has covered only the major points of interest to the layman. There is a search now going on for Imhotep's tomb, which is thought to be to the northeast of the Serapeum and the mastaba of Ti. In this area have been found the Anubieion, sacred to Anubis, with a gallery for dogs; the galleries of the Bubasteion, sacred to Bastet, filled with mummified cats; the Temple of Thoth, its galleries piled with thousands of mummified ibises, baboons and falcons; and the Isieion, the Temple of Isis, with underground galleries containing the sarcophagi of the sacred cows that had given birth to the Apis bulls. It is possible that these stacks of smaller mummified creatures were brought over hundreds of years by pilgrims as offerings to a favoured god, or as supplication by those seeking a cure. It is because of these associations with healing cults that Imhotep's shrine and tomb might be here; he was later worshipped as the god of medicine, the Egyptian equivalent of Asclepios. These cults continued into the Roman period and were only finally suppressed several centuries into our era by the victory of Christianity over paganism, when the fashion changed from dogs, cats, birds and baboons to collecting bits of martyrs' bodies.

Pyramids Farther South: Dahshur and Meidum

Dahshur
open 8–5; adm LE35

The necropolis of **Dahshur** is 6km south of Saqqara. Of its four pyramids, two date from the Middle Kingdom and are so badly ruined they are likely to be of interest only to the specialist. The Bent and Red pyramids are the chief attraction. For a good distant view of them, stand on the southern ramparts of Zoser's funerary complex to see these great pyramids resting upon an endless plain confronting only the cosmos.

The pyramid age began with Zoser, but his was a pyramid that rose in steps. The first attempts at building true pyramids with smoothly sloping sides were made by Snofru, the first pharaoh of the IV Dynasty, while it was his son Cheops who at Giza built the greatest of all Egyptian pyramids. Later generations looked back admiringly on Snofru for the prosperity and power that he brought to Egypt. He was portrayed as a beneficent ruler, good-humoured and pleasure loving, who spent idyllic hours in his royal barge being rowed across the palace lake by beautiful girls. But these were interludes in an exceptionally energetic 24-year reign marked by a far-seeing and vigorous foreign policy, campaigning against the Libyans and Nubians and in Sinai while greatly expanding trade with Lebanon, and the completion of not one but three massive pyramids, the Bent and Red at Dahshur and that at Meidum (for the story behind these, *see* p.180).

The **Red Pyramid**, so named for the colour of its limestone, is the more northerly of Snofru's two pyramids at Dahshur. This was the third, final pyramid built by Snofru and also his largest; it is the second largest pyramid ever built in Egypt, the Great Pyramid of Cheops only slightly exceeding it in volume. But Snofru's earlier ventures in pyramid building led him in this case to play safe, so

Getting to Dahshur and Meidum

Dahshur, 6km south of Saqqara and once a military area and therefore off-limits to foreign tourists, can now be freely visited. To get there you will need to take a taxi or you can make the long walk along the road from Badrashein or Memphis.

If driving to **Meidum**, 90km from Cairo and 55km from Saqqara, follow the road along the west bank of the Nile south towards El Wasta; the pyramid will appear on your right but you drive past it a bit until you come to a paved road signposted for the pyramid in English and Arabic. This heads off into the desert, at first passing south of the pyramid and then coming up to its northwest corner.

---

that the Red Pyramid, rising to a height of 104m at an angle of only 42.5°, looks squat compared to the bold outline of Cheops' Pyramid, which because of its steeper 52° angle rises to a height of 142m.

One and a half kilometres to the south is the aptly-named **Bent Pyramid**, whose sides rise evenly at 52° for part of the way but then bend to the flatter incline of 42.5°, so that instead of an intended height of 129m it is only 105m high. Nevertheless, this peculiarity makes it an impressive sight, as does its cladding of casing stones which has survived largely intact. Snofru seems to have gone on to build the Red Pyramid because he thought the Bent Pyramid was unstable, and indeed its two burial chambers show signs of having suffered some cracking under pressure, which lends some *frisson* to creeping about inside.

There are, uniquely, two entrances, one 33m up on the west face, the other 12m up on the north face, and it is by the latter that you gain access, making a steep descent through a passage 80m long but barely more than a metre high. This eventually reaches a short horizontal corridor amounting to a kind of vestibule with a high corbelled roof from which you climb by means of a ladder into the lower chamber, also corbelled, which is cut into the bedrock. From here a roughly hewn passage with a damaged roof leads to the upper chamber which was more directly reached by a steeply sloping corridor from the west entrance. In the western chamber are cedar beams, evidence of Snofru's trade with Lebanon, which presumably served as buttresses against lateral pressure on the walls which show signs of cracking.

Where Snofru finally chose to be buried is uncertain, though Egyptologists think that in spite of his earlier misgivings about the stability of the Bent Pyramid, it was there that he was laid to rest. Its only certain occupants, however, were an owl, whose dismembered remains were found inside, and five bats whose wrapped skeletons had been placed in a wooden box. Neither the Red nor the Bent pyramids have revealed any sign of a royal burial, except that Snofru's name was found written in red ochre on a block lying beneath the floor of the Bent Pyramid's upper chamber.

Meidum pyramid
can be visited at any time; adm free

Much farther south is the **Meidum pyramid**, or what remains of it. This was the first attempt at a true pyramid (*see* pp.179–80) and the lessons learnt from its monumental failure, if one accepts Mendelssohn's theory, led to the successful completion of those greatest pyramids of all at Giza. For that reason, but also for the spectacle of this abrupt tower on the desert's edge, the Meidum pyramid is as much worth visiting as any.

The Fayyum

'Cool are the dawns; prolific are the trees; diverse are the fruits; little are the rains.' This was how a Syrian emir described the Fayyum in the 13th century, comparing it to the luxuriant gardens which until recently have surrounded Damascus. A growing number of visitors, both foreigners and Cairenes escaping the oppressive heat and congestion of their city, are finding that the Fayyum still retains its charms.

It is a cultivated area occupying the northern part of a much larger depression surrounded by those low mountains you see from the Giza road. Here vegetables, cereals, fruits and flowers grow in remarkable abundance, watered by 2,300km of capillary canals – equivalent to the entire length of the Nile through Egypt.

08

Don't miss

1. Lake shimmering on the edge of the desert
Lake Qarun **p.221**

2. Abandoned Ptolemaic towns
Karanis **p.223** and Dionysias **p.227**

The Fayyum: the Garden of Egypt

The rich soil of the central Fayyum yields such crops as wheat, rice, melons and cauliflowers according to season, and in particular cotton, the main cash crop, which is planted in April and harvested in September. Around the periphery of the oasis where the soil is sandier, tomatoes are a favourite crop, as well as such medicinal and aromatic plants as camomile, mint, fenugreek and sesame. Palms, acacias, tamarisks and eucalyptus trees are loosely distributed across the level placid landscape. Groves of almonds, apricots, oranges, lemons, pomegranates, figs and olives screen the horizon.

The vine and the olive have been cultivated here since ancient times. Classical writers mentioned the deep red roses for which the Fayyum was famous, 'so lavishly strewn at the banquets of Cleopatra' (as Baedeker floridly put it in 1878), though now you will find only a humbler, pallid pink variety growing wild along the roadsides. Geraniums are grown for their essence, used in perfumes.

Lake Qarun, growing saltier with the centuries, is now nearly as saline as sea water and supports a dwindling stock of freshwater fish, notably a tastier version of the Nile bolti, but certain species of marine fish like sole, mullet, eel and shrimp are being introduced.

At places muddy and marshy and not suitable for swimming, the lake appeals to a wide variety of migratory birds, including the pink flamingo, and in winter its pearly surface is blackened by thousands of ducks. As throughout Egypt, egrets are a familiar sight, often roosting en masse and seeming to fill the trees with a sudden display of white blossoms. But the most common bird of the Fayyum is the chicken; under factory conditions five million are produced every year.

An excursion to the Fayyum can be accomplished in a day, starting early in the morning. For a longer stay it is most agreeable to overnight at Lake Qarun, though there is accommodation too at Medinet el Fayyum (106km from Cairo). Staying overnight is in fact the only way you would be able to cover the entire Fayyum as outlined in this chapter.

If you go there by the desert road from Giza, return via the Nile valley route. Note that it can be slow going on the roads within the Fayyum, and that at least 6 hours must be allowed for the excursion by boat and foot from the south shore of the lake to Soknopaiou Nesos on the north shore and back.

Getting to and around the Fayyum

Service taxis and **buses** arrive near the centre of Medinet el Fayyum, capital of Fayyum province. Service taxis and buses for getting round the oasis depart from depots at the eastern side of town, easily reached on foot. **Horse-drawn carriages** can also take you round Medinet el Fayyum.

By Service Taxi and private taxi

Service taxis depart round the clock from Midan el Giza on Sharia al-Ahram (Pyramids Road), which is in Giza, a few blocks west of the Giza Bridge from Roda. The journey will take about an hour and a half. Once in the Fayyum, most conveniently and ubiquitously, service taxis run along fixed routes from village to village. In Medinet el Fayyum and elsewhere, state where you want to go and you will be directed to the appropriate depot and taxi.

Private hire taxis are found in Medinet el Fayyum on the north side of the Bahr Yusef, three bridges west of the Cafeteria el Medina. For a taxi to the lake, ask for *el birka*, though Qarun or el Oburj (Auberge el Fayyum/Auberge du Lac) will also get you there. Taxis are also recommended for visiting Qasr Qarun, Medinet Madi, Omm el Borigat and the Hawara and Lahun pyramids.

By Bus

Fast, air-conditioned buses depart from Midan Ahmed Helmi situated behind Ramses Station in Cairo every half hour from 6.30am to 6pm, taking 2 hours to Medinet el Fayyum. You should book in advance. Avoid Thurs outbound, Fri and Sat back. There are also buses which go from village to village, but they are slow and invariably crowded.

By Car

The easiest, most direct approach to the Fayyum, and also the most striking, is by the desert road from Giza. You drive out of Cairo as though to the Giza Pyramids, but before reaching the Mena House Hotel you turn right onto the desert road for Alexandria. Follow this for 500m and then turn left; you are now on a good fast road all the way to Medinet el Fayyum, capital of Fayyum province. Behind you, to the east, there is a wonderful view of the Pyramids across the untrammelled sand; like a departed shore they sink into the horizon as you commit yourself to the desert. After 76km you approach the edge of the depression at Kom Aushim, the ancient Karanis, on your left. From here there is a fine panorama over the whole of the Fayyum, a surprise of green cultivation and blue lakewater surrounded by rocky hills and expanses of sandy desert. To hire a car, *see* p.88.

Tours

There are numerous one-day tours to the Fayyum, usually stopping at Karanis, the lake, Medinet el Fayyum and the Hawarat and Lahun pyramids. None of these, even if they return by the Nile valley route, stop at the Meidum pyramid, nor do they visit the Ptolemaic sites such as Dionysias and Narmouthis around the periphery of the oasis, or allow time to cross the lake to Soknopaiou Nesos.

Excursions from the Fayyum

Karanis can be reached by the Cairo/Fayyum bus; ask for the Mat'haf ('museum') Kom Aushim. Otherwise service taxis will get you to most the sites in the Fayyum, failing which you will have to hire a regular taxi. For the colossi bases near **Biahmu**, take a service taxi to Biahmu, and from there it is a 10 minute walk north out of the village.

The Hydrology of the Fayyum

★ Lake Qarun

Fayyum comes from the Coptic *phiom*, meaning sea. Yet the present-day lake clinging to the northwest edge of the cultivation is called merely Birket Qarun, literally Qarun Pond. For **Lake Qarun**, at 45m below sea level, is only a vestigial reminder of a once much greater expanse which stood at 40m above sea level. In that prehistoric time the lake was in free communication with the Nile, that is filling when the Nile flooded and then partly emptying itself back into the river when the Nile fell. For whatever reason – perhaps climatic or a change in the level or course of the Nile – by the period of the New Kingdom the lake was only about 2m above sea level and no longer exchanged seasonal waters with the river. Much of the lake now became swamp and marshland, the sort of hunting ground depicted in the Saqqara tombs, rich in wildlife and particularly in crocodiles, which were worshipped here throughout the pharaonic and Graeco-Roman periods.

Not until the Middle Kingdom did human agency really make an impression on the Fayyum, but then with massive effect. Ammenemes I (XII Dyn) widened and deepened the primeval channel between the depression and the Nile at a gap in the mountains near El Lahun. The river rushed through once more and the level of the lake rose to 18m above sea level. An immediate motive might have been to drain marshes along the western embankment of the Nile, but the grander conception was nothing less than to turn the Fayyum into a giant regulating reservoir which would moderate the effect on the Delta of high and low Niles. At flood the river would pour into the Fayyum; at other times the water could be refunded into the Nile to irrigate Lower Egypt. The regulator which Ammenemes I installed at El Lahun has its successor in the same place today.

Though water still enters the Fayyum through the Lahun Gap, it does so today via the canalized Bahr Yusef (River of Joseph) which sinuously parallels the Nile for over 200km from Deirut, nearly opposite Amarna, where it is fed in turn by the 19th-century Ibrahimiya Canal originating near Assiut. It is because of its ultimate dependency on the Nile that the Fayyum is not a true oasis. For 20 days every January the sluices at El Lahun are shut and the Fayyum's entire canal system dries up, 'to let the land rest' and to permit the clearing of waterways and the repair of bridges.

Rise and Fall of the Oasis

Succeeding pharaohs of the XII Dynasty developed an attachment to the Fayyum after Ammenemes I created Me-Wer (the Great Lake). Sesostris I built the pyramid at Lahun; Ammenemes III raised the colossi at Biahmu, and at Hawara he built both a pyramid and the famous Labyrinth.

But it was the Ptolemies, 1,500 years later, who developed the Fayyum as a major agricultural and population centre. The key once again was the level of **Lake Moeris**, as the Greeks called Me-Wer. Still at its Middle Kingdom level, it covered about three-fifths of the present cultivation. The Ptolemies now lowered Moeris to its Old Kingdom level of 2m above sea level, gaining a vast area of fertile land which was maintained by an elaborate irrigation system benefiting from such Greek inventions as Archimedes' screw and the *sakiya*. Ptolemy II named his new province after his sister-wife Arsinoe, and of all the provinces or nomes of Egypt, Strabo extolled the Arsinoite nome as 'the most remarkable of all, both on account of its scenery and its fertility and cultivation'. The settlers – Macedonians, Greeks and Jews – established new towns such as Crocodilopolis, Karanis and Dionysias, and the Fayyum became a centre of Hellenistic culture in Egypt. Later it was one of the early centres of Christianity, its relative isolation securing it against the extremes of persecution. Despite a large influx of Islamicized Bedouin following the Arab invasion, it remained a significant Coptic redoubt into the Middle Ages, with 35 monasteries recorded in the Fayyum in the 13th century.

During the Roman period the variety of the Fayyum was sacrificed to the demand that it supply Rome with corn, and the harsh imperial taxes led to the neglect of the irrigation system. By the 5th century AD Lake Moeris had fallen to 36m below sea level, and the salinity of the water, no longer adequately refreshed by the Nile, increased. The desert crept closer and once flourishing fields and towns were abandoned. The process accelerated under Turkish rule; remote, vulnerable to nomad raids and visited no more than once a year by the cadi, a kind of circuit judge, from Constantinople, the Fayyum's fortunes reached their nadir.

In 1874 a railway link tied the Fayyum once again to the Nile valley (the line has recently been torn up). Around the turn of the 20th century the British built roads and revived the irrigation system, encouraging major land reclamation. Once again the Fayyum is one of the most productive provinces in Egypt, though it has not yet regained the prosperity of Ptolemaic times.

Entering the Oasis

If you have come along the road from Giza, you first come to **Kom Aushim** on the edge of the desert overlooking the oasis. A small **museum** is by the roadside to the left. It is well laid out and contains finds from the Middle Kingdom to the Christian period from throughout the Fayyum.

Museum
open daily 9–4 , closed Mon; small fee

Immediately behind the museum are the extensive remains of **Karanis**, once set amid fields irrigated from the lake. Like other Greek towns of the Fayyum, it was founded in the 3rd century BC and abandoned to the sands late in the 4th or early in the 5th century AD. Once 3,000 people lived here, on or near the shore of Lake Moeris; you can walk along their streets and lanes, between the walls of their mud brick houses, noticing the millstones and granite olive presses often lying within. There are two limestone **temples**, the larger south temple standing on massive foundations

2 Karanis
open daily 9–4, closed Mon; adm LE35

in the middle of the town. It was built in the 1st or early 2nd century AD and dedicated to two crocodile gods, Pnepheros and Petesouchus. On its east face are Greek inscriptions from the time of Nero. There is a good view of the town and the Fayyum from atop the temple, and of the second smaller though otherwise almost identical north temple, dating to the 1st century BC and dedicated to Isis and the crocodile god Suchos.

The long low building between the town ruins and the museum was the **villa of Sir Miles Lampson** (later Lord Killearn), the High Commissioner and then British Ambassador to Egypt 1933–1946.

Continuing south from Kom Aushim on the road to Medinet el Fayyum, a turning off to the right (west) leads to **Lake Qarun** (50km east to west, 10km maximum north to south). The southeast end of the lake is developed for tourism, and it is from the Auberge el Fayyum or the village of Shakshouk that you can hire a boat for **Dimeh el Siba** up a steep 3km track from the north shore. This was the Ptolemaic settlement of Soknopaiou Nesos, Island of Soknopaiou, a local variant of the crocodile god Sobek, but by the time of its founding the level of Lake Moeris had been lowered and the town in fact stood on a promontory. It now stands 65m above the lake; a 400m processional way begins at what was the ancient lakeshore and by steps passes through the city gate and past two ruined pylons to the **Temple of Soknopaios and Isis**. The limestone temple preserves a few reliefs, one of Ptolemy II praying before Amun, and is surrounded by its original high mud brick enclosure wall. There are several well-preserved houses in the vicinity. The settlement was a fortified caravan station; goods would have been transported across Lake Moeris and here final preparations made before the caravans set off across the Western Desert for the more distant oases.

(Dimeh el Siba can also be reached by desert track from the Kom Aushim museum, leading first to Qasr el Sagha (28km), where at the foot of an escarpment there is a small unfinished Middle Kingdom temple built of irregularly shaped blocks, often cut at angles and fitted together like bits of a jigsaw. Nearby are the remains of an ancient quay. Soknopaiou Nesos is then a farther 8km south. Though this route is possible even without four-wheel drive, there is the danger of losing your way or getting stuck in the sand, and a guide is strongly recommended. Arrangements can be made through the museum, preferably the day before.)

Resuming the main road to Medinet el Fayyum, at 4km south of Sennouris near the village of Biahmu is the site where Ammenemes III (XII Dyn) erected two **colossal seated figures** of himself. Herodotus saw these from a distance, rising above the flooded fields, and thought they must have been sitting atop pyramids. Originally they may have stood on either side of a lakeside harbour. Both colossi were still in place in the 13th century when they were seen by an Arab visitor, and part of one was seen as recently as the 17th century by a European traveller. They were apparently hacked down in an ignorant search for treasure. Though 47 pieces are held at the Ashmolean Museum, Oxford (where a nose is on display), here only the bases remain – the statues rose another 12m above these, which would have made them as high as the famous Colossi of Memnon at Thebes, erected 400-odd years later.

A farther 7km south lies Medinet el Fayyum.

Medinet el Fayyum: Hub of the Oasis

Capital and market centre of the Fayyum, **Medinet el Fayyum** is also the point from which all roads radiate and where the waters of the Bahr Yusef are distributed throughout the oasis. The name means simply town of the Fayyum. The population of the entire oasis is about 1.6 million, of which about 350,000 live here. It is the antithesis of the surrounding countryside and is not an attractive place.

Nevertheless there are some points of interest within and near Medinet el Fayyum. As you enter the town on the Cairo road you pass the 13m **obelisk of Sesostris I** (XII Dyn) in the middle of a roundabout. This stood until the 18th century at its original site near the village of Abgig, but at the time of Napoleon's invasion of Egypt it was discovered lying on the ground broken in two. It has only fairly recently been reconstructed and erected here.

At the town centre, by the tourist information kiosk, is the large white Cafeteria el Medina, the obvious place to sit out at a table for something to eat – it all but embraces four **waterwheels** which groan like air-raid sirens during the London Blitz. The Fayyum is famous for its waterwheels, and there are said to be about 200 throughout the oasis. These are the heirs of those Ptolemaic *sakiyas* which brought the Fayyum to such a pitch of abundance. They are driven by the water itself which, because the oasis is higher in the south (26m above sea level) than in the north (45m below sea level), runs swiftly through its capillary canals, unlike the sluggish or stagnant canals of Upper Egypt and the Delta. Sitting in the Cafeteria el Medina, you notice the Bahr Yusef flowing from east to west in front of you; the wheels carry a portion of its flow into the Bahr Tanhala which runs off behind you to the north, while a block to the west there is the Bahr Sennouris, which also flows north. At the far west end of town, the Bahr Yusef divides into six other distributory canals which wend their way throughout the oasis. If you follow the Bahr Sennouris on foot for about half an hour northwards, first on the west bank, then on the east, you will come to the **Seven Waterwheels**, a Fayyum landmark. The first is at a farm, then you see a lovely group of four against a screen of mangoes, palms and willows, and then a final pair by a rustic bridge. It makes a delightful country walk.

Also northwards (20 minutes on foot), and now encroached upon by the town itself, is Kiman Faris, site of the original town, Shedet during the Middle Kingdom, **Crocodilopolis** or Arsinoe under the Ptolemies. This was the chief centre for the worship of the crocodile god Sobek, and in Graeco-Roman times tourists came from all over the Mediterranean to feed the sacred beasts with specially prepared food, a more exciting version of feeding the pigeons in Trafalgar Square. Now there is nothing to see but mounds, the occasional bit of mosaic, a fragment of sculpture, a foundation block poking out. Items of interest turned up by the construction of the Faculty of Engineering are in the Kom Aushim museum. But even before the mounds were built on, the *sebakhin* (those who work the mounds) had made a mess of the site, an interesting example of how Egypt lives upon its past. In a land where wood is a rarity, animal dung has traditionally been used for fuel and so other fertilizers have been sought. One of these has been the debris mounds of ancient towns which yield a kind of earth, called *sebakh*, containing as much as 12 per cent potassium nitrate, sodium carbonate and ammonium chloride.

You will find some remains of Crocodilopolis inside the **mosque of Qaytbey**, which stands on the south bank of the Bahr Yusef by the sixth bridge west of the Cafeteria el Medina. The mosque was in fact built at the end of the 15th century by Qaytbey's favourite concubine Khawand Asal Bey (by whose name it is often known). In 1892 the greater part of it fell into the Bahr Yusef, and so much of it is new. The south entrance with its heavy double wooden doors ornamented with greenish bronze is very fine, the portion below the trefoil arch being original; Asal Bey is mentioned in the inscriptions here, and she gave to the mosque its superb gilded teak minbar. Many of the marble columns within are clearly ancient, and would have been taken from the ruins of Crocodilopolis.

At the fourth bridge west of the Cafeteria el Medina on the south side of the Bahr Yusef is the **souk**, a warren of narrow and occasionally covered streets known as el Qantara. Behind it is el Sagha, the street of gold- and silversmiths, mostly Christians.

Excursions round the Oasis

The Arsinoite was the nome of the crocodile-god Sobek, who under various forms and names was worshipped in every village that could boast a temple of its own. In the Ptolemaic period, even after the extensive land reclamations from Lake Moeris, crocodiles must have still frequented the district in great numbers, and a pond or small lake full of the sacred animals was no doubt a common feature of the local shrines.

B.P. Grenfell, *Fayum Towns and Their Papyri* (1900)

When in late Roman times the irrigation system of the Fayyum began to fail through neglect, a number of Ptolemaic towns around the periphery of the oasis were left abandoned to the advancing sands. Two in particular are worth visiting from Medinet el Fayyum: **Dionysias** (at Qasr Qarun, 36km to the west) and **Narmouthis** (at Medinet Madi, 25km to the southwest). A third, **Tebtynis** (at Omm el Borigat, 26km to the south), can be visited if you have the time or as an alternative to Narmouthis.

Dionysias

Dionysias
adm LE35

Qasr Qarun (**Dionysias**) is at the western extremity of Lake Qarun. From here, caravans would set out for Bahariya Oasis in the Western Desert, and it was to secure this end of the route that a fortress of mud brick was built during Diocletian's reign, its walls now only 1m high, its interior filled with sand. The most noticeable feature of the site, a sandstone **Ptolemaic temple** dedicated to Sobek, is 200m to the southeast. Inside it is a maze of corridors, chambers, tunnels and stairways, including secret chambers within the thickness of the walls where the priests presumably hid themselves and made oracular noises. On either side of the sanctuary, spiral staircases lead to the roof, where there may have been a chapel similar in purpose to that at Dendera where the sun's rays revivified the cult statues, and from where you can enjoy far views over the oasis and the desert. Remains of the town in badly worn mud brick are evident, while here and there the shrivelled branches of small, long-dead trees trained up walls are reminders of a vanished fertility.

A visit to Qasr Qarun necessarily takes you through a hilltop farming village called **Tunis**, now an artists' colony with houses and pottery workshops built in the local style. You can stay here at the Zad Mesafa Guest House, **t** (084) 682 0180, a cheaply priced and pleasant place with simple rooms, a restaurant and a small pool.

Narmouthis

At **Medinet Madi** (Narmouthis) there is a **XII Dynasty temple** dedicated to Sobek and the serpent goddess Renenutet set in a sand-filled hollow. The work of Ammenemes III, it is one of the few surviving examples of Middle Kingdom religious architecture. Approached by a paved processional way lined with lions and sphinxes, the limestone temple consists of a pronaos with two papyrus bud columns and a sanctuary filled with hieroglyphics.

Among the numerous temple reliefs, there is a fine one of Sobek as a man with a crocodile's head on the outside back wall. The Ptolemies extended the temple at its south end. To the southeast of the temple are the mud brick remains of the town, while just to the north of the temple is a raised embankment which runs northwestwards, a natural formation marking the storm beach of Lake Moeris when it was 23m above sea level.

Tebtynis

The tombs of the large necropolis adjoining Tebtynis proved in many instances to contain only crocodiles... One of our workmen, disgusted at finding a row of crocodiles where he expected sarcophagi, broke one of them in pieces and disclosed the surprising fact that the creature was wrapped in sheets of papyrus. As may be imagined, after this we dug out all the crocodile-tombs in the cemetery... The most remarkable characteristic of the Greek papyri from crocodile-mummies is their great size. For enfolding crocodiles 3 or 4m in length small documents were useless, though they were employed as padding, in which case they had often not been unrolled or were hastily crushed together. For the outer layers the papyri used consisted of large unfolded rolls.

B.P. Grenfell, *Fayum Towns and Their Papyri* (1900)

Omm el Borigat (Tebtynis) is similar to Medinet Madi, with an even longer lion- and sphinx-guarded processional way leading up to the **Sobek temple**. A square tank in the courtyard may have been home to the sacred crocodile. The enclosure wall of mud brick is virtually intact, but the temple has been almost entirely destroyed. It was probably Middle Kingdom; the vestibule bears Ptolemaic reliefs, and it seems that the Ptolemies refounded Tebtynis, which then remained inhabited into the Arab period.

The site is best known for the treasure trove of **papyri** found here in 1899–1900 which did so much to throw light on Ptolemaic Egypt. B. P. Grenfell, who excavated here, has described the unusual circumstances of the discovery. Our own times excepted, there is no period or place better documented and understood, right down to the smallest details of everyday life, than Ptolemaic Egypt – thanks very largely to the papyrus-wrapped crocodiles of the Fayyum.

The Road towards the Nile

From Medinet el Fayyum the road southeastwards towards Beni Suef passes along the narrow corridor of cultivation which attaches like a stem the bud of the Fayyum to the Nile. From the village of Hawaret el Maqta (10km) a track runs north (1km) to the dilapidated mud brick **pyramid of Hawara** on the edge of the desert plateau. This was the tomb of Ammenemes III, and to its south are the remains of his once vast mortuary temple, now all but vanished at the hands of stone robbers, which so excited ancient travellers who knew it as the **Labyrinth**.

> *The Labyrinth has 12 covered courts – six in a row facing north, six south ... Inside, the building is of two storeys and contains 3,000 rooms, of which half are underground, and the other half directly above them. I was taken through the rooms in the upper storey, so what I shall say of them is from my own observation, but the underground ones I can speak of only from report, because the Egyptians in charge refused to let me see them, as they contain the tombs of the kings who built the Labyrinth, and also the tombs of the sacred crocodiles. The upper rooms, on the contrary, I did actually see, and it is hard to believe that they are the work of men; the baffling and intricate passages from room to room and from court to court were an endless wonder to me, as we passed from a courtyard into rooms, from rooms into galleries, from galleries into more rooms, and thence into yet more courtyards. The roof of every chamber, courtyard and gallery is, like the walls, of stone. The walls are covered with carved figures, and each court is exquisitely built of white marble and surrounded by a colonnade.*
>
> Herodotus

Herodotus, who saw the Labyrinth for himself in the 5th century BC, said, 'It is beyond my power to describe', and then warmed to the challenge: 'It must have cost more in labour and money than all the walls and public works of the Greeks put together – though no one would deny that the temples of Ephesus and Samos are remarkable buildings. The Pyramids too are astonishing structures, each one of them equal to many of the most ambitious works of Greece; but the Labyrinth surpasses them.'

It was at a desert cemetery near here that Flinders Petrie uncovered the remarkable painted **wax portraits** attached to mummies of the Graeco-Roman period, the best and greatest number now at Cairo's Museum of Egyptian Antiquities. They were painted in life and hung in the home until death when they were sent along with the body to the embalmer to be positioned over the face in the final wrapping. From observation of the mummies, Petrie thought that they were then kept in the house for a generation or two, where they were knocked about a bit and damaged like old furniture, until the descendants lost interest and gave them a perfunctory burial.

A farther 9km on is the small village of **El Lahun**, from the Coptic Lehune, mouth of the canal. It is here that the Bahr Yusef leaves the Nile valley and passes through a gap in the hills encircling the

(i) **Medinet el Fayyum** >
opposite the Cafeteria el Medina and the four waterwheels,
t (084) 634 7298

Lake Qarun:
(near the Auberge du Lac Fayyum),
t (084) 698 0707

(★) **Auberge du Lac Fayyum** >

Tourist Information in Medinet el Fayyum

At the tourist information kiosk you can pick up a simple map and enquire about travel and accommodation.

Where to Stay in and around Medinet el Fayyum

****Auberge du Lac Fayyum, t (084) 698 1200, *www.helnan.com* ($$$$). A former hunting lodge of King Farouk, situated at the southeast corner of Lake Qarun; now a small luxury hotel with swimming pool, tennis courts, health club, water sports, hunting, horseback riding and disco. Its restaurant serves such dishes as wild duck.

***Panorama, t/f (084) 830 757 ($$$$). A very attractive place, also on the lake in nearby Shakshouk el Fayyum. All rooms have bathrooms and air conditioning, and there are water sports facilities.

**Montazah Hotel, Sharia Ismail al-Medany, t (084) 348 662 ($). In the north part of Medinet el Fayyum; cheap, simple but clean. A 15min walk from the centre, near the Bahr Sennouris, but despite its starred category it's rather rundown.

Queen Hotel, Sharia Ata-Allah Hassan, t (084) 346 819, f (084) 346 233 ($). No stars but better; also in the north part

of town near the Bahr Sennouris, with clean spacious rooms, some with air conditioning and fridges. Its restaurant is good, too.

**Honey Day Hotel, Sharia Gamal Abdel Nasser, t (084) 634 1205, f (084) 634 0105 ($). A high-rise hotel near the central bus station; good rooms with air conditioning and TV, also restaurant and bar.

There is a youth hostel ($) at the extreme east end of town, but it is not worth staying there.

Zad Mesafa Guest House, t (084) 682 0180 ($). At Tunis, the artists' colony towards Qasr Qarun (Dionysus). Pleasant place, ecologically aware, with simple rooms, a restaurant and small pool.

Eating Out in Medinet el Fayyum

Cafeteria el Medina, by the water-wheels at the centre of town. An agreeable place.

Queen Hotel restaurant (*see* above) at the north of town is good.

Mokhimar Restaurant, 100m west of the tourist office. Cheaper and good.

Said on the Bahr Sennouris, where it leaves the Bahr Yusef. Still serves the best *kushari*.

Garden behind the Governorate Club, a short walk north along the Bahr Sennouris. Serves Western dishes. *Open till midnight or so.*

Fayyum depression; from the XII Dynasty to the present day there has been a regulator here to control its flow. A road turns north out of the village and in 3km comes to the **Lahun pyramid of Sesostris II** (XII Dyn), its limestone casing blocks long ago stolen and its mud brick core exposed and rotting away.

If you have not already visited the Meidum pyramid (*see* p.217), you can now look out for it towering in the desert to the west if you return to Cairo along the Nile valley road.

The Nile Valley

Lower Egypt is the Delta; Upper Egypt is the valley where the desert and mountains encroach on either side. But throughout Egyptian history the distinction has been as much cultural and political as geographical. In an ancient text the contrast between the two Egypts serves as a metaphor for the bewilderment of an Egyptian exiled to a foreign country: 'It was like a dream, as if a man of the Delta were to see himself in Elephantine, or a man of the northern marshes in Nubia.'

Lower Egypt in the north has been more open to foreign influences, more cosmopolitan; but along the Nile Valley from the south, from Upper Egypt, has come the periodic flood of national regeneration.

09

Don't miss

1. Going to the movies, ancient Egyptian style
Tomb of Kheti, Beni Hasan p.236

2. Capital of heresy
Amarna, the city dedicated to the sun by Akhenaten p.240

3. Noblest church in Egypt
White Monastery at Sohag p.251

Travelling through Time

In terms of pharaonic history, by following the Nile southwards you are – as nearly as geography and chronology in Egypt coincide – travelling from the Old Kingdom into the New. For the traveller flying from Cairo to Luxor, the chronology is simple and abrupt. Less than 60 minutes intervene between the Memphite pyramids and your first glimpse of the sprawling Theban temples below. Along the way there is the amazing and beautiful sight of the long blue ribbon of the Nile snaking through the scorched desert bringing a few kilometres, sometimes only a few metres, of land to life on either side. A life fragile like the delicate green wheat which waves against vast sand plateaux, a life – if you were close enough to know it – heavy with the mass of fellahin whose survival has depended on the constancy of their unending field labours and the varying generosity of the river's annual flood.

The traveller through time is isolated from the moment. From the air, this isolation seems no more than standing back from a charming tapestry to appreciate its overall effect. Travelling overland you are closer and you see the threads and knots; you long to feel for texture. If you are travelling by air-conditioned train, then outside the sealed windows, sealed against the sand, sealed against the heat, sealed against fragrance and life, Egypt passes in a series of *tableaux vivants*.

The pattern of older villages is a vestige of living 10,000 years with annual inundations: they sit on low mounds beyond the reach of a river which for nearly five decades has ceased to rise. Their mud brick houses pack against and on top of one another, a dense metropolis in embryo. At first their roofs are flat like houses of the Delta, but as you run southwards you see the dome and barrel roofs of Upper Egypt which so admirably deflect the heavy fall of heat. Camels, carts, donkeys and women troop along the road, enduring the flame-blue sky. An old man stands up to his knees in an irrigation ditch, washing himself, naked to the passing eyes and years, no longer ithyphallic Min.

These things pass beyond touch, beyond sound. You are an air-conditioned pharaoh riding with the sun, uncontaminated, unliving, kept company through eternity by wall paintings.

But though it is true that the major sites along this valley journey lead you away from the Old Kingdom pyramids to the Middle Kingdom tombs at Beni Hasan and then finally to the New Kingdom temples at Luxor, in fact there are many non-pharaonic interludes along the way. The traveller with more time, and who enjoys getting off the beaten paths of tourism and history, might like to explore some of the eddies en route. Not all are worth visiting; indeed at some there is nothing to see. But they are worth knowing about, to gain a greater appreciation of the many swirls

Getting to the Nile Valley

Distances given between major points are for journeys by rail – shorter than by road or river. A voyage between Cairo and Luxor follows the Nile for 740km; by road the journey covers 730km; while by rail the distance is 676km.

A road bridge is being built across the Nile from Mallawi to Deir el-Bersha on the east bank just north of Amarna. Otherwise there are no bridges across the Nile between El Wasta and Assiut, and so to get to sites such as Beni Hasan and Amarna on the east bank you have to take a boat across. There are regular ferry services at all towns and many villages. On the east bank you will usually have to continue on foot or by donkey or tractor.

Minya and Assiut have decent accommodation; if desperate you could also overnight at Mallawi and Sohag. Most hotels are to be found in the immediate area of the railway station.

By Boat

It is a rare and beautiful experience to sail all the way between Cairo and Aswan, normally a voyage of 11 to 13 days. Shore excursions below Luxor are usually limited to pharaonic and Ptolemaic sites such as Beni Hasan and Amarna (in this chapter) and Dendera and Abydos (in the next chapter); if you want to visit the monasteries, you will probably have to strike out on your own, hiring a taxi when the boat ties up at Minya, Assiut or Sohag (though it is as likely to attach itself to a palm tree in the middle of nowhere for the night).

By Train

The railway keeps to the west bank of the Nile between Cairo and Nag Hammadi (which lies between Abydos and Dendera, *see* p.259) before crossing over to the east bank to continue to Luxor and Aswan. The overnight sleeper or day express between Cairo and Luxor takes about 11 hours. The day train permits you to see the scenery en route and is recommended in at least one direction. But rail travel is also a good way to see the valley in stages, staying overnight, for example, at Minya and Assiut. For greater flexibility, rail journeys can also be combined with stages covered by service taxi or private taxi.

By Road

The main road follows the railway. There are also alternatives: a minor road along the east bank between Assiut and Nag Hammadi, where the gnostic gospels were discovered, and another along the west bank between Nag Hammadi and Edfu with its Temple of Horus, the best preserved and second largest temple in Egypt. The main road is good along the entire length of the valley; you can drive between Cairo and Luxor in as little as 12 hours, but if you want to explore anything along the way, you will have to make one or two overnight stops.

Long-distance service taxis from Cairo to Upper Egypt set out from the Ahmed Helmi depot near Midan Ramses and normally go as far as Assiut, where you must change for destinations south.

Long-distance buses are operated by the Upper Egypt Bus Company, and depart Cairo from Midan Ahmed Helmi near Midan Ramses, and from the al-Azhar station (towards the al-Azhar Mosque between Midan Ataba and Sharia Bur Said).

Service taxis, private taxis and local buses operate throughout the valley. **Service taxis** are particularly recommended as a quick, inexpensive and not uncomfortable way of getting from town to town. At Beni Suef, Minya, Mallawi, Assiut and Sohag (as indeed everywhere else along the valley), the service taxi and bus stations are almost next to or only a short walk from the railway station.

---

and layerings of time in Egypt. There are quite a few Christian sites along the way, and you will notice also many modern churches, for the stretch of valley between Minya and Sohag in particular is a stronghold of the Coptic faith.

Beni Suef to Minya

At the point where the valley is widest, 124km south of Cairo, is **Beni Suef** on the west bank of the Nile. Celebrated for its linen manufacture in the Middle Ages, it continues as a cotton-spinning and carpet-making town, at once crumbling and jerking into new forms as modern factories and housing blocks go up.

Fifteen kilometres west on the east bank of the Bahr Yusef, near the village of Ihnasya el Medina, a huge area of rubble marks **Heracleopolis Magna**, founded early during the Old Kingdom and surviving to Christian times. It achieved importance during the First Intermediate Period when its rulers governed most of northern Egypt. Opposite Beni Suef on the east bank of the Nile, **St Antony** first lived as a hermit before withdrawing deep into the Eastern Desert. Today a road strikes out across the desert to Zafarana on the Red Sea, passing near St Antony's Monastery from where monasticism spread throughout Christendom (*see* p.446).

Oxyrhynchus may have been one reason why St Antony felt he was one Christian too many in the valley. It lies 75km south of Beni Suef and 9km west of Beni Mazar, and is today no more than a mound of rubble atop which the present Muslim village of **Bahnasa** stands. But in the 4th century AD Oxyrhynchus was a hive of Christianity, with 10,000 monks and 20,000 virgins, 'enough to turn the town into a kind of holy city', according to the *Historia Monachorum*, 'where monks congested the streets and seemed to outnumber everyone else and monkish songs were heard in every quarter'. The ancient temples served as monasteries and there were 12 churches; a large Roman theatre has been excavated. Most importantly B.P. Grenfell, who later learnt so much about Ptolemaic Egypt from the sacred crocodile wrappings of Tebtynis in the Fayyum, uncovered here vast quantitites of papyri which included 3rd century AD fragments of the gospels of Matthew

An Egyptian Childhood: Taha Hussein

The river and canals were a world of wonder also for the writer Taha Hussein (1889–1973), born and raised a Muslim in a village between Beni Suef and Minya, as he describes in his autobiographical *An Egyptian Childhood*.

'A world that was inhabited by various strange beings without number, among which were crocodiles which swallowed people in one mouthful, and also enchanted folk who lived under the water all the bright day and during the dark night. Only at dawn and dusk did they come up to the surface for a breath of air, and at that time they were a great danger to children and a seduction to men and women.

And among these strange creatures also were the long and broad fish which would no sooner get hold of a child than they would swallow him up; and in the stomachs of which some children might be fortunate enough to get hold of the signet ring that would bring them to kingship. Now hardly had a man twisted this ring round his finger before two servants of the genie appeared in the twinkling of an eye to carry out his every wish. This was the very ring which Solomon wore and so subjected to his will genies, winds and every natural force he wished.

Now he liked nothing better than to go down to the edge of this canal in the hope that one of these fish would swallow him and so enable him to get possession of this ring in its stomach, for he had great need of it. ... On the other hand he shrank from the terrors he must undergo before he reached this blessed fish.'

and John, poems of Pindar and Sappho, and large portions of plays by Sophocles, Euripides and Menander, as well as summaries of the lost books of Livy. Oxyrhynchus declined during the Mameluke period.

A landmark you cannot fail to notice, whether you are travelling along this stretch of the Nile by rail or road, or best of all by ship, is the almost cliff-like hill of **Gebel el Teir** (Bird Mountain) on the east bank of the river, just south of the west bank town of Samalut (223km from Cairo). On the level summit is the Coptic **Deir el Adra** (monastery of the Virgin), inhabited by monks until the 19th century, its church of the Holy Virgin partly cut into the rock and said to have been founded by St Helena, mother of the Emperor Constantine, in AD 328. The legend has it that the Holy Family were sailing along the Nile when a rock nearly fell upon Mary and was only averted by the quick reaction of the child Jesus. 'This church is hewn out of the mountainside,' wrote a 12th-century Christian chronicler, 'and in the rock is the mark of the palm of the hand of the Lord Christ which was made when He touched the mountain.' Tens of thousands of pilgrims come here for the **Feast of the Assumption** on 22 August, mostly by felucca and from as far as Minya, Assiut and even Cairo. The doorway to the church is decorated in Byzantine style, and there are fine views over the Nile valley.

Minya and Surroundings

Beni Hasan, Hermopolis and Amarna (Akhenaten) with its new site museum all lie near **Minya** (247km from Cairo), a commercial town on the west bank, between the Nile and the Ibrahimiya Canal. Behind high iron railings, overgrown gardens quietly consume the ornate Italian-built villas of Minya's Greek and Egyptian cotton barons. The magnates and pashas have long since gone away, and their decaying villas have been taken over as government offices and army posts, but they lend charm and interest to Minya's shady squares and its winding tree-lined corniche. This together with a good range of hotels makes Minya an agreeable place to break a journey along the middle Nile.

Beni Hasan

On the east bank of the Nile, about 25km south of Minya, is **Beni Hasan**, a Middle Kingdom necropolis of 39 rock tombs belonging mostly to XI and XII Dynasty nomarchs. The excursion from Minya, taking in four of the tombs most worth visiting, will take about

Getting to Sites around Minya

To arrange excursions, book taxis, etc., it is a good idea to first ask at your hotel; they can usually fix something up for you.

West bank sites such as **Hermopolis Magna** and **Tuna el Gebel** are easily reached by service or private taxi to Ashmunein. **Deir el Muharraq** can be reached by service taxi via Mallawi to El Qusiya from where there are occasional minibuses to the monastery; otherwise private taxi direct.

Until the new bridge at Minya is completed, visiting east bank sites involves getting to the appropriate ferry landing. For **Gebel el Tier**, take a taxi north to the ferry crossing, asking for *il markib li Gebel el Tier* ('the boat to...'), which turns out to be no more than a canoe.

For **Beni Hasan**, take a private taxi south to the ferry crossing. Alternatively, take a service taxi (to find the depot turn right out of the Minya railway station and walk 500m south, following the railway tracks, until you reach a flyover coming in from the right) to Abu Qerqaz for a trifling sum, thence a pretty country walk of about 3km (or a ride in a pickup truck) to the ferry. Donkeys can be hired on the other side.

For **Amarna**, one approach is to take a train south from Minya to Mallawi and a taxi, service or private, to the ferry landing. There is also a local train from Mallawi to Deir Mawas from where you can walk (or take a pickup truck) to the ferry. Or you might prefer to set out from Minya, despite the greater distance, in which case you can either take a private taxi for the 1-hour journey, arranging for the driver to wait 3 or 4 hours, or go by service taxi (turn right out of the railway station and walk 500m south, following the railway tracks, until you reach a flyover coming in from the right). You can cross the Nile cheaply by felucca; the motor launch is much more expensive. On the other side you can walk, or hire a donkey or tractor. (With the eventual opening of the new bridge at Minya and the site museum at Amarna, getting there will become easier, organized and less adventurous than it is now.)

half a day, but less if you have come by cruise boat. A path leads up from the Nile to the tombs cut into the cliff.

The tombs are exceptional for their architecturally refined columns, including a fluted style designated by Champollion as 'proto-Doric', but most of all for the excellence of their paintings, done on stucco. Unfortunately, many of the paintings have been either damaged or obscured, though the Department of Antiquities has been cleaning them. Therefore, except for the specialist, only four of the tombs repay visiting – Tombs 17, 15, 3 and 2 (this being the order in which you will encounter them, to your left, after you have ascended to the cliff terrace). In them there is a great deal of satisfying detail: agricultural, craft, hunting and sport scenes are usual, and occasionally military scenes, for the princes of this nome were powerful in their own right.

Tomb 17 of Kheti (XI Dyn)

(1) Tomb of Kheti

Two of the original six **lotus cluster columns** with bud capitals survive and bear their original colouring. The stumps of the other four protrude from the ceiling. The left (north) and rear (east) walls are delightful for their **painted scenes** (*see* right) of small figures caught as though in the frames of a film at various stages of movement. On the rear wall men are wrestling; on the left wall the top register shows men hunting, the second register shows figures baking, and in the two registers below these, women and men dancing. At the rear end of the right (south) wall, Kheti is shown as high priest, wearing a leopard skin; closer to the entrance along the same wall Kheti is receiving offerings; while on the front (west) wall to the immediate right of the entrance he is shown making the final journey to Abydos – the symbolism of which is explained on p.256.

Tomb 15 of Baket (XI Dyn)

Baket was Kheti's father, and like his son was nomarch, that is governor of the nome. The tomb is very similar to 17 in decoration and proportion, but was intended to have only two columns, which are both missing.

Tomb 3 of Khnumhotep (XII Dyn)

Famous for its finely drawn **hunting, fishing and fowling scenes**, this tomb has fairly recently been cleaned and the colours enhanced. The four interior columns are missing, but the antechamber is marked by two proto-Doric **columns**. At the rear (east) wall, on either side of the shrine chamber, are wonderful scenes of Khnumhotep standing on a reed boat in a papyrus swamp, fishing and fowling (left), and harpooning fish in the Nile (right). Note the stars on the ceiling. Apart from being local nomarch, Khnumhotep was also governor of the Eastern Desert; on the left (north) wall he is shown receiving gifts of eye paint from a caravan of Semites, gaudily dressed and with beards and non-Egyptian hairstyles, who have crossed into Egypt with their women, their children and their goats and asses in tow.

Tomb 2 of Amenemhat (XII Dyn)

In plan this is very similar to Tomb 3, and it has three of its interior proto-Doric columns intact, and one nearly so. The antechamber is marked by two octagonal columns. The wall paintings too are similar to those in Tomb 3; there is a good scene here on the left (north) wall, top register, of an **antelope hunt**.

Tomb 17 of Kheti

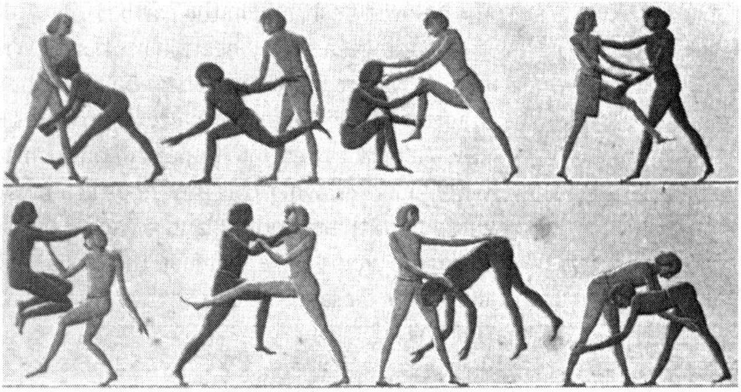

Speos Artemidos and Other Grottoes

On the way down from the necropolis you pass the entrance to a **wadi** on the left. About 500m along its south side is the rock chapel of Pakhet, the lioness goddess, assimilated by the Greeks to Artemis so that the chapel is better known as **Speos Artemidos** (Grotto of Artemis). Inside are scenes of offerings to various deities, but the chief interest of the shrine is the inscription over the entrance in which Hatshepsut (XVIII Dyn) implies that she has rid Egypt of the Hyksos invaders. That she certainly did not only heightens the belief that Hatshepsut wanted to be seen as the restorer of stability and the old ways of the Middle Kingdom in her struggle against Tuthmosis III's imperial ambitions (*see* p.321). As it extends deeper into the forbidding desert landscape, the wadi is cut with numerous other grottoes, once anchorite cells and early Christian tombs.

Antinopolis

Also on the east bank, 10km south of Beni Hasan at the village of **Sheikh Abada**, are the scanty ruins of **Antinopolis**. Antinous, the lover of Hadrian, accompanied the emperor on his journey to Egypt in AD 130. An oracle foretold that Hadrian would suffer a heavy loss, and it was to fulfill this and thereby forestall some greater calamity that Antinous drowned himself in the Nile. 'Everything gave way; everything seemed extinguished. The Olympian Zeus, Master of All, Saviour of the World – all toppled together, and there was only a man with greying hair sobbing on the deck of a boat' (Marguerite Yourcenar, *Memoirs of Hadrian*). The young favourite whose features are known to us from numerous antique sculptures was deified, with temples built and coins struck in his honour. Hadrian, according to Yourcenar, took Antinous, 'once so responsive', to the embalmers, knowing 'to what outrages I was submitting this body; but fire is horrible too, searing and charring the beloved flesh; and in the earth it rots ... All the metaphors took on meaning: I held the heart in my hands. When I left the empty body it was no more than an embalmer's preparation, the first stage of a frightful masterpiece.' Afterwards Hadrian founded this city: 'A check to death to impose upon such a sinister land a city wholly Greek ... where his [Antinous'] cult would be forever mingled with the coming and going on the public square, where his name would be repeated in the casual talk of evening.' Cities, like lovers, die, and the corpse of Antinopolis is not worth visiting. But it is a good story.

West Bank Sites South of Minya

Hermopolis Magna near the village of El Ashmunein on the west bank of the river, lies off a secondary road between Minya and Mallawi. The remains of the Middle and New Kingdom cities here are no more than uncertain mounds of earth and rubble, though a 5th-century Christian **basilica**, built with stones and columns from an earlier Ptolemaic temple, has been restored. It must have been of considerable size, comparable to the churches at Abu Mina and those of the Red and White Monasteries near Sohag, and was probably a cathedral, dedicated to the Virgin.

The surrounding palm grove lends a picturesque effect. An early association with Thoth, whom the Greeks identified with Hermes, accounts for its familiar name. Originally known as Khmun, meaning city of the eight primordial forces, it was said to have been built upon the primal hill from which the sun first rose

ⓘ **Minya >**
north along the Nile corniche towards the Governorate building, **t** *(086) 236 0150*

Train station, **t** *(086) 234 2044*

Tourist Information in Minya

The **Tourist Police**, **t** (086) 236 4527, are on the corniche at the centre of town in the building of the Security Department where they share a building with the regular police, **t** (086) 323 122 or simply **t** 123.

Where to Stay and Eat in Minya

Moderate ($$$)

****Aton**, Corniche el Nil, **t** (086) 234 2993, **f** (086) 234 1517, 1km north of town. Comfortable and friendly, this is the best hotel in Minya, with well-equipped bungalow rooms, many with marvellous Nile views. A pool, a bar and two restaurants – its **Banana Island restaurant** is very good.

Inexpensive ($$)

****King Akhenaton**, **t** (086) 236 5917, *www.kingakhenaton.8m.com*. Centrally located on the Nile corniche between Sharia Gumhuriya (which leads down from the railway station) and the Security Department building; has comfortable rooms with balconies and private bathrooms, some with air conditioning, satellite TV and fridge. It also has international fax and phone lines. A good **restaurant** on the sixth floor with a grand view over the Nile.

Cheap ($)

Dahabiyya, moored along the Minya Corniche, **t** (086) 236 0096. A lovely old houseboat run by a Coptic husband and wife who keep the craft spotlessly clean and serve up delicious meals. Reservations are essential as it has only three twin-bedded cabins.

****Lotus**, 1 Sharia Bur Said, **t** (086) 236 4500, **f** 236 4541, 200m north of the railway station. Has a bar, a top-floor restaurant with views and some air-conditioned rooms.

***Ibn Khaseeb**, 5 Sharia Rageb, **t** (086) 324 535, two blocks from the railway station towards the Nile. Despite its rating, this is a decent place with refurbished rooms of character and a pleasant garden.

****El Shatek**, 31 Sharia el Gumhuriya, **t** (086) 236 2307, **f** (086) 236 3117. On the main street running between the railway station and the corniche, just north of the Security Department building. Most of its rooms have air conditioning and private bathrooms.

The best place to eat is the **Banana Island restaurant** at the Aton Hotel.

above the waters to create the world out of Chaos – though the same claim was made for Medinet Habu and Heliopolis. The primal name, if not the hill or city, has tenaciously survived: from Khmun derived the Coptic Shmun, whence the Arabic Ashmunein.

Tuna el Gebel, 7km west of Ashmunein and beyond the Bahr Yusef, marked the western limits of Akhenaten's new city of Akhetaten. This side of the river was reserved for villages and farms. A boundary stele remains in situ, carved from the top of a cliff, showing the heretic pharaoh, Nefertiti and three of their daughters with upraised arms in adoration of the solar disc.

A necropolis to the south is riddled with underground passages used by the inhabitants of Hermopolis for burying mummified ibises and dog-headed baboons, sacred to Thoth. The most important building here is the Ptolemaic **tomb of Petosiris**, chief priest of Thoth at Hermopolis. It imitates the pronaos of a temple and is entered through a vestibule of four columns with floral capitals painted red, blue and turquoise, though bleached where exposed to the sun. Inside, the reliefs portray traditional Egyptian themes but Petosiris and his family wear Greek clothing. (His coffin is in the Egyptian Museum in Cairo, Room 49, ground floor.)

Amarna

Amarna

The beauty of Old Kingdom art and architecture lay in its restraint, in its simplicity and its confident mastery of form. There was a moment of discovery, of harmonization and integrity, and if the First Intermediate Period had instead marked the termination of pharaonic civilization we might now more eagerly respond to what had been lost.

But the centuries rolled on and too often carried with them only the embalmed culture of the past, integrity reduced to repetition, mastery to facility, the spirit salved with interminable formulae, authority justified and reassured with bombast. Even when using the old forms, there were brilliant exceptions as will be seen here and there farther upriver. But the general impression of tedium weighs heavily on the traveller. The breathtaking impact, then, of the Amarna period is all the more powerful, the sense of something wonderful, tragic and lost all the more acute.

Getting to Amarna (ancient Akhetaten)

Akhetaten is on the east bank, 67km south of Minya, 11km south of Mallawi, which are both on the west bank of the Nile and from either of which you can come by **taxi**, private or shared, and then – until the new bridge is built to the east bank from Minya – **ferry** across the river (*see* p.236). **Cruise boats** usually land you at the village of El Till towards the north end of the site, as do most ferries (though there are smaller ferries to the village of al-Hagg Qandil 3.5km to the south).

The palace and temple area lie between El Till and al-Hagg Qandil and can easily be visited on foot, but to reach the tombs and other outlying sights there are donkeys and tractors to haul you round. Allow at least half a day for the visit.

Akhetaten: Capital of the Heretic Pharaoh Akhenaten

Akhetaten belongs to Aten my father like the mountains, deserts, the fields, the islands, the upper lands and the lower lands, the water, the villages, the men, the animals and all those things to which Aten my father will give life eternally. I shall not neglect the oath which I have made to Aten my father for eternity.

Inscribed on boundary stelae by Akhenaten

The cattle are content in their pasture, the trees and plants are green, the birds fly from their nests.

Akhenaten's 'Hymn to the Sun'

The sensitivity and delight, the reverence and forcefulness conveyed in the painting, reliefs, sculpture and hymns of Akhenaten's reign are probably best appreciated in museums and books, for at his capital city of **Akhetaten**, or Amarna as it is known, very little of these things remain. Nevertheless, its site should be visited – in homage, perhaps; for the interest it does hold; and for its own beauty, spared the incursions of large numbers of tourists.

The ancient name Akhetaten means Horizon (or Resting Place) of the Disc, so that just as Amun dwelt at Thebes, Ptah at Memphis and other gods at their favoured places the pharaoh Akhenaten offered this as home to Aten. The site is incorrectly known as **Tell el Amarna**, a title which conflates the name of a local village, El Till, and the tribal name of the Beni Amran Bedouin who live here. In wrongly supplying Tell for Till it gives the impression that a mound created of centuries of human habitation and debris (tell) identifies the spot. It does not, and that is what makes Amarna archaeologically so interesting. It is all one layer, the largely mud brick remains of a complete royal city begun in the fourth year of Akhenaten's reign, his residence from about his sixth year, and abandoned for all time soon after his death in the 18th year of his reign.

From a strip of palm-spiked fields along the Nile, a plain, 12km from north to south, swells against a crescent ridge of the Arabian plateau. Sand fills the greater part of the arena, the remains of temples, houses and palaces traced upon it in bare outline. It is

Akhenaten's Counter-Revolution

For a moment, Egypt was offered spiritual and philosophical renewal. Akhenaten broke with a past whose search for stasis was leading to sterility. The sun and soul were recovered from their long dark voyage through the underworld and set in brilliant transit across the horizons of this life. Whether it was monotheism is uncertain and probably irrelevant; the universe was alive again. More important is whether Atenism was ever anything more than a royal cult. Akhenaten's hymn, phrased in demotic, suggests his intention was to place his revelation before all mankind. Yet, when he died, his religion was soon suppressed and, what is more, all mention of the heretic pharaoh was proscribed from the king lists and he went unknown until the 19th century of our era. Can it have been just a political reaction? Dynastic infighting led Tuthmosis III to obliterate all images and cartouches of Hatshepsut, but her memory remained. It seems as if Akhenaten offered something far more than a political threat – and more than the military and administrative failures he has been accused of. Possibly Egypt had so far lost its faith in life that it could accept no substitute for its long investment in death. That may explain the empty tombs at Amarna; cold comfort, for all their paeans, to a civilization lost to the hocus-pocus of formulae and solar boats. It is significant that with the coming of the Ramessids, tomb decorations concentrated less on the quality of this life or the next but on the rigmarole of passing from one to the other.

Like Akhenaten himself, those pharaohs who followed him and had shared at some time in their lives in the worship of Aten – Smenkhkere, Tutankhamun and Ay – were proscribed from the king lists at Saqqara and Abydos, and from that of Manetho. Akhetaten was never built on again. Horemheb's reign marked the full force of the reaction and cleared the decks for Seti I's classical renaissance. Something of Amarna art is found, straitjacketed and reduced to mannerism, in the works of Ramses II, especially in the fluid beauty accorded the female form, a touch of Nefertiti's Florentine elegance in those portraits of Nefertari, Ramses' queen, on the tomb walls in the Valley of the Queens at Thebes and inside the Temple of Hathor at Abu Simbel.

Nefertiti stayed on at Amarna after her husband's death. Living in exile at the north end of the plain, she had carved on the walls of her palace the names of Akhenaten and herself. And this **Northern Palace**, the foundations of which you can see 1.5km north of El Till, she called without compromise the House of Aten.

a lonely spot, of melancholy beauty, one of the most attractive in all Egypt.

The Museum

The site museum and visitor centre have been built on land reclaimed from the river beside the landing place for ferries at El Till. The museum combines displays of artefacts from the recent excavations at Amarna with models, photographs, reproductions and information panels, its purpose to acquaint visitors with the character of the site and with the way that modern archaeology can illuminate the past.

The Site

To appreciate the magnificence of the site you must go out to the cliffs and climb up to the tombs. But perhaps the most enjoyable part of the excursion is to wander along the east bank of the Nile between El Till and al-Hagg Qandil, the path leafy and shaded, the air sweet, water buffalo tied to trees, and numerous vine trellises – these last an agreeable continuity, as it has been suggested that

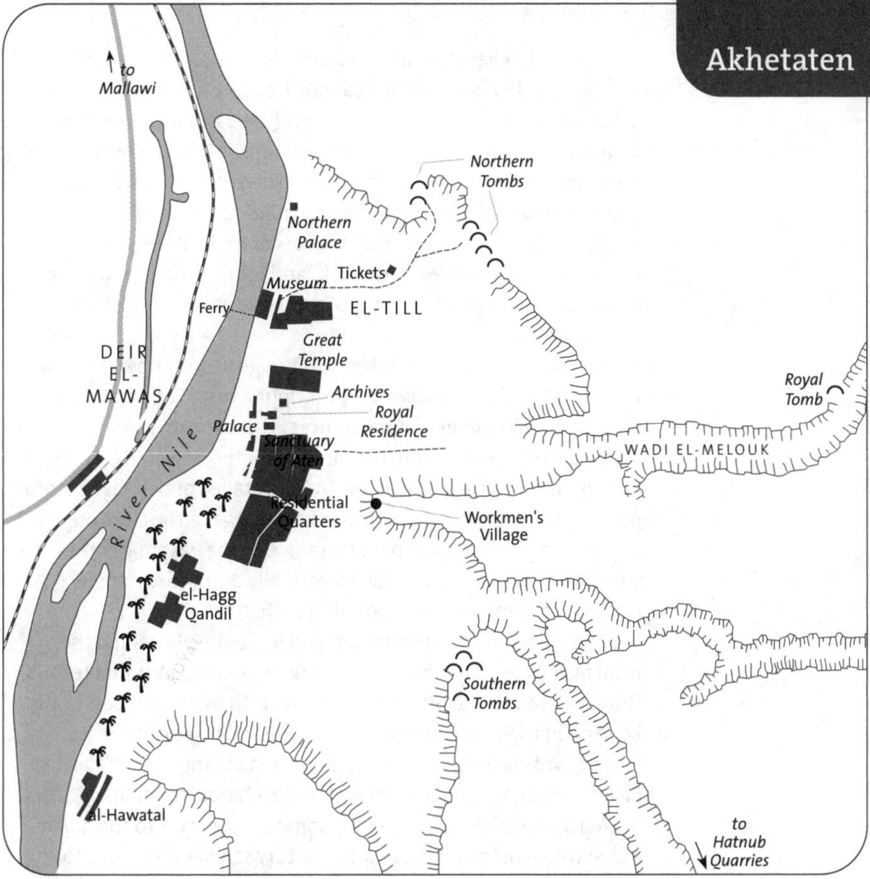

the square pillar bases of mud brick noticeable in the palace area might have supported grape trellises.

From your probable landing place at El Till the ancient **Royal Road** runs southwards through the administrative centre of the city. (If instead you have landed at the village of al-Hagg Qandil 3.5km to the south, you can pick up the Royal Road and walk north along it to the administrative centre.) Folk memory recalls the grandeur of this thoroughfare with the modern name Sikket-es-Sultan, Road of the Sultan. On your left (east) is a Muslim cemetery and traced in part beneath it is a vast rectangle, stretching 800m back towards the ridge, marking the **Great Temple of Aten**. It was deliberately desecrated and destroyed after Akhenaten's death and its foundations later quarried by Ramses II for his temples at Hermopolis Magna. Farther along on your left are the faint outlines of the temple's magazines. Then there are three **excavated rectangles**, again on the left. (Many of these features may be difficult to distinguish owing to a shifting veil of sand and broken stone.) The first was an extension of the royal palace and was the residence of Akhenaten and his queen, Nefertiti. It was divided into a walled garden (northwest quadrant), private apartments (southwest quadrant) and storerooms (the east half). Near the bedroom was found the celebrated picture now in the Ashmolean Museum at Oxford of Akhenaten and Nefertiti seated upon an embroidered cushion, face to face, surrounded by their six daughters. The entire residence was decorated with lively scenes, and the ceilings painted with ducks and other aquatic birds flying in all directions (seen in the Egyptian Museum in Cairo, Room 3, ground floor).

The royal residence was linked by a bridge across the Royal Road to the **main palace complex** on your right (west). Set within the bridge was a **Window of Appearances** where the royal family showed themselves before the public, as often depicted on reliefs and tomb paintings. (Indeed it is to the detailed and realistic tomb paintings at Amarna that so much knowledge of the city's original appearance is owed.) The next rectangle to the east marks the **Sanctuary of Aten** used by the royal family, and the rectangle beyond it the magazines associated with it.

Along a parallel road to the east and immediately behind the royal residence stood the Foreign Office where the **Amarna Letters**, those cuneiform tablets received from north Syrian princes now in Room 3 on the ground floor of the Egyptian Museum, were found in 1887. Writing in Babylonian, the diplomatic language of the day, Egypt's Syrian vassals complained to the pharaoh of military encroachments in their region by some great power to the north – a clue which helped the late 19th-century scholar A.H. Sayce to infer the existence of a previously unsuspected civilization, the Hittites of Anatolia. Sayce was able to identify them, too, as the adversaries who, a hundred years after these Amarna Letters were written, checked the ambitions of Ramses II at Kadesh (*see* the 'Temple of Luxor', pp.271–2, and 'Abu Simbel', p.397).

If you now walk south towards the village of al-Hagg Qandil you pass through the **residential quarters**. Much of this area has been sanded over and little can be discerned; however, here lived such dignitaries as General Ramose, Vizier Nakht (neither are to be confused with their namesakes in the Theban necropolis) and Vizier Panehsi. Also here were the **workshops** of the sculptor Tuthmosis where the exquisite bust of Nefertiti, now in the Berlin Museum, was found. There is a model of an Amarnan house in Room 8 on the ground floor of Cairo's Egyptian Museum. Other quarters, palaces and temples are scattered throughout the plain, their seemingly aimless distribution probably dictated by available well water, but exploration is unlikely to prove meaningful without the company of an archaeologist familiar with the site.

Visiting the Amarna Cliff Tombs

The necropolis at Amarna is in the eastern cliffs. Unlike at Thebes, the tomb decorations do not concern themselves with the afterlife: the Judgement of Osiris, for example, is absent, while instead there are vivid scenes of the everyday.

Many of the tombs were never finished and only a few reveal signs of burial, as if the collapse of the Amarna revolution outpaced mortality. Akhenaten's body has been vainly sought both here and at Thebes; one imagines him disinterred at the restoration of Amun and left to rot like Cromwell. The **royal tomb** lies far back in the wild valley, the Wadi el Melouk, dividing the north and south faces of the cliff. On founding Amarna, Akhenaten proclaimed: 'My tomb will be hollowed in the Eastern Mountain, my burial will be made there in the multitude of jubilees which Aten my Father has ordained for me, and the burial of the Great Royal Wife Nefertiti will take place there in the multitude of years.' Instead, like an ominous cloud on the Amarna horizon, it was their young daughter Makitaten who first died and was entombed here. Akhenaten and Nefertiti, joyful children of the solar disc, are shown on the walls of Makitaten's sarcophagus chamber in sad mourning. The tomb is closed to the public.

The Tombs

There are 25 tombs along the base of the cliff face, 1–6 to the north of the Darb el Malik, 7–25 to the south. Both to see the wall carvings and to avoid tumbling down the shafts leading to the burial chambers, a flashlight should be brought. The tombs are preceded by an open court, as at Thebes, and then usually run through two or three chambers, sometimes with papyrus-bundle columns, ending at a recess in the rear wall where a statue of the deceased (if it remains) stares in surprise at its infrequent visitors. The lyrical 'Hymn to the Sun' composed by Akhenaten is frequently incorporated into the decorations.

The tombs most worth visiting are those of **Huya (1)**, superintendent of the royal harem and steward to the queen mother, Tiy; **Merire (4)**, high priest of Aten; **Panehsi (6)**, servant of Aten with responsibility for his granaries and herds and also vizier of Lower Egypt; **Mahu (9)**, chief of police; and **Ay (25)**, royal confidant, Akhenaten's scribe and successor to Tutankhamun as pharaoh of Egypt. The outstanding tombs are those of Mahu and Ay.

Mahu's Tomb (9)

This is one of the best preserved tombs and is interesting for the detail it gives of Mahu's duties. He was responsible for certain desert frontier posts and is shown receiving a report of a nomadic incursion. Three offenders are brought before Mahu and the vizier for interrogation; the chief of police is true to his timeless type in accusing them of being 'agitated by some foreign power'.

Ay's Tomb (25)

This is the finest in the necropolis. In one scene, Ay and his wife are shown receiving golden collars from Akhenaten and Nefertiti while guards and onlookers outside the palace react to the honour and excitement of it all. There are street scenes, closely observed and marvellously true to life, and peeps of palace intimacy, with a lady of the harem having her hair done, some girls playing the harp and dancing, while others prepare the food and sweep the floor. Also, on the right-hand side of the doorway is the most complete and probably the most correct version of **Akhenaten's 'Hymn to the Sun'**. Here are some excerpts:

At dawn you rise shining in the horizon, you shine as Aten in the sky and drive away darkness by sending forth your rays. The Two Lands awake in festivity, and men stand on their feet, for you have raised them up. They wash their bodies, they take their garments, and their arms are raised to praise your rising. The whole world does its work.

The cattle are content in their pasture, the trees and plants are green, the birds fly from their nests. Their wings are raised in praise of your soul. The goats leap on their feet. All flying and fluttering things live when you shine for them. Likewise the boats race up and down the river, and every way is open, because you have appeared. The fish in the river leap before your face. Your rays go to the depths of the sea.

You set the germ in women and make seed in men. You maintain the son in the womb of the mother and soothe him so that he does not weep, you nurse in the womb. You give the breath of life to all you have created. When the child comes forth from the womb on the day of his birth, you open his mouth and you supply his needs. The chick in the egg can be heard in the shell, for you give him breath inside it so that he may live. You have given him in the egg the power to break it. He comes out of the egg to chirp as loudly as he can; and when he comes out, he walks on his feet.

Like the wall reliefs, the hymn portrays in remarkable detail and variety the cumulative incidents that give wonder to life. Convention, myth and abstraction are dispensed with, replaced by the sensate reality of Aten which creates, embraces and expresses existence.

South of Amarna: The Coptic Nile

From about the 4th century AD until the Arab invasion in the 7th century, Egypt was a Christian country which was then gradually Islamicized. In Upper Egypt the process worked slowest, the Nile valley being distant from the Arab centres of Fustat and Cairo and largely free from the wholesale settlement of Arab tribes, as happened in the Delta. Suffering less from persecution and with the moral and physical support of Christian Nubia south of Aswan, the Copts of Upper Egypt were probably not outnumbered by Muslims until the 14th century. Even today, as a proportion of the local population, Copts are most numerous between Minya and Sohag where they are about double the national average of around 10 per cent. So apart from early Christian sites along the Nile, you will also encounter the living faith.

Deirut is 10km south of Amarna but on the west bank. It is here that the Bahr Yusef, which waters the Fayyum, branches off from the Ibrahimiya Canal. The village of **Bawit** is 3km north of Deirut; 1km west of this village are the ruins of the 5th- or 6th-century **Deir Anba Abulu** (Monastery of St Apollo) in the desert. There is nothing to see among the mounds of debris, but it is worth mentioning that it was from St Apollo that one of the most famous and magnificent paintings of early Christianity was rescued for display in Cairo's Coptic Museum (exhibit 7118, Room 3): Christ enthroned, the four creatures of the Apocalypse in his fiery wings, and supported by the Virgin Mary and the Apostles.

About 20km south of Deirut is **Deir el Muharraq**, a large and functioning Coptic monastery built at what is by tradition the southernmost point of the Holy Family's flight into Egypt (*see* p.249 for details on how to get there). 'But when Herod was dead, behold, an angel of the Lord appeareth in a dream to Joseph in Egypt, saying, Arise, and take the young child and his mother, and go into the land of Israel' (Matthew 2:19–20). A church, **al-Adra** (the Virgin), was built over the cave where the Holy Family supposedly stayed; the altar stone is dated AD 747 but the claim is made that this is the oldest church in Egypt. Next to al-Adra is a three-storey keep, built in the 12th century. **Muharraq** ('Burnt') is unlike other still tenanted Coptic monasteries for being not in the desert but on the edge of the cultivation. It is reached by turning west off the main road at El Qusiya. Annually during the week of 21 June, upwards of 50,000 people attend the Feast of the Consecration of the Church of the Virgin.

Crocodile Grotto

Farther south on the opposite (east) side of the Nile from Manfalut and 5km northeast of the village of El Maabda is the **Crocodile Grotto**, contemptuously dismissed in old Baedekers as 'hardly worth visiting, as practically nothing is to be seen except the charred remains of the mummies of crocodiles.' Not only crocodiles, but human mummies too, as Flaubert, crawling about through the oozing bitumen and cracking bones, discovered. He returned to France with a human foot and kept it in his study as he wrote *Madame Bovary*; one day his servant shined it up with shoe polish. Flaubert's friend, Maxime du Camp, emerged with a head and a pair of hands and feet. He later wrote of his experiences in the quote below.

> *When you are standing on this bed of corpses, precautions cannot be too stringent: a bit of flame falling from a candle could instantly set fire to the dry debris, full of inflammable material, and then flight would be impossible and even useless. About 20 years ago an American visited the grotto with his dragoman and a guide. Some time after he went down, a loud noise was heard, and then black smoke poured from the opening. Neither American nor dragoman nor guide was ever seen again; the fire lasted 18 months and burnt itself out; for several years no one dared venture into the dangerous cave.*
>
> Maxime du Camp, *Flaubert in Egypt*

Assiut

Assiut, 378km from Cairo, with a population exceeding a quarter of a million, is the largest town in Upper Egypt. Its importance, like its name (from the ancient Egyptian Syut), goes back to pharaonic times, though it never achieved political dominance. Its prosperity has been owed to its position in the midst of an extensive and fertile plain on the west bank of the Nile, and to being the terminus of the Darb el Arba'in (Forty Days Road) which came up from Darfur in the Sudan and from the oases of the Libyan Desert. These circumstances filled its markets with produce as well as such craftwork as marquetry and carved ivory – and a supply of slaves which until well into the 19th century made Assiut the largest slave market in Egypt. Nowadays the export of wheat, cotton and soda is the main economic activity, though a busy souk (carpets are the speciality) survives in the old town west of the railway line. The newer districts extend along the tree-lined Nile corniche.

But Assiut is a city bubbling with frustration, important enough to be difficult to leave but lacking the horizons which would make staying worthwhile. Recently it was consumed by sectarian tension

Getting to Assiut

The **railway station** and the **service taxi** and **bus** depots (these last two for the oases of the Western Desert as well as for local and Nile valley destinations) are all in a line along Sharia el Geish which runs several blocks back from, and parallel to, the corniche.

To visit **Deir el Muharraq**, take a private taxi direct; otherwise take a service taxi to El Qusiya from where (unless you walk the final 5km) occasional minibuses run to the monastery.

---

and was a hotbed of fundamentalist violence. The strain has told on the Coptic population, who have visions. In September 2000 many people reported several sightings of the Virgin Mary hovering over the Church of St Mark. Her hands were outstretched, she glowed with light, and she was always seen among fluttering pigeons – though one priest who kept watch said he only saw the pigeons. Otherwise the lack of antique sights means that Assiut can gratefully be overlooked, and this exclusion from one of the most dynamic sectors of the Egyptian economy, i.e. tourism, probably contributes to the city's problems.

A City Ancient and Modern

The **barrage** at Assiut, built in 1898–1902, formed part of the British plan, which included the old dam at Aswan, for controlling the Nile. From here the amount of water entering the Ibrahimiya Canal is regulated for the irrigation of the valley all the way down to Beni Suef. Where Sharia Gumhuriya, the road leading from the railway station to the barrage, is about to cross the canal you will find the **museum** with a small but good collection of local finds. In the **souk** in the old town is the Hammam el Qadim (the old bath), dating from the earliest Muslim period. Cut into the hills, 2km to the west of the city, are a number of Middle Kingdom and Ramessid **tombs**, subsequently inhabited by Christian ascetics, but these are closed. Nevertheless, it is worth climbing up here for the view over the **Muslim cemetery** just below with its hundreds of domed mausolea, while from higher up, beyond a Coptic rock chapel, there is a magnificent panorama encompassing river, canal and desert.

Plotinus (AD 205–270), the great Neo-Platonist, was probably born in Assiut: 'No one could find out for certain because he was reticent about it, saying that the descent of his soul into his body had been a great misfortune, which he did not desire to discuss,' wrote E.M. Forster in *Alexandria: A History and a Guide*.

ⓘ **Assiut >**
t (088) 231 0010

Tourist Information in Assiut

The **Tourist Office** is on the second floor of the Governorate Building, which is north along the corniche just before the point where the the Ibrahimiya Canal joins the Nile. But in fact it has little to offer; you are likely to obtain more information at the better hotels.

Where to Stay and Eat in Assiut

***The Assiutel Hotel**, 146 Sharia el Nil, **t** (088) 231 2121, **f** (088) 231 2122 ($$). The best place to stay in Assiut. It is agreeably situated on the corniche towards the Governorate. Rooms have air conditioning, satellite TV and fridges.

***Hussein**, Sharia Mohammed Farid, **t** (088) 234 2532, **f** (088) 352 599 ($). Right by the bus station, which makes it convenient but also noisy – though by and large it's a comfortable place to stay.

The **Assiutel Hotel** has the best **restaurant** in town and the only one serving alcohol. There are plenty of easy-to-find low-budget restaurants around the railway station.

Sohag: Monasticism in Upper Egypt

A road crosses the Assiut Barrage and continues along the east bank of the river, but the main road and the railway follow the west bank with its broader cultivation and more frequent towns and villages. One of these is **Sohag**, a small agricultural town 470km from Cairo. Some 5km west along a country road to the edge of the desert hills is the **White Monastery** (Deir el Abyad), and another 5km north of that the **Red Monastery** (Deir el Ahmar), two of the most ancient Christian monuments in Egypt.

Though monasticism began early in the 4th century AD when Antony's followers gathered near him in the Red Sea hills, the first monasteries of Lower Egypt, including those in the Eastern and Western Deserts, were informal communities of individual hermits. No vow of obedience was taken, and the monks were free to develop their own way of practising the religious life. But in Upper Egypt monasticism was regulated from the start. **Pachom**, born to pagan parents at Esna in *c.* 292, served in the Roman army during the reign of the emperor Constantine before converting to Christianity. In *c.* 320, in response to a vision, he founded his own monastic community, followed by 11 more throughout Upper Egypt by the time of his death in 346. All were based on his military experience. Under the Pachomian rule, which with various modifications served as the model for monasticism in the West, the needs of the individual were subjugated to the requirements of the community, and the life of each monk was governed by a precise code of discipline. This coenobitic way of life, spiritually and economically self-sufficient, proved immediately popular.

The screw was further tightened by **Shenute** (334–452 *sic*, though some sources place his death a bit earlier), in a sense the true founder of Coptic Christianity. He was a fierce nationalist, and had no time for Greek philosophy or theological niceties; and he was a scourge of paganism, condemning the folk superstitions of the peasantry. As in the old Osiris religion, he emphasized judgement and inevitable punishment for even the smallest sin, rather than

Getting to Sohag

Sohag's **railway station** is on Sharia Mahatta, a block west from, and parallel to, the Nile. The **bus depot** is south along this same street, as is the depot for southbound **service taxis**, while local service taxis gather nearby. For northbound service taxis, walk a couple of blocks north along Sharia Mahattat.

From Sohag it is 53km to Abydos and 144km to Dendera; *see* pp.256 and 259.

---

atonement and redemption, which is manifested in the compact quoted below, made by each monk on joining the community. In 385 he became abbot of the White Monastery (though the monastic church to which that name now attaches was not built until *c.* 440) and instituted a far stricter regime than Pachom's over work, diet and prayer.

On joining the community, a monk made a compact: 'If I transgress that which I have vowed, may I behold the Kingdom of Heaven and not enter in thereto. May God, in whose presence I have made covenant, destroy my soul and my body in Hellfire.' Not that Shenute left God with a monopoly on punishment: when he discovered that a monk had slipped a woman into the monastery, he flogged him to death in a rage. Yet Shenute was regarded as a great reformer. He was working against the abuses, the laxity and the ignorance found among the fellahin, and was determined to build an enduring native Church.

The White Monastery

The White Monastery
adm free

The noblest church of which we have any remains in Egypt, the chief monument of the Christians.
Somers Clarke, *Christian Antiquities*

As you follow the road from Sohag you see a startling sight – at the edge of the cultivation, with its back against the Libyan hills, what seems to be an intact Egyptian temple. **Deir el Abyad** (the White Monastery) is the most remarkable instance of resemblance between Coptic and pharaonic architecture. Massive white limestone walls (hence its name) slope inwards and are finished off with a cavetto cornice of white marble. Two rows of small windows, like loopholes set in the flanks of a fortress, run round all four sides; but these are blocked up, as are five of the six gates, their jambs of red granite. It is through the one open gate on the south side that you enter.

'White Monastery' is a misnomer, for this is a church; the great edifice was only a part of a once vast monastery of 2,000 monks, its remains beneath the adjacent mounds of debris. The church is dedicated to St Shenute, so that Deir Anba Shenouda (monastery of St Shenute) is often heard, particularly locally, instead of Deir el Abyad. There is the medieval sight of tented stalls, a sprawling encampment pitched beneath the walls in the week leading up to the **saint's moulid** on 14 July. Thousands of pilgrims come then from all over Upper Egypt, and the night is filled with drifting laughter, the aroma of cooked foods, the sinuous sound of

Egyptian music, counterpoint to the incense, prayers and chantings inside the church in honour of the severe Shenute.

You enter a long **south hall**, which some authorities have thought housed the cells of the monks, assuming that the church was the monastery. Others say it was a refectory for the eating of the agape, the communal religious meal, literally love feast, of the early Christians. More likely it served as a secondary narthex, for the church was not reserved for the monks alone; Shenute opened it to the general populace on Saturdays and Sundays, and he invited people who could not make the pilgrimage to Jerusalem to look upon the church as a substitute. Along this hall to the right (east), notice that an architrave has made use of a block of stone bearing hieroglyphics.

You then enter the body of the church proper, a **basilica** in which broken columns of marble and granite mark off the aisles from the nave. Deep galleries above the aisles would have been reserved for women. Midway down the line of columns along the north side of the nave are steps which once rose to the ambon from where the scriptures were read. Much of the destruction you see before you can be dated to 1798, when both this church and Deir el Ahmar were fired by Mamelukes fleeing Napoleon's troops, though the timbered roof had already gone at least a century and a half before.

At the west end of the nave is the **narthex**, a baptistry at its southern extremity preceded by a vestibule, while at its northern extremity a chapel for first communion. Lord Curzon described this chapel in the 1840s: 'It is a splendid specimen of the richest Roman architecture of the later empire, and is truly an imperial little room. The arched ceiling is of stone; and there are three beautifully ornamented niches on each side. The upper end is semicircular, and has been entirely covered with a profusion of sculpture in panels, cornices, and every kind of architectural enrichment. When it was entire, and covered with gilding, painting, or mosaic, it must have been most gorgeous' (*Visits to Monasteries in the Levant*). The chapel has suffered greatly since, yet the semicircular recess at the north end with its diagonal patterning of bricks and its circlet of five slender Corinthian columns, bare though it is, remains exquisite. It is a moment to notice how strangely the interior of the church is in classical contrast to its enclosing pharaonic walls.

At the east end of the nave a wall of stuccoed brick, built not long before Curzon's visit, transforms what was the sanctuary into an entire church. Usually in Coptic churches there is one *haikal* (apse) or three in line, but in the oldest (pre-7th century AD) there is sometimes a **trefoil arrangement** as here and at the Red

Monastery, deriving ultimately from the throne chamber of the Byzantine emperors. The paintings in the semidomes, however, are 12th-century. In the south *haikal* Mary and St John flank a large blue cross draped with a red cloth and set within an oval frame; it represents the Resurrection. The central *haikal* has a large Christ Pantocrator. The subject in the semidome of the north *haikal* is impossible to determine; the Dormition of the Virgin has been suggested. On the wall of this *haikal* is a painting of a bearded saint, possibly Shenute himself. Higher up, note the shell niche and the floral and vine frieze, favourite early Christian motifs adopted from pagan Graeco-Roman decoration.

The Red Monastery

The Red Monastery
adm fee

The road north along the boundary between the cultivation and the desert brings you to a small village where patterns of crosses are worked into the otherwise plain brick façades of the huddled houses. Hiding behind these is **Deir el Ahmar**, the Red Monastery, itself built of red brick throughout. The monastery is smaller and in many ways less impressive than the White Monastery, which it closely resembles in plan and fortune. There is the same ruined nave and aisles, the same trefoil arrangement of the *haikals* now screened off by a wall to form a truncated church. You enter midway along the southern perimeter wall into what was probably a long southern hall, though only a suggestion of it remains at the east end. But whereas at Deir el Abyad this feature served as a supplementary narthex, an important difference between the two monasteries is that there is no evidence of a western narthex at Deir el Ahmar at all.

Built by a disciple of Shenute and dedicated to St Bishoi, the Red Monastery is also known as Deir Anba Bishoi. But the **Church of the Virgin**, built in the southwest corner of the enclosure, though ancient, is not part of the original foundation. Within the truncated church at the east end of the enclosure, that is the original sanctuary, the paintings in the semidomes are almost impossible to make out beneath the grime. But whereas at Deir el Abyad the sanctuary has been heavily plastered and whitewashed, here there is a richness of original decorative detail, with finely carved Corinthian columns, elaborate niches set into the semidomes, marble panelling and brick and stone inlay, and architraves and arches painted with curling patterns. It is in poor repair, but there is enough here to show what Curzon meant at Deir el Abyad by 'gorgeous'.

Where to Stay and Eat in Sohag

***Merit Amoun, t** (093) 460 1985, **f** (093) 460 2329 ($$). A good, air-conditioned hotel in Akhmim, opposite Sohag, just over the bridge on the east bank of the Nile and on the right-hand side of the road by the Governorate.

***Al-Safa**, in Sohag itself, on Sharia el Gumhurriya, 150m north of the bridge across to Akhmim, **t** (093) 230 7701, **f** (093) 230 7702 ($$). Large rooms with balconies facing the Nile, air conditioning, satellite TV. A good restaurant with a riverside terrace.

Andalos, t (093) 233 4328, unsigned opposite the railway station ($). If desperate, this is a shabby but clean place to stay; its rooms have air conditioning, fans and fridges.

The **al-Safa Hotel's restaurant** is the best place to eat. There are a few cheap restaurants near the Sohag railway station.

Abydos and Dendera

This chapter continues the southward journey along the Nile Valley, covering the area between Sohag and Luxor. But unless you are actually following this route by road, rail or river, it is best to treat the area as an excursion from Luxor.

The sites of greatest interest here are the temples at Abydos and Dendera. Of the two, the temple at Abydos, built and decorated by Seti I and his son Ramses II, is especially worth visiting for its finely carved and coloured reliefs.

Along this stretch the Nile sweeps to the east, bringing the Valley within convenient reach of the Red Sea.

10

Don't miss

1. **Exquisite New Kingdom reliefs**
   Temple of Seti I at Abydos **p.257**
2. **Primitive roots of Egyptian religion**
   Worship of the cow-goddess Hathor at Dendera **p.261**

Abydos: Shrine of Osiris

Let my name be called out, let it be found inscribed on the tablet which recordeth the names of those who are to receive offerings. Let meals from the sepulchral offerings be given to me in the presence of Osiris, as to those who are in the following of Horus. Let there be prepared for me a seat in the Boat of the Sun on the day whereon the god saileth. Let me be received in the presence of Osiris in the Land of Truth-speaking.

The Book of the Dead

One of the most sacred spots to an ancient Egyptian was the temple at **Abydos**, which is on the west bank of the Nile, 63km south of Sohag and about 200km north of Luxor. As most travellers visit Abydos and Dendera on day-trips from Luxor, these famous temples can seem something like footnotes to a stay there, and historically that is not altogether untrue.

History

The local god of Abydos had been a patron of the dead, and the identification of **Osiris** with him towards the end of the Old Kingdom was both natural and rapid. The crucial role Osiris played in the Egyptian conception of the afterlife soon turned Abydos into a national shrine. Rather like Mecca is to Muslims today, it became the goal of all Egyptians to visit Abydos during their lifetimes or, failing that, between death and burial. Frequently on the tomb walls at the Theban necropolis you see the mummy of some notable making the voyage by river to Abydos. Some were even buried here as Old, Middle and New Kingdom tombs testify. The appeal was to lie for eternity at that very spot where the head of Osiris was buried after Seth had cut him to pieces and scattered his remains (*see* 'Philae', p.379).

It is a measure of Akhenaten's assault on the established religion that not only did Aten supplant Amun but that the Judgement of Osiris did not appear on the tomb walls at Amarna. After Akhenaten and his successors were proscribed and Horemheb restored the old ways, the XVIII Dynasty was replaced by the XIX Dynasty from the northeastern Delta – by the brief reign of Ramses I and by Seti I who now had to consolidate. Ironically, **Seti** bore the name of Osiris' mortal enemy, Seth – his sensitivity on this point is demonstrated at Abydos where his cartouche reads Menmare Osiris-Merneptah rather than Menmare Seti-Merneptah – and both to remove any doubts about his loyalty to the past, and to identify his dynasty with the national god, Seti built a temple of fine limestone at Abydos. But Seti was more than a reactionary; he declared a renaissance, and in art he ignored both Akhenaten's expressionism and the overblown style of the XVIII Dynasty

Getting to Abydos and Dendera

For general information about travel in the valley, *see* the preceding chapter. Luxor is the best base for visiting both Abydos and Dendera. Thomas Cook and other travel agencies in Luxor offer **bus excursions** to both temples, which start early in the morning and cost about LE500 per person. You can also visit the temples either by taking **service taxis** or by **private taxi** (check first at the Tourist Police/Ministry of Tourism office in Luxor what the rate should be). For an early start, make arrangements the evening before.

Otherwise you can travel by **train**, linking with **local service taxis** or **buses**, but as these can be slow and with awkward connections, you will waste much time and most likely will be unable to visit Dendera on the same day. Abydos is 10km from Baliana, which is on the railway line midway between Sohag and Qena. Baliana is also served by buses and service taxis, and from there you can make the final leg of your journey by taking a service taxi or **minibus** out to the temple. Dendera (144km south of Sohag, 64km north of Luxor) is on the west bank of the Nile. It is 4km from the east bank town of Qena, from where you can catch a service taxi or hire a carriage or private taxi for the round trip.

Some of the **boats** cruising between Luxor and Aswan also come downriver to Qena, from where they are taken by coach to the sites.

---

empire. His **bas-reliefs** at Abydos are finely formed and beautifully coloured Old Kingdom revivals – though perhaps a touch effete: it is these one comes to see.

The Abydos Site

Abydos
open daily 7–6 summer, 7–5 winter; adm LE35; there is a simple restaurant

The pylon of Seti's **mortuary temple** has collapsed and the walls of the first and second courts are reduced almost to foundation level. You enter the temple by the central door of seven (the three on either side were sealed by Ramses II) and pass through the first hypostyle hall, completed by Ramses and of inferior work, into the second hypostyle hall which was the last part of the temple decorated before Seti's death. The seven doors are explained by the unusual feature of seven sanctuaries lying beyond, dedicated, from right to left, to Horus, Isis, Osiris, Amun, Re-Herakhte, Ptah (with fine though bleak profiles of the god) and Seti himself. But it is in the second hypostyle hall that you should pause, for this contains the remarkable **reliefs**. Seti appears in distinctive profile, a stylized but close likeness to his mummy (at Cairo's Egyptian Museum).

Temple of Seti I reliefs

Also unusual is the wing built onto the temple to the left of the sanctuaries. The first passageway on the left is known as the **Gallery of the Kings** for its famous list of Seti's predecessors. Though the list is incomplete (in particular, Hatshepsut, Akhenaten, Smenkhkere and Tutankhamun are all missing, for political reasons), the 76 cartouches from Menes onwards have assisted archaeologists in determining the correct order of pharaonic succession. The list is on the right wall, upper two registers; and represented as revering their ancestors are Seti himself and his son, the future Ramses II, with youthful side-lock and holding up two papyrus prayer rolls.

Immediately behind the temple is the **cenotaph of Seti I** or the Osireion. It stands on lower ground and was sunk within an

Abydos: Temple of Seti I

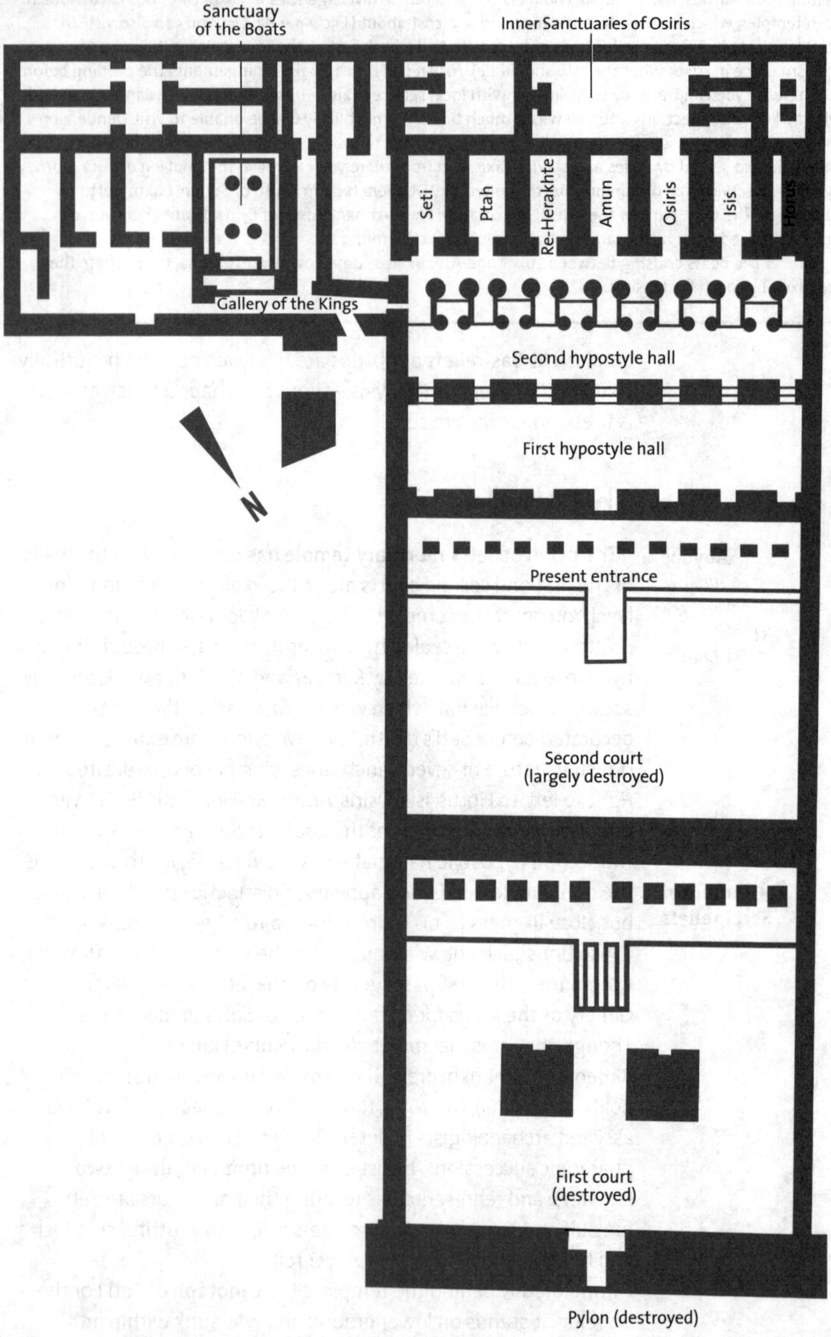
Sanctuary of the Boats
Inner Sanctuaries of Osiris
Seti
Ptah
Re-Herakhte
Amun
Osiris
Isis
Horus
Gallery of the Kings
Second hypostyle hall
First hypostyle hall
N
Present entrance
Second court (largely destroyed)
First court (destroyed)
Pylon (destroyed)

artificial mound, an association, perhaps, with a creation myth (*see* p.182). Funerary texts decorate the interior, and across the ceiling of the fine transverse chamber is a beautiful relief of Nut, goddess of the sky. But the whole place is waterlogged now.

The **temple of Ramses II** is 300m to the right of Seti's but is almost wholly destroyed above foundation level. The fine-grained limestone, architectural details picked out in red and black granite, and the bas-reliefs (Ramses normally employed sunk relief) suggest a standard of execution higher than was to be bothered with later in Ramses' prodigal reign.

Nag Hammadi

At Nag Hammadi (51km from Abydos, 556km from Cairo) on the Nile's west bank, the river sweeps round in a great bend to the east and the main road and the railway both transfer to the opposite bank – the road passing over the Nag Hammadi barrage, the railway carried by a bridge. Ten kilometres along the east bank 150 or so **ancient tombs**, later used by Christian hermits, are cut into the Gebel el Tarif. In one of these in 1945 the now famous Nag Hammadi codices were discovered – gnostic gospels in Coptic dating from the late 4th century but translated from Greek originals of the early 2nd century. One of them, the gospel of Thomas, might even date from AD 50 to 100 and therefore be as early as or even earlier than the gospels of Matthew, Mark, Luke and John.

'Gnosis' is Greek for 'knowledge', in this case the intuitive process of knowing oneself, and thereby knowing human nature and human destiny, and at the deepest level knowing God. In Judeo-Christian teaching the Creator and humanity are separate; in gnosticism the self and the divine are one. The Old and New Testaments discuss evil in terms of sin and repentance; the gnostics said the world was an illusion from which the escape was enlightenment. Jesus did not offer salvation by dying on the cross; he was a spiritual guide. 'If you bring forth what is within you,' said Jesus according to the gospel of Thomas, 'what you bring forth will save you. If you do not bring forth what is within you, what you do not bring forth will destroy you.'

Dendera

Some 19km northeast of Nag Hammadi on the 'east' bank of the Nile (actually on the north side of the river as it here runs east–west) is Faw Qibli; just south of it was Tabennese where Pachom founded the first coenobitic monastery, that is, where there are no private possessions and everything is shared. At **Qena** (612km from

The Worship of Hathor

The primitive roots of Egyptian religion – an animal fetishism that it never quite escaped and at the end, as seen at Saqqara, retreated to – are illustrated in Hathor, the cow goddess, goddess of joy and sexual love and identified by the Greeks with Aphrodite, despite her bovine features. One thinks of the Dinka and other Nilotic tribes of the southern Sudan, whose entire culture is based on cattle. The cow to them is the epitome of beauty; it is tended for its milk and aesthetic satisfaction, never for its meat unless it dies. The Dinka have contempt for agriculture, the nomad's disdain for those tied to the land. Perhaps it was so with the pre-dynastic Egyptians as their grasslands were swallowed by the desert and they were forced to labour for their existence along the Nile – a yearning for a stolen way of life expressed through Hathor, called also the lady of the sky, one of the most ancient and revered of their gods. At any rate, the worship of Hathor at Dendera went back to the earliest times.

Cairo) on the east bank, the Nile again bends sharply, resuming its flow from south to north.

On the west bank, opposite Qena, is **Dendera**. Cheops built, or rather rebuilt, here, as did numerous pharaohs throughout the Old, Middle and New Kingdoms. By Ptolemaic times the ancient cosmology had become much simplified. Deities, concepts and aspects were often assimilated to the dramatis personae of the **Osiris myth**. Through the incestuous working of mythology the fertility goddess Hat-Hor, literally castle of Horus, first suckled the son of Osiris and then lay with him at Edfu in culmination of a great pageant issuing each year from Dendera. As it was important that each pharaoh should trace his ancestry back to Horus (*see* 'Philae', p.378), it was especially necessary that the foreign Ptolemies should stress their links with the Osirid trinity and with the wet-nurse and bed-mate of Horus. The Temple of Hathor at Dendera was part of this Ptolemaic assertion, and the Romans too found it expedient to contribute stones to the story.

Cosmological simplification and single-mindedness of political purpose – and perhaps a Greek concern for harmony – gave unity to Ptolemaic temples in contrast to the sprawling accretions of earlier dynasties. The old motifs in architecture and decorations were retained to gratify the priesthood in exchange for their absorption into the machinery of Alexandrian rule, and perhaps to impress the

A scene from the second Dendera birth house, showing at the centre a figure of the child-god Ihy emerging from a lotus, observed on either side by Bes and Thoeris, both associated with childbirth. From Napoleon's Description de l'Egypte, *1798*

populace – though not to include them, as the abstruseness of Ptolemaic inscriptions makes clear. Non-pharaonic nationalism was shut out, though it intruded in the defacings of later centuries.

The Dendera Site

Dendera
open daily 6–6 summer, 7–5 winter; adm LE35; there is a simple restaurant

The temple **façade** is a pylon in outline, relieved by six Hathor-headed columns rising from a screen. A winged disc hovers at the centre of the huge cavetto cornice, an inscription above it, in Greek, from the reign of Tiberius – the façade and **pronaos** are Roman works. A central doorway admits to the pronaos, a great hypostyle hall, again with Hathoric columns. Its ceiling decorations include the signs of the Egyptian zodiac, the various deities traversing the heavens in their sacred boats amid bursts of stars. The columns bear reliefs of the ankh and sceptre in alternation – life and prosperity. The grooves at the column bases were made by the insistent fingers of the faithful. The divinity reliefs on the columns were once covered with gold, and it is possible that even the floor bore a veneer of gold and silver. The successive chambers become smaller, lower, darker. The second hypostyle hall of six columns is decorated with scenes concerning the temple foundation rites, such as turning the first spadeful of earth and laying the first stone. This was the **Hall of Appearances** where Hathor consorted joyfully with the gods and goddesses of her court before voyaging to Edfu. Beyond this is the temple proper, the sanctuary at its centre surrounded by a corridor lined with chapels. But first you pass through the Hall of Offerings and the Hall of the Ennead.

The **Hall of Offerings** marks the scene of the daily cult ritual in which offerings were laid out before the sanctuary, and from where the divine images were carried in New Year processions up the staircases to the roof to a kiosk where they made contact with the rays of Re – a spiritual emergence from darkness into light. The processions are depicted ascending and descending on both the east and west stairway walls. (See below for a description of the roof.) The **Hall of the Ennead**, immediately before the sanctuary, contained statues of Hathor's nine consorts, these being the primal elements or deities following on the creation (among them air, moisture, earth and sky) as opposed to the pre-creation forces (*see* p.182) – that is, the elements of cosmic order rather than the elements of cosmic disorder.

The **sanctuary** itself would normally be bolted and in complete darkness. It was opened and illuminated by torchlight to permit the pharaoh to adore the goddess, and for her consorts to dine in communion with her. These rituals are depicted on the inner walls: on the right, the top pictorial register shows, from right to left, the pharaoh opening the door after repeating four times 'I am pure'

Dendera: Temple of Hathor

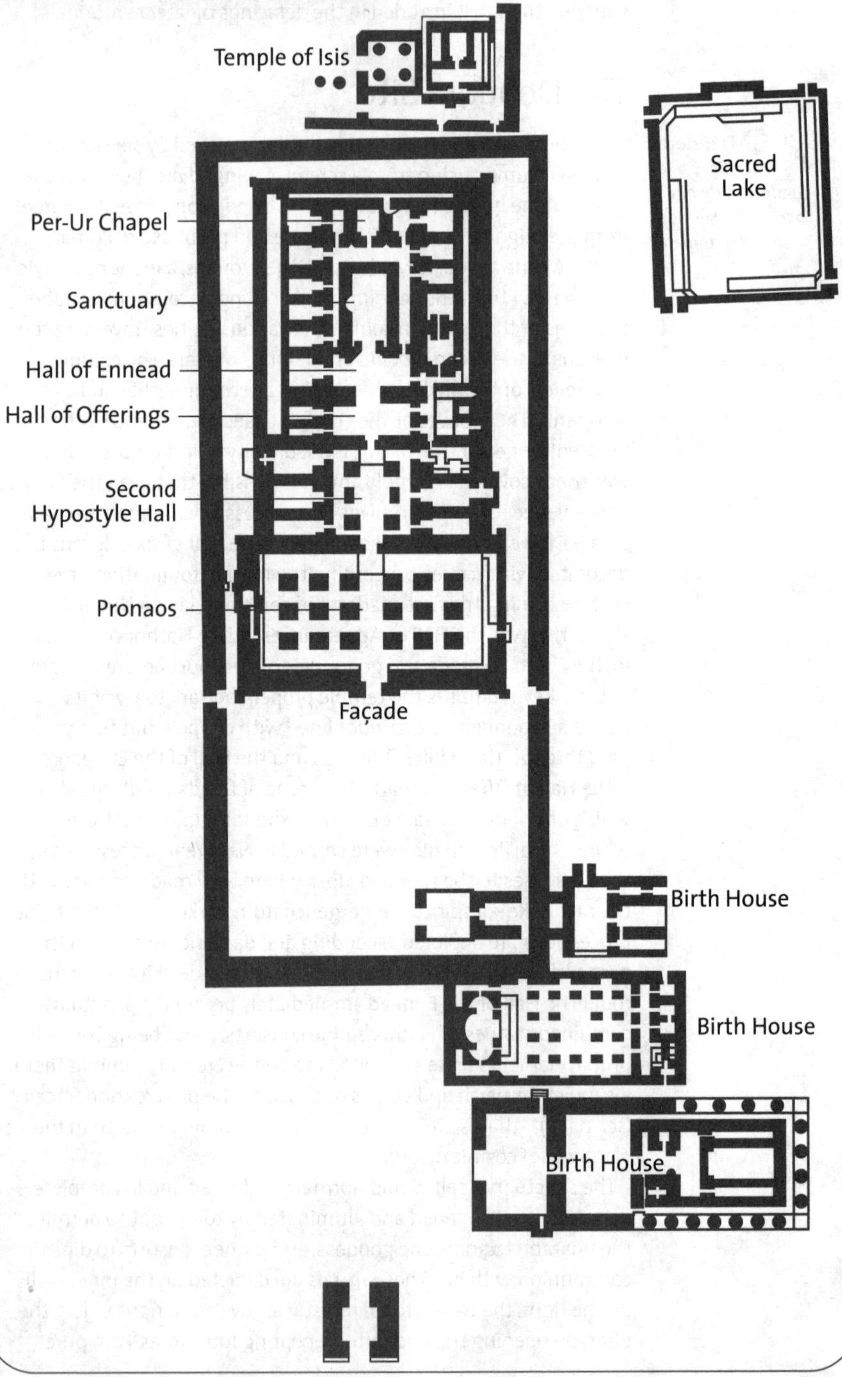

(frames 1 and 2), meeting Hathor (frame 3) and offering libations (frame 4); the same sequence is on the left wall. The surrounding chapels each had their different ritual and ceremonial functions. Most interesting are the three chapels immediately behind the sanctuary: at the centre the Per-Ur, to its left the Per-Nu, and to its right the Per-Neser. The **Per-Ur Chapel** was the starting point for the New Year procession and its decorations include the pharaoh offering the goddess a drink of intoxicating liquor, as Hathor was the goddess of joy. From the **Per-Nu Chapel**, Hathor embarked on her annual voyage to Edfu and congress with Horus. In the **Per-Neser Chapel** the goddess is represented in her terrible aspect, for example as a lioness goddess (by Ptolemaic times Hathor had assimilated the lioness goddess Sekhmet and the cat goddess Bastet, reflecting the terrible and gentle aspects of her nature). In the corridor outside the Per-Nu Chapel you can descend steps to the 32 treasure **crypts** beneath the temple.

To reach the roof you follow the west corridor back to the Hall of Offerings, pausing first about halfway along the length of the sanctuary to look at the **New Year Chapel** where rituals were performed preparatory to Hathor's communion with the sun. On the ceiling is a magnificent relief of Nut the sky goddess giving birth to the sun whose rays illuminate Hathor. The stairway, decorated with reliefs of the New Year processions, ascends to an elegant stone kiosk which was covered by a removable awning where Hathor was exposed to the sun's revivifying force. Also on the roof, but having nothing to do with the worship of Hathor, are the twin **chapels of Osiris** (one above the west stair, the other above the east). First there is an open court, decorated with a procession of priests; then a covered court, on its ceiling a zodiac, unique in Egypt (the original is in the Louvre), as well as two figures of Nut (the vagina of one well-worn by two millennia of fingers), with the boat of the sun shown at the different hours of night; and innermost an entirely enclosed room, representing the tomb of Osiris and decorated with resurrection scenes.

On the outside rear (south) wall of the temple colossal reliefs show **Caesarion**, son of Julius Caesar, with his mother, the great **Cleopatra** and the last of the Ptolemies, behind him, making offerings to a head of Hathor. The carvings are entirely conventional and in no way portraits. It is odd seeing Cleopatra in this anonymous form – for domestic consumption – when she is so much better known, or imagined, in flesh and blood, the centre-page fold-out who bedded the two most powerful Romans of her day. The **birth house** is a particular feature of Ptolemaic temples and served to legitimize the dynasty through its ritual association with the birth of Horus. At Dendera there are three birth houses. The Temple of Isis to the rear (south) of the Hathor temple was built by Augustus and is in ruins; a second monumental birth house, also built by Augustus, with reliefs completed under Trajan and Hadrian, is to the front of the Hathor temple court (a Coptic church built of stones from this birth house is squeezed between them); a third, bisected by the west wall of the court, was begun during the reign of Nectanebos I (XXX Dyn) and completed under the Ptolemies.

Beyond Qena

This part of the river is closest to the Red Sea. From **Qena**, across the Nile from Dendera, a main road runs for 160km through desert and mountain landscapes (beautiful during the second half of the journey) to **Port Safaga** on the Red Sea coast, from where you can head north to **Hurghada**. Flaubert journeyed by camel to **Quseir**, south of Safaga, in four days; on returning to Qena he sank into a bath and then into the arms of a prostitute: 'Dark eyes, much lengthened by antimony; her face held up by velvet chinstraps; sunken mouth, jutting chin, smelling of butter, blue robe'.

But the major starting point for caravans from pharaonic to more modern times was **Qift**, the ancient Coptos, located a little south of Qena (633km from Cairo). Expeditions such as Hatshepsut's (*see* p.325) would have set out for the Red Sea from around here and then continued by ship to the land of Punt; while throughout antiquity and until the Portuguese found their way around Africa, Coptos thrived on trade with Arabia and India. The Eastern Desert was once a busy place, criss-crossed by the Egyptians, and later the Romans, in search of gold, emeralds, granite and porphyry. The Romans turned it into a highway and maintained staging posts a day's march from each other along the way, charging a levy which rose from 5 drachmas for an able seaman or shipyard hand to 108 drachmas for luxury traffic like prostitutes. The Suez Canal, which made transshipment between the Red Sea and Alexandria no longer necessary, dealt the final blow to Qift's fortunes. There is now nothing of interest to detain you, and Luxor is only 43km away.

Some 10km south of Qift on the way to Luxor is **Qus**; opposite it, on the west bank, is the village of **Naqada**, where crosses outnumber crescents; about 75 per cent of the population is Christian. There are several ruined monasteries in the desert beyond it.

Where to Stay and Eat around Qena

Qena as well as **Sohag** (*see* p.254) have accommodation. Both have simple places to eat.

***New Palace Hotel**, Midan Mahattat, Qena, **t** (096) 532 2509. A bright blue edifice across from the railway station behind the Mobil garage. It should be carefully scrutinized first; it is dirt cheap but fairly clean, some rooms with bathroom, though not necessarily with hot water.

There are several other hotels, all sleazy, around the square.

Luxor, Karnak and the Necropolis of Thebes

'Luxor' is loosely applied by travellers to include three distinct places: the town of Luxor, population around 80,000, on the east bank of the Nile 676km south of Cairo; the village (suburb nowadays) of Karnak and its immense temple 4km north on the same bank; and the Theban necropolis on the west bank of the river opposite Luxor and Karnak. This chapter deals with each of these places in turn.

11

Don't miss

1. Temple with a mosque on top
   Temple of Luxor **p.269**
2. Gigantic temple to the great god Amun
   Temple of Karnak **p.279**
3. Enjoy having a temple to yourself
   Temple of Seti I **p.305**
4. Tombs of the great New Kingdom pharaohs
   Valley of the Kings **p.306**
5. Majestic temple of the woman who was pharaoh
   Deir el Bahri **p.320**

See map overleaf

Luxor, Karnak and the Necropolis of Thebes

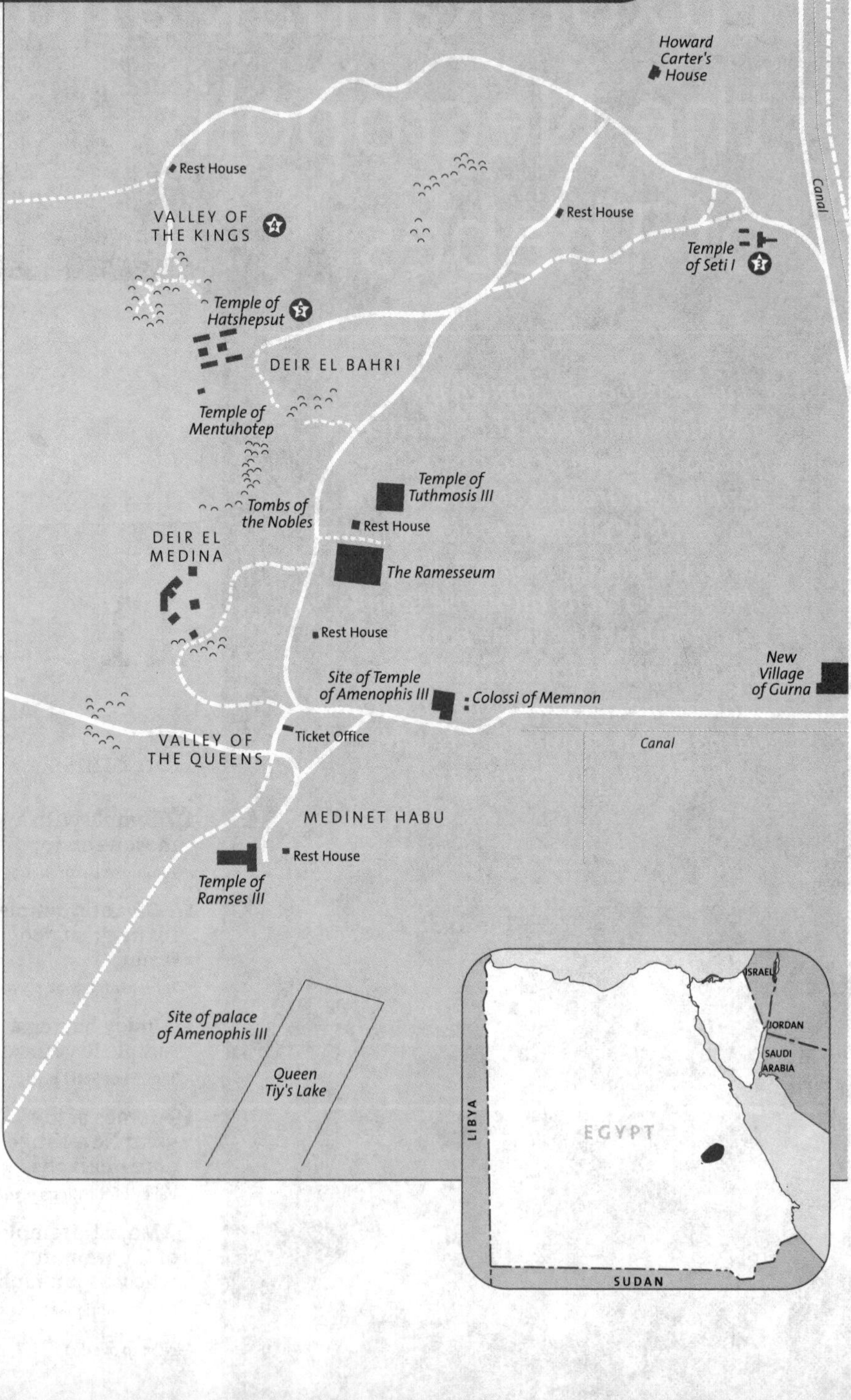
Howard Carter's House
Rest House
Canal
VALLEY OF THE KINGS
4
Rest House
Temple of Seti I
3
Temple of Hatshepsut
5
DEIR EL BAHRI
Temple of Mentuhotep
Temple of Tuthmosis III
Tombs of the Nobles
Rest House
DEIR EL MEDINA
The Ramesseum
Rest House
New Village of Gurna
Site of Temple of Amenophis III
Colossi of Memnon
Ticket Office
Canal
VALLEY OF THE QUEENS
MEDINET HABU
Rest House
Temple of Ramses III
Site of palace of Amenophis III
Queen Tiy's Lake
ISRAEL
JORDAN
SAUDI ARABIA
LIBYA
EGYPT
SUDAN

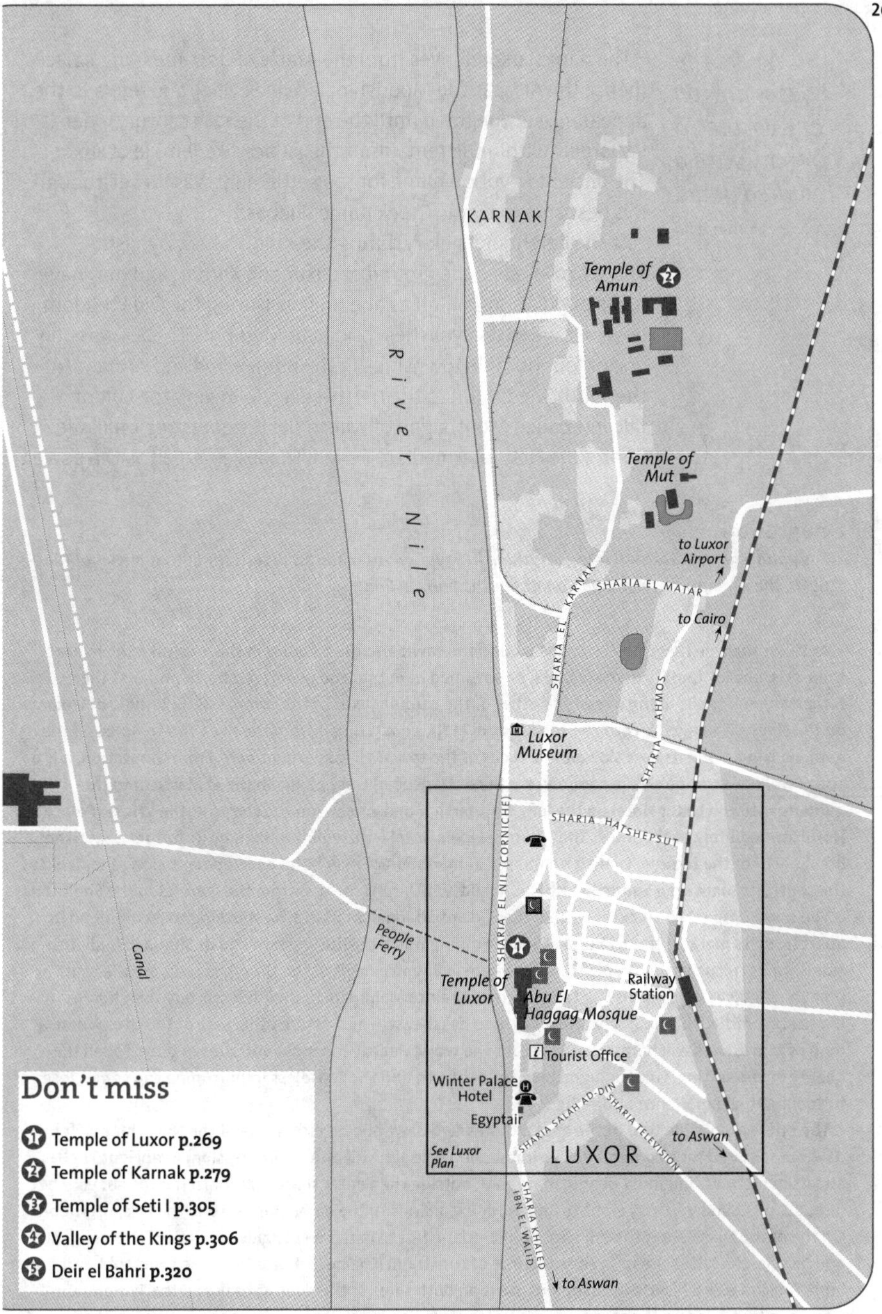
KARNAK
Temple of Amun
River Nile
Temple of Mut
to Luxor Airport
SHARIA EL MATAR
to Cairo
SHARIA EL KARNAK
SHARIA AHMOS
Luxor Museum
SHARIA HATSHEPSUT
SHARIA EL NIL (CORNICHE)
People Ferry
Canal
Temple of Luxor
Abu El Haggag Mosque
Railway Station
Tourist Office
Winter Palace Hotel
Egyptair
SHARIA SALAH AD-DIN
SHARIA TELEVISION
to Aswan
See Luxor Plan
LUXOR
SHARIA KHALED IBN EL WALID
to Aswan
Don't miss
1 Temple of Luxor p.269
2 Temple of Karnak p.279
3 Temple of Seti I p.305
4 Valley of the Kings p.306
5 Deir el Bahri p.320

> *Where the houses are full of treasures, a city with a hundred gates.*
>
> Homer, *Iliad*

The name **Luxor** derives from the Arabic *al-qasr*, meaning palace (hence the Alcazar, the Moorish palace in Seville), and refers to the appearance of the town until the end of the 19th century when it lay largely within the remains of the palace-like Temple of Luxor. The ancient Egyptian name for the settlement was Weset, though it is best known by the Greek name **Thebes**.

At the height of its glory during the XVIII and XIX Dynasties, Thebes covered all the ground of Luxor and Karnak, and may have had a population as high as one million. During the Old Kingdom, however, when its dynasties resided at Memphis, Thebes was only one of four humble townships in the nome – Tod and Armant to the south, Medamud to the north – each following the cult of falcon-headed Mont, a god of war. In the retreat to regional rule during the First Intermediate Period, Thebes emerged as the power

Orientation

The palm – an architectural tree. Everything in Egypt seems made for architecture – the planes of the fields, the vegetation, the human anatomy, the horizon lines.

Gustave Flaubert

At Luxor the Nile flows north-northeast and the town and the temples in the area take the river as their axis, but to simplify matters it will be assumed here that the river flows north and that the temples therefore lie along one or the other of the cardinal axes of the compass. The **Temple of Luxor** is on the Nile, with only the corniche road, **Sharia el Nil**, separating it from the river. The temple and the gardens lying along its east side are the focus of the town. All roads meet here. From the **station**, it is a 500m walk or carriage ride (a common means of transport) west along **Sharia el Mahatta** to the gardens with the **Luxor Hotel** on the left. A bit farther and you are on the corniche, the **Winter Palace Hotel** immediately to the south, the **Mercure Luxor Hotel** (still widely known by its former name, the Etap) north of the temple. There is an unappealing ribbon of new hotel development along the river to the south, its main drag **Sharia Ibn Khaled Walid**, which runs for 3km from the Iberotel to the Sheraton.

The town proper, which extends on either side of Sharia el Mahatta, has nothing to recommend it apart from its market street, **Sharia el Souk**, running north off the western end of Sharia el Mahatta. Nor is the corniche entirely a pleasure: nowhere in Egypt, except at the Giza Pyramids, are the touts as great a plague as here – insisting that you take their carriage, sail in their felucca, buy their home-made mummified ibis or at any rate give them baksheesh – and on the other side of the river where a mob of taxi drivers will harass you to accept the worst deal at the most outrageous price. For all the beauty of the setting, Luxor is a grasping tourist town and the ceaseless importuning can come close to spoiling the experience altogether.

The briefest possible tour of the area requires two days, one on either side of the Nile. Three or four days are required for a comprehensive impression (though still only an impression) of ancient Thebes and its necropolis. You must bear in mind that, outside the winter season, mid-afternoons get very hot (around 40°C) and you may want to limit your excursions to the early morning and the late afternoon. On the **east bank** there is the enjoyment of carriage rides; on the **west bank** the choice is between taxi and bicycle, the latter cheap, breezy and free of constraint, the best choice for those sound of heart and limb. You can **hire a bicycle** in Luxor and use it on both sides of the river. **Karnak** and the **Temple of Luxor** can be visited on the same day, the latter best seen in the late afternoon as it glows in the rays of the sinking sun, or at night when it is unsparingly and intelligently floodlit. Rising as early as possible, the whole of the second day should be devoted to the **west bank**, and the third day too, if you have the time. A fourth day will not only allow you to revisit Karnak, and perhaps one or two temples or tomb clusters on the necropolis side, but will also give you greater leisure to **shop** in Luxor and visit its excellent **museum**.

binding Upper Egypt together. After a struggle it reunited the country under its administrative and religious authority, inaugurating the Middle Kingdom. Thebes repeated the pattern when, following the disintegration during the Second Intermediate Period and the Hyksos invasion of Lower Egypt, it liberated the country and now also became the permanent residence of the pharaohs throughout the New Kingdom.

It is tempting to believe that apart from its prowess in war and its strategic position between the Delta and the cataracts, Thebes achieved ascendancy over the townships of its nome and eventually over all Egypt because of the special beauty of its situation. Certainly the great pharaohs of the New Kingdom responded, sometimes sensitively, sometimes grandiosely, to the architectural possibilities of the landscape, which is placid and horizontal, a broad plain on either side of the river cultivated mainly with sugar cane and maize. The desert to the east rises gently to the Arabian plateau, while to the west a low range of hills, the Theban Mountain, interpose themselves between the cultivation and the Libyan Desert. The Nile is majestic, at sundown an implacable lava flow. By day, feluccas seem to stride upon its surface like pond insects, and distant palms rise from the level stillness, distinct and exactly outlined in the clear air and brilliant light. For the ancient Egyptians, the richness and never-failing fertility of this landscape was a source of wonder. As capital of the New Kingdom it was the focus of an architectural activity so grand, and still so well preserved, that it can lay just claim to being the world's greatest outdoor museum.

The East Bank: Luxor and Karnak

The Temple of Luxor

Temple of Luxor
open daily 6am–9pm winter, 6am–10pm summer; adm LE50

Close to the more central hotels and to the landing stages for the Nile cruise boats, a visit to the Temple of Luxor can be casually arranged following a more rigorously organized morning. It is especially worth seeing in the evening when it is floodlit.

The temple is appealing: it is well preserved, its unity clearly stated, yet there is the intriguing irregularity of its plan. It was built largely under **Amenophis III** (XVIII Dyn) on the site of an older sanctuary. He also built the Third Pylon at Karnak and began the Hypostyle Hall there, and erected an enormous mortuary temple on the west bank of which only the colossi of Memnon remain: he was the first pharaoh of the New Kingdom to go in for the gigantism that broadcasts the imperial pretensions of the period. He would have been delighted with the reaction of the French

Getting to Luxor

By Air

Luxor airport, **t** (095) 237 4655, which lies 6km northeast of town, is small and user-friendly. The terminal has been designed to look like a temple pylon. The Egyptair office is in the arcade by the Old Winter Palace, **t** 0900 70000. The agents for British Airways are Eastmar, immediately south of the Old Winter Palace.

By Rail

The railway station is at the east end of Sharia Mahatta, 500m from the Temple of Luxor and the corniche. Trains link Luxor with Cairo to the north and Aswan to the south.

By Bus

The new bus station is 5km out of town, about 1km before the airport. Buses depart from here for Nile valley and Red Sea destinations. But the Upper Egyptian Bus Company has a ticket office immediately south of the railway station in Midan Mahatta, the square outside the railway station. Minibuses and taxis go from there to the bus station.

By Service Taxi

A good method of covering the distance between Luxor and Aswan, with the possibility of sightseeing along the way, is to take service taxis. The depot is beside the bus station, 5km east of town. You can go from Luxor to Esna, Esna to Edfu, Edfu to Kom Ombo and Kom Ombo to Aswan, paying leg by leg.

army in 1799: while in pursuit of the Mameluke Muradbey it rounded a bend in the Nile and came suddenly upon the temples of Karnak and Luxor. 'Without an order being given,' a lieutenant wrote, 'the men formed their ranks and presented arms, to the accompaniment of the drums and bands.'

Since 1885 when excavations began, the temple has been gradually cleared of the village once within it, the rubble blocking the pylon entrance, and the *kom* to the north which has revealed the **forecourt** and **avenue of sphinxes** leading to Karnak. It was from Karnak that Amun came during the annual Opet festival, but by water, amid a floating procession of great splendour to this harem of the South with his wife Mut and their son the moon god Khonsu. The forecourt wall is the work of Nectanebos I (XXX Dyn), as are the sphinxes which are set at a lower level to the excavated remains of post-pharaonic houses on either side. In the northwest corner of the forecourt is the restored **Serapeum** dedicated by the Emperor Hadrian on 24 January AD 126, his birthday.

Ramses II's Additions to the Temple

The Pylon and Obelisks

The obelisk that is now in Paris was against the right-hand pylon. Perched on its pedestal, how bored it must be in the Place de la Concorde! How it must miss its Nile! What does it think as it watches all the cabs drive by, instead of the chariots it saw at its feet in the old days?

Gustave Flaubert

Getting around Luxor

By Carriage

The most pleasant way to get about Luxor, and to Karnak, is by carriage (*calèche*). By law the rates must be posted on the sides of the carriages, although drivers will make attempts to hide them. Check at the tourist office if necessary. But this is only to arm you, for in the end it will all come down to bargaining. You are likely to wind up paying LE50 to LE60 an hour, about half that for a one-way trip to Karnak, and something more than that to have the carriage wait for you at Karnak and bring you back to Luxor.

By Bicycle

Bicycles can be hired for about LE15 per day from numerous places along Sharia el Mahatta, the street running between the railway station and Luxor Temple. These tend to be single-speed only. For something better, rent a bike from the Hilton, Sheraton, Mercure or other top hotel, which will cost LE20 per day. In all cases go for a brief test ride first to make sure the machine is in working order. Bicycles come into their own on the west bank and may be taken on board the people ferry.

On the 'People Ferry'

Though a bridge now spans the Nile 7km south of Luxor, the quickest and certainly the most agreeable way to reach the west bank is by the municipal ferry, or what the locals call the 'people ferry', which departs from a jetty near the entrance to the Temple of Luxor. The fare is LE1; you pay going over, and there's no charge for the return. The people ferry will also carry bicycles across the river.

In addition, there are small motor launches to be found moored all along the corniche. These are aimed at tourists in a hurry, and charge LE5 to LE10 a head.

In a Hot-air Balloon

Balloon flights over Luxor, Karnak and the Valley of the Kings are breathtaking. Most lift off in the early morning, with pick-up at 5am. Beware, though, that due to changing winds there is always a chance of cancellation. Operators come and go and charge anything from $80 to $150 per person; bookings can be made through travel agents or by contacting the operators themselves.

Sindbad Balloons, t (095) 227 29 60, *www.sindbadballoons.com*.

Hod-Hod Soliman, Sharia Television, **t** (095) 237 0116. The longest-running ballooning company in Luxor.

In a Felucca

A very pleasant time can be had by sailing about the Nile in a felucca. Bargain with any of the boatmen along the river (get advice on rates first by checking with the Tourist Office). You can sail all the way up the Nile to Aswan, although you will probably be able to get a better price coming downstream (*see* p.360).

Tours and Cruises

Jolley's, Eastmar, Misr Travel, American Express and Thomas Cook all offer tours, though these are geared mostly to groups. You can often join a group tour by going to one of these agents the evening before and asking if there is space.

For a Luxor–Aswan cruise you should already have made arrangements in Cairo or from abroad, though the tour operators named above might be able to help you out. Agents also offer a day-cruise tour to Abydos and Dendera.

Now turn south to look at the **pylon**: this and the court behind it were additions by Ramses II (XIX Dyn), the pylon a gigantic billboard advertising Ramses' dubious victory over the Hittites at Kadesh in Syria. The west (right) tower shows the Egyptian camp within a circle of shields and Ramses on his throne holding a council of war while beneath him two spies are being interrogated by beating. In the right light, or by floodlight, you can see that Ramses has been reversed on his throne, now facing east where he once faced west. (The floodlighting also attracts bats which enjoy

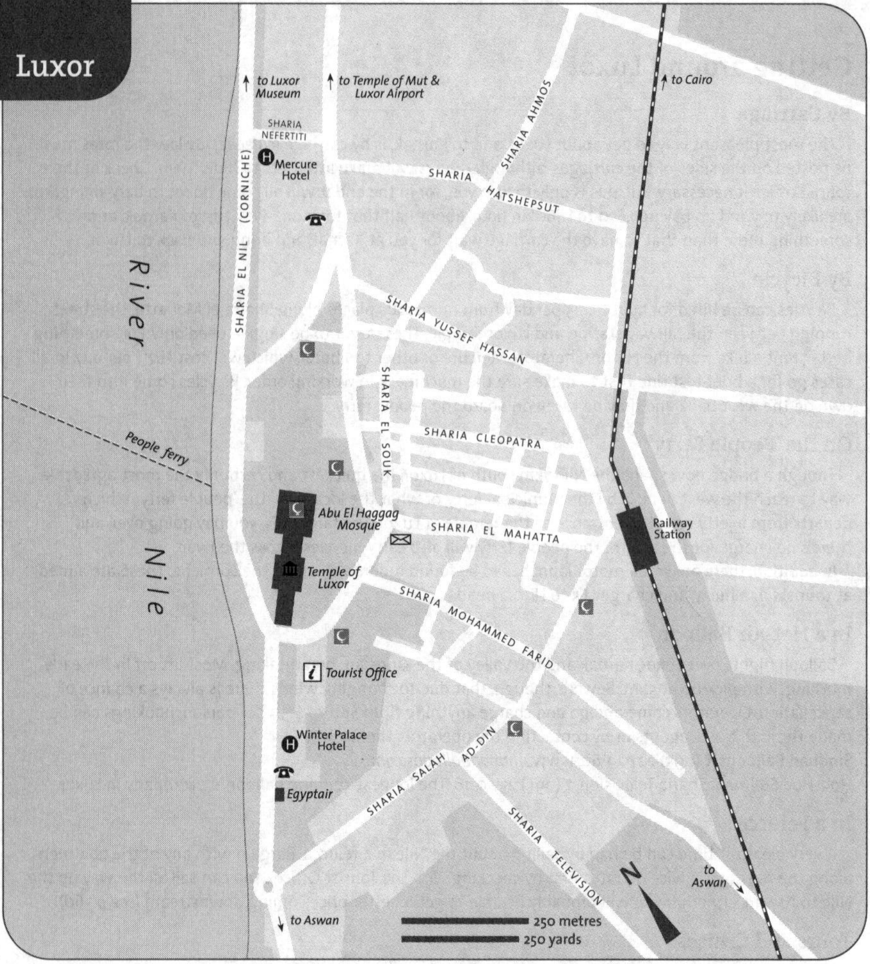

fluttering to rest upside-down within the deeper incisions of the drama.) The east (left) tower shows Kadesh on the left, surrounded by the waters of the Orontes, while to the right an heroically proportioned Ramses in his chariot is pursuing the broken enemy. In vertical lines below these scenes on both towers is the poem of Pentaur (*see* 'Abu Simbel', p.397, for partial translation), comparison of which with Hittite sources, and also taking into account the contemporary situation, including the superior iron weaponry of the Hittites to the Egyptian bronze, suggests that the battle was less glorious for the Egyptians than Ramses made out.

The vertical grooves along the pylon façade were for supporting flagstaffs, the apertures above to receive the braces securing the staffs and to admit light and air to the interior. Except at the corners above the entrance passage, the cavetto cornices are missing. Originally the pylon stood 24m high; its width is 65m.

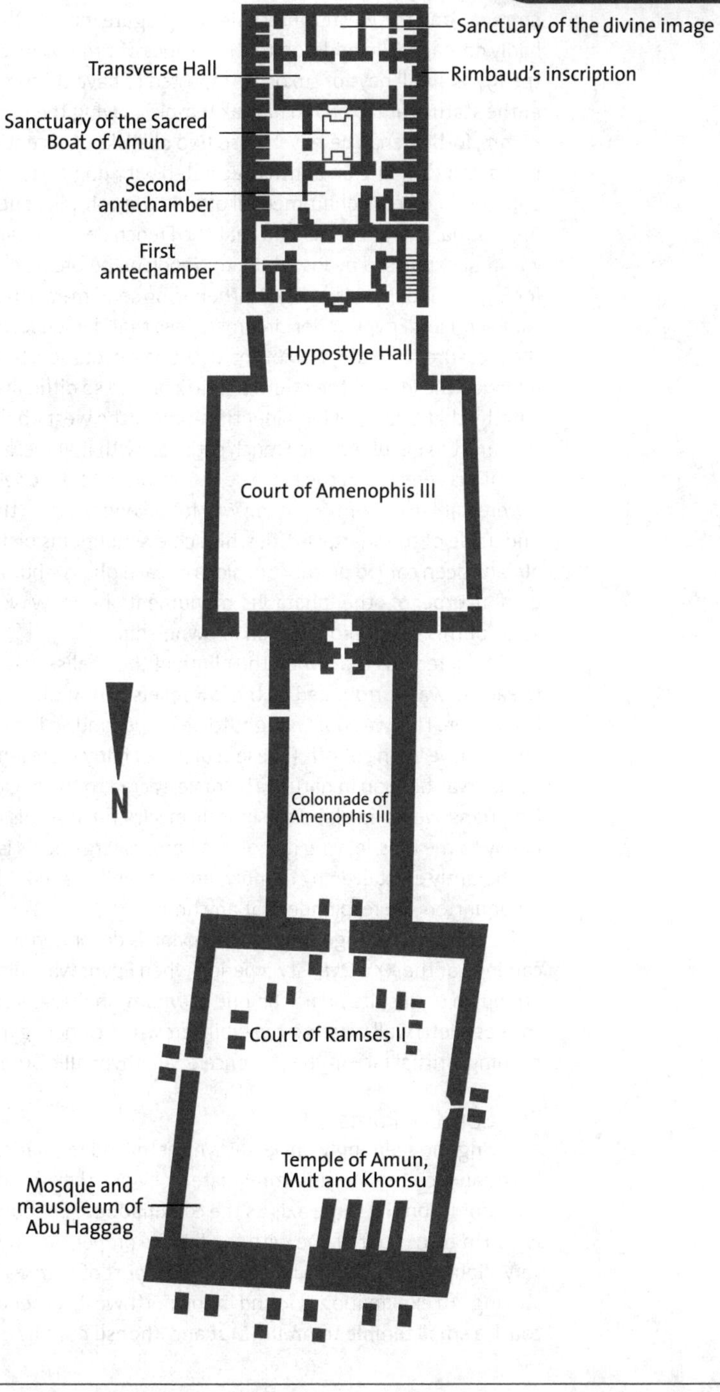
Sanctuary of the divine image
Transverse Hall
Rimbaud's inscription
Sanctuary of the Sacred Boat of Amun
Second antechamber
First antechamber
Hypostyle Hall
Court of Amenophis III
N
Colonnade of Amenophis III
Court of Ramses II
Temple of Amun, Mut and Khonsu
Mosque and mausoleum of Abu Haggag

In front of the pylon were six **statues** of Ramses, two sitting, four standing. Only the two seated figures on either side of the entrance and the westernmost standing figure remain; they are all badly damaged. (In addition to the ravages of time, as recently as the 1970s small boys of Luxor are reported to have thrown stones at the statues at Luxor and Karnak temples, saying their images are *haram*, forbidden.) There were also two **obelisks** of exceptionally fine detail standing on plinths decorated with dog-headed baboons in relief. Mohammed Ali offered the pair, plus one at Alexandria, to France. It is said that the French desire for an obelisk was first expressed by Josephine to Napoleon before he embarked for Egypt: 'Goodbye! If you go to Thebes, do send me a little obelisk.' Napoleon left Egypt under circumstances that denied Josephine the pleasure. In celebration of the Bourbon restoration, Louis XVIII renewed the idea. In the event, the task proved so difficult and lengthy that Champollion's identification of the west obelisk as the finest in Egypt left the French satisfied with it alone, and in 1836 it was erected in the Place de la Concorde. As the obelisk was lowered at Luxor, Ramses' name was found engraved on the underside of the shaft; his titles, his achievements, his piety had already been carved on the four sides of each obelisk, but being a great usurper of other pharaohs' monuments, he knew well the value of this secret protestation of ownership.

Cocteau records that when the plinth of the obelisk was removed to Paris it 'was surrounded by the low reliefs of dog-faced baboons in erection. This was not thought to be proper and so the monkeys' organs have been cut off'. (These sculptures fairly represent the hamadryas baboon in nature. The male, sacred to the ancient Egyptians, wears an elaborate mantle of silky fur; but this reaches barely to the hips, leaving its bottom bare. Its large penis is driven exuberantly erect even by friendly interest, while its red hindquarters are resplendent at any time.)

The **entrance passage** through the pylon is decorated with carvings of the XXV Dynasty, a period when Egypt was ruled by Ethiopian or Cushite pharaohs, one of whom, Shabaka, is shown on the east (left) wall wearing the white crown of Upper Egypt, running a ritual race in the presence of an ithyphallic Amun-Re.

The Court of Ramses II

Belying the seemingly universal symmetry and regularity of Egyptian architecture, it is immediately obvious that this court does not lie on the same axis as the colonnade of Amenophis III, which in turn is out of line with the temple proper, but these are very slight divergencies, while that of the court of Ramses II is striking. An explanation is found in the northwest corner of the court, a small **temple to Amun, Mut and Khonsu** built by

Tuthmosis III and Hatshepsut 100 years before Amenophis, 200 years before Ramses. The granite columns are original, while the carvings were redone by Ramses II who integrated the temple into his court, aligning his court to suit.

Sitting above the northeast corner of the court, surviving the clearance of the old village within the temple, is the **mosque and mausoleum of Abu el Haggag**, a Sufi sheikh born in Baghdad, who spent the last 50 years of his life at Luxor, dying here in his nineties in 1243. The mosque, however, is only 19th century, though the north minaret is 11th century.

Ramses' court is entirely surrounded by a double colonnade of bud-capital papyrus columns, while the interior walls are adorned with reliefs. Especially interesting is the representation of the pylon façade at the west end of the south wall, complete with colossi, obelisks and fluttering banners. Approaching this, along the west wall, is a procession led by 17 of Ramses' sons (he fathered over 100 in his 90-odd years) and followed by priests and sacrificial oxen. The unnaturally long hooves indicate the oxen have been fattened in their stalls for the occasion, while the model of an African's head between the horns of the fifth ox and the Asiatic head with long pointed beard between the horns of the sixth symbolizes the Egyptian triumph over Africa and Asia. The southern half of the court is further embellished with striding colossi of Ramses, and in an unexpected touch the slender figure of his beloved wife Nefertari between his legs, while the triumph motif is repeated round the bases of the black granite seated colossi on either side of the southern doorway: the shields and bound figures of vanquished Asiatics on the east base, of Africans on the west.

Amenophis III's Temple

The Colonnade and Court

Passing between these last two guardians of Ramses' memory, you enter the imposing colonnade of Amenophis III. The 15.8m-high papyrus columns with calyx capitals bearing massive architraves contribute gently to the serene profile of the temple when viewed from the river. Originally, however, this columnar rhythm would have been lost behind flanking walls, the upper three-quarters of which have collapsed. The remaining courses bear fine and fascinating reliefs from the reign of Tutankhamun, a celebration of the re-establishment of the Amun orthodoxy, depicting the god with Mut and Khonsu accompanied by the pharaoh and priests on their voyage from Karnak to Luxor at the height of the inundation period. Crowds of common folk follow by land, and there are scenes of rejoicing, of musicians and dancers, and of sacrifice. The series begins at the northwest corner with the pharaoh sacrificing to the boats at Karnak, and continues with the water-borne procession and, at the southeast corner, the arrival at Luxor. Starting at the southeast corner, the procession returns 24 days later to Karnak.

The colonnade leads into the **court of Amenophis III**, once enclosed on the east, north and west by double rows of clustered papyrus columns with bud capitals, an ensemble that appeals through its harmony. The east and west sides are well preserved and still carry their architraves. On the south side is the **Hypostyle Hall** with four rows of eight columns. On either side of its south wall are reliefs of the coronation of Amenophis by the gods. To the left of the central aisle, between the last two columns, is a **Roman altar** dedicated to Constantine.

The Temple

You now enter the temple proper. The first **antechamber**, which once had a roof supported by eight columns, bore reliefs on its walls of Amenophis. But in the 3rd or 4th century AD the walls were thickly whitewashed and covered with paintings. One view is that this became the chapel of a Roman imperial cult; others argue that it was a church. The only evidence are the paintings themselves, which must once have been very fine but are badly damaged and tantalizingly inconclusive. Those on the east wall are very faint; but on the south wall to the left of the arched niche there is a much clearer group of several figures. One figure, below the third from left, seems to be a woman. Also on the south wall, and on the north wall too, the reliefs of Amenophis worshipping Amun have been laid bare. The second antechamber is smaller, with four columns, and as the reliefs around the walls show – Amenophis driving calves to sacrifice, offering incense and sceptres to Amun – this was the offering chapel. Beyond that is the **sanctuary of the Sacred Boat of Amun**.

The sanctuary consists of a chapel open to north and south set within a chamber. The chamber walls are decorated with reliefs of Amenophis, while the chapel was rebuilt by Alexander the Great and both its exterior and interior walls bear reliefs of him before Amun and other gods. A subsidiary room with three columns to the east of the sanctuary has badly damaged scenes of Amenophis' coronation and on the north wall he is shown hunting in the marshes.

From this subsidiary room a doorway opens north onto the **Birth Room** with reliefs on the west wall referring to Amenophis' divine birth. At the left of the lowest register, Khnum is moulding the infant Amenophis and his ka on a potter's wheel. Moving from left to right across the middle register, Thoth foretells to Mutemuia, mother of Amenophis, the birth of her son; the pregnant Mutemuia is conducted by Isis and Khnum; her confinement; Isis presenting the infant to Amun; and Amun with the infant in his arms. The top register shows Amenophis and his ka nurtured by the gods and presented to Amun; to the far right, in the corner, Amenophis has become pharaoh.

The remaining rooms at the **south end** of the temple have suffered considerable damage and are without antique interest. The transverse hall with its 12 papyrus bud columns was an antechamber or hypostyle hall leading to the three southernmost chambers, the central one a sanctuary once containing the intriguingly described 'divine image of millions of years'. It was in this transverse hall that Cocteau noticed a more recent curiosity: 'Suddenly I was struck dumb. What could that be? High up, on top of the wall, Rimbaud had carved his name. He carved it, at the height of a man, and now that the temple is cleared, it shines forth like a sunflower. It blazes out, royal and sunlike, above suspicion, dreadful in its solitude.' Rimbaud gave up poetry by the time he was 21, in 1875; for the remaining 16 years of his life he travelled in the Far and Near East and into parts of Ethiopia where no European had been before, variously selling coffee, girls and guns – and making a mark for French culture at the Temple of Luxor.

The area outside the temple on the east serves as a storeyard for architectural fragments, pharaonic, Roman and Christian. The Christian friezes and fonts presumably came from the basilica which once stood outside Ramses' great pylon.

The temple is experienced most intensely at night when the floodlights throw the carvings into deeper relief and the black night rests like a roof on the brightness of the stone, enclosing you. On the dome of the mosque of Abu el Haggag, cursive green neon proclaims 'Allah'. Once a year at the saint's moulid a boat is carried in procession as was Amun's 3,500 years before. (For his moulid and the Ramadan celebrations which take place in front of the mosque, *see* p.294.)

For a magnificent view over the Temple of Luxor, especially at sunset, you should go to the mosque on Sharia el Karnak that overlooks the courtyard and the Avenue of the Sphinxes (not the mosque of Abu el Haggag which sits atop part of the temple itself). By asking permission and afterwards offering baksheesh you can ascend its minaret.

You can walk to Karnak from the forecourt at the north end of the Temple of Luxor, following the avenue of ram-headed sphinxes which lined the way of the ancient Opet procession.

The Mummification Museum

Mummification Museum
down steps off the corniche, halfway between the entrance to the Temple of Luxor and the Mercure Hotel; open daily in winter 9–1 and 4–9, in summer until 10pm; adm LE45

If you ever wanted to know exactly how the brain was removed from the skull via the nostrils, this is the place. The tools of the trade are on display with full explanations of how they were used, including techniques for desiccating and wrapping the bodies. There are mummies of a XXI Dynasty official, a cat, a baboon, a ram and a crocodile, as well as artefacts necessary for a successful transition to eternity, and a number of painted coffins in which one would pass the time.

Museum of Ancient Egyptian Art

Museum of Ancient Egyptian Art
on the corniche to the north of the Mercure Hotel; open daily 9–1 and 4–9 winter, 9–1 and 5–10 summer; adm LE60

The presentation of this museum is superb, with some well-chosen objects lit to best advantage. The exhibits include jewellery, furniture, pottery and stelae, almost all pharaonic though there are a few Graeco-Roman, Coptic and Mameluke pieces. Most outstanding in the general collection (quite apart from the Luxor Temple cache) are the **stone statues and busts.** The latter are most finely represented by granite and basalt works identified by the cartouches as Tuthmosis III, Amenophis II, Amenophis III (all XVIII Dyn) and Sesostris III (XII Dyn), any of which could stand in place of another for all they depict an individual (except for that of Sesostris with big ears). The craftsmanship is excellent, however, and the enjoyment of working with the graceful curves of crowns, necks and waists is clear. There is a marvellous alabaster statue of Sobek with crocodile's head and man's body, and one of Amenophis III, usurped by Ramses II by altering the cartouche – which shows how little the figure itself served to identify.

A series of **scenes in sunk relief** on limestone blocks found within the Ninth Pylon at Karnak show Akhenaten and Nefertiti worshipping Aten, but also the most ordinary daily palace tasks. At least when Akhenaten attacked the Theban priesthood, he obliterated images of their god Amun; the post-Amarna counterrevolutionaries reverted to the traditional method of defeating a predecessor's bid for immortality: for example, exhibit 150 is a block showing Akhenaten worshipping Aten – so clearly understandable and evidence of his heresy – yet it is defaced only to the extent that his cartouche is gouged. Always the name, the sign, rather than the idea.

Admission includes entrance to the hall containing a cache of 22 magnificent New Kingdom statues, including those of Amenophis III, Tutankhamun, Ramses II and his wife Nefertari, unearthed in

1989 at the Temple of Luxor where they had been buried at the outset of the Roman occupation.

Karnak

Karnak by starlight is peace; not peace and joy, but peace – solemn peace. You feel like spirits revisiting your former world, strange and fallen to ruins.

Florence Nightingale, 1849

27 Karnak Temple and Museum
open daily 7am–5pm winter, 7am–6pm summer; adm LE65; the Open Air Museum is LE25 extra; both tickets must be bought at the kiosk on the right-hand side of the parking lot outside. There are toilets by the son et lumière *grandstand at the far end of the Sacred Lake*

When Egypt stood at the height of empire, when Thebes ruled over Egypt, and when Amun was supreme over all, his temple here possessed 81,000 slaves and their families, 240,000 head of cattle, 83 ships, and from 65 cities and towns their vast annual tribute in gold, silver, copper and precious stones.

The Karnak site covers an enormous area, sufficient to accommodate 10 European cathedrals. The Hypostyle Hall alone is large enough to contain Notre Dame. At least two half-day visits are required to see the entire complex; if you can manage only one, then you will have to be content with walking through the main temple, that of Amun. A return can be made at night for the *son et lumière*. The size and complexity of the site, the arrangement of its structures on both an east–west and north–south axis, the multiple extensions to several of these structures by successive pharaohs, and in some areas its ruinous state, contribute to the lack of unity and proportion at Karnak. But this has probably always been so, even in its days of completeness. Karnak astounds, but does not awaken the sensibilities.

Apart from its size, Karnak represents a vastness of historical time. The main Temple of Amun, from the foundations of the original Middle Kingdom temple to the First Pylon, built (probably) during the XXV Dynasty, saw construction over 1,300 years. Comprehension of the site requires a brief historical review.

Son et Lumière

The *son et lumière* (sound and light) show costs LE75 (LE10 when in Arabic) and lasts 60 minutes. There are three shows nightly, in winter at 6.30pm, 7.45pm and 9pm; in summer at 8pm, 9.15pm and 10.30pm. The performances are in varying languages depending on the time and day of the week (check at your hotel or the Tourist Office): English, French, Italian, Spanish, German, Japanese and Arabic.

The best part is the walk deeper into the temple – the lights and voices lead you on and it hardly matters what is being said. The impression is magnificent and will enhance your earlier (or later) daytime visit. In the Hypostyle Hall, take the opportunity to wander off alone to one side or the other, until you are deep among the faintly illuminated columns – that is the most enjoyable.

Getting to Karnak

Karnak is 4km north of the Temple of Luxor. You can walk or take a taxi, but it can be pleasant to take a carriage (*see* 'Luxor', p.271) along the corniche to the First Pylon of the main temple at Karnak. When leaving, ask the driver to return you to Luxor by the road which passes the Gateway of Euergetes. Somewhere deep beneath this present roadway of your return journey lies the old sacred way, lined with sphinxes, that joined the temples of Karnak and Luxor, visible in now-excavated segments en route and at either end, where it leaves Euergetes' gateway, and where it enters the forecourt of the Temple of Luxor.

A Brief History: Thirteen Centuries in Stone

Although the war god Mont, associated with Thebes during the Old Kingdom, continued to be worshipped at Karnak, Amun achieved pre-eminence by the beginning of the Middle Kingdom and was honoured during the XII Dynasty by a series of temples facing west, the principal orientation throughout subsequent periods. All that remains of these are the alabaster foundations of what was to become the most venerable part of the extended Temple of Amun, and limestone blocks belonging to the White Chapel of Sesostris I, recovered from the foundations of the Third Pylon and re-erected in the Open Air Museum to the north of the Great Court.

With the expulsion of the Hyksos from Egypt and the elevation of Amun to victorious national god, the early pharaohs of the XVIII Dynasty set about turning Karnak into the principal sanctuary of their kingdom. Amenophis I and his son Tuthmosis I built chapels around the Middle Kingdom temple, while in front of it (to the west) the latter built the Fourth and Fifth Pylons and erected a pair of obelisks. Hatshepsut added two further obelisks between those of her father, chambers with carved decorations in front of the original temple, and initiated the north–south axis of the complex by building south. Her nephew Tuthmosis III continued building along the north–south axis with the Seventh and Eighth Pylons, and constructed the Festival Hall behind (to the east of) the Middle Kingdom temple.

In the century that passed between the Asian conquests of Tuthmosis III and the reign of Amenophis III, artistic and architectural restraint gave way to an overblown imperial style, expressed at Karnak by the Third Pylon built by Amenophis and his start on the great Hypostyle Hall. Empire introduced foreign influences and new wealth to the country, required an enlarged bureaucracy, and upset the status quo. Amun, who had lent his sword to pharaoh's victories, saw the coffers of his priesthood and of the old aristocracy from which it was drawn swell with tribute, and so their power grew. But another class, which owed its very existence to empire, grew up around the pharaoh. Tuthmosis IV married an Asian princess, and her son Amenophis III married Tiy, an Egyptian commoner. Tiy was given unusual artistic prominence

'Thebes, Karnak' by David Roberts

alongside her husband, and her parents, Yuya and Tuyu, were buried in splendour in the Valley of the Kings. Pharaoh and temple no longer represented identical interests. Before decamping to Amarna with his court of parvenus, Amenophis IV (Akhenaten as he became) did some building at the east of Karnak, where several of his statues now in the Cairo Museum were found, while some blocks now in the Luxor Museum were re-used in the foundations of later pylons and the Hypostyle Hall.

But the Amarna revolution did not survive the death of Akhenaten, and the reign of Tutankhamun marked the beginning of the counter-revolution which proceeded with a vengeance. The power of Amum was reaffirmed, and as though to sweep away all memory of heresy, internal conflict and the diminution of empire associated with the last pharaohs of the XVIII Dynasty, Seti I of the XIX Dynasty declared his reign the era of the repeating of births, literally a renaissance. Both he and his son Ramses II outdid all that had gone before, both in architecture and in military propaganda, to make good any deficiencies in this assertion. Between them they completed the Hypostyle Hall. It remained only for later dynasties to build the Great Court and the First Pylon for Karnak to assume the form it has today. The Ptolemies embellished, and the Copts cut crosses in stones.

The XIX Dynasty made its peace with Amun, but the cost in sacrificed wealth was greater than could be borne for long without the pharaoh becoming a mere creature of the priesthood. The Hypostyle Hall, the Ramesseum, Abu Simbel, may all have glorified Ramses II, but only through Amun who long survived that long-lived pharaoh. By the time Ramses IV (XX Dyn) came to the throne, 200 years after Akhenaten's resistance and only 60 years after the death of Ramses II, the Temple of Amun owned at least 7 per cent of the population of Egypt and 9 per cent of the land, with some estimates trebling those percentages, while the family of the high priest of Amun directly controlled the collection of pharaoh's taxes and management of pharaoh's lands. Pharaoh had become no more than an instrument of a ruling oligarchy, and Karnak was its juggernaut.

Entering Amun's Temple

You approach the maw of the beast along a short **processional way (1)** lined with ram-headed sphinxes with figures of Ramses II in mummy wrappings between their forelegs. This exactly expresses the new enveloping relationship between god and pharaoh, for the ram was identified with Amun. A now filled-in canal once linked the temple with the Nile, giving egress during the Opet festival for gods, priests and pharaoh aboard their boats.

The First Pylon, 113m wide and 43m high, is the largest at Karnak and nearly twice the size of the entrance pylon at the Temple of Luxor. It was probably built by Taharka during the XXV (Ethiopian) Dynasty, a trumpeting echo of XIX Dynasty bombast, but left unfinished, the south tower higher than the north and neither bearing any decoration.

The north (left) tower can be climbed for magnificent views over Karnak and the surrounding countryside.

The Great Court

The **Great Court (2)** was built by the rulers of the XXII Dynasty but encloses earlier structures. Columns with papyrus bud capitals line the north and south sides of the court, while a tall doorway in the southeast corner leads to the south end of the **Second Pylon** on which is cut a scene commemorating the victory of Sheshonk I (Shishak of the Bible) over Rehoboam, son of Solomon. The pylon itself was built by Horemheb, an XVIII Dynasty general who became military dictator and finally last pharaoh of the dynasty he had served. Like the Ninth and Tenth Pylons, also built by Horemheb, the Second Pylon made use of blocks that had once formed temples to Akhenaten's god, Aten. Continuing the palimpsest of politics, Ramses I and II cut their names on the pylon over that of Horemheb, and Ramses II installed two colossal figures of himself in pink granite on either side of the pylon entrance. Of the one on the left hardly anything remains; nor does that sector of the avenue of rams which once ran through the area that became the court, to continue beyond the First Pylon towards the Nile. Instead, at the centre of the court Taharka (XXV Dynasty) built a **kiosk (3)** with 10 enormous columns 21m high with papyrus calyx capitals, only one still standing. In the northwest quadrant of the court is the **Temple of Seti II (4)**, a simple arrangement of three chapels facing south, the one at the centre to hold the sacred boat of Amun, those to the left and right to hold the boats of Mut and Khonsu, during preparations for the Opet festival. The **Temple of Ramses III (5)** intersecting the south wall of the court similarly served as a station chapel during processions and is a fine example of a simple pharaonic temple. Its pylon, facing north, is decorated with the obligatory triumphal scenes on the outside and with jubilee scenes, assuring the pharaoh a long life, on the inside. An open court leads to a pronaos of four columns and then to a hypostyle hall of eight columns beyond which are the three boat chapels, Amun's at the centre.

A doorway on the north side of the Court leads to an outside staircase at the north end of the First Pylon for views from the top.

Open Air Museum
additional fee

Also through this doorway you come to the **Open Air Museum (6)** where statues, blocks and architectural fragments from around the

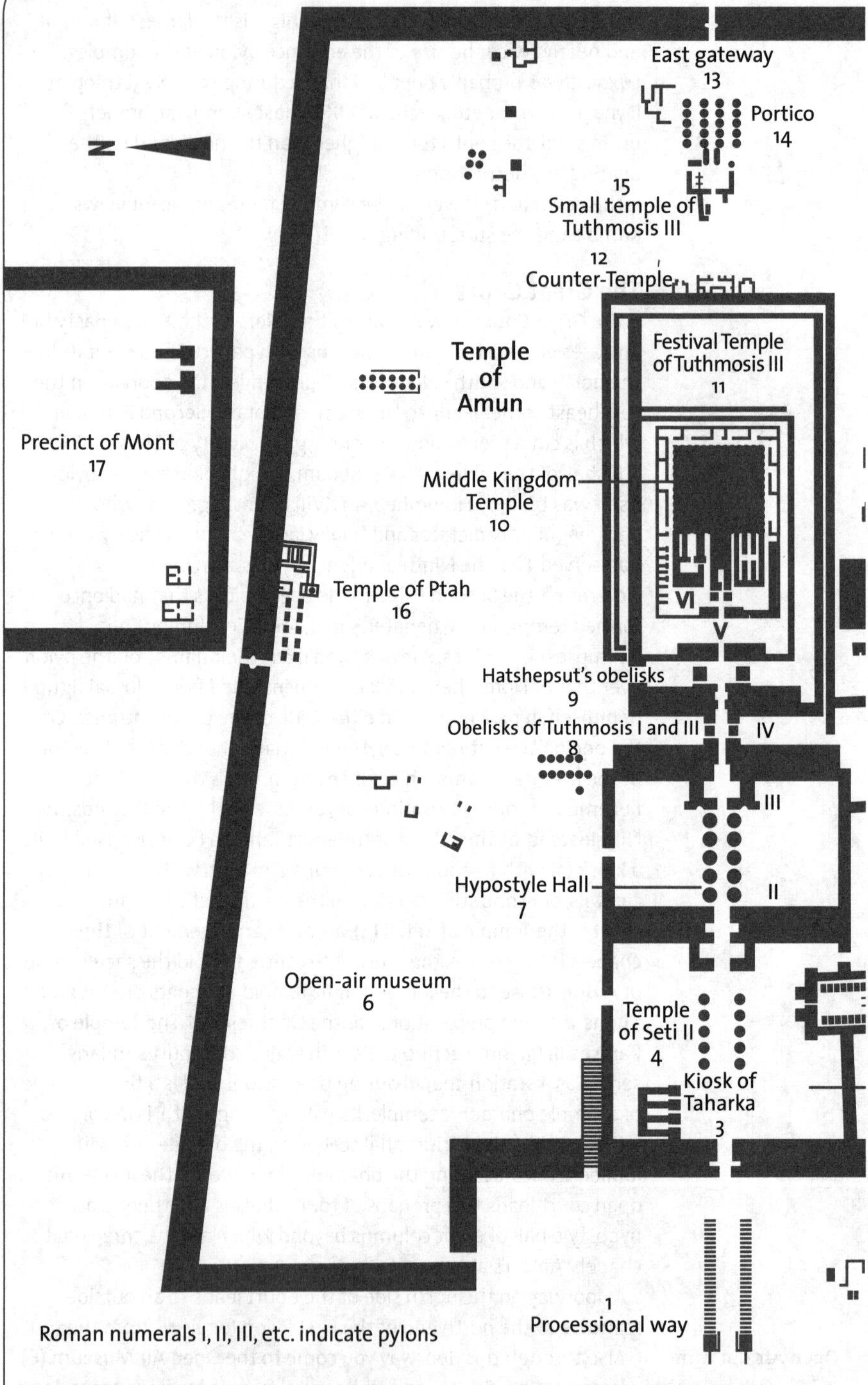

N
East gateway
13
Portico
14
15
Small temple of Tuthmosis III
12
Counter-Temple
Temple of Amun
Festival Temple of Tuthmosis III
11
Precinct of Mont
17
Middle Kingdom Temple
10
Temple of Ptah
16
VI
V
Hatshepsut's obelisks
9
Obelisks of Tuthmosis I and III
8
IV
III
Hypostyle Hall
7
II
Open-air museum
6
Temple of Seti II
4
Kiosk of Taharka
3
1
Processional way
Roman numerals I, II, III, etc. indicate pylons

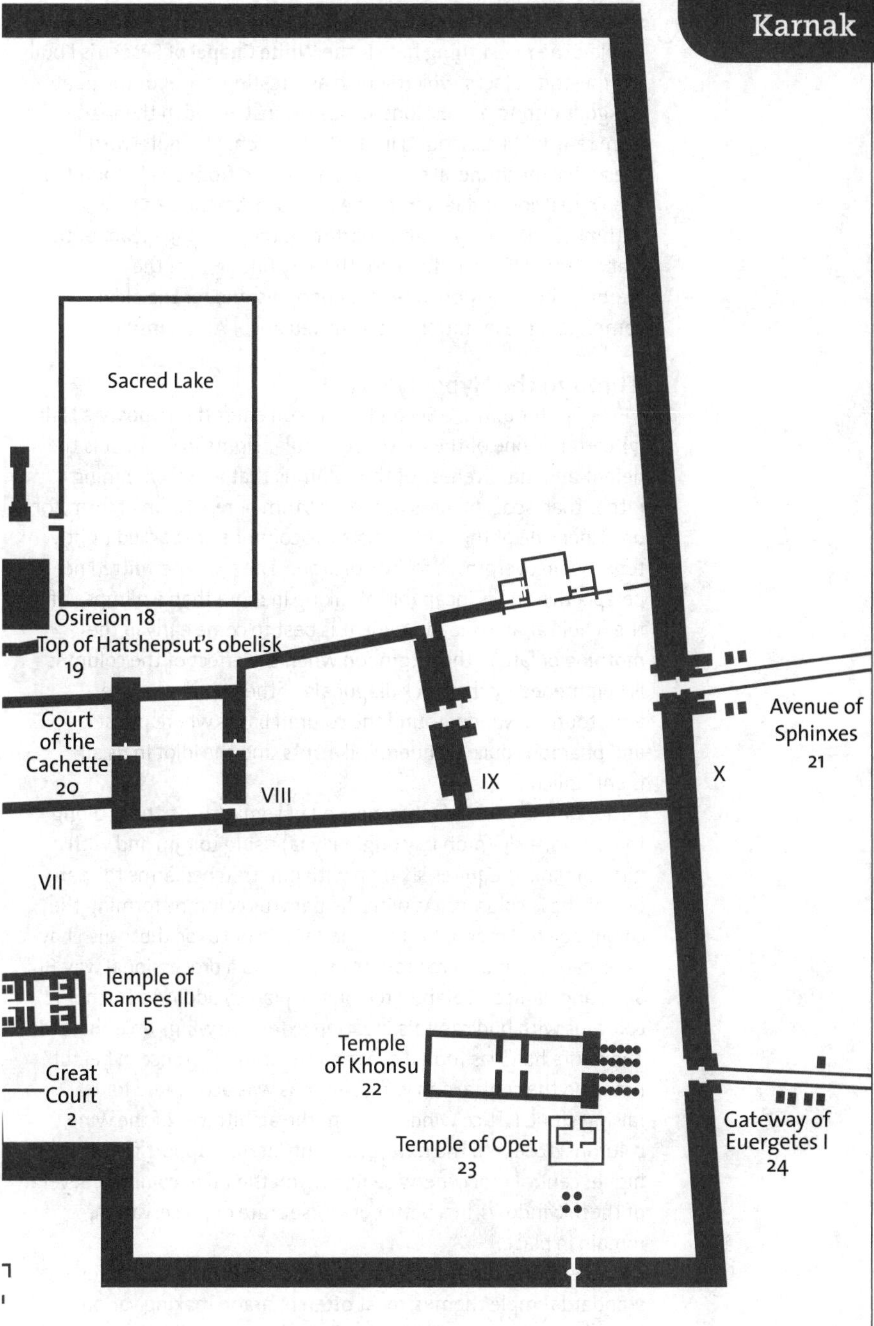
Sacred Lake
Osireion 18
Top of Hatshepsut's obelisk
19
Court
of the
Cachette
20
VIII
IX
X
Avenue of
Sphinxes
21
VII
Temple of
Ramses III
5
Temple
of Khonsu
22
Great
Court
2
Temple of Opet
23
Gateway of
Euergetes I
24

site were once gathered for private study but are now on public display. The finest thing here is the **White Chapel** of Sesostris I built of limestone blocks, which served as a resting place for the boats of the gods during processions. It was reconstructed in the 1940s from re-used blocks found in the Third Pylon. Also noteworthy is the **alabaster shrine**, likewise reconstructed from blocks found in the Third Pylon. It dates from the reigns of Amenophis I and Tuthmosis I (XVIII Dyn), and apart from the pleasing gleam of the alabaster itself it is notable for the very fine style of the hieroglyphics and portraits of Amenophis, and for the oldest complete representation of the sacred ark of Amun inside.

Through the Hypostyle Hall

Passing through the Second Pylon, you enter the **Hypostyle Hall (7)**, certainly one of the most spectacular sights in Egypt. It is the height and massiveness of the columns that is overwhelming rather than spaciousness or even rhythm or repetition of form, for on either side of the central aisle the columns are packed tightly together in overgrown forests of stone. The eye is permitted no perspective and is incapable of taking in more than a glimpse of the whole at any one moment. It is best to come early in the morning or late in the afternoon when the effect of the columns is heightened by the black diagonals of their shadows. Like ants, tourists wander round the column bases where priests and pharaohs once wandered, like ants, and the idiot in us all is enthralled.

The columns are in fact composed of semi-drums, the 12 along the central aisle (probably originally 14) rising to 23m and with a girth of 15m. It requires six men with outstretched arms to span one of these columns. As with the papyrus columns forming the colonnade of Amenophis III at the Temple of Luxor, these also have calyx capitals and were probably erected as a processional way. But Seti I and Ramses II elaborated on the plan by adding a further 122 columns with bud capitals, creating extensive wings on either side. The entire hall was roofed over and the 10m difference in height between the central and wing columns was accounted for by raising stone lattice windows from the architraves of the wing columns closest to the nave, providing lateral support for the higher central roof otherwise resting on the taller columns. Several of these windows, in a better or worse state of preservation, remain in place.

The central columns are richly painted and cut in sunk relief with standard temple themes, most often pharaoh making various offerings to Amun and other Theban gods. These cult scenes, with recurrent images of Amun in a state of erection (ithyphallic), are continued on the phallus-like columns of the wings, those in the north wing executed in bas-relief during the reign of Seti I, those in the south wing in the sunk relief preferred by Ramses II. The inside walls of the Hypostyle Hall are similarly decorated, but the outside walls proclaim the military exploits of Seti I in Palestine and Libya (north wall) and of Ramses II against the Hittites (south wall).

Of some romance in the study of ancient history is a stele standing upright against the west wall of the **Court of the Cachette (20)**, which runs into the south wall of the Hypostyle Hall: it records a treaty between Ramses II and the Hittite king. Not only is it one of the earliest codifications of international relations, but its cuneiform version (now in the Museum of the Ancient Orient, Istanbul) was found inscribed on clay tablets at the Hittite capital, Hattufflas, east of Ankara in Turkey. When independently translated, it served to confirm the accuracy of the labours of philologists in the two languages. A large votive pit in the Court of the Cachette was excavated early this century and found to contain several thousand bronze statues and 800 of stone. The best are on display in Cairo's Egyptian Antiquities Museum.

The intimate relationship between the structure of the Temple of Amun and the development of the Egyptian state has already been outlined (*see* pp.280–2). It is ironic that the great columns of the Hypostyle Hall stood on bases formed of re-used blocks from the time of Akhenaten (since removed and replaced mostly by concrete) and that these in turn stood on no firmer foundation than sand. Pretension was careless of the future, though a century of archaeological engineering has made good the past. Yet though grandiosity so suited the pharaohs of the XIX Dynasty, it is arguable that it was dictated by the temple itself. It was a canon of Egyptian temple architecture that, as you approached the innermost sanctuary, perspective should narrow, that pylons and columns should get smaller, ceilings lower, and that even the temple platform should rise so that you walked upwards towards the sanctuary as walls and ceilings funnelled in around you. Once Amenophis III decided to build his Third Pylon, it had to be larger than the one before, and the Hypostyle Hall, the Second Pylon and finally the First Pylon had to grow more massive still.

The Oldest Part of the Temple

A constricted court lies between the Third Pylon of Amenophis III and the Fourth Pylon of Tuthmosis I, a narrow gap of space and time between traditional and imperial Egypt. When the Fourth Pylon still marked the entrance to the temple, two pairs of **obelisks (8)** were erected before it by Tuthmosis I and Tuthmosis III. Only one obelisk survives. Of the pink granite pair raised by Tuthmosis I, originally tipped with electrum (a natural alloy of gold and silver), one fell as recently as the 18th century, some of its parts lying nearby, and the other leans a little but is still stable. Beyond the Fourth Pylon the outline of the temple becomes difficult to follow. The successive pylons are closely set, and the buildings have undergone repeated alterations and suffered extensive damage. But many beautiful details reward your exploration, and the absence of both overwhelming architecture and overwhelmed tourists encourages tranquil reflection

Hatshepsut and Tuthmosis

The numerous columns in the open space behind the Fourth Pylon suggest that this, at least in part, was a hypostyle hall. It was built by Tuthmosis III and may have been part of his extraordinary attempt to disguise the existence of Hatshepsut's two magnificent **obelisks (9)**. The lower shaft of one of these remains on its base, the upper shaft lying near the northwest corner of the Sacred Lake where you can closely examine its inscriptions. The second obelisk is in situ, the tallest completed obelisk in Egypt and of ancient obelisks second in height only to the Lateran obelisk in Rome. It stands 29.5m high and was covered in electrum not only at the pyramidion but also down half its shaft, so that as its inscription tells, 'Hatshepsut made as her monument for her father Amun two great obelisks of enduring granite from the south, their upper parts, being of electrum of the best of all lands, seen on the two sides of the river. Their rays flood the two lands when the sun-disc rises between them at its appearance on the horizon of heaven.' Stepmother to Tuthmosis III and originally regent to the young pharaoh, Hatshepsut soon proclaimed herself pharaoh and relegated Tuthmosis to the shadows for the remainder of her life. He later showed his resentment by chopping out her name wherever he found it, and here at Karnak went to the absurd length of building a now removed sandstone structure around her obelisks to a height of 25m.

The Fifth Pylon was also built by Tuthmosis I and leads almost immediately to the badly ruined Sixth Pylon, the smallest of all, built by Tuthmosis II. In the court beyond it he erected two tall pink granite pillars. Carved in high relief on their north and south sides are three lilies (south pillar) and three papyrus flowers (north pillar), the heraldic plants of Upper and Lower Egypt, beautifully stylized. At the north end of the court are two colossal sandstone statues of Amun and his 'grammatical consort' Amonet in the likeness of Tutankhamun. Farther along the main axis of the temple, on the spot where Hatshepsut's Red Chapel once stood (its quartzite blocks engraved with scenes of the procession of the sacred boats are in the Open Air Museum), is the granite **sanctuary**

of the Sacred Boats built by the half-witted half-brother of Alexander the Great. The interior decorations in bas-relief and the exterior ones in sunk relief are finely worked and vividly coloured in yellow, red and blue. High though the standard is, however, its mock-traditional Egyptian terms were adopted by the Ptolemies for political expedience and are sadly inferior to the terms governing the greatest period of Greek art only 100 years before.

Walls and Heroes

On the north side of the sanctuary, where there was much rebuilding, a **wall erected by Hatshepsut** was found concealed behind a later wall of Tuthmosis III, thus preserving the original freshness of its colouring. The wall has now been removed to a nearby room, and shows Amun, his flesh painted red and with one foot in front of the other, and also Amun in the guise of ithyphallic Min, a harvest god often amalgamated with Amun, his flesh painted black. The wall of Tuthmosis, known as the **Wall of Records**, was erected after the battle of Megiddo (Armageddon) in northern Palestine, fought in April 1479 BC. In *A History of Egypt*, James Henry Breasted wrote of Tuthmosis that 'he was the first to build an empire in any real sense; he was the first world-hero. He made not only a worldwide impression upon his age, but an impression of a new order.' Political history, in so far as it tells the story of territorial imperialism, began that April day when Tuthmosis, instead of destroying his enemies, organized the vanquished into agencies of tribute and annually recorded on this wall the share that was due to Amun.

Temples

The open space beyond the sanctuary marks the site of the original **Middle Kingdom Temple (10)**, its plan suggested by the remaining alabaster foundation stones.

To the east of the original temple is the **Festival Temple of Tuthmosis III** (11), and running north–south within it the Festival Hall of many columns and pillars where Tuthmosis celebrated his jubilees, those reinvigorations of temporal power and divine spirit. The pillars form a rectangular cloister around a central and taller colonnade. The two rows of ten columns are unique in Egypt, affecting the form of tent poles or upturned tree trunks (as in Minoan Crete), broader above than below. The capitals, like bells or inverted calyxes, are incised and painted in patterns of overlapping leaves or of vertical stripes. The architectural suggestion is of an outdoor tent or, as echoed in stone at the Heb-Sed Court at Saqqara, of a temporary timbered building. Early in the Christian era the hall was converted into a church, and the occasional haloed saint may be discerned on its columns.

A chamber at the southwest corner of the hall contained, until taken to the Louvre, the Table of Karnak, a list of 57 predecessors of Tuthmosis. It is probable that statues of ancient pharaohs carried in procession were also kept here. From the northwest corner of the hall, an antechamber leads into a corridor lined with fine reliefs of Tuthmosis in the presence of Amun. Without the hall but in the northeast area of the Festival Temple is a small room with four papyrus bundle columns with bud capitals still supporting the architraves, though the roof is gone. This is popularly known as the **Botanic Garden** for its bas-reliefs of plants and animals seen in and perhaps brought from Syria by Tuthmosis.

Towards the East Enclosure Wall

A footbridge leads east across the remains of enclosure walls, and against this wall, on the axis of the main temple, is a **counter-temple (12)** facing east. Beyond this is the **east gateway (13)** to the Karnak complex, set in an outer wall of mud brick and built by Nectanebos I (XXX Dyn). From the avenue of rams before the First Pylon to this gateway, it is 0.5km. Before exploring the breadth of the complex, have a look at the two structures standing between the counter-temple and the east gateway. The one to the east is a **ruined portico (14)** built by the same Taharka who built the kiosk in the Great Court; he placed similar structures at the north and south ends of the site, so covering the four cardinal points. Adjacent to this to the west is a small **temple (15)** built by Tuthmosis III. On the centre line of this temple is a large square base on which once stood the world's largest obelisk, the Lateran obelisk in Rome.

The Lateran Obelisk

It was a considerable achievement for the French to get the 22.5m-high obelisk of Ramses II from the Temple of Luxor to the Place de la Concorde in the 1830s, yet the giant 32.3m obelisk that stood in this small temple at Karnak was removed by order of the Emperor Constantine in the 4th century AD, consigned originally to Constantinople but having its course changed upon the emperor's death and delivered to Rome instead where it was erected in the Circus Maximus in AD 357.

It fell or more probably was toppled some centuries later, but in 1588 was re-erected in the Piazza San Giovanni in Laterano. Hieroglyphics on its shaft state that Tuthmosis III 'made as his monument for his father Amun-Re, Lord of the Thrones of the Two Lands, the setting up for him of a single obelisk in the Upper Court of the Temple in the neighbourhood of Karnak, on the very first occasion of setting up a single obelisk in Thebes.' It is stressed that the erection of a single obelisk was unusual, and it is probable that the Lateran obelisk comes from the same quarry of pink granite as that in which the great unfinished obelisk at Aswan still lies, and that the unfinished obelisk, until faults in the stone were discovered, was intended to complete the pair.

The North Complex Area

The Temple of Ptah and the Precinct of Mont at the north end of the Karnak complex are reached by a winding path that leads from the north wall of the Great Court of the Temple of Amun. The ground is overgrown and barely excavated.

Against the north enclosure wall and shaded by palms, the **Temple of Ptah (16)** is approached through an east–west series of five doorways. If the inner doorway is locked, call to what looks like a sentry tower atop the mud brick wall. Shout. The keeper is probably asleep and will have to put on his *galabiyya* before coming down to let you in. Each of the doorways is carved with scenes and texts of the Ptolemaic period. The fifth doorway leads into a columned vestibule; to the rear is a small pylon marking the entrance to the temple proper. Beyond the antechamber are three chapels dating from the reign of Tuthmosis III, and most unusually the cult statue of Ptah (with head missing) is still in the middle chapel; while in the chapel to the right is the startling apparition of Sekhmet, her bare-breasted body surmounted by the head of a lioness. The keeper will close the doors to enhance the eerie effect of the single shaft of sunlight from an aperture in the roof casting a greenish glow within.

A gateway (also often locked) leads through the enclosure wall to the **Precinct of Mont (17)** (god of war), its structures largely dilapidated and only of specialist interest. The main temple, totally ruined, was built by Amenophis III.

The South Complex Area

Exploration of the south end of the Karnak complex can begin at the **Sacred Lake**, restored and cemented. A grandstand at its east end is where visitors sit for the culmination of the *son et lumière*. Near the northwest corner is a giant scarab dedicated by Amenophis III to Atum, the god of the rising sun. Also here is the base with underground chambers of an **Osireion (18)** built by Taharka, and the broken-off top of Hatshepsut's other **obelisk (19)**. On the pyramidion a kneeling Hatshepsut is being blessed by Amun; his figure was recut by Seti I within the gouge caused by Akhenaten's attempt to obliterate the god of his priestly opponents.

Pylons along the Processional Way

At the south ends of the Third and Fourth Pylons of the Temple of Amun begins the second (north–south) axis of the Karnak complex, a **processional way** consisting of a series of open courts bounded by walls along their east and west sides and separated from each other by pylons. The Seventh and Eighth Pylons led originally to a Middle Kingdom temple and a temple of Amenophis I which both stood in what is now the court of the Cachette. The temples were taken down by Tuthmosis III, but not before he had erected the Seventh Pylon.

Considerable restoration work is being carried out along the north–south axis and the pylons may be closed off to the public. Nevertheless, the keepers will not hesitate to show you around for some baksheesh, and will lead you up the inner stairways to the tops of the pylons, or encourage you to follow them as they leap like goats across deep gaps in the towers and walls.

Seven statues of Middle Kingdom pharaohs stand or sit before the north face of the Seventh Pylon, while on its south side are the remains of two colossi of Tuthmosis III. On the outside of the east wall between this and the Eighth Pylon is an interesting **relief of the high priest** of Amenophis, his arms raised as though adoring Ramses IX (XX Dyn), who extends his palm in a reciprocal gesture. The very presence of the high priest, adoring or not, is unusual, but it is revealing that the priest is as large as the pharaoh and is even the focus of the composition. The relief is a vivid illustration of how much priestly power and arrogance had grown within a century after the reign of the great Ramses II.

The Eighth Pylon was built by Hatshepsut and, though the oldest part of the north–south axis, is well preserved. On its south side a relief shows Amenophis II slaughtering his enemies, while of the original six colossi on this side of the pylon, four remain, the figure of Amenophis I, on the left, the most complete.

The Ninth and Tenth Pylons were built by Horemheb in part with blocks from buildings erected by Akhenaten in honour of Aten. In front of the north side of the west tower is a stele erected by Horemheb proclaiming the restoration of the Amun orthodoxy. On the east side of the court between the Ninth and Tenth Pylons is a small temple built by Amenophis II, probably for his jubilee, with a graceful portico of square pillars. The fine bas-reliefs inside the hall, some of their colouring well preserved, show Amenophis before various deities. On the interior wall of the court between this temple and the Tenth Pylon, Horemheb is shown in relief leading captives from Punt bearing gifts for the Theban triad, and to the right of this he appears with fettered Syrian captives. Both claims of foreign triumph are almost certainly false, at best mere conventions, for Horemheb is known to have spent most of his energies imposing law, order and the old religion on post-Amarna Egypt, while there is no evidence at all that he led his armies abroad.

From the Tenth Pylon an **avenue of sphinxes (21)** runs for several hundred metres to the **Precinct of Mut,** still not entirely excavated and all the more picturesque for its ruins rising from the overgrown scrub. Consort of Amun and originally a vulture goddess, Mut was depicted during the New Kingdom with the skin of a vulture on her wig. Approached through a propylaeum cut with Ptolemaic cartouches, her badly ruined temple, built by Amenophis III, consists of two courts, a hypostyle hall and sanctuary. All around it, rising from the scrub, are figures of Sekhmet, the lion goddess, beautifully worked and with care taken to use the pink veins in the bluish granite to highlight certain features such as the ankh sign or the goddess's breasts. A sacred lake enwraps the temple and across it, to the west, is a temple of Ramses III. Another temple, of Amenophis III, is in the northeast corner of the precinct.

The Temples of Khonsu and Opet

But still within the main Karnak enclosure, in the southwest corner, is the **Temple of Khonsu (22)**, the moon god son of Mut and Amun. It faces south towards the Gateway of Euergetes and so towards the avenue of rams which disappears beneath village houses before emerging again in front of the entrance pylon of the Temple of Luxor. For the most part the Temple of Khonsu is in a good state of preservation, its simplicity and clarity of layout make it a classic of New Kingdom architecture. It was started by Ramses III, though possibly completed and certainly almost entirely decorated by his successors down to Herihor (XXI Dyn), who like Horemheb rose from the army to seize power as pharaoh, and went one better by making himself high priest of Amun as well (*see* p.302). The pylon of the temple is small but well proportioned, and decorated with a variety of religious scenes. On the rear wall of the first court, to the right, is a carving of the temple façade, banners flying. To the left is Herihor performing rites before the boats of the Theban triad. Beyond this is a small transverse hypostyle hall leading to the dilapidated sanctuary. Walking through its centre chapel, once containing the sacred boat of Khonsu, you come to a small hall of four columns with reliefs of Ramses IV, but also, on either side of the entrance, Augustus. From the southeast corner of the sanctuary a staircase leads up to the roof, from which there are good views of the ruins.

Immediately to the west is the smaller **Temple of Opet (23),** a hippopotamus goddess and mother of Osiris. It was left unfinished by Euergetes II, though otherwise finely decorated throughout the Ptolemaic period and into the reign of Augustus.

You can now leave the Karnak site through the **Gateway of Ptolemy III Euergetes I (24)**, its concave cornice adorned with a winged sun disc.

ⓘ Luxor > *at the Tourist Bazaar next to the New Winter Palace Hotel,* **t** *(095) 237 2215; open daily 8am–9pm*

***Airport*: t** *(095) 237 2306; open 8am–9pm in summer, 24 hours in winter*

Tourist Information in Luxor

At the Tourist Office, signposted as the Egyptian Tourist Authority, you can determine the official rates for car and carriage hire on both sides of the Nile, the cost of hiring a felucca or taking the ferry and the launches across the river, and the up-to-date entry fees for all temples and tombs. You will then be fully armed against the touts.

In an emergency, telephone **t** 123 – but do not expect anything to happen. Better to seek help at your hotel.

Visas can be extended at the Passport Office, **t** (095) 238 0885, on Sharia Khaled Ibn el Walid, about halfway down on the left (east) side (open 8–8, closed Fri).

Banks

The National Bank of Egypt is just south of the Old Winter Palace on Sharia el Nil (open daily 8.30am–2pm and 5pm-6pm; Fri 8.30–11; closed Sun). American Express and Thomas Cook, both in the arcade in front of the Old Winter Palace, can change money and traveller's cheques (open daily 8–8). All 5-star hotels and most other better hotels have exchange facilities.

There are ATMs at numerous points round town.

Communications

The main **post office** is on Sharia el Mahatta, and there's a branch in the Tourist Bazaar next to the Winter Palace Hotel.

The **central telephone office** is on Sharia el Karnak north of Luxor temple (open 24hrs). There are two further branches: in the arcade by the entrance to the old Winter Palace Hotel (open 8am–10pm) and at the railway station (open 8–8).

Internet access is widely available in Luxor, including at many hotels; ask and you will find.

Festivals

For the **moulid of Abu el Haggag** (the biggest in Upper Egypt, held on the 14th day of the Muslim month of Shaaban), and throughout the month of **Ramadan**, the mosque of Abu el Haggag is the focus of the nightly festivities. Hundreds of men gather in the gardens, some off to the sides playing cards, gambling, smoking hashish, many more listening raptly or dancing wildly to the drums, tambourines, ouds and violins, and to the teasing, climaxing, repeating passages of the imam's songs. They are religious songs, but passionate, or occasionally playful: a boy and girl are walking down a street hand in hand, they enter a house, they 'go to God together'. The audience laughs and shouts, but the lyrics are always secondary, and it is the narcotic beat and wailing of the music and the imam's exquisite phrasing that draws cries from the crowd. The imam twirls and sings, his eyes closed, his head shaking violently from side to side. A policeman in baggy khakis embraces him, rushes into the crowd to collect fistfuls of paper money and presses it into the imam's hands. Two or three dozen men begin to dance, arranging themselves in facing rows. First half-whirls, to the right, to the left, then hopping up and down, now jack-knifing, eyes closed, bodies sweating, shouting, whirling, hopping and jack-knifing in unison, beyond exhaustion. On the west bank the **moulid of Abu Kumsan** starts ten days before Ramadan and runs for three action-packed days and nights with horse-racing, stick-dancing, market stalls, entertainments, a funfair and prayer meetings. It takes place to the west of the mortuary temple of Seti I.

Shopping in Luxor

The principal market street in Luxor is **Sharia el Souk**, which begins north off Sharia el Mahatta as Sharia el Birka. *Galabiyyas* and spices and much else can be purchased here. Along the front of the Old Winter Palace are arcades of agencies and shops selling the usual souvenirs, among them A.A. Gaddis, with a good range of books, prints and old photographs. Immediately north of the New Winter Palace is the **Tourist Bazaar**. Here you will find Aboudi's shop, run by the successors of that wonderful dragoman-cum-poetaster (mentioned on p.304), which sells books (but alas not his guide), clothing, jewellery and souvenirs.

For **maps and guides**, try Aboudi in the Tourist Bazaar near the New Winter Palace Hotel, or A.A. Gaddis in the arcade in front of the Old Winter Palace Hotel.

If you are shopping for **souvenirs** there are any number of touts on both sides of the river who will importune you ad nauseam with pharaonic relics. None of it is genuine, and you should offer no more than one-tenth the asking price: it will be accepted with alacrity. Decent replicas of antiquities are on sale in the arcades by the Old Winter Palace.

Where to Stay on the East Bank

Luxor offers various luxury hotels, mostly built in the last 15 years. Courtesy buses, even boats, take you into town. Many of the newer places are aimed at the package tour market, and they can suddenly fill up when a group arrives. Standards however are at least decent throughout the range, and rooms are usually air-conditioned. Nevertheless you should check your room before accepting; standards can vary greatly within a hotel. Note also that many places are upgrading themselves. The pools at the 4- and 5-star hotels are usually open to non-guests for a fee. Also, the 5-star and some lesser hotels have oriental floorshows and discos.

Luxury ($$$$$)

★ Winter Palace >>

*****Winter Palace, Sharia el Nil, **t** (095) 238 0425, *www.sofitel.com/gb/hotel-1661-sofitel-winter-palace-luxor/index.shtml*. Just south of the Temple of Luxor, this is the place to stay for atmosphere. Winter Palace is the original name, but for decades this was known as the Old Winter Palace because in the 1970s the ugly New Winter Palace was tacked on alongside. Now both hotels have been taken over by the French Sofitel group, and this has reverted to being called the Winter Palace, while the New Winter Palace is now called the Pavillon Winter Hotel. The Winter Palace, built in 1886, is a living monument to the heyday of leisured travel. It has been refurbished and equipped with the usual modern in-room facilities. At the rear, the rooms overlook a well-planted garden, where there is a swimming pool, bar and outdoor restaurant, while the Nile-side rooms offer beautiful views across the river. The arcades on either side of the drive leading up to the Winter Palace are lined with shops and agencies.

*******Hilton Luxor Resort**, New Karnak, **t** (095) 237 4933, *www.hilton.co.uk/luxor*. Set in Karnak village on the east bank of the Nile. It offers four restaurants, three bars, with dining indoors and out. Lots of sports and activities, including squash, tennis, golf and horseback riding. Also there is a spa with such treats as Nile-side massages, 'holistic cocooning' and 'couple's serail mud experience'.

★ Maritim Jolie Ville Luxor Island Resort >>

*****Maritim Jolie Ville Luxor Island Resort, 4km south of town, **t** (095) 227 4855, *www.maritim.de/typo3/english/hotels/hotels/jolie-ville-luxor-island-resort.html*. Bungalow-style rooms each with private terrace located on richly landscaped Crocodile Island, with swimming pool, tennis courts, playground and mini-zoo; ideal for families, and a paradise for relaxing and enjoying nature.

Expensive ($$$$)

*******Pavillon Winter Hotel**, Sharia el Nil, **t** (095) 238 0425, *www.sofitel.com/gb/hotel-1662-pavillon-winter-luxor/*

index.shtml. Formerly called the New Winter Palace, this is a 1975 concrete eyesore adjoining the original Winter Palace and close by the Temple of Luxor. It should never have been built, and unfortunately it has withstood recent attempts to have it torn down; instead it is now the sow's ear in the Sofitel crown. It has a bank and shops, and there is a swimming pool in the gardens at the back.

*****Sofitel Karnak Luxor**, **t** (095) 237 8020, *www.sofitel.com/gb/hotel-5552-sofitel-karnak-luxor/index.shtml*. A luxury resort set in the countryside 6km north of town, 3km north of Karnak, with tennis, squash, two outdoor pools (one heated), boating trips, plus bars and three restaurants, one in the form of an Egyptian temple.

*****Pyramisa Isis**, **t** (095) 237 3366, *www.pyramisaegypt.com/pyramisaisis hotel/location.asp*. Overlooking the Nile on the nasty tourist strip immediately south of the Winter Palace, this is cheaper than the other modern 5-star hotels with the same facilities.

****Mercure Luxor**, **t** (095) 237 4944, *www.mercure.com/gb/hotel-1800-mercure-luxor/index.shtml*. On Sharia el Nil between the Temple of Luxor and the museum. This is an example of a hotel in which the architect clearly attempted to re-create the claustrophobia of a pharaonic tomb – and succeeded. You won't actually bang your head on the lobby ceiling, and perhaps because the area is crammed with shops and a 24-hour café there is a busyness here. The bars and restaurants are good, there is entertainment (disco, belly dancing) and a pool. In the main building, all rooms have Nile-side balconies; in the rear annexe, all look at other rooms.

★ Luxor Hotel >>

****Iberotel**, formerly the Novotel, on the hotel strip, Sharia Khaled ibn el Walid, 500m south of the Temple of Luxor, **t** (095) 238 0924, *www.jaz.travel/ English/Iberotel_Luxor_discover.asp*. A concrete box built round an atrium with vaguely the feel of a caravanserai, it has a pool and terrace restaurant overlooking the Nile, and small but well-equipped rooms, some overlooking the river.

Moderate ($$$)

***Emilio**, Sharia Yussef Hassan, **t** (095) 237 6666, *www.emiliotravel.com*. On the corner of Sharia el Karnak, back from the corniche and just north of the Temple of Luxor. Rooms are comfortably furnished and include video TV; some have balconies with views over the temple, and there is a shaded roof terrace restaurant. This is a popular place.

***Philippe**, Sharia Nefertiti, off the corniche north of the Mercure Luxor, **t** (095) 237 2284, *www.philippeluxor hotel.com*. A newish hotel, clean and friendly, with a good reputation – try to book ahead. There is a downstairs restaurant and bar, and a pool and rooftop garden. All rooms are air-conditioned; those to the front, with a glancing view of the Nile, have balconies.

***St Joseph Hotel**, Sharia Khaled ibn el Walid, 350m along the strip south of Luxor Temple, **t** (095) 238 1707, (095) 238 1727. A modern and friendly family-run hotel with well-equipped rooms including private bathrooms and satellite TV, heated rooftop pool, cellar bar and excellent breakfast buffet. It also features popular evening entertainments with local music.

***New Pola Hotel**, Sharia Khaled ibn el Walid, 350m south of the Temple of Luxor, and just before you reach the St Joseph Hotel, **t** (095) 236 5081, *www.newpolahotel.com*. A new and friendly hotel with basic clean rooms equipped with minibar and satellite TV and balconies looking out towards the Nile. Excellent value for money.

Inexpensive ($$)

Luxor Hotel, **t** (095) 238 0018, **f** (095) 238 0017, facing the Temple of Luxor. Another survivor from the good old days, though survivor may be saying too much for this thoroughly decrepit place, whose broken down magnificence is likely to appeal only to enthusiasts and connoisseurs. Dating back to the 19th century, this is the oldest of Luxor's old hotels. It is built in Moorish style with *ablaq* arches and columns along the verandah (where a plaque commemorates Luxor's turn-of-the-century vicar to the English community who went off to Messina in Sicily where he died in the great 1908 earthquake which took 200,000 lives). The hotel is set back in its gardens from the Nile and so lacks river views, but it does look upon the Temple of Luxor, especially if you get a room with a terrace at the northwest corner, one of the finest spots in town. The front gardens, once private and secluded, where you could enjoy late afternoon tea and evening drinks, have been squatted upon by several popular cafés. Behind the hotel is another garden, which is lovely, but its pool is empty and its bar and restaurant no longer function. The cause of this neglect has been the outrageous behaviour of the Egyptian government towards Wena Hotels, a British company set up by an Egyptian, which obtained the lease to operate the hotel. Wena has won a $20 million judgement against the government in compensation for its behaviour which included sending in thugs to harrass staff and guests and to trash the building, but the government continues to obstruct. When finally somebody fixes this place up, you will not be able to afford to stay here.

****Horus**, Sharia el Karnak, **t** (095) 237 2165, **f** (095) 373 447. A few metres north off Sharia el Mahatta as it reaches the Temple of Luxor. The hotel overlooks the temple but also the Abu el Haggag Mosque, so you will benefit from the dawn call to prayer, and the four that follow throughout the day. Gaudy from the outside, simple and decent within, the Horus is a refurbished old-style hotel offering a range of rooms and prices, including air conditioning and bathrooms, so you should ask to be shown a few first. The hotel has laundry service, a currency exchange desk, a bar and restaurant.

****Mina Palace**, Sharia el Nil, **t/f** (095) 237 2074. On the corniche immediately north of the Temple of Luxor and opposite the Mummification Museum, with most of its balconied rooms overlooking the Nile, those on the south corner with a second balcony overlooking the temple as well. Rooms have comfortable beds, are spotless, and have bathrooms and satellite TV. Watch the sun go down behind the Theban Mountain while having a drink on the rooftop terrace. Excellent value.

*****Tutotel**, 1 Sharia Salah al-Din, just off the roundabout soon after the Winter Palace Hotel, **t** (095) 237 7990. A well-located and comfortable hotel with a homey Egyptian feel. Disco in the cellar. Most rooms with a Nile view but sometimes lacking in cleanliness. You may do better at some of the hotels in the cheap category.

Cheap ($)

Most of Luxor's cheap hotels and pensions are clustered in three areas: near the railway station (Sharia el Mahatta), on and in the streets off Television Street (Sharia Television) in the south of town, and along Sharia Yussef Hassan near the souk. Standards, even from room to room within a place, vary considerably. Some might insist on half-board, especially during the winter season. And some may have upgraded themselves by adding facilities, lifting them out of the cheapest price bracket by the time you get there.

★ Little Garden >>

***Little Garden**, Sharia Radwan, off Television Street, **t** (095) 227 9090, *www.littlegardenhotel.com*. Spacious, clean and comfortable rooms, rooftop sunbeds and showers, and a garden. A delightful place and very good value.

***Happy Land**, Sharia el Kamrr, off Television Street, **t** (095) 237 1828, *www.luxorhappyland.com*. Small and quiet, its rooms are spic and span clean, all with fans, most with private baths. Rooftop terrace. A friendly place.

***Anglo Hotel**, **t/f** (095) 238 1679, Midan Mahatta, just south of the station. A clean and friendly place, with new rooms equipped with air conditioning and private bathrooms.

Nefertiti >

*Nefertiti, Sharia el Karnak, **t** (095) 372 386, *www.nefertitihotel.com*. Centrally located amid the Luxor souk and overlooking the avenue of sphinxes leading north from Luxor Temple. The hotel has been run by a welcoming Bedouin family for generations. Rooms are clean and have baths. Meals are served on the rooftop terrace. Also part of the family business is the El Sahaby restaurant (*see* opposite), spilling out onto the street next door, which is the oldest in Luxor, with excellent local cuisine.

*__Venus__, Sharia Yussef Hassan, **t** (095) 238 2625. A favourite with back-packers; a bit shabby but centrally located, cheap, and has lively views over the souk. The rooms are clean, simple and have fans; most have private baths, some are air-conditioned. Meals are cheap and good, beer is served in the bar, and the atmosphere is liberal.

Hostels and Camping

You will not save much by staying at a hostel or campsite, nor are they conveniently situated – all are in the north of town and something of a lonely exile. The Rezeiky Camp at least has a swimming pool, but otherwise these places will only suit those with a passion for tents and curfews.

Youth Hostel, on a side road off Sharia el Karnak near the Luxor Museum, **t** (095) 237 2139. Membership is not obligatory but makes your stay cheaper still. There are dorms with bunks and also family rooms with double beds and private baths. It fills up quickly with Egyptian students in winter. Lockout is from 10am to 2pm, and curfew is at 11pm.

Rezeiky Camp, a couple of hundred metres farther north along Sharia el Karnak from the youth hostel, **t** (095) 238 1334, *www.rezeikycamp.com.eg*. Has a swimming pool, bar and restaurant. You can pitch your tent in the partly shaded grounds, seek a roof over your head in one of their grotty cabins with shared toilets and showers, or shell out for a room with bath.

Eating Out on the East Bank

There is a certain earnestness about Luxor: so many antiquities lying on either side of the river, requiring early risings to see them before the day grows too hot. Accordingly, visitors go to bed early and there is not a great deal of choice, nor are the standards particularly high for eating out.

The expensive restaurants are, as you might expect, to be found in the top hotels; the finest is the **1886 restaurant** in the Winter Palace Hotel, a superb experience and not necessarily all that pricey. A selection of less expensive options follows.

Expensive ($$$$)

El Nakheel >>

El Nakheel restaurant, Winter Palace, in the garden by the pool, offers light refreshments. *Open 12–4pm.*

Moderate ($$$)

El Kababgy >>

El Kababgy, Corniche el Nil. Opposite the Winter Palace and down the steps to a waterfront terrace where the feluccas tie up, providing a picturesque backdrop as you enjoy a cold beer, light snack or full meal. The cuisine is traditional Egyptian. In summer a mist machine keeps you agreeably cool.

Ali Baba restaurant. Next to the Luxor Hotel, entrance in the side street, Sharia Mohammed Farid, one flight up to the open terrace, its chief amenity the view towards the Temple of Luxor.

Sofra >>

Sofra, 90 Sharia Mohammed Farid, towards the railway line in the old part of town called Manshiya, **t** (095) 235 9752, *www.sofra.com.eg*. Sofra occupies a traditional Egyptian house of the 1930s, its three private dining rooms and the main salon on the ground floor filled with antique oriental furniture, colourful copper lamps and beautiful mirrors.

Oasis Café >>

Oasis Café, Sharia Labaib Habachi. Facing the Mercure hotel, this is the street that runs along it on the left. On the same side as the hotel you come to a tall pink building; the Oasis Café is on the ground floor. Similar to

Sofra but not so ornate, its 1940s music and décor might remind you more of Rick's Café in *Casablanca*. No cards accepted. *Open 10am–10pm.*

Inexpensive ($$)

El Sahaby ›

El Sahaby restaurant in Sharia El Sahaby, which runs alongside the Nefertiti Hotel in Sharia el Karnak. With tables spilling out into the street, this is the oldest restaurant in Luxor, serves excellent local cuisine, and is run by the same Bedouin family that runs the hotel.

There are numerous inexpensive restaurants serving simple dishes at tables both indoors and outdoors (but no alcohol) just north of the Abu el Haggag Mosque. Beyond these and heading into Sharia el Souk there are several agreeable local cafés where tric trac is played. Here between Sharia el Souk and Sharia el Karnak you will find the **New Oum Khalsoum Café**, where you can perch out on the terrace and enjoy a coffee or juice or puff on a *narghileh* to recover from a hard stint of bargaining in the bazaar while a mist machine keeps you cool.

King's Head Pub, about two-thirds of the way along Sharia Khaled Ibn el Walid. The pub sign, a head of Akhenaten, hangs from the building, and the pub itself is on the second floor above a carpet bazaar. Good food (from curries through chips to Yorkshire pudding), good bar, excellent service, jazz and reggae music, a pool table, darts, and a wide selection of newspapers and magazines to read. *Open all day and most of the night.*

The West Bank: The Necropolis of Thebes

During the New Kingdom, when Thebes was the opulent capital of Egypt, a vast necropolis was founded across the river, on the west bank of the Nile. A **tour** of the necropolis involves following a north–south arc, starting at either end. If you are feeling adventurous and want to follow the path from the Valley of the Kings to Deir el Bahri for its marvellous views, you should start at the north, visiting first the Temple of Seti I, continuing to the Valley of the Kings, Deir el Bahri, the Tombs of the Nobles, the Ramesseum, Deir el Medina, the Valley of the Queens, Medinet Habu and back to the river via the Colossi of Memnon. This guide describes the tour in that order.

At least two days are required to complete this tour, but if you have only one day you will have to pick among the highlights, e.g. the Valley of the Kings (2 hours), Deir el Bahri (30 minutes), the Tombs of the Nobles (30 minutes–1 hour) and either the Ramesseum (30 minutes) or Medinet Habu (30 minutes). If you have a second day, visit those sites you missed the first time round.

A warning, taken from a newspaper report: 'The mystery of a Canadian woman's disappearance two years ago at Luxor was unravelled this week when police located her remains in an archaeological ditch. Before dying she had scribbled on a postcard that she fell inside the labyrinth after losing her way, and she was preparing herself for death from thirst and hunger. The police

Getting to the West Bank

Because of the intense heat of the afternoon, it is usual to take the **ferry** across from Luxor to the west bank of the Nile very early in the morning and to complete your explorations by about 1pm. However, if you do not mind the heat, stay until the tombs close when there are fewer fellow tourists (especially fewer tour groups, coachloads of whom pound over the bridge 7km upriver from Luxor). The long incline to the Valley of the Kings is best done by car, followed by a walk over the escarpment and down to Deir el Bahri, the Temple of Hatshepsut; the driver will leave you at the Valley of the Kings and collect you later at Hatshepsut's temple. The rest of the west bank can be covered by **bicycle** if you are up to it; it gives you more time and frees you from the impatient harassment of a driver. Those in search of the perversely picaresque can still ride a donkey on the West Bank, but only as an organized trek, not for visiting the sites. Horses and camels can be hired for romping about the open spaces behind Medinet Habu, etc., but likewise not for exploring the necropolis.

Note that before even crossing over to the west bank you should go to the Tourist Office in Luxor (*see* p.294) and arm yourself with the official rates for hiring taxis. Drivers will often try to tie you down to a schedule or a route, saying that their price will cover such and such in half a day or a full day. This should be resisted. Better that you pay by the hour, or if necessary by the half or full day, but reserve to yourself the absolute discretion as to which sites you will visit, in which order, and how long you will spend at each. Always agree clearly on the price beforehand, and do not pay a single piastre until the driver has fulfilled his side of the bargain.

Crossing the Nile

The 'people ferry' as the municipal ferry is known (*baladi* in Arabic) departs from the corniche by the Temple of Luxor Winter Palace and lands you on the West Bank where there will be a hoard of waiting taxis and their drivers (though you may also be approached by a driver on the ferry itself). These ferries cost LE1 on the way over and make no charge for the return journey; they carry bicycles for free. There are also private launches all along the corniche which sail on demand, cost LE5 to LE10 return, and do not carry bicycles.

The recent construction of a bridge (no toll) 7km south of Luxor has had an unfortunate effect on the west bank. Ferries were once the only way across, and this preserved something of its traditional character and tranquillity. Now that unlimited numbers of tourist coaches can thunder their way across, the west bank is becoming increasingly developed and commercialized. The independent traveller can likewise join the rat-run, hiring a taxi in Luxor to take one over the bridge and round the west bank sites, but it is a dull thing to do and will prove more expensive than hiring a taxi on the other side.

---

located her skeleton this week, her clothes still on, in a distant area behind the pharaonic temples where archaeological digs were under way.' Now, while not wishing to inhibit the curiosity of travellers, it is worth mentioning that care should be taken at excavations and you should not get off the beaten track if exploring on your own.

A Historical Background

A Case of Looting in Pharaonic Times

Under the powerful pharaohs of the XVIII and XIX Dynasties local officials were closely supervised and tomb looting kept in check. But under the weaker rulers of the XX Dynasty tombs were robbed. A picture of surprising detail can be built up from surviving papyri of the necropolis workers enduring food shortages and late payment of wages, of riots, pay disputes and strikes. There are also documented accounts of bribery and collusion among workers, priests and officials. One papyrus describes a major Theban law case during the reign of Ramses IX (XX Dyn), in which the mayor of

Tickets

Tickets for the mortuary temples (except Deir el Bahri), Deir el Medina and most of the Tombs of the Nobles are sold at the kiosk next to the Tourist Police headquarters by Medinet Habu. Tickets for Deir el Bahri are sold at the site. Tickets for the Valley of the Kings and the tomb of Ay in the Western Valley are sold at the Valley of the Kings, while there is a special ticket booth at the Valley of the Kings for the tomb of Tutankhamun.

And we made the gold which we had found on these two gods – from their mummies, amulets, ornaments and coffins – into eight shares. And two kilos of gold fell to each of us.

A XX Dynasty tomb robber

Thebes brought to the vizier's attention stories of tomb robbing at the necropolis. The matter was investigated by the chief of the necropolis police and the stories denied; the vizier then ensured that the mayor of Thebes was disgraced for making malicious and politically inspired accusations. Some years later, however, as the tomb robbings continued, the case was reopened and it became clear that both the vizier and the chief of police were up to their eyeballs in corruption. Examined by birch and screw, the stonemason Amun-pa-nefer admitted tunnelling into a royal tomb and stripping the pharaoh and his queen of gold, silver and precious stones.

Amun-pa-nefer then described the chain of corruption: 'We then crossed over to Thebes. And after some days, the agents of Thebes heard that we had been stealing in the west, so they arrested me and imprisoned me at the mayor of Thebes' place. So I took the two kilos of gold that had fallen to me as my share, and gave them to Kha-em-Opet, the District Clerk of the harbour of Thebes. He let me go, and I joined my companions, and they made up for me another share. And I, as well as the other robbers who are with me, have continued to this day in the practice of robbing the tombs of the nobles and people of the land who rest in the west of Thebes. And a large number of the men of the land rob them also.' Presumably the bribe was shared out among other officials higher up the ladder, though no share fell to the mayor of Thebes, who was either an honest man or complained because he was being cut out of the action.

Iron Age Economic Crisis

The case has its anecdotal interest, but it throws light too on the causes underlying the enfeeblement of the New Kingdom from the XX Dynasty. In describing Karnak it was mentioned how an ever greater proportion of the nation's wealth went to the priesthood; much gold and silver was also literally buried underground in the tombs, taken out of circulation. Yet it was precisely at this time that the world was shifting from the Bronze Age to the Iron Age, and while Egypt had copper mines, she had no iron – the essential metal for weapon superiority. Under the Egyptian Empire, iron could be expropriated abroad; as the rule of the pharaohs weakened and the empire shrank, Egypt was forced to buy iron

Getting around the West Bank

By Taxi

Expect to pay about LE150 for half a day (4hrs); proportionately more per additional hour. This is regardless of the number of people carried, which depending on the car can be from 4 to 7 persons. For this price the taxi is exclusively yours throughout. If during winter there is a lot of business, the driver may ask that he be free to zoom off when you do not need him, and if you agree then a discount is in order.

For odd journeys, try your luck by hiring a taxi to the Valley of the Kings, walking over the ridge to Deir el Bahri, and then catching a taxi from there to somewhere else.

By Pick-up Truck

A recent innovation, and a variation on taking a taxi, is the use of small pick-up trucks or vans with flat backs and bench seats arranged along each side. They are as roadworthy as taxis, much cheaper and more fun. You can usually flag one down to take you from one site to another, or to ride between the ferry landing and the ticket office (about LE5 each leg).

By Bicycle

Bicycles, hired for about LE15 or so per day in Luxor or on the west bank, are the best way to get around – if you are fit. As you pedal along past tombs and temples you are surprisingly cool and sweatless in the dry air (though beware of sunstroke); the instant you stop the sweat pours off you in buckets. Bring plenty of drinking water. The one disadvantage of a bicycle (apart from heart attacks and sunstroke) is not being able to walk from the Valley of the Kings to Deir el Bahri – this walk is highly recommended.

Bicycles can be hired at a number of places on the west bank. There are many places dotted about the west bank that will mend punctures and do general running repairs.

If you have a problem or get too tired, you can always flag down a taxi and put your bike in the back.

By Horse, Camel and Donkey

Horses, camels and donkeys are not for hire to visit the sites. But riding a horse or camel along farm tracks and the edge of the desert is enjoyable, especially if you are staying on the west bank and have the time. The best riding is early in the morning and during the late afternoon. Camel drivers wait amid the scrum at the people's ferry landing, while both camels and Arab horses can be hired from the stables on the left of the road leading away from the landing. These include Pharaoh's Stable, **t** (095) 231 2263, and the Arabian Horse Stable, **t** (095) 231 0024. Expect to pay LE40 per hour.

Donkeys are good for climbing over difficult terrain, and for that you will have to join a trek taking you over the Theban Mountain, usually lasting five hours, or hire the donkey with a guide. Pharoah's Stables has donkeys for about LE20 per hour. But donkeys are uncomfortable and are a perversely picaresque form of travel, best avoided.

Horse, camel and donkey treks can be arranged at most of the smaller hotels in Luxor.

---

abroad, making payment in gold and silver. The value of these precious metals rose during the period 1150 to 1110 BC (Ramses V–Ramses X, approximately). Food shortages and wage delays followed; the necropolis workers struck and many of them turned to tomb robbing. The bonanza of precious metals and stones they clawed back from the tombs and put into circulation, however corrupt the channels might have been, soon relieved the situation. By that time the Empire was finished, the moral authority of the administration had been sapped, and power fell to Herihor, a general who became military dictator, assumed the high priesthood of Amun and made himself pharaoh. His power extended only over Upper Egypt however; Lower Egypt was ruled by merchant princes at Tanis and the country was never long united again.

Access and Fees

Sites on the west bank are open 7–5 in winter, 7–6 in summer, with no lunchtime closure. The ticket kiosk is open 6–4 in winter, 6–5 in summer. Tickets are valid on the day of purchase only. Nefertari's tomb has been closed for some years; check to see if it has reopened, but if it has note that tickets are likely to be severely limited as in the past.

It is often said that you should start early to avoid the crowds. But the crowds all have the same idea, giving you good reason to start late.

Tickets are required for almost all sites and must be purchased in advance. Tickets for the mortuary temples (except Deir el Bahri), Deir el Medina and most of the Tombs of the Nobles are sold at the kiosk next to the Tourist Police headquarters by Medinet Habu. Tickets for Deir el Bahri are sold at the site. Tickets for the Valley of the Kings and the tomb of Ay in the Western Valley are sold at the Valley of the Kings, while there is a special ticket booth at the Valley of the Kings for the tomb of Tutankhamun.

Tickets are sold for specific sites and normally can only be used for that site (though sometimes you can haggle your way in to a site with a different but same-price ticket). As the opening times for the various sites can change from time to time, you should check at the ticket kiosk near Medinet Habu, where the latest information is clearly displayed.

As tickets are valid on the day of purchase only, you should ration yourself to what your time and energy will allow: it is easy to be over-ambitious, especially in the heat and more especially so if you are intending to walk over the mountain path between the Valley of the Kings and Deir el Bahri. You could either make a selection from the highlights, e.g. the Valley of the Kings, Deir el Bahri, the Tombs of the Nobles and the Ramesseum or Medinet Habu, or you could first buy tickets for a selection of sites in the northern part of the necropolis and then return to the kiosk to buy tickets for those in the southern part.

Tickets are generally LE30 per site, but there are exceptions. The Tombs of the Nobles range from LE15 to LE30. The Valley of the Kings is LE80 for three tombs (a further LE80 must be paid for each additional set of three tombs you wish to visit); the tomb of Ramses VI costs an additional LE50 while Tutankhamun's tomb is likewise charged separately at LE100. There is no charge for seeing the Colossi of Memnon, nor for wandering around Deir el Medina (the Workmen's village), though LE30 is payable to enter the tombs there. These prices are set annually and are likely to increase with each passing year, so expect to pay a bit more.

Photography in all tombs is forbidden. **Toilets** are found at the Valley of the Kings, at the restaurant in front of Deir el Bahri, near the Ramesseum and at the restaurant opposite Medinet Habu. There are also 'mobile' toilets in the car parks at most sites. There is a **pharmacy** about 400m along the main road running west from the people's ferry landing stage. There are also two good pharmacies near the mortuary temple of Seti I; the hospital is close by.

From the west bank landing stages the road runs to the new village of Gurna and continues on past the Colossi of Memnon towards the Theban Mountain. At the village another road runs north towards the Temple of Seti I.

The New and Old Villages of Gurna

The work of an architect who designs, say, an apartment house in the poor quarters of Cairo for some stingy speculator, in which he incorporates various features of modern design copied from fashionable European work, will filter down, over a period of years, through the cheap suburbs and into the village where it will slowly poison the genuine tradition.

Hassan Fathy, *Architecture for the Poor*

Aboudi and his Guidebook

In the bad old days when donkeys were the only means of getting about the west bank, there was a wonderful Thomas Cook dragoman called Mohammed Aboudi, who later opened a shop in Luxor and published a near-to-useless and vastly entertaining guide. Alas, neither is extant. But for a while Aboudi was private secretary to Cole Porter both in Europe and Egypt, and it was perhaps this connection which encouraged Aboudi to leaven his guide book with his own poetry. It deserves what further lease on life this present guide can provide; for example:

O East is East and West is West in Luxor or in London town;
But Aboudi, our faithful Aboudi, will never let us down.
Through all the plagues of Egypt, donkey-boys, the flies, the sand,
This trusty modern Moses leads us towards the Promised Land.
Weird tales of long dead ages come tripping from his tongue,
With him through tombs and temples we pass in wondering throng.
And when foot and brain are weary with the sights we've come to see,
He calls our patient donkeys up to bear us home to tea.
Surely in future ages the tourists all will stand,
An unabridged edition of Rosetta in each hand,
And read the hieroglyphics which proclaim how Pharaoh's Cook,
By his henchman, great Aboudi, mighty hosts through Egypt took!
There's one thing more, if you can stick it:
The law of this land is very intricate.
At each temple gate is an Arab picket,
So please don't forget your little ticket;
And galloping donkeys is not allowed!

New Gurna was built in the late 1940s by the Egyptian architect Hassan Fathy. Employing the almost forgotten art of forming vaults and domes in mud brick without the use of timber centring, his aim was to reintroduce 'a way of building that was a natural growth in the landscape, as much a part of it as the palm tree.' He died in 1989, disappointed in his hope that traditional methods could solve urgent housing needs in the Third World, avoiding extravagant and climatically unsuitable Western technology. In his famous testament *Architecture for the Poor*, he objected to the bastardization of Arab architecture as applied to recent hotel design and the interior decoration of restaurants and nightclubs.

Though the project was commissioned by the government, bureaucratic red tape and the erratic provision of funds ensured that New Gurna was never entirely finished, though the houses all have plumbing, and a theatre and recreation centre were provided. One reason for this lies in Luxor's oldest profession. Over the past 3,000 years or more, easy access to the Theban tombs has provided villagers on the west bank with an extra source of income. It was partly to check this that the new village was built, and for this same reason that New Gurna has been so much resented. However, a locally-based group has now turned Hassan Fathy's house, next to the theatre, into a museum and a study centre dedicated to his work, while the *khan* provides workshops and serves as a showcase for traditional crafts.

Meanwhile the Ministry of Antiquities has now ejected the inhabitants out of the string of hamlets that made up the village of **Old Gurna** (properly Sheikh Abd el Gurna) at the foot of the Theban Mountain. Almost all traces of old Gurna have been destroyed and the population has been moved into a modern housing estate to the north (which locals will sometimes, confusingly, call new Gurna), just past the turning to the Valley of the Kings. The villagers offered strong resistance, objecting to leaving the houses in which they have lived for generations and having to move away from the land they farm close by. They objected also to losing the income from robbing the tombs over which many of their houses had been built.

Temple of Seti I

13 Temple of Seti I

Even more so than Karnak, the tombs and mortuary temples of the Theban necropolis tell of the rise and fall of the New Kingdom and the Egyptian Empire.

The Mortuary Temple of Seti I (XIX Dyn) lies off the road to the Valley of the Kings and is usually bypassed by tourists in haste. This in itself should recommend it; also that the works of Seti's reign – famously his temple at Abydos – are among the finest and most restrained of the New Kingdom. The temple was founded in honour of Amun but was also devoted to the worship of Seti's father, Ramses I. The first two pylons and courts have been destroyed; what remains is the temple proper and a tour of it is made both at ground level and, the better to see certain reliefs, by leaping goat-like after the resident guide, from architrave to broken architrave.

A colonnade facing east towards the Nile admits, through a central door, to a **hypostyle hall** with six columns decorated with reliefs of Seti and Ramses II making offerings to divinities. On either side of the hall are small **chapels** with very fine reliefs of Seti, his ka, his sacred boat, Thoth and Osiris, as he offers sacrifices and performs ceremonies en route to the afterlife. The **sanctuary**, once containing Amun's sacred boat, lies beyond. Reliefs show Seti offering incense before the boat. To the left (south) of the hypostyle hall is the **chapel of Ramses I**. On the side walls of the central chamber, Seti is again depicted offering incense to Amun's boat, and anoints a statue of Ramses I with his finger. The chambers on either side were given inferior reliefs by Ramses II. The right (north) side of the temple is ruinous; a larger hall, dedicated to Re-Herakhte, was built by Ramses II and decorated with crude reliefs.

The obsessive appropriations of Ramses II and their inferior quality stand out among the works of Seti I who consciously sought a renaissance in taste and values. But then Seti's own reliefs suffer from the New Kingdom preoccupation with gaining access to the afterlife: they are reassuring encounters with the gods at death, but do not concern themselves with the quality of life. If not yet in empire, certainly in spirit Egypt was in retreat.

The Valley of the Kings

4 Valley of the Kings

The flat alluvium suddenly quits and it is utter desert to the Valley of the Kings. Set amid trees on a hill where the road from Seti's temple is joined by the road from Deir el Bahri is the **house where Howard Carter lived** during his search for the tomb of Tutankhamun. (Above it, on the barren summit of the hill, is another house, often identified as Carter's, but it is not.) The road climbs towards the oven of white sand and sun that is **Biban el Muluk** – the 'Gates of the Kings'. Unblinking tomb entrances stare vacantly from the close valley walls. Each ramp is cut and swept, each doorway numbered in order of discovery: the most exclusive suburb in the world, where the mightiest dead once lay in silent, motionless expectation of awakening. Anxious priests, covetous archaeologists, and robbers caring more for life than life after, carried them away. Anubis and Osiris remain, paintings on the wall.

Burials at the Valley of the Kings date from the XVIII to the XX Dynasties, with Tuthmosis I being the first to select the site. Though the pharaohs and, rarely, certain exalted but non-royal personages were entombed here, offerings to the dead were made at the mortuary temples built on the plain. The tombs therefore were entirely private receptacles for the sarcophagus, and their decoration concentrated exclusively on the formulae efficacious in transferring the deceased from this world into the next. The tombs and their decorations can be impressive, and their contents of course were staggering, but they do not speak of life, of humanity, or even of personal death and resurrection – they are monuments of state and of ideology, and less vivid, less revealing than the tombs of the lesser dead elsewhere in the Theban necropolis.

The Tombs of the Pharaohs

In all, 62 tombs are known in the Valley of the Kings. A few of these were known and visited by tourists in Ptolemaic times as indicated by Diodorus and Strabo and the occasional Greek and Latin graffiti. Most are of little interest except to scholars and are closed to the public. Only tombs 2, 6, 8, 9, 11, 16, 17, 34, 35, 57 and 62 have electric lighting, and most visitors will be content to see those of **Tutankhamun (62)**, **Ramses VI (9)**, **Seti I (17)**, **Ramses IV (2)**

Valley of the Kings

1	Ramses VII	34	Tuthmosis III
2	Ramses IV	35	Amenophis II
3	Intended for Ramses III	36	Maherpra, fan-bearer to Hatshepsut (contents in Cairo Museum)
4	Ramses XII	37	No inscriptions
5	Sons of Ramses II	38	Tuthmosis I
6	Ramses IX	39–41	No inscriptions
7	Ramses II	42	Possibly Tuthmosis II
8	Merneptah	43	Tuthmosis IV
9	Ramses VI	44	No inscription
10	Amenmeses	45	Private tomb
11	Ramses III	46	Yuya and Tuya, parents of Queen Tiy, wife of Amenophis III (contents in Cairo Museum)
12	No inscriptions	47	Siptah
13	Intended for royal functionary	48	Vizier Amenemopet
14	Tausert, wife of Seti II	49–54	No inscriptions
15	Seti II	55	Tiy or Smenkhkare
16	Ramses I	56	No inscriptions
17	Seti I	57	Horemheb
18	Ramses X	58	Tutankhamun annex
19	Son of Ramses IX	59–61	No inscriptions
20	Hatshepsut	62	Tutankhamun
21	Unfinished		
22	Amenophis III (in the Western Valley)		
23	Ay (in the Western Valley)		
24, 25	No inscriptions (in the Western Valley)		
26–33	Unfinished		

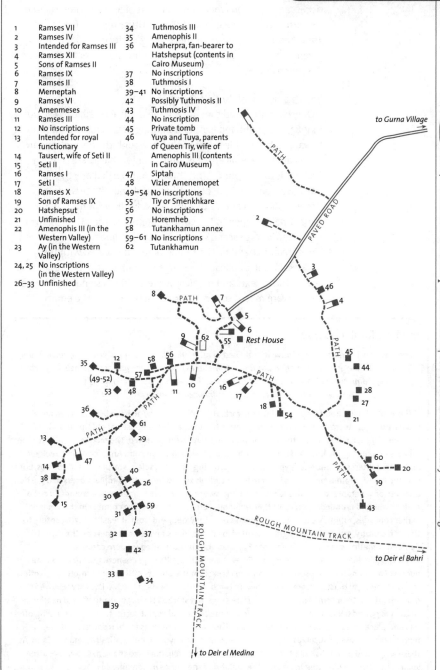

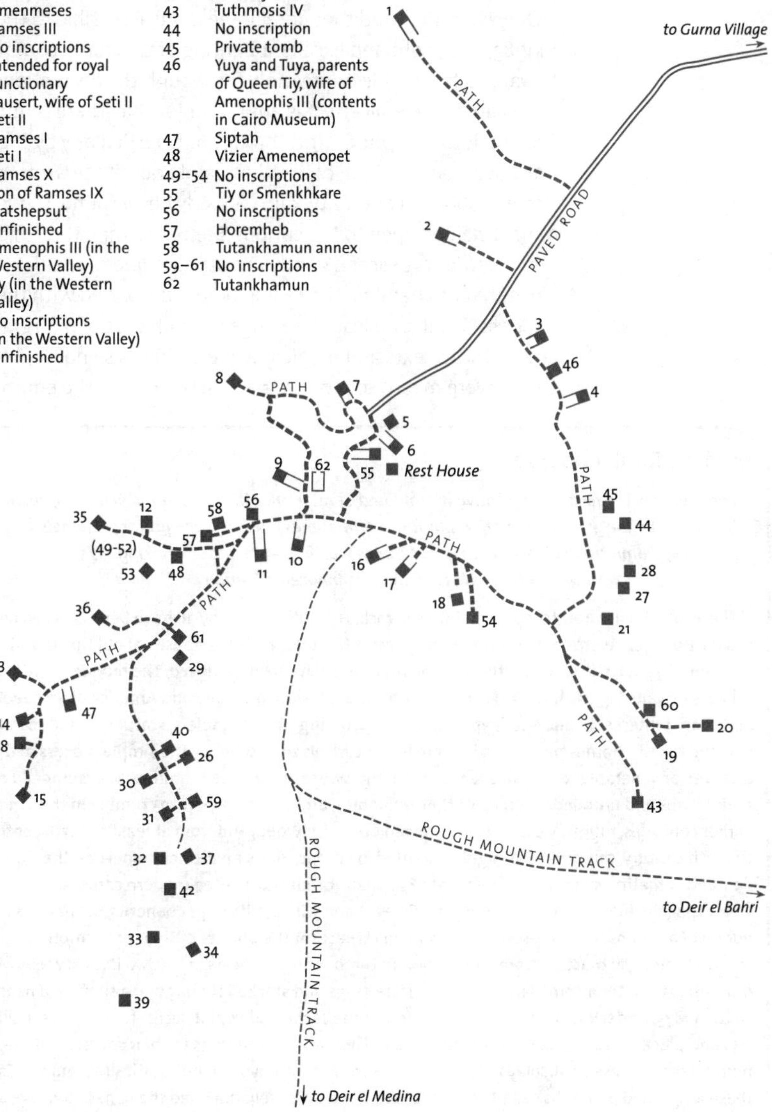

and **Tuthmosis III (34)**, and then possibly the tombs of **Amenophis II (35)** and **Horemheb (57)**. Not all of even these tombs will necessarily be open when you visit; that of Seti I has been closed for some time. There are plans to substitute replicas for Tutankhamun's tomb and others. The identity of all 62 tombs is given on the accompanying map, but only those electrically lit are described below.

Tomb 2: Ramses IV (XX Dyn)

Only electrified and therefore made more accessible to the public in 1983, the bright and excellent lighting of this tomb contributes towards a favourable impression, for though the decorations are third-rate the overall effect is entirely enjoyable. There is much Ptolemaic and Coptic graffiti throughout, particularly by the entrance – on the right, two haloed saints raise their arms in prayer. Robbed in antiquity, Ramses' body never found, the tomb long remained open to the curious. Steps and then three high white corridors descend gently in a straight line to the sarcophagus chamber. The ceiling here is decorated with the goddess Nut in duplicate. The huge sarcophagus of pink granite is covered with texts and magical scenes, while Isis and Nephthys on the lid were meant to protect the hijacked body – the empty

Modern Tomb Robbing

The fuel they use for the locomotive is composed of mummies three thousand years old, purchased by the ton or by the graveyard for that purpose ... Sometimes one hears the profane engineer call out pettishly, 'Damn these plebeians, they don't burn worth a cent – pass out a king.'

Mark Twain, *The Innocents Abroad*

There are at least 900 tombs built into the rock. The authorities say all have been checked and locked. But there were constant rumours of secret finds beneath the houses of old Gurna and occasionally even the wall paintings in known tombs have been removed. The modern heyday for tomb robbers was during the late 19th century with the explosion in Europe and America of archaeological and tourist interest in ancient Egypt. Luxor saw a roaring trade in tablets, statuettes and scarabs, both real and faked – home-made scarabs were fed to turkeys to 'acquire by the simple process of digestion a degree of venerableness that is really charming', wrote one visitor. Mummies were dragged out of their tombs and unrolled, stripped of their valuables, broken up and left to crumble in the sands. In earlier centuries, mummy cases were chopped up for firewood, and from at least the 13th century to the 19th century 'mummy' was highly regarded in Europe for its medicinal properties, the export demand sometimes proving so great that Egyptians often substituted modern corpses.

Not that the humble quest for loot has always been without its larger benefits, or that even the poorest Egyptians have not sometimes shown respect for the objects of their peculations. In an effort to save their royal masters from contemporary tomb robbers, priests in the XXI Dynasty removed the mummies from their tombs in the Valley of the Kings and stacked them, 30 in a shaft, in a nearby rocky cleft. In 1875, Abdel Rasul, sheikh of Gurna, found the cache and kept it secret for six years, selling off bits and pieces as he needed money. Archaeologists traced these clues to their source, and the mummies are those on display in the Mummy Room of the Egyptian Antiquities Museum in Cairo. As these long-dead pharaohs sailed down the Nile by steamer, fellahin lined the banks at village after village, the women ululating in lament, the men firing their rifles in homage.

Tomb Construction and Decoration

A similar pattern of construction and decoration is followed in each of the tombs. Three corridors lead to an antechamber giving onto the main hall with its sunken floor for receiving the sarcophagus. The tombs were cut into the soft limestone by two teams of 25 men working alternating ten-day shifts. They normally lived at Deir el Medina, but when on shift stayed in huts within the valley. Construction of a tomb began at the beginning of a reign and never took more than six years to complete. Once the interior surfaces were prepared, the designs and inscriptions were sketched in black; the designs filled in, the hieroglyphics outlined in red; the decorations carved and finally painted. In some tombs, notably that of Horemheb (57), these various stages of decoration are evident.

The dead pharaoh, absorbed in the sun god, sailed through the underworld at night in a boat, with enemies and dangers to be avoided along the way. This is the recurrent theme of the decorations, the inscriptions being extensive quotations from the Amduat or Book of the Underworld and the Book of the Gates which provide instructions for charting the course; the Book of Day and Night is also sometimes employed. Pictorially, there are three registers, the middle one showing the river of passage, the top and bottom registers depicting the shores with their inhabitants of deities and demons. The registers are divided into 12 sections for the 12 hours of the night. After this nocturnal voyage the naked body of the goddess Nut gives birth each morning to the sun. This is beautifully represented on the ceiling of the sarcophagus hall of the tomb of Ramses VI.

sarcophagus has been retrieved from the tomb of Amenophis II where the priests had hidden it. Throughout the chambers and corridors of the tomb, against all the whiteness, are small patterns of red, blue, yellow and some green pastels and this is pleasing, despite the poor carving and line and the sloppy application of colour. Indeed this slapdash effect has a quality of *gaieté*, as though the whole affair was a French reproduction.

Tomb 6: Ramses IX (XX Dyn)

A flight of steps on either side of an inclined plane leads you down to the tomb door, its lintel decorated with the solar disc, the pharaoh worshipping it on both sides. Behind him stands Isis (left) and Nephthys (right). The tomb is of near-model design: three corridors, an antechamber, but then a pillared hall and short passage before the final sarcophagus chamber. The decorations are similar to those in Tomb 9.

Tomb 8: Merneptah (XIX Dyn)

Merneptah, the possible pharaoh of the Exodus, was the son of Ramses II by his secondary wife Istnofret. His tomb, which descends steeply through corridor steps, is typical of XVIII and XIX Dynasty tombs; those of the XX Dynasty are shallower. Over the entrance, Isis and Nephthys worship the sun disc, while the entrance corridors are decorated with scenes from the Book of the Gates and other texts. In the small antechamber is the huge granite lid of the outer sarcophagus; a further flight of steps leads down to a pillared hall with barrelled roof containing the pink granite lid of the inner sarcophagus. Carved on the lid is the

Tomb 9: Ramses VI and Tomb 17: Seti I

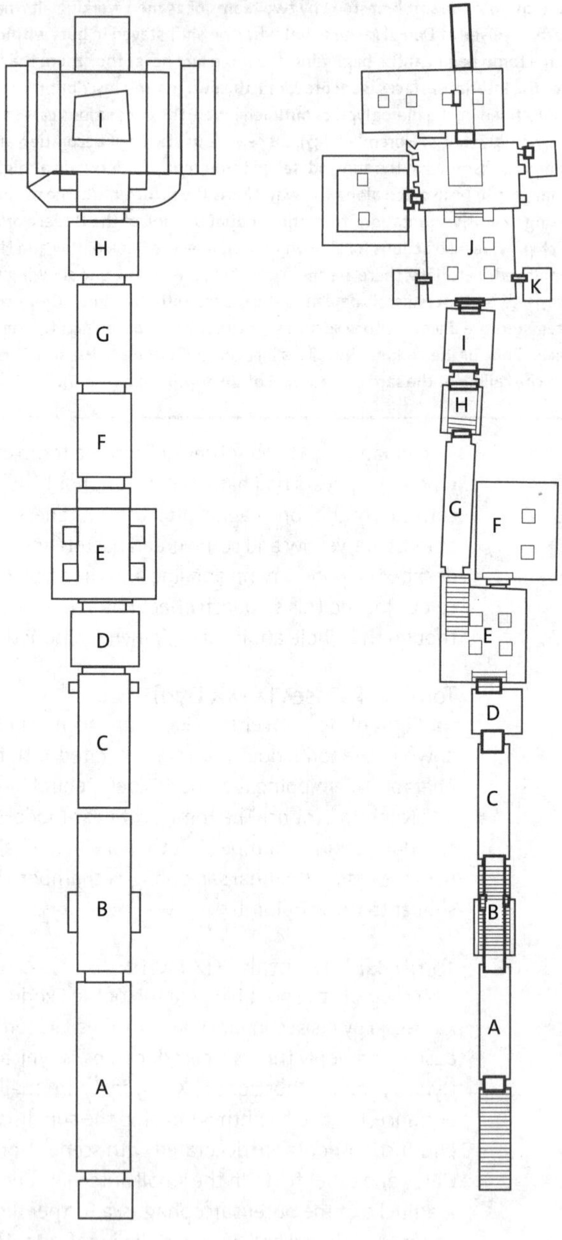

recumbent figure of Merneptah as Osiris, and on the underside is the goddess Nut.

Tomb 9: Ramses VI (XX Dyn)

Though decorated in sunk relief of workmanship inferior to that of the previous dynasty, the colouring remains fresh. The tomb was originally constructed for Ramses V and ended with Chamber E. On the left walls of this part of the tomb is the complete text of the Book of the Gates with a summary of the creation of the world on the left part of the rear wall of E. Another text, the Book of Caverns, decorates the right walls, while the ceilings of C, D and E are decorated with the Book of Day and Night. Corridors F and G show the hours from the Amduat on their walls. In Chamber H are portions of the Book of the Dead; on the left wall is the negative confession. The admission of any transgression would have prevented entry into the afterlife, and so the 'confession' was a series of denials ('I have not done this or that'). The pillared Chamber I contains fragments of the great granite sarcophagus. Its vaulted ceiling is splendidly painted with the Book of Day and Night, the sky goddess Nut appearing twice, back to back, framing the Book of Day on the entrance side, and on the far side the Book of Night.

Tomb 11: Ramses III (XX Dyn)

One of the largest tombs in the valley, the second half is ruinous and not illuminated. Once again the decorations are inferior sunk relief, but they are exceptionally varied and remain freshly coloured. This is sometimes called the 'Harpers' Tomb' after the two harpers playing to divinities in the last of four small chambers opening off the left-hand side of the second corridor. This tomb is unique in having ten side-chambers off its entrance corridors; where they do occur in tombs, they were for receiving tomb furniture. Beyond these the tomb turns to the right and then to the left and the third chamber along is a sloping passage with side galleries and four pillars: the perspective through here to the rooms beyond is impressive.

Tomb 16: Ramses I (XIX Dyn)

Though founder of his dynasty, Ramses I reigned for only a year or two and was interred in a simple tomb. A sloping corridor and steep flight of steps leads to a single almost square chamber containing the open sarcophagus. The decoration – painted, not carved – is brilliantly coloured on grey ground. The pharaoh is variously shown with Maat, Ptah, Osiris, Anubis and other deities, and portions of the Book of Gates are depicted (on the left wall, notice the 12 goddesses representing the hours of the night).

The 'Harpers' Tomb' of Ramses III (Tomb 11)

Tomb 17: Seti I (XIX Dyn)

At 100m, this is the longest tomb in the valley. Its **reliefs** are wonderfully preserved and so beautifully executed that they rival the famous decorations in Seti's temple at Abydos. Beneath a ceiling painted with vultures flying towards the back of the tomb, the walls of Corridor A are decorated on the left with Seti before the falcon-headed Re-Herakhte, god of the morning sun. The sun in other forms, as disc, scarab and ram-headed god follows, and the text of the Sun Litany continues on the right wall. This and other texts are continued in Corridor B with staircase. On the upper part of the recess in the left wall are represented 37 forms of the sun god. Corridor C is decorated with the fourth (right) and fifth (left) hours of the night from the Amduat. In Chamber D Seti is shown on four walls in the presence of various deities. Chambers E and F show Seti on each side of the square pillars with a deity. The wall decorations are various hours from the Book of the Gates.

The pattern of construction and decoration of the tomb so far is now in a general sense repeated, with G, H and I corresponding to B, C and D. Corridors G and H are decorated with the **Ritual of the**

Opening of the Mouth which ensured that the mummy's organs were functioning, particularly to permit eating and drinking. The decorations in Chamber I are similar to those in D. Chamber J is in two parts, the first a pillared hall with hours from the Book of the Gates on the walls, the second with the Amduat on the walls and astronomical figures on the vaulted ceiling. The northern constellation here was intended to permit Seti to orient himself with the sun. The sarcophagus (now in the Sir John Soane Museum, London) rested in the depression in this second part; a passage behind runs for 46m, apparently to nowhere. A side room, K, to the right, is known as the **Chamber of the Cow** for its representation of the sky goddess Nut in the form of a cow. The texts here recount the myth of the destruction of mankind, the Egyptian equivalent of the Mesopotamian and biblical story of the Flood.

Tomb 34: Tuthmosis III (XVIII Dyn)

At the far end of the rising valley and requiring a steep climb up metal steps to reach the entrance, and then a steep descent within, this tomb is unusual for the rounded shape of the **sarcophagus chamber**. A pit (A) that you now cross by footbridge in one of the approach corridors was probably meant to deter tomb robbers, though later the priests removed Tuthmosis' mummy to a rocky cleft (*see* box, p.308) for safekeeping; it is now in the Cairo Museum, though the red granite sarcophagus remains in situ.

The tomb is worth visiting for its unusual paintings. In the room (B) preceding the sarcophagus chamber the walls are decorated with a repeating pattern of stars, and below them what appear to be potted plants. They are potted plants: papyrus, symbol of the south, being grown in pots. The spareness of the decorations is carried through into the sarcophagus chamber (C). The walls are painted in black and red only; the black stick-figures have the stylishness of 1930s magazine illustrations. Note, on the first pillar you come to, Tuthmosis being suckled by his mother in the form of a tree.

Tomb 35: Amenophis II (XVIII Dyn)

This tomb is unadorned except for the sarcophagus chamber, approached by a long corridor and steep flight of steps. A shaft at A is crossed by a modern gangway leading to Chamber B with unfinished walls. The walls of the Sarcophagus Chamber C are painted yellow in imitation of papyrus and bear the complete text of the Amduat as though inscribed on a continuous scroll. The blue ceiling is painted with yellow stars. The tomb was not discovered until 1898. Amenophis' mummy was found in situ, a floral garland still round its neck, and only in 1934 was it removed to the Cairo

Museum. The quartzite sarcophagus was left in the tomb. Three mummies were found in side room D, and nine royal mummies, hidden there by priests, were found in room E. These last included Tuthmosis IV, Amenophis III and Seti II, now all in the Egyptian Museum in Cairo. It is to the late discovery of the tomb that the survival and identification of these mummies is owed.

Tomb 57: Horemheb (XVIII Dyn)

The plan is almost identical to that of Tomb 17 (Seti I) and some of the decorations are finely executed. The principal interest, however, is in the partially finished work, showing the various stages of decoration.

Tomb 62: Tutankhamun (XVIII Dyn)

This most famous of Egyptian tombs is neither large nor impressively decorated. It bears all the marks of hasty burial following the early death of Tutankhamun while in his late teens. Even its fabulous contents, seen by millions of people around the world, cannot have compared to the funerary treasures of far greater pharaohs entombed in the valley. This relative lack of

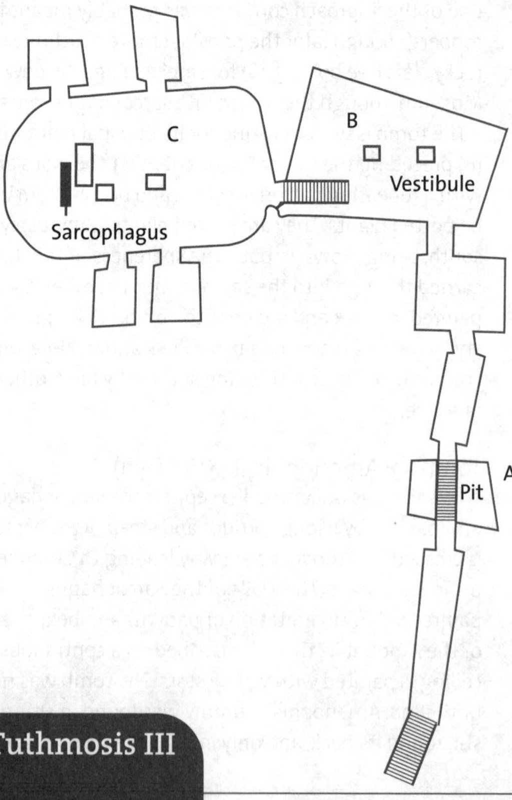

Tomb 34: Tuthmosis III

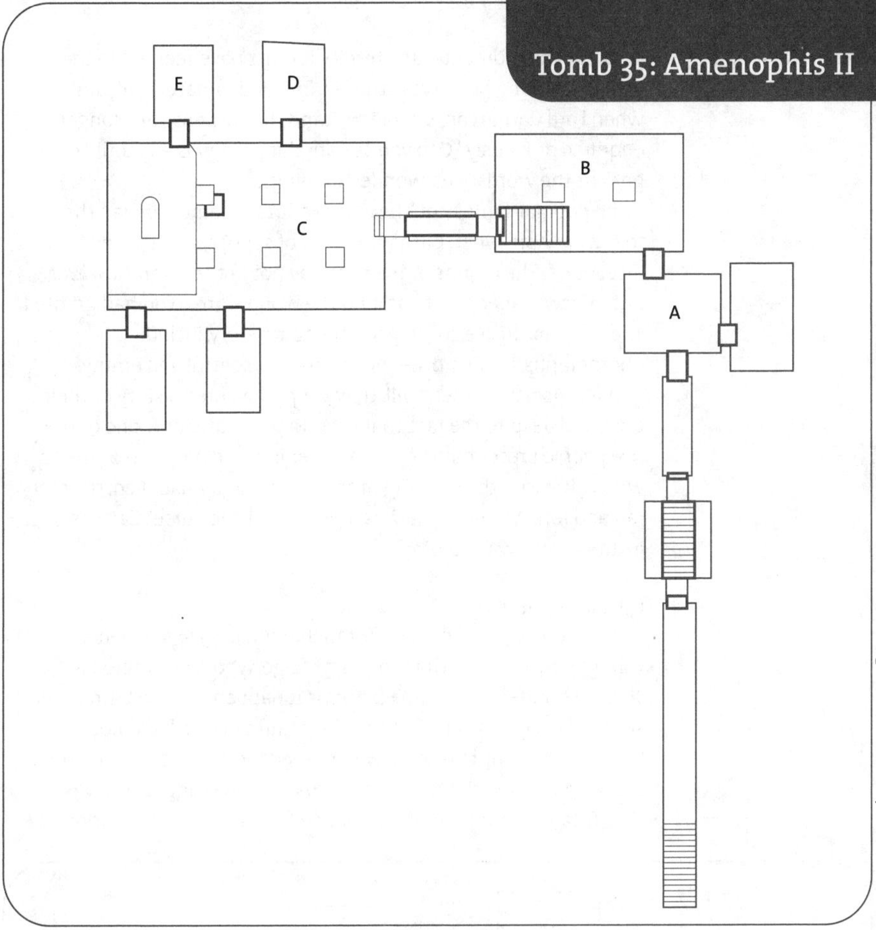

importance of a briefly reigning pharaoh caught up in the Amun priesthood's counter-revolution probably assisted in the long secrecy of the tomb's existence and whereabouts. Also, nearly above it was the entrance to the grander tomb of Ramses VI (Tomb 9), the debris from which early on covered the entrance to the young pharaoh's tomb.

Discovery and Curse

Gold – everywhere the glint of gold.
Howard Carter

The tomb was discovered on 4 November 1922 by Howard Carter and opened by him and his patron Lord Carnarvon on 26 November. In *The Tomb of Tutankhamen* (his spelling), Carter described his famous landfall on that ancient world: 'At first I could see nothing, the hot air escaping from the chamber causing the candle flames to flicker, but presently, as my eyes grew accustomed to the light, details of the room within emerged slowly from the mist, strange animals, statues and gold – everywhere the glint of gold. For the moment – an eternity it must have seemed to the others standing by – I was struck dumb with amazement, and when Lord Carnarvon, unable to stand the suspense any longer, enquired anxiously, "Can you see anything?" it was all I could do to get out the words, "Yes, wonderful things."'

The popular fantasy of 'the curse of Tutankhamun' began the following April when Carnarvon died of septicaemia caused by an insect bite. The origins of the curse lay not in the tomb, however, but in newspaper offices around the world. Carnarvon had granted *The Times* exclusive coverage of the tomb story, including photographs, leaving other newspapers resentful and empty-handed. As newspapers will, they simply invented a story of their own, and despite the fact that even 10 years later only one of the five people present at the tomb's opening, and only two of the 22 who witnessed the opening of the sarcophagus, had died, the story ran and ran. Whenever he was asked about the 'curse', Carter's own irritable reply was 'tommy-rot'.

Cause of Death

The autopsy performed on Tutankhamun in 1926 showed a young man, no more than 19 years of age, who had suffered a cheek wound – in the same place, as it happens, where Carnarvon suffered his insect bite. But the likely cause of death did not become clear until his torso was X-rayed for the first time, in 1968, showing that his chest had been crushed. One suggestion was that Tutankhamun might have fallen from his hunting chariot and

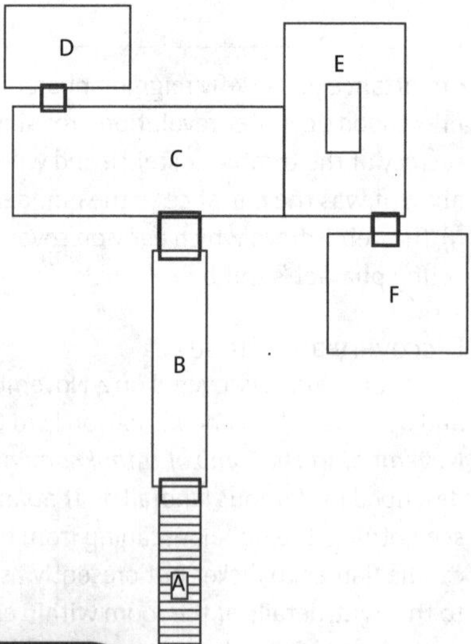

Tomb 62: Tutankhamun

got caught up by his reins beneath its wheels. No mystery surrounds Carter's death at 65 of Hodgkin's disease and cardiac failure. He lies obscurely in grave 45, block 12, of Putney Vale Cemetery, London. His headstone reads simply: 'Howard Carter, Archaeologist and Egyptologist, born May 9, 1874, died March 2, 1939.'

The Chambers and Tomb

The door at the bottom of the entrance stairway A was found walled up and sealed with the royal seal. The entrance corridor B was found filled with stone debris through which a tunnel had been dug soon after interment in an unsuccessful attempt to rob the tomb. The undecorated Chambers C, D (now walled up) and F contained most of the funerary objects now on display at the Cairo Museum. Chamber E, originally walled off from C and at a lower level, contained the four gilded wooden shrines, one inside the other, within which lay the rectangular stone sarcophagus, then three mummiform coffins, the innermost of solid gold, and then finally the mummy of Tutankhamun himself. The wall has now been replaced by a railing beyond which visitors cannot venture.

From here you can view what remains in the tomb. The sarcophagus turned out to be a second-hand retread. A 1993 study revealed that it had been intended for Tutankhamun's predecessor, Smenkhkere – the wings of the figures at the four corners were carved later to obscure the original inscriptions. The largest of the mummiform coffins is within the sarcophagus, and, unseen within, the mummy of Tutankhamun. (Minus, as it happens, his penis – photographs taken in 1926, before the body was reinterred, show it in situ, but when the remains of Tutankhamun were examined again in 1968 the penis was missing, perhaps having found its way onto somebody's mantelpiece.) This chamber was the only one decorated, its paintings betraying signs of haste. (The paintings have been suffering damage, perhaps from visitors' humid exhalations.) On the right wall, the coffin is transported on a sledge. To the rear from right to left, Ay, the young king's successor, performs the rite of the opening of the mouth (note a suggestion of the Amarna style); Tutankhamun sacrifices to Nut; again the young pharaoh, this time with his ka, before Osiris. On the left wall is the sun god's boat, while on the all-but-impossible-to-see entrance wall, Tutankhamun, accompanied by Anubis and Isis, receives life from the goddess of the west.

The Plight of Tutankhamun's Widow

Perhaps among the last people to have left this tomb before Carter entered it 3,300 years later was Tutankhamun's young widow, Ankhesenamun, and to her attaches a romantic tale. Like her husband, she had only recently changed her name – he from Tutankhaten, she from Ankhesenpaaten, as both had been raised at Amarna during the Aten cult of Akhenaten (indeed she was Akhenaten's daughter by Nefertiti and he may have been Akhenaten's son by a lesser wife). 'I have no son, and my husband is dead,' Ankhesenamun is said to have written to the Hittite king. 'Send me a son of yours and I will make him king.' The story, as Carter unfolds it, goes that Ankhesenamun found herself faced with the political ambitions and, possibly, the nuptial intentions of her grandfather Ay, retainer to her late husband and power behind the throne. In answer to her letter, Suppiluliumas, far off in the Hittite capital of Hattusas, east of present-day Ankara in Turkey, sent one of his sons to be Ankhesenamun's husband and rule as pharaoh. But, as a later Hittite text informs us, 'they killed him as they were conducting him to Egypt', while Ay, beneficiary of two deaths, hastily installed Tutankhamun in this small tomb. As Horus buried Osiris, so he who buried the pharaoh became pharaoh in turn, though whether Ay also married his own granddaughter is disputed by scholars.

However, a different scenario is put forward by some scholars, who say that the letter-writer was not Tutankhamun's widow but Nefertiti after Akhenaten's death, and that the villain of the piece was Smenkhkere ... but then yet other scholars say Smenkhkere may have been none other than Nefertiti herself, making an attempt to rule in masculine guise after her husband's death, as had Hatshepsut. Possibly it is better just to stick to reading Agatha Christie.

At any rate, somebody wrote a letter to Suppiluliumas, whose son was killed on his way to Egypt – and that in itself is one of those fascinating might-have-beens of history. For instead of an alliance between the two superpowers of the day, the murder of the Hittite prince contributed to nearly a century of enmity that encompassed the later battle of Kadesh fought between Ramses II and Suppiluliumas' grandson Muwatallis and found its reconciliation only in the marriage of Ramses II to a Hittite princess.

In the Western Valley: Tomb 23: Ay (XVIII Dyn)

Ay was the successor to Tutankhamun, and though he first had a tomb made for himself at Amarna, he ended up here in the Western Valley. Ay's tomb is similar to that of Tutankhamun and both were probably decorated by the same artists. When discovered by Belzoni in 1816, it immediately became apparent that

Surprise Discovery of Massive Tomb for Ramses II's Sons

Recent archaeological work at Tomb 5 shows that surprises may still lie in store at the Valley of the Kings. The entrance to the tomb was discovered in the 19th century, but inquisitive Egyptologists, including Howard Carter early in the 20th century, were prevented by flood-borne debris from exploring more than the front three chambers – what lay beyond was entirely unknown.

Then in 1995 a team from the American University in Cairo penetrated beyond the debris, finding a T-shaped arrangement of galleries. The stem of the T is a corridor leading past 20 chambers to a statue of Osiris from where the arms of the T are lined with more chambers, each arm ending at stairs that perhaps lead to yet further rooms. In all, 67 chambers have now been found, making this the biggest rock-cut tomb ever found in Egypt.

Tomb 5 was looted in ancient times, but the various finds, including fragments of sarcophagi and mummies, inscribed stone vessels, and pottery and jewellery, prove that this was the burial place for many of Ramses II's sons. 52 of his sons are known by name (he had over 100, and another 100 or so daughters, variously by his chief queen Nefertari, his associate chief queen Istnofret, and an extensive harem) but the burial places of only three sons have been identified: Tomb 8 of Merneptah, his son by Istnofret and his ultimate successor, in the Valley of the Kings; what is thought to be that of Khaemwas found in 1993 at Saqqara; and a chamber in Tomb 5 where Amen-hir-khopshef, Ramses' first-born son by Nefertari and intended heir, has long known to have been interred. It is now thought that Ramses' remaining 49 sons may have been buried in Tomb 5 also. Egyptologists have been taken aback by this unexpected discovery and are now asking themselves what else lies hidden within the tomb and indeed elsewhere in the Valley of the Kings.

Ay's tomb had been entered in antiquity, and that most of his representations were hacked out at the time. His sarcophagus too was smashed. The tomb is unique for its marsh hunting scene, often found in the tombs of nobles but the only one on the walls of a New Kingdom royal burial. It has now been ruthlessly restored to the detriment of archaeology but for the commercial benefit derived from tourism. The tomb can be reached from the car park at the Valley of the Kings by following a 2km dirt path along a desolate valley past sheer rock cliffs where you are surrounded by a silent and haunting atmosphere long since gone from elsewhere in the Theban necropolis – the visit is worth it more for that than for the tomb itself.

Mountain Paths to Deir el Medina and Deir el Bahri

You can leave the Valley of the Kings by the road you came, that same ancient road along which the bodies of the pharaohs were drawn here on sledges. Or you can leave on foot, climbing the path to the right of Tomb 16, opposite the resthouse. As it gains the ridge, there is usually a donkey boy waiting but the donkeys should be declined. Almost certainly, a guide will fasten himself on you in hope of baksheesh. He can be useful for those who are not footsure, but otherwise he is not necessary either. On the ridge, the path divides. One heads south, rising slowly over the mountain; the other runs to the left, level along the ridge. The first leads to Deir el Medina and is the same path the workmen used when returning home from their shift at the tombs. There are sweeping views of the Nile valley, magnificent in the afternoon with the sun in the west. The second path soon creeps high along the edge of the amphitheatre of Deir el Bahri and offers changing angles and elevations of Hatshepsut's temple, and views towards the Nile. You continue along round the north flank of Deir el Bahri and then pick your way down, to be met by your driver after visiting the temple. Both walks are highly recommended, but the second (about 30 minutes) is a must for a full appreciation of Hatshepsut's architectural achievement.

Hatshepsut's Mortuary Temple at Deir el Bahri

Deir el Bahri

The Mortuary Temple of Hatshepsut at Deir el Bahri is the finest building in Egypt. Elegant, revolutionary, it satisfies and provokes in whole and in detail. Along with the Parthenon, the Taj Mahal, the interiors of Chartres and Hagia Sophia, it is one of the great buildings of the world. Not that the temple has received its fullest due: though far older than the others, it was unknown in modern times until Mariette made preliminary excavations in the third quarter of the 19th century. The temple was only entirely cleared in 1894–96 and has undergone sporadic restoration since then.

Hatshepsut's Reign

Interpretation of the events following the death of Tuthmosis I (XVIII Dyn) is marked by controversy among archaeologists which mimics, even if it does not rival, the original dynastic struggle played out between Hatshepsut, his daughter, and Tuthmosis III, his grandson. By any interpretation, Hatshepsut emerges as one of the most formidable figures in Egyptian history, only the third woman to rule as queen, the first to rule as king. In the ruthlessness and romance the story implies, and the high policy at stake, parallels between the reigns of Hatshepsut and Elizabeth I easily suggest themselves to the imagination.

Hatshepsut married her father's son and successor, Tuthmosis II, and during the lifetime of her husband her full titles were 'pharaoh's daughter, pharaoh's sister, god's wife and pharaoh's great wife'. But Tuthmosis II died before Hatshepsut could bear him a child, and it was one of her husband's secondary wives who became 'pharaoh's mother' to Tuthmosis III. But for her sex, Hatshepsut's claim to the throne through her father was at least as good as Tuthmosis III's and through her mother she was descended from the Ahmose family who had thrown the Hyksos out of Egypt. But as Tuthmosis was later to advertise, his future as pharaoh was proclaimed by no less a god than Amun who, while

Tuthmosis I was sacrificing at Karnak, stood the young prince in the place usually occupied by the sovereign. This conveniently has Tuthmosis III designated heir in the lifetime of his own father, but betrays the more pedestrian likelihood that the priests of Amun eventually sided with the army in its support of Tuthmosis and his imperial designs against Hatshepsut and her party in the civil service who preferred a peaceful domestic policy.

Tuthmosis III, when finally he became sole pharaoh well into his manhood, launched Egypt upon her period of conquest abroad and bloated magnificence at home, so often celebrated in stone at Thebes. Yet as powerful a pharaoh and warrior as he was to become, Tuthmosis was no match for Hatshepsut in her prime. In the first few years following her husband's death, Hatshepsut reigned as widow-queen, but she soon took the momentous step of assuming the title of pharaoh, co-reigning with but entirely overshadowing her stepson. She went so far as to pose and dress as a man – at least on reliefs – and to wear the pharaonic beard. In this way she ruled for about 20 years.

Elizabeth I had her Essex; Hatshepsut had her **Senmut**, a man of modest birth who rose to occupy a score of high offices, including steward of Amun, probably giving him control over the vast wealth of the Karnak temple, and minister of public works, with the suggestion that he was the architect at Deir el Bahri. As such favourites often do, Senmut overstepped the mark. He used his royal mistress's temple for his own purposes, introducing reliefs of himself in niches that would be concealed behind opening doors and, though building himself a tomb at Gurna, planned secretly to be buried within the great court at Deir el Bahri. Most of his reliefs were hacked out and his sarcophagus smashed, yet in his secret tomb the name of Hatshepsut was left untouched, suggesting the destruction was wrought not by Tuthmosis III, who in malice destroyed so much that was Hatshepsut's, but by Hatshepsut herself in rage at this attempt to extend familiarity into the eternal. The last record of Senmut comes about five years before the end of his mistress's reign. In those last years she was alone.

How Hatshepsut's reign ended is not known. Perhaps she fell victim to a coup d'état, or merely died a natural death. In any case her inward-looking peace policy was suddenly eclipsed and Tuthmosis III, obliterating her name and her image wherever he found them, within 75 days of her death was leading his army into Palestine (*see* 'Karnak', p.289).

The Conception of Hatshepsut's Temple

Into the rugged eastern flank of the Theban Mountain nature has cut an immense amphitheatre facing Thebes. Its sheer golden walls embrace the site like the wings of some mighty hovering solar disc. Just off centre, to the left and rising from the cliffline, is a pyramidal peak. A magnificent backdrop, it invites a performance, and would condemn any but the most brilliant to insignificance before it. The Middle Kingdom pharaoh Mentuhotep II (XI Dyn) built a temple here; you can see its ruins to the south of Hatshepsut's. What impression it made cannot fairly be judged from its remains. Like Hatshepsut's temple, it rose in terraces but then was surmounted by a pyramid, a Memphite legacy perhaps. Mentuhotep II and III were both entombed here. But a pyramidal structure set against the pyramidal peak seems superfluous, and any structure vying with the cliffs for height can only have been overwhelmed.

Mentuhotep's temple was already in ruins when 500 years later Hatshepsut was drawn to the holy site. (Whether out of convenience or some similar feeling of awe, Hatshepsut's temple was taken over by early Christians as a monastery: Deir el Bahri, the Northern Monastery). She was obviously influenced by the earlier temple, and in all probability would have replicated it on a larger scale: the foundations suggest a pyramid was intended. One purpose of a pyramid is to protect the tomb, but her father Tuthmosis I had abandoned this idea for the greater security of discreet entombment in the Valley of the Kings. It remained necessary therefore to build only a mortuary temple at which the appropriate ceremonies would be performed. At some point Hatshepsut decided to build wide instead of high.

If it is true that circumstances dictated this decision, or suggested that the alternative was now pointless, it is no less true that the new form was seized upon with conviction and executed with genius. The terraces of Hatshepsut's temple emphasize the stratification of the cliff behind and the line between rock and sky. At the same time, the bold rhythm of the pillared colonnades, vertical shafts of light-reflecting stone framing and contrasting with the shadowed ambulatories, reflect the dark gashes of gullies and fissures in the cliff face itself. Even the peak seems brought into the conception: a pyramid offered by nature. The temple mediates between the wildness of the mountain and the cultivation of the valley. The power and contradiction of the landscape is gripped and tamed with a confidence and elegance that is breathtaking, and then played throughout the structure so that as you walk round the temple you feel it, never too much, but to a measure that insists on the spiritual nature of man.

A Tour of Hatshepsut's Temple

The Lower Terrace

The main temple complex may originally have been preceded by a valley temple near the Nile; if so, it has been lost beneath the

Hatshepsut's Mortuary Temple

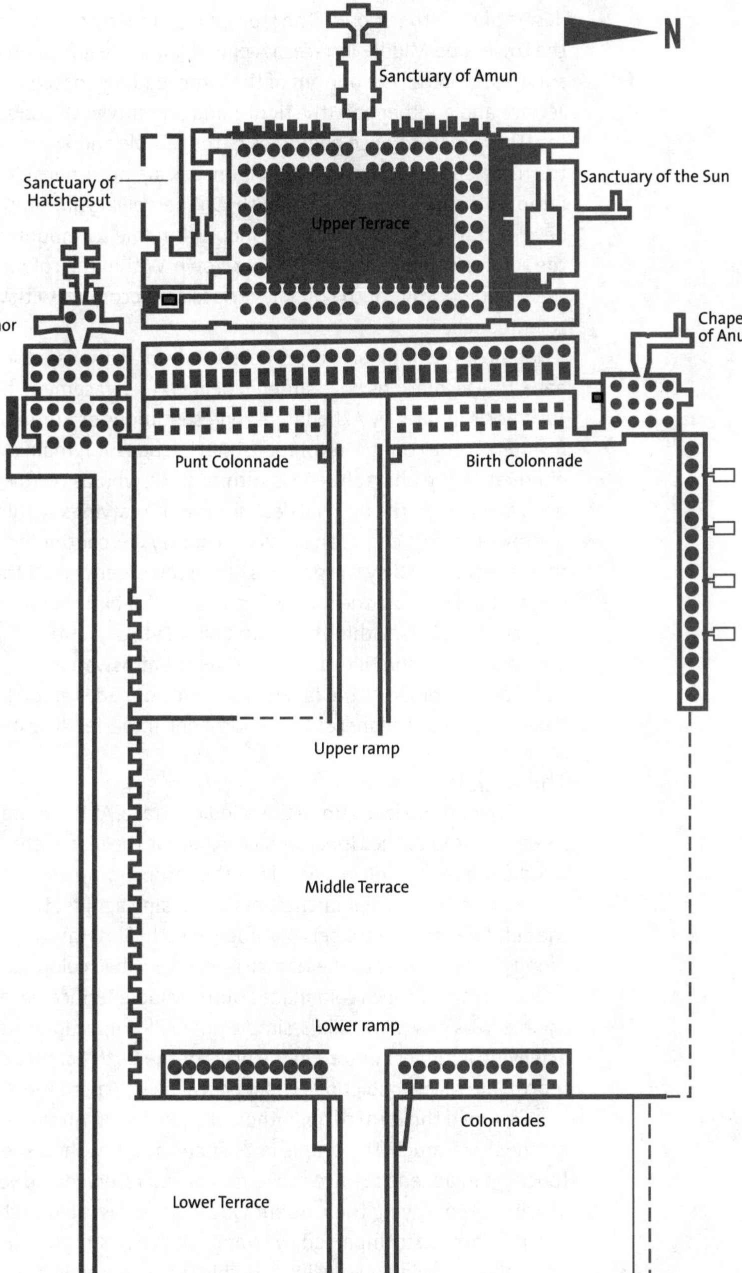

tilled alluvium. From this temple ran a promenade lined with sphinxes to the Lower Terrace, a zone of transition between the profane and the sacred. This was a garden with myrrh trees and fountains, as though a foretaste of that life which endures in the desert of the other world. (The stumps of some trees are visible on the Lower and Middle Terraces.) A pair of lions (the left-hand one survives) stood at the bottom of the ramp leading up to the Middle Terrace and another pair (the right-hand one survives) stood at the top. These were at once guardians of the temple and witnesses to the rising sun, proof of rebirth. Colonnades are on either side of the ramp, to the north and to the south. On their pillars are simple devices stating a variation of Hatshepsut's name surmounted by the solar falcon wearing the double crown. Within the colonnades, the retaining walls of the Middle Terrace are decorated with vividly coloured reliefs.

Not all of the original courses have survived and, where they have, the decorations have suffered deliberate defacement, first by Tuthmosis III, later by Akhenaten. Representations of Amun were restored at the counter-revolution, but Hatshepsut remains obliterated; the pharaoh seen is Tuthmosis III, who, as co-ruler, had been included in the original decorations. The carvings within the North Colonnade depict an idealized country life, continuing the theme established by the gardens of the Lower Terrace. Of the greatest delicacy are the scenes (right) of water birds being caught in nets. The reliefs within the South Colonnade depict the transport down the Nile of two obelisks cut at Aswan at Hatshepsut's order. At the far ends of the colonnades stood large Osiris statues of Hatshepsut (the north one imperfectly restored).

The Middle Terrace

The lower ramp leads up to the Middle Terrace. At its centre rises a second ramp to the Upper Terrace. Again, at the rear of the Middle Terrace and on either side of the second ramp are colonnades and at their farthest ends, pressing against the rock of the cliff face, are the chapels of Anubis (north) and Hathor (south). Along the north side of the terrace is an unfinished colonnade.

The north and south colonnades of the Middle Terrace have double rows of square pillars, simple but well-proportioned and achieving a modest grace. On the walls of the **Birth Colonnade** (north) are reliefs depicting Hatshepsut's divine parentage: Amun has assumed the form of her father who sits facing Ahmosis, her mother, on a couch. The couple gaze at one another, their knees touching in a scene at once conventional and reserved and yet sensitively conveying their ardour. Queen Ahmosis is led to the birth chamber, accompanied by strange deities, a smile of suffering and delight playing on her lips. The child, conventionally shown as a boy, is fashioned by Khnum on his potter's wheel, and also its ka. Just as Tuthmosis III justified his claim to the throne with the story of Amun's selection of him at the Temple of Karnak, so these reliefs serve the same purpose for Hatshepsut. Not that we should think that either pharaoh was simply cynical; overriding the political propaganda was probably a sincere belief in their divine birth, and these beliefs certainly have all the delicacy and feeling of a belief honestly integrated in Hatshepsut's character, sustaining her in her rule. On the lateral faces of the pillars, Tuthmosis is shown with Amun; on front and back it is Hatshepsut (defaced) with Amun.

The façade of the **chapel of Anubis** continues the line of the colonnade, but with columns (fluted, with simple capitals, like Doric columns). From a distance, the columns are indistinguishable from the pillars, but stand in the northwest corner of the terrace and look along the façades towards the ramp: that almost unnoticed variation creates a subtle yet entirely harmonious contrast. There is a touch of Greece here, and in the discreet widening of the distance between the central columns as if inviting the visitor into the sanctuary within. The walls of the hall are brilliantly coloured and show the co-rulers (Hatshepsut hacked out), Anubis, protector of the dead, and facing each other at either end, the falcon-headed sun god (north wall) and his wife Hathor (south wall). Cut into the rock in a series of right angles are several chambers with vaulted roofs of brick, though lacking the wedge-shaped keystones of true weight-bearing vaults which do not appear in Egypt until the 8th century BC (and not universalized until taken up by the Romans).

On the south side of the ramp is the **Punt Colonnade**, named after the decorations on its rear wall of the expedition to the land of Punt (probably the coastal region of the modern Somali Republic) instigated by Hatshepsut. Amun had told her: 'It is a glorious region of god's land, it is indeed my place of delight; I have made it for myself in order to divert my heart.' Hatshepsut's ancestors had often sent expeditions there to procure the precious myrrh necessary for the incense in temple services, but now, as she recorded, Amun desired her 'to establish a Punt in his house'. So the purpose of the expedition was to obtain for the first time living myrrh trees; and to plant the terraces of this temple dedicated to Amun with them.

The walls illustrate and relate the story. After presumably crossing the desert to a Red Sea port, the expedition sailed southwards in five ships. The Egyptians are shown being greeted on the shore by the chief of Punt and his extraordinarily corpulent wife – a rare instance of humorous caricature, the rolls of fat from her body reaching right down to her ankles. In exchange for gifts, the beached ships are laden 'very heavily with marvels of the country of Punt; all goodly fragrant woods of god's land, heaps of myrrh resin, of fresh myrrh trees, with ebony and pure ivory, with green gold of Emu, with cinnamon wood, with incense, eye cosmetic, with baboons, monkeys, dogs, with skins of the southern panther, with natives and their children. Never was the like of this brought for any pharaoh who has been since the beginning.' Back at Thebes, Tuthmosis III and Hatshepsut are shown offering incense to Amun's sacred boat, his offering paltry compared to hers. But later he had Hatshepsut defaced; Tuthmosis' portrait, however, is beautifully carved, his individuality realized in a way lacking in the idealized representations on the pillars.

At the far south end of the colonnade it is the **chapel of Hathor** that continues the façade. This time there are pillars, not columns, but still, and unnoticed from any distance, they differ from the rest in having the cow-eared head of Hathor serve laterally as capitals. Beyond the first pillared chamber, and then the second, decorated with a procession of boats along the Nile, is the **sanctuary of Hathor** with vaulted roof. After all the hacking out of Hatshepsut's figure you yearn to see one intact and here, in the farthest recess of the sanctuary, that desire is satisfied. Either because the room was sealed or because at least here in Hathor's sanctuary Tuthmosis respected Hatshepsut's right to some modest remembrance, she survives, albeit in stylized and masculine form. She meets Amun, she suckles regenerating milk from Hathor, and above a recess in the left wall she and Tuthmosis III are shown kneeling, she to the left with an offering of milk, he to the right with wine. Also within this chamber, in a little alcove on the right and towards the floor, is a portrait of Senmut, Hatshepsut's favourite.

The Upper Terrace

The second ramp leads to the Upper Terrace, which was badly ruined but has recently been restored. A portico of Osiris pillars stood a short distance from the edge; their restoration is well under way. On what remains of the rear wall are reliefs of boats accompanied along the Nile banks by a festive procession of soldiers, and of the Festival of the Valley during which Amun visited the necropolis.

Passing through the last wall against the cliffs is a granite doorway leading into the **sanctuary of Amun** hewn out of the rock. The walls are decorated as elsewhere in the temple but are blackened with smoke. In Ptolemaic times the sanctuary was cut deeper and was dedicated to the healing cults of Imhotep, counsellor to Zoser, and Amenhotep, son of Hapu, counsellor to Amenophis III.

At the left (south) end of the Upper Terrace is the **sanctuary of Hatshepsut**. The reliefs are of high quality and show processions of priests and offering-bearers. At the right (north) end of the terrace is the **sanctuary of the Sun**, an open court with an altar in the centre. A flight of steps on its west side permitted a priest to mount the altar gaining a magnificent view of the valley and river below and the rugged horizon to the east, and to await the rising of the sun.

The Noble Tombs

Over 400 private tombs have been discovered at the Theban necropolis, dating from the Old Kingdom to the Ptolemaic period. These include the workmen's tombs at Deir el Medina (*see* p.334), and the tombs of the nobles (in fact nobles, priests and officials) found in clusters from near the Temple of Seti I at the north end of the necropolis to Medinet Habu at the south end. The noble tombs are interesting because they often give a vivid picture of contemporary life instead of the impersonal ritual decorations of the royal tombs. The artists have been more free to express themselves and the sensitivity of their work has been greater. The limestone on this side of the mountain is of poor quality, generally not suited to cutting reliefs; usually the decorations are paintings on stucco walls of white, grey or yellow ground. The tombs are, strictly, mortuary chapels; a filled-in shaft led to a deeper chamber containing the sarcophagus.

Seven of the most outstanding tombs of the nobles are described here, all XVIII Dynasty, all near the old village of **Gurna** (Sheikh Abd el-Gurna). They are signposted from the Ramesseum and fall into three groups (ticket for each group): Rekhmire (100) and Sennufer (96); Menna (69) and Nakht (52); and Ramose (55), Userhat (56) and Khaemhat (57).

To visit all seven tombs would take two hours or so. For a good sample of differing types of tomb, you should visit **Rekhmire (100)**, **Sennufer (96)**, **Nakht (52)** and **Ramose (55)**.

Tomb 100

Rekhmire was vizier under Tuthmosis III and Amenophis II, and the decorations therefore concentrate on foreign policy, and matters of justice and taxation. The tomb is cruciform, i.e. a transverse chamber extending far to left and right, and a long corridor leading straight ahead, its ceiling steadily rising to 5.5m at the far end where there is a false door. *Left arm of transverse chamber*: on the far left wall Rekhmire is shown being installed as vizier; on the far right wall tribute is brought to Egypt. This is delightful: from the top register the tribute is shown from Punt, Crete and the Aegean, Nubia, Syria and Cush (on the western shore of the Red Sea), including a wonderful procession of African beasts, among them a giraffe, and precious goods, including elephants' tusks. *Right arm of transverse chamber*: on the left wall scenes of hunting, fowling and the treading of grapes; on the near right wall taxes and offerings; on the far wall Rekhmire's ancestors. *Corridor*: on the near left, Rekhmire is shown inspecting the workshops of Amun; centre left, the voyage to Abydos (*see* 'Abydos', p.256); right wall, the afterworld, with trees and lake, and a funerary feast.

Tomb 96

Up the hill from Rekhmire's tomb. **Sennufer** was mayor of Thebes and overseer of the gardens of Amun during the reign of Amenophis II. It is likely that he was also chief vintner, and you wonder whether his tomb is not his last laugh on that theme. You go down steep steps to an antechamber, the highly irregular surface of its ceiling seeming to give deliberate relief to a painted arbour with vines and grapes. But when you step into the chamber beyond, you see that everything – ceiling, walls, pillars – wobbles before your eyes as though you were drunk. It is possible that the rock here was difficult to cut. It is also possible that Sennufer said what the hell. In either case the effect is extremely pleasing. The walls in both chambers are painted with religious scenes, Sennufer repeatedly depicted with his daughter, his sister and his wife.

Tomb 69

This and 52 are across the road from one another. **Menna** was an estate inspector under a mid-XVIII Dynasty pharaoh, and so the decorations emphasize country life. The paintings are finely executed and excellently preserved. In the entrance passage, Menna, his wife and daughter are shown worshipping the sun. In the left wing of the first chamber are a variety of rural scenes, while the right wing depicts various ceremonies, with the dead man and his wife receiving offerings, Anubis facing Osiris, Re and Hathor. A lively hunting and fishing scene occupies the centre of the right-hand wall of the second chamber, though generally mourning and burial scenes are depicted.

Tomb 52

Across the road from 69. **Nakht** was a scribe and astronomer of Amun in the middle of the XVIII Dynasty. A short passage leads to a transverse first chamber, the only decorated part of the tomb. The paintings are well preserved and brilliantly coloured, and like those of Menna depict country life: the supervising of field labours by Nakht; the deceased and his wife banqueting and making offerings. Note that Nakht is frequently defaced, his eyes gouged, even the upper part of his body destroyed; also the name of Amun is everywhere obliterated – acts committed, presumably, during Akhenaten's reign. The chamber beyond, as was the custom, contained a statue of the dead man with his wife: it was shipped to America but the boat sank. A shaft here runs down to the sarcophagus chamber.

Tomb 55

To the south of 69 and 52; to the east of 100. A relatively grandiose structure with wall carvings, the unfinished tomb of **Ramose** is one of the most fascinating in the necropolis. Ramose was governor of Thebes and vizier in the early years of Amenophis IV's reign and took pains to honour himself with two hypostyle chambers (only the first is open) decorated in the most exquisite classical Egyptian style.

From an open court you enter the first chamber and follow the decorations from the near wall of the right wing: classical reliefs show Ramose and his wife in several offering ceremonies. These scenes are continued along the near wall of the left wing. The groups of seated figures are friends or relatives of the dead man. Continuing clockwise, the south wall bears a painting of the procession to the tomb with bearers of offerings, mourning women and priests; to the right, the dead man and his wife worshipping Osiris; and below, four representations of the dead man before his tomb. The west wall in the left wing resumes the reliefs and shows Ramose four times offering flowers to Amenophis IV seated under a canopy with the goddess Maat. At the very south (left) end of this wall you can see that prior to cutting the relief the figures were drawn in black outline over a red

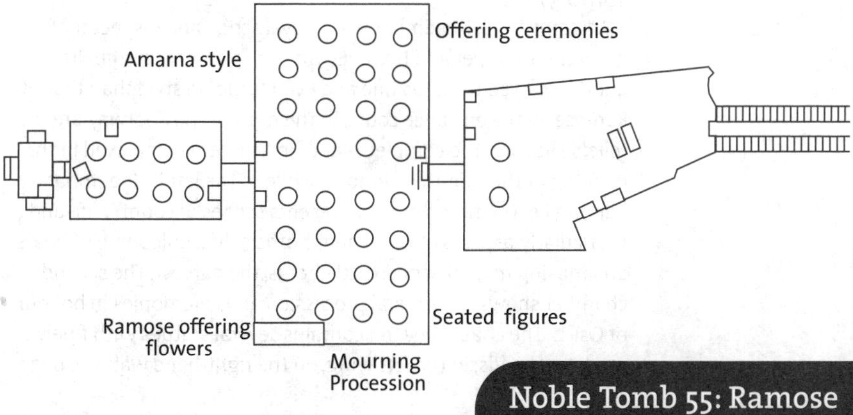

Noble Tomb 55: Ramose

grid, suggesting the usual artist's concern to transfer the scene in the same detail and proportions as it appeared on the (perhaps smaller) original sketch.

Now passing across the closed entrance to the second chamber you come to the north end of the west wall and suddenly the style has changed from the classical to the Amarnan. The explanation is that while Ramose was working on his tomb, Amenophis IV had become Akhenaten, introducing both Aten and a new art. Ramose never did finish his tomb here because he followed Akhenaten to Amarna. This wall shows Akhenaten and Nefertiti at their palace window under the rays of Aten, receiving homage from Ramose. In sketch form you can see Ramose receiving a decoration (a gold collar, as at Ay's tomb at Amarna) and acclaimed by courtiers and representatives from Nubia, Libya and Asia, and also Ramose receiving bouquets in the temple. It is interesting to compare these new-style portraits of Ramose to his classical portrait at the north side of the east wall. And it is significant to note that not only Akhenaten and Nefertiti are depicted with elongated heads, but now Ramose (though not quite so much) is too – in some measure countering the argument that Akhenaten and his family were portrayed in this way because they were afflicted by some deforming disease or gene.

Tomb 56

Immediately south of Ramose's tomb. **Userhat** was a royal scribe and tutor during the reign of Amenophis II. The walls and ceiling are finely painted, and there are some interesting scenes of barbers cutting hair and of Userhat hunting gazelle from a chariot, and fowling and fishing in the marshes. The tomb was later used by Coptic hermits who here and there added their own curious creatures and crosses.

Tomb 57

Adjacent to 56. **Khaemhat** was a royal scribe and inspector of granaries in Upper and Lower Egypt under Amenophis III. His is another carved tomb, as fine and even firmer in style than that of Ramose. In the entrance court, to the right of the doorway, are reliefs showing the complete set of instruments employed in the opening of the mouth ceremony, while to the left is Khaemhat adoring Re. The first chamber presents scenes of country life and, particularly, aspects of Khaemhat's official life: unloading of boats, an amusing market scene, cattle herds, the harvest. The second chamber shows the funeral procession and ceremonies in honour of Osiris. The chapel beyond contains several statues with finely modelled heads; in the left wing, on the right-hand wall, the dead man in the act of worship; in the right wing, on the right-hand wall, the cast of a portrait of Khaemhat.

A coffin was traditionally carried through a banquet, giving the lie to an unending feast of life. Macabre it might seem to us; to the Egyptians it must have carried with it some promise against time: 'You live again, you live again for ever, here you are young once more for ever' – the final benediction of the priests as the desiccated mummies of these titled dead were interred in their tombs.

The Ramesseum

The Ramesseum, the mortuary temple of Ramses II, is part of a still larger rectangular complex enclosed by its original brick wall. The area was filled with vaulted brick storehouses, now entirely ruinous, which were once invaded, as is known from an extant papyrus, by desperate tomb workers who had not been paid for two months: 'We have reached this place because of hunger, because of thirst, without clothing, without oil, without fish, without vegetables! Tell pharaoh, our good lord, about it, and tell the vizier, our superior. Act so that we may live!' So that the great Ramses should live for ever this grandiose temple was built, and enough of its stones remain piled atop one another to remind us of his hunger.

The 1st century BC Greek historian Diodorus was impressed. Coming upon the granite colossus of Ramses he fancifully interpreted its inscription, corrupting the pharaoh's praenomen, User-maat-Re, as he went: 'I am Ozymandias, king of kings. If any would know how great I am, and where I lie, let him excel me in any of my works.' To which Shelley offered time's reply:

I met a traveller from an antique land
Who said: Two vast and trunkless legs of stone
Stand in the desert ... Near them, on the sand,
Half sunk, a shattered visage lies, whose frown,
And wrinkled lip, and sneer of cold command,
Tell that its sculptor well those passions read
Which yet survive, stamped on these lifeless things,
The hand that mocked them, and the heart that fed.
And on the pedestal these words appear:
'My name is Ozymandias, king of kings:
Look on my works, ye Mighty, and despair!'
Nothing beside remains. Round the decay
Of that colossal wreck, boundless and bare
The lone and level sands stretch far away.

Pylons and Courts

You approach the temple at its north flank and so to reach the **First Pylon**, measuring 67m across, you must turn left through the ruined First Court. The outer wall of the pylon is as intelligible as a quarry face, but on the pylon wall facing the court there are excellently carved reliefs, albeit of Ramses' all too familiar exploits against the Hittites (*see* p.271). It is possible to enter the First Pylon from the north: an ascending passage emerges at the top amid a heap of fallen stones, and by clambering over these (it is best to have someone with you for assistance) you can gain a towering view over the First Court. A double colonnade on the south side of the court formed the façade of the royal palace of which little remains. A colonnade of Osiris pillars runs along the north side of the court, their folded arms a reminder of Ramses' mummy in the Egyptian Museum at Cairo, where he seem to be uncrossing his arms as though reaching out to life.

At the far (west) end a flight of steps leads to the Second Court; on the left, as you ascend, is the fallen **Ozymandias**. Weighing more than 900,000 kilos and once standing at 17.5m, this was one of the largest free-standing statues in Egypt, surpassed by the Colossi of Memnon only by virtue of their pedestals. The index finger alone is 1m long. A nearby stand of trees gives the spot an Arcadian touch, and it is pleasant to linger here, though the trees may soon be cut down as their roots are said to be causing structural damage.

The inner surface of the north tower of the **Second Pylon** is decorated, again, with the Battle of Kadesh, though the top

The Ramesseum, as depicted in Napoleon's Description de l'Egypte, *1798*

register more peacefully portrays the festival of the harvest god Min. The front and back of the **Second Court** is lined with Osiris pillars, and where three stairways rise to the west portico, another granite colossus, not quite so large as the first, lies in fragments, the head in good condition with only the nose smashed. On a nearby throne, next to the name of Ramses, Belzoni carved his name. An Italian artist and one-time seminarian, in the early years of the 19th century Belzoni appeared on the stage of Sadler's Wells and elsewhere in England with his famous human-pyramid act, 'bearing on his colossal frame, not fewer, if we mistake not, than 20 or 22 persons'. He later turned serious explorer and succeeded in removing from the Ramesseum the giant bust of Ramses II now in the British Museum.

The Portico and Great Hypostyle Hall

On the rear wall of the **portico** (reached by stairways at the rear of the Second Court) between the central and left-hand doorways, are three rows of reliefs: the bottom register shows 11 of Ramses' sons; the middle shows Ramses with Atum (a Heliopolitan sun god) and falcon-headed Mont who holds the hieroglyph for 'life' to the pharaoh's nose, while to the right Ramses kneels before the Theban triad and Thoth inscribes the pharaoh's name on a palm branch; the top shows Ramses sacrificing to Ptah, and to the right offering incense to an ithyphallic Min. Against the outside north wall of the portico and the Great Hypostyle Hall are the scant remains of an earlier temple of Seti I, its alignment probably accounting for the overall alignment of the Ramesseum which accordingly skews to the south instead of fitting squarely within the rectangular walls of the complex.

The **Great Hypostyle Hall** had 48 columns of which only 29 still stand. It was similar to the one at Karnak (to which Ramses II made a major contribution), a higher ceiling over the central aisle allowing illumination through windows set upon the architraves of the adjoining row of shorter columns. The First Small Hypostyle Hall of eight papyrus bud columns still retains its ceiling, decorated with astronomical signs. Only four out of eight columns survive in the Second Small Hypostyle Hall, while of the shrine beyond nothing remains.

Here, as elsewhere beneath the glaring sun of Egypt, the columns, the reliefs, the sculptures are streaked with white. Ramses boasted and Shelley cut him down to size; and Flaubert dispassionately observed: 'Birdshit is Nature's protest in Egypt; she decorates monuments with it instead of with lichen or moss.'

The Workmen's Village at Deir el Medina

From the Valley of the Kings there was a mountain path that led down to Deir el Bahri, or if you had continued along the crest southwards it would have brought you to the village of the ancient tomb workers, Deir el Medina. This is more usually reached by road, travelling 700m or so west from the Ramesseum. There are rows of **humble houses**, 70 in all, mud brick walls rising on stone foundations along straight and narrow alleys. They had a second storey or at least a living area on the roof, reached by stairs. Some have simple wall decorations inside.

The men who worked at the Valley of the Kings (which they called the Place of Truth) were not mere labourers but artisans and freemen whose food was delivered to the village by serfs, and whose houses were swept by slaves. They fashioned their own **tombs**, and decorated them not so much with scenes of the everyday as did the nobles but with the afterlife, borrowing from their experience in the pharaonic tombs. And over their tomb entrance they would construct a man-size pyramid.

Several of the tombs, which like the village date from the XVIII to XX Dynasties, can be visited. A favourite is **Tomb 1 of Sennedjem** (contents in Cairo's Egyptian Museum), a vaulted chamber down steep steps, with reliefs and paintings on religious themes, including a fine funeral feast and, in the passage that opens onto the final chamber, a nicely observed cameo of a cat killing a snake under the sacred tree. Also worth visiting is **Tomb 3 of Peshedu** (in the burial chamber, note Peshedu praying beneath the tree of regeneration) and **Tomb 217 of Ipy** (unusual for its scenes of everyday life).

Deir el Medina means the monastery of the town, for the workmen's village and the small **Ptolemaic temple** just north of it were occupied by monks during the early years of Christianity. Dedicated to Maat and to Hathor whose head adorns the pillars between the outer court and pronaos, this elegant temple is worth a look if you have the time, though other more considerable Ptolemaic temples await you upstream at Edfu, Kom Ombo and at Philae.

The Valley of the Queens

Beyond, in the Valley of the Queens, Biban el Harem, there are over 70 tombs of queens, princes and princesses of the XVIII though mostly XIX and XX Dynasties. These dead, however, were not gods and so their tombs were not built on the same scale as

A reconstruction of the temple at Deir el Medina from Napoleon's Description de l'Egypte, *1798*

those of the pharaohs. Nor did the friable limestone at this end of the Theban Mountain permit much carved decoration; the tombs are more often only painted, though many were left unfinished and have merely the appearance of caves. An exception is the tomb of Nefertari (*see* below), but it has been closed for some years now.

Tombs 43, 44 and 55 belong to sons of Ramses III. A smallpox epidemic towards the end of Ramses' reign killed several of his sons, and in **Tomb 55 of Prince Amun-herkhopshef** in the hall at the bottom of the entrance steps it falls to the father to introduce his son to the gods. The sarcophagus chamber at the end of the corridor contains a mummiform sarcophagus and, in the far right corner, in a glass case, a **six-month-old foetus**. It is perhaps the foetus that makes this tomb so popular, though its real interest is the well-preserved colours of the **paintings**, and you can have the benefit of this with fewer tour groups getting in the way by visiting **Tomb 44 of Prince Khaemweset**. **Tomb 52 of Queen Titi**, a first wife of one of the Ramessid pharaohs (which one is not known), is one of the few queens' tombs that can be visited without special permission. There is no descent into the tomb; everything is on ground level, particularly exposing it to damage over the centuries by floods, Copts and tourists. That said, however, much remains of its delicate colouring and detailed relief, which make this tomb well worth close observation. In particular have a look in the rear chamber off the main tomb chamber, where you will find scenes of a feast, where the guests include some remarkable figures of sacred bulls, baboons and crocodile-headed gods.

Tomb 66: Nefertari

The outstanding tomb in the Valley of the Queens is **Tomb 66 of Nefertari,** wife of Ramses II, which had suffered greatly from salt deposits and since its discovery in 1904 could be visited only by special permission. Following painstaking restoration work it was opened to the general public in 1995 with visitors limited to 150 a day and for no more than 10 minutes each. However, for the past few years it has again been closed. Nevertheless, the tomb is described below in the event that it reopens to visitors soon.

Entering the tomb of Nefertari, you go down a staircase leading to a hall, on the outer lintel of which are Nefertari's titles with a winged sun disc between Isis and Nephthys. Stepping into the hall you see on the left near wall inscriptions from the Book of the Gates and on the right near wall Nefertari before Osiris. The left side wall is blank, having been too much damaged to restore. On the projection to the near right are Anubis and Neith, while on the projection to the far right are Selket and Osiris. Here in this hall and throughout the tomb the ceilings are painted deep blue and scattered with gold stars. Above the door on the opposite side of the hall are the sons of Horus and again the queen's titles. From here runs a staired corridor; on the upper parts of its walls, to left and right, Nefertari is shown making offerings to various deities,

Nefertari, the Beautiful Lady

No other woman of ancient Egypt has been so honoured by monuments as Nefertari, the wife and chief queen of Ramses II, yet her life is veiled in mystery. Ramses was still heir-apparent, his father Seti I still on the throne, when he married Nefertari, the girl who was to share the first 24 years of his 66-year reign, those daring, dangerous and glorious years when he took to the field against the Libyans, the Nubians and most famously the Hittites at Kadesh. We see her in the third year of his reign in the first court of the temple of Luxor, the graceful high-breasted figure standing between Ramses' striding legs; she is at Abydos, Karnak and the Ramesseum also, but she is most celebrated at Abu Simbel. There at the temple of Hathor, completed in the 24th year of Ramses' reign, Nefertari appears as often as her husband, who dedicated the temple to her, to 'Nefertari for whose sake the very sun does shine' (*see* p.399).

It was a poignant dedication, for it is the last we hear of Nefertari. She was then in her mid-40s and had borne Ramses seven or eight children, and it was one of these, their eldest daughter Meryetamun, who stood by her father at the dedicatory rites at Abu Simbel. If Nefertari made the long river voyage into Nubia, perhaps she was ill and unable to leave the royal barge to attend the ceremonies herself. At any rate she very soon after was brought to this tomb in the Valley of the Queens.

Looted already in ancient times, neither her treasure nor her body was found when the tomb was discovered in 1904. What remained were the carvings of Nefertari, delicately modelled in low relief and beautifully painted, but even then suffering from water containing sodium chloride (table salt) seeping through the limestone walls. Once exposed to the dry air, the solution formed crystals between the walls and the surface plaster, reducing sections of murals to thousands of pieces scattered about the floor. In 1985 the source of the seepage was identified and technology used by space scientists, geologists and biologists was prescribed to prevent any further penetration. Then starting in 1989 and taking six years, each of the thousands of dislodged pieces of mural were dusted and cleaned, revealing their vivid original colours, and by referring to photographs taken at the time of the tomb's discovery were refixed in place using paper-thin slivers of Japanese mulberry bark.

The result is a startling freshness of colour, as brilliant as it was on the day Ramses laid his queen to rest, all other tombs seeming dim by comparison. Here indeed is Nefertari, whose name means Beautiful Lady, elegant, gracious, charming and luminous, 'for whose sake the very sun does shine'.

while along the lower parts of the walls are Isis and Nephthys kneeling in mourning. You come now to the large pillared burial chamber containing Nefertari's sarcophagus, at the entrance to which the queen is shown making offerings to Osiris and Atum. Within the chamber the walls on the left-hand side are inscribed with the Book of the Gates, while the walls on the right-hand side show Nefertari adoring the Book of the Gates. On the pillars are symbols of Isis and Osiris. In the small chamber opposite are Isis and Selket, and Nefertari's cartouche between two uraeuses.

Mortuary Temple of Ramses III at Medinet Habu

I caused the woman of Egypt to walk freely wheresoever she would unmolested by others upon the road. I caused to sit idle the soldiers and the chariotry in my time, and the Sherden and the Kehek [Sardinian and Libyan prisoners, or their children, who were recruited to the royal bodyguard] in their villages to lie at night full length without any dread.

Ramses III

Though built by Ramses III of the XX Dynasty, the temple complex of Medinet Habu is in the great building tradition of the XIX Dynasty pharaohs and has many points of similarity with the Ramesseum and is better preserved. Not long after the reign of Ramses III, the power of the pharaohs declined and Egypt herself became divided once more. Medinet Habu is the last major architectural work of the pharaonic period. Though Egypt was threatened by foreign invaders early in Ramses' reign and a palace conspiracy against him and the succession of his son was uncovered, the greater part of his 30-odd years of rule seems to have passed in peace, as recorded in the quote above which was probably part of the palace archives.

Ramses at Work and Play

In nomen and praenomen, Ramses III imitated his great predecessor of the XIX Dynasty and the designers of Medinet Habu freely borrowed from the Ramesseum. They sometimes cut reliefs celebrating triumphs by Ramses III over Asian foes who had either long since perished on the field of history, or who since the reign of Ramses II lay beyond the enfeebled might of Egypt. This motif is echoed in the lofty **gatehouse**, a unique feature in Egyptian architecture, through which you enter the site. It was meant to resemble one of those Syrian fortresses which the Egyptian armies had met with so often in their Asiatic campaigns, but here the purpose was not military, the **upper storeys** serving as a resort where the pharaoh could amuse himself with the women of the harem. The carved heads of captured prisoners enlivened the view from the east window above, reached now by a staircase on the south (if this is closed, offer baksheesh). Scenes inside the top apartment show Ramses waited on by harem girls, their bodies bared of even their transparent dresses once suggested by a light wash of paint. To the left of the west window the pharaoh is stroking one of the girls under her chin.

The Primeval Hill

To the north (right) of this gateway is an earlier **XVIII Dynasty temple** built and partly decorated by Hatshepsut. Her image and name were obliterated, as elsewhere, by Tuthmosis III; Akhenaten scratched out all reference to Amun but Horemheb and Seti I replaced them; and Ramses III then decorated the north and south walls to suit his own purposes. This temple stood on one of the most sacred spots in Egypt, the primeval hill which first rose clear of the receding waters of Chaos. An inscription identifies it as the burial place of the four primal pairs – Ocean and Matter, the Illimitable and the Boundless, Darkness and Obscurity, and the Hidden and Concealed ones – who preceded even the creator god, Re-Atum. While preserving this older temple, Ramses III levelled the ground behind to build his own mortuary temple dedicated to 'Amun united with Eternity', and a palace and other structures, set within gardens, surrounded by walls, and linked to the Nile by a canal.

Chapels and Campaigns

Through the gateway and to the south (left) are the **mortuary chapels** of the Divine Adorers, princesses who were the chief priestesses of Amun at Thebes. The chapels are late additions, dating from the XXIII to the XXVI Dynasties.

Straight ahead (to the west) is the **First Pylon** of Ramses' mortuary temple. The pylon would have almost the same dimensions as that at the Temple of Luxor except that it has lost its cornice. A stairway at the north end leads to the top for an excellent view across the temple towards the Theban Mountain. The pylons, columns and chambers are smaller as you gaze westwards; the platforms at each stage of the temple are higher; an architectural funnel pointing towards the final sanctuary – as at Karnak, and with Egyptian temples generally. The reliefs on the pylon towers depict campaigns against the Nubians and Syrians, campaigns never fought by Ramses III and probably copied from the Ramesseum.

Battle with the Sea Peoples

A net was prepared for them to ensnare them, those who entered into the river-mouths being confined and fallen within it, pinioned in their places, butchered and their corpses hacked up.

Inscription on relief

In the eighth year of his reign, Ramses III was in desperate struggle with the Sea Peoples, a coalition of northerners including Sardinians, Cretans, Philistines and others, not all of whom have been identified. By sea and by ox-carts carrying their women and children overland, these peoples were bent on permanent settlement in the rich Delta pasturelands. One group, whom the Egyptians called the Danu, the Danaoi of the *Iliad*, here emerged into history for the first time. The invasion is recorded in dramatic detail by reliefs along the outer north wall of the mortuary temple (walk round to it before passing through the pylon) and should not be missed. It is the only Egyptian relief portraying a sea battle. In a single sweeping picture the artist has combined the various phases of the engagement: the Egyptians stand on their decks in steady order; an opposing vessel is held fast with grappling irons, the enemy in confusion, many of them falling into the water; while from the shore Ramses standing upon the heads of captives joins with his archers in shooting volleys of arrows at the invaders. In places, deep grooves have been cut into the wall by ancient visitors seeking to obtain stone dust from this sacred place for use in magical charms.

Proceeding Through the Temple

The **First Court** was the scene of ceremonies and entertainments which would have included sword fights and wrestling. The east wall celebrates Ramses' victory in his eleventh year against the Libyans: trophies of enemy hands and genitals are counted by scribes, and soldiers are rewarded for their valour. The pharaoh himself might have distributed rewards from the window in the south wall, decorated on either side with reliefs of prisoners' heads. This was the façade of the **royal palace**; its central hall surrounded by six columns was for holding audiences; the private apartments were on the south side.

The mortuary temple continued in use for only 200 years, though the smaller temple of Hatshepsut remained a place of worship throughout Ptolemaic times. In the Ptolemaic and Roman periods, the First Court was filled with houses and a monastery, the **Second Court** with the principal church of what was now a town of some size. Traces of the church can still be seen, for example the base of an octagonal font on the south side. Osiris figures against the pillars along the east and west sides were removed in building the church, and the central pillar on the north side was taken down to make way for the apse. A few of the **Osiris figures** remain at the north end. Along the west colonnade, which is also the façade of the temple proper, the colours on the **reliefs** are especially bright. In the central register on either side of the doorway, Ramses is shown variously with Atum and Mont entering the temple; being crowned in the presence of the Theban triad; and being purified before receiving the emblems of his rank from the gods of Heliopolis. In the lower register on either side, Ramses' name is written in alternation with figures of his sons. None of their names, however, is inscribed as there appears to have been some uncertainty over the succession. On the architrave over the doorway is a brightly painted winged solar disc.

Hypostyle Halls

Beyond is the **First Hypostyle Hall**, roofless now but once with a raised ceiling over the central aisle as at the Ramesseum and Karnak. To the right are a series of sanctuaries, the first for the cult of the living pharaoh. To the left are treasure chambers, still with

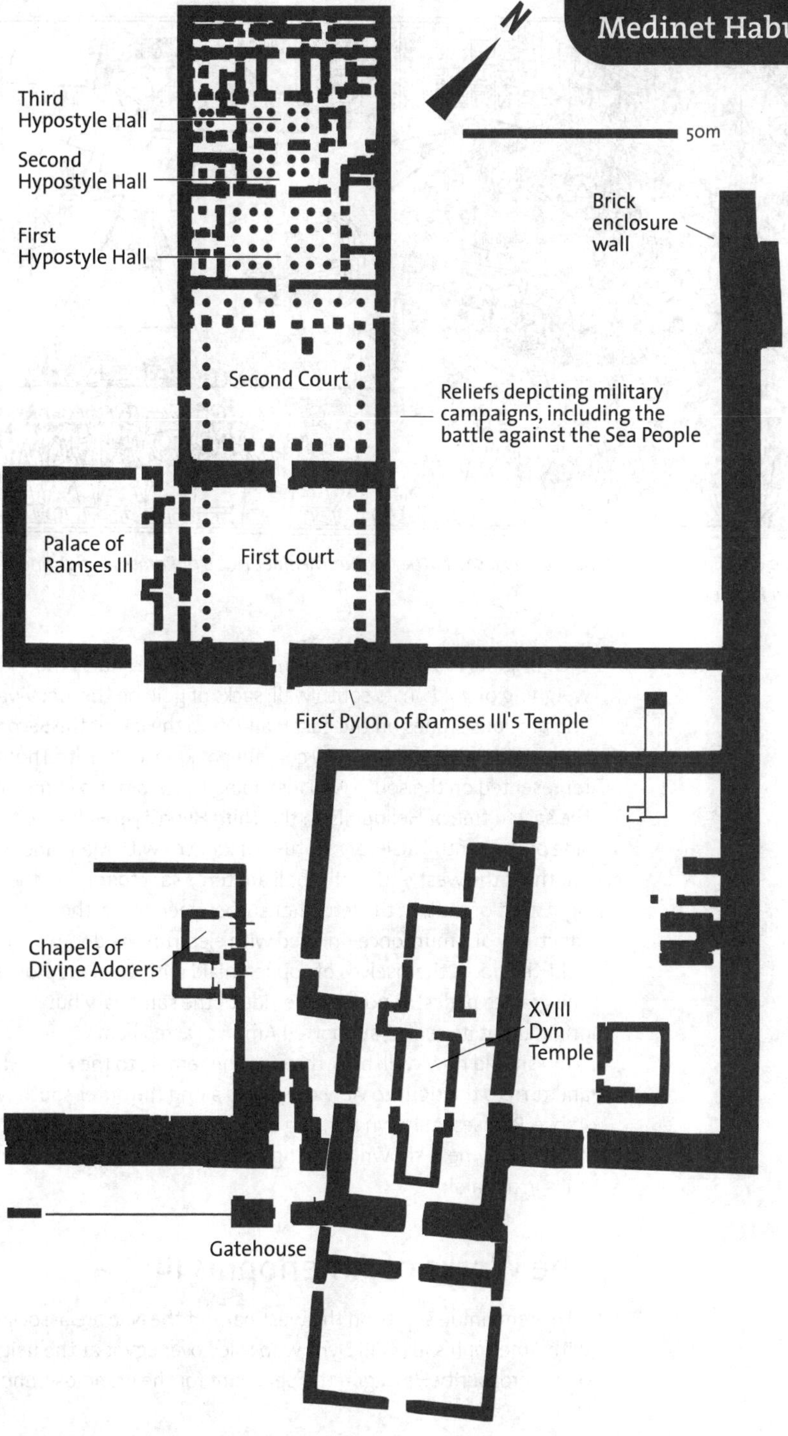
N
50m
Third Hypostyle Hall
Second Hypostyle Hall
First Hypostyle Hall
Brick enclosure wall
Second Court
Reliefs depicting military campaigns, including the battle against the Sea People
Palace of Ramses III
First Court
First Pylon of Ramses III's Temple
Chapels of Divine Adorers
XVIII Dyn Temple
Gatehouse

The only Egyptian relief portraying a sea battle, that at Medinet Habu of Ramses III fighting the Sea Peoples

their original roofs. The central chamber of these shows the weighing of gold on its south wall; sacks of gold on the west wall; and precious stones on the east wall. Off to the left of the **Second Hypostyle Hall** is the funerary chamber of Ramses III with Thoth represented on the south wall inscribing the pharaoh's name on the sacred tree of Heliopolis. In the **Third Hypostyle Hall**, on either side of the central aisle, are statues of Ramses with Maat and with Thoth. At the west end of this hall are three sanctuaries: to the right, that of Mut; to the left, Khonsu; between them, the sanctuary of Amun, once finished with electrum, its doorway of gold, the doors themselves of copper inlaid with precious stones. The granite pedestal, now to one side of the sanctuary but originally at its centre, supported Amun's sacred boat.

You should now walk back through the temple to the First Pylon and turn to the right to view the reliefs along the outer south wall. Above, Ramses is shown hunting various desert animals; below, most vividly, he is shown impaling with his hunting spear writhing bulls in a marsh.

The Works of Amenophis III

The remaining sights on the west bank of the Nile are associated with Amenophis III (XVIII Dyn), who ruled over Egypt at the height of her prosperity. He began the penchant for the grandiose, and though it later served pharaonic bombast, in the works of Amenophis there is always a more tolerable touch of grandeur and opulence. It is unlikely that he was ever personally engaged in any military exploits, though some inscriptions make this claim by way of convention; rather he comes across as a man who enjoyed life to the full, and had the means to enjoy it more fully than any other man of his times. A smile of contentment plays upon his lips as he sits with Queen Tiy in the colossal group at the Cairo Museum; a stele found at Amarna and now at the British Museum shows him in later years, his weary frame and jaded expression suggesting that he had known pleasures beyond even his ability to enjoy them.

The House of Joy

Though the ancient Egyptians built their temples of stone, their homes and even their royal palaces were built merely of mud brick and so have barely survived the millennia. **Amenophis' palace** lies about 1km south of Medinet Habu. Though badly ruined and rarely visited, it is one of the few royal residences in Egypt of which substantial portions remain. The palace contained living and state apartments for Amenophis, a separate residence for Tiy, a large festal hall built for the pharaoh's jubilee and quarters for courtiers and for the harem. When excavated, traces of plastered walls were found, bearing lovely paintings of birds and water plants prefiguring the art of Akhenaten. These have now disappeared.

Though Tiy clearly enjoyed her husband's love and confidence, and was often represented as his equal in size, Amenophis did not deny himself the delights of an extensive harem. The dowry of a Hittite princess whom Amenophis married as a secondary queen included 317 damsels for most of the other nights of the year. Another text shows that having already married the sister of a Babylonian king, he was now clamouring for the king's daughter as well. And in his old age Amenophis is known to have married one of his own daughters by Tiy. Little wonder he called his palace the House of Joy.

To the east of his palace Amenophis shared his bounty by digging for Tiy an enormous **lake**, 370m broad by 1940m in length, whereon the imperial couple might sail in the royal barge named Aten Gleams – again suggesting that in spite of his indulgence Amenophis played some role, insensible though he might have been of the effect, in raising his son to Aten and bringing religious revolution to Egypt. Amenophis claimed, improbably, that the lake was dug in 15 days, though signs of haste are apparent in the mounds of excavated earth still lying along its western boundary.

The Colossi of Memnon

Amenophis also built a **mortuary temple** which has now vanished beneath ploughed fields between the Ramesseum and Medinet Habu. Responsibility for its destruction lies principally with Merneptah, possible pharaoh of the Exodus, who used it as a quarry for building his own temple immediately to the north. All that remains are the two famous **Colossi of Memnon** which once guarded its outer gates. The Colossi are along the road leading back to the new village of Gurna and are visible from some distance. They are in fact gigantic statues of the enthroned Amenophis himself, rising 19.5m from the plain. At one time they wore the royal crown and were even higher. Both are damaged and are lacking their faces; the one on the right (north) broke at the waist during an earthquake in AD 27 and was later crudely repaired, the top having been sawn into blocks. Cocteau described them as victims of rainless thunder storms: 'Crucified, sitting against great crosses; the lightning has left nothing untouched except their legs.'

The Colossi of Memnon, from Napoleon's Description de l'Egypte, *1798*

If it was lightning that crucified them, it was Greek and Roman tourists who cut graffiti into the legs of the figure on the right. The inscriptions reach as high as a man can stretch and were usually cut by visiting notables, including eight Roman governors. The Colossi had early on been accorded the wonder due to the divine, perhaps because of their imposing size, perhaps because Amenophis was recognized as both pharaoh and god. But their cult status was too elaborate: a commoner, Amenophis, son of Hapu, was architect of his pharaoh's mortuary temple and raised the Colossi. The vast undertaking impressed both king and public and, like Imhotep at Saqqara, he was divinized. In Ptolemaic times the Colossi this son of Hapu erected and the wise sayings attributed to him attracted followers throughout the Graeco-Roman world. All memory of Amenophis III was forgotten, and the Greeks decided the statues were of Memnon, son of Tithonus, a legendary king of Egypt, and Eos, the Dawn, who went to fight in defence of Troy and was slain by Achilles.

But it was the **north colossus**, with its diminutive figures of Amenophis' mother Mutemuia on the left and Queen Tiy on the right, that eventually attracted so much curiosity, for after it was shattered by the earthquake it would sometimes emit a musical note as the sun rose over the eastern mountains. The Emperor Hadrian came in AD 130 with his wife and a large retinue, and camped for several nights at its feet to hear the phenomenon. He was at last rewarded with three performances on a single morning and was declared to have been exceptionally favoured by the gods. The association with Memnon was expanded to account for the sound: fallen at Troy, he now greeted his mother Eos with a sweet and plaintive sound when she appeared at dawn, and she in turn wept tears of dew upon her beloved child. Nowadays it is thought that the rapid change in temperature as the sun rose caused splittings off of quartzite particles which resonated within the fractures. Certainly, once the colossus was repaired in AD 199, it cried out no more.

Where to Stay on the West Bank

Accommodation on the west bank is generally of a more basic standard than at Luxor or Karnak, but there is a degree of tranquillity and the sense of being close to rural Egypt (though this is rapidly changing, especially since the construction of the bridge upstream) – and for those serious about exploring the sites there is considerable convenience too.

Inexpensive ($$)

****Nile Valley**, near the ferry landing, **t** (095) 231 1477, *www.nilevalley.nl*. Owned by a Dutch-Egyptian couple, this is a friendly and well-run hotel with a pool and a rooftop restaurant which sells alcohol and has a wonderful view across to the Temple of Luxor.

****Gezira**, **t/f** (095) 231 0034, *www.el-gezira.com*. A small hotel near the people ferry landing with a roof garden restaurant giving good Nile views.

****Amun el Gezierat, t** (095) 231 0912, **f** (095) 231 1353. A few hundred metres up from the people ferry landing stage behind the horse-hire stables; a pleasant small hotel set in a garden.

****Pharaohs, t/f** (095) 231 0702, near the entrance to Medinet Habu. An older hotel, more like a villa set in gardens, with comfortable rooms, some with air conditioning and private bathrooms.

Cheap ($)

Habu, t (095) 237 2477, near the entrance to Medinet Habu. Built in traditional village style, this offers insulation against extremes of temperature. Rooms have fans, and there are shared bathrooms. The situation is lovely, but the place is less than clean.

Mersam Hotel, t (095) 237 2403, *www.luxor-westbank.com/marsam_e_az.htm*, behind the Colossi of Memnon on the road running towards the Ramesseum. A rustic place amid lush fields. Run by a Czech-born woman, the rooms (doubles and triples only) are clean and are cooled by fans, and there are shared hot-water bathrooms. An extension will offer rooms with private baths.

Eating Out on the West Bank

Soft **drinks** and bottles of mineral water are sold at the major sites.

Meals can be had at the **Tutankhamun** and **African** restaurants by the people's ferry landing, both serving good Egyptian food. Also try either of the **two café-restaurants** on the corner opposite the temple at Medinet Habu. The restaurant at the **Marsam hotel** is highly recommended for its atmosphere and good Egyptian fare. The rooftop restaurant at the **Nile Valley hotel** near the landing stage serves alcohol and has good food and the world's best view across to the Temple of Luxor. The three-star **Hatshepsut Restaurant** opposite Deir el Bahri is identified by signs mysteriously reading No Galag (the place turns out to be run by Mr Sayed No Galag); open all day and evening, it is a white domed building covered with Hajj-style paintings and has both a 1st-floor air-conditioned restaurant and a rooftop restaurant and bar.

A River Journey between Luxor and Aswan

Like a string of citadels extending Alexandrian power towards Nubia, the Ptolemies built temples along the Nile at Esna, Edfu and Kom Ombo. Cruise boats ply between Luxor and Aswan throughout the year and offer an agreeable way of enjoying the lush valley scenery and visiting the temples en route. The experience can only be improved, for the more adventurous, by hiring a felucca and entrusting yourself to the power of the current and the winds.

12

Don't miss

1. **Best preserved temple in Egypt, with traces of the original colouring throughout**
   Temple of Horus at Edfu
   p.350x
2. **A touch of Greece in Egypt**
   Temple of Sobek and Haroeris at Kom Ombo
   p.353

It is godly to cruise the Nile through Egypt. Before the roads and the railways there was only this river, and as the pharaohs and the hoi polloi sailed upon it and watched their world unroll it cannot have failed to make a special impression on them all. The echoing silence of the deserts spoke of the void beyond the grave. But here along the river was the rhythm of bright green fields perpetually tender, small brown figures absorbed in their patch, fishermen like spiky water insects poling through the reeds. A flap of egret wings as you glide by, distant, breeze-blown, upon the artery of life itself. It is like the most beautiful murals in the ancient tombs, too sweet not to carry into eternity.

Esna

A short walk up from the quayside through the constricting streets of **Esna**, 54km from Luxor, and beside an awning-shaded market is the temple, squatting in a pit. It had been covered over with houses; now it is partly laid bare behind railings and you descend a staircase into the excavations. Ptolemy VI rebuilt this **Temple of Khnum**, the god who fashioned man on his potter's wheel, over the ruins of earlier structures, but almost all that remains to be seen is the later hypostyle hall begun by the Emperor Claudius in the 1st century AD. The carvings within are of a poor standard, but the roof is intact and supported by 24 columns with 16 different capitals, bearing their original colours well. It is these you come to see. It is best to stand, slowly revolving, looking upwards at the myriad palm and composite plant capitals, arranged without order or symmetry, but with the most pleasing effect, as though you were standing among trees, admiring the subtle and powerful architecture of a forest.

Temple of Khnum
open winter 6–5.30, summer 6–6.30; adm LE25

In the forecourt of the temple there are several blocks from an **early Christian church**, recalling a time when Esna was an important centre of Christian activity. Notice the lion-headed font carved from an ancient block bearing fine hieroglyphics on the reverse. The Emperor Decius (reigned AD 249–51) decreed that all Christians should sacrifice to the Roman gods or suffer death. His is the last cartouche carved on the temple walls, but he is commemorated too in a sense by Deir Manaos wa al-Shuhada 6km southwest of town, the **monastery of the Three Thousand Six Hundred Martyrs**, whose 10th-century church is one of the most beautiful in Upper Egypt.

Esna was once a terminus for caravans picking their way from oasis to oasis across the desert from the Sudan, but this trade virtually expired with the passing of the last century. It remains though a merchant town and weaving centre, and can be

Getting around between Luxor and Aswan

For additional travel information, *see* the Luxor and Aswan chapters.

The temples at Esna, Edfu and Kom Ombo can be seen in a day if you **hire a car** with driver at either Luxor or Aswan, arriving in the evening at the other. If you're relying on **train, service taxi** or **local bus**, count on seeing only two temples en route, returning to the third from your new base – though you may find you are able to manage all three. The temple you would most kick yourself for not visiting is that at Edfu.

Reaching **El Kab** is more difficult and the effort will only repay the enthusiast; you either take the train or a service taxi to El Mahamid, from where it is a 2.5km walk to the site. Most cruises do not stop here.

---

interesting to wander about. It is worth walking south a bit through the covered **market street**, where lengths of fabric are sold or made up into clothing, and then back along it (north), passing the temple, into a quarter of old houses with fine brickwork and *mashrabiyya* screens. Where the street opens up into a little square, turn right towards the Nile and look in on the **Coptic church**. Along the corniche, north of the church, are more fine old houses. A barrage crosses the Nile here, built in 1906; it is busy with trucks and carts trundling from one side of the river to the other, and in the morning with barges and cruise boats waiting to pass through its locks. Back at the stone quay along that part of the corniche nearest the temple, notice the carved cartouches of the Emperor Marcus Aurelius.

Flaubert Entertained in Esna

At Esna Flaubert was propositioned aboard his boat by an *almeh* followed by her pet sheep, its wool spotted with yellow henna. He went with her to the house of Kuchuk Hanem, 'a tall, splendid creature, lighter in colouring than an Arab; she comes from Damascus; her skin, particularly on her body, is slightly coffee-coloured. When she bends, her flesh ripples into bronze ridges. Her eyes are dark and enormous, her eyebrows thick, her nostrils open and wide; heavy shoulders, full, apple-shaped breasts.' She danced the Bee, which required that the musicians be blindfolded, and slowly removed her clothes. 'When it was time to leave I didn't leave. I sucked her furiously – her body was covered with sweat – she was tired after dancing – she was cold – I covered her with my pelisse, and she fell asleep with her fingers in mine. As for me, I scarcely shut my eyes. Watching that beautiful creature asleep (she snored), my night was one long, infinitely intense reverie – that was why I stayed. I thought of my nights in Paris brothels – a whole series of old memories came back – and I thought of her, of her dance, of her voice as she sang songs that for me were without meaning and even without distinguishable words. That continued all night. At three o'clock I got up to piss in the street – the stars were shining ... As for the coups, they were good – the third especially was ferocious, and the last tender – we told each other many sweet things – towards the end there was something sad and loving in the way we embraced.' (*Flaubert in Egypt*).

Back in France, while he was writing *Madame Bovary*, he wrote to Louise Colet, his jealous mistress: 'You tell me that Kuchuk's bedbugs degrade her in your eyes; for me they were the most enchanting touch of all. Their nauseating odour mingled with the scent of her skin, which was dripping with sandalwood oil. I want a touch of bitterness in everything – always a jeer in the midst of our triumphs, desolation even in the midst of enthusiasm.' And he reminded Louise that 'you and I are thinking of her, but she is certainly not thinking of us. We are weaving an aesthetic around her, whereas this particular very interesting tourist who was vouchsafed the honours of her couch has vanished from her memory completely, like many others. Ah! Travelling makes one modest – you see what a tiny place you occupy in the world.'

It was perhaps here that Flaubert landed in 1850, though his interest was not antiquarian: by an edict of Mohammed Ali's in 1834 prohibiting prostitution and female dancing in Cairo, the *almehs* (literally, learned women) of Egypt had concentrated in Qena, Esna and Aswan. Flaubert entertained a mystique about prostitution: 'A meeting place of so many elements – lust, bitterness, complete absence of human contact, muscular frenzy, the clink of gold – that to peer into it deeply makes one reel. One learns so many things in a brothel, and feels such sadness, and dreams so longingly of love!'

Continuing Upriver: El Kab

El Kab
open daily 8–6; adm LE20

Thirty kilometres south of Esna on the east bank of the Nile, right on the water's edge, is **El Kab**, the ancient Nekhab, important from Pre-Dynastic to Ptolemaic times. A massive mud brick enclosure wall surrounds the ruins, 11.5m thick and pierced by gates approached by ramps on the north, east and south. Of the two temples here, the finest is the small **Temple of Nekhbet**, the work of Amenophis II and later Ramses II, and next to it, also within an inner enclosure, a **Temple of Thoth** built by Tuthmosis III. Nekhbet was the white vulture goddess, the 'mistress of the valley' and cult goddess of Upper Egypt. The importance of the site as a national shrine is evidenced by the fact that the innermost mud brick wall was rebuilt at least ten times.

Edfu

Temple of Horus
open winter 7–4, summer 6–6; adm LE50

On the west bank of the Nile, equidistant from Luxor and Aswan (105km), **Edfu** is spread upon the mound of an ancient city. The **Temple of Horus** is on the western outskirts of the present town, at a spot where Horus and Seth met in titanic combat for the world (*see* 'Philae', p.379). The temple, the second largest in Egypt after Karnak, is suitably monumental and the best preserved in the country. You see evidence of the original colouring everywhere both inside and out. Construction began under Ptolemy III Euergetes and it was completed, down to its decorations, by the mid-1st century BC. It is therefore hardly a century or two older than the many technically superior imperial ruins in Rome. But you forget this and applaud the Ptolemies' phoney archaic style, for this is pure theatre. Remembering Justinian's boast that with Hagia Sophia he had surpassed Solomon's temple, at Edfu despite a mouthful of popcorn you cry out, 'Cecil B. DeMille, they have outdone you!'

On the **pylon** Neos Dionysos, in New Kingdom gear, snicker-snacks among the Bandersnatch, while in the colonnaded **court**,

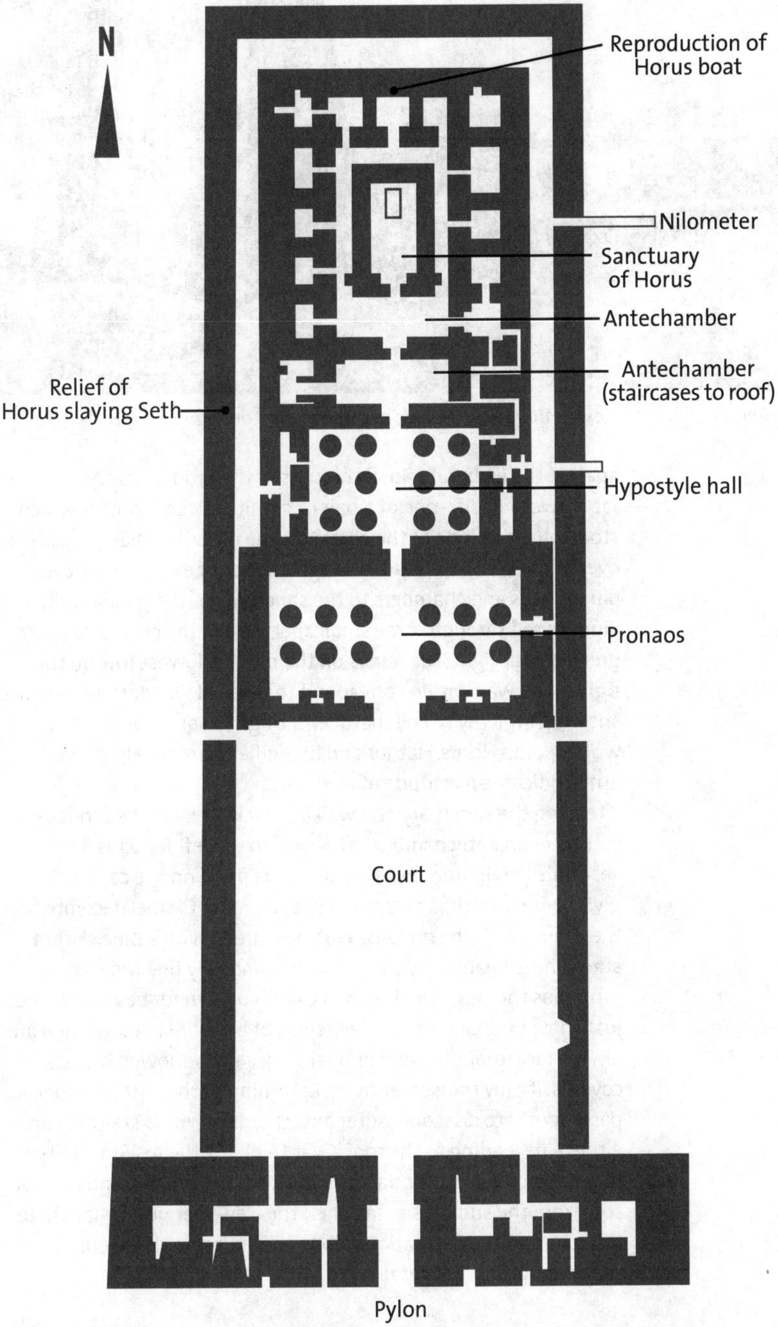
N
Reproduction of Horus boat
Nilometer
Sanctuary of Horus
Antechamber
Antechamber (staircases to roof)
Relief of Horus slaying Seth
Hypostyle hall
Pronaos
Court
Pylon

The temple of Edfu before excavation, from Napoleon's Description de l'Egypte, *1798*

against the elaborate floral columns of the pronaos, is the Jabberwock itself – one of a pair of granite falcon-Horuses which stood on either side of the entrance (the other, headless, has keeled over in the dust). You walk through a series of ever smaller, ever darker halls and chambers to the **sanctuary** of the god, weirdly illuminated through three small apertures in the ceiling by a dim green Nilotic light. The reliefs on the next-to-lowest row on the right-hand wall within correspond to those at Dendera, in this case showing Ptolemy IV Philopator entering the sanctuary and worshipping Horus, Hathor and his deified parents. His pendant arms indicate an attitude of reverence.

Leaving the sanctuary and walking back towards the pronaos, you enter an **antechamber**, off which, to the left (east), is a vestibule (a fair amount of red and blue paint on the capitals) giving onto (north) an elegant little New Year Chapel decorated on the ceiling with the goddess Nut, pale green with a blue skirt of stars. She is beautifully shaped, with unusually fine breasts and profile, as though here there is a Greek concern for beauty and not just conventional form. Indeed reliefs of bare-breasted women are always Ptolemaic; the earlier pharaonic reliefs showed breasts covered, if only transparently so. Returning to the antechamber you pass (south) to a second, outer antechamber with a staircase on either side leading to the roof. As at Dendera, the residing deity required at least an annual dose of sunshine, a reimpregnation of soul from the sun. This occasioned the New Year procession up to the roof, and the decorations along the staircase walls reproduce the ceremony in full detail.

Other **rites** celebrated annually were the conjugal visit of Hathor (*see* Dendera, p.260); the triumph of Horus over Seth (*see* the inner face of the west enclosure wall); the coronation in the main court of a live falcon as the living symbol of Horus on earth; and the re-enactment of the divine birth of Horus and the pharaoh at the Birth House outside the pylon (with episodes of the ceremony carved on its walls).

The Changing Landscape: Edfu to Kom Ombo

Southwards beyond Edfu the palms and cultivation on the east bank give way to the **Eastern Desert** and at **Silsileh** (145km from Luxor) the Nile passes through a defile, now with only hills on either side but thought once to mark a cataract. The rock bed of Egypt changes here from limestone to the harder sandstone used in almost all New Kingdom and Ptolemaic temple building. During the reign of Ramses II, the Silsileh quarries were worked by no fewer than 3,000 men for the Ramesseum alone.

Above Silsileh the mountains again recede from the river and the desert is kept at bay by canals. Irrigation and the fellahin bring harvests of cane and corn to the fields. The reclaimed land on the east bank around **Kom Ombo** (164km from Luxor, 46km from Aswan) supports a large Nubian population displaced from their homeland by the rising waters of Lake Nasser. The village is on the Luxor–Aswan road; nearby is a sugar refinery supplied by barges landing near the temple 4km to the west.

Kom Ombo: the Temple of Sobek and Haroeris

Temple of Sobek and Haroeris
open daily 7–5.45; adm LE35

The **Temple of Sobek and Haroeris**, which is Ptolemaic, stands on a low promontory overlooking the Nile, 4km outside the town of Kom Ombo. Its elevation, its seclusion, the combination of sun and water flowing past as though in slow but determined search for the Mediterranean, suggests something of Greece. It has ruined well, and there is something in its stones of that Hellenic response to light, the uncompromising noonday glare, the soft farewell to the setting sun without fear of night.

The usual Ptolemaic (and Roman) appeasement of the fossilized Egyptian priesthood is apparent, however, as soon as you abandon mood for detail – even Marcus Aurelius must stoically appear on an outer corridor wall in pharaonic garb offering a pectoral to Sennuphis, divine wife of Haroeris. The naos was begun by Ptolemy VI Philometor; the hypostyle hall and pronaos were added by Neos Dionysos; and Augustus added the court, the outer enclosure wall and the now destroyed pylon. It is a symmetrically twin temple, the

The temple of Kom Ombo was largely obscured by rubble and sand at the time of the French expedition in 1798 (from Napoleon's Description de l'Egypte*)*

left side dedicated to falcon-headed Haroeris (the older Horus), the right to Sobek, the crocodile god. The two parts of the temple are physically divided, however, only at the two sanctuaries.

Mention of seclusion needs to be qualified, however. Until fairly recently the site was occupied by the temple alone, but now there are souvenir stalls and tacky tourist shops hogging the ground. If somebody is making a few piastres out of these, it is at the cost of rapidly destroying the idyll of the site.

A Tour

The temple faces more or less west, towards the Nile. You approach from the south, past a massive ruined gateway built by Neos Dionysos. In front of you, between an ancient mud brick enclosure wall and the outer temple wall, is a small chapel of Hathor, the gift of a wealthy Roman woman. Through its gratings you can see sarcophagi and piled up crocodile mummies – not belonging here, merely tossed in after being dug up in a nearby cemetery.

Only a few courses of the temple **pylon** remain, and the stumps of the 16 columns once surrounding the court – at its centre is the stone altar used in sacrifices. Except for the three centre columns framing the dual passageways leading to the twin sanctuaries, the pronaos façade has lost the upper parts of its columns where they rise above the screen. But there is no loss of effect. The surviving columns burst in floral capitals, and above them, across the remaining section of the cavetto cornice, are two winged discs emphasizing again the duality of the divine presence here. Within the pronaos the ceiling is decorated with flying vultures and the supporting capitals proclaim the unity of Upper and Lower Egypt, some the lily, some papyrus – and one eccentrically a palm. On this side of the screen are coronation reliefs showing various Ptolemaic

Kom Ombo: Temple of Sobek and Haroeris

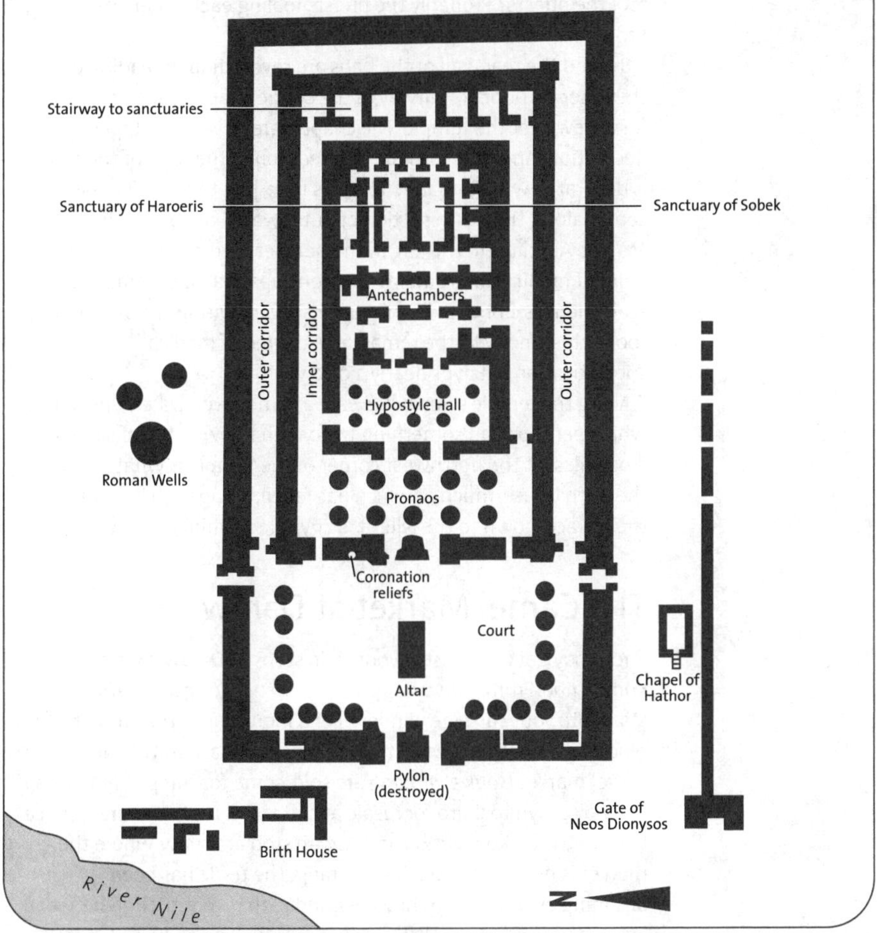

pharaohs receiving the blessings of Egypt's high gods and the double crown of the Delta and the valley.

In the hypostyle **hall** beyond, and in the three rising antechambers after that, are more reliefs. One, between the doors into the sanctuaries, shows Ptolemy Philometor and his sister-wife before Sobek, Haroeris and Khonsu who inscribes the pharaoh's name on a palm stalk, the equivalent of St Peter confirming entry into Heaven. Philometor wears a full Macedonian cloak, a rare exception to the traditional guise. Little is left of the sanctuaries, but they are all the more revealing for that. Between them, at a lower level, is a **crypt** which communicates with one of the chapels to the east. The crypt is now exposed but was once covered with a sliding slab. It is not difficult to imagine someone creeping down there from the chapel to make spectral noises at appropriate moments – the priests to fool pharaoh, or one of pharaoh's men to fool the priests? Probably the priests fooling each other, the Ptolemies having the last laugh.

Beyond the rear wall of the naos are **seven chapels** leading off the inner corridor. A stairway in the centre chapel leads upwards for a view over the temple. The chapels are at various stages of decoration. An **outer corridor**, entered from either end of the court, is decorated with Roman reliefs. It is here, just to the left of dead centre along the north section of outer wall that you will find Marcus Aurelius. To the left, in the northeast corner, is a display in relief of **medical instruments**: suction cups, scalpels, retractors, scales, lances, bone saws, chisels for surgery within the skull, dental tools – testimony to the remarkable degree of medical sophistication in Egypt nearly 2,000 years ago.

Along the temple's north flank are a Roman well, cistern and basin, which perhaps had something to do with the worship of sacred crocodiles. At the northwest corner of the temple is what is left of the birth house, much of which has fallen, along with its portion of the terrace, down to the Nile. It is Egypt reclaiming her own.

The Camel Market at Daraw

You may get a surprise if your train stops at **Daraw**, 5km south of Kom Ombo. From railway wagons drawn up alongside, camels stare into your carriage window. For a month or so they have been plodding across the desert from northern Sudan, and at the Daraw camel market (*souk el gimaal*) are sold, some for trans-shipment all the way down to Cairo for resale at the camel market there. Service taxis between Kom Ombo and Aswan stop at Daraw, where the market is held every Tuesday morning. The trade has been declining over the years, however, and with recent friction between Egypt and fundamentalist Sudan it may well be on its last legs.

Where to Stay and Eat between Luxor and Aswan

You should stay at **Luxor** (*see* p.295) or **Aswan** (*see* p.380); the only alternative is **Edfu**, though this should be avoided if at all possible. Accommodation at Edfu is confined to the shabby and distinctly no-star **El Medina**, Sharia Gumhuriya, **t** (097) 471 1326, though the breakfasts are generous. Sharia al-Maglis runs east–west from the Nile to the temple; about two-thirds of the way towards the temple is the main town square; turn north here into Sharia Gumhuriya and you reach the hotel in about 50m. Just outside Edfu temple there is a café serving refreshments.

Otherwise the basic **Zahrat el Medina** restaurant on Sharia al-Maglis serves decent chicken and vegetable meals. Refreshments can be obtained by the Kom Ombo temple and at the market adjoining the temple at Esna.

Aswan

Aswan is where the valley closes upon the river, no more buffer of cultivation on either side, instead a universe of desert sundered by the pulsing Nile flowing out of Africa.

Following the day's fierce sun and dry desert heat, there is the beauty at evening of sand, sky and water fading imperceptibly through deepening violet, a lift of breeze on the Nile, a movement of palms, a flight of hoopoes, and the graceful glide of swallow-tailed feluccas.

The final pleasure is to know that when morning comes at Aswan there is so little to do. Those who insist on doing it can easily do it all in a couple of days. Those who want to do nothing will want to stay far longer.

13

Don't miss

1. Camel ride to an evocative Christian monastery in the desert
   St Simeon's p.369
2. Boat journey to the island of Isis
   Philae p.375
3. Drifting with the currents on the Nile
   Felucca journey to the Botanical Island p.367
4. Evening walk along the street of the bazaar
   Sharia el Souk p.360

See map overleaf

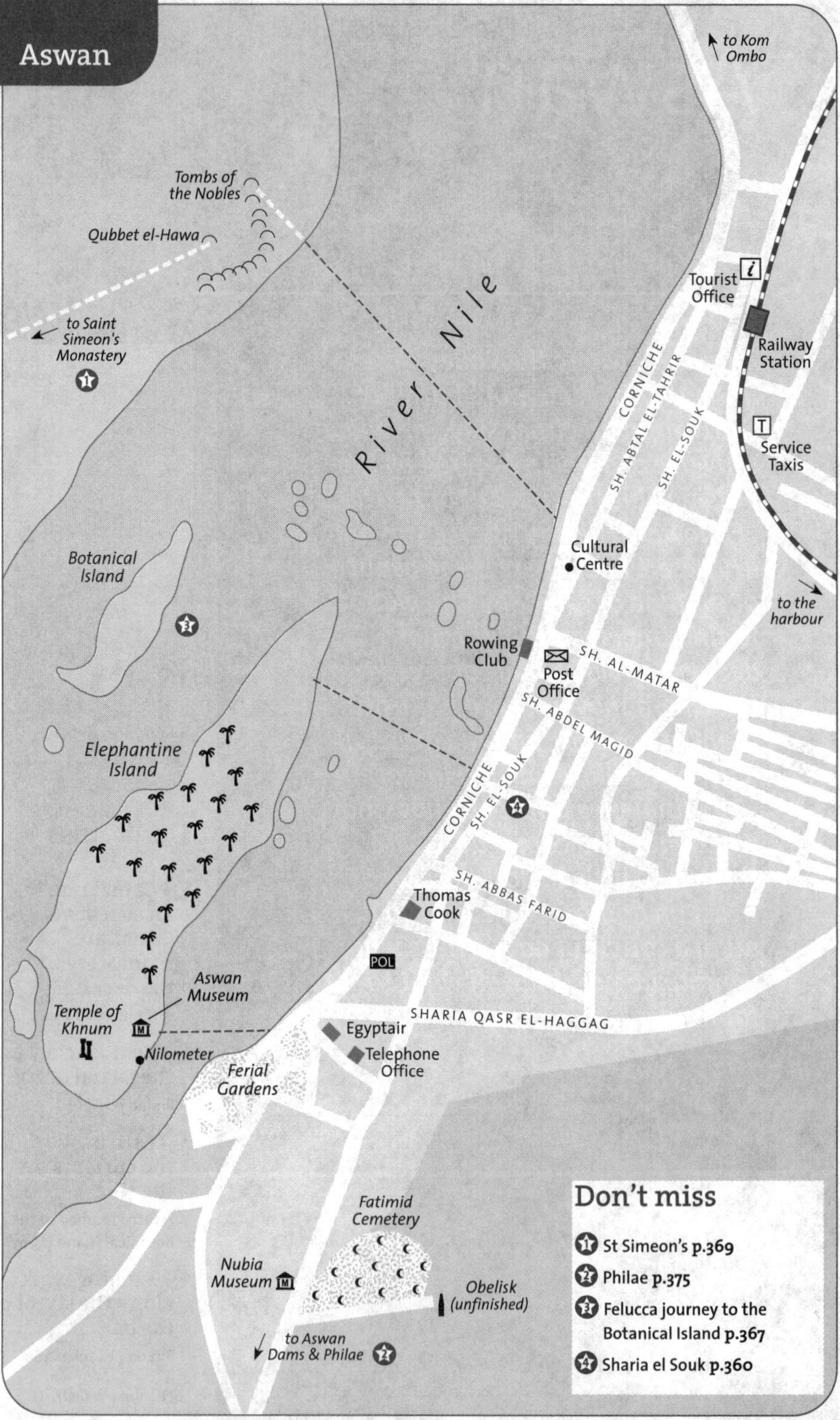
to Kom Ombo
Tombs of the Nobles
Qubbet el-Hawa
to Saint Simeon's Monastery
River Nile
Tourist Office
Railway Station
Service Taxis
CORNICHE
SH. ABTAL EL-TAHRIR
SH. EL-SOUK
Cultural Centre
to the harbour
Botanical Island
Rowing Club
Post Office
SH. AL-MATAR
SH. ABDEL MAGID
Elephantine Island
CORNICHE
SH. EL-SOUK
SH. ABBAS FARID
Thomas Cook
POL
Aswan Museum
Temple of Khnum
Nilometer
SHARIA QASR EL-HAGGAG
Egyptair
Telephone Office
Ferial Gardens
Fatimid Cemetery
Nubia Museum
Obelisk (unfinished)
to Aswan Dams & Philae
Don't miss
1 St Simeon's p.369
2 Philae p.375
3 Felucca journey to the Botanical Island p.367
4 Sharia el Souk p.360

At Aswan the Nile is only 87m above sea level, so low a height for so massive a river you would think it would disdain the 87m inducement to go farther, but there is a continent of water behind, urging it on through the cataract above Aswan, and the current is strong. The layer of sandstone covering Upper Egypt from Edfu southwards is ruptured here by the thrust of underlying granite which the river has hewn into the rocks and islands of the First Cataract. Even before construction of the British dam at the turn of last century and the giant hydro-electric dam in the 1960s, this was where traffic on the Nile stopped. Camels transported cargoes round the rocks while lightened boats took their chances through the granite passage. The more intrepid passenger might stay aboard:

> *We see the whole boat slope down bodily under our feet. We feel the leap – the dead fall – the staggering rush forward. Instantly the waves are foaming and boiling up on all sides, flooding the lower deck, and covering the upper deck with spray. The men ship their oars, leaving all to helm and current; and, despite the hoarse tumult, we distinctly hear those oars scrape the rocks on either side.*
>
> Amelia Edwards, *A Thousand Miles Up the Nile*

Frontier Outpost

Aswan, 210km from Luxor and 886km from Cairo, is where Egypt ends. Beyond lie Nubia and the Sudan, and the traditional routes of invasion and trade. The ancient Egyptians garrisoned the 500km stretch of river to the Third Cataract, and the fleet patrolled the Nile between the First Cataract and the Second at Wadi Halfa. An uprising or an attack on a caravan, and signal fires relayed the summons for help to Aswan. Two thousand years and more later, Aswan marked the southernmost margin of the Roman world, and when Juvenal fell into disfavour at Rome for writing satirical verses against the emperor's court, it was to Aswan that he was posted, to guard the empire he had mocked. It is the High Dam that accounts for the modern military presence: its breach would send a tidal wave down the whole length of the Nile Valley and inundate half of Cairo. But that presence and the object of its protection lie out of sight some kilometres south of the town, which for all of its growth and the influx of workers in recent years retains an atmosphere of remoteness and tranquillity.

Long favoured as a winter resort with daytime temperatures around 23–30°C, the increase and changing style of tourism in Egypt has led greater numbers of travellers to challenge the summer heat which usually ranges from 38–42°C during the day, though it can climb much higher. Air conditioning and a siesta during early afternoon, and the low humidity, make even the hottest July and August days bearable.

Getting to Aswan

By Air

Egyptair (national call centre **t** 0900 70000) has direct flights between Aswan and Cairo, Luxor and Abu Simbel. The airport is 16km southwest of Aswan beyond the High Dam. Egyptair runs buses back and forth between the town and airport; its office is on the roundabout at the south end of the corniche, with another at the Aswan Mövenpick. There are also taxis costing about LE60. For more information on flights, *see* **Planning Your Trip**, p.59.

By Train

Several trains a day link Aswan with Luxor and Cairo (*see also* **Planning Your Trip**, p.59), with travel times and frequencies set to increase when a second track is completed between Luxor and Aswan. The train station is at the north end of the town, several blocks back from the corniche. A taxi or carriage from the station to anywhere in town will cost about LE10.

By Bus and Taxi

The bus and service taxi depot is 3.5 km north of the train station. By **service taxi** it is quite practicable to visit Kom Ombo, Edfu and Esna in a day, ending up in Luxor, though a change of taxi is required at the end of each leg. Before hiring a **private taxi**, try a bit of negotiating to get a feel for prices; but you could also try making arrangements through one of the agents along the corniche, thereby ensuring reliability and often obtaining a better price than you could manage yourself.

By Boat

Numerous **cruise boats** ply between Aswan and Luxor, some also sailing downriver as far as Qena for excursions to Dendera and Abydos (*see also* **Planning Your Trip**, p.61).

A more adventurous way of visiting places between Aswan and Luxor is by **felucca**. It is better to sail downriver from Aswan than upriver from Luxor as you will have the current with you. Prices depend on how far you are going, the duration, the number of passengers (usually six), time of year, demand – and also whether you deal directly with a captain or make arrangements through an agency or hotel. Assuming six passengers, you can expect to pay about LE60 per person per day. Sailing to Kom Ombo will take two days; the entire journey can take four or five days. First check the official rates with the Tourist Office, then either strike a bargain direct with the boatman or arrange things through an agent. Make sure there are plenty of blankets aboard, as it gets chilly at night (in winter it can get very cold) and that there is sufficient bottled water for drinking and cooking (though drinking from the Nile down as far as Esna is perfectly all right).

The Town

The chief purposeful activity in Aswan is the visit by motor launch to the island of **Philae**. Mixing purpose with the pleasure of sailing about in a felucca, call at **Elephantine Island** and the **Botanical Island** and then land on the west bank to visit the **tombs of the Nobles** and **St Simeon's Monastery**. But for sheer pleasure, simply sail about aimlessly in a **felucca**, or sit on the terrace of the **Cataract Hotel** and let the world float peacefully past. In the evening take a stroll along **Sharia el Souk**, Aswan's sinuous market street, the best bazaar outside Cairo.

(4) Sharia el Souk

The railway station is at the north end of the town, some distance back from the river. The temperature, often 10°C higher at Aswan than in Cairo, hits you as you step off the train, and darker skins and lighter builds introduce you to the tropics. You may also notice Nubian spoken, if not here then when you are floating on a felucca and hear the boatmen calling to one another. A taxi, or

Calculating the Earth's Circumference

Over the centuries the Tropic of Cancer has shifted slightly to the south, but in classical times it fell across Aswan, proved by a famous well into which the sun's rays plunged perpendicularly at midday during the summer solstice, leaving no shadow. Hearing of this, Eratosthenes (276–196 BC) of the Mouseion at Alexandria set out to measure the Earth. His method was as follows. He already knew that the Earth was round and that Aswan and Alexandria lay on the same longitude, but at that same moment in Alexandria the sun cast a shadow of seven and one-fifth degrees, that is, one-fiftieth of a complete circle. Estimating the distance between Alexandria and Aswan as 805km, he concluded that the circumference of the Earth was 40,250km, an error of only 242km, and its diameter 12,819km, an error of only 77km. A triumph of constructive thought inspired by a place whose genius lies in the inducement to idle contentment.

better yet a carriage, will take you to your hotel and provide you with your first glimpse of the setting. As you emerge onto the corniche, you see a bare hill rising from the opposite bank and cut into its face the small dark openings of the ancient tombs of Aswan's governors and princes.

The façades at this end of the corniche are new and concrete, but the sweep of the Nile is impressive. The **older town** lies behind. A few streets back, running parallel with the corniche, is the best **bazaar** outside Cairo, alive with Egyptians, Nubians and blacks from the south trading in gum, spices, ebony and other exotic prizes out of Africa, as well as local weaves and manufactured goods. Although Aswan is not the crossroads of trade it once was, and the days of the caravans are gone, the flavour remains and the imagination recalls magnificently shawled and turbaned guards, huge scimitars dangling at their sides, accompanying a hundred camels laden with elephant tusks out of Ethiopia, driving the dust before them in clouds. This picturesque **inner town** deserves exploration, especially at evening. There are a few simple but **good restaurants**, and a large **Coptic church**.

In ancient times this area on the east bank was known as Syene and famous for its nearby quarries of pink granite, but it was always secondary to the main commercial and administrative settlement of Yebu, which stood at the southern end of the long palm-covered island opposite the corniche. Yebu was Egyptian for elephant, and the island today bears the Greek translation, **Elephantine**. Perhaps in the earliest millennia of their history, before the desert had crept down to the Nile, the Egyptians first encountered elephants here, though it is more likely that Yebu owed its name and much of its importance to the ivory trade from the south. The most obvious feature at this northern end of Elephantine is the unfortunate bulk of the **Aswan Mövenpick Hotel**, like a control tower without an international airport, and, if that were not bad enough, an even larger hotel is under construction just north of it (though now abandoned) . On the far side of Elephantine, and largely obscured by it, is the **Botanical**

Getting around Aswan

By Taxi

Unless you join a tour, you will need to hire a taxi for journeys to the granite quarry, the old Aswan Dam, the new High Dam, Philae and Kalabsha. All of these can be visited in one half-day's excursion (though including Kalabsha, especially if you also visit the Nubia Museum and the Open-air Museum of Sculpture, is pushing it). It is best to arrange for a taxi the day before through your hotel or a travel agent. Sometimes an agent will know of other interested people with whom you can share, so reducing the cost per person.

By Carriage

For journeys within town it is most agreeable to clop along in a carriage – perhaps taking one up to the terrace of the Cataract Hotel to enjoy the sunset, and then walking back, joining the promenaders along the corniche.

By Ferry

You can cross to Elephantine Island and to the tombs of the Nobles by ferry, the former from the southern end of the corniche, the latter from the northern end of the corniche. Also it is worthwhile taking the free hotel ferry to Isis Island for the views en route and from the island itself.

By Felucca

Getting to the **Botanical Island**, and also landing on the **west bank** of the Nile below the Aga Khan's mausoleum and at the closest point to the monastery of St Simeon means hiring a felucca along the corniche or below the Cataract Hotel. Whatever price you agree to after bargaining – you will do better in summer and if you do not hire at the Cataract – expect to be hit for baksheesh afterwards. Instead of rushing things, arrange to have the felucca for 4 hours. Note that at Aswan feluccas are often owned by one man and operated by another. The lion's share of what you pay goes to the owner. Therefore drive the hardest bargain for the cost of the felucca, but after the journey, and without being seen by his boss, pay extra to the man who sails it.

By Camel

Once on the west bank of the Nile, you can hire a camel to save you the trudge up to St Simeon's Monastery; you can also ride between there and the tombs of the Nobles.

To Abu Simbel

Abu Simbel can be reached by air (a 25-minute flight), road (about 3 hours by bus or taxi), or by cruise boat. For detailed information, *see* p.xxx.

Island; it was from Aswan that Kitchener set out to conquer the Sudan in 1896–98 and the island is a botanical garden begun by him.

All along the **corniche**, cruise boats are tied up at the quayside, and towards the north end are many feluccas, while midway along it the Aswan Mövenpick's ferry, designed to look like a pharaonic barge, makes frequent crossings to the hotel. At the south end of the corniche is a roundabout with the **Egyptair** office, behind which is a seldom-visited small Ptolemaic temple of Isis; it is here that the road from the airport enters town. **Ferries** leave from here to the southernmost Nubian village on Elephantine. **Feluccas** for hire concentrate here too. One arm of the Nile runs through the narrow channel between the massive embankments of ancient Yebu and the great dough-like outcrops of pink granite on the east bank, the road rising round the shaded **Ferial Gardens** that overlook the river here, with the vast new Coptic cathedral opposite. Surmounting the outcrop is the Cataract Hotel.

Devotees of nostalgia must make a pilgrimage to the **Cataract Hotel**, a russet pile atop a loaf of pink granite, surrounded by gardens, with beautiful views along the Nile in either direction and across the tip of Elephantine Island to the mausoleum of the Aga Khan and against the distant desert horizon the old monastery of St Simeon. John Fowles in *Daniel Martin* describes the interior as it was until the early 1970s: 'Pierced screens, huge fans, tatty old colonial furniture, stone floors, silence, barefooted Nubian servants in their red fezzes; so redolent of an obsolete middle class that it was museum-like' – it has since been refurbished to the tastes of the *nouvelle bourgeoisie*, though not spoilt. The exterior features in the film of Agatha Christie's *Death on the Nile*; the terrace, cocktail in hand, amid the calm, is the perfect place to plot an elegant murder.

The Nubia Museum

Nubia Museum
open daily 9–1 and 6–10; adm LE50

The **Nubia Museum**, opened at the end of 1997, is a striking modern sandstone building on the slope of a granite outcrop at the southern end of town. Its entrance is opposite the Basma Hotel on a road running up from the Cataract Hotel.

In the museum garden is a reconstructed cave in which prehistoric rock carvings have been set; there is also a village house characteristic of those upriver from Aswan until the whole of Nubia was drowned beneath Lake Nasser. The entire span of time between cave and house – about 25,000 years – is represented within the museum.

You enter the museum on its upper level, where there are lecture rooms, a gift shop and a hall for temporary exhibitions. Steps descend to a vast lower hall illuminated by a dim subaqueous light so that like Nubia itself it seems under water. The exhibits, however, are picked out brightly. These are arranged chronologically, starting from the left and continuing round clockwise. All of the exhibits here have been salvaged from Nubia since the beginning of the 20th century and have been brought together from Cairo's Egyptian, Coptic and Islamic museums and from the Aswan Museum on Elephantine Island. Everything is labelled in Arabic and English.

From the **prehistoric period** there are cosmetic palettes, delicate pots turned almost as thin as ostrich eggs (of which there are also several) and human and animal figures worked in ivory and other materials. These are the finest objects in the museum and repay close attention.

Throughout almost all subsequent periods, Nubia was dominated politically by Egypt, whose culture it crudely aped. **Statues** show that eminent Middle and New Kingdom Nubian personages felt honoured to dress up like their foreign masters;

this was no less true, as his statue shows, of Taharka (XXV Dynasty), who as a pharoah of the 'Ethiopian' (i.e. Nubian) dynasty which ruled Egypt for nearly a hundred years built the last and largest of the pylons at Karnak. Also from the pharaonic period are a **mummified ram** with a golden mask, found at the temple of Khnum on Elephantine Island, and a colossal **statue of Ramses II,** rescued from his temple at Gerf Hussein, now submerged beneath the lake.

It was in its **folk art** that Nubian culture reasserted itself and is most interesting, stimulating and entertaining: in the tiny ceramic frogs used as playthings during the Graeco-Roman period, in the boldly painted murals of saints of the Christian period, and best of all in its domestic architecture. This last is found in the final **ethnological section** recreating village houses and community life during the 20th century until all was lost with the construction of the High Dam. In the burning heat of Nubia, everything was done to promote the cooling flow of air. The reconstructed houses are shown built round open courtyards, walls are pierced by a latticework of triangles, and reception rooms are wide open to the north to catch the prevailing breeze. But as in their prehistoric artefacts, nothing was ever simply functional: the Nubians would express their strong decorative sense by setting china plates into the façades of their houses and painting their exterior walls in brightly coloured geometric patterns.

Elephantine Island

The purposeful excuse for visiting Elephantine is to see the scant ruins of **Yebu**, the ramshackle **museum** and the ancient **nilometer**. For a few piastres, a small ferry will take you over to the island from the corniche; you cannot get to the rest of Elephantine from the Mövenpick compound towards the north end of the island.

The Nilometer

The **Nilometer** is under a sycamore tree, a few boat-lengths north of embankments bearing inscriptions from the reigns of Tuthmosis III and Amenophis III (XVIII Dyn) and Psammetichus II (XXVI Dyn). Its square shaft can be entered directly from the river or down steps from above. Though probably dating from an earlier period, it was rebuilt by the Romans, the scales marked in Greek. It was restored in the last century, when Arabic and French inscriptions were added. Strabo records that 'on the side of the well are marks, measuring the height sufficient for the irrigation and other water levels. These are observed and published for general information. This is of importance to the peasants for the management of the water, the embankments, the canals, etc., and to the officials on

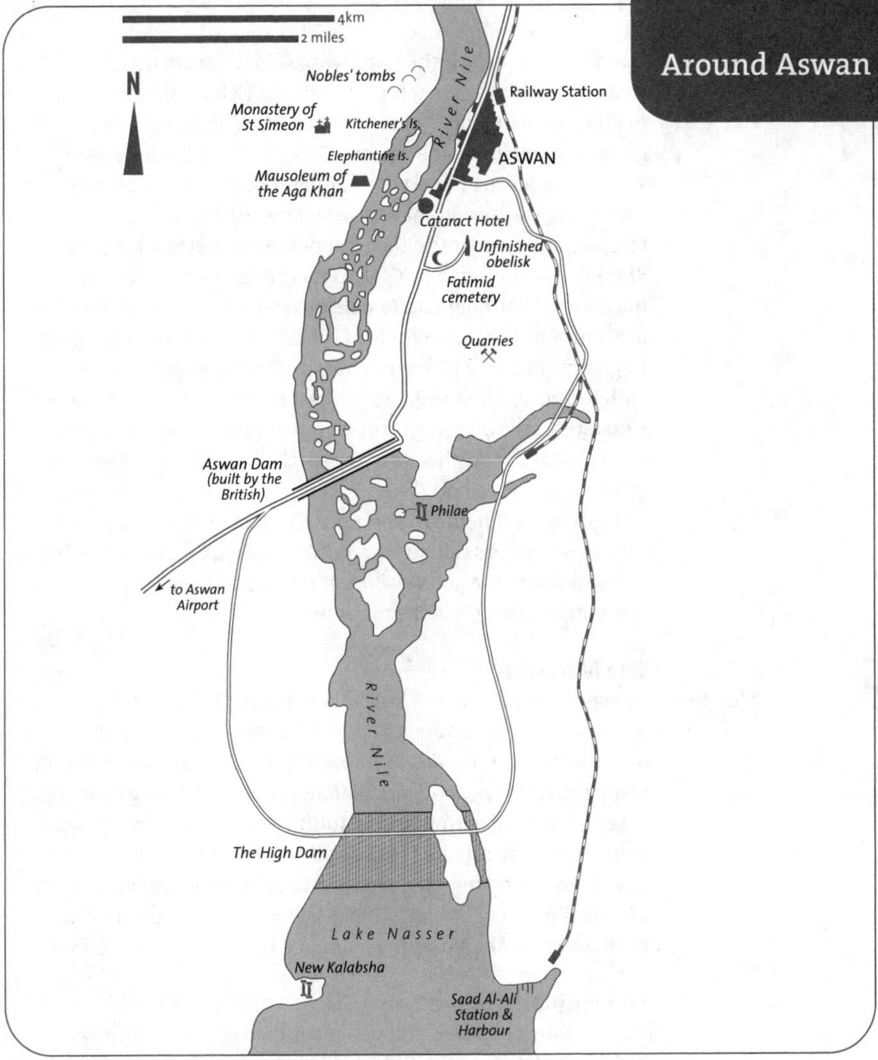

account of the taxes. For the higher the rise of water, the higher are the taxes.' The High Dam put an end to the annual inundation, and under Nasser this ancient basis of taxation was abolished. The more modest fluctuations in the level of the Nile are still measured, however. An American aid-sponsored satellite communications system now tells irrigation engineers in Cairo the level of every waterway in the country.

Yebu

The ancient town of Yebu stood at the southern end of the island. Its mound is being picked clean of debris by archaeologists, revealing mud brick structures of successive levels of occupation. Excavations began early in the 20th century after the discovery that there had been a sizeable Jewish colony here in the 6th century BC with its own temple to Yahweh (Jehovah). From a military order of King Darius II in 419 BC permitting his Yebu garrison to celebrate the Passover, it is clear that the Jews here served in defence of the Persian Empire's southernmost border. The continuing excavations have revealed the existence of several temples, among them, to the west of the nilometer, a **Temple of Khnum** built during the XXX Dynasty and, to the north of the museum, a **New Kingdom Temple of Satet**, the female counterpart of Khnum. At the southern tip of the island by the water's edge the fragments of a small Ptolemaic temple have been reassembled with the aid of much yellow brick. Just to the west of the temple is a granite statue of an elephant with part of its head missing, excavated 250m northwest of the small **Ptolemaic temple** of Isis behind the Egyptair office.

The island was home to Khnum, a ram-headed god of the cataracts who was said to have fashioned man on a potter's wheel. Rams sacred to the god were mummified, and the sarcophagus of one, with mummy, is in the museum.

The Museum

Museum
open daily 8–4; adm LE30 (also admits you to the ruins)

Originally the villa of Sir William Willcocks, designer of the first Aswan dam, this is a verandahed old house on high ground overlooking the ruins and set in well-kept gardens. On view are an assortment of jewellery, pots, granite statues of island governors, weapons, bronze mirrors and beautiful slate palettes for cosmetics in the form of fish, birds, buffalo and hippopotamus – all of them local finds dating from the predynastic through Byzantine periods, and labelled in English and Arabic. Many of the best exhibits have been moved to the Nubia Museum (*see* p.363).

The Nubian Villages

The greatest pleasure of the island is to follow the pathways which wander off through the fields and luxuriant palms to the three Nubian-speaking villages on the island. The houses are pale yellow or brilliant blue, the eyes of the young girls alluringly black. Some doorways are carved with crocodiles at the foot, fish in the middle and a man on top, a woman's hand between fish and man, a statement of ideal proximities. The woman's hand is brass and serves as a door knocker, a ring on one finger. The Kaaba, the sacred black cube at Mecca, is painted on some housefronts to show that its owner has been on the *hajj*, and sometimes to show how he got there a boat will be added, or fancifully a single-engined propeller plane with open cockpit, or more likely a wide-bodied chartered jet.

Towards the north end of the island is the **Aswan Mövenpick Hotel**, but as it is entirely surrounded by a fence you cannot pass directly from the hotel to the rest of the island, or vice versa. At the very northern point of the island is the unfinished concrete hulk of Elephantine Island Hotel. Work stopped on it a few years ago, but the reasons are unclear – perhaps because it exceeded the five-storey limit, or because it ran out of money.

The Botanical Island

3 Botanical Island
open daily 7–5 in winter, 7–6 in summer; adm LE10; refreshments available

The **Botanical Island** can be reached only by felucca, and you may wish to include it in a tour of west bank sites. On the way to the island, Aswan disappears behind Elephantine Island and you could be almost anywhere along the Nile, except that few stretches of the river are as lovely as this. Still widely known as Kitchener's Island, it was presented to Kitchener (*see* the Khartoum Column, p.508) early last century when he was Consul-General in Egypt and here he indulged his passion for flowers, ordering plants from India and all over the Middle and Far East. Though it is not what it was, a visit is still enjoyable, and you should allow a guide to attach himself to you; he will skip about like one of Peter Pan's boys among the trees and plants in his sandals and *galabiyya*, picking leaves, flowers and fruits and crushing these in his fingers for you to smell, awakening all the pungency and variety of your surroundings. The island attracts birds of remarkable pattern and colour, and it is also a favourite resort for cats.

The Noble Tombs

Noble Tombs
open daily 7–5; adm LE30

Interred in the noble tombs on the **west bank** of the Nile opposite the north ends of Elephantine and the Botanical islands were the governors, princes and priests whose lives revolved around the control of the Nubian trade. Though more modest than those at Beni Hasan, the tombs are similar in style, and like them date mostly from the end of the Old Kingdom through the First Intermediate Period and the Middle Kingdom. They can be reached by ferry from near the Tourist Office or as part of a felucca cruise. They can also be reached by camel or on foot from St Simeon's Monastery.

A slog up a sandy path from the landing stage brings you to the line of tombs cut into the cliff face. The tombs were originally approached by those steep **ramps** you see etched into the hillside, with steps on either side and a channel at the centre for dragging up the sarcophagi. Those ramps that are exposed are nevertheless sometimes partly sanded over; the more nimble visitor can afterwards pick and slalom his way back down to the Nile pretty quickly.

The tombs are numbered in ascending order from south to north. The path brings you up to the northern (high-numbered) tombs;

after working your way south you can then zip down a ramp, or otherwise retrace your steps and return to the river by the path.

Tomb 36

This is the tomb of **Sirenput I**. It is about 60 years older than that of his namesake in Tomb 31, though both are XII Dynasty. These are the two finest tombs. Sirenput I was governor and overseer of the priests of Khnum and Satet. A limestone doorway leads to a six-columned courtyard decorated with the makings of a contented afterlife: a large figure of the deceased followed by his sandal bearer and two dogs; another of his bow bearer, dog and three sons; and other paintings of fishing, women bringing flowers and two men gambling.

Tomb 31

This tomb of **Sirenput II**, who was also a governor, is one of the largest and best preserved. It was constructed at the apogee of the Middle Kingdom, when Egypt extended its power beyond the Second Cataract. Beyond a six-pillared hall without decoration is a corridor with three niches on either side with Osiris statues of the deceased cut from the rock. The dead man appears with his son in a brightly coloured painting to the left of the first niche; he appears again on each of the four pillars in the small hall beyond, the artist's grid lines for setting out the pictures still visible on some. At the back of this hall is a recess with good paintings on stucco and very fine hieroglyphics. On the left wall Sirenput is shown with his wife and son; on the right wall his mother sits at a table while he stands to the right. On the centre wall Sirenput sits at a table and his son stands before him clutching flowers. Notice the wonderfully coloured and detailed hieroglyphics here, particularly of birds and animals, including (upper left) an elephant.

Tombs 25 and 26

These tombs of **Mekhu** and his son **Sabni** date from the VI Dynasty, a period of decline, and are crude both in construction and decoration. It is the entrance of Tomb 26 that is noteworthy, for an inscription on it states that Sabni, governor of the south, mounted an expedition against the Nubians who had killed his father; that he recovered the body which was then mummified by embalmers sent by the pharaoh; and that Sabni went to Memphis to thank him and offer presents. Apart from instancing an occasion of Yebu's military role on Egypt's southern border, the inscription shows how much importance was attached to the outpost by Memphis.

The summit of the hill is crowned with the **Kubbet el Hawa**, the shrine of a local sheikh and holy man, and commands a magnificent view of the Nile valley, the cataract and the desert that more than compensates for the difficult climb. A path runs from here across the desert to **St Simeon's Monastery**, about 45 minutes by foot.

The Mausoleum of the Aga Khan and St Simeon's Monastery

Unless you cross the sands from the nobles' tombs, you must take a felucca to reach the west bank landing for the Aga Khan's Mausoleum. At a corral by the landing stage you can hire a camel for St Simeon's (about LE50, including waiting for an hour at the monastery); otherwise it is no more than a 20-minute walk. A paved path runs between the mausoleum and the monastery, but a wall has been erected across it at the mausoleum end.

The Mausoleum

Mausoleum of the Aga Khan
closed to visitors

Aga Khan is the title assumed by the dynastic spiritual leader of the Nizari branch of the Ismailis, a Shi'ite sect (as were the Fatimids) centred on India but with large communities in East Africa and elsewhere. Aga Khan III was an important figure in international affairs and in 1937 became president of the League of Nations. He was also a man of considerable bulk and was of such wealth that on his diamond jubilee in 1945 he was weighed in diamonds, which were then distributed to his followers. The succession passed over his playboy son Ali (who was briefly married to Rita Hayworth) and went to his more earnest grandson Karim, Aga Khan IV.

Closed to visitors since 1997, the mausoleum is built above the white villa where, until his death in 1957, Aga Khan III spent the winter months and where his French-born wife, the Begum, lived for three months each year until her death in 2000. Now she lies beside her husband in the mausoleum. Apart from its beauty, the Aga Khan associated himself with the spot after he found a cure there for his leg trouble by immersing himself up to the waist in the sand. The restrained proportions and the granite and sandstone of the domed mausoleum are entirely in keeping with the surroundings. The tomb within is of white Carrara marble, beautifully carved in Cairo with geometric patterns and Koranic inscriptions in high relief. Each morning in winter the Begum would lay a red rose on the tomb; the ritual was taken over in summer by the gardener. There is a story that one July not a single rose was to be found in Egypt and on six successive days a red rose was flown in by private plane from Paris.

St Simeon's Monastery

St Simeon's Monastery
open daily 7–5; adm LE35

The monastery of St Simeon (Deir Amba Samaan) with its towers and walls looms like a Byzantine fortress on a ridge at the head of a desert valley once cultivated with fields and gardens down to the Nile. Built in the 7th century and rebuilt in the 10th, it is the finest example of an original Christian monastery in Egypt, and is highly evocative. Little is known of St Simeon – he was not the Stylite – and in any case the monastery was first dedicated to Anba Hadra, a bishop of Aswan and saint of the late 4th century, who the day after his marriage encountered a funeral procession and decided to give up the world for a desert cave. The saint's tomb may have been here, a pilgrims' rest and monastery growing up afterwards. Fearful that the monastery might serve as a refuge for Christian Nubians during their forays into southern Egypt, Saladin destroyed it in 1173.

St Simeon was built on a grand scale, with dressed stone walls 10m high. A small city lay within the walls, with cells for 300 resident monks and dormitories for several hundred pilgrims, as well as bakeries and workshops to support the community. The hills and desert around offered solitude and godly communion for probably thousands of monks and hermits.

The lower storeys of the monastery are stone; the upper are mud brick and it is these that have most fallen into decay or vanished altogether.

You enter the portal, and before you, on a height, is the three-storey keep, open to the sky, cells on either side of the long corridors. Stucco seems to have been applied throughout the monastery, and on it, in the apses of the basilica to your left, are badly damaged paintings. There is a Christ Pantocrator in the central apse; on the sides, the faces of saints have been cut out. Names are carved right into the paintings by Arabs and tourists alike – it is not only time that has taken its toll. The monastery has never been systematically excavated, and repairs have been slight; it is largely a confusion of vaults, staircases, walls, workshops and quarters. From the tops of the walls there is a glimpse of Aswan, of green, but around 350 of the other degrees there is only the desert sea, luridly red at sundown. Yet there is an evening breeze, and amid the gardens and within the shadow of the towering walls it must have been cool. It is strange to wander round these arches, vaults and apses of familiar shape and significance; and even before the Arabs came it must have been like that, this comforting bastion against the fierce landscape.

Aswan's Outlying Sights

Aswan's Outlying Sights

all open daily 7–5 in winter, 7–6 in summer

A visit to the granite quarry with its **unfinished obelisk** (LE30), to the old **Aswan Dam** and the new **High Dam** (LE15), as well as a trip out to **Philae** (LE50, plus about LE30 per boat load) can be done in a morning starting early. Additional time will be needed to include the **Open-air Museum of Sculpture**. Taking an hour or two longer will allow you also to visit the **New Kalabsha** site (LE35).

The Fatimid Cemetery and Ancient Quarries

A road leading off the roundabout by the public gardens turns south towards the **Fatimid cemetery** with its domed mausolea of holy figures, some local, others – such as Sayyida Zeinab, Ali's daughter and granddaughter of the Prophet – more widely revered. A turning to the left brings you to an **ancient granite quarry**. From this and similar quarries around Aswan came the prized pink or red granite used for statues, columns and obelisks throughout Egypt and indeed throughout the ancient world. And here, still in place, is the **unfinished obelisk**. Roughly dressed and cut nearly free from the surrounding bedrock, in its finished state it would have weighed over 1 million kilos (2.3 million lbs) and would have been the largest piece of stone handled in history. But work stopped after a flaw was discovered in the stone; it may have been intended to complete the pair of which the lone Lateran obelisk, removed from the temple of Tuthmosis III near the east gateway of Karnak to Rome, was the other half.

The Open-air Museum of Sculpture

Continuing along the road past the quarry and also past the turning for Philae you come to the **Open-air Museum of Sculpture** in the hills above the First Cataract. On this stunning site are displayed the works from the International Sculpture Symposiums held annually in Aswan since 1996. Each year twelve sculptors who work in granite, from Egypt and around the world, are invited to spend two months in Aswan where they create their own large pieces from granite specially chosen from the local quarries. You can watch them at work during the early months of the year on the terrace outside the Basma Hotel on the hillside behind the Cataract Hotel.

The Aswan Dams

Back on the road south and 5km from town you come to the **old Aswan Dam**, built by the British between 1898 and 1902. The road passes over it and across the **First Cataract**; the water swirls round the jagged stones, plays white, but has lost its boil. The height of the dam was twice raised to increase irrigation and its hydroelectric capacity was multiplied, but Egypt's fast growing population and the need both to increase her cultivable land area and to provide vast new supplies of power for a necessary industrialization programme, led to work beginning in the mid-1960s on the High Dam 6km upriver. The road linking the two runs through disturbed desert on the west bank, a giant disused sand pit it seems; you cannot imagine that this is the shore of an uncharted sand ocean going on forever. Numerous electricity pylons add to the impression of it being a manmade litter ground. At the west approach to the dam there is a giant lotus-shaped monument originally commemorating Soviet-Egyptian co-operation. The police here take the opportunity to check your papers and impose a charge.

The **High Dam** has commanded world attention. Its construction became a political issue between East and West. Its sheer size, its effect on the economic potential of the country, and the sudden attention it forced on the Nubian antiquities threatened by the rising waters of Lake Nasser, have all been extraordinary.

The dam was completed in 1971 and since then the water contained by it has reached a height of 182m and has backed up 500km to the Second Cataract within the Sudan. Evaporation from the artificial lake amounts to 5,000 million cubic metres annually (about seven per cent of the lake's volume) and is causing unusual clouds and haze in the surrounding area, and even occasional rain. But the lake also retains the silt that once renewed Egypt's fields. Chemical fertilizer plants running off the dam's hydroelectric power are filling that gap, while it is estimated that in 500 years' time the silt will have filled the lake. By then, however, some other means of water conservation may have become available, or the wasteland to the south may have reverted to the lushness of long distant millennia. The water table beneath the Sahara has already risen noticeably as far away as Algeria.

Though Egypt's population explosion and mistakes in economic policy have in some measure offset the dam's immediate benefits, it has already averted catastrophe. The droughts that have brought starvation to Ethiopia and the Sudan have recently seen the Nile fall to its lowest level in 350 years, and the same scenes of famine would be repeated in Egypt were it not for the High Dam. The British dam regulated the flow of the Nile during the course of the year; the High Dam can store surplus water over a number of years, balancing low floods against high and ensuring up to three harvests a year. The god Khnum has answered Zoser's prayer (*see* box opposite).

The structure that achieves this contains the equivalent in material of 17 pyramids the size of the Great Pyramid of Cheops, and enough metal has been used in its gates, sluices and power plant to build 15 Eiffel Towers. The road runs across the top back to the east bank. In merely driving along, somehow the hugeness of the enterprise is lost upon you, and because it is not ancient, and because it is functional and it works, it is easy not to be impressed. It is even possible for some to complain that it was not worth the

Sailing on the Nile: to Sehel and Back

By now you have become addicted to sailing in a felucca on the Nile, and the only cure is to have more of it. The longer journey upstream to the island of **Sehel** is recommended. The round trip takes about 3 hours and you will have to bargain over the price (expect to pay at least LE80, but first check for the official rate at the tourist office). The current is against you but the prevailing wind is in your favour and the gaff is extended upwards giving great height and grace to the sail. Sehel is just below the First Cataract, and even at the north end of the island the boat is shoved about by turbulent whirlpools. Hawks hovering above the cliffs wheel and dive for fish.

You land on the east side and walk southwards over the sands to a granite outcrop streaked with bird droppings and covered with inscriptions from the IV Dynasty to the Ptolemaic period. Up top and towards the south is one of the most interesting (no. 81), Ptolemaic in date but depicting Zoser and the god Khnum. The inscription relates to a famine lasting seven years through Zoser's reign. Zoser asks the governor of Aswan why the Nile has not flooded and is told that it is in the power of Khnum to whom Zoser then erects a temple. From here there is a view of the rocks and swirling waters of the cataract, but the pounding Nile and foam passed into history with the construction of the British dam. It is cool as you sail upon the river, though the sun can be dangerous; on the island there is no mistaking its ferocity. You need to be well shod, for the sand and piles of rock are blisteringly hot. A **Nubian village** lies off to the west and here you may be invited into a house and invited to enjoy a refreshing cup of mint tea. The walls are thick and insulating, and the barrelled or domed roof reflects the heat at every angle; it is very cool inside.

The felucca tacks back down the Nile, taking advantage of the current. Nubians in passing feluccas are singing and beating drums, ancient sounds on the waters. The boatmen drink directly from the Nile, pointing out that there is no bilharzia above Esna and certainly not in the middle of the river where the current flows swiftly. It is said that to drink from the Nile is to ensure your return; the water has a fresh and slightly organic taste. Nor, with bilharzia no nearer than Esna and the crocodiles held at bay by the High Dam, need you resist plunging into the river altogether and opening your eyes in the almost impenetrably green water. Afterwards, you smell like the Nile, but a shower admits you once again onto the terrace of the Cataract. Just as they are designed to catch the slightest breeze, so in the last faint blue of sunset the felucca sails catch that glimmer of light off the horizon, and like crescent moons glide among the rocks in the Nile below.

drowning of so many Nubian monuments. The same was said when the British built their dam, to which Churchill replied:

> *This offering of 1,500 millions of cubic feet of water to Hathor by the Wise Men of the West is the most cruel, the most wicked and the most senseless sacrifice ever offered on the altar of a false religion. The state must struggle and the people starve, in order that the professors may exult and the tourists find some place to scratch their names.*

Some feeling for the controlled energy of the place is realized at the **viewing platform** over to the eastern end of the dam. The green water rises in eddies, like large bursting bubbles from somewhere below the visible tops of the sluices. The generators hum as the river is put through its paces. Scores of lesser pylons flick currents of electricity towards the larger pylons striding across the desert, and bound by thick cables this energy is delivered into Egypt. Downstream, the Nile slips its harness and runs free beneath a glassy surface.

The Source of the Nile

It is an ancient belief that the source of the Nile was at the First Cataract. The waters so swirled and seemed to flow in different directions that it was thought the river rose here from underground, flowing north to the Mediterranean and south into Africa. The belief hinged, as most beliefs do, on laziness and the desire not to spoil a good story: the most cursory examination of the river's flow at any point south of the First Cataract would have revealed, as no doubt it did reveal a thousand times, that the Nile always flows north. Herodotus, who enjoyed a good story himself, nevertheless dismissed the notion expressed in this relief. He traced the northerly flow of the Nile back deep into Africa, and even reported a theory, based almost certainly on lost knowledge, that the source of the Nile, and the cause of its floods, lay in distant snowfalls – a theory he rejected (though 2,000 or so years later it was proved right) because he could not imagine high snow mountains somewhere in the hot interior of Africa.

New Kalabsha

The newly created archaeological site of New Kalabsha is a kilometre south of the High Dam on the west bank of the Nile. Three temples were removed here to save them from the rising waters of Lake Nasser, but considering the effort that went into the project, little encouragement was given to visiting these stone-by-stone reconstructions. Until fairly recently, special permission was required; this is a military area (the fear in essence is that somebody might pull the plug out of the High Dam and drown all Egypt). Now you may visit the site without restrictions.

The original site of the **Temple of Kalabsha** was 50km farther into Nubia. It was built during the reign of Augustus to the familiar blueprint of his Ptolemaic predecessors, though as the temple was being dismantled, evidence of earlier structures dating from the time of Amenophis II and Ptolemy IX were found. Considered to rank second only to Abu Simbel as the finest monument south of Philae and enjoying a harmony of proportion, nevertheless the temple was never completely adorned with reliefs and inscriptions, and the reliefs are generally of poor workmanship. Dedicated to Mandulis, a Nubian god associated with Isis, the Kalabsha temple later became a Christian church.

An imposing causeway of dressed stone leads westwards to the pylon which is slightly askew to the axis of both the causeway and temple. This admits first to an open court and then a hypostyle hall (the roof has fallen in), both with columns bearing elaborate floral capitals. Three chambers lie beyond, the last being the sanctuary. All three are decorated with reliefs of Augustus making offerings to just about every god in the Egyptian pantheon, which would have made him laugh had he ever come here to see for himself – after defeating Cleopatra and Antony, Octavian (as he then was) was content to gaze at Alexander's preserved corpse but refused to visit any Egyptian temples, dismissing native beliefs and practices as bizarre. But you, earnest traveller, can admire here the nicely preserved colours on these propaganda reliefs of Augustus. Within the first two chambers, stairways on the left lead up to the roof and walls for the wonderful **view** across the vast blue of Lake Nasser.

Also at New Kalabsha are the **Kiosk of Qirtasi**, a Ptolemaic edifice from 40km upriver, and the **Temple of Bayt al-Wali** rescued from near the original site of the Kalabsha temple. Bayt al-Wali is Arabic for House of the Governor, and the temple was built by the Viceroy of Cush for Ramses II.

Philae: Island of Isis

2 Philae

Before the construction of the British dam, you could winter at Aswan and visit the **Temple of Isis** standing proud on its sacred island. But the dam all but submerged the temple for half the year during the winter, and Philae became a name only, hardly a place to visit. Yet there was romance in that visit, a romance, once established, far greater for some than any satisfaction gained from seeing the Temple of Isis raised again on new and profane ground. In *Daniel Martin*, John Fowles records the experience many travellers enjoyed in the 20th century:

> *Then they drove to see the temple of Philae; a long row out into the lake, followed by the slow gondola-like tour round the submerged columns, shadowy shafts in the translucent green water. An exquisite light shimmered and danced on the parts that rose into the air. They and the guide were rowed by two old men, with scrawny wrists and mummified bare feet. Every so often, on the long haul, the pair would break into a strange question-and-answer boating-chant, half sung, half spoken. Work on transporting the temple to its new site, the guide proudly told them, would begin within the next few months; very soon sunken Philae would be abusimbelised.*

The annual rise and fall of the Nile, elevated behind the British dam, slowly wore on the inscriptions and reliefs of the temple and eventually, though perhaps after only hundreds of years, would have brought the whole thing down. But then the High Dam was built and the Temple of Isis, between the two, was permanently almost completely submerged, and worse, where it rose just clear of the river, suffered swift daily tide-like movements that would have destroyed it (and Philae's other monuments) far sooner. With Hathor doubly gratified, it has now been the turn of professors and tourists to avenge Churchill's words.

Now Philae has been recreated. The nearby island of Agilqiyyah has been carved and sliced to replicate the original island, so that it is 450m long and 150m across, and the Temple of Isis, as well as the Temple of Hathor and the Kiosk of Trajan, have been placed in positions corresponding as nearly as possible to their previous relationship. (The plan shows the disposition of monuments on the original island of Philae, but those at the northern end of the island, in particular the Roman gate and the ruined Temple of Augustus, and also two Coptic churches and the remains of a monastery, were left where they stood. The intention is to transfer them later.) The present site was opened to the public in 1980.

Approaching the Temple of Isis

The logical starting point for a tour of the Temple of Isis is the **Vestibule of Nectanebos I** (XXX Dyn) at the southwest corner of the island (the landing stage is just below). The temple it once led to was washed away by the Nile, but this vestibule was rebuilt by Ptolemy II Philadelphos. Nearly every other monument on the island dates from the Ptolemaic and Roman periods, and Herodotus, who visited Elephantine *c.* 450 BC, seems to have found no reason to make any mention of Philae, though it is probable that older temples stood on the island then. Northwards extends the outer temple court, the first pylon of the Temple of Isis at its far end, **colonnades** on either side. The East Colonnade is unfinished, with many of the columns only rough-hewn; the West Colonnade follows the shoreline, its columns bearing reliefs of Tiberius offering gifts to the gods, the capitals of varying plant motifs, no two alike.

The **First Pylon**, 18m high and 45m wide, consists of two massive towers with a gateway between them. The towers were begun by Ptolemy II Philadelphos and completed by Ptolemy III Euergetes, though the decorations were carried out over a long period. On the front of the right or **eastern tower**, Ptolemy XII Neos Dionysos is shown in the traditional pharaonic pose of seizing his enemies by the hair, about to bash their brains out with a club; Isis, Hathor and the falcon-headed Horus of Edfu look on placidly. Above and to the right, Neos Dionysos offers the crowns of Upper and Lower Egypt to Horus the child. On the left or **western tower**, Neos Dionysos is again sacrificially braining his foes while above he appears before Unnefer (the name given to Osiris after his resurrection) and Isis, and before Isis and Harsiesis, a form of Horus. The reliefs have been severely damaged by the Copts. The vertical grooves on the towers were for holding flagstaffs. The main **gateway** was built earlier by Nectanebos and bears reliefs of his as well as Coptic crosses and, as you pass through, a French inscription on the right commemorating the victory of General Desaix over the Mamelukes in 1799 (‘*L’an 6 de la République*’).

Son et Lumière

There is a *son et lumière* programme at Philae, costing LE75. Shows are in English, French, German, Italian, Spanish and Arabic, depending on the day of the week and the time of evening. There are three shows a night, 8pm, 9.15pm and 10.30pm in summer, and 6.30pm, 7.30pm and 8.30pm in winter.

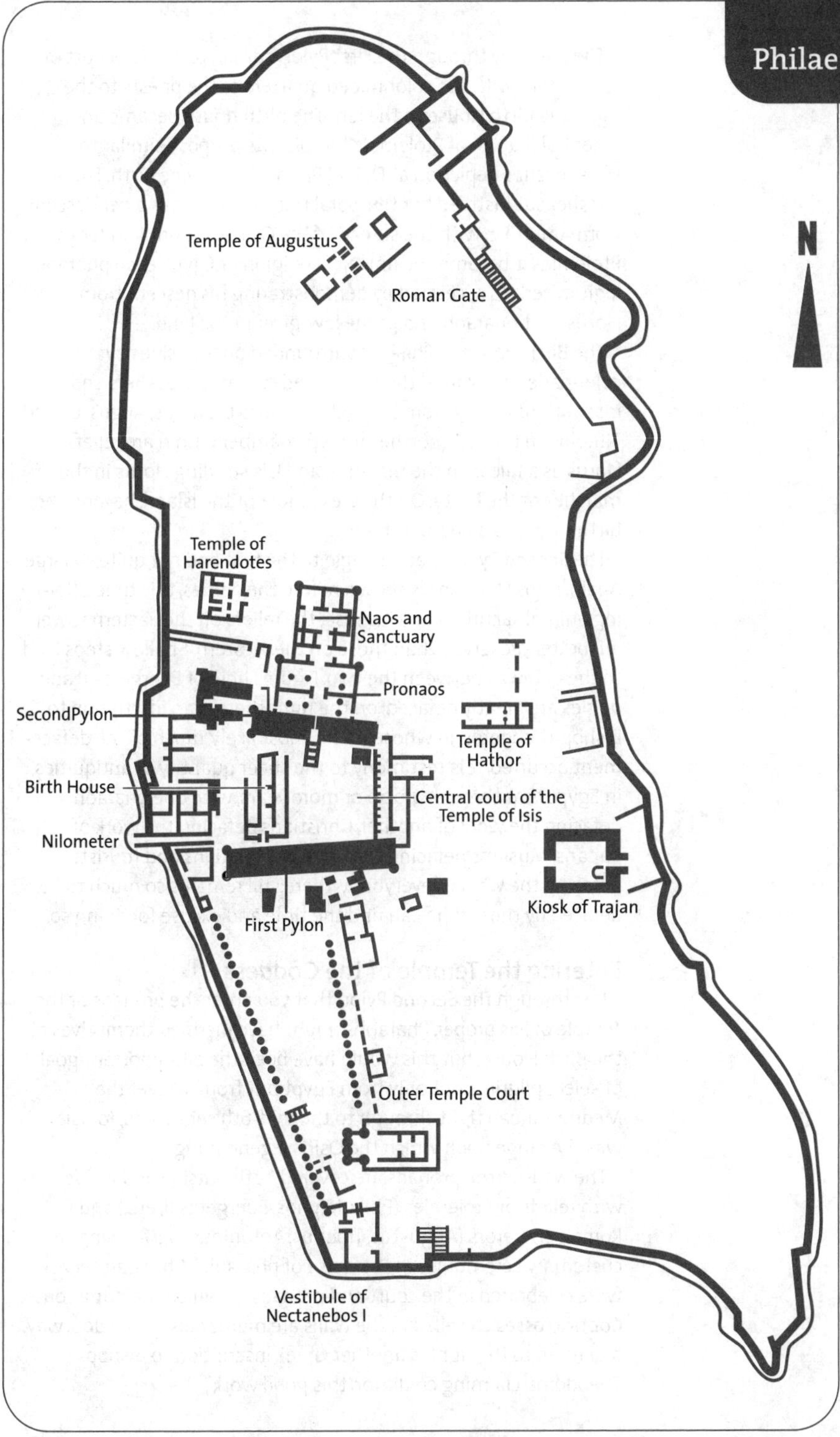
N
Temple of Augustus
Roman Gate
Temple of Harendotes
Naos and Sanctuary
Pronaos
SecondPylon
Temple of Hathor
Birth House
Central court of the Temple of Isis
Nilometer
Kiosk of Trajan
First Pylon
Outer Temple Court
Vestibule of Nectanebos I

The gateway through the First Pylon admits to the forecourt of the temple, with the colonnaded quarters of the priests to the right, the **Birth House** to the left. The birth house became an essential feature of Ptolemaic temples, its purpose similar to Hatshepsut's depiction at Deir el Bahri of her divine birth. There, Hatshepsut justified her temporal rule by proclaiming her descent from Amun-Re; with the spread of the Osiris cult until under the Ptolemies it became the universal religion of Egypt, each pharaoh legitimized his accession by demonstrating his descent from Horus, first pharaoh and prime law-giver in the land.

The Birth House at Philae is surrounded on four sides by colonnades and round their walls and columns are reliefs and inscriptions dating from Euergetes II, Neos Dionysos, Augustus and Tiberius. In the last (northernmost) chamber within are reliefs of Horus as a falcon in the marshes, and Isis suckling Horus in the marshes of the Delta. On the west shore of the island, beyond the Birth House, is a **nilometer**.

The **Second Pylon** is at an angle to the first and not quite so large. Again, Neos Dionysos is shown before the deities, this time offering animal sacrifices and incense; the reliefs on the eastern tower are better preserved than those on the western. Shallow steps lead to the gateway between the two. Figures here of Euergetes II and deities are greatly defaced; on the right there is an inscription to Bishop Theodoros, in whose name, most likely, much of the defacement occurred. It is testimony to the sheer quantity of antiquities in Egypt that through 4,000 or more years, with one pharaoh defacing the work of another, Christians defacing the work of pagans, Muslims defacing the work of Christians and tourists defacing the work of everybody, there still remains so much to be defaced by those who can find the time and excuse for doing so.

Entering the Temple of the Goddess

It is through the Second Pylon that you enter the pronaos of the **Temple of Isis** proper. Pharaohs might have justified themselves at the Birth House, but this would have been the all-important goal of select pilgrims not only from Egypt but from all over the Mediterranean right through to the mid-6th century AD, for Isis was the hinge upon which the Osiris legend hung.

The walls of the pronaos are covered both outside and inside with **reliefs** of Ptolemies (Philadelphos, Euergetes II, etc.) and Roman emperors (Augustus, Tiberius, Antoninus) performing the customary ceremonies in the guise of pharaohs. Christian services were celebrated in the court and pronaos, of which the numerous **Coptic crosses** chiselled in the walls are memorials. In the doorway of a room to the right is another Greek inscription to Bishop Theodoros, claiming credit for 'this good work'.

The Cult of Osiris

There are many strands to the Osiris legend, and many accretions to the story and levels of meaning. Osiris, son of Re, was a king who ruled and was greatly loved in distant times. Isis was his sister and wife, Seth his brother. When Seth killed Osiris and dismembered his body, Isis searched out the pieces and put them together again, wondrously restoring Osiris to life in the underworld where he reigned as judge and king. Isis' son Horus was secretly raised to manhood in Lower Egypt and after a long and desperate struggle overcame Seth and established order over all Egypt. Historically, this may recall the subjection of the south by the north in pre-dynastic times. Mystically, Horus is the incarnation of his father, while Isis is the agent of both resurrection and reincarnation. Celebration of the rites relating to the legend, and in particular to the birth of Horus, took place at birth houses such as this one at the Temple of Isis, the pharaoh proclaiming his legitimacy through his involvement in them.

The three antechambers of the naos lead through to the **Sanctuary** with two small windows and a pedestal on which stood the sacred boat with the image of Isis. On the left wall is a relief of a pharaoh facing Isis whose wings protectively embrace Osiris; on the right wall (above) Isis enthroned suckles the infant Horus, and (below) Isis standing, her face gouged out by Christians, suckling a young pharaoh. Of course these pharaohs were Ptolemaic kings in pharaonic guise.

Christianity, with its male-orientated antecedents in the Judaic and Greek religions, may never have given the prominence it did to the Virgin Mary had not a figure been needed to absorb in turn the great popularity and success of the rival Isis cult. It was a rivalry that continued well into the Christian era. In spite of the edicts of the Roman Emperor Theodosius I, which succeeded in terminating the Olympic Games after a thousand years in the 4th century AD, pagan Philae continued as a centre of Isis worship till the reign of Justinian in the 6th century, while farther into Nubia the worship of Isis probably persisted until the Arab Islamic conquest.

West of the Temple of Isis

West of the second pylon is **Hadrian's Gateway** (which can be reached by leaving the naos of Isis' temple through a west doorway). It is preceded by a badly ruined vestibule which nevertheless preserves an interesting relief on the inside of its north wall (second register from the top), depicting the source of the Nile: the Nile god, entwined by a serpent, pours water from two jars.

North of Hadrian's Gateway are the foundations of the **Temple of Harendotes**, built by the Emperor Claudius.

East of the Temple of Isis

East of the Second Pylon is the **Temple of Hathor**, a goddess comparable to the Greek Aphrodite despite the usual convention of cow's ears, built by Ptolemy VI Philometor and Euergetes II. The colonnade was decorated during the reign of Augustus with **amusing carvings** of music and drinking – apes dancing and one

The Cult of Isis

Through her suffering and her joy the goddess offered an emotive identification so powerful and satisfying that she became identified too with all other goddesses of the Mediterranean, whom she finally absorbed. Isis was the Goddess of Ten Thousand Names, Shelter and Heaven to All Mankind, the House of Life, the Great Mother of All Gods and Nature, Victorious over Fate, the Promise of Immortality, Sexuality and Purity, the Glory of Women when all else failed, she still could save. She was passionately worshipped by men and women alike. Cleopatra deliberately identified herself with Isis, and called herself the New Isis, casting Antony as Dionysos, the Greek equivalent of Osiris, so that on earth they affected the already existing cosmological bond.

playing a lute, dwarfish Bes beating a tambourine, while Augustus offers a festal crown to Isis.

To the south stands the unfinished **Kiosk of Trajan**, a rectangular building of 14 columns with beautifully carved floral capitals. On the only two screen walls between the columns that have been completed are scenes of the Emperor Trajan offering incense and wine to Isis, Osiris and Horus. The elegance of the kiosk has made it the characteristic symbol of the island.

As you return to the landing stage, look south at the larger **island of Bigah**: this was the legendary burial place of Osiris. The original island of Philae, now submerged, lay alongside it to the east – in other words, the ancient priests and votaries of Isis would once have gazed westwards into the setting sun to see the resting place of the lord of the underworld.

Tourist Information in Aswan

ⓘ Aswan >
Railway station, **t** *(097) 231 2811; open daily 9–3 and 6–8*

Before doing anything, visit the **Tourist Office**, a small domed building just by the north corner of the railway station. A helpful and friendly mine of information – in English, German and French. Here you can obtain in advance the official prices for taxis, carriages, feluccas and camels. The **Tourist Police** have an office on the south side of the railway station, **t** (097) 223 3163, and another not far away at the north end of the corniche, **t** (097) 230 3436, just north of the Ramses Hotel; both branches 24hrs.

It can also be useful to make enquiries at the various **travel agencies**. Sometimes they can fix things up for you on an ad hoc basis, or they might have a tour which will suit your purposes. There are various travel agencies along the southern end of the corniche, for example Misr, Eastmar, Wagons-lits and Thomas Cook, together with several **banks** where you can change money.

The **post office** is on Sharia Salah el Din, one block in from the centre of the corniche, nearly opposite the Aswan Mövenpick Hotel.

Shopping in Aswan

The **Aswan Cultural Centre**, on the corniche between the Philae and Abu Simbel hotels, sells Nubian handicrafts. A couple of blocks back from the river is **Sharia el Souk**, Aswan's sinuous market street, the best bazaar outside Cairo, still with an atmosphere and an array of goods suggesting trade with Africa deeper south. Woven blankets and rugs are particularly good here and cheaper than elsewhere in Egypt; also there is silver, turquoise, ebony, spices, *galabiyyas* and much else. As you wander along, have a glass of pressed cane juice.

Where to Stay in Aswan

Like Luxor, Aswan's high season is from October to May when it is best to make reservations in advance. Summer can be slack and the heat should not deter you – it is a dry heat, and all but the cheapest places will have air conditioning.

Luxury ($$$$$)

Cataract Hotel >

*****Cataract Hotel**, Sharia Abtal el Tahrir, is beyond the Ferial Gardens south of the corniche. Standing on a great outcrop of granite overlooking the Nile, the Cataract enjoys the most magnificent view in Aswan. Now operated by Sofitel, the hotel was closed for extensive refurbishment for two years from May 2008. Contact details were not available when this guide went to press, so check the Sofitel website for an update and contact details: *www.sofitel.com/gb/home/index.shtml*. Next door is the characterless modern eyesore until recently called the New Cataract to distinguish it from the old, but Sofitel are likely to give it a new name after they have finished gutting it and rehabilitating it as a Frenchified characterless modern eyesore.

*****Mövenpick Resort Aswan**, on Elephantine Island, **t** (097) 230 3455, *www.moevenpick-hotels.com/en/pub/your_hotels/worldmap/aswan/overview.cfm*. Formerly the Aswan Oberoi, this looks like an airport control tower rising absurdly from the north end of the island. It is reached by regular ferries designed like ancient Egyptian royal barges (free for guests and the curious alike). Deplorable though its concrete monumentality is, this architectural calamity offers some fine views for those on the inside looking out, particularly westwards at sundown from the rear terrace across to the Botanical Island. It has a bank, bookshop, hairdresser, café, nightclub, pool, boutiques and other trappings. Egyptair has a branch here.

Nile >>

Expensive ($$$$)

****Basma Hotel**, **t** (097) 231 0901, *www.basmahotel.com*. On the hillside near the Nubia Museum and above the Cataract Hotel with fine views over the Nile. Rooms are large, comfortable and fully equipped, and there is a good-sized swimming pool. Distance is a bit of a problem, and so a free shuttle bus runs hourly to the Isis Hotel in town.

*****Isis Island Aswan**, **t** (097) 231 7400, *www.pyramisaegypt.com/pyramisaisisisland/location.asp*. A 400-room resort hotel on a island in the Nile well to the south of Elephantine. In reality it is an ecological disaster which encroaches upon a stretch of the river where several supposedly protected islands preserve the only original vegetation growing in Egypt. Indeed Isis island was one of these special habitats but has been ruined by the hotel. The architecture is in the style of Saddam Hussein. The largest of the chalets, at the north tip of the island, is of course called Villa Mubarak. The man behind the hotel is Alaa Mubarak, President Hosni Mubarak's oldest son. Here was the opportunity for a man with the best contacts to build something worthy, an example. Instead he has built something awful and depressing, and he has destroyed the ecology of the island and has threatened the ecology of neighbouring islands too. All the same, it is worth the free trip to Isis Island in the hotel launch for the views along the way, while from the northeast part of the island there are good views towards Yebu and the Aga Khan's mausoleum.

***Marhaba**, a new hotel at the north end of town, a short walk from the railway station and overlooking the al-Salam Gardens along the Nile corniche, **t** (097) 233 0102, *www.marhaba-aswan.com*. Rooms nicely furnished, with TV, all with Nile views, and a great rooftop. But rather expensive for what it is.

Moderate ($$$)

***Nile**, a new hotel at the southern end of the Nile corniche near the Egyptair office, **t** (097) 231 4222, *www.nilehotel-aswan.com*. All rooms with satellite TV, private bath, and huge windows, often with balcony, giving magnificent panoramic Nile views taking in Elephantine Island and the far bank with the Aga Khan's Mausoleum and St Simeon. Good service, friendly staff. Excellent value.

***Sara**, hanging on a pink granite clifftop overlooking the Nile at Sharia El Fanadek, Nasr City, 2km south of the Nubia Museum, **t** (097) 232 7234, *www.sarahotel-aswan.com*. This is a peaceful place to stay with wonderful views over the river. The hotel runs an hourly shuttle bus into town. Well-equipped rooms, disco, Internet café, bar and dining terraces with river views, pool.

Inexpensive ($$)

****Ramses**, Sharia Abtal el Tahrir, **t** (097) 230 4000, **f** (097) 231 5701, at the north end of town near the train station. Comfortable rooms, most with balconies overlooking the Nile, all with air conditioning, private bathroom, fridge and TV. There is a bar, restaurant and disco.

****Horus**, Corniche el Nil, **t/f** (097) 231 3313, 232 3323. Near the ferry landing for the Mövenpick. Rooms are clean, air-conditioned, and have private bathroom, TV and Nile views.

****Philae**, Corniche el Nil, **t** (097) 231 2089, **f** (097) 232 4089, south towards the Thomas Cook office. Recently renovated and has small, clean rooms with air conditioning and private bathrooms. Avoid the first floor, which suffers from noise off the street.

****Keylany**, in Sharia Keylany, east of the lower end of Sharia el Souk, **t** (097) 231 7332, *www.keylanyhotel.com*. Clean, air-conditioned rooms, almost all with private bathrooms. In the middle of things, but quiet; restaurant, Internet café, and a pleasant rooftop café.

Cheap ($)

***Hathor**, midway along the Corniche el Nil, near the post office, **t** (097) 231 4580. All rooms with private bathrooms and most with air conditioning; but get a room facing the Nile as those at the back are gloomy. There is a pool and sundeck on the roof.

***Rosewan**, Sharia Kamel Nour el Din, **t** (097) 230 4497. A clean and friendly place popular with backpackers; turn right out of the train station, walk north one block, then left towards the corniche. The rooms are large and all have fans; private bathrooms extra.

***Yassin**, a short walk south from the train station along Sharia el Souk, then left, **t** (097) 231 7109. Next door to and better than the Noorhan. Rooms are cheap and clean; some with private bathrooms.

***Noorhan**, next door to the Yassin (*above*), **t** (097) 231 6069. Clean but rather shabby rooms with air conditioning or fans, some with baths.

Eating Out and Entertainment in Aswan

★ 1902 Restaurant >>

The **1902 Restaurant** at the Cataract Hotel is a sight in itself: a spacious chamber beneath a high dome supported by pillars and arches in *ablaq* style like a palace from the time of the Mamelukes – very impressive. Breakfast (included) is served here to guests; it is open to all for lunch and dinner.

The **Sunset Café**, on the roof of a mall opposite the Cataract, gives good views towards the corniche, across to the desertic hills of the west bank, while to the immediate right is the Coptic cathedral. The café is a popular local trysting place.

★ Al Saeda Nafesa >>

Apart from dining at the hotels, there are several Egyptian restaurants along the corniche, sometimes with live Nubian music. Among these are the **Panorama**, near Egyptair; **Aswan Moon**, a floating restaurant, opposite the Mövenpick; **Salah al Din**, a multi-level restaurant serving beer and wine, just north of Aswan Moon; and **Emy**, a hangout for felucca captains just south of Aswan Moon. All are inexpensive. Tucked away in the centre of town just east off the main market street, Sharia el Souk, is **El Masri** on Sharia Abu Zid, a traditional place with excellent food. South of Sharia Sayida Nafisa and up an alleyway east off Sharia el Souk is **Al Saeda Nafesa** (as it is written on the sign), a very friendly place with tables in the street and likewise inexpensive. Ask for directions.

The Cataract and Mövenpick hotels have **nightclubs** with Western and Nubian music, perhaps a belly dancer too; the dancing is usually Nubian and worth seeing. In winter the **Palace of Culture**, south of the main post office, presents Nubian dancing.

Nubia

South of the First Cataract at Aswan lay the ancient land of Nubia which extended along the valley of the Nile as far as the Fourth Cataract, a distance as the crow flies of about 700km. But much of Nubia now lies beneath the waters of Lake Nasser, 510km long. A third of southern Nubia, called Cush by the pharaohs and Ethiopia by the Greeks and Romans, which today lies in Sudan, has disappeared beneath the lake, while northern Nubia, which lies in Egypt, has been entirely submerged.

When the High Dam was constructed at Aswan, many monuments were moved to higher ground. The grandest of these, Abu Simbel, can be visited by air, while New Kalabsha involves nothing more than a short trip in a motor launch from the Aswan High Dam. Several other monuments have been gathered at New Sebua and New Amada and can only be visited by joining a Lake Nasser cruise, calling in at New Kalabsha and Abu Simbel too, and mooring off the strange site of Qasr Ibrim.

14

Don't miss

1. **Ramses triumphant**
   Temple of Re-Herakhte at Abu Simbel **p.396**

2. **Nefertari, the woman for whom the sun does shine**
   Temple of Hathor at Abu Simbel **p.398**

3. **Inside the bubble of reality**
   Inside the artifical dome enclosing the temple of Re-Herakhte **p.399**

See map overleaf

Nubia and Lake Nasser

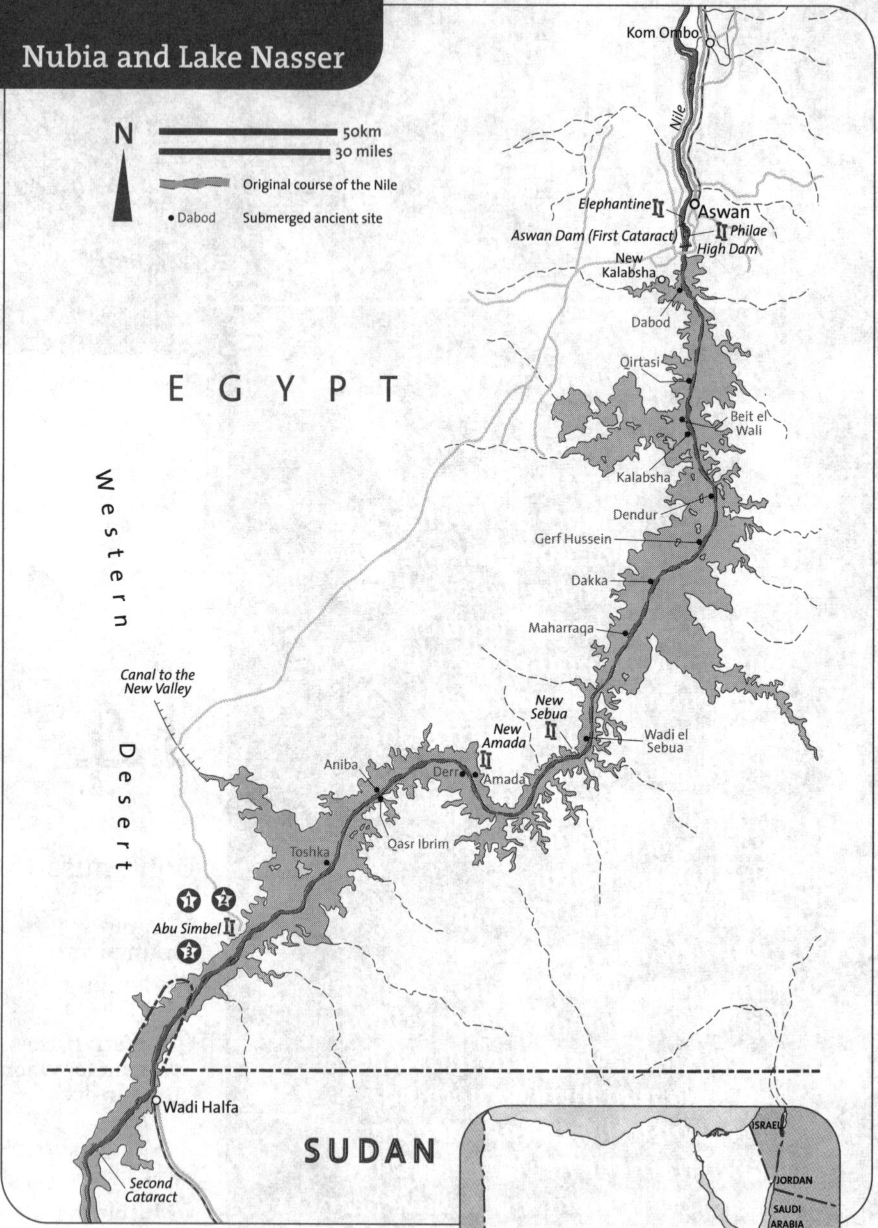

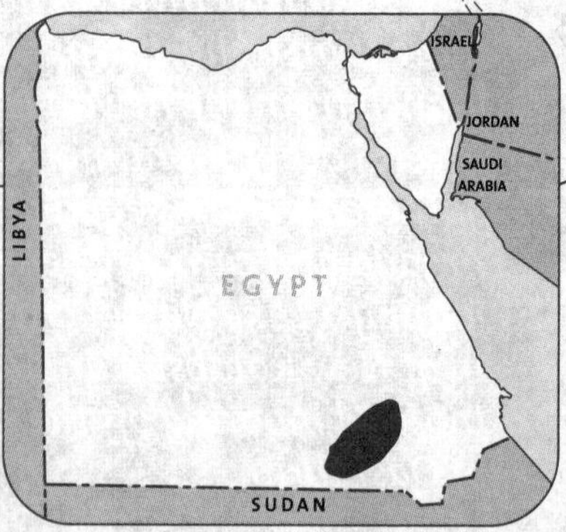

Don't miss

1. Temple of Re-Herakhte at Abu Simbel **p.396**
2. Temple of Hathor at Abu Simbel **p.398**
3. Inside the artifical dome enclosing the temple of Re-Herakhte **p.399**

You feel you are now beyond the reach of history.
Dean Stanley in Nubia, 1852

Both Nubians and ancient Egyptians were originally of the same Mediterranean stock, but their languages were distinct and the Nubians, as depicted in Egyptian art, had darker skins and curlier hair. Nubia tended to be dominated by Egyptian culture, and neither its resources nor its degree of centralized organization were as great as Egypt's, so that from the time of the Old Kingdom the Egyptians looked down on the Nubians as their poor provincial relations and regarded Nubia as theirs to exploit by right.

The pharaonic name for Nubia was To-Kens, meaning Land of the Bow, for the Nubians were famous as archers. The name Nubia itself came into usage only in Graeco-Roman times and seems to have been derived from the ancient Egyptian *nbw*, meaning 'gold'. Indeed, it was as a source of gold and of bowmen and other military recruits that Nubia was attractive to the Egyptians; also for its minerals, wood, incense and slaves, and because it was an avenue of African trade.

With the Middle Kingdom Nubia came under direct Egyptian military control as far south as the Second Cataract, near Egypt's present-day border with Sudan (that is, about 60km south of Abu Simbel), while during the New Kingdom the Egyptian presence was further asserted by the construction of numerous rock-cut temples, most of them during the reign of Ramses II. A thousand years later the Ptolemies, and the Romans who followed them, built in Nubia in their turn.

Therefore New Kingdom, Ptolemaic and Roman temples were the principal monuments that faced drowning beneath the waters of Lake Nasser as the High Dam at Aswan neared completion in the 1960s. Under the aegis of UNESCO, fifty countries contributed money and expertise, and, though some monuments were left to their fate, as many as possible were removed to other sites – some abroad, others on higher ground in Nubia itself; it is these latter you come to see.

What is almost entirely missing in Nubia, however, is Nubians. Their country began to be sacrificed to the larger needs of Egypt with the completion of the British dam at Aswan in 1902 when the drowning of Nubia began. At first the Nubians moved their villages to higher ground, and each time the height of the dam was increased, in 1912 and 1934, they moved their villages again. But with the construction of the High Dam in the 1960s, they had no choice but to accept relocation altogether. Their lives had always been bound up with the river, far more closely than the Egyptians were: 'We have lost our land, our way of life. We used to live entirely by the riverside, planting, fishing and hunting.' Apart from the few living on the islands of Elephantine and Shellal, most have been resettled in government housing well back from the Nile at Aswan,

Kom Ombo, Daraw and towards the airport at Abu Simbel. 'We have lost nature,' they will tell you. 'This is what we miss.'

Some of them return, as one man did after nearly thirty years in 1989, when the drought in the Sudan caused the level of the lake to drop by nearly half, exposing his village with its mosque, its houses – he recognized his own – and the cemetery where his grandparents lay. Now he works on a cruise boat plying Lake Nasser, and to the passengers who have come to see ancient temples salvaged from its depths, he speaks from his memory: 'Here we are moored above a date grove'. The monuments are set in a spectacular landscape, but a landscape even more beyond the feel of human life and history than a hundred and fifty years ago. Not even memories grow in Nubia now.

Cruising Lake Nasser from Aswan

Cruises
see p.63 for cruise operators

The cruise boats for Lake Nasser are at **Sadd al-Ali**, which is Arabic for the High Dam and is also the name of the railway station and of the small harbour facility, both to the east of the dam. The Sudan ferry also puts in here. This harbour lies 12km south of Aswan; you will need to hire a taxi to reach it.

Even before you set sail you will be taken by motor launch from your boat across the south face of the High Dam to New Kalabsha on the far side of the lake (*see* p.374). The cruise boat then heads south on a long journey of 150km before reaching New Sebua. At 10km you sail over the original site of the Graeco-Roman temple of Isis at Dabod (it now stands in parkland in Madrid). At 35km you are over the original site of the Kiosk of Qirtasi and at 50km the original site of the temples of Kalabsha and Beit al-Wali – all three now removed to New Kalabsha. At 60km you cross the Tropic of Cancer, and at 70km you pass over the one-time home of the Roman Temple of Dendur, which has now been fostered out to the Metropolitan Museum of Art in New York. At 85km you are floating above the rock-cut temple of Gerf Hussein from which the colossal statue of Ramses II now in the Nubia Museum at Aswan was rescued. The temple itself, however, lies submerged in a realm of darkness; the average depth of the lake is 180m.

At one of the broadest expanses of the lake, 95km and 105km south of Sadd al-Ali, you sail over the original sites of the temples of Dakka and Maharraqa, which have been removed to New Sebua. All along this stretch and nearly to New Sebua the lake is very broad, generally 20–35km across, and there is no sense at all of Nubia as it was when it hugged the Nile.

New Sebua

But that changes as you arrive at the west bank site of **New Sebua**, 150km south of Sadd al-Ali, where the lake narrows to the width of a broad river and the Nubian landscape in all its strangeness fills your eye. The launch brings you in over shallow marshes, where three temples are ranged on a ridge above you, rugged rock outcrops burst from the orange sand and low pyramidal peaks crouch darkly against the horizon.

The leftmost monument as you land at the site, standing apart from the other two, is the **Temple of Wadi el Sebua**. Moved here in the early 1960s from 4km further upstream, it was built for Ramses II in the middle years of his reign by his viceroy of Cush, who also constructed the almost identical and now drowned temple at Gerf Hussein. *Wadi el Sebua* in Arabic means 'valley of the lions' and refers to the **avenue of lion-bodied sphinxes** that leads up through the two ruinous mud brick outer courts of the temple. The sphinxes in the first court bear the heads of Ramses II, while those in the second are falcon-headed. A stairway rises out of the second court and brings you before a sandstone pylon leading into the **hypostyle hall**, where Ramses appears in the form of Osiris on its ten crudely carved pillars, most of them headless – the hypostyle hall and the rock-cut part of the temple beyond it later served as a church, where the Christians hacked away or plastered over the pagan images. The sanctuary is at the most interior point and until the Christians got at them contained statues of Amun-Re, Re-Herakhte and the godly Ramses himself, the triad to whom the temple was dedicated. The temple was carved with dedicatory scenes throughout, and these have been laid bare again as most of the plaster has come away. But on the back wall of the sanctuary some of the plaster has survived, bringing the pharaonic and the Christian periods into surreal conjunction, for you see Ramses offering flowers not to a god but to St Peter.

Camels run a shuttle service for those who prefer not to walk between the Temple of Wadi el Sebua and the temples of Dakka and Maharraqa, about a kilometre to the north.

The rebuilt **Temple of Dakka**, dedicated to Thoth, has been faithfully aligned north–south, the pylon therefore facing downstream just as it was at its original site (*see* above), in contrast to the east–west alignment of most temples in Nubia. Though substantially of Ptolemaic construction, the temple was begun by a Nubian king based near the Fourth Cataract and received its sanctuary and its disproportionately large though elegant **pylon** during the reigns of the Roman emperors Augustus and Tiberius. Each tower of the pylon has an internal staircase

A Cruise Too Far?

When the sun goes down and the silence falls is the time to pick up a copy of Sir Arthur Conan Doyle's *The Tragedy of the Korosko*, published in 1898. The *Korosko* is a cruise boat not unlike your own, dear reader, and even in those days the landscape was bleak enough, deserts rising on either side, with Nubia writhing 'like a green sand-worm along the course of the river. Here and there it disappears altogether, and the Nile runs between black and sun-cracked hills, with the orange drift-sand lying like glaciers in their valleys. Everywhere one sees traces of vanished races and submerged civilisations. Grotesque graves dot the hills or stand up against the skyline: pyramidal graves, tumulus graves, rock graves – everywhere, graves... It is through this weird, dead country that the tourists smoke and gossip and flirt.'

Kitchener has not yet taken Khartoum and avenged the death of Gordon at the hands of the Mahdi and his fundamentalist Dervish followers, who threaten Egypt along its southern frontier. But the passengers of the *Korosko* form 'a merry party' as 'even Anglo-Saxon ice thaws rapidly upon the Nile', so that when the boat has tied up for the evening and from somewhere in the distant shadows there is 'a high shrill whimpering, rising and swelling, to end in a long weary wail', only the ladies give a start and are laughingly reassured that they have heard nothing more than the howl of a jackal. There are no Dervishes for miles about, one gentleman insists, as everyone goes to their cabins and shuts their doors to cheery calls of goodnight. The *Korosko* now lies tethered, silent and motionless against the bank, while 'beyond this one point of civilisation and of comfort there lay the limitless, savage, unchangeable desert, straw-coloured and dream-like in the moonlight, mottled over with the black shadows of the hills'.

Of course what happens to the passengers is not what will happen to you. Even after the lights go out on the temples at New Sebua, you have always sunrise and croissants to look forward to – assuming nothing befalls you before the dawn.

leading up to the roof from where you gain a commanding view of the strange beauty of the landscape. Beyond the pylon is an open court, its side walls gone; then begins the temple proper, with a pronaos leading to a transverse chamber which in turn leads into the original Nubian-built sanctuary, offering reliefs of generally high quality throughout. The final chamber, the added-on Roman sanctuary, is crudely decorated.

The northernmost and smallest of the three temples at New Sebua, also moved here from the north (*see* above), is the Roman **Temple of Maharraqa**, which is believed to have been dedicated to Serapis. Its decorations were never completed, yet it is this that makes it interesting. Climb the spiral staircase (possibly a unique feature in ancient Egyptian building) at the northeast corner of the main hall so that you can look down on the unfinished floral capitals of the columns. They remind you of the story of the man who, presented with a solid block of stone, said that anyone could carve an elephant: 'You just cut away everything that doesn't look like an elephant'. Here a first attempt was made to cut away everything that did not look like a lotus, palm and papyrus bouquet, but the task was soon abandoned, leaving you full of admiration for the skill of those who elsewhere went beyond the preliminary outline phase seen here to produce capitals of astonishing delicacy.

From the top of the stairway at the Maharraqa temple you gain a wonderful view – including, if they are still at it, the work of the farming family who have raised a crop of tomatoes, courgettes and melons in a well-watered field just to the north, a gauze of green against the burning sand. This family here at New Sebua and a few others near New Amada have come from the Delta to Nubia where they earn a premium price for producing crops two months earlier than their season in the rest of Egypt.

You might think that the shores of Lake Nasser would be brimming with enterprises such as these, for the sandy soil is ideal for crops of this type and water is unlimited. But the government makes it almost impossible for individuals to purchase land in Nubia, as that would involve investment in infrastructure – roads, electricity, markets, schools and security. Similarly, though Lake Nasser abounds in fish, next to nothing has been done to build up a local fishing-based economy. Instead the fishing rights have been leased to two large companies operating refrigerator boats to which local fishermen are obliged to sell their catch at a knockdown price, about one-tenth that paid in the Cairo market.

But the traveller gazing from the deck of his cruise boat can content himself with the vacancy of Nubia's austere and beautiful landscape. You watch the sun go down to the sudden cry of birds and then listen to the perfect silence. Moored out in the lake you look across to New Sebua, where after darkness falls the temples are illuminated, and this is magical. Then the switch is flicked and the shore goes black and the sky above goes thick with stars, bright ones, dim ones, some no more than dust and powder.

New Amada

The sensation of voyaging along a broad river continues for nearly the whole 45km or so to **New Amada**. After New Sebua there is a bend in the lake towards the west, but soon you are sailing southwards again with high mountains closing in along the eastern shore. Then the lake sweeps away to the north at the place that was once Korosko, which until the beginning of the 20th century was the starting point of the great caravan route that struck south across the desert, avoiding the Second, Third and Fourth Cataracts and further windings of the Nile, and in eight to ten days reaching Abu Hamed, 400km north of Khartoum.

New Amada, like New Sebua, lies off to starboard, but because the lake is now running north you land on its eastern shore. Crocodiles are an occasional hazard. Large numbers of them inhabit the lake, where they can grow to the length of a living room, and sometimes they like to bask on shore, forcing tours to be postponed. Judging from sightings of their tracks, they are especially fond of New Amada.

At New Amada there are two temples and a tomb to see, all within a few minutes' walk of one another. The **Temple of Amada** was built during the reigns of Tuthmosis III, Amenophis II and Tuthmosis IV of the XVIII Dynasty and is the oldest surviving monument on Lake Nasser. Though its exterior is unprepossessing, the interior, partly restored under Seti I (XX Dynasty), is decorated with high quality raised reliefs which largely owe their preservation to having been plastered over when the temple served as a Christian church. For the sake of the reliefs the main body of the temple, instead of being dismantled like its forepart, was moved in a single piece – jacked up and placed on flatcars, then hauled along railtracks 2.5km away from its original location, now 60m below the lake. Many of the reliefs show the various pharaohs making offerings to Amun-Re and Re-Herakhte, to whom the temple, like most others in Nubia, was dedicated.

But most interesting historically is the hieroglyphic inscription on the rear wall of the sanctuary, where Amenophis II describes a victorious military campaign in Syria: 'His Majesty returned in joy to his father Amun after he had slain with his own mace the seven chiefs of the district of Takhesy, who were then hung upside down from the prow of the boat of His Majesty'. After battering out the brains of his enemies, Amenophis displayed six of their bodies from the walls of Thebes, while the body of the seventh was suspended upside down from the prow of a ship which sailed the entire length of Nubia as far as the Fourth Cataract to impress the inhabitants with his power. And indeed, if you count four registers up from the bottom and look about a third of the way from the left, there he is, the upside-down man, after three thousand four hundred years, suffering still an unwanted fame.

The rock-cut **Temple of Derr** was removed here from its original site 11km away to the southwest where it stood on the opposite bank of the Nile. Built during the second half of Ramses II's reign, it served the familiar purpose of associating his deified self with Amun-Re and Re-Herakhte, and also in this case Ptah. Their four statues, carved out of solid rock at the rear wall of the sanctuary, were hacked out by Christians when they made the temple into a church. In plan and decoration it resembles Ramses' great temple at Abu Simbel but on a smaller scale and without the colossal statues of himself set against the façade. The chief attractions are the painted carvings, in sunk relief, which though poorly executed are unusually bright and vivid.

From Aniba, which was 40km further along the Nile, comes the **Tomb of Pennut**, who was the chief administrator of northern Nubia under the viceroy of Cush during the reign of Ramses VI

(XX Dynasty). He would seem to have been an Egyptianized Nubian, for he was buried at Aniba with other members of his family, whereas Egyptians usually made sure they were buried in their homeland. The tomb was already recorded as dilapidated in the 1920s, and half its painted reliefs had fallen or been hacked from the walls by the time it was moved to New Amada, but those that survive are delicately carved and often retain their colour, as for example on the rear right-hand wall of the tomb where his sons are shown bearing offerings to Re-Herakhte.

Qasr Ibrim

Soon the lake broadens and bends to the south, and 40km beyond New Amada, when you are hovering over what Baedeker described in 1929 as 'the pretty village of Aniba, shaded by palms' (and, long before that, Pennut's hometown), you see an island off to the east which was once a towering promontory overlooking the Nile. Your boat will slowly glide past the island, allowing you a leisurely look, but you will not be permitted to land: this is the only surviving original site in Nubia, and its rich and complex remains are reserved exclusively for archaeologists.

Where Baedeker could describe upon this 'lofty' pinnacle the 'extremely picturesque ruined fort of **Qasr Ibrim**, dating from Roman times', you now see only a jumble of stones and at the centre a collapsing cathedral. Founded in the 7th or 8th century, the basilica stands on the remains of a still earlier church, while off to the northwest stood a temple in the Egyptian style. These were the two most prominent buildings, standing among houses of the Ottoman period which completely filled the Roman fortress walls, which had replaced earlier Ptolemaic fortifications. But the history of the site goes back well beyond that, for incised in the steep west slope of the headland were several XVIII and XIX Dynasty stelae variously proclaiming the authority of Hatshepsut and Tuthmosis III, Amenophis II and Ramses II (these have been removed to New Sebua). Taharka (XXV Dynasty) also built a mud brick temple at what became the southwest corner of the fortress; converted to a Christian church, it remained a place of worship for 2,000 years.

Indeed from pharaonic times through to the 19th century, Qasr Ibrim alternated between roles as a military bastion and a religious centre. Here, even later than at Philae, the worship of Isis persisted long after Egypt became a Christian country; this also became the last place in northern Nubia to fall to Islam when, following the Ottoman conquest of Egypt, a garrison of Bosnian mercenaries occupied Qasr Ibrim in 1528 and the cathedral became a mosque. During her return voyage from the Second Cataract in 1874, Amelia

Edwards encountered their descendants who had intermarried with the local Nubians: 'At Ibrim, as at Derr, there are "fair" families [whose] light hair and blue eyes... date back to Bosnian forefathers of 360 years ago. These people give themselves airs, and are the *haute noblesse* of the place'.

Sailing on: Qasr Ibrim to Abu Simbel

From Qasr Ibrim to Abu Simbel the voyage is 60km, and here the lake becomes very broad again. At Toshka, halfway between the two, work has begun on a **canal** which will eventually be over 300km long and will link the lake with the oases of the Western Desert. The oases form a region known as the New Valley, so called in the expectation that its development will some day match the valley of the Nile for fertility. Until now the New Valley has relied entirely on local artesian water supplies, but the addition of canalized water from Lake Nasser could prove decisive in doubling Egypt's agricultural area. The canal is being financed by the sale of land along its projected path in lots of not less than 50,000 *feddans* to private companies of 'trusted' countries such as the United States and Saudi Arabia.

Finally the lake narrows again and the shore to the west runs flat against the sky – except for a pale mound into which you can just make out that something has been etched: the colossi of Ramses II set in the façade of his great rock-cut temple at Abu Simbel. The scene grows ever more imposing as you draw nearer, and you notice ant-like people scurrying about the site: these are the tourists who have arrived by air. By late afternoon the planes have taken them away, and with your boat tied up before the colossi, you have Abu Simbel to yourself. At night there is a *son et lumière* which is something like a drive-in movie: projected onto the façades of the temples, Ramses sighs for Nefertari, Nefertari sighs for Ramses, and chariots go galloping by. You are watching it all as you dine on deck by candlelight: it is wonderfully artful, thoroughly stupid and entirely delightful.

Abu Simbel

Originally the rock temples of **Abu Simbel**, located 280km south of Aswan and just 40km north of Wadi Halfa on the Sudan border, stared from the sandstone cliffs which rose like gigantic temple pylons over the narrow Nile. In 1812, John Lewis Burckhardt, the first European since classical times to visit Abu Simbel, was not immediately impressed; he had come upon the cliffs from above, and only as he gained the river and turned upstream was he struck

Getting to Abu Simbel

By Air

Abu Simbel can be reached by air direct from Cairo, Luxor or Aswan. Many seats are booked up six to twelve months in advance by tour companies, so you should reserve a seat at the earliest opportunity. Rather than expect your flight to Abu Simbel to fit in with your overall plans, you may well have to make your overall plans fit in with when you are able to book a flight to Abu Simbel. Nevertheless it is always worthwhile trying at the last moment. Egyptair's national call centre number is **t** 0900 70000.

The fullest way to enjoy Abu Simbel is to spend two days there, giving you the opportunity to see the temples in the afternoon when all the crowds have left, also to see the sound and light show at night, then to come back for sunrise in the morning, again before all the crowds have arrived.

If you are doing it just as a day trip and want the sun shining full on the temple façades it is better to fly to Abu Simbel in the morning, though that is also when the temples are most likely to be crawling with people. For day-trippers a two-hour stay at Abu Simbel is sufficient, and indeed you are usually issued with flight tickets timed to that assumption.

If you are flying from Aswan, the flight will take 25 minutes. Add to that the need to check in early and the likelihood that the flight will be delayed, and you can reckon that the expedition will take 5 hours in all. A bus will take you to the temples from the airport and back.

Thomas Cook, Misr Travel and others offer inclusive air tours from Aswan.

By Cruise Boat

Six cruise boats sail the waters of Lake Nasser between Sadd el-Ali (the port for Aswan) and Abu Simbel, calling at New Kalabsha, New Sebua, New Amada and Qasr Ibrim, the voyage taking three to four days. By far the two finest boats on the lake are the luxurious five-star MS *Eugénie* with *fin de siècle* décor, and the Art Deco MS *Kasr Ibrim*, each charging from $200 per person per day, all meals, site charges and the services of an excellent guide included. Both are operated by **Belle Époque Travel**, with offices in Cairo, **t** (02) 2516 9649, *www.eugenie.com.eg* and *www.kasribrim.com.eg*. Cruises are also included in packages by tour operators abroad. For more information *see* p.61.

By Road

A road from Aswan to Abu Simbel was opened in 1985 and it has since been extended to Sudan. Private taxis, luxury coaches and cheaper public buses, as well as giant international trucks, ply the 250km route from Aswan, taking three hours. Journeys can be arranged at travel agents or sometimes at your hotel in Aswan.

---

by the four colossal statues of Ramses II. 'Could the sand be cleared away,' he said, 'a vast temple would be discovered.' The sand was repeatedly cleared away during the 19th century. Remarkable photographs were taken in the early 1850s by, among others, Maxime du Camp, Flaubert's travelling companion, of the sand rising over the faces of the two right-hand colossi. On Holy Thursday, Flaubert noted, 'We began clearing operations, to disengage the chin of one of the exterior colossi.' It was only later in the century, with the coming of the British, that Abu Simbel and so many other monuments were properly cleared. Then, usually by Cook's steamer, tourists came. Laid bare in all their glory, and enhanced by the unique and striking beauty of the setting, the temples of Abu Simbel excited the enthusiasm of early visitors. Baedeker allowed himself a large adjective: they 'are among the most stupendous monuments of ancient Egyptian architecture'; and he went on to say: 'The temples produce a very grand effect by moonlight or at sunrise. The interior of the great temple is

Access and Fees

The site is open daily from 6am to 5pm, though if there are late-arriving flights it will stay open longer. Unless included in your air or coach tour, admission to both temples is LE80. The advantage of getting there early is that, as the temples face east, that is when the sun is shining on them. The disadvantage is that everyone else has the same idea. If the season seems busy and you want the place more to yourself, either stay overnight and see it at dawn, or consider coming later in the day. Note that cameras are not allowed in the temples.

illuminated at night by electricity provided from the steamer.' Those were the days.

Rescuing the Temples

As the waters of Lake Nasser rose during the mid-1960s, the original site of the temples was protected temporarily behind a coffer dam while the friable sandstone was injected with synthetic resin and then hand-sawn into 1,050 blocks. The first block was cut in spring 1965; by autumn 1967 block had been replaced upon block at the new site 210m from the old one and 61m higher up. The $42 million operation was organized and funded by UNESCO. The temples were saved, the dam was breached, and the sacred site, which had known human activity since prehistoric times, was swallowed by the lake.

If there is such a thing as spirit of place, it now lies behind and below you somewhere beneath the waters as you stand facing the colossi of Ramses. The reconstruction has been impeccable; you knock your knuckles against Ramses' foot and are assured it is stone, not plaster; you look for the filled-in joins in the torsos but cannot detect them; and if you are there at dawn you will see that the sun's rays fall flat upon the pharaonic faces and, if the temple door is open, penetrate to the innermost sanctuary. Everything is as it was before, except that it is here and not where it used to be, and that greatly weakens the force of the new Abu Simbel.

The genius of the place lay in working with the living rock, the temple façades set into cliff faces seemingly prepared by nature for the purpose, the colossi of Ramses at the south temple and those of Nefertari at the north temple seeming to step out from the mountain, liberated from the imprisoning rock by the divine force of the rising sun.

But when the cliffs are themselves reconstructions, that dramatic relationship between architecture and topography, and that mystical emergence of man from nature, suffers and perhaps is lost. To have left those ancient and powerful links intact would have meant surrendering the temples to the waters. Instead, it was decided to save the body and risk losing the soul. We now examine what remains.

Abu Simbel

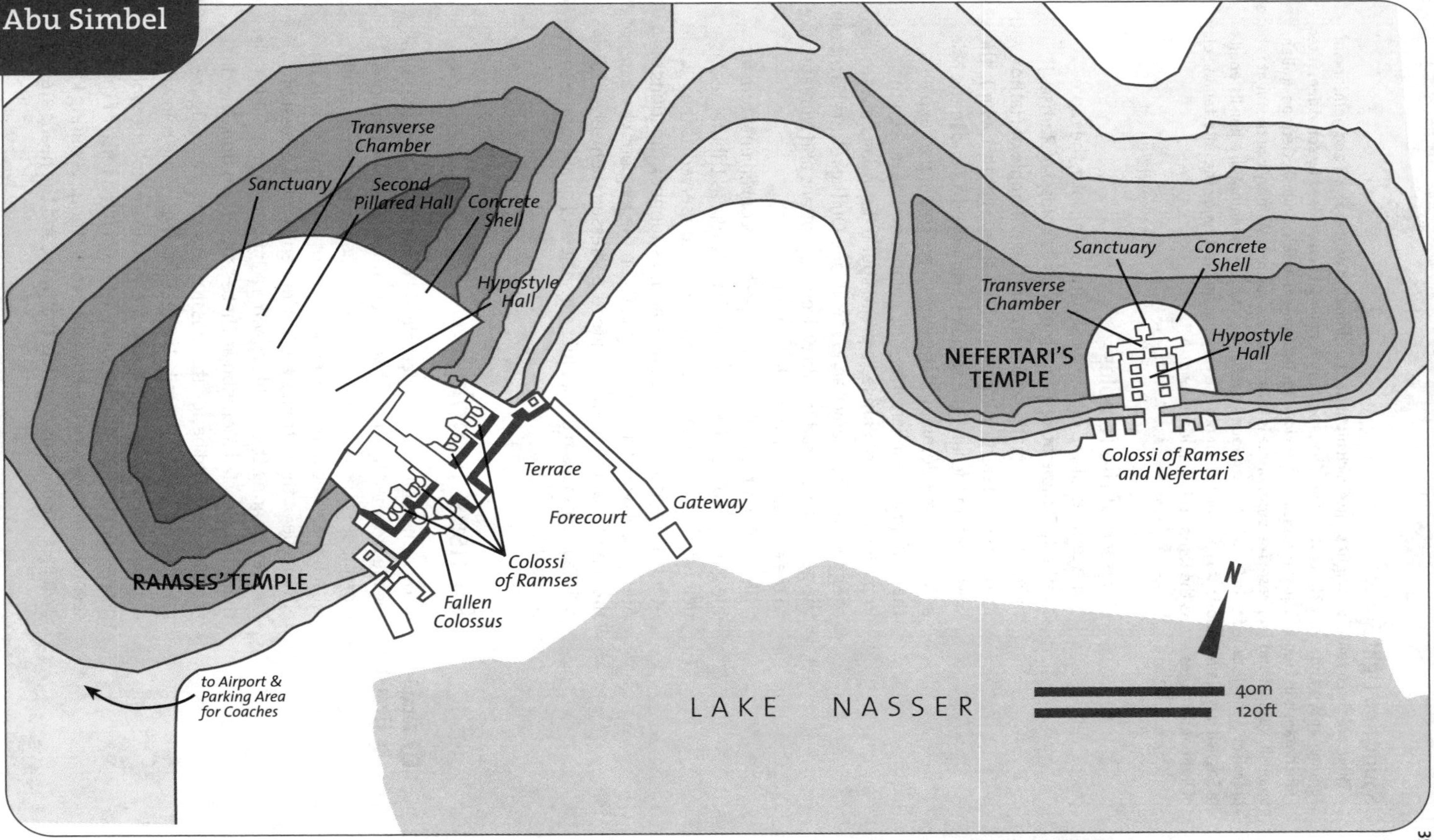

Transverse Chamber
Sanctuary
Second Pillared Hall
Concrete Shell
Hypostyle Hall
RAMSES' TEMPLE
Terrace
Forecourt
Gateway
Colossi of Ramses
Fallen Colossus
to Airport & Parking Area for Coaches
Sanctuary
Concrete Shell
Transverse Chamber
Hypostyle Hall
NEFERTARI'S TEMPLE
Colossi of Ramses and Nefertari
N
LAKE NASSER
40m
120ft

Sound and Light Show

There are three sound and light shows each night at Abu Simbel, in winter at 7, 8 and 9pm, and in summer at 8, 9 and 10pm. The cost is LE90. The programme, having been devised by some demented Frenchman, is in French, but earphones are provided for listening in Arabic, English, German, Italian, Spanish, Russian and Japanese. The programme is full of phrases such as 'Memory like the night is but a promise'. When listened to in French this can sound poetic and vaguely meaningful; when listened to in English it is plainly idiotic. It is probably better to use earplugs and just enjoy the entertaining play of light and images across the temples; this at least is worth it.

Purpose of the Temples

The temples stand on the west bank of the lake, the more southerly **Temple of Re-Harakhte**, with its **colossi of Ramses II**, facing east, the smaller and more northerly **Temple of Hathor**, with its **colossi of Nefertari**, Ramses' wife, angled slightly towards the south. Before the lake, the temples overlooked a bend in the Nile and must have dominated the landscape. This in part explains their purpose. Travellers into Africa would first have seen the imposing colossi of Ramses, a proud spur to Egyptians, a warning of Egypt's might to any fractious Nubians. On the return, Hathor, in the guise of Nefertari, would welcome Egyptians and Nubians alike to the embrace of a great civilization.

Also, the temples would have served as a convenient store for the gold and other riches exacted from Nubia as tribute, just as nearly a thousand years later the Parthenon served as the Athenian treasury. But the political and strongbox functions of Abu Simbel would have relied greatly on the religious character of the temples, and that the architects addressed themselves to religious symbolism of magnificent scale and quality there can be no doubt.

Ramses' Temple

Temple of Re-Herakhte

You come first upon the **Temple of Re-Herakhte**, its trapezoidal façade crowned by a cavetto cornice surmounted by baboons worshipping the rising sun. The falcon-headed sun god stands within the niche above the entrance door. Arranged in pairs on either side of the entrance are the four enthroned **colossi of Ramses** wearing the double crown. Each figure is 20m high, taller than the colossi of Memnon at Thebes, and hewn from the cliff face. Between and beside the massive legs are smaller figures of members of the royal family. The feet and legs of the colossi are crudely carved, as though deliberately inchoate, but the work grows finer up through the torsos (the head and torso of the second colossus from the left fell in an earthquake during Ramses' own lifetime and has been left that way), and the heads are excellently executed. This is most true of the first head on the left, of which Burckhardt remarked, 'a most expressive, youthful countenance, approaching nearer to the Grecian model of beauty than that of any ancient Egyptian figure I have seen'. The sides of the **thrones** on either side of the entrance are decorated with Nile gods symbolically uniting Egypt, while below are fettered prisoners: those to the left black Africans; those to the right Syrians.

Also to the left of the entrance, on the nearest colossal leg, notice the Greek **inscription** which reads, 'When King Psammetichus came to Elephantine, this was written by those who sailed with Psammetichus the son of Theocles, and they came beyond Kerkis as far as the river permits. Those who spoke foreign tongues were led by Potasimto, the Egyptians by Amasis.' The reference is to the Nubian campaign of Psammetichus II (XXVI Dynasty), but the point is that already in the 6th century BC Greeks were operating in Egypt, albeit as mercenaries. At sea, however, they were in control of the Egyptian navy. With the arrival of Alexander 260 years later, they would be in control of Egypt itself.

Entering the Temple

The first room is the **Hypostyle Hall**, corresponding to an open court with covered colonnades. There are four pillars on either side, against which and facing the central aisle are 10m-high Osiris-type figures of Ramses, though this is Ramses alive, not dead, in athletic near-nudity showing a process of heroization at work. The best is the fourth figure in the north row. Heroic martial deeds are depicted in sunk relief around the walls. If you face the entrance you will see on the left (north) entrance wall a vigorous account of the **battle of Kadesh** in the fifth year of Ramses' reign. It was a battle Ramses endlessly boasted about, and boast he needed to do as it was no more than a Pyrrhic victory. Ramses cut himself out of a Hittite trap, but he failed to take Kadesh. Above Ramses is a vulture, and behind him his ka, who acted as guardian angel in the struggle. On the right (south) entrance wall a corresponding scene shows Ramses in the presence of Amun, to whom (as the inscription known as the **poem of Pentaur** tells it) the king appealed at his most desperate moment: 'What ails thee, my father Amun? Is it a father's part to ignore his son? Have I done anything without thee, do I not walk and halt at thy bidding? I have not disobeyed any course commanded by thee... What careth thy heart, O Amun, for these Asiatics so vile and ignorant of God?... What will men say if even a little thing befall him who bends himself to thy counsel?'

Facing again the interior, the left (south) wall of the hall bears an **epic masterpiece** depicting (below the top five reliefs showing Ramses making offerings to the gods) Ramses in his chariot storming a Syrian fortress, in the centre the pharaoh piercing a Libyan with his lance, and to the right his triumphal return from battle with black captives. On the opposite (north) wall are further scenes from the Hittite campaign while on the rear wall Ramses is shown leading Hittite and black captives. Lateral chambers leading off from this top end of the Hypostyle Hall were probably used for storing the Nubian tribute.

In the next hall of four pillars, reliefs on the left (south) wall show Ramses and Nefertari before the sacred boat of Amun, and on the opposite (north) wall a similar scene before the boat of Re-Herakhte. Three doors lead from here into a transverse chamber from which in turn three doors lead off, the central one into the **Sanctuary**. Four seated mutilated figures are carved out of the rear wall: Ptah, god of Memphis, Amun, god of Thebes, the divinized Ramses, and Re-Harakhte, god of Heliopolis. Before them is a stone block on which would have rested the sacred boat. The symbolism is one of unity, the pharaoh and gods of Egypt's three greatest cities as one; but there is also Ramses as the living and visible god, perhaps again to awe the Nubians. The entire temple leads to this central message: Ramses as conqueror, hero and then god, the awesome progression enhanced by the heightened perspective of ever-smaller chambers, ever-smaller doorways, and at dawn when the sun rose exactly opposite the temple, a brilliant shaft of light pointing to the sacred boat and Ramses with his fellow gods in the sanctuary. Leaving the temple you should stand before the façade again, before the entrance with its falcon-headed sun god, and imagine that effect.

You now walk on to the Temple of Hathor. Nearby there is a refreshment stand with trees and welcome shade. A while ago, and perhaps now too, there was a low mud rectangle beneath these trees, hardly more than an outline on the ground with a gap at one end, a niche at the other. It was a mosque, just broad enough for two prostrate figures, so great a contrast to the massive temples, so great a witness to the immanence and power of Allah.

The Temple of Hathor

2 **Temple of Hathor**

The **Temple of Hathor** is secondary and complementary to the larger Temple of Re-Herakhte, and in some ways more symbolically satisfying. Hathor was wife to the sun god during his day's passage and mother to his rebirth. As Ramses is identified with the god of the first temple, so his wife Nefertari is identified with the goddess of this, and so god, goddess, pharaoh and wife are each mated with one another.

The façade is again a pylon, though the cavetto cornice has fallen. A series of buttresses rise into the cliff, and between them six **colossal statues of Ramses and Nefertari**. You should get up close to them. There is the uncanny impression that they are emerging from the rock, that they are forming and will at any moment stride out towards the sunrise. The royal children stand knee-high in the shadows. Ramses framed these figures with a bold hieroglyphic inscription cut into the façade: 'Ramses II, he has made a temple, excavated in the mountain, of eternal workmanship, for the chief queen Nefertari beloved of Mut, in Nubia, forever and ever, Nefertari for whose sake the very sun does shine' (*see* p.337).

Inside the **Hypostyle Hall** with its crudely carved heads of Hathor on the six pillars, turn to examine the entrance wall. Ramses is smiting his enemies; Nefertari's hands are raised, perhaps as part of the ritual, though she seems to be seeking to moderate her husband's fury. In any case, she cuts a delightful figure, a slender form in flowing dress, appealing, graceful, dignified. The side walls show Ramses before various gods, while the rear wall shows Nefertari before Hathor (left) and before Mut (right), consort of Amun and the pre-eminent goddess of Thebes. Three doors lead to a transverse chamber. On either side is a further chamber above the entrance to which is Hathor's cow in her boat.

In the **Sanctuary** there is the startling sight of the divine cow emerging from the rear rock wall, a suggestion of the world beyond where her milk brings life to the souls of the dead. Also have a good look at the reliefs of Nefertari on the wall which faces the emerging cow; they are exquisitely carved, the lines freely drawn, her figure trim and sensual, very AD 1920s.

The Bubble of Reality

Artificial dome

If you enter the small door leading into the rock face to the right of Re-Herakhte's temple, the atmosphere is suddenly air-conditioned. You climb some stairs at the back and with even more surprise than at seeing a cow coming at you from a stone wall you enter a vast echoic dome.

It is the bubble that surmounts the major temple and over which fill has been dumped and shaped to recreate the contour of the original bluff. A walkway runs right round the inside where there are abandoned displays and sheets of data explaining how it was all done. There is much to be said for this bubble. It is the one thing at Abu Simbel that is real.

Where to Stay and Eat at Abu Simbel

You can no longer spend a windy night sleeping out at the temples themselves to catch the magnificent dawn; you will have to stay at a hotel. As for eating places, you can have lunch at the **Seti Abu Simbel hotel**, or best of all at the traditional Nubian-style **Eskaleh** restaurant and hotel; there is little that is appealing in town.

******Seti Abu Simbel, t** (097) 400 720, *www.setifirst.com*, near the temples ($$$$). Comprises 142 chalets set in a luxuriant garden with three swimming pools and overlooks Lake Nasser. Its individual chalets, all with bathrooms, are air-conditioned and have refrigerator, minibar, DVD and satellite TV.

★ **Eskaleh ›**

Eskaleh (also ask for Beit el Nubi, meaning the Nubian House); it lies between town and temples; best is to make direct contact with its owner Fikry Kachif, **t** (097) 340 1288 or mobile **t** 0020 012 368 0521, *eskaleh@tele2.ch* ($$$). Fikry Kachif is a well known Nubian musician who has established this hotel-restaurant-cultural centre on a quiet spot along the shore of Lake Nasser. The building is traditional Nubian style with domed rooms set about a central courtyard which keeps things shady and cool. Relaxing, friendly, atmospheric, this is a charming place to stay, especially when Fikry and his friends get together for an impromptu musical session. It is best to book in advance as there are only six rooms.

***Abu Simbel Village, t** (097) 400 092 ($$). In town; a pink cluster about 200m from the main intersection and heading away from the temples. Its simple vaulted rooms built round a concrete courtyard have air conditioning and bathrooms.

The Western Desert

Egypt is a land of pairs – arranged as opposites, as complementaries, as identities. There is this life and the afterlife; the river and the sky; the cultivated land and the desert; and there is the desert and the sea. It is the desert and the sea, described in this and subsequent chapters, that bound Egypt, protect it, preserve it, sometimes suddenly change it, and with the Nile determine its fortunes.

This chapter covers first the oases of the Western Desert, beginning with Siwa which lies farthest west and has always been on the outermost fringe of the Egyptian world, then from south to north the inner oases of Kharga, Dakhla, Farafra and Bahariya with their much closer links to the civilization of the Nile. The latter part of this chapter deals with the Christian monasteries of the Wadi Natrun, which lie off the Desert Road between Cairo and Alexandria, and finally places of interest west of Alexandria where the desert meets the Mediterranean.

15

Don't miss

1. **Date palms, olive and fruit trees, streams and meadow grasses in the desert**
   Siwa Oasis **p.403**
2. **Devils, scorpions, eternity and God**
   Ancient Coptic monasteries of the Wadi Natrun **p.419**
3. **Putting Rommel on the run**
   Alamein **p.434**

See map overleaf

The Western Desert

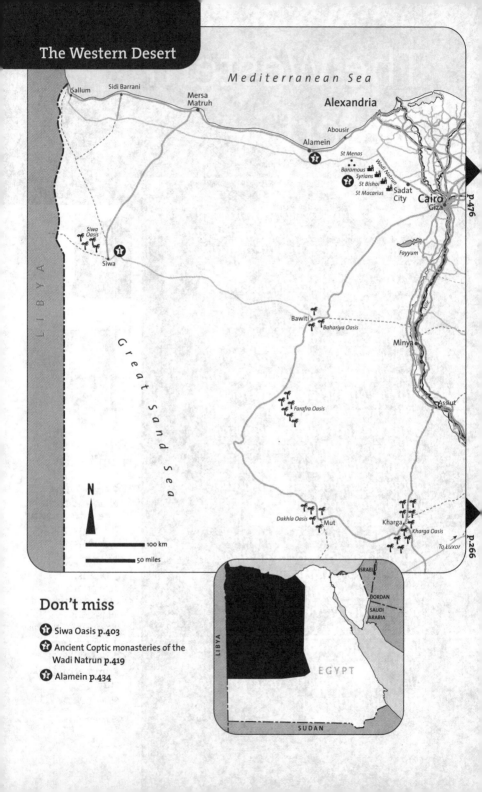

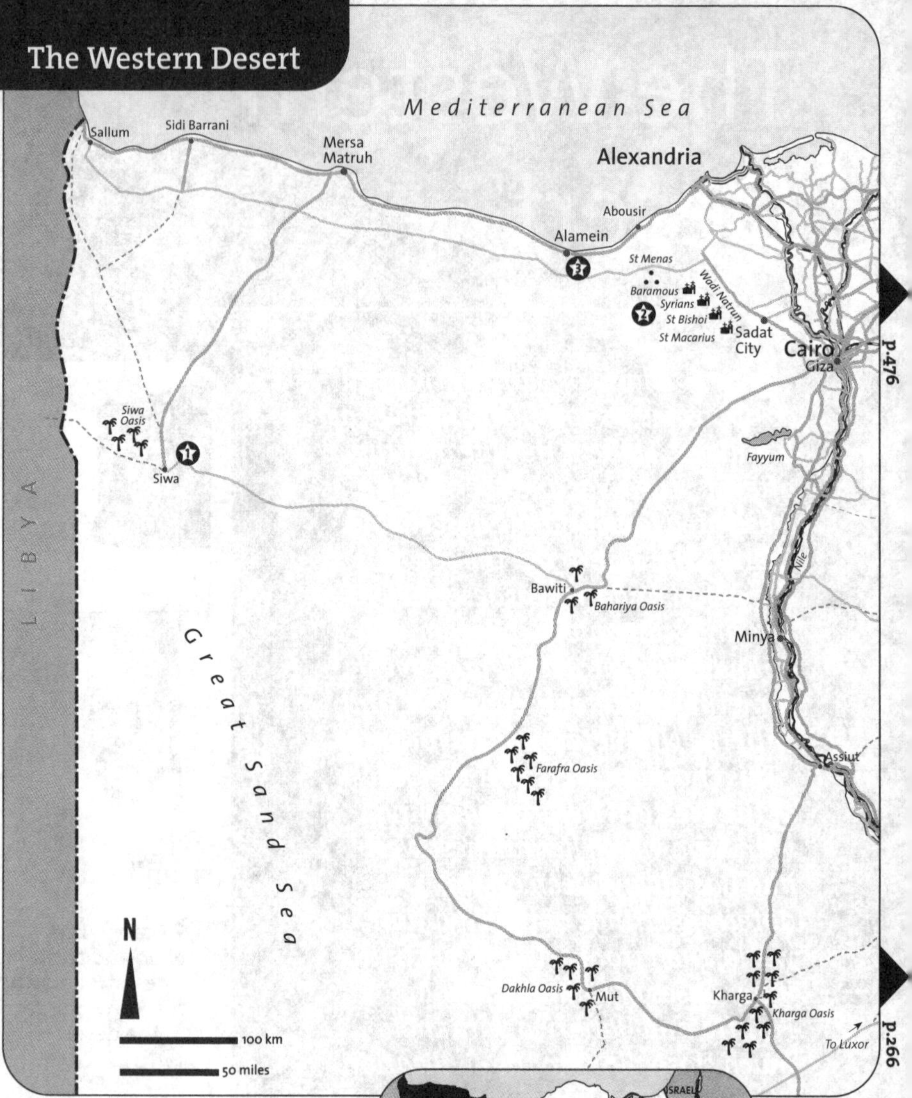

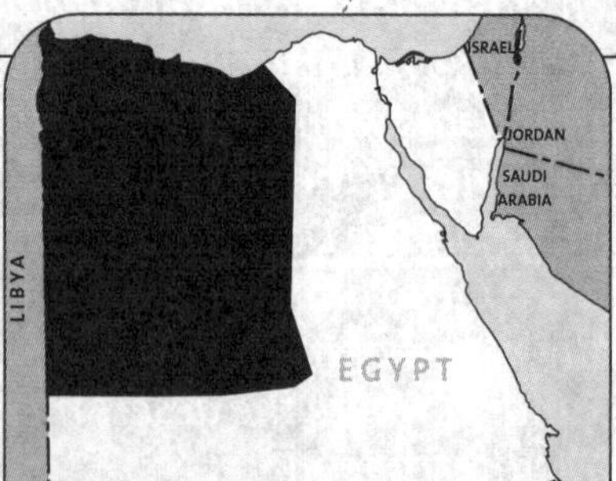

Don't miss

1. Siwa Oasis p.403
2. Ancient Coptic monasteries of the Wadi Natrun p.419
3. Alamein p.434

The deserts and the sea have always provided Egypt with its security, but have provided its conquerors with avenues of attack. It has generally been the forces of the West that have come by sea or at least secured themselves by Mediterranean routes of supply. Alexander marched into Egypt from Gaza, but founded his city by the sea, his Ptolemaic successors governing from Alexandria. The Crusaders landed repeatedly at Damietta. The French and British came by sea and prized Egypt less for itself than for its strategic position on the route to India. They underlined this by building and operating the Suez Canal, and as recently as 1956 fought in vain along with Israel to keep it under their control. The Germans attacked across the desert and met defeat at Alamein, one of the most important battles of the Second World War; they had come in tanks to break British naval power in the Mediterranean, and that naval power broke them in turn.

In its effects, the greatest desert attack on Egypt came in AD 640–41 when Amr swept across the sands under the banner of Islam. He had with him only 3,500 men. Today barely half as many men are waging from the deserts a jihad of another kind: in the world's oldest monasteries they are leading Christianity in Egypt towards a spiritual renaissance.

Siwa Oasis

Siwa Oasis

Siwa, an oasis in the Western Desert, is 550km from Cairo as the crow flies, and 300km from the sea. From Mersa Matruh on the Mediterranean (*see* p.435) the road climbs gradually onto the desert plateau, a barren expanse of limestone bedrock that is hardly the desert of your imagination: apart from the heavy fall of heat it could be the Siberian tundra, featureless and dreary, the only relief against the level waste an occasional black Bedouin tent crouching off in the distance. Yet the plateau has this peculiarity: from its height of 200m it suddenly falls away to the south in a continuous line of cliffs running west from the Nile and far into Libya. Below, the ground sinks away well below sea level, forming the vast and lifeless Qattara Depression, before rising again, ultimately reaching its greatest height of 1,800m at the mountains of Uweinat in the southwest corner of Egypt, a thousand kilometres from the sea.

The road from Mersa Matruh comes to the line of cliffs just west of the Qattara Depression from where you look down and see not lifelessness but the remarkable and joyous sight of the Siwa oasis, a vastness of date palms, of olive and fruit trees, streams and meadow grasses, 82km long from east to west, between nine and 28km broad. Like Qattara, Siwa lies below sea level (though its

Getting to the Western Desert

Particular travel details are given with each oasis account. What follows here is a general summary.

By Road

All the oases can be reached by paved road and are served by **bus**. The inner oases of Bahariya, Farafra, Kharga and Dakhla are served by the Upper Egyptian Bus Company from Cairo Gateway. For buses to Siwa you first must go to Alexandria or to Mersa Matruh.

Note that the road from Dahkla through Farafra to Bahariya gets potholed and sandswept; the bus service can be erratic, and if driving your own vehicle, check on road conditions in advance. Four-wheel-drive vehicles can be hired with driver/guide, but an ordinary two-wheel-drive car will do unless you want to camp off in the desert.

If travelling by **car** between Bahariya and Farafra, or between Bahariya and Siwa, at least two vehicles should travel together with adequate supplies of water and petrol. **Petrol** is available at Siwa, Kharga, Dakhla and Bahariya, but there is no petrol between Mersa Matruh and Siwa, nor any between each of the inner oases. If you break down, stay by the road and wait until someone comes along; do not go wandering off in the heat.

Desert **excursions** can be booked at each of the oases.

Further Reading

Two books by Dr Ahmed Fakhry, *Siwa Oasis* and *Bahariya and Farafra Oases*, have been published by the American University in Cairo Press. Also published by The AUC Press is *The Western Desert of Egypt: An Explorer's Handbook* by Cassandra Vivian. All three can be purchased at the AUC bookshop in Cairo or ordered at competent bookshops abroad or online.

depression is not so deep: 18m against as much as 134m for Qattara). But unlike the Qattara Depression where there is no fresh water, only a narrow salt marsh at the foot of the cliffs, Siwa sits upon a seemingly inexhaustible source of underground water which bubbles up everywhere, much of it running off to form peripheral lakes of piercing blue, their shallows towards the desert's edge encrusted with shimmering sheets of salt. To the south you see the Great Sand Sea, the legendary ocean of caravans, explorers and lost oases, its rolling dunes like gigantic waves set to crash down upon and drown this green and fragile island.

Some Background to Siwa

Like Aswan to the south and the isthmus of Suez to the east, Siwa marks a natural limit to Egypt. Though it is unknown if Egyptian influence extended this far until the XXVI Dynasty, the oasis has long been a gateway to the world beyond, and together with the coast road it has offered the only sand-free passage between the Shark and the Gharb, the east and west halves of the Muslim world which differ so profoundly. This is evident in the Siwan language, a dialect spoken by the Berbers of North Africa long before the Arabs came this way; at Siwa Arabic is still a second language – the language of the occupation. It is evident too in the way Siwans speak of Egypt as another land, Egyptians as another people; and though they may say we are all Egyptians now, they will also tell you that they are Siwans first. A significant Sudanese minority, the descendants of slaves, lends a further dimension, for

Getting to Siwa

It is no longer necessary to obtain a **permit** from the military authorities to visit Siwa. But to visit the outlying oases of Girba to the northwest of Siwa or Qara to the northeast, or the oases of al-Areg or Sitra along the way to Bahariya, and indeed to travel to Bahariya itself, you will need to apply to Military Intelligence in Mersa Matruh (*see* p.436) or to the Ministry of the Interior in Cairo (*see* p.76).

There are several **buses** a day to Siwa from Alexandria (*see* p.488) in about nine hours: Alexandria to Mersa Matruh takes four hours; there is a one-hour layover at Mersa Matruh for refreshments and taking on passengers, then four hours to Siwa. The best service is the air-conditioned luxury bus (with video, snack service and onboard toilet) operated by the West Delta Bus Company and costing LE35 each way. Departures are daily at 8.30am, 11am, 2pm and 10pm from the al-Moaf al-Gedid station which is near the start of the Alexandria-Cairo Desert Road. Tickets should be bought some hours, preferably a day, in advance. You can also take a bus to Mersa Matruh and then at your convenience, take another bus to Siwa.

Service taxis will cost a bit more and go a bit faster but are likely to be less comfortable and more hair-raising than taking air-conditioned buses. Petrol is available at Siwa. The **train** between Alexandria and Mersa Matruh is not recommended, but if you are coming from Cairo then you might like to travel to Mersa Matruh by the Abela Egypt **sleeper**.

---

they are a reminder that Siwa also once stood at a crossroads of the old trans-Saharan caravan routes.

Until recently the Siwans built on rocky outcrops using a mixture of mud and salt which dries as hard as cement, their mosques and houses piled atop one another like a gigantic African termite mound. The original settlement was at **Aghurmi**, crawling up the flanks of the rock towards the Temple of Ammon at its summit, but it suffered greatly from Berber and Bedouin attacks during the Middle Ages. In 1203, according to the Siwan Manuscript, a local history kept by one of the families of the oasis, the family elders

Itineraries and Practical Matters

The four inner oases – **Kharga, Dakhla, Farafra** and **Bahariya** – lie along a 1,000km circuit road that loops through the desert between Cairo and either Assiut or Luxor. But if you are relying on public transport, you will have to follow the Assiut–Kharga road; there is no bus from Luxor. In either case, allow a week to complete the circuit.

Kharga especially but also Dakhla are fairly developed and modern places at their centres, their interest lying more in their ancient ruins and outlying villages. Bahariya and Farafra are more what you imagine oases to be, and there is the wonderful journey across the White Desert that lies between the two. Bahariya is more in touch with Cairo and the more developed of the two; Farafra is more remote and traditional. These four inner oases have had cultural and political links with the valley of the Nile since ancient times. The most rewarding of all the oases, however, is **Siwa** where they speak of Egypt as almost another country.

It is difficult to combine a visit to the outer oasis of Siwa with the inner oases owing to the bad and unfrequented road between Bahariya and Siwa. This is also true, and especially when travelling from Bahariya to Siwa, because of **military red tape** on this particular leg; the military requires forms to be filled in and fees to be paid, which usually takes longer and is more arbitrary if coming from Bahariya. Otherwise getting to Siwa means a separate journey and involves travelling first to **Mersa Matruh** on the Mediterranean coast.

There is a range of **accommodation** at all the oases from simple huts to air-conditioned hotels. Most of the hotels also serve as local expedition centres which offer tours round their own oasis and often to other oases too; Bahariya in particular is the safari centre of the inner oases. There are **banks** in the main towns of the oases but not ATMs except at Kharga. All the oases are in touch with the outer world by telephone but not necessarily by Internet.

decided to remove a kilometre west to a larger outcrop where they built their new settlement within a strong girdle wall. This was **Shali**, as they called it, the Siwan for town, and entering the oasis along the road from Mersa Matruh it is at the base of Shali that you arrive. To guarantee the security of the population, the Siwan elders forbade anyone to build outside the walls of Shali, but as security also meant an increase in numbers, so storey upon storey was added to the original houses until some were seven and eight storeys high, the houses packed so closely together that the alleyways between them were barely wide enough for a single loaded donkey to pass – if two met, one of the donkeys had to retreat into a house.

The occupation of Siwa in 1820 by soldiers sent by Mohammed Ali ensured that the oasis would be safe against Bedouin raids, so that in 1826 the elders gave permission for houses to be built outside the walls, fanning out around the base of the rock, the origin of the **modern town of Siwa**, while some were built amid the fields and gardens of olives and date palms.

Marriage: Homosexual and Heterosexual

Landownership, however, remained with the heads of families (as it still largely does today), their groves worked on a feudal basis by the *zaggalah*, labourers by day, guards by night (*zaggalah* means club-bearer) – poor young men who in the days when Shali was still inhabited were forbidden to enter within the walls lest they struck up a relationship with a woman, for the *zaggalah* were also forbidden to marry before the age of 40. Instead the *zaggalah* gathered for parties in the fields by night, getting drunk on *labgi*, a fermented juice made from the heart of the date palm, and to the music of flutes, pipes and drums danced with expressively erotic movements and enjoyed homosexual affairs.

Homosexuality was practised among the *zaggalah* to the point of marriage contracts being drawn up between men, which though outlawed in 1928 remained common enough, even if secret, until the end of the Second World War. Older Siwans who recall those days profess to do so with 'shame'; instead young men's fancies are meant to turn to the girls – whom however they rarely get a chance to see and never a chance to speak.

Women live utterly secluded lives, usually staying indoors and emerging only if entirely veiled and robed in blue. For young men wishing to marry, the custom is to go to the annual Siyaha festival at **Jebel Dakrur**, a feast held at the October full moon attended by all the males and the unmarried females of the oasis. The oldest man of Siwa climbs to the top of Mount Dakrur and calls out that God is great, at which moment the gathered thousands break open their parcels of food and begin to eat. This is the moment, too, when a young man spots his girl; she will probably be 12 to 14 years old. He speaks not to her ('she has no idea', as one Siwan put it), rather to his own mother who in turn calls on the mother of the girl, who if she says 'our door is open' means the matter can be carried further.

Over the course of the engagement, lasting perhaps five years, the young man must assemble a dowry, nowadays fifty to a hundred dresses, also ornaments, that he has gone into Alexandria to buy. Likewise the girl's family spends at least as much on clothing and ornaments, but the days of that heavy and elaborate silver jewellery for which Siwa was famous are now gone. Already the 1950s saw the demise of the last silversmiths in the oasis, who lost out to competition from Alexandria and Benghazi, and who lost out also to a flashy new taste for gold. More recently almost the entirety of Siwa's traditional silver jewellery was bought up by a Swiss couple who have opened a museum in their own country. Any 'Siwan' jewellery sold in Khan el Khalili or elsewhere has probably never been anywhere near the oasis.

On the wedding day a tremendous blow-out is laid on by the groom's family, perhaps an entire street of houses taken over for the feast to which several thousands are invited, each guest making a gift of money to help the couple get started. In effect this is a community loan, as in the course of a lifetime the man will in turn be invited to enough weddings to refund the money back into the community. While everyone is partying, the women of the groom's family go to the bride's home to carry her away, to which her female friends and relations offer resistance which is not always feigned. More usually the girl is successfully captured and locked into the bedroom with her husband, the women of his family hovering about outside listening for her virginal scream which together with blood on the sheets confirms the marriage. The groom then joins the party, only returning to his bride some days later. Given all this rigmarole it is perhaps surprising that divorce is common, men boasting that they have been married several times in succession, while many of the girls have been married and divorced once or twice by the time they are 18.

The Changing Oasis

Today the oasis has 15,000 inhabitants, of whom 11,000 live in the town of Siwa that now sprawls round the base of old Shali. Landownership is still feudal and the *zaggalah* still work in the fields, but the prohibition on marriage before 40 has long since lapsed and when a Siwan is asked if homosexuality is still widespread, he will shrug and say it is neither more nor less common than elsewhere in Egypt. This comparison with the rest of the country is significant, as for all the Siwans' sense of apartness they are being drawn quickly and relentlessly into Egyptian ways.

Alexander's Journey to Siwa

Alexander the Great stood scanning the oasis from the heights above Siwa 2,300 years ago. Rocky outcrops rise here and there from among the palms, and atop one stood – and still stands – the Temple of Ammon. It was to consult its oracle, famous for its truthfulness, that Alexander came.

After founding Alexandria, in 331 BC Alexander made the long and dangerous journey, attended only by a small number of men, to consult the Oracle of Ammon, a ram-headed Libyan god associated with Egyptian Amun and Greek Zeus. Only twice in his career did Alexander's route diverge from strategic dictates; the first time he went to Troy, the site of his hero Achilles' glory; the second he went to Siwa.

Writers ancient and modern have adduced a variety of reasons why he should have made the journey, but there is the recurring theme that he went to seek confirmation that he was the son of Zeus. Alexander himself never explained his motive, nor did he ever reveal what he had asked the oracle, nor what he had been told, though from that time on he was shown on coins with the horns of a ram.

Before entering Egypt, Alexander had defeated Darius at the battle of Issus, appropriating the fleeing king's 365 concubines. After Egypt, Alexander would strike at the heart of the Persian Empire, march to the Indus, and appropriate the world. In doing so, he would combine East and West, and the journey to Siwa may have been an early example of this policy of amalgam. Alexander the son of Ammon; the son of Amun; the son of Zeus. It was a usefully embracing pedigree for a young man on the threshold of universal domination.

Even today on an asphalt road the journey to Siwa takes four hours or more from Mersa Matruh on the Mediterranean coast, 230km west of Alexandria. Alexander and his guides and companions took eight days to cover the distance from the coast, getting lost in a sandstorm and after four days having exhausted their water; then clouds gathered and a sudden storm broke, 'not without the help of the gods', and they were able to refill their leather water bottles. They travelled by night along a chain of hills, their way rising and falling through valley after valley and into a final pass which wound down a ravine to the sandy plains beyond. In this pass, beneath the light of the moon and desert stars, the ground was covered with shells which reflected the moonbeams till the whole path sparkled. Bayle St John, a 19th-century traveller, followed Alexander's route and described it at this point: 'A gorge black as Erebus lies across the path, and on the right stands a huge pile or rocks, looking like the fortifications of some vast fabulous city.... There were yawning gateways flanked by bastions of tremendous altitude; there were towers and pyramids and crescents and domes and dizzy pinnacles and majestic crenellated heights, all invested with unearthly grandeur by the magic beams of the moon but exhibiting, in wide breaches and indescribable ruin, that they had been battered and undermined by the hurricane, the thunderbolt, the winter torrent and all the mighty artillery of time.'

Here Alexander lost his way again, but was rescued by a pair of crows, some writers say also by a pair of talking snakes, that set him on the proper track. Bayle St John also saw crows here, and the valley is still known to the Berbers of the region as the Pass of the Crow. Finally he came to the tiny northeastern oasis of Qara almost encircled by cliffs and then, working his way round the blinding whiteness of a salt lake, entered the Siwa oasis.

For both Alexander and the people of Siwa, the sudden arrival must have been momentous. Alexander had survived the phantasms and perils of the desert and was lucky to be alive; the natives had never seen a pharaoh, but here was a Macedonian conqueror. Desert caravans and the occasional pilgrim were its only link with the outside world and, after the oasis was visited by Pausanias in AD 160, it was not visited by a European again until 1792.

In 1985 something astonishing happened. On average it rains in Siwa every 50 years, and then at worst it might rain for a day. But in 1985 it rained for three days running, dissolving the salt that stiffens the Siwans' mud-built houses and reducing 260 homes to ruin. Even so, in years past they would soon have been rebuilt in the old way, not least because their materials and design keep them cool and airy in the most punishing heat. But the year before saw the completion of the paved road from Mersa Matruh, and in 1988 television was introduced. Increasingly exposed to outside influences, the younger men of Siwa refused to 'live in caves' anymore and began slapping up the breeze block houses seen increasingly throughout the oasis.

Despite these changes, Siwa is a conservative place where whatever the *zaggalah* might get up to in the fields, the consumption of alcohol is forbidden as are public displays of affection, while women visitors are asked to cover their arms and legs (and are advised not to wander about in the fields alone).

Oasis Excursions

Buses arrive in the market square of **Siwa town**, which itself presents no mysteries. Almost all the hotels and eating places, also shops selling books and film and a pharmacy, lie immediately round the square or within a few minutes' walk, and after taking a room you can begin to explore. Off to the west of the square and opposite (north) the modern mosque of Fuad, a traditional house entered through a garden serves as a modest **folk museum**, while to the south of the mosque rises the old fortified town of **Shali**, floodlit at night, where you can wander about at will.

Folk Museum
open daily 9–noon, closed Fri; small fee

Bicycles can be hired round the square for excursions about the oasis, or you can arrange for a car at the tourist office (usually cheaper than the tours offered by safari operators based at the hotels). By these means you can reach the salt lakes such as **Birket Siwa** 6km to the west of town, where on **Fatnas island** there is a pool for bathing, or Birket Zeitun 25km to the east. Beyond Birket Siwa, in all about 25km northwest of Siwa town, is **Maraqi** where at a temple some time ago Liana Souvaltzi, an inexperienced and overenthusiastic Greek archaeologist, claimed to have found the tomb of Alexander the Great. Though ancient chroniclers have recorded Alexander's wish as he lay dying in Babylon in Mesopotamia to be buried at Siwa, it is a well attested fact that his body was buried in Alexandria. The discovery at Maraqi was therefore treated sceptically, to say the least, by archaeological authorities throughout the world, and indeed it was soon found that the Greek archaeologist's claim was based on her over-interpretive misreading of a Greek inscription. But of course the Siwans are reluctant to let go of so great a prize and still repeat her nonsense. You can also get to the edge of the **Great Sand Sea** which lies only a few kilometres to the south of Shali, though if you enter it you must make sure not to lose sight of the oasis. Several of these places, such as Birket Siwa and the Great Sand Sea, and all of the sites described below can also be easily visited on foot.

Walking gets you into the rhythm of the place and except perhaps in the middle of the day at the height of summer is comfortable.

A kilometre north of town along the Mersa Matruh road and then off to the right (east) is **Jebel el Mawta**, the Hill of the Dead, a bare orange outcrop pockmarked with tombs dating originally from the XXVI Dynasty to Ptolemaic times but often reused by the Romans. Bits of mummies and shrouds litter the site, and quantities of pottery shards; simply to scuffle about makes the visit worthwhile, and to climb to the top for the view. The **four tombs** at all worth visiting for their murals are on the north side of the hill. The tomb of Niperpathot (XXVI Dyn), the largest in the necropolis, belonged to a man styled 'prophet of Osiris'; on the wall facing the entrance he is shown adoring the god. The tomb of the Crocodile, late Ptolemaic or early Roman, depicts not only the reptilian god Sobek but also gazelles browsing at a tree. The unfinished 4th- to 2nd-century BC Ptolemaic tomb of Mesu Isis was discovered intact in 1940 when during Italian bombing raids the people of Siwa sought refuge at Jebel el Mawta. The most interesting tomb is that of Si-Amun, that is Man of Amun, which belonged to a merchant of the 3rd century BC who, judging from his beard (Egyptians were clean-shaven), was probably a Greek. Though never entirely completed and robbed in Roman times when its paintings were also mutilated, the tomb is well preserved and decorated.

Four tombs
open daily 10–1, closed Fri; free but baksheesh expected by the custodian who will appear if you give a shout

The Temple of Ammon and Jebel Dakrur

A kilometre or so northeast of Siwa town on the road passing by the Siwa Safari Paradise Hotel is the old settlement of **Aghurmi** (signposted on the right) with its crumbled and melted houses. Immediately on entering through the mud-built gate by the towering mud-built minaret you see at the top of the rock the fairly well preserved XXVI Dynasty **Temple of Ammon**. Here because the temple is so small you can be certain of standing exactly on the spot where Alexander himself stood 2,300-odd years ago. Alexander entered into the innermost shrine, a small room about 3m wide and 6m long, and put his questions directly to the god. As at Kom Ombo in Upper Egypt you can see here – unlike Alexander – the means by which the god replied: a narrow passage ran behind the right-hand wall and was linked to the shrine by a series of small holes. Through these the priest could speak as though the god were answering in person. But it was on the temple steps, as Alexander entered or departed, that the words which came to establish Alexander's divinity were spoken. Accounts and interpretations differ. Alexander had come to Siwa via Memphis and Alexandria, and the priest in welcoming him may simply have called him 'son of Amun', that is 'Pharaoh', and this

Lost At Lunch

One of the more foolhardy ventures into the Western Desert occurred in about 524 BC when the Persian king Cambyses, who had conquered Egypt, sent his army across the sands from the Nile valley to subdue the Ammonians at the Siwa oasis. Herodotus tells the story: 'The force which was sent against the Ammonians started from Thebes with guides, and can be traced as far as the town of Oasis [Kharga], which belongs to Samians supposed to be of the Aeschrionian tribe, and is seven days' journey across the sand from Thebes. The place is known in Greek as the Islands of the Blessed. General report has it that the army got as far as this, but of its subsequent fate there is no news whatever. It never reached the Ammonians and it never returned to Egypt. There is, however, a story told by the Ammonians themselves and by others who heard it from them, that when the men had left Oasis, and in their march across the desert had reached a point about mid-way between the town and the Ammonian border, a southerly wind of extreme violence drove the sand over them in heaps as they were taking their mid-day meal, so that they disappeared forever'.

translated into Greek would have been 'son of god'. Another story is that the priest, who would not have known much Greek, addressed Alexander as 'my boy', but saying '*o paidios*' for '*o paidion*'. To Alexander and his Macedonians this would have sounded like the two words '*pai dios*', 'son of Zeus'. In any case, Greeks attached great significance to slips of the tongue, so even if they realized the error it would happily have been taken as a truth. What is historically important is not what was said that day, but what was believed in the four years between Siwa and the Indus, and it is true that Alexander did come as close as any mortal might to being the son of Zeus.

Looking out from the temple of the oracle at Aghurmi you have a wonderful panoramic view of the oasis. A little to the southwest at **Umm Ubaydah** you see a portion of ancient wall, all that remains of another temple of Ammon, this one XXX Dynasty and fairly intact until 1897 when the local governor blew it up for stones to build his house. Farther south you see **Jebel Dakrur**; indeed if you are at the summit of Aghurmi at about midday you will see little white tents suddenly popping up all over its yellow flank. The mystery is explained by following the road from Aghurmi past Umm Ubaydah and the so-called spring of Cleopatra (with whom it has absolutely nothing to do – a dull pool in the middle of the road where people go bathing) to Mount Dakrur (about 4km). Body-sized holes, like shallow graves, are dug in the sandy slope of Dakrur early in the morning so that they grow hot with the mounting sun. Between about noon and 2pm the bodies are put in, 50 or 60 at a time, each stripped naked, Israelis, Libyans, Egyptians, neither nationality nor religion mattering at a time like this, nor sex for they are both male and female, and each is covered over with sand. Only their heads pop out, and this explains the miniature tents which are there to protect their heads from the sun, for these are not corpses; rather, each belongs to a willing supplicant in search of a cure for rheumatism, arthritis and the like.

You would think there was sand enough in Libya, in Israel even, or elsewhere in Egypt, but no, it must be here, for it is not the sand but the method. The method is applied by Abou el Kassem Shouraik, a great bull of a man with a great pot of a belly, who describes himself as a 'professional for burial curing purposes' but looks more like a bordello bouncer. Nice Mr Shouraik's patients will first have spent the night at his adjacent and grotty Amun Hotel and have fasted. Then when they are exhumed after 20 minutes or so, sweating profusely, each must wrap himself in a towelling robe and drink an unpalatable herbal liquid. Nor may they shower for 30 days after. But *voilà*, their pains are relieved, or so they all swear, the men telling you also, *sotto voce*, that they become fantastic lovers.

Tourist Information in Siwa

ⓘ Siwa >
for address, see right;
t (046) 460 2338;
open Sat–Thurs 8–2,
Fri 6pm–8pm

The Tourist Office is near the entrance to Siwa town as you come in from Mersa Matruh, set back a bit on the right-hand (i.e. west) side of the road, near the post office and opposite the Arous el Waha hotel. The Banque du Caire and the Tourist Police are near by.

The Tourist Office is run by the knowledgeable and patient Mahdi Hweiti, who is a native Siwan, a fluent English-speaker and a sociology graduate of Alexandria University. Mahdi has put together a well-presented and useful booklet on the oasis and provides a continuously updated map. If you have questions about hotels, travel, trips round the oasis, Siwan customs, see Mahdi Hweiti. Also ask him about Siwa's future: he fears that growing tourist numbers could have a disastrous impact on both the community and the landscape. For example, tourist numbers are placing considerable demands on Siwa's water supply, which is worrying farmers on whom the Siwan economy depends; locals are also concerned that a lack of fresh water could see Siwa swallowed up by a vast salt lake.

Where to Stay in Siwa

Luxury ($$$$$)

********Adrère Amellal Ecolodge, t** (02) 2736 7879 (this is a Cairo number), *http://adrereamellal.net*. In the lee of the White Mountain (which is what Adrère Amellal means in Siwan) and nestling within its own oasis at Sidi Jaafar, 15km north of Siwa town, this is eco-chic for the rich, among them Prince Charles; extremely expensive even after allowing that room rates include meals, beverages and day trips into the desert. Built by Cairo architect and environmentalist Mounir Nematalla, the Ecolodge is a huge complex resembling a medieval palace constructed out of mud brick with the walls engrained with natural salts so that they shimmer in the candlelight (there is no electricity). For those able to pay for the privilege, this is a relaxing and utopian experience, though next to nothing of the price you pay feeds into the local community.

Moderate ($$$)

*****Al-Babinshal, t** (046) 460 1499. Another of Mounir Nematalla's enterprises, it is constructed in the traditional mud brick style and sympathetically incorporated into the ruins of the old town of Shali. A labyrinth of passageways and stairways connect the cool cavernous rooms which have wooden floors, wooden shutters and exposed palm log supports.

*****Shali Lodge, t** (046) 460 1299. Yet another of Mounir Nematalla's efforts, the Shali Lodge is a mud-brick hotel made with local materials and beautifully designed with arched doorways, terracotta or carved olive wood light shades, and hand-carved furniture with traditional motifs. A bit tricky to find, it is nestled in a lush palm grove a three-minute walk from the main square, down a quiet unpaved road that winds through palm trees – central yet secluded, by day the sounds of chickens, donkeys and the call to prayer, and come darkness the great silence of the night.

***Siwa Safari Paradise Hotel, t** (046) 460 1290, *www.siwaparadise.com*. On the right-hand side and 100m or so along the road to Aghurmi, which runs off from the northeast corner of the market square. Set amid date palms, the place has a variety of accommodation ranging from delightful huts, with fans or heaters available at extra cost, to villa bungalows which cost a little more or less depending on whether you have air conditioning or a fan (a fan is sufficient). There are also proper hotel rooms in the main building with air conditioning and satellite TV. There is a good moderately priced restaurant and a beautiful swimming pool behind, overhung by palm fronds and fed by a natural spring. Rates include half board.

Cheap ($)

There are several cheap and basic hotels on or within a few minutes' walk of the market square in Siwa town.

***Arous el Waha, t** (046) 460 0028. A refurbished and formerly state-owned hotel on the east side of the road from Mersa Matruh and opposite the tourist office, with clean carpeted rooms with fans and bathrooms. Larger suites come with refrigerators. In all cases breakfast is included, and the hotel has a restaurant.

***Palm Trees, t** (046) 460 1703. Situated just where the road to Jebel Dakrur heads off from the east side of the market square, many of its rooms having fan and bath, those to the rear overlooking a small palm garden.

***Cleopatra, t** (046) 460 0421, just to the south of the market square and across from the east flank of Shali. Rooms are clean, some have baths and balconies, fans are available in summer, but as there is a stagnant pond nearby, mosquitoes can be a problem.

You can **camp** almost anywhere in the oasis, but first check at the tourist office.

Eating Out in Siwa

Moderate ($$$)

Al-Babinshal Restaurant on the roof of the al-Babinshal hotel. Chic, romantic and with marvellous views.

Kenouz on the rooftop of Shali Lodge. Has the most extensive menu in town.

Tanta Waa, Cleopatra's Bath. A chic café and restaurant with fruit juice bar and roof terrace, built in mud brick. It serves good food, both local and Italian, salads and chilled smoothies and the like. Walid, the Alexandrian entrepreneur who set up Tanta Waa, cheerfully explains how all this is helping to ruin Siwa: 'In 10 years this will be like Dahab, with Hilton hotels and many tourists.'

Cheap ($)

There are several little restaurants, all cheap, on and immediately off the market square in Siwa town.

The Inner Oases of the Western Desert

A road over 1,000km in length loops far out into the Western Desert from Giza, at first southwest to **Bahariya** and **Farafra Oases**, continuing southeast to **Dakhla Oasis** and then due east to **Kharga Oasis**, finally turning northeast to join the **Nile Valley** near Assiut. The distance between each stage is about 200km, except between

Getting to the Inner Oases

Kharga Oasis

From Cairo (via Assiut) the Upper Egypt Bus Company runs several **bus** services a day from the Cairo Gateway terminus. The journey can take up to 12 hours. In Assiut the bus terminus is a couple of blocks south from the train station. There are at least six buses a day; journey time is 5 hours. Also from Assiut's bus depot you can catch a **service taxi**. Journey time is 3–4 hours. There is no bus service along the road between Luxor and Kharga which, though new, varies in condition from good to poor.

Dakhla Oasis

There are several **buses** per day to Mut from Cairo (15–16 hours) or Assiut (8–9 hours). Also, **service taxis** go to Mut from both Assiut and Kharga. Mut Talata is reached from Mut by taxi or van in 5–10 minutes, or it is a 40-minute walk.

Farafra Oasis

Buses run daily, the journey taking 5 hours, but the service can be erratic, as it can be onwards to Bahariya, in part due to sandstorms. However, there is usually a daily **service taxi** or **minivan** running between Dakhla and Farafra. It starts early, and if there is sufficient demand there may be a second later in the day. From Cairo the bus journey is 5 hours to Bahariya and a further 3 hours to Farafra.

Bahariya Oasis

The Upper Egypt Bus Company runs a daily **bus** to Bahariya from Cairo Gateway, with an additional service on Monday, Wednesday and Friday. The journey takes 5 hours. From Farafra there are daily buses to Bahariya. **Service taxis** make the run if there is demand. Bahariya is the safari centre of the inner oases; most hotels run expeditions into the desert.

Giza and Bahariya where the distance is about 350km. The entire journey can be done by ordinary **car** or, erratically, by **public bus**; the Dakhla–Farafra stretch of the circuit is least well served by any form of transport.

Kharga Oasis

Kharga and Dakhla, being closest to the Nile Valley, have been under greater control by the central authority and this is reflected in the number of monuments and relative prosperity of these areas. The ancient Egyptians were in full control of Kharga Oasis from the XVIII Dynasty; it was an area of exceptional fertility, and the Greeks and Romans called it the Great Oasis. Decline set in during the Middle Ages, though Kharga remained an important centre on the *Darb el Arba'in*, the **Forty Days Road** – named for the time it took camel caravans to reach the Nile from Darfur, Sudan.

Today attempts are being made to raise the water table, and wells, some of them 1.5km deep, have been drilled. The water is estimated to have been in the ground 25,000 years, the time it has taken to percolate through from Lake Chad. The New Valley project has proved more difficult and costly than anticipated, and the intended mass transfer of population, mostly landless fellahin from the Delta and the 'Old' Valley, too ambitious. Nevertheless, at Kharga Oasis there is a population of around 60,000; model villages have been built, new roads laid, and electricity (which often blacks out) installed. Kharga is not the most romantic of the oases, but it is the easiest to get to and there is much of interest nearby.

In the town itself there is the **Museum of the New Valley**, containing finds ranging from VI Dynasty stelae to 12th-century Islamic pottery from Dakhla and Kharga. Just to the north of Kharga, on the west side of the Assiut road, lie the ruins of the ancient town of **Hibis**. The site has not been excavated except for the central **Temple of Amun**, dedicated to the god by Darius I, whose soldiers met defeat at Marathon and whose namesake Alexander would defeat 150 years later. It has been reconstructed and makes a picturesque scene amid groves of date palm, in contrast to the edge of desert situation of so many temples along the Nile. On a ridge 1km to the north is the Christian **necropolis of al-Baqawat**. The mud brick mausolea, some surmounted by domes, were painted inside with symbolic figures or biblical themes, and a few are well preserved.

It is a 3- or 4-hour journey from Kharga to Dakhla, with spectacular scenery en route – cliffs, wadis and crescent dunes.

Dakhla Oasis

Dakhla Oasis is visited for the sheer beauty of the place, its peace, its pleasant walks and the kind-heartedness of its people. For this reason it is enough to arrive at **Mut**, one of the two main towns of the oasis, and sit around in the spacious central square.

There are a few ruins in the area but you need not trouble yourself with these; every other building in Mut contains a **coffee house** where men sit playing backgammon and smoke waterpipes

The New Valley

Ninety-three per cent of Egypt lies on either side of the Nile Valley and the Delta and overwhelmingly this is desert wasteland. No more than one per cent of the country's population inhabits these regions, and the oases, found only in the Western Desert, are home to the majority. The four inner oases are artesian depressions and obtain their water from vast though local underground supplies. More romantically however they have been thought to mark the line of a prehistoric branch of the Nile and in 1958 the government decided to bring this area back to life, to create a New Valley in parallel with the present Nile Valley. Things really got underway in 1997 just north of Abu Simbel when the digging of the Toshka canal began, its purpose to carry overflow water from Lake Nasser towards the oases of Kharga, Dakhla and Farafra, with the intention of turning the Western Desert into a 'New Valley' which would increase Egypt's arable area by 28 percent, and where there are plans to grow cotton, wheat and early-season grapes and citrus fruits. Power stations, factories, packing plants and housing estates have been built with the intention to extend Egypt's agricultural land by many thousands of square kilometres. But some experts have expressed serious doubts about the viability of the New Valley project, and indeed the unintended consequences of the High Dam are a warning. Meanwhile the way of life at the inner oases remains for the most part simple and traditional, though change is accelerating, not least because of the increase in tourism.

and the muezzin wails to the sudden Saharan darkness from his crenellated mosque.

There are **springs** nearby at Mut Talata, one above blood temperature, the other a little cooler, where you can join the local people for a pitch-dark wallow under the desert stars.

Still within the oasis, 27km to the west, is the other principal town, **al-Qasr**. This is the original fortified settlement, silent and ageless, where the Mamelukes rebuilt the main mosque on Ayyubid foundations and its misshapen domes rise over low mud brick and white plaster houses.

A kilometre southwest of al-Qasr there is a **Roman cemetery**, and 2km farther, at **Deir al-Hagar**, there is a picturesque ruined **Roman temple** dedicated to Amun, Mut and Khonsu, the Theban Triad.

Farafra Oasis

Unlike the other oases, **Farafra** does not give the impression of sitting in a depression but, instead, of standing on an endless plain of light-coloured limestone rocks. The impression is owed to the fact that of all the major oases Farafra is the smallest, yet it sits within one of the largest depressions in the Western Desert. From the south the descent is hardly noticeable, but there are steep cliffs along the northwest rim. The limestone landscape all round dazzles, and much of the depression is filled with blown sand which here forms *seif* dunes.

The one habitation is **Qasr el Farafra**, a village of mud brick that stands on an island rising out of the surrounding desert flatness. It is pleasant to follow its narrow streets to the olive groves and gardens. At the centre is the mud-brick fortress, *qasr*, which gives the place its name; it partly melted away during a fierce rainstorm in 1950. East of the fortress is **Badr's Museum**, a fanciful desert mansion in which Badr exhibits his strange paintings and sculptures; he has shown in Britain, Germany and France. **Bir Sitta**

The Sex Life of Sand Dunes

The dunes in the northern end and western parts of the desert form in long continous ridges or 'swords' (*seif*), but here in the southeast are the crescent (or *barchan*) dunes – the two are never found together. The barchan is a remarkable phenomenon, weighing up to 450 million kilos, standing perhaps 30m high and advancing forward in the direction of its horns which may be as much as 365m apart. The two widely separated horns always remain exactly level with one another, and the dune keeps its simple crescent shape intact with extraordinary persistence even while it is on the move, and while it is passing over such large obstacles as rocks, small hillocks and villages. It is seemingly an organism existing in a slow elementary way, and there is evidence that it is capable of a sort of reproduction whereby baby dunes are formed in the open 100m or so downwind of the horn of a fully grown parent. (As to how dunes form, why they assume one shape and not another, and for details of their sex lives generally, see *The Physics of Blown Sand and Desert Dunes* by R.A. Bagnold; also there is his *Libyan Sands: Travel in a Dead World*.)

(Well Six), 4km west of town, is a lovely spot to swim and camp out. Despite New Kingdom inscriptions found in the Nile valley referring to both Bahariya and Farafra, the oldest sites at Bahariya date only from the XXVI Dynasty, while there are no ancient remains at Farafra at all. That leaves you with nothing else to do except at evening to gaze upwards and let the black sky transfix you with its milliard stars.

Bahariya Oasis

Leaving Farafra towards **Bahariya**, the scenery is spectacular as you pass through the vast and brilliant 'white desert' with its weirdly eroded sandstone outcrops. In the near rainless environment of Bahariya Oasis, dates, olives, citrus fruits and onions of high quality are grown. The administrative centre is **Bawiti**, a village of white-walled houses decorated with patterns in blue and red, and with a 6th-century Coptic church.

A ridge overlooking Bawiti to the southwest, called **Qarat al-Farargi** (Ridge of the Chicken Merchant), contains subterranean galleries of bird burials, mostly hawks and ibises, the detritus of a Thoth and Horus cult which flourished here from the XXVI Dynasty through to Roman times. The locals, who these days raise turkeys, imagined the galleries were filled with chicken bones. Farther southwest at a separate community called Qasr al-Magisbah there is a **Temple of Alexander the Great** with reliefs of the conqueror.

About 40km south of Bahariya, just off the main road to Farafra, is the small **oasis of al-Hayz**, with a Coptic church, all that remains of a once thriving Christian community. The dunes here are blackened with stones containing ferrous oxides. Beyond lies the 'white desert'. **Excursions** run to all these places from Bahariya; ask at the Tourist Office or any hotel.

ⓘ **Kharga >>**
at the north end of town, by the Mabrouk fountain and near the Tourist Police; **t** *(092) 792 1206,* **f** *(092) 792 1205; open Mon–Thurs and Sun 8.30–2, and sometimes eves 7–10 Fri*

Tourist Information in the Inner Oases

For information on accommodation, safaris, money exchange and so on, visit the local tourist offices at Kharga, Dakhla and Bahariya.

The Kharga **Tourist Police, t** (092) 792 1367, are at the north end of town, near the tourist office and the Museum of the New Valley, on Kharga's Sharia Nasser, as are the Bank Misr and the Banque du Caire (ATM).

Mut is the chief town of the **Dakhla oasis**. Bank Misr, near the Tourist Office, is where you can change money or draw cash on a Visa card.

Bawiti, the chief town of **Bahariya**, has a bank, post office and police station by the bus stop. The **Tourist Police, t** (02) 847 3900 (open daily 8–8), are 1km to the east along Sharia Gamal Abdel Nasser. The Tourist Office can point you to safari operators; many hotels in the Bahariya oasis double as expedition centres.

Where to Stay and Eat in the Inner Oases

Kharga Oasis

All accommodation falls within the cheap ($) range.

Mut (Dakhla) >
Midan el Tahrir, t (092) 782 1686; open 8–2 daily and some eves 6–9

Bawiti (Bahariya) >>
by the bus stop, t (02) 847 3039; open daily 8.30–2 and some eves 5–8

****El Kharga Oasis**, Sharia Nasser, **t** (092) 792 4940, at the north end of town (the end at which you enter from Assiut) near the tourist office. Kharga's best hotel. Rooms are large, comfortable and air-conditioned, have bathrooms and also balconies overlooking a palm garden. Its **restaurant** is also the best place to eat. Also you can **camp** in the hotel grounds and use the hotel's showers.

****Hamadalla**, **t** (092) 792 0638, Sharia Abdel Moniem Riad, east off Sharia Nasser. Clean and comfortable, though rooms are often dark. Its double rooms have private bathrooms, and some rooms have air conditioning, others balconies.

The Waha, Sharia el Nabawi, off Sharia Nasser in the south part of town, **t** (092) 792 0393. The cheapest place in town, basic and a bit dingy; pay extra for your own bathroom.

Dakhla Oasis

Al Tarfa Lodge, at Al Mansura, midway between Mut and al Qasr (15km from each), **t** (092) 9105 007, *www.altarfa.travel* ($$$$$). An eco-friendly lodge and spa set within a desert sanctuary; highly sophisticated and aimed at the top-most reaches of the international market. Built in rustic Saharan style, the lodge nevertheless has all the comforts of a luxury hotel, including a courtyard **restaurant** set round an ancient Roman well, an outdoor pool, a spa with sauna and heated indoor pool. The lodge also offers guided walks, horseback and camel riding, desert excursions by beast or 4-wheel-drive vehicle, and many other activities. Al Tarfa can arrange travel to the lodge from anywhere in Egypt.

***Mebarez**, 2 Sharia El Tharwa el Khadraa, **t/f** (092) 782 1524 ($$). The best hotel in the vicinity of Mut, situated just outside town on the main road west towards Mut Talata, with clean rooms, fans, and some with private bathrooms. The **restaurant** is one of the better places to eat in Mut.

Anwar Hotel, Sharia Basateen, **t** (092) 782 0070 ($); in Mut, facing the gardens immediately north of the old town. A friendly family-run place, its clean rooms are above the popular Anwar restaurant.

Gardens Hotel, **t** (092) 782 1577 ($), a couple of blocks from the bus station in Mut. Popular with backpackers. Shared bathrooms.

Farafra Oasis

Badawiya, **t** (092) 751 0060, *www.badawiya.com* ($$$). 300m north of town, this is a lovely place with 12 loft-style and 8 single-floor rooms with bathroom, fan and mosquito net as well as 13 newly-built suites with living and sleeping area, bathroom, some with fireplace, mosquito net and air conditioning. The hotel has a swimming pool, a restaurant with rooftop terrace, which is supplied with organic food from its own farm.

El Waha, **t** (satellite) 012 720 0387, near the post office and Badr's Museum ($). Small hotel, basic rooms, some with bathrooms.

White Desert, **t** (satellite) 012 255 7263 ($). A former government rest house, 1km north of Qasr el Farafra. Its six triple rooms are tolerably clean, some with bathrooms but no fans.

Bahariya Oasis

*****International Hot Spring**, **t** (satellite) 012 321 2179, *www.whitedeserttours.com* ($$$), on the eastern edge of Bawiti, north of the Tourist Police. Large rooms with bathrooms, also dorm rooms, and a **restaurant**.

Western Desert, **t** (02) 3847 1600 ($$$). New German-run hotel in the centre of Bawiti, opposite the Popular Restaurant. Large rooms with bathrooms, satellite TV, air conditioning or fans, and balconies. Internet access.

***Alpenblick** (meaning 'Alpine View'), **t** (02) 847 2184 ($). The oldest hotel in Bawiti, German-run, clean, pleasant garden, centrally located just south of the post office and tourist office, but running to seed.

El Beshmo Lodge, on the edge of the palm groves on the north side of town, **t** (02) 3847 3500, *www.beshmolodge.com* ($). Comfortable rooms with bathrooms, restaurant, spring-fed swimming pool.

Monasteries of the Wadi Natrun

The place called Scete is set in a vast desert, and the way to it is to be found or shown by no track and no landmarks of earth, but one journeys by the signs and courses of the stars. Water is hard to find. Here are men made perfect in holiness, for so terrible a spot could be endured by none save those of austere resolve and supreme constancy.

A pilgrim's account of the late 4th century, *Historia Monachorum*

Coptic Monasteries of the Wadi Natrun

Christian asceticism first most widely flourished at a place once known as Scetis or Scete, now the **Wadi Natrun**, its famous monasteries standing as citadels of the Coptic faith through all the adversities of the past 1,700 years. After years of decline, all four monasteries (St Macarius, St Bishoi, the Syrians and Baramous) are now thriving monastic communities.

The 200km **Desert Road** between Cairo and Alexandria, completed in 1936, passes within sight of the Wadi Natrun, and it is only a 90-minute drive from either city. A depression 35km long running southeast–northwest and never more than 8km wide, the wadi takes its name from the salt lakes lying 6m below sea level; drying up in summer, they leave a deposit of sodium carbonate (natron), once used in mummification and glass making.

Evolution of the Monastic Communities

As you approach, the monasteries give the impression of enormous arks for the faithful sailing in a desert sea. But their high walls were raised only in the 9th century to protect them from Bedouin raids. The original communities, at one time about 50 in all, were much humbler foundations. St Macarius the Great, a disciple of St Antony, retreated here *c.* 330 and soon had his followers. About ten years later, on the site of Deir el Baramous, they established the first *laura*, that is an unenclosed settlement of scattered cells around a central nucleus, each nucleus providing a church for monks and hermits to visit on Sundays and feast days, a bakehouse and common eating place, and perhaps a hostel for pilgrims. This pattern reflected the individualistic approach of St Antony and his followers to the ascetic life, and stands in contrast to the highly regulated coenobitic monasticism which Pachom instituted from the start in Upper Egypt (*see* 'Sohag', p.250). There the need for each community to possess a wall was laid down in the Pachomian rules, its purpose probably to reinforce the sense of community as excavations at the White Monastery reveal that it would have had only limited defensive capabilities. In the Wadi Natrun, as at the Red Sea monasteries of St Antony and St Paul, the centripetal attraction of each nucleus, abetted by the need for defence, drew

Getting to the Monasteries

The **Desert Road** runs between Cairo and Alexandria – though nowadays 'Desert Road' is something of a misnomer, for cultivation has been developed along much of its route, and tomatoes, bananas and olives are a common sight. About equidistant from the two cities is the **Rest House** where you turn off to the west for the Wadi Natrun. From Cairo, the Desert Road is reached by turning off the Pyramids Road just before the Mena House Hotel. The Rest House is 95km away. Just beside it, a road runs west 3km to the village of **Bir Hooker**; there you keep right for the northernmost of the monasteries, **Deir el Baramous** (14km), or you go left for **Deir Anba Bishoi** and **Deir el Suriani** (both 7km). The signs may not be obvious and you might have to ask. The southernmost monastery, **Deir Abu Maqar**, can be reached from the last two (8km), though it is easier to turn west off the Desert Road 13km south of the Rest House – the road goes straight to the gate (8km).

Buses and **service taxis** plying between Cairo and Alexandria normally stop at the Rest House; in any case you can ask to be dropped off there. You can then get a taxi from the Rest House to the monasteries; otherwise it is a very long walk. But for several people travelling together it makes more sense to hire a taxi in Cairo or Alexandria and go for a half or full day.

Further Reading

For a history and description of the monasteries, read *Monks and Monasteries of the Egyptian Deserts* by Otto Meinardus, published by The American University in Cairo Press.

---

the communities together and gave them their present aspect. As well as the eventual walls, fortifications included a central keep (*qasr*), the earliest extant that of Baramous dating possibly from the 7th century, followed by the 9th-century keep at Suriani, and those at Bishoi and Maqar from the 11th or 12th century.

The Monasteries Today

The monasteries have compromised with the encroaching world to varying degrees, none more so than Deir Anba Bishoi and Deir

Access and Fees

There is no charge to visit any of the monasteries (make a donation), nor is permission required except in the case of St Macarius (Deir Abu Maqar), which requires that you present yourself with a letter from the Coptic Patriarchate in Cairo (next to St Mark's Cathedral, 222 Sharia Ramses, Abbassiya, **t** (02) 282 5374) or the Coptic Patriarchate in Alexandria (at the St Mark's Cathedral enclosure, Rue Eglise Copte, **t** (03) 483 5522).

The Coptic Church goes in for a great deal of fasting and a monastery may be closed or partly closed during a fast: the 43 days preceding Coptic Christmas (7 January); the 3 days commemorating Jonah in the whale (the Monday, Tuesday and Wednesday of the second week before the Fast of Heraclius); the 55 continuous days of the Fast of Heraclius and Lent (the one runs into the other); from Pentecost (seventh Sunday after Easter) to 12 July; and the 15 days (7–22 August) commemorating the Assumption of the Blessed Virgin Mary. Normal opening times are given for each monastery below, but if you intend visiting during a fast, phone their Cairo bureaux to check if there are any restrictions.

St Macarius: Open daily but only by permission of the Patriarchate in Cairo or Alexandria (*see* above); closed during Lent; **t** (02) 577 0614.

St Bishoi: Open daily: in summer, 7am–8pm; in winter, 7am–6pm; **t** (02) 592 4448.

Suriani: Open in summer Mon–Fri and Sun 9am–7pm, Sat 9am–5pm; in winter Mon–Fri and Sun 9am–6pm, Sat 9am–3pm; **t** (02) 592 9658.

Baramous: Open daily: in summer 7am–8pm; in winter 7am–6pm; **t** (02) 592 2775.

Each of the monasteries is open to both men and women, but neither shorts nor revealing clothes should be worn by either sex. Men, but not women, can stay overnight; written permission must be obtained from the particular monastery's Cairo bureau.

Monasteries of the Wadi Natrun

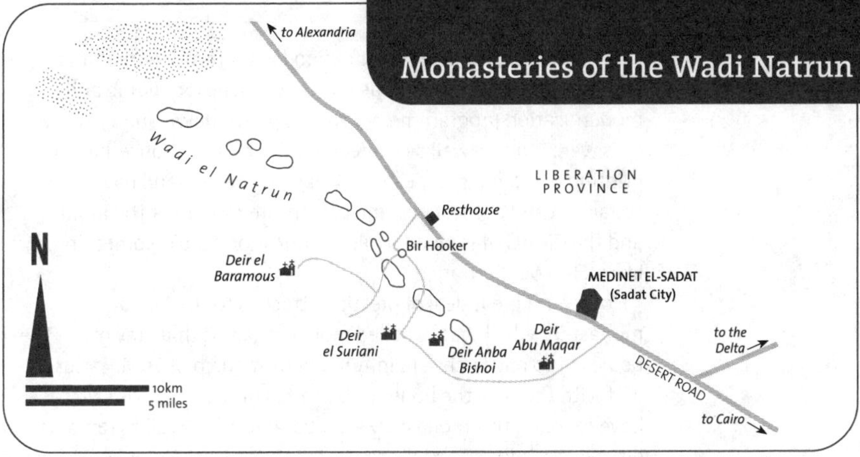

The Monasteries Today

The monasteries have compromised with the encroaching world to varying degrees, none more so than Deir Anba Bishoi and Deir Abu Maqar, though the latter has recently taken to shutting itself off from tourists by demanding a letter of introduction from the Patriarchate. Deir el Suriani and Deir el Baramous give a greater sense of the monasteries' isolation in the past. The Desert Road, and now the surfaced roads which lead up to all four monasteries, have made change inevitable. But change has been deliberate as well, instigated by Pope Shenouda III, enthroned in succession to St Mark the Evangelist as 117th Patriarch in 1971. Responding to a renaissance in Coptic consciousness last century, Shenouda (who was himself a monk at Deir el Suriani and for several years lived the life of a solitary in desert caves) has encouraged monastic involvement in parish life. The days when monks were characterized by their anti-intellectualism and occasionally even gross ignorance are over: today they are recruited from the universities and the professions, many of them having been doctors, chemists, engineers or architects. If anything, however, there has been an increase in spiritual discipline, and it is as though, even here in the Wadi Natrun with its Antonian origins, the Pachomian Rule has taken new hold. Shenouda is responsible too for the revival of the traditional black cowl embroidered with 12 crosses representing the 12 apostles. A stitched-up tear running from the crown to the forehead recalls St Antony's expulsion of the devil. The design of the stars is different for each monastery. Only one monastery resists the cowl; that is Maqar, where the monks wear a simple round cap.

it was inhabited by only six monks; today there are more than 100 monks and the monastery has seen a full-scale rebuilding and modernization programme. Much was pulled down and 150 new cells were built, as well as a refectory, library, guesthouse, bakery, printing press and garages. Great tracts of desert land have been reclaimed and cows, sheep and poultry are raised. For the monks and the Church it is wonderful; to the visitor it looks something like a Club Méditerranée.

However, a great deal of prestige attaches to the Maqar monastery, which has supplied more patriarchs than any other. The bodies of 10 patriarchs are interred in the church of St Macarius, and with them lie the bones of Macarius himself (who is said to have founded this monastery after Baramous) as well as remains discovered in 1978 and felicitously identified by the monks as those of John the Baptist.

After entering the courtyard of the monastery, you pass beneath a pointed arch down steps to the earlier level. Straight ahead is the much rebuilt **church of St Iskhirun**, what is left of the original dates from the 14th century, and to your right is the **church of the Forty-Nine Martyrs**, commemorating those monks who in 444 freely submitted themselves to death at the hands of Bedouin rather than hide. Wider than it is long, it is a church without a nave and may once have been a western extension of the church of St Macarius, which from the arch is on your left.

Though the **church of St Macarius** too has been extensively rebuilt, it is clear that it was once a magnificent structure. There were marble columns and decorations of fine stucco work and painted frescoes, though now the pillars are of brick, and plaster covers everything. The site may well have been the nucleus of the original *laura*; the central sanctuary of St Benjamin and to its left the sanctuary of John the Baptist are the oldest survivals, dating from the 7th to 9th century. The **central sanctuary** deserves a close look for its large dome and on a squinch beneath it the winged cherub surrounded by the four creatures of the Apocalypse. This is probably 11th-century, and of similar date to the finely painted medallions on the wooden frame of the arch at the entrance to the sanctuary; the first illustrating the embalming of Christ, the second showing his body being carried to the tomb, the third with the heads of Christ, St Peter and possibly St John the Evangelist, and the fourth showing Christ and another figure.

Beyond the churches is the three-storey **keep**, entered at second-storey level across a drawbridge from an adjacent building. Over 20m square and 16m high, it is a massive crenellated structure with inward sloping walls pierced occasionally by small windows. At almost every monastery you go to, you will be told that the keep

God's Eternity in the Desert

Many of the fundamental doctrines of Christianity were first shaped within sight of the sea at Alexandria. For about 250 years, from the end of the 2nd century AD to the break between Egypt and the wider Church at the Council of Chalcedon in AD 451, Alexandria was the great centre of theological learning and controversy. At first Greek in outlook, a part of the wider Mediterranean world, Alexandria's voice was heard throughout the Roman Empire.

With the translation of the Bible into Coptic during the 3rd century, Christianity spread beyond the metropolis and other Greek-speaking communities to the native population throughout Egypt. It was a century and more of persecution, beginning in 202 under Septimius Severus, continuing in 250 under Decius, and reaching its most awful climax under Diocletian from AD 303. Nowhere in the Roman Empire suffered more than Egypt, where hundreds of thousands were martyred in a final holocaust.

So many were killed on a single day that the axe, blunted and worn out by the slaughter, was broken in pieces, while the exhausted executioners had to be periodically relieved. No sooner had the first batch been sentenced, than others from every side would jump on to the platform in front of the judge and proclaim themselves Christians. They paid no heed to torture in all its terrifying forms, but undaunted spoke boldly of their devotion to the God of the universe and with joy, laughter and gaiety received the final sentence of death.

Eusebius (an eyewitness), *History of the Church*

A few sought refuge in the desert, but it was only after Constantine's Edict of Toleration in AD 313 when the need to flee had passed, that the great exodus began. Martyrdom had offered a direct route to God; now the way would be found in the desert. This was a peculiarly Egyptian response, for the first solitaries and monks were natives nearly to a man. In an astonishing act of anarchy, Egyptians in their thousands, rejecting any interference by the hierarchy of state or church, deserted the towns and cultivation for the barren wilderness with the aim of shedding all worldly possessions and distinctions, wishing if possible even to shed their sense of self, the better to unite with God. Through them Christianity explored another dimension, as they strove to embody eternity in their lives. St Antony said, 'Let no one who hath renounced the world think that he hath given up some great thing. The whole earth set over against heaven's infinite is scant and poor.' That quiet voice from the Egyptian desert, which said that each living moment carried its eternal freight, was to have as profound an impact on the Western imagination as all the Greek sophistication of Alexandrian thought.

is Justinian (6th century) and in every case they are wrong. At Maqar they go one better and claim 5th-century origins; in reality it is 11th- or 12th-century. As you enter you notice the recess in the outer wall for receiving the drawbridge, and above it, within the keep, the winch for raising it. On the ground floor were oil and wine presses, a mill and access to a deep well. On the first floor is the **church of al-Adra** (the Virgin) of recent date, though the screen is perhaps 12th-century. As is the case in almost every monastic keep, the top storey (the second floor here) has a **church of the Archangel Michael**; it is at the north end nearest the stairway, and possesses a beautiful 14th- or 15th-century screen. But the church is especially notable for its paintings: on the north wall St Michael, on the south wall a gallery of saints martyred under Diocletian. Next along the corridor is the **church of SS Antony, Paul and Pachom**, founders of the eremetic and monastic life, with their paintings along the north wall. Last is the **church of the Hermits**, with portraits of nine on the walls, among them the exceptionally hirsute Anba Nofer who during the 4th century wandered the desert for 60 years, covering his nakedness with his beard.

The Monastery of St Bishoi

At **Deir Anba Bishoi** lies the uncorrupted and unwithered body of the monastery's 4th-century founder, reported to extend its arm to shake the hands of true believers. St Bishoi, in turn, had once washed the feet of Christ when the Saviour appeared before him, and was permitted to drink the water afterwards. Next to him in the church of St Bishoi (dating to the 9th century but thoroughly restored in 1957) lies the body of his friend, Paul of Tamweh, who achieved a reputation for sanctity after seven times carrying his ascetic practices to the point of death. Six times he was restored to life; on the seventh he was left to rest in peace. Otherwise the monastery is unremarkable, with much new building and an air of administrative bustle. The entire monastery has been so often restored as to be without interest, and almost all the iconography is blandly modern; the oldest paintings are of the 12 apostles in the **church of St Michael** at the top of the keep.

Deir Anba Bishoi became famous when Pope Shenouda III was incarcerated here by President Sadat in September 1981, its gates sealed and guarded by soldiers. Sadat had been facing growing dissent against his rule; now he arrested over 3,000 people, mostly rank and file Islamists, but also leading lawyers, journalists, politicians and religious figures from whatever quarter. A month later Sadat was assassinated by Muslim fanatics. Only in January 1985 did President Mubarak allow Shenouda his freedom, though the pope's attachment to the place has since been evident and he often comes here on retreat. The number of monks has increased to about 100, additional cells have been built, new chapels opened in the keep, conference facilities and administrative offices built, and guest rooms refurbished.

The Monastery of the Syrians

Deir el Suriani was founded later than the other monasteries of the Wadi Natrun, in the 6th century, after a quarrel within Deir Anba Bishoi in which the greater number of monks adopted the Gaianite heresy which undermined the human nature of Christ. This in turn reflected on the status of the Virgin Mary, for her popular devotional title of Theotokos, Mother of God, depended on Christ taking his human flesh from his human mother.

The minority decamped and established their opposing monastery half a kilometre to the northwest, stressing their

Deir Anba Bishoi, from Napoleon's Description de l'Egypte, *1798*

orthodoxy by calling it the Theotokos Monastery of St Bishoi. Later, when their cause had won through, they returned to their original monastery; in the 7th or 8th century the Theotokos monastery was purchased by a Syrian for the use of his devout countrymen, hence its familiar name, though its association with the Virgin Mary remains close.

It is Deir el Suriani that most suggests a desert ship, its undulating ochre walls riding a wave of sand. Domes, towers and crosses make the superstructure, and palms wag within like prizes bound for Kew Gardens. Unfortunately, the graceful line of the northern wall has been spoilt at its western end by the abutment of a tatty block of guest rooms built in the 1980s. You pass through this northern wall by a small doorway into a forecourt, then left into the courtyard before the 10th-century **church of the Virgin**, al-Adra, remarkable for its doors across the choir and central sanctuary, and the frescoes in the semidomes of the choir.

During all periods of Egyptian history wood has been a precious commodity, and has nearly always had to be imported. The **doors** here at al-Adra are ebony and have been further enriched with ivory inlay. Inscriptions date the doors to the early 10th century; the work is probably Egyptian. Along the top row of the four door panels leading on to the choir are holy figures, from left to right St Paul, the Virgin, Christ and St Mark. The sanctuary doors have six panels, Christ and the Virgin on the central pair, St Mark the Evangelist and St Ignatius (representing Alexandria and Antioch) on the second and fifth panels, while on the first and sixth panels, badly damaged, are the patriarchs Dioscorus of Alexandria (444–54) and Severus of Antioch (512–18), champions of the monophysite cause.

During restoration work that has been going on since 1995 it has been discovered that **wall paintings** in the church have covered older layers, four layers in all, dating from the 7th to the 13th century. Taken all together, the layers of paintings uniquely illustrate the development of Coptic art over the course of six centuries. The oldest layer has been painstakingly restored *in situ*, while the overlaid paintings have been removed to a specially-built exhibition place which mimics the form of Al-Adra and stands just behind it. Among the scenes painted on the semidomes of the church itself, and the later versions in the mimic church behind, are beautifully rendered and richly coloured versions of the Annunciation, the Nativity and the Dormition of the Virgin.

At the west end of the south aisle is a **grotto**, said to have been the cell of St Bishoi long before the church was built; supposedly a tunnel leads from here to Deir Anba Bishoi. According to legend, the hook in the ceiling here is where the saint attached himself by the hair to keep him upright through four days of prayer until he saw Christ and washed his feet. In an ebony reliquary, which a monk might show you, the bits and pieces of numerous Desert Fathers are kept company by the hair of Mary Magdalene.

The church of the Forty-Nine Martyrs abuts al-Adra; ancient paintings have been uncovered there too. Farther east is the church of Sitt Mariam, the Cave Church, with good **icons**; while as usual the keep has a church of the Archangel Michael on the top storey.

Pope Shenouda III was a monk at Deir el Suriani. In fact, for a while he was the librarian.

Lord Curzon's Visit

It was in the keep that Lord Curzon, a visitor to Suriani in 1837, discovered a number of ancient manuscripts now in the British Museum. He recorded his stay in his *Visits to Monasteries in the Levant*.

Seeking permission to explore, Curzon resorted to strategem: 'Next to the golden key, which masters so many locks, there is no better opener of the heart than a sufficiency of strong drink. I have always found it invincible; and now we sat sipping our cups of the sweet pink rosoglio, and firing little compliments at each other, and talking pleasantly over our bottle till some time passed away, and the face of the blind abbot waxed bland and confiding; and he had that expression on his countenance which men wear when they are pleased with themselves and bear goodwill towards mankind in general.'

At last the key was turned, and on the top floor Curzon discovered 'a superb manuscript of the Gospels, with commentaries by the early fathers of the church; two others were doing duty as coverings to a couple of large open pots or jars, which had contained preserves, long since evaporated'. Curzon broached the subject of money. '"Ah!" said the abbot. "Another cup of rosoglio," said I; "help yourself". "How much will you give?" asked the abbot. "How much do you want?" said I; "all the money I have with me is at your service". "How much is that?" he enquired. Out came the bag of money, and the agreeable sound of the clinking of the pieces of gold or dollars, I forget which they were, had a soothing effect upon the nerves of the blind man, and in short the bottle and the bargain were concluded at the same moment.'

The Monastery of Baramous

About 14km west of Bir Hooker is **Deir el Baramous**, the oldest monastery of the Wadi Natrun. Baramous is Coptic for 'the two Romans', Maximus and Domitius, sons of the emperor Valentinian, who came to Scetis to find God. In their cave they ate little and prayed all day, and indeed hardly slept, praying through the night as an angel with a sword of fire fought off demons darting round the younger brother's head like flies. As they sang the Psalms, flames rose to heaven from their mouths. Achieving perfection first, the older brother died; for the younger the battle was waged three days longer, then he too died. St Macarius witnessed their fearful struggle, and it was for these two young Roman 'martyrs without blood', as he called them, that Baramous was named.

SS Maximus and Domitius are said to be buried beneath the **church of al-Adra**, parts of which date to the 9th century. Recent restoration has meant large areas of the church being covered with new plaster, though as layers of old plaster are removed in the nave ancient frescoes are being laid bare. Parallel to the church is the old refectory. There are four other churches too, one of St Michael in the 7th-century keep, but none are of much interest.

What is special about Baramous is its atmosphere. From the parapet along its 11m-high walls there is the contrast of views, down into the monastery with its central courtyard shaded beneath a vine arbour, and out into the vastness of the desert.

Of Devils, Scorpions and God

The monks rise at four in the morning for five hours of chanting and liturgy before beginning the day's work, some of them in the fields they have brought to life near the monastery walls. It is only then, late in the afternoon, that the monks are free. Some return to their cells for personal devotions, others sit talking and smoking beneath the grapes, as accomplished in idleness as they are in the discipline of prayer. You do not realize it at first, but they are like soldiers only momentarily resting on their swords.

A monk attaches himself to you as your guide and shows you a shirt emblazoned with blood, dotted here and there with unmistakable crosses, explaining that a troubled man had come to the monastery, and approaching the altar – 'the womb of Mary' – had shrunk back in horror. In a strange voice the man cursed the monks, who anointed him with oil on his wrists and head ... and then witnessed the devil erupt from his body, splattering the shirt with blood as he went. 'I saw this', says the monk, the shock and struggle made real by his trembling words.

It is wonderful to be a child and to be told incredible bedtime stories. It is even more wonderful to be an adult and to sit beneath a vine trellis sipping tea within ancient walls as the sun falls into the Western Desert and to hear the incredible from a bearded man in a long black robe with a starry cowl pulled over his head.

With the monk you might then walk 2km out into that desert to the cave of Shenouda's predecessor, Pope Kyrillos VI. It is now something of a shrine, marked by wooden crosses and adorned inside with icons. It stands on the edge of an escarpment, where your guide, his black robe flapping in the desert wind that rises before nightfall, points westwards into the featureless void. 'We have five hermits out there, 15km to 20km into the desert, each one out of sight of the other. They are very holy; they speak with scorpions.' You then recall those demons flitting about the head of the young Roman 1,600 years ago, the fiery sword, the Psalms flaming from the brothers' mouths. 'It is very beautiful out there, very spiritual', says the monk, and you know he is not talking about the view, but about those solitaries he had pointed to, lifetimes spent alone in caves where apart from scorpions there is nothing to talk to except God and the devil. 'Would you become a hermit?' you ask him. 'To live with yourself in the desert and to find God you must have humility. I am trying.'

Behind you the monastery is sinking rapidly into the darkness and with a momentary shiver you feel how desperately your detachment depends on something to cling to. You turn to go, and at Baramous you push some money into your guide's hand. He gives it back and reproves you: 'We do not ask for money.' 'You didn't ask; it is a gift,' you reply, but he will not take it. 'Money comes to us by miracles; God provides for us.' You wonder how consciously disingenuous he is being and you think of the farm

Where to Stay and Eat at the Monasteries

To stay overnight at the monasteries (for which there is no charge, though a donation would not go amiss) you should enquire at the Coptic Patriarchate (*see* p.420). Otherwise there is accommodation at the **Rest House** or one of the nearby **motels** ($$$$–$$$) on the Desert Road.

It is possible to **eat** at the **monasteries** if you are staying there. There is also a **restaurant** and **café** in the Rest House, and a **café** on the opposite side of the road, as well as many stands selling fruit, sweets and drinks.

equipment and the water pumps which even the monk would not have said were delivered from heaven down a pillar of flame. And then you think also why you had offered it – in payment, to balance the account between your world and his, and you see the impossibility.

The City of St Menas

Farther along the Desert Road from Cairo to Alexandria, at Bir Abu Hush, a turning (west) is signposted in English and Arabic for the **monastery of St Menas**, that is Deir Abu Mina. About 30km northwest the modern Coptic monastery with its two belfry towers hoves into view. Built in 1959, the relics of St Menas were transferred here three years later. The monastery sits within high stone walls, its building concrete and ugly though luridly decorated inside. But it is not for this that you come, rather for the early Christian site near by.

The Cult of St Menas

Menas was a young Egyptian officer who was martyred in 296 during his service with the Roman army in Asia Minor because he would not abandon Christ. When his legion moved back into Egypt his friends brought his ashes with them, but at this spot the camel carrying the burden refused to go farther. Menas was buried and forgotten, but later a shepherd noticed that a sick lamb that crossed the spot became well. Then a sick princess was healed. The remains were exhumed and a church built (350) over the grave. The church was incorporated into the great Basilica of the Emperor Arcadius, added at the beginning of the 5th century, and soon houses, walls and cemeteries were built, a city in the desert. The secret of this rapid growth was water; there were springs in the limestone that have since dried up. But in its heyday the cult was carried by caravans across the deserts (Menas is always shown between two camels) and extended throughout the Mediterranean, pilgrims coming from as far as Italy and France

Getting to St Menas

There are several **bus** departures each Friday and Sunday between 7.30am and 1pm (journey time: 1 hour) from the square in front of Alexandria's Misr Railway Station, which will bring you right up to Deir Abu Mina (the monastery of St Menas). On other days the service terminates at Bahig from where you have to take a taxi.

In Alexandria an agent such as Misr Travel or Thomas Cook can tailor-make something for you – or you can hire a **taxi** – perhaps including a trip along the Mediterranean coast west of Alexandria to Abusir and Alamein.

---

for 'the beautiful water of St Menas that drives away pain'. Souvenirs of these pilgrims' visits, little earthenware flasks with the saint depicted between the camels, have been found all over Europe and Africa – and even in the Thames at Windsor.

The City Lost and Found

As the water gave out, the city declined, though in the 11th century the Arab geographer El Bekri could still describe 'superb and beautifully constructed palaces' and 'the cathedral of St Menas, an enormous building ornamented with statues and the most beautiful mosaics ... Over the church is a dome covered with paintings which, they say, represent the angels ... The whole countryside round about is planted with fruit trees which produce excellent fruit and there are also many vines which are cultivated for wine' – this when water was already scarce. A century later, when the wells finally did dry up, the city and its vineyards simply disappeared beneath the sands. For nearly 1,000 years El Bekri's description was regarded as the fantasy of an oriental geographer, until, in 1905, the site was excavated almost single-handedly by Monsignor Kaufmann.

Since then Menas has enjoyed a revival. In 1943, the Coptic pope issued an encyclical letter ascribing the saving of Egypt from invasion at the Battle of El Alamein to 'the prayers to God of the holy and glorious martyr Menas, the wonderworker of Egypt', which was something else Rommel never counted on. Menas has been, in fact, a very practical saint. A paralytic man and a dumb woman both happened to implore his help at the same time. During the night, the saint came to the man in a vision and said, 'Do not be afraid, but fasten your lips to the dumb woman's. Then get into bed with her and you will be cured.' Although astonished, the paralytic followed instructions: the dumb woman awoke and screamed; the paralytic, alarmed at being caught, fled.

Visiting the Remains of the City

The remains of the city of St Menas appear at first as slight mounds and clearings a few hundred metres beyond the monastery. The ground is littered with fragments of marble paving, granite and basalt columns and shards. The foundations of the primitive church and the encompassing basilica are clear, though little rises to any height.

The **crypt** in which St Menas was buried is down a marble staircase in the original church which is incorporated into the portico of the Basilica of Arcadius. A baptistry, octagonal within a square, its walls standing to 14m with a font in the central courtyard, is to the west. North of the basilica are the hospice and sacred baths with hot and cold cisterns. Surrounding the whole area are the remains of the pilgrims' town. Most of the artefacts and decorations found during excavations can now be seen at the Graeco-Roman Museum in Alexandria (*see* p.502).

The Mediterranean Coast West of Alexandria

But what impresses me most in the scene is the quiet persistence of the earth. There is so little soil about and she does so much with it. Year after year she has given this extraordinary show to a few Bedouins, has covered the Mareotic civilisation with dust and raised flowers from its shards. Will she do the same to our own tins and barbed wire? Probably not, for man has now got so far ahead of other forms of life that he will scarcely permit the flowers to grow over his works again. His old tins will be buried under new tins. This is the triumph of civilisation, I suppose, the final imprint of the human upon this devoted planet, which should exhibit in its apotheosis a solid crust of machinery and graves.

E.M. Forster, *Pharos and Pharillon*, 1923

Alexandria stands on a limestone ridge that runs westwards parallel to the coast, on one side the burning turquoise of the Mediterreanean, on the other the marshy greens of **Lake Mariut**, the ancient Mareotis. A luxuriant civilization flourished here in Ptolemaic and in Roman times, plantations of papyrus and the giant water bean, its stalks three metres high with great cup-shaped leaves, growing round the margins of the lake, vineyards, fruit trees and olive groves planted along the lakeside slope and towns and villages strung along the spine. The wealthy had their summer villas here, and at holidays the lake was aflutter with the sails of pleasure-seeking Alexandrians, who would ply from island to island to refresh themselves at simple tavernas on beer made from local barley and the sweet white Mareotic wine before drifting off to the shallows where the giant bean leaves offered shade and privacy for their amusements.

The lake had been filled by fresh water from the Canopic branch of the Nile but as this and the connecting channels silted up,

Getting to the Mediterranean Coast

Buses and **service taxis** run along the coast road to points west of Alexandria; you could ask to be put down at Abousir (not that anyone will have the slightest idea that there is a temple near by; it is just before the road which turns left, south, for Bahig).

By Air

Egyptair flies from Cairo to Mersa Matruh twice a week in summer only.

By Train

From Alexandria a slow and grotty train runs west to Alamein (4 hours) and Mersa Matruh (8 hours). From Cairo direct to Mersa Matruh there are daily air-conditioned trains, while Abela Egypt runs a sleeper service 3 times a week (9 hours).

By Bus

For Alamein take the non-express bus from Alexandria to Mersa Matruh (departures every one to two hours) from Midan el Gumhuriya outside Mahattat Misr, the main railway station in Alexandria; get off at the Rest House. Getting back can be a problem, however, as the buses are usually full. For reaching Mersa Matruh, *see* 'Siwa', p.xxx; note that in summer there are also additional services running to Mersa Matruh only.

By Taxi

From Midan el Gumhuriya outside Mahattat Misr (Alexandria's central railway station) service taxis depart frequently to points along the coast (about 4 hours to Mersa Matruh). If going to Alamein insist on being dropped at the Rest House near the museum, not dumped on the main road.

Tours

Misr Travel and Thomas Cook in Alexandria run full-day tours to **Alamein**, the former returning via Ikingi Mariut, a desert resort on the south side of the lake, the latter taking you on (20km) to the beach resort of **Sidi Abdel Rahman**.

---

communication with the interior, water supply and irrigation all suffered, and by the 12th century Mareotis had become a salty swamp, the soil of centuries of vegetation eroded by wind and rain, leaving the hills stony and bare. Though briefly flooded with sea water by the British at the beginning of the 19th century to isolate the remains of Napoleon's army holed up in Alexandria, the lake remained dry until 1892. Plantations of olives, carob and date palms were afterwards established and programmes initiated to improve the Bedouins' barley yield.

Otherwise for a few weeks in February and March after a light touch of rain the landscape exploded with wildflowers, a display described by Forster as 'one of the finest in the world', and so it has continued into recent years. But now there is a new desolation, not the tins and barbed wire that Forster had feared (that happened farther west at Alamein), rather an explosion of unregulated development both all around Lake Mariut and along the coast, not that long ago pristine and beautiful, now all the way from Alexandria to Mersa Matruh an unbroken calamity of holiday resorts for the army, professional guilds (lawyers, doctors, etc.) and others for whom money is no bar to tastelessness.

Abousir

Following the coast road about 40km west from Alexandria you come to **Abousir**, or rather you see on your left atop the limestone ridge an ancient stone tower and then a few hundred metres along the rectangular bulk of a temple enclosure wall. A road running south just west of the temple leads off to Bahig for the City of St Menas.

The tower, though called **Burg el Arab** (the tower of the Arabs), is in fact Ptolemaic and was a giant funerary monument (the burial chambers are underneath) but which also served either as a lighthouse or as a watchtower and signalling station. Similar aids to shipping were built all along this coast from Alexandria to Cyrenaica (eastern Libya) during Ptolemaic times as an aid to shipping. Its interest is that it was modelled on the Alexandrian Pharos, square at the base, then rising as an octagonal shaft and cylindrical at the top, but only one-tenth the size of its gigantic contemporary. It was restored just after the Second World War, and a spiral wooden stairway has been put in, allowing you to climb to the top. Where the ridge falls away southwards into the expiring extremity of Mariut, you can discern on its slope the indifferent remains of **Taposiris Magna**, its name preserved in Abousir, and traces of a causeway that connected the town with the desert, probably pierced with arches like the Heptastadion at Alexandria to allow the passage of boats.

A short walk west along the crest of the ridge brings you to the high enclosure walls of the Ptolemaic **temple of Osiris**, the finest monument to have survived north of the Pyramids (and like the tower visited only rarely). The vine was first discovered at Mareotis, according to Greek writers, from where its cultivation spread throughout the Mediterranean, the story perhaps linked to the worship here of Osiris whom the Greeks identified with their wine-loving god Dionysus, and who like Osiris had undergone death, dismemberment and resurrection. Alexander stopped at an earlier temple on this site on his way to Siwa, and Cleopatra and Antony, she dressed as Isis, he as Dionysus, would sail from Alexandria along the length of the lake to celebrate the Osiran festival. You enter through the intact east pylon whose interior stairway takes you to the top of the walls, but looking down into the court you see that except for a few remnants the temple itself has disappeared, instead at this near end are the foundations of an Early Christian church. On the opposite side of the lake off the road to Bahig is the **model village of Burg el Arab**, built by an Englishman just after the First World War like a miniature medieval Italian town, circular and fortified (and incidentally the inspiration for Justine's 'summer palace' at Burg el Arab in *The Alexandria Quartet*). The place was originally intended as the capital of the eastern district of the Western Desert Province frontier administration, where the Bedouin could congregate to market and their women could gain an income making carpets for sale in Alexandria, while the desert round about was planted with olives, vines, carobs and other trees of commercial value – the purpose all in all to provide a means for the tribes to gradually meet the dread of civilization face to face. You may have difficulty finding it, for civilization has lately arrived in full force, and the place, now falling apart, is hidden behind a clutter of suburban tattiness. Near by, the president of Egypt has a summer house.

Alamein

On 17 July 1942, Auchinleck had won a historic battle. It had been as desperate, difficult and gallant as Wellington's repulse of Napoleon at Waterloo... He saved the Middle East, with all that this implied for the general course of the war. It was the turning point.

Corelli Barnett, *The Desert Generals*

Alamein

Alamein is 106km west from Alexandria, and scene of that series of battles which from July to November 1942 halted Rommel's thrust to the Delta and reversed the tide of war in northern Africa. On 1 July, as the Afrika Korps arrived at Alamein, the British fleet left Alexandria and withdrew through the Suez Canal into the Red Sea or sailed to Haifa; clouds of smoke rose from the chimneys of the British military headquarters in Cairo as their files were hastily burned; Cairenes, certain that the British were fleeing Egypt, besieged the railway station in a rush to get away; and the outside world took it to mean that Britain had lost the Middle East. But Rommel was overextended, his men exhausted, and the majority of his supplies consigned by the British Navy to the bottom of the sea. General Auchinleck coolly gauged the situation and won the historic battle.

Later, Montgomery took command of the Eighth Army: 'a man of dynamic personality and of supreme self-confidence ... a past-master in showmanship and publicity; audacious in his utterances and cautious in his actions ... He was the right man in the right place at the right moment', and from 23 October to 5 November he decisively defeated the Germans and put Rommel on the run. Within little more than six months the Germans and Italians were cleared from Africa altogether.

Alamein museum
adm LE15

There is a **museum** at Alamein (café adjoining), with tanks, heavy artillery and other debris left behind after the battles, displays of uniforms and tableaux showing how soldiers of the contending armies lived in desert conditions, though best are the photographs of the time. There is also some guff about the Egyptian contribution to the war, which as a noncombatant neutral with fascist sympathies at the highest political and military levels was, fortunately, next to nil. Just to the east is the starkly beautiful British and Commonwealth Cemetery, while immediately east is the small Greek memorial; farther west is the grandiose tower marking the Italian cemetery and a suitably monstrous gothic blockhouse put up by the Germans for their dead.

The Bedouins, in the wadis near the shore, watching the battle wage backwards and forwards along the tableland, consider the protagonists mad. They see first one army and then another retiring in haste, leaving behind a wonderful amount of loot. The Bedouins steal forward and they sell this loot to the conquering army. A few months later the victors are vanquished; again the Arabs find great booty ... After the battle, in which tanks are set on fire and their occupants fried alive, and the fluid field of battle moves on, the Arabs arrive to pick up, among the useless relics and impedimenta of destruction, the gold rings, wristwatches, cameras and souvenirs from the stiffened bodies lying in the sun ... Occasionally they are punished with the loss of an eye, hand or arm; for the Germans sometimes leave behind them fountain pens and thermos' which, when opened, ignite the secret fuse, so that an explosion follows.

Cecil Beaton, *Near East*, 1943

Mersa Matruh

If we consider Egypt a book as poems we can say that Marsa Matrouh is the best poem in that book. If we consider Egypt a musical symphony we can say that Marsa Matrouh is the best tune in that symphony. If we look at Egypt as an exhibition of world painting we can say that Marsa Matrouh is the best tableau. In short Matrouh has the best beautiful sceneries in Egypt.

Matrouh Governorate: The Prospect & The Future, The Sharm & the Baeuty [sic] (government tourist brochure)

Mersa Matruh is an ugly and depressing place, the final blot on this once magnificent Mediterranean coastline before you escape inland to the relatively untarnished (for a few years yet) delights of **Siwa** (*see* p.403) – about the only place of 'sharm and baeuty' in the entire Mersa Matruh governorate which takes in the whole of northern part of the Western Desert. Nor are the beaches at Mersa Matruh a pleasant experience unless you like garbage and watching women bathe fully clothed or are a woman who is dying to be like them. The one exception to this rule, and the only really pleasant place to stay, is the Hotel Beau Site whose private beach is open to non-residents. On the tip of the harbour arm is the **Rommel Museum**, where the Desert Fox, when the going was good and the beaches were clean and Mersa Matruh was a pretty little fishing port, is said to have gone for a dip. On this slender pretext there are maps, a desk and his greatcoat to see (possibly the one he went bathing in).

Rommel Museum
open daily 10–5; small fee

In fact you have to get well away west from Mersa Matruh to stand any chance of enjoying the **beaches**, though nowadays even Ubayyad Beach (14km), where the army has built one of its dreadful resorts, and Agiiba Beach (24km), an otherwise lovely cove, are both crowded throughout the summer – but come out of season and you will have them to yourself.

Tourist Information on the Mediterranean Coast

It is no longer necessary to obtain a permit from the military authorities to visit Siwa but you do need to apply to the **military authorities** in Mersah Matruh to visit the outlying oases of Girba to the northwest of Siwa or Qara to the northeast, or to take the road between Siwa and Bahariya, or to visit the oases of al-Areg or Sitra along the way, or to take the difficult road south from there to Bahariya. The Tourist Office can direct you, but it is easy enough to find: at the far eastern end of Sharia el Shatta, one block back from and parallel to the corniche (open daily 8–2 and 8–11pm). You will need a photocopy of your **passport**, including your Egyptian visa, which you can have done along Sharia Iskandariya. No charge is made for the permit. Or you can go to the Ministry of the Interior in Cairo (*see* p.76).

ⓘ Mersa Matruh >>
Corniche (at the junction with Sharia Iskandariya, the main drag running north–south through the town), **t** *(046) 493 1841; open daily 8.30–7 summer, to 5pm winter*

Where to Stay and Eat on the Mediterranean Coast

Alamein

****El Alamein, **t** (046) 468 0140, **f** (046) 468 0341 ($$$$$). This is in fact located in Sidi Abdel Rahman and is the best place to stay in the area: a resort hotel with a beautiful white sandy beach on your doorstep and Alamein 20km to the east. Reserve as far ahead as possible during summer.

***Atic, **t** (046) 410 6183, **f** (046) 410 6182 ($$$). On the coast road 90km west of Alexandria and 16km east of Alamein, with its own beach and pool.

Mersa Matruh

All you need to know to find your way around Mersa Matruh is that the **corniche** runs along the Mediterranean and that Sharia Iskandariya runs perpendicular to it through the centre of town. Most hotels are on the corniche or in the first three parallel streets behind.

***Beau Site, Sharia el Shatee, **t** (046) 493 2066, **f** (046) 493 3319 ($$$$). On the corniche 2km west of Sharia Iskandariya. This is the most agreeable place to stay in Mersa Matruh. Its **restaurant** is first-rate, and the hotel has its own private, and clean, beach.

***Riviera Palace, Sharia Gallai on the corner of Sharia Iskandariya, **t/f** (046) 493 3045 ($$$). A comfortable place with a good **restaurant** situated a block back from the corniche.

Arous el Bahr, Sharia Corniche, **t (046) 493 4420, **f** (046) 493 4419 ($$). Balconied rooms overlooking the Mediterranean and a decent **restaurant**.

Ghazala, Sharia Alma Rum, **t** (046) 493 3519 ($). A basic but very clean place about eight blocks back from the corniche, immediately east off Sharia Iskandariya. No hot water, and for a shower they provide a bucket of cold water to pour over your head.

The Suez Canal and the Red Sea

In days gone by, many visitors to Egypt were not more than passers-through the Suez Canal, disembarking from their ship at one end, racing to Cairo to see the Pyramids, then racing back to board ship as it reached the other end of the canal. Today, the process is reversed and visitors who have flown into Cairo will sometimes take a day trip to the canal to watch the ships sail through. Otherwise, one or more of the canal cities of Port Said, Ismailia and Suez might be visited en route to the Red Sea coast or Sinai.

The Red Sea is famous nowadays for its crystalline waters, its coral reefs and multitudes of beautifully coloured fish; it has become a centre for diving and watersports. But it also has a much older history, and it is worth going back into the mountains to visit some of the most ancient Christian monasteries in the world.

16

Don't miss

1. Hypnotic proces?sion of ships sailing through the desert
   The Suez Canal at Ismailia or Port Said **p.441 and 443**
2. Trudging down for water, beans and dates, and trudging up again for God and the view
   Cave of St Antony **p.449**
3. Watch tourism destroy the environment
   Hurghada **p.452**

See map overleaf

The Suez Canal and the Red Sea

p.402

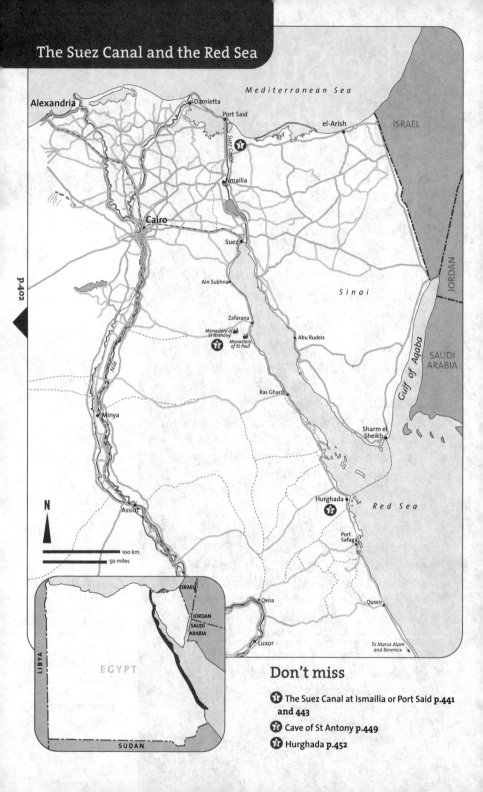

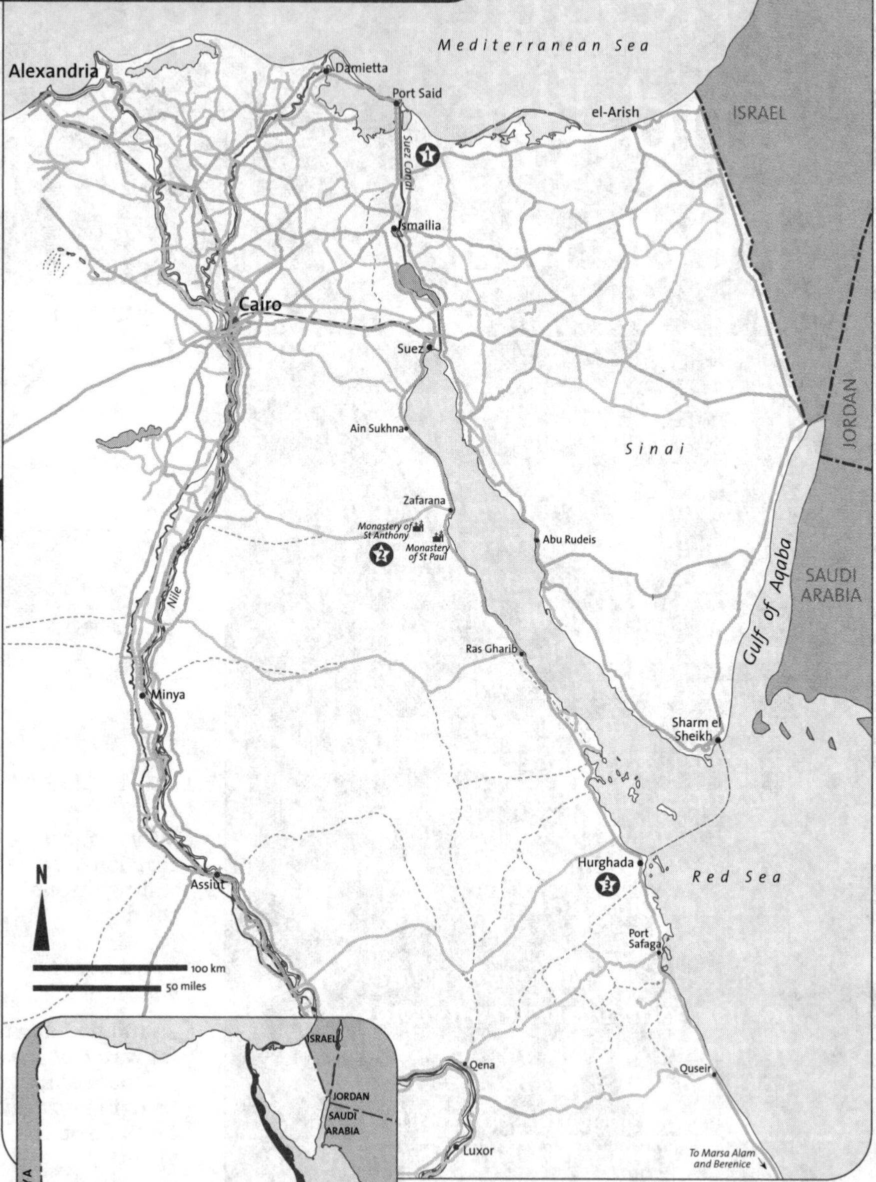

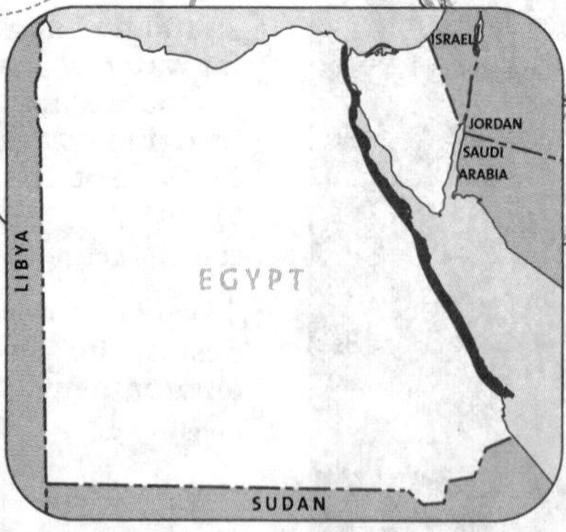

Don't miss

1. The Suez Canal at Ismailia or Port Said **p.441 and 443**
2. Cave of St Antony **p.449**
3. Hurghada **p.452**

The atmosphere, temperature and colours have been so exquisite and fresh; compared to India, where all is aged and complex, it is like a world in its morning. I always did argue Suez is beautiful, and today it agreed with me, and hour after hour we have stolen through white desert, edged with pale pink or purple hills.

E. M. Forster, passing through the Suez Canal on his return from India, 1922

At its narrowest, the Isthmus of Suez is 144km long and apart from dividing the Mediterranean from the Red Sea is also the divide between two ancient patriarchal sees, those of Alexandria and Jerusalem, the one becoming ultimately Coptic, the other remaining within the Greek Church – which explains why St Catherine's Monastery in Sinai is, unlike all those Egyptian monasteries west of the canal, Greek Orthodox.

The Suez Canal

The History of the Canal

The idea of a Suez canal is by no means a modern conception. The earliest authenticated attempt to connect the Red Sea with the Nile, and thereby with the Mediterranean, was made by Necho (XXVI Dyn). Herodotus says that 120,000 Egyptians perished while engaged in the work which was abandoned when an oracle warned that only the Persians would profit by it. And indeed it was Darius I (he of Marathon) who completed it a century later, *c.* 500 BC. Tradition, however, reports a canal as early as the reign of Tuthmosis III (XVIII Dyn). Darius' canal (which ran from the Red Sea to the Great Bitter Lakes and then westwards to Bubastis, modern Zagazig) was maintained by the Ptolemies and improved by Trajan. It was later restored by Amr, the Arab conqueror of Egypt, in order to supply Arabia with corn, but was abandoned a hundred years later to starve out Medina which had risen in revolt against the caliph. The Venetians, the Ottomans and the French under Louis XIV all contemplated its renewal. It was during Napoleon's sojourn that for the first time a canal was proposed direct from the Red Sea to the Mediterranean, but his engineer wrongly calculated a difference of 10m between their two levels and the plan was dropped.

Construction of the Modern Canal

The present canal, at 167km, is the third longest in the world and the longest without locks. Its construction is owed to **Ferdinand de Lesseps**, formerly French consul in Cairo, who obtained a firman from the khedive Said (whence Port Said) granting a concession to run 99 years after the canal's completion. Work began in 1859, two-

Getting to the Suez Canal

By Train

Trains depart from Cairo for Ismailia (2hr 30min), Port Said (4hr) and Suez (2hr 30min), but they are dirty, crowded and slow – you would do better to travel by bus.

By Road

Frequent **buses** from Cairo to the Canal cities are operated by the East Delta Bus Company (Sharq el Delta) and leave from the Cairo Gateway terminal; they knock at least half an hour off the train times. Costs are LE12 to Ismailia and Suez, LE16–20 to Port Said. There are also buses from Alexandria (al-Moaf al-Gedid station) to the Canal cities costing LE20.

Service taxis from Cairo cost a little less than the buses; they depart from the al-Kulali terminal.

From the Canal cities you can continue into Sinai or along the Red Sea coast by frequent buses or service taxis.

thirds of the finance coming from private investors, one-third from the new khedive, Ismail (after whom Ismailia was named). Twenty thousand Egyptians dug the canal and many thousands died from cholera and accidents. The official opening took place on 17 November 1869 amid much fanfare. The Empress Eugénie, wife of Napoleon III, was the principal attraction after the ditch itself. The expense of the canal contributed largely to Ismail's bankruptcy, his shares purchased by the British government in 1875, and Egypt falling under the authority, in effect, of British and French bankers. It was this event which led Ismail to speak the words which serve as an ironic commentary on the canal's significance: 'My country is no longer in Africa; we are now part of Europe. It is therefore natural for us to abandon our former ways and to adopt a new system adapted to our social conditions.'

The Suez Canal Crisis

Nasser wanted to build a new dam at Aswan which would increase farming land by one-third, and went to Britain, France and the United States for loans. These were refused because of Nasser's willingness, during the height of the Cold War, to deal with both East and West. In July 1956 Nasser surprised Egypt and the world by sending Egyptian troops into the Canal Zone and announcing the **nationalization** of the Suez Canal Company. The lease on the Canal still had twelve years to run, and nationalization of the Suez Canal Company made little financial sense for Egypt. Once compensation had been paid to its mostly French and British shareholders, there would not be sufficient revenue from Canal users' fees to finance construction of the High Dam at Aswan, yet that was the excuse Nasser gave for seizing the company.

In fact Nasser's motives were political, for by challenging the Western powers and realizing Egypt's last great nationalist aim of gaining operating control of the Canal, he hoped to bolster his own position which as yet was far from secure. Britain and France were alarmed; most of their oil supply came through Suez, and they also feared for their other interests in the region. Israel was fearful over the loss of a buffer. Action against Nasser became a shared aim, and Israel, France and Britain formed a secret alliance to invade Egypt with the intention of regaining control of the Canal and overthrowing Nasser's regime. The military operation was a success, but when the new postwar superpowers America and the Soviet Union humiliated Britain and France by demanding their withdrawal, Nasser was handed an unexpected triumph and became the hero of the entire Arab world. As for the Aswan High Dam, in the event it was paid for with loans from the Soviet Union to which Egypt was obliged to give due allegiance.

The **Six Day War** in 1967 closed the canal for eight years. This time the British, French and American governments proved more cooperative and aided in its dredging. But meanwhile the canal towns were impoverished by the closure and devastated by Israeli shelling, Suez even being entirely evacuated. This was one reason for the massive increase in Cairo's population. In 1975 President Sadat officially re-opened the canal. As many as 90 ships pass through every 24 hours with an average transit time of 15 hours. They carry with them 14 per cent of the world's trade. There are plans to double the canal's width, and the Egyptian-Israeli peace has permitted the canal cities to get back on their feet.

To Ismailia

Suez Canal

From Cairo the most direct route to Ismailia is across the desert (128km), though in one direction it is worth taking the slower road via Bilbeis, following the course of the **Ismailia Canal** (which in part follows Darius' ancient canal) through well-cultivated countryside for fascinating glimpses of Delta life. This was the biblical land of Goshen. About 50km along the desert road is **Medinet Ramadan** (Ramadan City), one of the new desert cities intended to relieve the capital's overpopulation. It is a good example of the inanity of city planners. Where traditional architecture would be cheap, familiar and insulating against the fierce heat, here amid the desolate expanse are pointless highrises. One knows that the lifts will break down, the air conditioners will fail, and these poor pioneers will have to sweat their way to the uppermost storeys, there to roast alive in their oven-like rooms. Farther along on the right, a **tank monument** indicates the farthest advance of the Israeli counter-attack during the 1973 war.

Ismailia is the most agreeable of the canal cities, at least towards the canal where you will find the old and well-tended European quarter; on the other side of the railway line is the broken down and fetid part of town where the greater number of Ismailia's 500,000 people live. The **bus and service taxi stations** are opposite one another on Sharia Gumhuriya in the shabby part of town not far from the **railway station.** Immediately opposite the railway station is Sharia Ahmed Orabi which leads straight down to Sharia Mohammed Ali. At the intersection of Sharia Mohammed Ali and Sharia Ahmed Orabi is **de Lesseps' house**, a small villa and supposedly a museum, though as it is now encompassed by a larger villa used as a government rest house you may have to talk your way in through the side entrance. His carriage is in the garden, and one small room contains his effects – a bed, desk, cross and picture of Empress Eugénie. In the entrance hall bookshelves there is a complete *Description*, that famous survey of Egypt published by Napoleon's savants.

Sharia Mohammed Ali parallels the Ismailia or Sweetwater Canal (dug in the 19th century and successor to Darius' ancient canal) through town; with the canal on your right after leaving de Lesseps' house head east and after 250m you come, on your left, to Sharia Sultan Hussein with George's restaurant (Greek, good fish) on one side and the Crocodile Inn on the other. Continuing along Sharia Mohammed Ali, the Ismailia Canal veers off to the right, as does a road which brings you to the Mercure Forsan Island Hotel and several beach clubs on the Suez Canal; if instead you continue straight on, you soon come to the interesting **museum** designed like a Ptolemaic temple, with pharaonic and Graeco-Roman artefacts, and with exhibits concerning Darius' canal. In front of it is a garden with stelae, describing Darius' conquest of Egypt and the digging of his canal between the Nile and the Red Sea. In this favoured waterside quarter along the edge of Lake Timsah and the canal are the suburban villas of a tropical England. Here among the neat gardens, the clean and silent streets, drawn shutters keep time at bay, as though the English were still inside, drinking tea and gin. At the **beach clubs** on the canal you can loll on the sand, enjoy some refreshment, and if you are feeling energetic take the opportunity to dodge the passing supertankers for a swim to Asia and back. A plume of black smoke rises from behind a ridge of sand, then you see the bridge of a ship and slowly its vast form slides into view; the constant procession is hypnotic.

Ismailia Museum
open daily 9–4, closed Fri 11–2; adm LE3

6 October 1973

Only when looking across the canal at the steep sand embankments on the other side do you realize what a bold achievement it was for the Egyptians to have overrun the Israeli positions on 6 October 1973. Even with surprise and meticulous preparation it would seem suicide. In preparation, the Egyptians had ordered from abroad powerful water cannon for the Cairo fire department. The Bar Lev (Israeli defence) line was least well defended at those points where the embankments were steepest, and against these sand slopes the Egyptians trained their hoses, carving gullies up which they scrambled. The pride they won back that day, after their humiliating 1967 defeat, allowed them ultimately to sign the peace treaty with Israel.

Where to Stay in Ismailia

****Mercure Forsan Island, t (064) 391 6316, *www.mercure.com* ($$$$). As much a resort as a hotel – has fully equipped rooms, plus tennis courts, pool and private beach, with waterskiing and windsurfing facilities.

Crocodile Inn, 179 Sharia Saad Zaghloul at the intersection with Sharia Sultan Hussein, t (064) 391 2555, f (064) 391 2666 ($$). The one decent hotel in the centre of town, it has air-conditioned rooms with balconies, a **restaurant and a 24-hr coffee shop.

**Nefertari, 41 Sharia Sultan Hussein, t (064) 391 2822 ($$). With air conditioning and private bathrooms.

**Isis Hotel, Midan Orabi opposite the railway station, t (064) 392 2821 ($). Has brightly decorated clean rooms with fans.

Port Said

In 1860 it did not exist, but by 1890 it had achieved the distinction of being called the wickedest town in the East, and vice and evil were rampant in the streets. It was always used by writers of sensational novels as the setting for Oriental romances, and it was at Port Said that the hero became hopelessly entangled with a female vampire, the heroine was ravished by an oily Sheikh or Bey in flowing robes, and even the villain met his match in depravity and bestiality.

Major C.S. Jarvis, *Oriental Spotlight*, 1937

Suez Canal

Port Said ('Bur Said' in Arabic), 80km from Ismailia at the north end of the canal, has a population of 600,000 and is the busiest of the canal cities. The place is attempting to cultivate itself as a resort among Egyptians – there is some good swimming along its Mediterranean beaches – but it is principally owing to its status as a **duty free port** (from drink and digital cameras upwards) that it flourishes. In theory you must pass through customs on your way in and out, though this is rarely enforced; but be sure to have your passport with you.

Buses arrive by the Ferial Gardens, a few blocks in from the canal at the centre of town. The **railway station** and the adjacent **service taxi depot** are a bit south of centre but still only a short walk from the southern end of Sharia Filastin which runs along the canal, where you will find the **Tourist Office**.

Military museum
open Sat–Thurs 9–4; adm LE5

Much of the city was destroyed during the wars with Israel and has been rebuilt. A small **military museum** on Sharia 23 July (the date of Nasser's coup in 1952; Farouk abdicated on 26 July), just south of the New Corniche which parallels the Mediterranean beaches, commemorates these and the 1956 Anglo-French-Israeli attack. But a few fine buildings survive from Port Said's earlier and somewhat dubious heyday (when it was more than digital cameras that went cheap). Though Port Said is very much a canal city with a plain grid pattern, there is a touch of the picturesque

Where to Stay in Port Said

*****Helnan Port Said, New Corniche, t (066) 332 0890, *www.helnan.com* ($$$$$). A luxury resort hotel overlooking both the canal and sea, with private beach.

***Panorama, 72 Gumhuriya, t (066) 332 5101, f (066) 332 5103 ($$$). Lives up to its name in providing good views from its comfortable rooms, all with balconies, air conditioning and bathrooms.

Hotel de la Poste

****Hotel de la Poste**, 42 Sharia Gumhuriya, **t** (066) 322 9655 ($$). A recently renovated relic of Port Said's heyday, and excellent for a two-star hotel. Good service, restaurant, clean rooms with hardwood floors and private bathrooms, some with balconies.

***Akri Palace**, 24 Sharia Gumhuriya, **t** (066) 221 013 ($$). A charming old Greek-run place at the southern end of the street near the harbour and with views of the canal.

*****Holiday**, 23 Sharia Gumhuriya, **t** (066) 322 0711, **f** (066) 322 0710 ($$). With pavement café, has comfortable rooms with air conditioning and fridge.

along Sharia el Gumhuriya, which runs parallel to the canal but a couple of blocks back, where there are many beautiful old **wooden buildings** with balconies dating from the 19th century and reminiscent of the French Quarter in New Orleans. The most famous building, known to many sea travellers, is the **Suez Canal Building** on Sharia Filastin, right on the canal, its two-storey gleaming white colonnade crowned with three brilliant green domes. Farther north along the canal quay is the new and pleasingly cool **National Museum**, with exhibits from the pharaonic period onwards, including the coach used by Khedive Ismail at the opening of the canal. At the northern end of the quay is a statue of Ferdinand de Lesseps.

National Museum
open Sat–Thurs 9–4; adm LE20

Across the Canal is Port Fuad, which is a suburb of Port Said; together they form a single metropolitan area straddling Africa and Asia, and they are connected by frequent free ferries. Taking a ferry back and forth across the Canal is an ideal way to watch the ocean-going ships go by.

Suez

Suez is at the southern end of the canal and, like Ismailia, is easily reached from Cairo (134km, or from Ismailia 88km). It was the worst affected by the 1967 and 1973 wars and the sporadic shelling in between; three-quarters of the town was razed and has since been rebuilt. The population has climbed up to 500,000, and Suez is now a major industrial centre producing cement, fertilizer and petrochemicals. It is also the point of embarkment for the Mecca pilgrimage, explaining why it is an especially conservative place, with **no alcohol** to be had. The only reason to be here is to overnight to or from Sinai, which you can see stretching away to

Where to Stay in Suez

Note that during Zoul Hagga, the month of pilgrimage, you might have difficulty finding a place to stay in Suez.

***Green House Hotel** on Sharia Port Said where Sharia el Gaish runs off to Port Tewfiq, **t** (062) 333 1553, **f** (062) 333 1554 ($$$). A new, friendly and clean hotel with a pool and good restaurant. The air-conditioned rooms have views over the Gulf of Suez.

***Red Sea**, 13 Sharia Riad, **t** (062) 333 4302, **f** (062) 333 4301 ($$$). At Port Tewfiq, on an island at the mouth of the canal and connected by a causeway to Suez. Rooms are comfortable, air-conditioned and have balconies and satellite TV. The 6th floor **Mermaid restaurant** is good and offers a panoramic view of the Canal.

Arafat, off Sharia el Gaish, Port Tewfiq, **t** (062) 333 8355 ($). The cheapest decent hotel in the area, but being close to the port it is just a little rough and women on their own might want to give it a miss. Rooms are clean with balconies and fans; some have bathrooms.

the south, via the 1.4km Ahmed Hamdi Tunnel, 11km to the north. The Arba'in **bus and service taxi station** (where there is a tourist information kiosk) is just off Sharia Salaam (El Gaish), 1.5km west of the canal, while the railway station is 50m farther west.

When you think about it, Suez's **Ahmed Hamdi Tunnel** is bizarre. Normally a tunnel is dug beneath or through some natural obstacle, but in this case you must journey through a hole in the desert to avoid a man-made trench in the desert which has been filled with water so that ships can sail through the desert. You hold your breath and hope that a ship filled with sand bound for Saudi Arabia does not come sinking through the ceiling.

Along the Red Sea Coast

The Red Sea is part of a great rip in the Earth's surface extending from the Jordan Valley in the north to East Africa's Rift Valley in the south. Sinai divides the sea into the Gulf of Suez, which opens on to the Red Sea proper only just to the north of Hurghada (395km south of Suez) and the Gulf of Aqaba with its apex at Eilat in Israel. At its southern end the Red Sea is constricted by the Bab el Mandeb (Gate of Lamentation), a strait 26km wide, which gives access on to the Gulf of Aden and the Indian Ocean. From Suez to the Bab el Mandeb the Red Sea is 2240km long, while its greatest width is 355km. Being so enclosed, the Red Sea is considerably saltier than other seas; also its water temperature is high, the climate hot and dry, and the surrounding landscape barren. (During winter the prevailing north wind can make the Gulf of Suez clear down to Hurghada distinctly cooler, however.) It was first called 'red' in Roman times, but the reason is not certain; some say it is from the colour of the mountains, sometimes 2,000m high along this coast.

The mountains and the stretches of sandy beaches offer whatever interest the otherwise largely unindented coastline holds, though beyond Zafarana the coast road is dull. The road runs 1,100km south from Suez to the border with Sudan, deteriorating halfway along at Quseir. In fact the traveller is unlikely to go farther than Port Safaga, where a road heads off across the Eastern Desert to Qena in the Nile valley. The real attractions lie beneath the surface of the Red Sea for scuba divers, or back within the mountains.

At 55km south of Suez is **Ain Sukhna**, meaning Hot Springs, a developing resort with a good sandy beach where the desert plateau comes close in to the sea. (It can also be reached direct from Cairo by a good road which touches the coast just to the north.) The mountains continue to press against the sea all the way to **Zafarana** (120km from Suez), a nondescript port marked by a lighthouse at the mouth of the Wadi Araba. A road runs east from here, rising onto the plateau and meeting the Nile valley at El Wasta (badly potholed in places, it is manageable by car but four-wheel-drive would be safer), while another branch reaches the Nile farther south at Beni Suef. From Zafarana it is 30km west along this road that a paved left-hand turning brings you after 10km to St Antony's Monastery.

The Monastery of St Antony

From the base of the shorn flank of the desert plateau, here rising to 1,500m, **Deir Anba Antunius** looks out across the broad flat Wadi Araba. It is a dramatic situation, best appreciated by climbing up to St Antony's cave or from the parapet of the 12m-high monastery walls, 2km in circumference, which enclose what could almost be a village in some more hospitable part of Egypt, with gardens and palms watered by a spring flowing out of the rock. Until the beginning of the 20th century the monastery's only contact with the outside world was the monthly camel caravan carrying food and other necessities for the monks from the Nile valley. That journey took three or four days, with only two wells along the way. At that time, too, visitors were hoisted into the monastery by a windlass which you can see above the present entrance. Even after the coast road south from Suez was built in 1946, very few visitors came; over a five-year period in the mid-1950s the total was less than 500. Now coachloads of Copts and tourists draw up before the walls.

St Antony and the Origins of Monasticism

The problem of visitors, both pilgrims and gawkers, would have been familiar to St Antony, though on a lesser scale. A well-to-do

Getting to the Monastery of St Antony

There is no public transport to St Antony's Monastery. You could hire a **taxi** for the day from Cairo, Suez or Hurghada, or arrange something through Misr Travel, which in any case operates tours from Hurghada. You could join a **pilgrimage** organized by the Coptic Patriarchate in Cairo (*see* p.420). **Buses** running along the coast road stop at Zafarana; as a steady trickle of Copts visits the monastery, it is likely that they or a service taxi will then take you farther.

young man living on the banks of the Nile (*see* 'Beni Suef', p.233), it was during the 3rd century that St Antony heard in church the gospel words, 'If thou wilt be perfect, go and sell that thou hast, and give to the poor, and thou shalt have treasure in heaven' (Matthew 19:21). At first he retired to the bottom of his garden, but then withdrew to a more distant tomb. There he attracted the devout and the curious, and so joined a caravan bound eastwards across the desert, and by the beginning of the 4th century he was living in a cave above the rock spring, the first historically documented Christian hermit. Even here he was pursued by followers, who after his death in 356 (at the age of 105) founded the monastery that bears his name. It is often said that this is the oldest monastic settlement in the world, though Deir el Baramous in the Wadi Natrun, founded by a disciple of Antony's, would dispute the claim. What is certain however is that it was St Antony's life (which was written up by his friend, the great Athanasius of Alexandria) which inspired the monastic movement, and so in a sense it did begin here, from where it spread not only throughout Egypt but within a very few years was taken by Egyptians to Ireland and was from there carried to Britain and across northern Europe, implanting Christianity even beyond the bounds of the Roman Empire.

Nowadays, when you visit a monastery, a monk often comes forward to show you round. Appropriately, in view of his founder's act of renunciation, one of these at St Antony's used to work in a New York City bank. 'I returned to Egypt,' he will tell you, 'to be with God', as though for God too this was home ground. Ask him what he thinks of these invasions of his monastery, and he will politely misunderstand your question, answering that several times St Antony's had been overrun by Arabs, Mamelukes and Bedouin.

Visiting and Staying at the Monastery of St Antony

Open 9am–5pm daily but closed during Christmas and Lent. For exact dates of closure, check first with St Antony's residence in Cairo (*see* below). Visitors should not wear shorts or too-revealing clothes.

A guesthouse, open to both men and women, has been built outside the walls. If you want to stay overnight, you should first enquire at the Cairo residence of St Antony's and St Paul's monasteries, 26 Sharia el Kenisa el Morcosia, Kolet Beck, Cairo, t (02) 590 0218. You will normally need written permission in advance. Note that you will need to bring food and bedding; drinking water is supplied, but there are no showers nor cooking facilities.

'We Copts, you see, have suffered. It is the cross we bear. But it is the monasteries that keep Christianity alive in Egypt; here suffering does not lead to despair but to spirituality. Our people come to us, to learn of their heritage, and to find God here. But to be honest I prefer peace and prayer, and I hate that road which now brings the world to our door.' At the suggestion that tourists are also his cross, he replies, 'You goddit in one,' in fluent New Yorkese, then adding, as he anticipates your departure, 'but after the cross comes the resurrection.' Duly abashed, you can now look round the monastery.

Within the Walls of St Antony's

Once within the 10th-century walls (rebuilt and strengthened in the 16th and 19th centuries), you see at the end of the north–south street ahead of you the 16m-high **keep** of four storeys with a church of St Michael at the top. The lower courses are of rough stone, the upper courses of mud brick bound with timber; the original was probably built in the 10th century but the present structure dates from the 16th century. In fact it is likely that there is nothing within the monastery, except the church of St Antony next to the keep, that is older than the 16th century, for the reason you discover in its **sanctuary**. It is blackened with smoke. One night late in the 15th century, Bedouins who lived and worked within the walls (Muslim slaves iniquitously purchased, goes one version) turned against the monks and killed them all, setting up a kitchen here in the church and fuelling their fires with ancient scrolls from the library. The devastation was general and the loss is brought home when you read the words of a 14th-century French traveller who described St Antony's as 'even more beautiful than the monastery of St Catherine'.

The **church of St Antony** is entered through the north wall of the nave, so that to your left is the choir giving on to the sanctuary with two side chapels, while to your right is the narthex off which is a small chapel with an apse. There are paintings throughout, dating from pre-13th-century to 16th-century. The paintings in the **small chapel** all date to before the 13th century and include Christ enthroned and Mary with her hands slightly raised in wonderment. Around her are the four creatures of the Apocalypse (man, lion, ox and eagle). In the **narthex** the figures on the north and south walls are difficult to make out; on the north wall the beardless, haloed figure wearing a red cloak and riding a white horse may be St George. On the west wall are four warrior saints, Claude, Victor, Menas and Theodore. Note the camels between the legs of St Menas' horse (*see* 'The City of St Menas', p.429). All these figures date from the 16th century. In the nave is a series of monastic figures and a bishop.

The **archway** leading into the choir has a painting of the Archangels Gabriel and Michael, thought variously to be 10th-century, in which case they are among the oldest of Coptic frescoes, or 14th- to 15th-century. On the south wall of the choir is the one painting carrying a date, that of St Macarius, AD 1233. On either side of the arch leading into the chamber containing the **sanctuary** and **side chapels** are paintings relating to the Resurrection; they show three women coming to anoint Christ's body (Mark 16:1), and the two Marys with the risen Christ at the tomb. These are 15th-century. On the south wall of the right-hand chapel are four patriarchs, while on the arch of the central sanctuary are busts of Jeremiah, Eli, Isaiah, Moses, David and Daniel. All these are pre-13th-century, as are the busts of St Mark and St Anastasius in the far left and far right corners of the central sanctuary, and the depiction of Abraham sacrificing Isaac on the right side of the dome.

Claims have been made that the **refectory** to the northwest of the church is 7th-century, but it cannot be dated accurately. In the same building is a **church of the Holy Virgin** (recent). Among other churches within the monastery are the **church of the Apostles**, east of St Antony's Church, and the **church of St Mark** towards the east enclosure wall. Both are 18th-century. The new **library and museum** is against the northwest enclosure wall. Against the south enclosure wall is the **spring of St Antony** which provides 100 cubic metres of water daily, until recently the monastery's sole source; a spring of St Mark has now been revealed near by. Around the west side of the monastery a path begins its gradually stiffening ascent up to the **Cave of St Antony** (a climb of 270m over 2km) where, it is said, the saint spent the last decades of his life, trudging down for water, beans and dates, and trudging up again for God and the magnificent view.

Cave of St Antony

The Monastery of St Paul

Deir Anba Bula is reached by continuing 25km south along the coast from Zafarana. There a road winds northwestwards for 15km through the narrow Wadi el Deir to the monastery, snug within a mountain cirque. For all the remove of St Antony's in the past, you feel it always kept one eye on those caravans crawling along the Wadi Araba; but St Paul's is truly an outpost in the wilderness, at once hostage and challenge to the imposing landscape. You have in fact driven almost in a circle for if you were to climb the mountains behind the monastery of St Paul you could look down into the monastery of St Antony.

Getting to the Monastery of St Paul

There is no public transport to St Paul's Monastery. You could hire a **taxi** for the day from Cairo, Suez or Hurghada. The Coptic Patriarchate in Cairo arranges **pilgrimages**, which you could join, or you could arrange something through Misr Travel, which in any case offers tours from Hurghada. Otherwise you could get off the **coast-road bus** at the turning for St Paul's and pray for a lift.

St Paul, St Antony and the Crow

Walking over the mountains between the present sites of Deir Anba Antunius and Deir Anba Bula is what Antony did at the age of 90. There had come suddenly into his mind the proud thought that there was no better hermit in the desert than he, and almost as suddenly the humbling dream that he was wrong. After three days of aimless wandering, it was at this spot that he discovered Paul, aged 113, living in a cave and waiting for him. The story is told by St Jerome, who describes how a crow, which for 60 years had brought Paul a half-loaf of bread each day, now brought a full loaf for the two. Crows fly about the monastery, attracted by its gardens amid the desolation, but notwithstanding a crow appearing in almost every icon of their founder saint, the monks shoo them away. Also a pair of lions are associated with him, for no sooner had the two hermits met than Paul died: Antony was 'very unhappy', says Jerome, at the prospect of having to walk back over those mountains to fetch a spade, but the lions appeared, 'wagging their tails', and scratched out a grave with their paws.

A modern scholar has written that Paul 'is at best a symbolic figure and at worst a pious fraud', his supposed existence thereby saving Antony from the sinful pride of being the first hermit – but the word has not yet travelled up the Wadi el Deir where the saint's cave and his remains are as tangible as the faith of the monks.

Inside the Monastery of St Paul

St Paul's is only a seventh the size of St Antony's, which further heightens its sense of being an enclosed village. To the left of the present-day gate is the rope and pulley in use till early in the 20th century to hoist visitors into the walls. If anything, St Paul's is more pleasingly antique, though this is because it is more decrepit. It too suffered from the Bedouins late in the 15th century and was rebuilt by monks from Deir el Suriani – and then had to be reconstructed again in 1701 after lying desolate for over 100 years. Remoteness and poverty have probably been as much its enemies, yet perhaps they have contributed to the friendly atmosphere you encounter here. Visitors are not so many, and a novice will make you sweet mint tea while a monk is found to show you round. Unusually, the four-storey **keep** has a church of the Virgin rather than of St Michael on the top floor. Near by is the old **refectory**, adjacent to

Visiting the Monastery of St Paul

Visitors should not wear shorts or too-revealing clothes. Note that monasteries sometimes shut themselves off from the world during fasts, and that St Paul's is generally closed to visitors from 25 November through 7 January (pre-Christmas fast) and throughout Lent; check with the monastery's residence in Cairo (*see* below). A new **guesthouse** for both men and women has been built outside the walls. If you do want to stay overnight, you should first enquire and then obtain written permission from the residence of the monasteries of St Paul and St Antony in Cairo, 26 Sharia el Kenisa el Morcosia, Kolet Beck, Cairo, **t** (02) 590 0218.

the triple-domed 17th-century **church of St Mercurius** or Abu Saifain, with a good sanctuary and indifferent icons.

Almost below this is the **cave church of St Paul**. As you go down the steps a dome above you is painted with warrior saints on horseback. These are 18th-century. Below, to the east (left), are three **sanctuaries** marking an enlargement of faith over time. The farthest is dedicated to St Paul and is indeed meant to be the very cave in which St Antony found him. Near it is a modern marble sarcophagus containing, you are told, his remains. The central sanctuary, dedicated to St Antony, is perhaps 8th-century, possibly as late as 13th-century. The nearest sanctuary was built of stone in the 18th century and is dedicated to the Twenty-Four Elders of the Apocalypse. The **paintings** in the older portions of the church may well have dated originally from the 13th century, but most were repainted, according to a French pilgrim here in 1716, by a monk who 'informed us that he had never learnt to paint. His work is evident proof of that.' And it is true that he seems to have painted with a sure touch for the stilted and bland. On the west wall are four archangels, Raphael, Suriel, Zaqiel and Sathiel; also Shadrach, Meshach and Abednego in the fiery furnace. But you might confess your pleasure at the grotesquely prawnlike cherubim on either side of the Virgin and Child, and to delighting in the composition decorating the left-hand sanctuary, the Elders with what appear to be half a gigantic moustache each, Christ Pantocrator amid a swirl of Fauvist colour (the monk ground up the local rock to make his paints) from which peep the cubistic heads of the four creatures of the Apocalypse all tenth-rate Braque, perhaps, but it would not have been out of place seen from the very back row as a backdrop to a Diaghilev ballet.

Farther into the monastery is the 17th-century **church of St Michael** containing an icon of the Virgin painted, you are assured, by St Luke in AD 40, and an extraordinary **icon** of the head of John the Baptist staring at you horizontally from a dish, dated 1760. (St Luke's more famous icon of the Virgin, painted it is said from life, was lost at the fall of Constantinople in 1453. John the Baptist has been more fortunate; his actual head is kept at Venice, Aleppo, Damascus and the monastery of St Macarius in the Wadi

Natrun.) Towards the western end of the monastery is the **spring of St Paul** with a meagre outflow of 4 cubic metres of water daily (compared to St Antony's 100 cubic metres).

South to Hurghada and Beyond

All down the coast after the turning for the monastery of St Paul the mountains stand well back from the sea and the road runs through featureless desert on both sides, offering no more than distant views of occasional offshore oil rigs. Only at Hurghada do the mountains close in again around the bay. Off the coast road 30km north of Hurghada a track runs back into the Eastern Desert to **Mons Porphyrites**, the porphyry quarries, where at terrible human cost the Romans hewed so much of that magnificent red stone for the adornment of their basilicas, baths and private houses. The ruins of a settlement and unfinished Ionic **temple** of Hadrian's reign can be seen here, but you will need a four-wheel-drive vehicle.

Hurghada

Hurghada

Once a fishing village, Hurghada (395km from Suez or 214km from Qena on the Nile) has become the centre of Egypt's Red Sea oil operations, which are second in importance only to those in Sinai. This, but even more so the rampant tourist development occasioned by the attraction of nearby coral reefs and islands set in turquoise waters, have made Hurghada ugly and squalid. It is a familiar story, but here amid a vacant landscape the intrusion is all the more offensive. The converse of the traditional Egyptian genius for building civilization out of mud is their modern talent for contaminating much that is not mud with the rubbish of civilization.

Ghardaka, as it is known in Arabic, is useful as a place to overnight between Sinai or the Red Sea monasteries and the Nile in Upper Egypt, and there is the bonus of a refreshing splash at one of the resort hotels. **Tours** to the Roman quarries (and to the monasteries) can also be arranged. Otherwise only those with a fondness for Russian prostitutes and mafiosi types or those dedicated to sticking their head underwater and keeping it there for the duration would want to spend more than a few hours of daylight here.

Near the town the sea is too polluted with sewage and oil to **swim** in. Instead you must check into one of the resort hotels several kilometres south of town for their clean beaches and ostrich views (a small mountain between the Sheraton and

Getting to Hurghada

By Air

Egyptair has frequent flights throughout the day to Hurghada from Cairo, Alexandria, Aswan and Sharm el Sheikh.

By Sea

Recently the high-speed ferry between Hurghada and Sharm el Sheikh has been replaced by a smaller vessel. The Red Sea Jet, operated by the United Company for Marine Lines, only carries passengers and no longer motor vehicles. The voyage takes three hours.

The one-way fare for tourists is LE300. For departures from Sharm el Sheikh, *see* p.460. Departures from Hurghada are at 9am on Sat, Mon, Tues and Thurs; and at 4am on Wed. Tickets are sold at the Red Sea Jet office at Hurghada harbour two hours before departure or through travel agents. Passengers should be at the harbour an hour before departure and must carry their passport.

By Road

Super Jet and the Upper Egyptian **Bus** Company run services a day from the Cairo Gateway terminal (7 hours), and the latter also runs services from Suez and Luxor.

Boats Trips and Tours

Boat trips can be arranged and snorkelling and scuba diving equipment hired at any of Hurghada's 80 or so **dive shops**, including those at resort hotels. However you should use only those that are members of HEPCA (*see* p.454). Among these are Aquanaut, Shedwan Golden Beach, **t** 012 248 0463; Easy Divers, Triton Empire Beach Resort, **t** 012 230 5202; James & Mac, Giftun Beach Resort, **t** 012 311 8923; Jasmin Diving Centre, Jasmin Village, **t** (065) 346 0475; Orca, Tariq el Nasr, between El Dahar and Sigala, **t** 012 239 4784; and Sub Aqua, at the Sofitel Hotel, **t** (065) 346 4101.

Another way of seeing the underwater world is aboard the **Sindbad Submarine**, moored off the Sindbad Beach Resort, **t** (065) 344 4688. Though the submarine can safely dive to 45m it rarely goes below 10m, at a cost of $50 for adults, $25 for children.

The monasteries of St Antony and St Paul, and the Roman quarries of Mons Claudianus and Mons Porphyrites, can be reached by joining **tours** organized by Thomas Cook, **t** (065) 344 3338, and other agents.

Aquarium
open daily 9am–10pm; adm LE5

Hurghada serves to provide pressure for the hotel's water supply which is stored in a tank on top, but more importantly shuts out the landward blot). From there you can hire a boat out to the reefs and deserted islands and submerge yourself in crystalline waters to enjoy a brilliantly coloured submarine world. The **Aquarium** on the Corniche north of Three Corners Village presents a sampling of what you might find beneath the sea, excluding turds but including sharks.

The Ruin of the Red Sea Coast

As recently as the early 1980s, only a few hundred people, their lives based on fishing, inhabited what was then the village of Hurghada. Today its population stands at 300,000 and the numbers are fast rising daily, as does the volume of sewage and rubbish pumped and dumped into the sea, polluting the marine environment. Even in the early 1990s, when Hurghada was already established as a resort, there were 3,000 hotel beds and 40 dive centres; by 2000 there were more than 12,000 hotel beds and 80 dive centres. These numbers too are rising unchecked, with enormous new hotels constructed every season, each adding an average of 1,000 beds. Between them the dive centres operate well over 1,000 boats, each dropping and sometimes dragging its anchor at one of Hurghada's 30 dive sites and damaging the coral below, each also unloading its share of the many thousands of divers who daily descend onto the reefs where inevitably, if only by carelessness and sheer numbers, they contribute to the destruction of nature. 'Even if the boats were operated properly,' says one resident diving expert, 'the number of dive centres in Hurghada is exorbitantly high for such a limited area. At some dive sites I have seen more divers than fish.' With so many hotels and restaurants catering to the overwhelming number of beach-lovers and divers, the local fishermen have joined in the depredation, increasing their catch by blowing up fish with dynamite, which can damage coral within a radius of 700m. Though this is illegal, the law is hardly enforced.

Even so, broken soft coral can grow back in a few years. But what coral cannot recover from is the relentless landfilling that is part and parcel of the building boom on shore. Hoteliers dump sand into the sea to increase beach space, but when the sand settles on the nearby reefs it suffocates and kills them. So far over two million square metres of beach has been gained at Hurghada in this way. The law forbids it, but the law is not enforced. There is a law too prohibiting contruction closer than 220m to the shoreline, but numerous hotels obtained their permits when they were free to build within 50m of the shore – and all along the already blighted 65km stretch of coast between Hurghada and Safaga there are countless more projects underway or planned, in each case the owner possessing a permit obtained under the old legislation and still valid.

What has happened here is happening along the coasts of Sinai and along the Mediterranean west of Alexandria too, the destruction of the environment by the unregulated activities of Egyptians and foreigners alike. Ugliness and overdevelopment on shore are a warning and a cause of devastation beneath the surface of the sea.

The Hurghada Environmental Protection and Conservation Association (HEPCA) was founded in 1992 by a group of concerned foreign divers. It has since received millions of dollars worth of backing from USAID towards installing hundreds of buoys costing $500 each to which dive boats can moor themselves rather than drop anchor, and towards creating a ranger service with its own boat and four-wheel-drive vehicle to monitor the observance of good marine practice and environmental legislation. But HEPCA is not the law and can only raise environmental awareness. Visitors should make sure that they only have truck with member organizations of the HEPCA.

South of Hurghada

Port Safaga (65km south of Hurghada) would no doubt be offensive if it could muster a pretention to being anything more than a road junction. Its primary function these days is as a port for offloading imported wheat from Australia (a complete reversal of Egypt's fortunes, which until recently was a major exporter of wheat). Here you can turn west for Qena on the Nile (160km); then at about 40km en route to Qena you can follow a newly paved road northwest to within 2km of the ancient **Mons Claudianus** where through the reigns of Nero to Hadrian condemned prisoners were set to work to provide the prized Claudian granite for Rome's public buildings. As at Mons Porphyrites, the remains of a settlement and **temple** are evident, and a number of unfinished columns and blocks are lying about.

Alternatively you can continue south along the coast, in 85km reaching **Quseir**, a small inlet sheltered by a coral reef, but in medieval times a flourishing port through which Egypt exported wheat from the Nile valley and imported precious Eastern wares. Until the 19th century it was the favoured transit point for pilgrims to Mecca, and a number of caravanserais serving this traffic survive. The Suez Canal destroyed its trade. A 16th-century **Ottoman fortress** built against the Portuguese dominates the harbour, and there is the interest of local Bedouin life, a **souk**, and **boat trips** on the Red Sea.

Until recently **Marsa Alam** (145km south of Port Safaga) was nothing more than a fishing village with good offshore coral reefs, but with the opening of its small airport it is beginning to burgeon as a tourist resort. Beyond Marsa Alam you come to **Berenice** (375km from Port Safaga) on the same latitude as Aswan. Founded by Ptolemy II and named for his mother, it handled trade with Arabia, East Africa and India throughout the Graeco-Roman period, disappearing from history in the 5th century AD and rediscovered only in 1818 by the amazing Belzoni (*see* Ramesseum, p.331). There is the ruinous **Temple of Serapis**, built under Trajan during the Roman imperium, and offshore the island of **Topazos** which gave its name to topaz, once abundant here. Bir Shalatayn, 75km south, is the administrative border with Sudan.

Where to Stay in Hurghada

There are plenty of places to stay in Hurghada, in all categories, and a dozen more are being built at any one moment. Places in the lower categories are in town; touts will try to get you to their place, and there is no reason why you should not go along for a look. The resort hotels are well out of town; once ensconced in one you will be entirely catered for and need never venture beyond the walls. Those wishing to dive will almost certainly find it cheaper to take a package including both diving and accommodation.

Oberoi Sahl Hashish >

Luxury ($$$$$)

*****Oberoi Sahl Hashish, **t** (065) 344 0777, *www.oberoisahlhasheesh.com*. South of Hurghada and a 20-minute drive from the airport (guests are met by chauffeur-driven car), this is without doubt the very finest beach resort along the Red Sea coast. Its private beach is 850m long, and there are special facilities and courses for snorkelling and diving. Each party is accommodated in its own individual villa built in beautiful Arab style with domes, arches, columns and courtyards, all with views of the sea; if that is not luxurious enough, there are deluxe villas which have their own swimming pool and outdoor dining pavilion. A central building, reminiscent of a princely caravanserai, contains the reception, a shop, a library and a bar; its **restaurant**, which serves oriental and continental cuisine, offers magical views of the Red Sea, while at the nearby swimming pool the Pergola provides light meals throughout the day. Sahl Hashish (the name means Valley of Grass) has an open-air jacuzzi, a floodlit tennis court, a gymnasium, steam bath and sauna, and also a spa providing holistic treatments based on Western and ancient Egyptian therapies. You check in here and you turn off the world; it is the perfect idyll to combine with an Oberoi Nile cruise.

Expensive ($$$$)

*****__Hurghada Marriott Beach Resort__, **t** (065) 344 6950, *www.marriott.co.uk/hotels/travel/hrgeg-hurghada-marriott-beach-resort*, 11km south of Hurghada. Has a private beach, marina, pool and all the usual watersports facilities.

*****__Sonesta Pharaoh Beach Resort__, 18km south of Hurghada, **t** (065) 346 1001, *www.sonesta.com/Hurghada*. A modern pharaonic-style resort hotel with both rooms and bungalows, private sandy beach, dive centre, outdoor and indoor pools.

****__Sofitel Hurghada__, **t** (065) 346 4646, *www.sofitel.com*, 12km south of town. A stylish Moorish complex with a restrained atmosphere and all facilities.

*****__Hilton Hurghada Plaza__, **t** (065) 354 9745, *www.hilton.com*, 4km south of the city centre. Set within a lavish garden, excellent private beach, impeccable service, all rooms overlooking the sea.

Moderate ($$$)

***__Gezira__, in town just off Sharia el Bahr, **t** (065) 354 7785, **f** (065) 354 3708. Has spacious rooms, air-conditioned and with private bathrooms, set about a leafy courtyard. There is a bar, restaurant and nightly disco.

***__Triton Empire Hotel__, Hospital Street, **t** (065) 354 9200, *www.threecorners.com/hurghada_hotel/empirehotel.php*. A large Belgian-run place at the centre of downtown near the nightlife, with four restaurants, two pools and its own private beach. Rooms have balconies, satellite TV and private bathrooms.

Inexpensive ($$)

Snafer, on the Corniche, **t/f** (065) 354 0260. Friendly well-kept hotel with good sea views from the upper floors.

Four Seasons, **t/f** (065) 354 5456. On the street that runs off the Corniche behind the Three Corners Village. Rooms are simple and clean with private baths and balconies, some with air conditioning and satellite TV.

Cheap ($)

Happy House, 200m north of the bus station along Tariq el Nasr, and between the post office and the El Dahar Mosque, **t** 012 358 5016. A good, friendly budget place of long reputation, only four rooms.

Happy Land, **t** (065) 354 7373, on Sharia Sheikh Sebak on the north side of the tourist bazaar, north of the bus station. Rooms a bit shabby, with fans, extra for private bath.

Sinai

When you cross the Suez Canal into Sinai there is the sense of having crossed a border. By geographical convention you have entered Asia, but that means little. Certainly you have left behind the placidity that characterizes so much of the Egyptian landscape; here in the Sinai peninsula mountains rise in violent revolt. Nor is there that sense as along the Nile of the land and people being one; only 400,000 people inhabit an area the size of Sicily, most of them huddled along the coasts with their backs to the forbidding interior. Bedouin account for 80,000, eking out an existence by growing dates or scratching the barren foothills with their flocks.

Curiously, Hathor was anciently worshipped here, but that must have had less to do with her bovine qualities than with her association with the sky; it was on a mountain top that Moses rendezvoused with God. In Sinai neither man nor deity seem quite to touch the ground.

17

Don't miss

1. **Off-road into the ancient wilderness**
   Serabit el Khadim turquoise mines and the Wadi Moqattab rock-carved inscriptions **p.462**
2. **The Burning Bush, ostrich eggs and a fine mosaic**
   St Catherine's Monastery **p.464**
3. **Sunrise on the holy mountain**
   Mount Sinai **p.468**
4. **Best diving in the Red Sea**
   Ras Mohammed nature reserve **p.471**

See map overleaf

Sinai

p.476

p.438

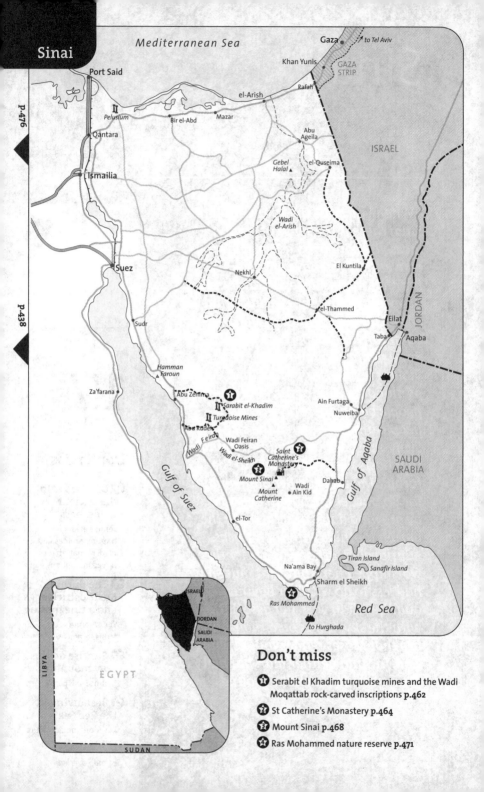

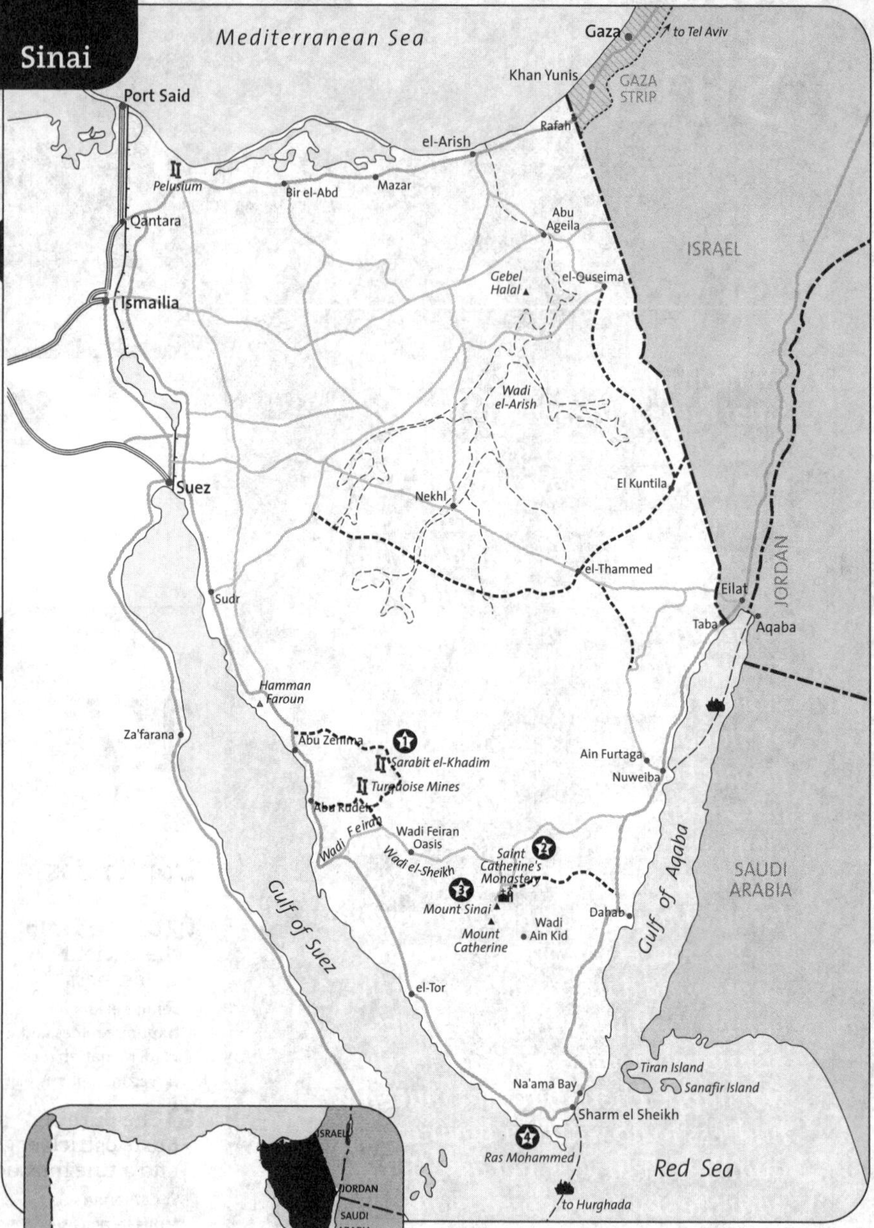

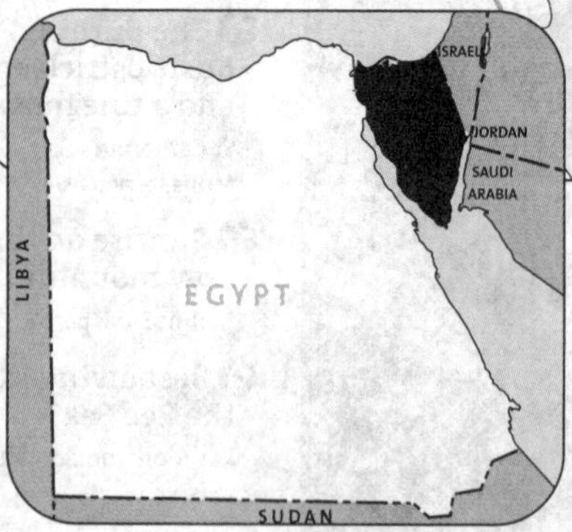

Don't miss

1. Serabit el Khadim turquoise mines and the Wadi Moqattab rock-carved inscriptions p.462
2. St Catherine's Monastery p.464
3. Mount Sinai p.468
4. Ras Mohammed nature reserve p.471

Sinai has long been a holy place, and its most fixed inhabitants for 1,500 years have been those neither born here nor permitted to procreate – the monks beneath Moses' mountain at the monastery of St Catherine. And being ethnic Greeks (mostly from Crete and Cyprus), they remind you of another border crossed, into the patriarchal See of Jerusalem, created at the Council of Chalcedon in AD 451 when Alexandrian monophysitism was declared a heresy. At St Catherine's you leave behind the battered fortunes of Coptic Egypt and enter one of the most magnificent strongholds of Byzantine Orthodoxy.

Urban Development

After Egypt's reocccupation of the whole of Sinai in 1982, Cairo ministries quickly unleashed scores of plans for the peninsula's rapid exploitation. The government's intention to settle two million immigrants here from the Nile valley by the year 2000 fell far short of target, with hardly more than a quarter of million induced to make the move. **El Arish** on the Mediterranean coast and **El Tor** on the Gulf of Suez are the new administrative centres of north and south Sinai; urban development is meant to be concentrated here. (El Tor was formerly a quarantine station for pilgrims returning from Mecca. 'It is exceedingly difficult to please a returning pilgrim,' Colonel Jarvis observed in *Oriental Spotlight* in 1937, 'as he has been so near to Heaven that he expects to live in something that closely resembles it, and it would take an optimist to call Tor Heaven.') Manganese, copper, phosphates and offshore oil and gas are intended to provide the industrial base, while fishing and agriculture are also being encouraged. But this fetishism for development requires heavy capital investment; it is cheaper and quicker to attract tourism, and that is really where the boom is. Along the Gulf of Aqaba at **Sharm el Sheikh**, **Dahab** and **Nuweiba** the Egyptians, abetted by the lowest form of foreign tourism, have let development rip without any regard for the beauty and quality of the land or marine environment. The interior of Sinai, however, remains for the time being one of the least touched places in the world.

Across Northern Sinai

There is a cultivable strip along the Mediterranean coast, but behind this are broad sand valleys rising towards the limestone plateau of central Sinai. Across this undulating northern half of the peninsula, migrants, caravans and armies have passed since before recorded time.

Getting to Sinai

By Air

Egyptair flies to Sharm el Sheikh from Cairo, Alexandria, Hurghada and Luxor.

By Road

You can cross into Sinai by the Suez Canal Bridge at Qantara, north of Ismailia, or pass under it via the Ahmed Hamdi Tunnel north of Suez.

From the Cairo Gateway terminal in Cairo the East Delta Bus Company and Super Jet run frequent **bus** services to Sinai, including destinations such as El Arish, St Catherine's Monastery, Sharm el Sheikh, Dahab and Nuweiba.

Service taxis for Sinai leave from the al-Kulali station near Midan Ramses, Cairo.

By Sea

The high-speed ferry operating between Sharm el Sheikh and Hurghada has been replaced by a smaller vessel which carries passengers only, no motor vehicles, and takes 3 hours. The one-way fare for tourists on Red Sea Jet is LE300. For departures from Hurghada, *see* p.453. Departures from Sharm el Sheikh are at 5pm on Sat, Mon, Tues, Thurs; and at 6pm on Wed. You can purchase tickets at the Red Sea Jet office in Sharm el Sheikh harbour 2 hours before departure or through your local travel agent. Passengers should be at the harbour one hour before departure and must have their passport.

There are regular ferries between Aqaba in Jordan and both Taba and Nuweiba in Sinai.

Tours and Safaris

Misr Travel, American Express and other agents offer tours to **St Catherine's** and the **Gulf of Aqaba resorts. Four-wheel drive safaris** can be arranged in Cairo through the above agents, as well as at the various Sinai resorts themselves, which do **camel treks** too. Likewise you can hire a four-wheel-drive car locally or, in Cairo, from various car hire firms.

The main east–west thoroughfare is the coastal road, usually reached by going first to Ismailia and then crossing the Suez Canal to the north at **Qantara**, where in the late 1980s the remains of a **fortress city** were discovered, 400m square, with initial excavations undertaken by the Egyptian Antiquities Organization indicating a temple and palace, and 12 gigantic granaries. From here you are following the ancient **Horus Road**, the military route taken by Tuthmosis III and Ramses II as they marched towards Armageddon and Kadesh (*see* 'Karnak', p.289, and the 'Temple of Luxor', p.271. respectively). At about 30km northeast of Qantara where the road draws near the sea are, just north, the rubble mounds called **Tell el Faramah**, the ancient Pelusium. Founded as a frontier town and port in the 6th century BC, it was abandoned in the 8th century AD when the easternmost (Pelusiac) branch of the Nile on which it stood dried up. Known as the 'key to Egypt', here Alexander received the Persian surrender in November 332 BC, and here too in AD 640 Amr marshalled his Arab horsemen before invading Egypt, beginning the long slow process of severing its people from their ancient cultural inheritance.

El Arish

El Arish, 158km from Qantara, is the largest town on the peninsula. Until fairly recently merely a Bedouin settlement

Where to Stay in Northern Sinai

El Arish's better hotels are on the beach road, Sharia Fuad Zakri, which as it runs east also comes to a fork, the left-hand road continuing eastwards past the museum (in 2km) and on towards Rafah (for the Gaza Strip and Israel). The right-hand road, Sharia 23 July, curves off southwards and in 2km terminates in Midan Baladiya. The cheaper hotels are along Sharia 23 July and along its lower end is the Bedouin souk, while the *midan* itself is a raucous place, with a loud mosque, a loud bus station and a loud service taxi station. Service taxis and minibuses shuttle between Midan Baladiya and the beach.

*****Swiss Inn Resort**, at Al Nakheel Beach, **t** (068) 335 1321, *www.swissinn.net/arish* ($$$$). Offers complete resort facilities right on the Mediterranean. All rooms overlook the beach, and facilities include fresh- and salt-water pools, a health club, tennis and squash courts, windsurfing, waterskiing and fishing trips.

*****Semiramis**, Sharia Fuad Zakri, **t/f** (068) 336 4167 ($$$). Has air conditioning and TV in all rooms, and its facilities include a gym, tennis courts and a pool. Pricier suites are on the beach, otherwise singles and doubles are in the compound across the road, some distance from the sea. If you can stretch your budget a bit, it is far better to stay at the Swiss Inn.

*****Sinai Beach**, Sharia Fuad Zakri, **t/f** (068) 336 1713 ($$). On the beach and offers watersports facilities. Rooms have air conditioning and private bathrooms.

****Mecca Hotel**, Sharia el Salam, off Sharia Fuad Zakri, **t/f** (068) 335 2632 ($). A friendly place on a quiet street.

Yet cheaper places than this can be found towards Midan Baladiya.

surrounded by groves of date palms and making a living too from the sea, some industry has now been established and tourists accommodated in new luxury hotels along its magnificent beach.

Apart from a small **museum** (2km east on the Rafah road) devoted to the natural and human history of Sinai, and a **Bedouin souk** on Thursdays, the sole attraction of El Arish is its watersports. You can hire diving equipment at the hotels. The place is favoured in fact by Egyptians rather than foreigners, so that, unlike the Gulf of Aqaba resorts, both mood and dress are conservative and the nightlife close to sober.

To be banished in Ptolemaic times to Rhinocolura, which once stood here, was to suffer the ultimate loss of face: the name means 'severed nose', the mark by which its prisoners were distinguished.

Into Southern Sinai

A great granitic massif dominates the southern part of the peninsula, an eruption of jagged peaks with remarkably convoluted and mineral-coloured veins. **Gebel Musa** (Mount Moses or Mount Sinai) at 2,285m and **Gebel Katerin** (Mount St Catherine) at 2,642m, both overhanging **St Catherine's Monastery**, are the highest mountains in Egypt and can be capped with snow in winter. The journey to the monastery introduces you to this wild and chaotic landscape, with its ever-changing views and the surprise of green as you pass through the **Feiran Oasis** between mountain walls along the way. The road is perfectly suitable for ordinary vehicles, but to venture up the remoter wadis, in the footsteps of those ancient Egyptians who from the I Dynasty onwards searched for copper and turquoise, requires a 4-wheel-drive vehicle or a camel.

Just north of Suez, at El Kubri, the Ahmed Hamdi Tunnel passes beneath the canal and puts you on the coast road running south. 25km after the tunnel, on the right side of the road, are the springs of **Ain Musa** (Moses), which tradition associates with the Children of Israel's successful escape across the Red Sea (Moses' song, Miriam's dance, in Exodus 15) – mere stink holes in fact, turbid and littered with plastic mineral bottles. At 115km beyond the tunnel, Gebel Hammam Faraun (the Mountain of Pharaoh's Bath) is another wretched place, where sulphurous hot springs dribble into the sea and people come to swim and make a mess.

Abu Rudeis (166km from the tunnel) has the look of a broken-down military camp; it is in fact a settlement founded by an oil company for its workers. For the passer-by it has the virtue of a shop selling cold drinks and with a toilet round the side; also, it stands at the mouth of the **Wadi Sidri** which leads to ancient turquoise mines.

Off-Road to the Turquoise Mines

The **Wadi Magara turquoise mines** are reached by following an ancient track eastwards up the Wadi Sidri from Abu Rudeis. You need to be in a 4-wheel-drive vehicle, or go by camel. At 25km the Wadi Magara opens off to the north and it is then a short distance to the mines. They are round the final leftwards bend, 40m above the valley floor on the left. The mines were worked as early as the I Dynasty, and as you walk deep into the valley wall you sometimes notice small turquoises, though these are of little value. If you climb up higher you come to **carvings** on the rock face depicting IV and V Dynasty pharaohs. Directly across the valley on the hill opposite are the remains of workshops, workers' houses and a fort, all pharaonic. Back down on the sandy wadi floor you can picnic beneath the shade of an acacia tree; the acacia survives in these most arid parts of Sinai by sending down roots as deep as 100m.

Serabit el Khadim turquoise mines

Back in the **Wadi Sidri** and following it southeastwards for a few kilometres, there is a choice of following wadis north or south. Heading along the northwards track for about 50km you come to the larger **turquoise mines of Serabit el Khadim**. (These can also be reached by turning off the coast road north of Abu Zenima into the Wadi el Homur: go east for 21km, then south for 4km, then east again for 7km where a track south brings you to Serabit el Khadim in 5km.) Here there is a rock-cut XII Dynasty **sanctuary to Hathor** with inscriptions to Hatshepsut and Tuthmosis III. But the great importance of this site is that it lays claim to being the place where the alphabet was invented.

Inscriptions using hieroglyphics but serving to write some other language, probably Semitic, have been found at Serabit el Khadim. Only 30 signs are used, indicating an alphabetic system. Found frequently are a set of modified hieroglyphic signs bearing a resemblance to Hebrew, Phoenician and Greek letters, and which can be read as 'Baalat', the Mistress, the name always given by the Semites to the Egyptian goddess Hathor who was worshipped here.

Wadi Moqattab

If instead of heading north to Serabit el Khadim you take the wadi running southwards, you enter the broad **Wadi Moqattab**, the Valley of Inscriptions – Nabataean and Greek mostly, but also Coptic and Arabic, dating from the 1st to 6th century AD, as well as more recent Hebrew inscriptions telling of the Israeli advances in Sinai in 1956 and 1967. Most delightful are the presumably **Nabataean depictions** of various creatures and horsemen, and the somewhat later inscription, 'Mozart'. The Wadi Moqattab runs south into the Wadi Feiran.

The Road to the Feiran Oasis and St Catherine's

The **Wadi Feiran** with magnificent mountain scenery along the way has a good paved road which is normally joined by turning off the main road at 32km south of Abu Rudeis. At 22km along the Wadi Feiran road is the Wadi Moqattab to the left (*see* above), while continuing straight on the valley walls narrow and rise to imposing granite peaks. In another 30km you enter the **Feiran Oasis** (84km from Abu Rudeis, 250km from the tunnel).

The Travels of Mt Sinai

On the plain of Raha, where the Children of Israel are said to have camped, the Egyptians have thoughtfully built a tourist complex of small chalets, somebody's idea of Bedouin tents in stone. The view is up the Wadi el Deir, with two mountainous shoulders on either side. The scene seems pure Cecil B. DeMille and is familiar. Then you realize it is familiar because it *is* Cecil B. DeMille: here Charlton Heston came down from the mountain clutching the Ten Commandments. For once a gigantically imposing set did not have to be built; the location chosen by God and Moses for their famous encounter had satisfied a Hollywood film producer's demand for spectacle.

But it may be that the mountain came to the monastery rather than the monastery to the mountain. Some historians have argued that an earlier Christian tradition claimed Gebel Serbal in the Feiran Oasis as Mt Sinai, and that Pharan became a Christian centre for that reason. Driven away from the oasis by Bedouins and Muslims, what remained of the community retreated here. The Emperor Justinian had founded a church dedicated to the Virgin part way up Gebel Musa, and at the base of the mountain built a fortress which gradually drew the monks and hermits of Gebel Serbal, and along with them the early Christian legends. Yet another scholarly squib denies the site of the Ten Commandments to the Sinai peninsula altogether, saying that the fire and smoke and quaking on Mt Sinai (Exodus 19:18) must refer to the activity of now extinct volcanoes in the northern Hejaz on the eastern side of the Red Sea. However, here you are and here is the tradition.

The largest oasis and most fertile area in the whole of Sinai, the Feiran Oasis offers the most pleasant scenery of the entire journey. It is a secret garden of amazing lushness, filled with palms, tamarisks and wheat. The Alexandrian geographer Ptolemy mentions a town here, **Pharan**, in the 2nd century AD, and later it became a great centre of Christian eremetic life, antedating the community beneath Gebel Musa (site of St Catherine's Monastery). The remains of monasteries and hermit cells are evident both in the valley and on the rocky slopes of **Gebel Serbal**, at 2070m the third highest mountain in Sinai. At the Council of Chalcedon in 451 Pharan became the seat of an archbishop subject to the patriarch of Jerusalem, but late in the 7th century, following repeated Bedouin attacks and the Muslim conquest, the town was abandoned. A plantation belonging to St Catherine's was established here in 1898; amid it is a **chapel** dedicated to Moses, approached by an avenue of column drums and capitals salvaged from ancient buildings. A handful of nuns (often from the Greek community in Egypt) have lived here since 1978 in quarters built partly of stones taken from the 4th-century **bishop's palace**, the ruins of which you can see behind; and so they tend to palms and prayers.

The Greek Orthodox Monastery of St Catherine

(2) Monastery of St Catherine
open Mon–Thurs and Sat 9–12 noon, though it sometimes opens up to groups a half hour or so earlier; closed on Fri, Sun and public and Greek Orthodox holidays; adm free

The road climbs steadily (800m to 1,500m) through the Wadi el Sheikh, over the granite-flanked Watiya Pass, and onto the **plain of Raha**. On the left a white **chapel** on a small mound marks the place where the Israelites are said to have worshipped the golden calf; just beyond this, running off to the southeast, is the Wadi el Deir and, a kilometre within it, **St Catherine's Monastery** (133km from Abu Rudeis, 299km from the tunnel). The site of the monastery is explained by early Christian tradition: it lies against the flank of Gebel Musa, claimed as the Mt Sinai of the Bible.

A short distance up the Wadi el Deir you notice St Catherine's Monastery, **Deir Sant Katerin**, overwhelmed by its surroundings. As you near, you pass up through a terraced garden of cypresses and flowers which bloom in March and April. Here too is the **Charnel House** heaped with piles of monkish bones, sorted into skulls, arms, legs, hands and feet, while more collectedly sits St Stephen the Porter, a 6th-century monk, dressed in a purple robe and holding a staff in his skeletal hand. The monks are buried in the cemetery near by; as the latest corpse goes under, the oldest is exhumed and his bones transferred to the ossuary. This is common

Greek practice, for the laity too, and saves space where good land is scarce.

It is worth having a walk round the fortress-like granite **walls**, 12 to 15m high, before entering the monastery. Those on the west (through which you enter) and south date from the original founding in *c.* AD 530: the north and east walls were destroyed by an earthquake early in the 14th century and later rebuilt. Here and there along the walls are ancient **Christian symbols** in relief. Until recently, access to St Catherine's was by basket and pulley into an elevated doorway in the west wall, above the sealed up gate with its massive lintel. Now you enter through the small postern to the left.

The Church of the Transfiguration

Ahead of you and dominating the other buildings within the monastery is the **church of the Transfiguration** (its original name, though later dedicated to St Catherine). Apart from the chapel of the Burning Bush, which it encloses, the **basilica** is the oldest structure within the walls and now stands 4m below ground level. It was built of massive granite blocks in the mid-6th century by Justinian in memory of his wife Theodora. You enter the narthex, added in the 10th or 11th century, through carved wooden 11th-century doors; then through 6th-century Byzantine doors magnificently carved from cedar from Lebanon with crosses, birds, date palms and other designs, you pass into the main body of the church.

Granite **columns** with richly decorated foliage capitals mark the aisles off from the exceptionally high nave which is illuminated by clerestory windows. Against each of the 12 columns is a calendar icon portraying the saints venerated within each month. The patterned marble floor and chandeliers are 18th-century, as is the flat wooden ceiling. This last now hides the original trusses which support the roof, though you can see their 6th-century bracing **beams**, elaborately carved with animals, plants, cherubs and scenes of life along the Nile. Suspended from the ceiling are **ostrich eggs**, seen in Greek, Coptic and Muslim places of worship alike. The explanation is given that the ostrich is remarkable for the ceaseless care with which she guards her eggs, and this, becoming proverbial, reminds the believer that his thoughts should be fixed on spiritual things.

The choir is separated from the nave by a gilded **iconostasis** adorned with large icons of John the Baptist, Mary, Jesus and St Catherine, all Cretan work of 1612. Behind the iconostasis, to the right and beneath a marble canopy, is the **reliquary** of St Catherine, said to contain her skull and left hand (*see* 'St Catherine's Mount', p.470).

In the apse is the 6th-century **mosaic** of the Transfiguration, one of the finest works of Byzantine art. It is exceptional too for having survived the destructions of the iconoclasts (the figurative mosaics of Constantinople are 9th-century or later) and for being untouched by restorers. (Part of the effect of a mosaic is the subtle way in which it refracts light, whether the moving beams of light entering through windows or the flickering of candlelight, which is achieved by setting the individual tesserae at random angles. Restoration involving the removal of the mosaic with its plaster backing tends to flatten the angle of the tesserae and reduce their refractive quality.) The Transfiguration is notable too for the painterly manner of its execution, unlike the more graphic style of its mosaic contemporaries at Ravenna.

The subject of the mosaic is taken from Matthew 17:1–3, after Jesus asks his disciples who they think he is:

And after six days Jesus taketh Peter, James, and John his brother, and bringeth them up into a high mountain apart. And was transfigured before them: and his face did shine as the sun, and his raiment was white as the light. And behold, there appeared unto them Moses and Elias talking with him.

To the left of Christ are Elias and St John, to the right Moses and St James, while kneeling below is St Peter. The gold ground is surrounded by 31 portraits of saints, apostles and prophets, while above the arch are medallions of John the Baptist (left) and the Virgin (right) and a pair of angels. On either side of the windows at the top are scenes of Moses taking off his sandals before the Burning Bush (left) and receiving the Ten Commandments (right).

Put off thy shoes from off thy feet, for the place whereon thou standest is holy ground.

Exodus 3:5

Which is what God said to Moses at the Burning Bush and what you must do when you pass behind the apse and down to the very earliest and lowest level within the monastery, and so enter the Chapel of the Burning Bush. Though it goes against all logic, not to mention spiritual ecology, the altar has been placed above the roots of the bush, but in order to do so the bush itself had to be yanked out. But it is an accommodating bush and has allowed itself to be transplanted a few metres off (but outside the church) where, with your shoes back on, you can look at it flourishing if not flaming.

The Icon Gallery and the Library

To reach the bush you have to walk back through the church and out through the narthex which, recently anyway, has served as the

icon gallery (though a new Icon Gallery is next to the library at the southeast corner of the monastery). Wherever you find them, the icons should be looked at closely: they are a sampling of the 2,000 icons in the monastery's collection and are wonderful. One is of St Peter, 5th- or 6th-century, in encaustic, that same melted coloured wax technique of the Fayyum portraits seen in the Egyptian Museum in Cairo, and indeed of a similarly striking realism. In the same technique is a 7th-century Christ Pantocrator, the New Testament in his left arm, his right hand raised in benediction and, weirdly, one eyebrow raised as though he might be peeping through a crack in the universe.

In the **Library**, with a collection second in importance only to that of the Vatican, are 5,000 books and 3,000 manuscripts, the rarest of the manuscripts once in its possession being the 4th-century *Codex Sinaiticus*. Borrowed by a German scholar in the 19th century, it was given to the Czar of Russia and never returned; the Communist government instead sold it on to the British Museum. Understandably the monks are reticent about showing their manuscripts to all and sundry, and what you see and when you are allowed to see it will be limited. You may get a look at the Library's most valuable remaining possession, the 5th-century *Codex Syriacus*, the monk obligingly turning over the pages, each time licking his thumb.

Returning from the Library, pass behind the church towards the transplanted Burning Bush; near it is the medieval **Refectory**, on its east wall a 16th-century Last Judgement by a Cretan artist, and its wooden furnishings incised with mostly 15th-century graffiti.

The Monastery's Protectors

From Justinian's time St Catherine's Monastery has enjoyed the special protection and patronage of rulers. The monastery possesses what it claims is a copy of a document from Mohammed granting security; later the Crusaders took St Catherine's into their care, as did the Ottoman sultans, the Russian czars (who saw themselves as the inheritors of Byzantium) and Napoleon during his Egyptian expedition.

Since 1782 the monastery has enjoyed autonomy within the Greek Orthodox Church and today its archbishop is normally resident in Cairo. Though it is sometimes said that St Catherine's is the oldest continuously inhabited monastery in the world, in fact it was sacked in the 10th century and abandoned for some time in the 15th century when relations with the Mamelukes were bad. Generally, however, it has been respected both as a refuge for wayfarers – including those making the *hajj* – and as a protector of shrines holy to the religions of the book. So it is not surprising that opposite the narthex of the church is what was a hospice built in

Where to Stay near St Catherine's Monastery

Apart from staying at the airport, 20km from the monastery (by taxi or St Catherine's Tourist Village bus), accommodation and other facilities, including a petrol station, supermarket, restaurant and bank, cluster in St Catherine's village before the entrance to the wadi leading up to the monastery. And there is the monastery's own magnificently sited guesthouse.

Expensive ($$$$)

****St Catherine's Tourist Village**, on the plain of Raha, 1km from the monastery, **t** (069) 347 0325, **f** (069) 347 0326. Has comfortable air-conditioned rooms and is an agreeable place to stay. Run by the Misr Sinai Tourist Company, bookings can be made through any branch of Misr Travel, its sister organization. Accommodation is in fully equipped bungalows looking like Bedouin tents, and meals are in a central restaurant.

Moderate ($$$)

St Catherine's Monastery Guesthouse >

St Catherine's Monastery Guesthouse, just outside the monastery walls and dramatically set beneath the towering cliffs, **t** (069) 347 0353. You are paying for the view, as the rooms are small and simple, though they do have private bathrooms, and basic meals are included.

***Catherine Plaza**, **t** (069) 347 0289, *www.catherineplaza.com*. A large complex of over 150 rooms just outside St Catherine's Village, 3km from the monastery. Rooms have air conditioning, heating, terrace, and there are several restaurants, a bar, and a swimming pool.

Daniela Village, 1km from the monastery, **t** (069) 347 0379, *www.daniela-hotels.com*. A 70-odd room bungalow complex though hardly an imaginative one. Rooms with private bathrooms; restaurant and 24-hour café.

Cheap ($)

El Malga Bedouin Camp, **t** 010 641 3575 (mobile), close to the bus stop and 3km from the monastery. You can get simple rooms here, private or dorm, or camp outside. It also does trekking tours with a bedouin guide.

You can also sleep out atop **Mt Sinai**, but it is chilly at any time of year and extremely cold in winter; a sleeping bag is essential.

the 6th century for pilgrims, but converted to a **mosque** in 1106. The free-standing **minaret** was added in the 12th century. From here you can look up at the church's **bell tower** in its northwest corner, built by a monk in 1871, its bells gifts of the czar of Russia.

Gebel Musa

Gebel Musa (Mount Sinai)

It is worth walking up **Gebel Musa** (the Mount of Moses), claimed as the Mount Sinai of the Bible, to be there like Moses for dawn. Later, with the sun up, the way will be hotter and the colours flatter. At the autumnal equinox (21/22 September) the sun rises at about 6.30am, though the sky begins turning light a good half hour before that. So depending on the season you should time your arrival a bit earlier or later, bearing in mind that in Egypt there is only about a 2-hour difference between a summer and winter sunrise. Also, before even a summer's dawn it gets chilly on the top; in winter it is bitter and there might be snow. Allow about two hours to get up, and keep at least half an hour in hand to ensure a good position. You will not be alone. Some people camp out on the peak for the night, and others begin the ascent at 2am.

The mountain is 2,285m high, but the monastery is already at an altitude of 1,500m. There are two ways up. The shorter and more difficult, established perhaps as early as the 6th century, is 3,750 **rock steps** built by the monks and starting immediately to the south of the monastery. The easier and longer route follows the road cut by the Egyptian government in the last century: this passes alongside the monastery and loops off behind it in a gradual ascent until, near the top, you must follow the ancient way for the final few hundred steps. This route is perfectly easy to follow in the dark, though sometimes you might trip over a camel. The Bedouin lie in wait, hoping you will hire their beast. And there are little **stalls** along the way, selling coffee, mint tea and biscuits. Were you expecting to meet God, you would feel shamefaced with all these indulgences; then again, you might think it best to take what you can get. The not so wicked could go up by the road and down by the steps.

At **dawn** there is first a gentle seepage of blue into the black sky and the stars go out. The mountain forms go mauve. The sun slips up from behind the horizon like a levitating egg yolk. It is very good, and there is applause, the occasional shout of 'Do it again!' The jagged peaks run through a violent range of reds and oranges. There is the silvery glint of the Red Sea and Gulf of Aqaba far in the distance. From within the chapel, built in 1934 on 6th-century foundations, there are the sounds of a mass.

The Argument between God and Man

What might come to mind as you watch the dawn up here is not so much the handing over of the Ten Commandments as the extraordinary exchange between God and Moses beforehand (Exodus 32). For 40 days and 40 nights, Moses had been on the mount, receiving God's detailed instructions for the construction of the tabernacle, the clothing of the priests, the dedication of the altar. But the people below, believing they had been abandoned, came to Aaron who made for them the golden calf, round which they sang and danced naked. 'Go, get thee down,' God says to Moses, 'for thy people have corrupted themselves. Let me alone, that my wrath may wax hot against them, and that I may consume them.' To which Moses replies: 'Wherefore should the Egyptians speak, and say, For mischief did he bring them out, to slay them in the mountains, and to consume them from the face of the earth? Turn from thy fierce wrath, and repent of this evil against thy people.' Considering that God had already once drowned the world and had promised the fire next time, you have to admire Moses' audacious attempt to shame God into forgiveness. And it worked, for 'the Lord repented of the evil which he thought to do unto his people'. It is the great theme that develops through the Bible, this covenant, this civilizing relationship, between God and man, and between man and man, and it is on the mount that it takes its first step forward. It is indeed an impressive dawn.

Gebel Katerin

Gebel Katerin or St Catherine's Mount, at 2,642m, is the highest mountain in Egypt and requires greater exertion than Mount Sinai. From the monastery to the summit via the plain of Raha it is a 5-hour walk, ascending a path marked out by cairns. Camels are available for going up (be prepared to bargain), but you will have to walk down. Effort aside, you appreciate the difference 357 additional metres of height can make when you find snow lying in crevices about its summit well into summer. Carry something warm. The view extends as far as the mountains of Arabia.

The story is that 500 years after her martyrdom in Alexandria during the Diocletian persecutions, monks found St Catherine's body glowing on the summit (notice the depressions in the rock by the chapel). Beautiful, high-born and learned, she had publicly protested her Christian belief to the emperor, who responded by sending 50 pagan philosophers to point out the error of her ways. Instead it was she who converted them to Christ, for which the emperor had them burnt alive. He then asked to marry her but was refused. Thrown into a dungeon and tortured, she converted 200 of the imperial guard. These were beheaded. Put on a spiked wheel, it fell apart, killing several onlookers. Finally when her head was chopped off, milk flowed from her veins. Angels carried her away, no one knew where, until in the 9th century she was discovered atop this mountain, whence she was placed in a casket within the Monastery of the Transfiguration, renamed St Catherine's in the 11th century. There her bones oozed sacred oil, and to this day, say the monks, 'the sweet fragrance of her sacred remains is a continuous miracle'.

That 11th-century date of the renaming of the monastery is significant. E.M. Forster observed that 'St Catherine of Alexandria is said to have died under Diocletian, but it is improbable that she ever lived; she and her wheel were creations of Western Catholicism, and the land of her supposed sufferings has only recognized her out of politeness to the French.' It was indeed precisely at the time of the First Crusade, when the monastery found itself with new protectors, that it took on St Catherine's name: certainly the story made a great impression on the Crusaders, mostly French, who carried it back to Europe.
St Catherine is recognized by churches of the Greek and Latin rites, but she does not appear in the early martyrologies. She was probably invented by some Greek writer who intended her life as an edifying romance. The Copts ignore her.

Along the Gulf of Aqaba

From St Catherine's you can head east for the resorts on the **Gulf of Aqaba**, turning south for Dahab or north for Nuweiba (79km and 126km from St Catherine's). Either serves as an alternative to spending the night in accommodation near the monastery.

But for most people the prime reason for staying anywhere along this coast is to enjoy its **diving**, which from Ras Mohammed at the southern tip of Sinai to Taba, only a kilometre from the Israeli border, is rivalled only by Australia's Great Barrier Reef for offering the finest dive sites in the world. It gets chilly in the winter however, the water too cold for swimming unless you wear a wetsuit.

Sharm el Sheikh, Na'ama Bay and Ras Mohammed

Sharm el Sheikh is 370km from the canal tunnel along the Gulf of Suez road, 171km from St Catherine's and 240km down the Gulf of Aqaba from Eilat in Israel. Many people find themselves in the resort, which lies near the very bottom of the eastern side of the Sinai peninsula, because of its good transportation links with the rest of Sinai and Egypt. When you are outside the area, Sharm is often used to refer to Sharm el Sheikh and also to **Na'ama Bay**, 7km to the north, but when you are there, then Sharm means Sharm el Sheikh only. Sharm el Sheikh is big, boring, has limited accommodation and has all the atmosphere and attitudes, once you step outside your hotel, of an Egyptian provincial town. Na'ama Bay has better reefs, an excellent beach and top flight facilities (most of the best hotels are here) – and is sanitized to the extent that you would not think that you were in Egypt at all. But the whole strip is overbuilt and ugly, an aesthetic and ecological disaster. From Sharm you can make the 30-minute drive (no public road transport, so take a taxi or hire a car) or take a boat to **Ras Mohammed National Park** at the southernmost tip of Sinai, an undeveloped **nature reserve** (no fresh water, food nor petrol), where there are superb views across the Gulf of Suez to the Red

Ras Mohammed National Park
adm $5 per person, $5 per car, camping $5 per person per night

Diving in the Gulf of Aqaba

Most diving centres are attached to hotels, but usually you do not have to stay at the hotel to join a course or expedition. The many diving spots in the **Sharm** area include **Ras Umm Sid** for dolphins and turtles, **The Tower** for barracuda, **Na'ama Bay** for turtles, and the **Near**, **Middle** and **Far Gardens** for sea fauna. Even without experience, you can enjoy snorkelling in the shallow waters of Na'ama Bay off the corniche. At **Dahab** diving is off the shore, though much of the sea bed at **Asilah** is so covered in rubbish (especially plastic bags which turtles swallow, thinking they are jellyfish, and choke to death) that you can barely make out the coral, which is meagre anyway; instead divers head some kilometres north along the coast, usually taken there on trips arranged by local dive centres. **Nuweiba** is only good for shallow snorkeling just offshore; for something more serious, dive centres will take you to points south or north of Nuweiba.

Remember it is illegal to take **coral** from the sea and export it, nor should you buy it.

Getting to and around the Gulf of Aqaba

You can fly to Sharm el Sheikh from Cairo, Alexandria, Luxor and Hurghada with Egyptair.

By Ferry to Jordan

Nuweiba is linked with the Jordanian port of Aqaba by both **ferry** (passengers and cars) and **catamaran** (passengers only). Nuweiba's port is just south of town; you should be there two hours before sailing.

The ferry departs daily at noon and midnight and takes three to five hours; tickets cost $60 and are bought at the port. The catamaran departs daily except Saturday at 4pm and takes 60 to 90 minutes; tickets cost $70.

There is also a ferry between Aqaba and Taba; it takes 45 minutes and costs $55.

Tickets can be purchased through an agent in advance or on the day of travel at the ferry ticket office near the port where you must pay in dollars (though possibly euros will be accepted), and you will need to show your passport. Visas for Jordan can normally be obtained on board either craft by North American, Australian and New Zealand, British and most Western European passport holders.

Tours and Excursions

Most hotels in Sharm el Sheikh area, or in Dahab or Nuweiba, can fix you up with **4-wheel**, **camel** and more conventional excursions (some lasting a few hours, others lasting several days) into the **mountains**, to the **turquoise mines**, and to **St Catherine's** and up **Mt Sinai**.

Sea Mountains and across the Gulf of Aqaba to Arabia. But the real spectacle is its underwater views; the best diving in the Red Sea is here, and includes rocky, sandy and reef dives, though the sea can be rough out at the reefs, where diving is not really suitable for beginners. Everyone, however, can enjoy the underwater **Shark Observatory** here.

Dahab, Nuweiba and Taba

If you are not wholly dedicated to diving, but want more of a beach holiday, Dahab (101km north of Sharm el Sheikh) and Nuweiba (72km north of Dahab) might suit you better. Strikingly set against a backdrop of bare russet mountains, **Dahab** has two lifestyles: to the south is the tourist town with its deluxe resorts, while 3km to the north is Asilah, a hippie colony on the edge of the pre-existing Bedouin village of date palms and grass huts – though this too is developing fast. The great attraction are the reef fishes, and it is the tourist town which offers the best reefs and the best dive shops. At **Nuweiba**, though mountains also loom behind, its situation is less attractive than Dahab's, with few diving facilities for exploring its fine reefs, though the diving is easy here and good for novices. The mood is changing, though, with the construction of several new luxury resort hotels.

At the northern end of the Gulf of Aqaba, next door to Eilat in Israel, is the beach resort of **Taba**, handed back to Egypt early in 1989. Offshore is **Geziret el Faraun** (Pharaoh's Island), bearing along its crest the ruins of a Crusader castle. Built roughly and in haste in about 1115 by King Baldwin I of Jerusalem, this castle on what the Franks called the Isle de Graye marks the farthest point of Crusader expansion.

Where to Stay in the Gulf of Aqaba

Sharm el Sheikh and Na'ama Bay

Luxury ($$$$$)

*******Sonesta Beach Resort**, **t** (069) 360 0725, *www.sonesta.com/SharmResort*, on the beach at the north end of Na'ama Bay. A series of beautifully designed Arab-style chalets. In addition to all the expected 5-star facilities, it has tennis courts, seven swimming pools, a water gym and a club for children, a scuba service and a diving centre.

*******Jolieville Sharm el Sheikh Resort and Casino**, 7km from Na'ama Bay (free shuttle) **t** (069) 360 3200, *www.jolievillehotels.com*. A fully equipped luxury resort hotel, spacious rooms, a variety of restaurants, health club, large water theme pool, tennis courts, and the only 18-hole championship golf course in the region.

*******Hilton Fayrouz Resort**, **t** (069) 360 0136, *www.hiltonworldresorts.com/Fayrouz*. Right on one of the largest beaches in Na'ama Bay, it has squash and tennis courts, pools, dive courses, a kids club, several restaurants serving seafood and Italian and Egyptian cuisine; its rooms are spacious, all with private balconies.

Moderate ($$$)

******Camel Dive Hotel**, boutique hotel attached to one of the best dive centres in the area, located at the centre of Na'ama Bay, **t** (069) 360 0700, *www.cameldive.com*. Comfortable rooms overlooking courtyard with pool, most with terraces. Lively Camel Bar and subdued Roof Bar, several restaurants serving Egyptian, Italian and Indian cuisine.

*****Sanafir Village**, **t** (069) 360 0197. One of the earliest hotels at Na'ama Bay, it is towards the southern end of the bay and several hundred metres from the shore. It has air-conditioned huts and also rooms within the domed Moorish-style hotel. Altogether it is a relaxed place to stay, with pool and lively nightlife.

*****Halomy Sharm Village**, **t** (069) 360 0681, **f** (069) 360 0134. A string of air-conditioned chalets arranged along a clifftop at the southern end of the bay with good views over the gulf. Access to the centre of town and the private beach via steps from the hotel (otherwise it is a 2km taxi drive to the centre), private coral reef, excellent snorkeling. Rooms have bathroom, satellite TV, and most have a private balcony or terrace. A good place, but a bit worn.

Inexpensive ($$)

****Sharks Bay Umbi Diving Village**, **t** (069) 360 0942, *www.sharksbay.com*. A Bedouin-owned place 6km north of Na'ama Bay (say 'Sharks Bay Bedouin' to the taxi driver). Budget bamboo huts at the top of the cliff are the cheapest option here, but there are also wooden cabins right on the beach and rooms built into the cliffside. A friendly place, terrific location on the sea, and a good Bedouin restaurant too.

Dahab

*******Hilton Dahab**, **t** (069) 364 0310, *www.hiltonworldresorts.com/Resorts/Dahab/index.html* ($$$$). White Nubian-style bungalows built round a saltwater lagoon, creating the ambience of an oasis entirely lost to the world. All rooms with balconies or patios and marvellous views; tennis court, pool, private beach, dive and windsurfing centre.

*****Christina Beach Hotel**, 1km south of Dahab Bay, **t** (069) 364 0390, *www.christinahotels.com* ($$$). A beautiful, friendly and clean place run by an Egyptian-Swiss couple. Rooms are spacious and tastefully furnished, all with bathrooms and fans (air conditioning is available), and wonderful views. The hotel will help arrange treks, diving, etc.

****Blue Beach Club**, at the north end of Dahab, a five minute walk from the Eel Garden dive site, **t** (069) 364 0411, *www.bluebeachclub.com* ($$$). Spacious rooms with an Arabian feel; all have bathrooms and either a balcony or a terrace looking on to stunning views. Good restaurant and a popular bar.

Bedouin Moon, in the desert foothills just north of Dahab on the Blue Hole road, **t** (069) 640 695, *http://hosting.menanet.net/~bedouinmoon/bedouin moon* ($$). A small Bedouin-run hotel with restaurant, shop, laundry and dive centre; it also organizes treks into the mountains. The rooms are pleasant with sea or mountain views, all with balconies and bathrooms.

Bedouin Moon ($; *see* above) has dormitory rooms, 3 people per room, with private bathroom.

Nuweiba

Accommodation is found in three areas: at Nuweiba town; Maagana Bay south of town; and Tarabeen, the Bedouin area north of town.

********Hilton Coral Nuweiba**, **t** (069) 520320, *www.hiltonworldresorts.com/Resorts/Nuweiba/index.html* ($$$$). A luxury resort on Maagana Bay with heated pools (it gets chilly in winter) and full watersport activities.

Swisscare Resort Hotel, **t** (069) 352 0640, *www.swisscare-hotels.com* ($$$). Run by the same Swiss-Egyptian family as the Christina in Dahab. The comfortable rooms are in fact suites comprising a living room and bedroom, two bathrooms, two satellite TVs, and two terraces for views overlooking the pool, the sea and the mountains of Sinai and Saudi Arabia.

Nuweiba Village Resort, **t** (069) 350 0401, *www.nuweibavillageresort.com* ($$$). A good, laid back, comfortable place, where all rooms have satellite TV, private terrace frontage, air conditioning, private bathrooms, and direct access to the resort's kilometre-long stretch of private beach.

Nakhil Inn, at the north end of Tarabeen beach, **t** (069) 350 0879, *www.nakhil-inn.com* ($$$). Has air-conditioned rooms with private bathrooms and satellite TV.

There are usually cheap **campgrounds** at Tarabeen, though they come and go with the seasons.

Taba

*******Taba Hilton**, **t** (069) 353 0140, *www.hiltonworldresorts.com/Resorts/Taba* ($$$$). Offers the works.

****Salah el Din**, **t** (069) 353 0340, **f** (069) 353 0343 ($$$). A decent place run by Misr Travel.

The Nile Delta

From the beginning of the dynastic period through Ptolemaic times, the Nile Delta played a role of gathering importance, politically, economically and culturally. Already by the New Kingdom the draining of the Delta marshes had provided Egypt with an area of cultivation double that of the entire Nile valley. But whereas the course of the Nile from the First Cataract down to Cairo has remained almost unchanged throughout recorded history, the play of the river across the alluvium of Lower Egypt has erased history itself.

18

Don't miss

1. **See the sails of feluccas billow across fields furrowed with canals**
   Travelling by train through the Delta **p.478**
2. **Tombs and temples of the golden pharaohs of the 'Thebes of the North'**
   Tanis **p.480**
3. **Joyous October *moulid* of a Sufi saint**
   Tanta **p.482**

See map overleaf

The Nile Delta

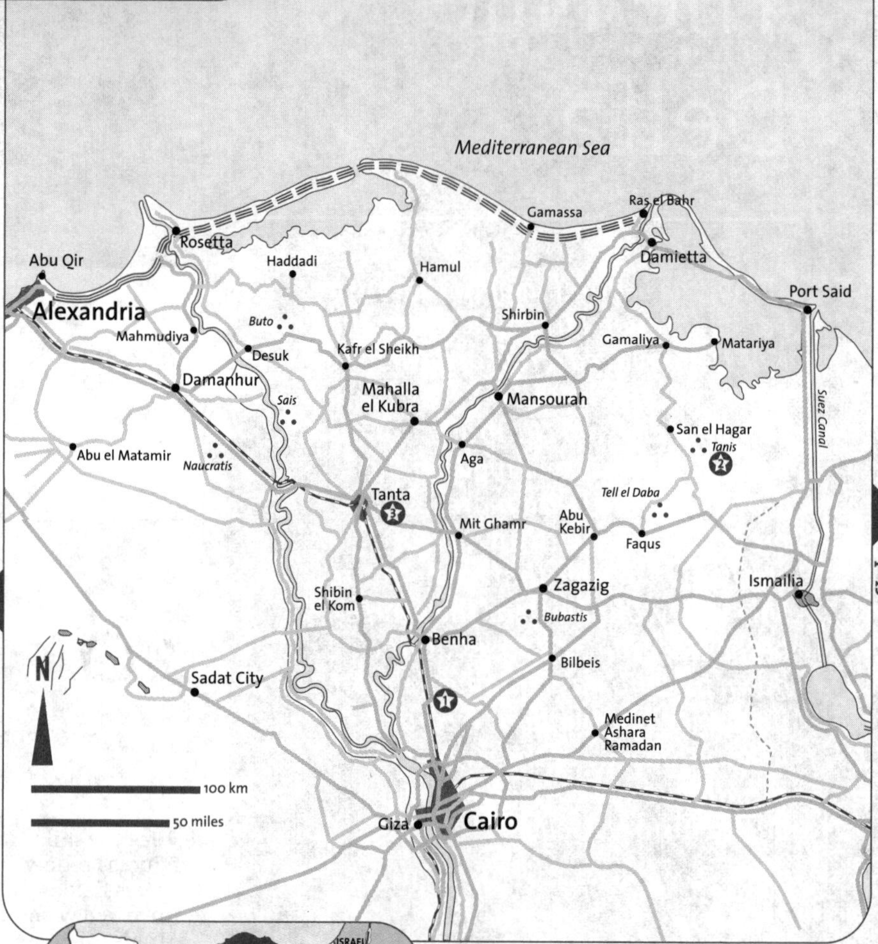

p.402

p.438

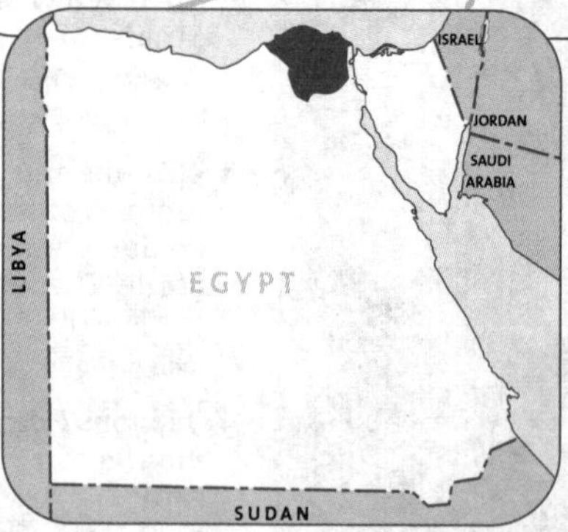

Don't miss

1. Travelling by train through the Delta **p.478**
2. Tanis **p.480**
3. Tanta **p.482**

That odd mixture of 'the country' and 'the East' that is typical of this part of Egypt – at one moment an ordinary Cambridgeshire/ Surrey effect of crops and ditches and trees, at the next vignettes from the Arabian Nights.

E.M. Forster, 1915

In antiquity the Nile had seven arms, from east to west the Pelusiac, the Tanitic, the Mendesian, the Phatnitic or Bucolic, the Sebennytic, the Bolbitine and the Canopic. Now it has only two; one (the ancient Phatnitic) flowing into the sea at Damietta, the other (the ancient Bolbitine) at Rosetta.

As arms dried up or changed course, cities were abandoned; often they disappeared; and even today, when Egyptologists discover a site, the arguments rage over its identification, unhelped by the shifting topography.

A Great but Vanished Past

The wealth of its soil and the Delta's proximity to the Mediterranean and nearby coastal lands attracted foreign settlement, both by military and peaceful means. From their capital in the eastern Delta, the Hyksos ruled over the whole of Egypt during the Second Intermediate Period, and in the eastern Delta too was the Land of Goshen, mentioned in Genesis and Exodus. The Sea Peoples, recorded on the wall of Ramses III's funerary temple (*see* 'Medinet Habu', p.339), fought to establish themselves in the Delta estuaries, and in the 7th century BC Naucratis in the western Delta became a flourishing Greek trading centre. The Ramessids had their roots in the Delta and Ramses II built his capital, Pi-Ramses, here. Throughout the first millennium BC the Delta dominated the affairs of Egypt. The XXI Dynasty came from Tanis; the XXII Dynasty was founded at Bubastis; the XXIII Dynasty came also from Tanis; and the XXIV, XXVI and XXVIII Dynasties all came from Sais. Its importance became all the greater when the Ptolemies built their capital, Alexandria, between the Delta and the sea.

Yet the Delta, for all its rich and cosmopolitan past, its important sanctuaries and great cities, almost entirely lacks the historical survivals of the deserts and the valley. Where the aridity and limited cultivation of the south has preserved the past, in the north the shifting Nile, the fanning mud, abundant harvests, repeatedly ploughed fields and Mediterranean rainfall have all but obliterated it.

Where the Past has Gone

The Delta people often built in limestone and granite, but the blocks had to be brought great distances from the deserts and the

Getting to and around the Nile Delta

To appreciate the Delta landscape, it is enough to travel by rail or road between Cairo and Alexandria. These also make good bases for excursions.

By Train

There is a frequent service between Cairo and Alexandria, with most trains stopping at Benha, Tanta and Damanhur. There is a less frequent service between Cairo, Tanta, Zagazig and Damietta.

By Road

Service taxis to all the Delta towns depart from Cairo's Ahmed Helmi terminus near Midan Ramses, and from Alexandria's al-Moaf al-Gedid station which is on the start of the Desert Road to Cairo, and in some cases from Midan el Gumhuriya in front of the main railway station.

The East Delta Bus Company has frequent daily **bus** services to Zagazig, Faqus, Mansura, Damietta, Ras el Bar (summer only) from the Cairo Gateway in Cairo, and from Alexandria's al-Moaf al-Gedid station at the start of the Desert Road to Cairo. Sites in the western Delta are best visited by first taking a train to Tanta or Damanhur and then hiring a taxi.

Tours

Agencies like Misr Travel sometimes offer tours (or could arrange one for you) to major Delta sites like **Bubastis** and **Tanis**.

valley. It was common already in pharaonic times for the stone of earlier structures to be reused in later ones rather than to go to the far-off quarries for more. The disassembling of the past was even more intense during the Middle Ages when the Delta people would plunder ancient buildings, burning the limestone in their kilns and using the granite for foundations or grindstones. Right up until recent decades the *sebakhin* (*see* 'Medinet el Fayyum', p.226) would work the tells (or *koms*, to use the particularly Egyptian word for those great mounds of debris marking the sites of ancient settlements) for fertilizer, so that some that were 10m high in Napoleon's time are near-level today. In any case, mud brick was more often used, and where these remains have been excavated, they have immediately begun to suffer weathering. Finds from the famous sites of the Delta have been taken away to the museums of Cairo, Alexandria or abroad, and what remains in situ does no justice to their historical renown.

Green and Watery Landscape

Travelling by train through the delta

Whatever your interest in the ancient sites, it is fascinating to travel through the Delta landscape with its extraordinary flatness and vast fields of cotton, rice and maize; buffalo with sleek oily coats and down-turned horns like large floppy ears, grazing or ploughing or turning wheels for grinding or pumping; also sheep, donkeys, camels, and huge dovecotes like Cambodian temples. High clouds blow in from the Mediterranean, a reminder that here in the north during the winter months it is advisable to have a raincoat, and along the coast a warm sweater for evening breezes throughout the year. And spectacle though it is to see a tanker seemingly plough through the desert at Suez, it is enchanting to see the sails of feluccas billow across fields furrowed with canals.

Ancient Sites in the Eastern Delta

The most significant ancient sites in the eastern Delta are **Bubastis** near Zagazig (85km northeast of Cairo), the sites claimed as **Avaris** and **Pi-Ramses** adjacent to one another at **Tell el Daba** and **Qantir** (just beyond Faqus and 45km northeast of Zagazig) and **Tanis** near San el Hagar (74km northeast of Zagazig). Only Tanis, and possibly Bubastis, would be of interest to the non-specialist.

Zagazig, founded only in the 1820s, is a chief centre of the corn and cotton trade. It stands on the Muweis Canal, once the Tanitic arm of the Nile.

Bubastis

At 3km south along the road to Bilbeis is **Tell Basta**, the site of Bubastis, one of the most ancient cities in Egypt. Bubastis means House of the Goddess Bastet, who was represented as a lioness, later as a graceful domestic cat. Below the southwest side of the tell is her much ruined temple, founded during the Old Kingdom but given its final form by the pharoahs of the XXII Dynasty, who resided here – the festival hall, dating from this last period, is the most evident feature of the temple. Where now there are only some granite blocks and columns to see, some with inscriptions and reliefs, and a few statues, Herodotus said that of all the temples of Egypt, this gave the greatest pleasure to look at, both for its own merits but also because the city all round it had been raised to a higher level, so you could look down upon it where it stood amid shade trees on almost an island formed by two embracing canals which stopped short without meeting.

Near by are **underground galleries** for the burial of cats, where many fine bronzes of cats or of Bastet have been found. Many artefacts from here, if they have not been taken to the Egyptian Museum in Cairo, can be seen in Zagazig's **Orabi Museum**, named after Ahmed Orabi, leader of the 1882 revolt against foreign influence, who was born here.

Orabi Museum
open 9–4 daily, closed Fri 11.30–1.30

Once, a licentious festival was held at Bubastis.

They come in barges, men and women together, a great number in each boat. On the way, some of the women keep up a continual clatter with castinets and some of the men play flutes, while the rest, both men and women, sing and clap their hands. Whenever they pass a town on the riverbank, they bring the barge close inshore, some of the women continuing to act as I have said, while others shout abuse at the women of the place or start dancing, or stand up and hitch up their skirts. When they reach Bubastis they celebrate the festival with elaborate sacrifices, and more wine is consumed than during all the rest of the year. The numbers that meet there, are, according to a native report, as many as 700,000 men and women.

Herodotus

Tell el Daba and Qantir

Avaris was the Hyksos capital and **Pi-Ramses** was the Delta capital of Ramses II. But though it has long been accepted that Pi-Ramses stood on or near the site of Avaris, their location has been disputed since the beginning of modern Egyptology. For much of that time, Tanis was favoured; but then starting with Egyptian excavations at Qantir in the 1920s and 1950s, and culminating with Austrian excavations just south of it at Tell el Daba in the 1960s and 1970s, opinion has swung round to accepting the former as the site of Pi-Ramses and the latter as the site of Avaris. Both are situated along the ancient course of the Pelusiac arm of the Nile.

What has always given this question a heightened interest is the mention of Pi-Ramses in Exodus 1:11 and 12:37 as the city built for the pharaoh by the afflicted children of Israel and, under Moses' leadership, their point of departure out of Egypt.

In fact the excavations look like an exposed underground car park, and as a recent report on the sites says, 'The old splendour of the two cities has vanished completely because of quarrying, plundering and later land reclamation'. But once, as Ramses II himself said when he had founded Pi-Ramses, 'His Majesty has built himself a residence whose name is Great of Victories. It lies between Syria and Egypt, full of food and provisions. It follows the model of Upper Egyptian Thebes, its duration like that of Memphis. The sun arises in its horizon, and even sets within it. Everyone has left his own town and settles in its neighbourhood.'

Tanis

27 **Tanis**

The site of Tanis, for all its fall from biblical grace, is the most outstanding in the Delta from the layman's point of view. It is a huge *kom*, 3.5km from north to south, 1.5km broad and rising to 35m above sea level. A number of excavations since 1825 have still only turned up a small portion of the whole, revealing structural remains from the XXI Dynasty through Ptolemaic times. But also a great quantity of stone, originally statues, stelae, carvings and blocks from the time of Ramses II and frequently bearing his cartouche, have been found incorporated into later buildings or littered about. It was on this basis that the French excavators here from 1927 to 1956 argued that this was Pi-Ramses – and certainly as much statuary has been found here as anywhere else in Egypt except Thebes, causing it to be known as the '**Thebes of the North**'.

Several points went against its identification with Avaris and Pi-Ramses, however; one being that it was too far inland, on the Tanitic rather than on the Pelusiac arm of the Nile, and therefore too far from the edge of the Delta to have been a suitable military base for incoming Hyksos or an outward bound Ramses II; another, more importantly, being that for all its Ramessid statuary, the earliest structural level belonged to the XXI rather than to the IXX Dynasty. In fact what seems to have happened is that in building Tanis, Pi-Ramses was pilfered of its stones.

From the road a track leads up to the excavation headquarters from where there is a good view of the walled temple precinct and the rubble mounds beneath which a great deal of the city still lies. The completely ruined **Temple of Amun** is nevertheless spectacular for its fallen colossal statuary and architectural fragments, though the most important pieces have been taken to the Egyptian Museum in Cairo, along with the splendid gold masks, inlaid jewellery and silver sarcophagus found at the royal necropolis towards the southwest of the enclosure. Discovered in 1939, these XXI and XXII Dynasty royal tombs were at least as important a find as that of Tutankhamun's. The coming war, however, overshadowed the discovery and it received little public attention at the time. The best preserved tomb is No.3 of **Psusennes I** (XXI Dyn). A sacred lake and the remains of two other temples are evident within the enclosure walls.

Damietta and the Crusades

Dumyat (210km northeast of Cairo), as Damietta is known in Arabic, lies 15km from the Mediterranean on a narrow strip of land between the Nile (the ancient Phatnitic arm) and Lake Manzala. With a population of around a million, Damietta is a thriving port and industrial centre, and has some interesting houses of the Ottoman period comparable to those at Rosetta (which being near Alexandria is much easier to visit).

Damietta's heyday was before the revival of Alexandria and the opening of the Suez Canal when it was a prosperous Arab trading city. But its fame rests in its struggle against the Crusaders, and that Damietta stood farther north, to be razed to the ground in 1250 by Shagarat al-Durr's Mamelukes after the site had yet again proved its vulnerability to foreign attack. (*See* Cairo, 'To the Northern Walls', p.134.) The old port was taken in 1218, principally by Germans, and abandoned again in 1221, but not before its townspeople were sold into slavery. Its inhabitants fled when in 1249 St Louis landed near by, but Damietta was returned to Egypt a year later as part of St Louis' ransom.

One of those among the besiegers of Damietta in 1218 was **St Francis of Assisi**. Seeing that the attack was at first going badly, he courageously crossed the enemy lines to confront Sultan Kamil in person. He informed the sultan that he had come to convert him and his people to Christ, apparently unaware that Kamil was surrounded with Coptic advisers and fully familiar with the Christian faith. St Francis offered to enter a fiery furnace on the condition that should he come out alive, Kamil and his people would embrace Christianity. The sultan replied to the saint with a lesson in humanity and common sense, saying that gambling with one's life was not a valid proof of one's god, and saw St Francis on his way with oriental courtesy and lavish gifts.

Between Lake Manzala and the sea a narrow spit of land carries a poor road to Port Said (66km). Pelicans, storks, flamingos and egrets inhabit its brackish waters and southern marshes. The **lagoon** was caused by the subsidence of the northern Delta; from the time of Augustus the Mediterranean began its incursion, destroying good land and disrupting the drainage system (the Mendesian and Tanitic mouths were once here), a process completed by the end of the 4th century AD. There is a summer beach resort, **Ras el Bahr**, at the tip of land north of Damietta where the Nile debouches into the sea, and another, 45km west at **Gamassa**.

The Western Delta

So little remains of antiquity in the western Delta that it is not worth visiting except as a passer-by between Cairo and Alexandria. The Cairo–Alexandria railway and Agricultural Road parallel one another all the way, passing through Benha, Tanta and Damanhur.

Tanta

Tanta is a nondescript city of 450,000, but annually it jumps to life when as many as two million people from the Delta and all round the Arab world attend a joyous **moulid** centred round the mosque and tomb of Said Ahmed el Badawi, a Sufi saint who died in 1276. The origins of the celebration clearly antecede Badawi, for unlike so many other Muslim festivals, this one at Tanta is linked not to the lunar calendar but is fixed to coincide with the cotton harvest towards the end of October. During the week-long festival large quantities of sugar-coated nuts called *hubb el Azziz* ('seeds of the Beloved Prophet') are consumed – a delicacy popular in Egypt since ancient times. A burlesque sideshow to the more serious ritual of the moulid, known locally as *zeffa el Sharamit*, the procession of the prostitutes, recalls the licentious celebrations at Bubastis described by Herodotus.

Such is the potency of the saint that throughout the year both Christians and Muslims come to pray for favours or offer thanks for some stroke of good fortune at his tomb inside the 19th-century mosque built by the khedive Ismail in a square at the centre of the city, the arcaded front façade and its minaret added only in 1979. This is far from being the only case in Egypt of ecumenism arising from the presumed efficaciousness of some holy figure; at Deir el Muharraq, for example, Muslim women wanting to become pregnant will pray at the spot where the Virgin Mary dwelt with the infant Jesus after their flight from Herod.

Sais is to the northwest of Tanta; once a royal capital, but now in part due to the activities of the *sebakhin* no more than a waterlogged hole in the ground, it was sacred to the goddess Neith who protected the embalmed bodies and entrails of the dead and is often depicted on sarcophagi and at the entrances to tombs.

Buto lies to the east of Desuk and is most conveniently reached via Damanhur; its deity was the cobra goddess Wadjet, represented as the uraeus on the pharaonic crown.

Naucratis was founded in the 7th century BC as a Greek trading city, and until the founding of Alexandria three centuries later was the pre-eminent commercial centre in Egypt. It is now a level and desolate patch of ground to the left of the Tanta-Damanhur road.

Damanhur stands on the site of the Roman Hermopolis Parva, no remains of its past surviving.

Rosetta (Rashid) and **Abu Qir** (ancient Canopus) are covered later as excursions from Alexandria (*see* pp.523–4).

Where to Stay in the Nile Delta

The only places offering accommodation in the Delta are Tanta, Damietta, and a few coastal resorts to the west of Damietta. For Rosetta, *see* the Alexandria chapter.

Damietta

****Soliman**, 5 Sharia el Galaa, **t/f** (057) 377 050 ($$). Rooms with air conditioning, TV and fridge.

***El Manshy**, 5 Sharia el Nokrashi, **t** (057) 323 308, **f** (057) 345 050 ($). Well equipped and comfortable, with a good restaurant.

Ras el Bahr

****El Mina**, Sharia 61, **t** (057) 252 9290 ($$).

****Abu Tabl**, 4 Sharia 17, **t** (057) 252 8166, **f** (057) 252 6650 ($$).

There are many other hotels along the seafront.

Gamassa

****Amoun**, **t** (050) 760 660, **f** (050) 761 710 ($$). In the souk area.

****Beau Rivage**, **t** (050) 760 268 ($$).

Tanta

*****New Arafa**, Midan Mahatta, **t** (040) 340 5040, **f** (040) 335 7080, by the railway station ($$$). Rooms have

air conditioning, TV, minibar; restaurant and 24-hour snack bar.
***Green House, Sharia el Borsa, t (040) 333 0761, f (040) 333 0320 ($$$). Off Midan Gumhuriya and similarly equipped. Both hotels should be booked well in advance if you want to stay during the moulid.

Alexandria

Even the most determined seer of sights will be able to catch the evening train back to Cairo. A Roman theatre, Pompey's Pillar, the catacombs at Kom el Shogafa; these and a medieval fortress squatting on the foundations of the Pharos lighthouse are the principal but paltry remains of Alexandria's resplendent past. Some will see nothing. Others will voyage through the phantom city and listen to its voices and its music.

For all the commonplace surface of the modern town, Alexandria is haunted by its past. There was a time when it was the greatest city in the ancient world and the capital of Western civilization. If more survived, that past would haunt you less.

19

Don't miss

1. **Greatest poet of the 20th century**
   Cavafy Museum p.498
2. **Roman life revealed**
   Roman theatre and the Villa of Birds p.500
3. **Eastern Harbour view**
   Fort Qaytbey p.515
4. **One of Egypt's weird?est places**
   Catacombs of Kom el Shogafa p.518
5. **The great Library reborn**
   Bibliotheca Alexandrina p.520

See map overleaf

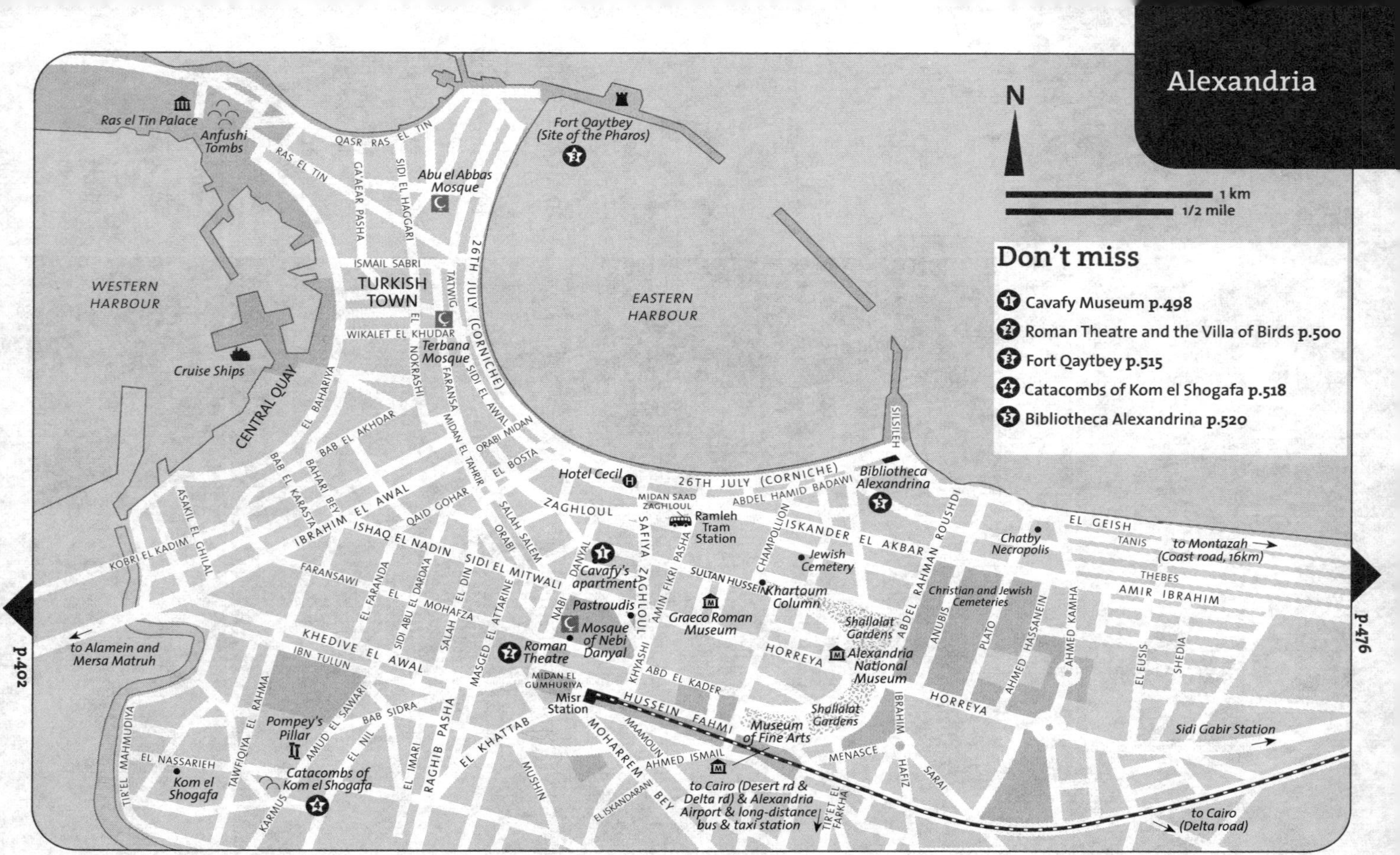
Alexandria
N
1 km
1/2 mile
Don't miss
1 Cavafy Museum p.498
2 Roman Theatre and the Villa of Birds p.500
3 Fort Qaytbey p.515
4 Catacombs of Kom el Shogafa p.518
5 Bibliotheca Alexandrina p.520
Ras el Tin Palace
Anfushi Tombs
Fort Qaytbey (Site of the Pharos)
WESTERN HARBOUR
EASTERN HARBOUR
TURKISH TOWN
Abu el Abbas Mosque
Terbana Mosque
Cruise Ships
CENTRAL QUAY
Hotel Cecil
26TH JULY (CORNICHE)
Bibliotheca Alexandrina
SILSILEH
Ramleh Tram Station
MIDAN SAAD ZAGHLOUL
Cavafy's apartment
Pastroudis
Mosque of Nebi Danyal
Roman Theatre
MIDAN EL GUMHURIYA
Misr Station
Graeco Roman Museum
Khartoum Column
Jewish Cemetery
Shallalat Gardens
Alexandria National Museum
Museum of Fine Arts
Christian and Jewish Cemeteries
Chatby Necropolis
Pompey's Pillar
Catacombs of Kom el Shogafa
Kom el Shogafa
to Alamein and Mersa Matruh
to Montazah (Coast road, 16km)
Sidi Gabir Station
to Cairo (Delta road)
to Cairo (Desert rd & Delta rd) & Alexandria Airport & long-distance bus & taxi station
p.402
p.476
QASR RAS EL TIN
RAS EL TIN
GA'AEAR PASHA
SIDI EL HAGGARI
ISMAIL SABRI
TATWIG
WIKALET EL KHUDAR
EL NOKRASHI
FARANSA
SIDI EL AWAL
MIDAN EL TAHRIR
ORABI MIDAN
EL BOSTA
EL BAHARIYA
BAB EL AKHDAR
BAB EL KARASTA
BAHARI BEY
EL AWAL
IBRAHIM
QAID GOHAR
ISHAQ EL NADIN
SIDI EL MITWALI
SALAH SALEM
ORABI
ASAKIL EL GHILAL
KOBRI EL KADIM
FARANSAWI
EL FARANDA
SIDI ABU EL DARDAA
EL MOHAFZA
SALAH EL DIN
MASGED EL ATTARINE
NABI DANYAL
ZAGHLOUL
SAFIYA ZAGHLOUL
AMIN FIKRI PASHA
SULTAN HUSSEIN
KHYASHI
ABD EL KADER
KHEDIVE EL AWAL
IBN TULUN
TIR'EL MAHMUDIYA
EL NASSARIEH
TAWFIQIYA EL RAHMA
AMUD EL SAWARI
BAB SIDRA
EL NIL
KARMUS
EL IMARI
RAGHIB PASHA
EL KHATTAB
MUSHIN
MOHARREM BEY
MAAMOUN
AHMED ISMAIL
EL ISKANDARANI
TIR'ET EL FARKHA
HUSSEIN FAHMI
HORREYA
ABDEL HAMID BADAWI
CHAMPOLLION
ISKANDER EL AKBAR
ABDEL RAHMAN ROUSHDI
ANUBIS
PLATO
AHMED HASSANEIN
AHMED KAMHA
EL GEISH
TANIS
THEBES
AMIR IBRAHIM
EL EUSIS
SHEDIA
IBRAHIM
HAFIZ
SARAI
MENASCE

Alexandria is not an obvious city; she requires, before revealing herself, time, study and love.

Sir Ronald Storrs, *Orientations*, 1937

Unlike Rome or Athens with their monuments extant, Alexandria is all intimation: *here* (some spot) is where Alexander lay entombed, *here* Cleopatra committed suicide; *here* the Library, the Serapeum ... yet almost nothing is there – a stone, a broken column, an unsuspected chamber, but nothing substantial to root the city's phantom personages to their place, and they wander through Alexandria's streets, intruding on your waking thoughts.

Overlaying the ancient city and resonating with it is the architectural fantasia of 19th- and early 20th-century Alexandria, that fevered cosmopolitan town celebrated by Constantine Cavafy, E.M. Forster and Lawrence Durrell. The departed cast of this more recent Alexandria joins the ghostly pageant, haunting the cafés, barber shops, hotels and apartments of a gently disintegrating stage set.

Until the 1950s Alexandria was truly a cosmopolitan city; now only a few Armenians and Syro-Lebanese relieve the relentless homogeneity of the town, which has become conservatively Islamic. The Mediterranean corniche, once set with villas and gardens, has been mercilessly developed and its beaches spoilt, and five million people fill a city built in more spacious times for 500,000. Yet Alexandria (Iskandariya in Arabic) is a city of resonances, where even the lift of a summer sea breeze reminds you of its past and possibilities. Alexandrian façades are lighter than those of Cairo, the rooftops almost white and gleaming in the morning sun. Instead of brushed by desert sand, the city seems frosted by the salt air of the Mediterranean. The sea weather gives freshness to Alexandria and sets it apart from the rest of Egypt, while even the city's name recalls its founder from a foreign shore.

Significantly, the two most interesting projects in Alexandria today pay homage to the past, when thanks to the Greeks the city belonged to the wider Mediterranean world. One project is the underwater archaeological investigations in and around the Eastern Harbour where Greek and French teams are rediscovering Cleopatra's city. The other is the new Bibliotheca Alexandrina, built in emulation of the Library of the Ptolemies, which housed the greatest collection of knowledge in the ancient world.

History

When **Alexander the Great** entered Egypt in November 332 BC he marched straight to Memphis. But early in 331 BC he sailed northwards down the Nile, and there, prompted by a dream, he made his most lasting contribution to civilization. As he slept, a grey-haired man of venerable appearance seemed to stand by his side, reciting these lines from the *Odyssey*: 'There is an island in the surging sea, which they call Pharos, lying off Egypt.' The next morning, Alexander went to Rhakotis, then a place of goatherds

Getting to Alexandria

By Air

Alexandria is served by two airports. **Nouzha Airport** (which is coded ALY) is just south of the city, 6km from the centre, 13km from Montazah. One of the pleasures of flying out from or (especially) in to Nouzha are the wonderful daytime or nighttime views of Alexandria. Nouzha Airport has flights to Cairo (though these are hardly worth it as the train and bus services are so frequent and quick, and are also more reliable – flights are occasionally cancelled) as well as a few international flights, such as Olympic and Royal Jordanian airlines. Increasingly, however, international airlines are shifting their flights to the far less convenient **Burg el Arab Airport** (coded HBE), a former RAF airfield 60km west of Alexandria.

Airline offices are centrally located. **British Airways** is at 15 Midan Saad Zaghloul, **t** (03) 487 6668, while **Olympic**, **t** (03) 486 1014, and **Egyptair**, **t** (03) 486 5937 or their national call centre **t** 0900 70000, are both at 19 Midan Saad Zaghloul. All three are on the north side of the Ramleh tram station. **Lufthansa**, **t** (03) 487 7031, is at 6 Sharia Talaat Harb, which lies between Sharias Saad Zaghloul and Salah-Salem.

By Train

The Alexandria railway station, **Mahattat Misr** (which means Cairo railway station, i.e. the station for trains going to Cairo) is the main railway station, facing Midan el Gumhuriya at the south end of Sharia Nebi Danyal, though all Alexandria-bound trains stop first at Sidi Gaber, a secondary station 4km to the east. There are frequent trains to Cairo (2–3 hours) via Sidi Gaber, Damanhur, Tanta and Benha. Trains also leave here (or from Sidi Gaber) to Rosetta in the east and Mersa Matruh in the west, but these are slow, filthy, uncomfortable, non-air-conditioned third-class journeys that are not recommended; go by bus or service taxi, or hire a car or taxi instead.

There is a Tourist Information Office on platform 1 at Alexandria railway station, 9am–6pm, **t** (03) 392 5985. The station also has a good clean bright coffee shop at the head of the platforms, but it is pricey.

By Long-distance Service Taxi

Service taxis for Cairo and Aboukir are found in Midan el Gumhuriya in front of Mahattat Misr, the main railway station. Service taxis for all other destinations are at the al-Moaf al-Gedid bus station which is on the start of the highway to Cairo, close to Carrefour and the City Centre Mall, several kilometres south of the centre of town – you will need to take a taxi to get there.

By Long-distance Bus

All long-distance buses arrive at and depart from the al-Moaf al-Gedid station, which is on the edge of Lake Mariut at the start of the highway to Cairo, close by Carrefour and the City Centre Mall.

West Delta Bus Company has services to Cairo, Mersa Matruh and Siwa; it has a kiosk at al-Moaf al-Gedid station and also at Midan Saad Zaghloul near the Cecil in town.

Super Jet has services to Cairo and Sinai; it has a kiosk at al-Moaf al-Gedid station and also opposite the Sidi Gaber railway station.

Tickets are best bought a day in advance.

West Delta and Super Jet operate air-conditioned buses with onboard toilets. The journey to Cairo (Giza, Cairo Gateway, Cairo Airport) takes about 3 hours and follows the Desert Road. The journey along the Mediterranean coast to Mersa Matruh takes about 4 hours and continues after an hour's stopover for the 4-hour ride to Siwa.

There are also cheaper, slower long-distance buses which do not have air conditioning or onboard toilets.

Travel Agents and Tours

The best all-round travel agent is **Annie Travel,** 30 Sharia Ahmed Orabi (also known as Sharia Tewfiq), which runs parallel with Sharia Salah-Salem, **t** (03) 483 0007, **f** (03) 483 5586. With courtesy, efficiency and reliability, they can fix up flights, train tickets, cruises, excursions, accommodation – you name it. Also good are **Thomas Cook**, 15 Midan Saad Zaghloul, **t** (03) 487 5118; and **Misr Travel**, 33 Sharia Salah-Salem, **t** (03) 484 6001.

---

and coastguards, opposite the island, and seeing the advantages of the site, declared that Homer, besides his other admirable qualities, was a far-seeing architect.

Two limestone ridges running parallel to the coast give Alexandria its permanence. The inner ridge holds Alexandria fixed against the shifting alluvium of Egypt; the outer breaks the waves. It is a feature unique in Egypt, but vision was required to realize its potential. By ordering that a causeway join the ridges, Alexander at a stroke gave his city its two sea harbours, while another harbour on Lake Mareotis behind, linked to the Nile, drew all the riches of Egypt to Alexandria. But he did not stay long enough to see a single building erected. Instead he made his mysterious visit to Siwa (*see* p.408) and then back across the desert to Memphis before committing his life to the conquest of Asia. Eight years later, at the age of 33, he was dead. His body was brought to Memphis, but the priests refused it, saying: 'Do not settle him here, but at the city he built at Rhakotis, for wherever this body must lie the city will be uneasy, disturbed with wars and battles.' So he descended the Nile again, wrapped in gold and enclosed in a coffin of glass, and was buried at the centre of Alexandria, by its great crossroads, to be its civic hero and guardian spirit. Memphis has slipped into the mud. Alexandria after many battles survives.

When Alexander died, one of his Macedonian generals took Egypt as his portion of the divided empire and made Alexandria his capital, ruling as Ptolemy I Soter and founding a dynasty that was to end with the suicide of Cleopatra VI – 'It is well done and fitting for a princess/Descended of so many royal kings'. Under Cleopatra and Antony, the city very nearly supplanted Rome, which both strategically and culturally was Alexandria's inferior.

During the reign of the Ptolemies Alexandria became a resort of artists, poets and scholars, and was outstanding particularly in its mathematicians and scientists. Among these were Euclid, who in his theories of numbers and plane and solid geometry demonstrated how knowledge can be derived from rational methods alone; Eratosthenes (*see* **Aswan**, p.361), who determined the earth's circumference; Aristarchos of Samos, who, anticipating Copernicus by 1,800 years, was author of the heliocentric theory; and Erasistratos, who came close to discovering the circulation of blood and first made the distinction between motor and sensory nerves. Later, in Roman times, philosophy flourished too; so that here, between desert and sea, men enquired into the problems of the universe in a way unknown before in Egypt, though, unlike some of their predecessors in Greece, never doubting the existence of God.

The Christian City

As the outstanding centre of Graeco-Roman philosophy, Alexandria developed much of the theological basis of early Christianity, even as native Egypt provided the new religion with many of its images, among them the resurrection of Osiris, Isis with Horus her child, and the cross-like pharaonic ankh, symbolizing life. But these early Christians suffered heavily for their faith: early in the 4th century the Emperor Diocletian demolished all churches, demoted all Christian officials and enslaved the rest, also killing 60 a day over five years, according to the Coptic Church. His persecutions made such an impression, that the Copts date their calendar from his accession in AD 284, and his reign is known as the Era of the Martyrs. This struggle between Egyptian Christianity and imperial paganism understandably gave rise to a kind of nationalism – indeed Copt derives from *Aigyptos*, the Greek for Egypt – so that even after the emperors at Constantinople had themselves become Christians, their political and religious interference in Egyptian affairs was resented.

At first Alexandria maintained its pre-eminence in theological matters, monopolizing the arguments both pro and con. The issue which most exercised the intellects and passions of the day was the nature of Christ. All agreed that he was the Son of God: that is, the link between the human and the divine. But if emphasis was put on the divinity of Christ, then he would be almost as remote as God himself; while if Christ's human nature was emphasized, again man would be lost and abject in the vast gulf between himself and the Almighty. Defining the nature of Christ was crucial in comprehending the condition of man, and it was a problem which Alexandria was particularly suited to solving. On the verge of sea and land, Greece and Egypt, neither simply one nor the other, Alexandria was practised on account of its geography and culture in mediating between opposites and reconciling the irreconcilable. Early in the 4th century, in a controversy that was taken up throughout the Christian world, Arius, an Alexandrian priest, devalued the divinity of Christ by arguing that as the Son of God he must in some way be less than God. His great opponent was Athanasius, also of Alexandria and later patriarch, whose efforts led to the Nicene Creed, used to this day in the Eucharist in the Eastern and Western Churches, which anathematized the Arians for denying that the Son and the Father were of the same essence and which asserts the unity of the Trinity.

But meanwhile Greek culture and thought were losing their hold on Egypt, and increasingly native Egyptians made the Church their own, so that in AD 451 at the Council of Chalcedon, nationalism as much as theology placed Alexandria on the opposite side to Constantinople and Rome in another Christological argument. A majority in the Council decided that Christ had two natures, the human and the divine, and that these were unmixed and unchangeable but at the same time indistinguishable and inseparable. This is the view of almost all Christian churches to this day, but the Egyptian Church, while not denying the two natures, put emphasis on their unity at the Incarnation. For this the Copts were called monophysites (*monophysis*, single nature), and were charged with the heretical belief that Christ's human nature had been entirely absorbed in the divine, a charge the Copts deny.

What exactly the parties to the dispute meant when they talked of the nature of Christ was affected by shades of language and culture, and these were taken to the limits of contrast by opposing political ambitions. The three great apostolic sees had been Rome, Antioch and Alexandria. But with the founding of Constantinople in AD 330, the lesser see of Ephesus was translated to the new imperial capital, which at Chalcedon (conveniently just across the Bosphorus) sought to achieve supremacy along with Rome, and to humble Alexandria.

Apart from its theological import, the argument over the single or dual nature of Christ provided slogans by which the opposing political groupings denounced one another. The hatred between Constantinople and Alexandria was so intense that when in AD 641 the Arab general Amr rode into Egypt with his 3,500 Bedouin horsemen, the Alexandrians signed an armistice and in the following year admitted him into their city as a lesser evil than the evacuating Byzantine Greeks. They were soon regretting their decision, however, according to John of Nikiou, the 7th century Coptic bishop and historian, who described the forced labours imposed by the Arabs on the Egyptians: 'The yoke they laid on the Egyptians was heavier than the yoke which had been laid on Israel by Pharaoh. Him God judged by a righteous judgement by drowning him in the Red Sea after He had sent many plagues both on men and cattle. When God's judgement lights upon these Muslims, may He do unto them as He did aforetime unto Pharaoh!'

The Copts Embraced by the Wider Church

In a new spirit of ecumenism the old theological differences are coming to be accepted as a misunderstanding, and by means of agreements such as the following (signed in 1988 at Deir Anba Bishoi in the Wadi Natrun by Pope Shenouda III and the Roman Catholic Nuncio) the Copts are being reintegrated into the wider fold: 'We believe that our Lord, God and Saviour Jesus Christ, the Incarnate-Logos, is perfect in His Divinity and perfect in His Humanity. He made His Humanity One with His Divinity without Mixture, nor Mingling, nor Confusion. His Divinity was not separated from His Humanity even for a moment or a twinkling of the eye. At the same time, we Anathematise the Doctrines of both Nestorius [the original proponent of two separate natures in the Incarnate Christ] and Eutyches [the original proponent of two natures before but only one after the Union, which is true monophysitism].'

The Islamic formula brought by Amr, that 'there is no God but God', swept away all that stood between the human and the divine in favour of direct submission. For Alexandria, which had thrived on mediation, it was the end of an era. It was still recognizably the city of its glorious past; colonnades of marble lined Amr's triumph along the Canopic Way; the tomb of Alexander rose to his left, the Pharos to his right. But in the flat tones of an inventory, as though denying Alexandria's history, its culture, its ideas, its very essence, Amr reported back to the caliph in Arabia: 'I have taken a city of which I can only say that it contains 4,000 palaces, 4,000 baths, 400 theatres, 1,200 greengrocers and 40,000 Jews.'

Alexandria declined, though it remained an important trading centre until late into the 15th century, and throughout the Crusading period Venice and Genoa did more trade with Alexandria than with all the Crusading ports put together. But it had long ceased to matter as a city of the intellect, and during the Turkish period it collapsed altogether.

The Rise and Decline of Modern Cosmopolitan Alexandria

When Napoleon landed near Alexandria in 1798, the city was hardly more than a village. What brought it back to life was Mohammed Ali's construction of the Mahmoudiya Canal, completed in 1821, which gave it access to the vital Egyptian hinterland and brought Egypt again face to face with the Mediterranean. Within a century Alexandria's population grew to nearly half a million, about what it had been in Cleopatra's time, and many foreigners, mostly Greeks and Italians, but also Jews, Syro-Lebanese and others had settled here, so that all central Alexandria and the coast eastwards towards Montazah became a cosmopolitan town.

British and French investment in the construction of the Suez Canal, which opened in 1869, greatly increased foreign interest in the country, especially that of Britain which was concerned for its route to India. In 1882, Colonel Ahmed Orabi led a revolt against his own government, which he opposed for its Turkish and European leanings. Riots broke out in Alexandria, where over 150 Europeans were killed. This was met by the bombardment of Alexandria's harbour defences by the British fleet, which in turn incited further riots during which much of the European city was burnt to the ground. The British then landed forces in Egypt, Orabi was defeated, and the country, though notionally governed by Egyptians, remained under British control until 1922 and did not achieve complete self-determination until 1936. The half-century between 1882 and 1936 was the heyday of cosmopolitan Alexandria, its life temporarily extended by the Second World War when it was the base for the Royal Navy's Mediterranean Fleet and a staging post for the Western Desert campaigns.

Alexandria was the foremost port of Egypt, and a hive of activity for the country's cotton brokers ... with wide streets flanked by palms and flame trees, large gardens, stylish villas, neat new buildings, and above all, room to breathe. Life was easy. Labour was cheap. Nothing was impossible, especially when it involved one's comfort.

Jacqueline Carol, *Cocktails and Camels*, 1960

Nasser's seizure of power, the 1956 Suez fiasco involving Britain, France and Israel, and finally the expropriation of property and businesses, meant the departure or ejection of almost all Egypt's Jews and foreigners. This left the Egyptians in possession of no more than the carapace of cosmopolitan Alexandria, a city 'clinging to the minds of old men like traces of perfume upon a sleeve: Alexandria, the capital of Memory' (Lawrence Durrell, *The Alexandria Quartet*).

'Core of nostalgia steeped in honey and tears', is how Naguib Mahfouz, in his novel *Miramar*, describes the city, and he continues with this dialogue between an Egyptian and an elderly Greek woman who has stayed behind:

'Monsieur Amer, I don't know how you can say there's no place like Alexandria. It's all changed. The streets nowadays are infested with canaille.'

'My dear, it had to be claimed by its people.' I try to comfort her and she retorts sharply.

'But we created it.'

The passage of time and a massive increase in population, which now stands at about five million, have brought changes to the city. Alexandria has lost its cosmopolitan flavour and is now a culturally homogeneous city, also something of a backwater in which Islamic extremism flourishes. Yet it has not entirely lost its sparkle. There is a sense of well-being; Alexandrians stream about the streets late into the night, shopping or simply walking, sitting at cafés talking. And there is the breeze that licks sudden plumes of water against the Corniche and carries an Aegean tang and freshness into Africa. This much has not changed since Alexander ordered his Greek metropolis to be built on this Egyptian shore.

Around Midan Saad Zaghloul

A good place to begin exploring Alexandria is **Midan Saad Zaghloul**, which opens onto the magnificent sweep of the Eastern Harbour. Overlooking the square is a statue of Saad Zaghloul (1860–1927), who led the nationalist campaign against the British after the First World War, which culminated, though only after his death, with their evacuation from all but the Canal Zone in 1936.

Getting around Alexandria

By Taxi

Taxis, which are orange and black or yellow and black, are inexpensive, especially as you stand a slightly better chance of running on the meter than in Cairo. Otherwise, LE10 is adequate for central Alexandria (you will be asked for more, Egyptians will pay less) – except from the main railway station to a central hotel (for example the Cecil) when, as the driver has been waiting, and he has you over a barrel, he will expect a premium. Along the Corniche between the centre of town and all the way out to Montazah it is worth flagging down any taxi you see, regardless of whether it is already carrying a passenger. This is almost like a service taxi route, with drivers picking up and letting off people along the way. A taxi from Nouzha Airport should not cost more than LE60 and a good deal less when travelling *to* the airport. A taxi to or from Burg el Arab Airport will cost about LE120.

Outside the Hotel Cecil on Midan Saad Zaghloul is a good place to hire a taxi (usually a big Peugeot) for excursions to Rosetta, Abu Mina, Alamein, Wadi Natrun, or even Cairo, Mersa Matruh and Siwa. The best of all the drivers on station there, a charming and exceptionally knowledgeable man with a good command of English, is Reda Mohammed El Shenawy (ask the Cecil doorman or among the drivers on the rank), who can also be reached at home, **t** (03) 574 9926, mobile **t** 0122 759153.

By Bus and Tram

Central Alexandria is best covered on foot, but buses and trams are very cheap and can get you to some of the more distant sights, although they can get very crowded and you might not think it worth travelling on them. The two principal stations for catching city buses and trams are Midan Orabi, which lies between Midan el Tahrir and the Eastern Harbour Corniche, and the Ramleh tram station in Midan Saad Zaghloul near the Corniche at the north ends of sharias Nebi Danyal and Safiya Zaghloul.

Buses 120, 220 and 320 ply the Corniche as far out as Montazah;
Bus 129 goes from Midan Orabi to Aboukir;
Tram 16 from Midan Orabi goes to Pompey's Pillar;
Tram 15 from the Ramleh tram station goes to Fort Qaytbey;
Tram 14 from Midan Orabi goes to Moharrem Bey;
Trams 1 and 2 both go eastbound from the Ramleh tram station via Sidi Gaber to Victoria (Al-Nasr). Tram 1 takes a somewhat inland route via Bacos, while tram 2 goes via Glymenopoulo (Glym), close to though not within sight of the sea.

By Carriage

Carriages are the most delightful way of being transported about the city. Hail them on the trot; also they can be found waiting at the main railway station (Mahattat Misr) and in Midan Saad Zaghloul outside the Hotel Cecil. The fare has to be bargained over and will usually work out a little more than a taxi would cost.

By Car

Car hire, with or without driver, is available from **Avis** at the Hotel Cecil in Midan Saad Zaghloul, **t** (03) 485 7400. *See also* taxis, above.

On this spot 2,000 years earlier Cleopatra began a stupendous temple in honour of Mark Antony. Before its completion their fleet was defeated at Actium off the west coast of Greece, and in the following year, 30 BC, they each committed suicide in Alexandria. Rededicated to their conqueror, who was worshipped here as Caesar Augustus, the Caesareum remained in imperial hands until Christian times. Athanasius made it a church in the 4th century AD, but it was soon destroyed during his struggles with the Arians. On its ruins rose the cathedral of Alexandria; here in AD 415 Christian monks won a victory over paganism, dragging the neo-Platonist philosopher Hypatia into its precincts and tearing her to pieces with tiles. The building was destroyed in AD 912, but two obelisks which had stood in front of it remained in place much longer, one falling over in 1301, but neither being removed until the 19th century. These became known as **Cleopatra's Needles**, though they bear the names of Tuthmosis III, Seti I and Ramses II and were brought here from Heliopolis by the Romans 20 years after her

Orientation

Note that many street signs in Alexandria still bear the old French style, hence *rue* for *sharia* (French was the lingua franca of the cosmopolitan city). And whatever the street signs say, the old names often persist. For example, Alexandria's main east-west thoroughfare is offically Sharia Horreya, meaning Liberty Street, but as often as not it is still known as Rue Fuad, named for the father of King Farouk.

Running from east to west through ancient Alexandria was the Canopic Way, its route followed by today's **Sharia Horreya** (Rue Fuad). This is intersected by Sharia Nebi Danyal (Rue Nebi Daniel), at the southern end of which is the **main railway station** for Cairo (Mahattat Misr). Near here are the Kom el Dikka excavations where the **Roman theatre** has been discovered. Sharia Nebi Danyal runs northwards into Midan Saad Zaghloul, with the Ramleh tram station, which opens up onto the Corniche along the Eastern Harbour.

About a third of the way northwards, Sharia Nebi Danyal is intersected by Sharia Horreya which you can follow eastwards to the **Graeco-Roman Museum**, **The Alexandria National Museum** and the **Shallalat Gardens** or westwards to Sharia Salah-Salem (Rue Chérif Pasha) which in turn runs northwest into Midan el Tahrir (Place Mohammed Ali), planned by Mohammed Ali as the centre of his new city.

There are many hotels, eating places and travel offices within the area described above, particularly between Sharia Horreya and Midan Saad Zaghoul.

Alexander's causeway, the Heptastadion (meaning seven stades long), left the mainland somewhere in the vicinity of what is now Midan el Tahrir. To either side of the Heptastadion were the two **ancient harbours**, the Eunostos or Harbour of Safe Return to the west and the Great Harbour to the east. Their roles have been reversed in modern times; Mohammed Ali developed the Western Harbour for commerce so that it now hides behind its docks and warehouses, but under the Ptolemies it was the less important of the two. (A third harbour, on Lake Mareotis to the south, took the Nile traffic and was said to clear a bigger tonnage than both the sea harbours combined.) The causeway has long since silted up; it is now the neck of land occupied by the old houses and mosques, the souks and lanes, of the so-called **Turkish town**.

The **Eastern Harbour** makes a graceful sweep and with its 6km-long Corniche, Sharia 26 July, is the most pleasing attraction of the city. Fort Qaytbey, which stands on the site of the ancient **Pharos lighthouse**, marks the tip of its western arm; the lesser promontory of Silsileh, now a military compound, completes the eastern arm. From Silsileh westwards towards Midan Saad Zaghloul ran the royal quarter of the Ptolemaic city – the foundations, pavings and fallen columns of what is claimed to be **Cleopatra's palace**, have recently been found beneath the harbour waters (*see* below).

At the southwest corner of the city, about 2km from the Corniche, is **Pompey's Pillar**, marking the site of the Serapeum, and nearby are the **catacombs of Kom el Shogafa**.

Southeast of the centre is the **Moharrem Bey** district, and well east of this are the **Nouzha**, **Antoniadis** and **Zoological gardens** overlooking the **Mahmoudiya Canal**, which undulates round the south side of the city. Also to the south is **Lake Mariut**, the ancient Mareotis.

From the Eastern Harbour to **Montazah**, the former summer residence of the royal family 12km eastwards, runs Sharia el Geish, the **Mediterranean corniche road**. The stretch from Sidi Gaber eastwards is called **Ramleh**, meaning sands, where from the late 19th century Alexandrians built suburban villas amid extensive gardens; but since the Second World War the area has become entirely built up. From west to east along the coast or not far inland from it are Chatby, Camp-Cesar, Ibrahimiya, Sporting, Cleopatra, Sidi Gaber, Roushdi, Stanley Bay, Fleming, Bacos, Bulkeley, Glymenopoulo, San Stefano, Gianaclis, Sarwat, Sidi Bishr, Victoria, Asafra, Mandarah – and finally Montazah.

Cleopatra's Palace Beneath the Waves

Earthquakes and a sinking coastline are part of the reason why so little of the ancient city survives: much of it has simply slipped into the sea. Over the last few years, however, a Greek and two French archaeological expeditions have made some exciting finds beneath the waters off Alexandria. Already in the last quarter of the 19th century, as maps and studies of the time show, archaeologists had a pretty good idea of where the royal port and palaces were under the waters of the Eastern Harbour. If only the seabed could be properly explored, Cleopatra's palace and Antony's hideaway, the Timonium, could perhaps be exactly identified, but the right equipment and technology were not then available.

That is precisely what the Greek and French expeditions have brought to bear. The Greeks under Harry Tzalas are working off the eastern edge of the Silsileh promontory where they believe they have found the remains of a shrine to Isis where Cleopatra privately worshipped. Like the French, however, one of their great problems is pollution. In 1995, under the direction of Jean-Yves Empereur, divers using underwater lights and video cameras (capable of seeing more than the naked eye in the murky sewage-filled harbour) found hundreds of blocks, some estimated to be as heavy as 70,000 kilos, lying in the water round Fort Qaytbey, almost certainly the remains of the Pharos lighthouse which a succession of earthquakes sent tumbling into the sea. Numerous columns, presumably the remains of attendant temples, and huge granite and marble statues of sphinxes, deities and Ptolemaic kings and queens have also been found. Some have been lifted to the surface and are being given lengthy fresh-water soakings at various spots round Alexandria before being exhibited at the Graeco-Roman Museum or in one case erected outside the Bibliotheca Alexandrina.

A second French expedition under Franck Goddio has been working from a launch off the western edge of Silsileh to pinpoint the royal port and palaces. In 1996 it announced the definitive discovery of the palaces of Cleopatra and Antony, which seem to have been submerged suddenly by an earthquake and tidal wave in AD 335, most of the marble and limestone statuary, obelisks and blocks remaining where they fell, on top of the limestone paving. That Goddio has found palaces, piers and temples is without doubt, but his ascription of this one to Antony, that one to Cleopatra, seems suspiciously and melodramatically too certain at this stage.

Goddio is bringing to the surface only those pieces that might be stolen or damaged if left in situ. 'We want people to be able to see the site as it is,' he says, 'but I have to say that at the moment visibility in the water is very bad.' The Alexandria Governorate has undertaken to move sewage disposal from the Eastern Harbour, though they are years behind schedule, and if and when they do the intention is to turn the Eastern Harbour, from Silsileh to Fort Qaytbey, into a vast underwater museum that can be surveyed from glass-bottomed boats or, better yet, visited by means of transparent tube walkways winding across the harbour bed. If that could be done, then Alexandria, where for so long there has been almost nothing to see, would become, along with the Pyramids and the Valley of the Kings, one of the biggest draws in Egypt.

death. In 1877 the fallen one was removed to the Thames Embankment in London, and two years later the other – which stood on the site of the present Metropole Hotel and Trianon Café – was taken to New York where it now stands in Central Park.

Overlooking the square and the Corniche is the **Cecil Hotel**, built in 1929, an Alexandrian institution in which Moorish, classical and Art Deco styles mingle. Its architect was Alessandro Loria (1880–1937), an Egyptian-born Italian Jew, who during his career built many of the finest buildings in Alexandria, among them the nearby Venetian-style palazzos (1920) that overlook the Corniche and back on to the Ramleh tram station, and the neo-Islamic Bank of Egypt (1925) in Sharia Talaat Harb between sharias Salah-Salem and Saad Zaghloul, which like the Cecil but more so display his taste for fantasia with their brightly patterned brickwork and the colourful mosaics that decorate their façades. The Cecil was a haunt of Justine in Lawrence Durrell's *The Alexandria Quartet*: 'In the gaunt lounge of the Cecil Hotel she would perhaps be waiting, gloved hands folded on her handbag, staring out through the windows upon which the sea crawled and sprawled, climbing and subsiding, across the screen of palms in the little municipal square which flapped and creaked like loose sails.'

Something of Alexandria's cosmopolitan past is also recalled in a number of restaurants, cafés and patisseries around town, two of them on Midan Saad Zaghloul. Facing the Ramleh tram station is **Athineos**, formerly a Greek café filled with mirrors and Corinthian columns, with a yet more ornately decorated restaurant within. Diagonally opposite, with entrances on the square and Sharia Saad Zaghloul, is the **Trianon**, with orientalist murals in its patisserie and Art Deco panels and screens in its restaurant. Above it, in what were once the offices of the Third Circle of Irrigation, worked the poet Constantine Cavafy: 'Kings, emperors, patriarchs have trodden the ground between his office and his flat,' wrote E. M. Forster, who described encountering Cavafy, 'at a slight angle to the universe', making his way between the two.

A short way west along Sharia Saad Zaghloul there is a turning on the left, Rue de l'Eglise Copte, which brings you to the handsome patriarchal **church of St Mark**, its nave spanned by gracefully curving arches lifted upon high Corinthian columns. It was reconstructed in 1952 from its 19th-century predecessor and does not (whatever the Copts might tell you) stand on the site of the original church supposedly founded by St Mark. (That church, founded by the Evangelist or otherwise, was by the sea just east of Silsileh at Chatby; and it was there that Arius was deacon.) In fact the seat of the patriarchate is in Cairo, at St Mark's Cathedral, Abbassia, but in title the Pope remains the Patriarch of Alexandria and the See of St Mark. It is impressive to read on the plaque here the names of all the patriarchs, including the great Athanasius, and to recall that Alexandria was once the most important city in the Christian world.

Synagogue
open daily 10–1 and Sat 8–10

Close by, at the north end of Sharia Nebi Danyal (entrance from the street to the left), is Alexandria's chief **Synagogue**. In Ptolemaic times perhaps as many as 200,000 of Alexandria's half-million inhabitants were Jews (they also represented an important part of the community more recently until the wars with Israel). Now they have trouble raising 10 men to form a *minyan* (quorum for prayer).

Literary Alexandria

The streets in the vicinity of Sharia Horreya and Sharia Nebi Danyal housed most of **Lawrence Durrell**'s characters in his

Alexandria Quartet. Darley and Pombal shared a flat in the Rue Nebi Daniel (now Sharia Nebi Danyal); Clea's studio was in the Rue St Saba; Justine and Nessim lived in a town house set back from the Rue Fuad (now Sharia Horreya) – and Balthazar lived in the Rue Lepsius, in 'the worm-eaten room with the cane chair which creaked all night, and where once the old poet of the city had recited *The Barbarians*'. The Cervoni's house, where at the carnival ball Narouz drove a hat pin through Toto de Brunel's skull, thinking he was killing Justine, was not far from the Greek Patriarchate; and many of them would find themselves sitting at the tables at Pastroudis.

Durrell refers to 'the city's exemplars – Cavafy, Alexander, Cleopatra and the rest', giving pride of place to one of this century's greatest poets, who inspired E. M. Forster and Durrell himself to discover the dream-city Alexandria. **Cavafy** (and later Durrell's fictional Balthazar), lived at 10 Rue Lepsius as it was early last century, now 4 Sharia Sharm el Sheikh. You get there by turning east off Sharia Nebi Danyal into Sharia Sultan Hussein (also called Sharia Estanbul), which is parallel to and just north of Sharia Horreya. Once in Sharia Sultan Hussein, ignore the first turning on the right, which is a foot-alley, and instead take the second turning on the right, a narrow street which is Cavafy's. A dusty plaque in Arabic and Greek reads: 'In this house for the last 25 years of his life lived the Alexandrian poet Constantine Cavafy (1863–1933)'. His apartment, two floors up, was for many years the seedy Pension Amir, but in 1992 it was turned into a **museum**. Here the literary apotheosis of Alexandria began.

11 Cavafy Museum
days and hours of opening unreliable, though in theory 10–3 Tues, Wed, Fri and Sat, also 10–5 Thurs and Sun, closed Mon; adm LE15

There is a death mask of the poet, and his desk. His bed has been put in the wrong room, as you can tell by looking at the photographs on the walls, and much of its furnishings, and with them much of its atmosphere, is missing. But in a city that has changed hands so completely since Cavafy's day, it is remarkable that the museum exists at all, and it manages to be a noble and affecting monument to the man.

Unfortunately, a squatter has been foisted on Cavafy, for one room displays mementoes of Stratis Tsirkas, the Alexandrian-born Greek novelist (author of *Drifting Cities*, a trilogy set in Jerusalem, Cairo and Alexandria during the war). A dogma-ridden marxist, he was the sort of person Cavafy would have shown to the door. His connection with the poet is to have written a study claiming, against all evidence to the contrary, that Cavafy was secretly a highly politicized anti-imperialist opposed to the 'Hitlerian' activities of the British in Egypt. The best thing you can do is to stand out on the balcony and, like Cavafy, catch a glimpse of the passing city. In his poem 'In the Evening', Cavafy describes rereading an old love letter and murmurs to himself, 'It wouldn't have lasted long anyway/ ... Yet how strong the scents were,/ what a magnificent bed we lay in,/ what pleasures we gave our bodies'.

Then, sad, I went out on to the balcony,
went out to change my thoughts at least by seeing
something of this city I love,
a little movement in the streets, in the shops.

On the ground floor of 10 Rue Lepsius was a brothel. 'Poor things!' Cavafy said to a friend who had accompanied him to his door one night. 'One must be sorry for them. They receive some disgusting people, some monsters, but' – and here his voice took on a deep, ardent tone – 'they receive some angels, some angels!' His English friends called the street the Rue Clapsius, though indeed the entire quarter was ill-famed. Cavafy satisfied his homosexuality by picking up boys in the cafés along the Rue Missala (now Sharia Safiya Zaghloul). With the Greek Hospital opposite and the Greek patriarchal church round the corner, Cavafy was fond of saying, 'Where could I live better? Below, the brothel caters for the flesh. And there is the church which forgives sin. And the hospital where we die.' He did die in that hospital; his funeral service took place at St Saba's, and his body was buried in the Greek Cemetery at Chatby.

E.M. Forster, who had already written *A Room With a View* and *Howards End* (but was still struggling with *A Passage to India*), was working for the Red Cross in Alexandria during the war when he first met Cavafy in 1916. 'It never occurred to him that I might like his work or even understand it ... and I remember the delight to us both, one dusky evening in his flat, when it appeared that I was "following". When he was pleased he would jump and light a candle, and then another candle and he would cut cigarettes in half and light them and bring offerings of *mastica* [a liquor flavoured with the resin of the mastic tree] with little bits of bread and cheese, and his talk would sway over the Mediterranean world and over much of the world within.' It was Forster who introduced Cavafy to the English-speaking world, and years later he remarked, 'I did a little to spread his fame. It was about the best thing I did.'

St Saba's is in the parallel street to the east, Rue du Patriarchate Grec. An inscription over the door announces that it was rebuilt in 1975 under Nicholas VI, Pope and Patriarch of Alexandria and All Africa, a reminder that ever since the Coptic Orthodox Church became separated from the Greek Orthodox Church in AD 451 at the Council of Chalcedon, both Churches have laid claim to the title of Patriarch of Alexandria.

By walking south to the end of Rue du Patriarchate Grec you come to Sharia Horreya, and by turning west (right) you return to the intersection with Sharia Nebi Danyal. On the way, you pass an archway on the north side of Sharia Horreya which leads to the

Mohammed Ali Opera House, its façade decorated with grimacing Dionysian masks. Carriages would roll up here of an evening and the audience would take their seats beneath the dome still emblazoned with the names of Berlioz, Wagner, Verdi, Gounod, Mozart, Bizet, Gluck and Rossini. Indeed, opera and ballet, concerts and plays, continue to be performed here. Outside the Opera House is a statue of Nubar Pasha, an Armenian Christian who was foreign minister and then prime minister of Egypt at various times during the 1860s, 70s and 80s. It originally stood in the Shallalat Gardens but was hidden away after Nasser's coup d'état, only recently being erected here, half hidden from the world.

The Roman Theatre and Baths at Kom el Dikka

22 Roman Theatre and Baths at Kom el Dikka
open daily 9–4; adm LE20, plus LE20 for the Villa of the Birds

If you now walk southwards to the top of Rue Nebi Daniel, so that Midan el Gumhuriya (the square in front of the railway station) is ahead of you, and turn left so that you are walking beside a high wall, you will soon arrive, on your left, at the entrance to the Kom el Dikka excavations. It is likely that a great deal of Alexandria's past could be uncovered, and the work here, begun by the Polish Centre of Mediterranean Archaeology in 1959, marks a start.

Kom el Dikka, meaning Mound of Rubble, describes the centuries of debris that had piled up over the site of various Byzantine and Roman foundations, and yet deeper traces dating from the Ptolemaic period. The archaeologists first cut through layers of 9th- to 11th-century Muslim tombs and then discovered a large complex of 3rd-century AD Roman baths. The spur to further and intensive excavation came in 1964 with the unearthing of a small 2nd-century AD Roman theatre. Encouraged by these finds, methodical excavations have continued, exposing the remains of streets, houses and a school.

The **Roman theatre**, the only one so far found in Egypt, may at one point have been roofed over to serve as an odeon for musical performances. Inscriptions suggest it was sometimes also used for wrestling contests. Rising in 13 semi-circular tiers of white marble imported from Europe, it could seat up to 800 people. Its columns are of green marble from Asia Minor and red granite from Aswan. The wings on either side of the stage are decorated with geometric mosaic paving. It is pretty but has none of the excitement of an excavation in progress.

That is provided by the ever deepening and broadening trenches being dug to the northeast of the odeon. The dusty walls of the trenches are layered with extraordinary amounts of potsherds, and as you peer down from the surface of the *kom*, you can see the

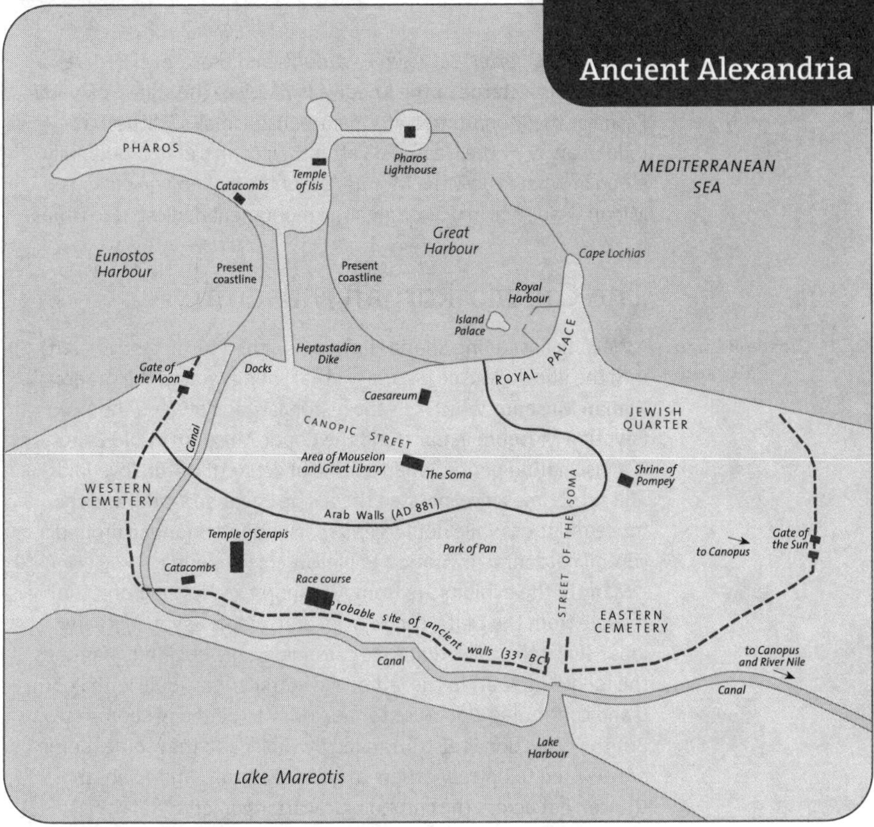

substantial arches and walls in stone and brick of the **Roman baths**, and beyond this the remains of houses. For a sensation of immediacy rare in Alexandria, you should climb down into the excavations and wander about, and though a watchman may tell you not to, you can sometimes buy yourself a bit of freedom with an offer of baksheesh. In any case you can visit the **Villa of the Birds** named for its beautiful mosaic floors dating to the 2nd century AD.

Villa of the Birds
a separate ticket must be purchased when entering Kom el Dikka

You can now leave the Kom el Dikka excavations by the way you came in, but turning left (east) to walk counterclockwise round the perimeter of the site, so that you will turn left again (north) at the first street you come to, in a few moments coming again to Sharia Horreya. Here, on the south side of Sharia Horreya, formerly the Rue Fuad, near the intersection with Sharia Safiya Zaghloul is **Pastroudis**, established by Greeks in 1923 though Egyptian-run now, where it is pleasant to sit with a drink, a coffee, a rich pastry (there is also a restaurant), and let time pass. Pastroudis used to occupy this entire triangular corner but it has recently been amputated, the part facing Sharia Horreya becoming a bank. This was once one of the smartest rendezvous in Alexandria and a favourite haunt of Lawrence Durrell who mentions it in his

Alexandria Quartet. Between Pastroudis and the Kom el Dikka excavations is a **statue of the Khedive Ismail**. Like the statue of Nubar Pasha at the Mohammed Ali Opera House, Ismail's statue was hidden away by the Nasserists after their coup d'état; it originally stood in what is now the Monument of the Unknown Soldier in Midan Orabi, which was originally a monument dedicated to Ismail.

The Graeco-Roman Museum

Graeco-Roman Museum
open daily 9–4 , closed Fri 11.30–1.30; adm LE40

Walking east along Sharia Horreya and then turning north (left) into the Rue du Musée (Sharia Mathaf) brings you to the **Graeco-Roman Museum**, which fills the historical gap between the Egyptian Museum in Cairo and the Coptic Museum in Old Cairo. It is a fascinating period, when a familiar Western culture overlaid and sometimes incorporated the native Egyptian world; and the museum itself, while not large, is spacious and arranged around a central garden, an invitation to pleasurable lingering.

Many of the exhibits are from Alexandria and its environs; the rest are from the Delta, the Fayyum and Middle Egypt. In a very loose sense the collection runs chronologically, beginning (as does the following tour) to the left of the entrance vestibule with Room 6 and continuing clockwise to the Christian period in Rooms 1 to 5. But the collection is also arranged by subject, so that some rooms are devoted to pottery, others to glass, sculpture, and so on, and this can cut across the chronological arrangement.

Note that the rooms are numbered but not always the exhibits, or their numbers are hard to find. Nor is everything labelled, though usually the most important exhibits are. Furthermore the museum is undergoing a considerable refurbishment programme, and meanwhile some of its exhibits are in the Alexandria National Museum. In short, take what follows with a sense of adventure.

A Tour

To the left of the entrance vestibule is **Room 6**, and at its centre is a fine diorite statue of the **Apis bull**, erected at the time of Hadrian and found towards the end of the 19th century at Pompey's Pillar. It had probably been buried there when a Christian mob sacked the Serapeum in AD 391. Against the left-hand wall is a statue of **Serapis** (22158) with a bushel on his head representing plenty. The great wealth of the Ptolemies was founded on the river of wheat which poured into Alexandria. Its trade was a royal monopoly and made the Ptolemies the richest grain merchants in the world. Later, Rome's dependence on Egyptian wheat was total.

Serapis was the most successful god made by a modern man. Egyptians at Memphis had worshipped Osiris in his Apis form as Osarapis; Ptolemy I combined this deity with Dionysos and made

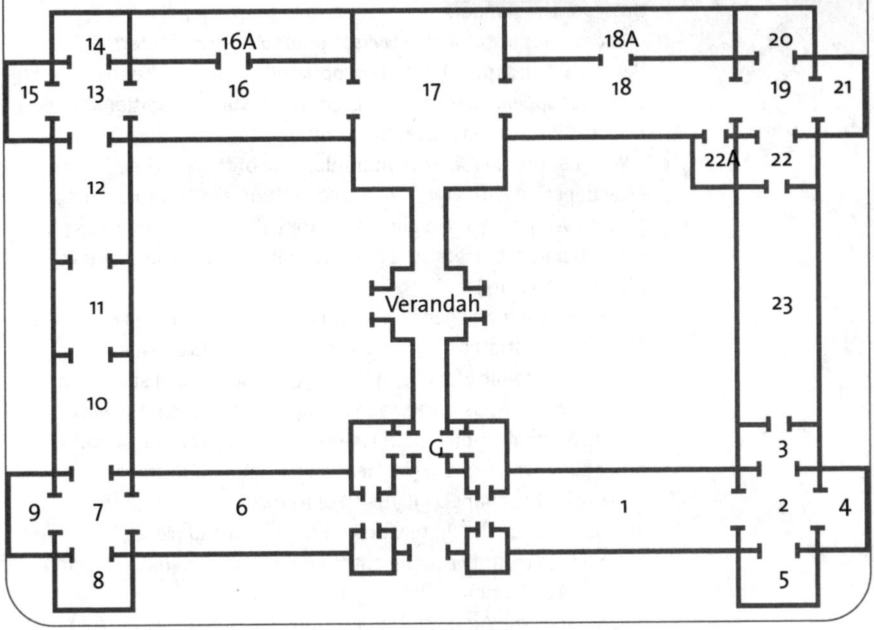

what was in effect a new god. The intention, probably, was to unite Greeks and Egyptians in a common worship, but the Egyptians would not accept him and he became the Greek god of Alexandria. His cult statue (this is a contemporary copy) of white marble was painted blue, his gilt head and jewelled eyes gleaming from the darkened recess of its shrine, the Alexandrian Serapeum. His worship spread throughout the Aegean, his cult was established at Athens and particularly at Delos, though he was venerated as far away as India. His importance can be gauged by the fact that when Bishop Theophilus destroyed the Serapeum and its statue in AD 391, it was taken by the world as the definitive triumph of Christianity.

Also in this room you will find a **bust of Isis**, that yet greater deity with whom Cleopatra identified herself, and so naturally, and with useful effect, Antony was identified with her consort Serapis, or at least with Dionysos. This may have assisted Roman propagandists (from whom Shakespeare took his cue) in depicting Antony as a debauched Bacchic figure – more a measure of Roman methods and Philistine contempt for Greek culture (and fear of Antony's alliance with Greek Alexandria) than any true reflection on Antony the man. Romans admired and copied things Greek, but Greeks themselves, and those like Antony who immersed themselves with genuine understanding in Greek culture, were despised. There was a ready Roman audience for a 'scheming' and 'treacherous'

Cleopatra, a 'cowardly' and 'besotted' Antony, and history, particularly the Battle of Actium, was easily distorted to provide proof for the slanders.

Room 7 has a statue of a **Hyksos pharaoh** (Second Intermediate Period) at the centre. It was appropriated by Ramses II and on its shoulder appears Ramses' daughter Hout-Ma-Ra, traditionally the princess who found Moses in the bulrushes.

Room 8 contains several **mummies**, one of them a Greek of the Roman period with an encaustic portrait mask, elaborate diamond-pattern wrapping and a glimpse of toes. (See the reference to the Fayyum portraits, p.229; the best are in Room 14 of the Egyptian Museum in Cairo.)

In **Room 9** is a wooden stretcher bearing a **mummified crocodile**. The room illustrates the Ptolemies in their Egyptian aspect, and here it is crocodile worship in the Fayyum. Because of such mummified crocodiles as these, found wrapped in and stuffed with papyri, we know more about Graeco-Roman Egypt than about any other past time or place (*see* 'Tebtynis', p.228). There are the remains of the chapel (19678–81) of a crocodile god with the wooden door of the first pylon and the coffin and bier of the sacred animal (2nd century BC). The entire chapel has been reconstructed in the North Garden of the museum.

Room 10 is the Antoniadis Collection of various objects. Most strange is the **mummy of a baby**. Apart from its smallness, no concession is made to its babyness: the face mask is the usual stereotype. There is also a headless, sensuous piece, a fragment of diorite breast (3221), similar to a statue of Queen Arsinoe, wife of Ptolemy II Philadelphos, in the Vatican, which is magnificent.

Room 11 has objects in which the Greek and Egyptian influences mingle – never very well. There are some curious blocks with footprints, votive offerings to Isis and Serapis.

At the centre of **Room 12** is a dull statue of Marcus Aurelius; a sea-worn marble head of Alexander is on the left, as is a limestone head of Cleopatra VII (21992) in Egyptian guise – though this may be a misattribution. Compare this to the **Cleopatra head** nearby (3239) in which she appears in her Greek guise and bears a resemblance to her coin portraits, albeit sucked by the sea like a jujube.

Rooms 13 and 14 contain miscellaneous sculptures: bodies without heads, heads without bodies, including Julius Caesar, Augustus, Tiberius, Hadrian, Vespasian, Claudius and Septimius Severus.

In **Room 15** is a portion of tomb wall, late Ptolemaic period or early Roman, painted with a delicately lifelike rural scene of oxen turning a *sakiya* or waterwheel.

Room 16 is devoted to sculpture. Against the wall at the far end is the repulsive **Mithras** (24407), sun god of the Persians, his virile cult carried by the legions to the corners of the Roman Empire during the early centuries AD. Initiation involved climbing down into a pit and being bathed in the blood of a bull which was sacrificed upon a grille above. This statue comes from near Minya. He is lion-headed, cloven-hoofed and winged, with hairy legs, and is draped with snakes. The foundations of one of his temples lie exposed along Queen Victoria Street in the City of London.

In **Room 16A** are the finest pieces of **Hellenistic sculpture** in the museum. The large torsos at the left end of the room are particularly impressive: two unclothed male torsos (3923 and 3925); and a female torso (3924) wearing a light tunic.

In **Room 17** is the **largest known statue** (5934) carved from a monolithic block of porphyry; some authorities say he is Diocletian, others that he is Christ Pantocrator – about as wide a split as you could hope for. Among the six marble sarcophagi is one (17927) showing the sleeping Ariadne surprised by Dionysos on Naxos.

Room 18 has pottery, terracotta and funerary urns. In the centre is an urn (16152) from the Chatby necropolis which still retains its wreath of artificial leaves and berries, bright green and gold (4th century BC). Also in the centre is a caseload of bronze wreaths, their flowers gilded. These are ugly and were probably more ugly at the time, but they are impressive for being so old. In Case X against the wall is a crude terracotta oil lantern in the shape of the Pharos. In other wall cases are terracotta figurines, and these are mostly stupid and vulgar.

But in **Room 18A** are the finest objects in the museum: miniature **Tanagra terracotta figures** of great delicacy and charm. These come from Alexandrian cemeteries, late 4th- to early 2nd-century BC, and occur only in tombs of children, adolescents or young women. The best are the figurines of women in Cases K, L, M, N and O, full of detail and dignity. These works were prompted by the sadness of death in youth; they are entirely sincere and noble, and they live. On the opposite side of this room is a statuette of Isis-Aphrodite (23936), her dress hitched up to reveal her bounty.

Rooms 19, 20 and 21 contain more terracottas and pottery, including much from the Chatby and Ibrahimiya necropolises in Alexandria.

Room 22 displays some beautiful examples of glass vases, plates and all manner of pots and vials for perfumes and wines – mostly Graeco-Roman, but also belonging to the Islamic period.

Rooms 23 and 3 contain coins, jewellery and assorted treasures. The most beautiful items are the **torso of Aphrodite** (24042) in silver and the silver gilt **goblet** (24201) decorated with cupids gathering grapes. The most important, however, are the foundation plaques (8357–66 and 9431–40) in gold, silver, bronze, Nile mud, green faïence and opaque glass, carved with Greek and hieroglyphic inscriptions, each recording Ptolemy III's dedication of the Temple of Serapis. Only when these were found in 1943–45 was it established with certainty that the Serapeum had stood on the plateau where Pompey's Pillar stands.

At the centre of **Room 2** is a Christian capital; in **Room 4** are delightful fragments of Coptic textiles, with rabbits, centaurs and dancing women, full of movement and sensuality; in **Room 5**, in painted stucco, are Christian designs and saints from the environs of Alexandria.

In **Room 1** there is the surprise of a **Christian mummy** – an each-way bet on immortality – note the black cross painted at his neck. In wall cases there are many objects associated with St Menas (*see* p.429), including little souvenir flasks (13953 and 13922) once filled with oil and taken by departing pilgrims all over the Christian world. Note the recurrent motif of the saint between two camels.

As in their textiles, so in their carving, the Egyptians of this period were capable of great delicacy and sensuousness. You see this for example in the case containing bone and ivory pieces with exquisite female forms, most definitely not the Virgin Mary, for decorating furniture and weapons. (Though identified as 'Christian period', clearly not everyone was yet a Christian, while some who were, like that mummy in the centre of the room, also had their fingers in other pies.) And you see this combination of delicacy and sensuousness with less technical finesse but in the almost Indian style of the limestone relief (14145) of two women sitting in the shade of a tree with a basket of fruit between them. But then look at the two architectural fragments in high relief (23779 and 23776): these are definitely Christian work, from Bahnasa, which is the modern name for Oxyrhynchus, the great monastic centre. There is that same lusciousness in their vine motifs, even while in 23776 the leaves form a cross within the encircling vine. Also from Oxyrhynchus is the low relief fragment of plant and cross motif (23565), the cross in this case very much based on a pharaonic ankh, the sign of life.

From the vestibule, enter the gardens encircled by the museum. To the right is the **South Garden** with two reconstructed **rock-cut tombs**. One (21004) of the 3rd century BC contains a sarcophagus in the form of a bed. The other (20986) of the 1st century AD has an arched entrance with shell decoration in relief. To the left is the **North Garden** with the three reconstructed pylons and chapel of the crocodile god whose furnishings are in Room 9. Against the far wall is a head, supposedly of Mark Antony, though the attribution is doubtful. It is so stylized that it could also be Dionysos, or almost anyone else. A composite capital sprouts from the grass like a giant flower, its top surface hollowed out to serve as a baptismal font.

There is a café in the garden and a shop with books, postcards and souvenirs.

Alexandria National Museum

Alexandria National Museum
open daily 9–4, closed Fri 11.30–1.30; adm LE40

Farther east along Sharia Horreya you come, on the north side, to a palatial villa which has recently been transformed into the state-of-the-art **Alexandria National Museum**. Its interior has been strikingly designed, with spotlighted artefacts suspended in hanging glass cases. You ascend from the dim tomblike basement devoted to the pharaonic period through the ground floor Graeco-Roman period with its sky-blue walls and finally to the top-floor Coptic and Islamic eras where the green walls are meant to represent paradise.

But the city's 19th- and 20th-century cosmopolitan period is ignored completely, as the very brilliance of Alexandria at that time offends the centralizing and nationalistic mentality of the government and bureaucracy in Cairo. In keeping with this bias, a notice in the Islamic rooms of the museum advances the absurd claim that Alexandria's heyday occurred not during the Ptolemaic period nor in the modern cosmopolitan period but during Mameluke times.

The highlights of the museum are some of the recent archaeological finds in town and offshore. One of these, from a neighbourhood of sprawling Ptolemaic and Roman houses that have been excavated just south of Ramleh Station, is the exquisite **Medusa mosaic**, which once decorated a dining room floor and perhaps meant to turn unwanted guests to stone with her stare. Also there are several **statues** brought up from the Eastern Harbour and elsewhere along the coast, accompanied by ceiling-to-floor photographs of the sites which almost make it seem that you are underwater too.

Around the Shallalat Gardens

Continuing east along Sharia Horreya you come to the Shallalat Gardens. Alternatively you can reach the gardens by turning right out of the Graeco-Roman Museum and walking north along Sharia Mathaf (Rue du Musée), which will bring you to the leafy Sharia Sultan Hussein (also called Sharia Estanbul) with the Khartoum Column off to your right.

Ancient Alexandria was enclosed by **walls** which on the east and west extended southwards to Lake Mareotis, now Mariut, where there was an important harbour linked by canals to the city's sea harbours. But by the 9th century AD the city had shrunk to less than half its size, and the new walls built by the Arabs in AD 881 no longer included the southern quarters nor the former palace area which extended inland from the Silsileh promontory. From the Khartoum Column to the Gate of the Sun, which perhaps stood where the gardens are now bisected by Sharia Horreya, and then round to the stadium, the Shallalat Gardens describe an eastward-bulging curve that indicates the eastern course of the Arab walls. All this area between Sharia Horreya and the curve of the Shallalat Gardens was known during the late 19th and the first half of the 20th century as the **Quartier Grec**, for this lovely neighbourhood was renowned for its concentration of wealthy Greeks, mostly cotton brokers, who had their palatial villas here; and not only Greeks, but Egyptians, Jews, Lebanese, English and other members of Alexandria's cosmopolitan community.

At the centre of a roundabout near the northwest tip of the Shallalat Gardens is the **Khartoum Column**, a huge Ptolemaic shaft which was found near this spot and raised to commemorate the retaking of Khartoum by General Kitchener in 1898, 13 years after Gordon had been overwhelmed there by the forces of the Mahdi.

Ibn el Nabih cistern
adm free

A block eastwards through the widening gardens, a sign indicates the **Ibn el Nabih cistern**, one of 700 underground reservoirs that the 15th-century historian al-Maqrizi recorded in the city, many of them dating from Graeco-Roman times and later rebuilt. Beyond this a string of **small lakes** follows the curve of the gardens round to Sharia Horreya: these are all that remain of the ancient canal which once linked Mareotis to the Eastern Harbour. There is a ruined **Arab tower** here too and you can trace sections of the Arab walls right round to the stadium which incorporates a segment of wall at its eastern end.

Plutarch records that the night before Antony's final battle against Octavian 'a marvellous sound of music' was heard passing 'through the middle of the city towards the outer gate, which led to the enemy's camp'. It was the god Dionysos, who was loved by Antony and who loved him, passing along what is now Sharia Horreya to the Shallalat Gardens and the now vanished Gate of the Sun. Cavafy recalls the nocturnal procession in his poem, 'The God Abandons Antony', though in his version it is the divine spirit of Alexandria that is departing.

When at the hour of midnight
an invisible choir is suddenly heard passing
with exquisite music, with voices –
Do not lament your fortune that at last subsides,
your life's work that has failed, your schemes that have proved illusions.
But like a man prepared, like a brave man,
bid farewell to her, to Alexandria who is departing.
Above all, do not delude yourself, do not say that it is a dream,
that your ear was mistaken,
Do not condescend to such empty hopes.
Like a man for long prepared, like a brave man,

like to the man who was worthy of such a city,
go to the window firmly,
and listen with emotion,
but not with the prayers and complaints of the coward
(Ah! supreme rapture!)
listen to the notes, to the exquisite instruments of the mystic choir,
and bid farewell to her, to Alexandria whom you are losing.

Returning to more recent history, you discover that not all the inhabitants of cosmopolitan Alexandria left the city: many have stayed behind in its **cemeteries**. On the north side of the Shallalat Gardens near the Khartoum Column is a Jewish cemetery, and there is another off Sharia Abdel Rahman Roushdi to the east of the gardens, adjoining those of the Catholic, Protestant, Armenian, Greek Orthodox, Syrian Greek Orthodox and Coptic Orthodox communities. All of them are carefully tended and can be fascinating places to wander about. Cavafy is buried in the Greek Orthodox Cemetery; the Protestant Cemetery is moving for its simplicity; while several monuments in the Syrian Greek Orthodox Cemetery portray the embrace of Death in the most sensuous terms, a reminder that in matters funereal 19th- and early 20th-century Alexandria had lost none of that ancient flair found in such places as the catacombs of Kom el Shogafa. Incidentally, this main road running alongside the cemeteries and north towards the promontory of Silsileh has been shown by archaeologists to have been one of the widest crossroads in the ancient city and may well have been the **Street of the Soma**.

The **Alabaster Tomb**, which some think indicates the vicinity of Alexander's tomb (*see* box below), is in the Terra Sancta Catholic

The Whereabouts of Alexander's Tomb

Before dying at Babylon in Mesopotamia in 323 BC, Alexander the Great expressed the wish to be buried at the oasis of Siwa where he had been declared a god (*see* p.408). Instead Ptolemy Soter, one of his generals who soon made himself master of Egypt, brought the body to Alexandria where it was placed in a tomb, the Soma, at the crossroads of the city somewhere along the Canopic Way. There 500 years later, in AD 215, the Roman Emperor Caracalla paid homage to Alexander at his tomb – the last record of its existence that has been preserved. The tomb with its body are thought to have been destroyed in city riots of the late 3rd century AD, or possibly they fell victim to that same earthquake of AD 335 that submerged the royal palaces (*see* p.496). Certainly by the late 4th century AD the mystery of the whereabouts of Alexander's tomb had become proverbial.

Important finds have been made which confirm that Sharia Horreya does indeed follow the course of the Canopic Way. Numerous ancient crossroads have also been identified, but it is not certain which of these might have been the Street of the Soma. The position of the Serapeum, the Caesareum and the royal palaces are all known, and excavations in the 1960s at Kom el Dikka laid bare a Roman theatre and baths, but the location of Alexandria's most famous landmarks, the famous Mousieon and its Library, and the tomb of Alexander, continue to elude conclusive discovery. The growing archaeological consensus, however, places the Museion and Library somewhere very close to the new Bibliotheca Alexandrina, and the tomb of Alexander not far from the Alabaster Tomb in the Catholic Cemetery (*see* below).

Cemetery – not the main one on the corner of Sharia Horreya and Sharia Abdel Rahman Roushdi, but in the overflow cemetery behind. To reach it walk east along Sharia Horreya to the first turning on your left, the appropriately named Sharia Anubis, and then enter the first gate on your right. The Alabaster Tomb is in a large excavation pit surrounded by a wall at the north end of the cemetery. The tomb is certainly impressive, a great hollow alabaster cube, a beautiful waving pattern running through the stone. It is thought to date to the early Ptolemaic period and its grandness obviously suggests that its owner was a person of considerable means. Some authorities believe it is the tomb of an exceptionally wealthy Greek; others are convinced that it belongs to a member of the Ptolemaic dynasty. In either case such persons are known to have placed their tombs round that of Alexander, so it follows that Alexander's tomb, the Soma, would have stood somewhere near this spot. There is sense to this, as the Alabaster Tomb is near enough to Silsileh, the ancient Cape Lochias on which the Ptolemies' royal palaces stood and from which the royal precincts of the city extended southwards.

Around Midan el Tahrir

A short walk west along Sharia Horreya from Sharia Nebi Danyal brings you to Sharia Salah-Salem, which leads off at an angle on your right towards Midan el Tahrir (but return to this a bit later). Beyond this point, Sharia Horreya becomes Sharia Sidi el Mitwalli, and in two blocks you come to Sharia Mesgued el Attarine, referring to the triangular Attarine Mosque at the intersection. Here, but occupying a much larger site, once stood the **church of St Athanasius**, dedicated to the patriarch soon after his death – the church of St Theonas where Athanasius preached was farther west near the Gate of the Moon. Between Athanasius on the Western Harbour and Arius at the original church of St Mark at Chatby, the two Alexandrians tore the Christian world apart during the 4th century AD.

All along Sharia Mesgued el Attarine to the south, and off its sidestreets (the general area is called Souk el Attarine), are numerous **junk and antique shops** where it can seem that the whole of cosmopolitan Alexandria is up for sale. Most are open from 9 or 10am to 10pm and close from 2 to 4pm.

Return now to **Sharia Salah-Salem**, formerly Rue Chérif Pasha, in which Constantine Cavafy was born. Once Alexandria's most fashionable shopping street, it is not as smart as it was. Nothing in Alexandria is.

A brass plaque at No.33, on the left, announces 'Fayed & Co Shipping, Fayed de Castro & Co Shipping Successors, Member of

Fayed Group of Companies'. These are the three Fayed brothers, sons of an Alexandrian school teacher. One of them, Mohamed al-Fayed, went on to own Harrods in London and the now notorious Ritz Hotel in Paris. At No.30 on the right is the **National Bank of Egypt**, once the Banco di Roma (the wolf of Rome can still be seen over the left doorway); it is a modified copy of Rome's 16th-century Palazzo Farnese built by Antonio da San Gallo and Michelangelo. During the Second World War the British Information Office was lodged nearby at 1 (now 2) Sharia Toussoun, and in a letter to Henry Miller Lawrence Durrell wrote: 'I am in charge of a goodish-sized office of war-propaganda here, trying to usher in the new washboard world which our demented peoples are trying "to forge in blood and iron". It's tiring work. However, it's an office full of beautiful girls, and Alexandria is, after Hollywood, fuller of beautiful women than any place else. Incomparably more beautiful than Athens or Paris; the mixture of Coptic, Jewish, Syrian, Egyptian, Moroccan, Spanish gives you slant dark eyes, olive freckled skin, hawk lips and noses, and a temperament like a bomb.'

Farther along, on the right, is **Sharia Adib**; a short walk along it, on the left, is **Cap d'Or**, a good seafood restaurant with an Art Nouveau bar which is worth a look. The place dates from Alexandria's heyday when bankers and brokers and businessmen would pop in here for refreshment. But, like the **Bourse**, they are gone now: the Bourse was at the end of Sharia Salah-Salem, on the left as it issues into Midan el Tahrir, and housed the Cotton Exchange, once the second most important in the world. 'The howls and cries that may be heard here of a morning proceed not from a menagerie but from the wealthy merchants of Alexandria as they buy and sell,' Forster wrote. It was put out of business by Nasser's nationalization measures and then set alight and gutted during food riots in 1977, since when it has been demolished.

Midan el Tahrir (Liberation Square) was formerly Place Mohammed Ali and was laid out by him in 1834 as the centre of his new cosmopolitan city. On the left (southwest) are the Law Courts built in 1884 and until 1947 the Mixed Tribunals which mediated between foreigners and natives. Next to the courts is the Passage Menasce, dating from 1885 and built in imitation, though on a smaller scale, of the famous Galleria in Milan. On the right (northeast) of the square is the Anglican church of St Mark. Built in 1855, its façade can be loosely described as Islamo-Byzantine. Its architect was James Wild who fifteen years earlier built the now restored Christ Church on Brixton Hill in Streatham, south London, a wonderfully eclectic work combining Romanesque, Ottoman, Mameluke, Alhambran, Sevillean and ancient Egyptian elements. The inscription along the frieze of St Mark's is from Psalm 100: 'The Lord is gracious, his mercy is everlasting and his truth endureth from generation to generation.' As though by foresight, the fine **equestrian statue** of Mohammed Ali at the centre of the square, a French work of 1872, was raised upon an exceptionally high plinth, preserving him both from changes of regime and from the mêlée of traffic which now fills the square where once there were fountains and gardens. From the balcony of the Bourse on 26 July 1956, the fourth anniversary of the abdication of King Farouk, Nasser announced to a crowd in Midan el Tahrir the nationalization of the Suez Canal. With the expulsion or departure of what was left of the foreign community following the Anglo-French attack on the canal that November, and Nasser's expropriations of both foreign and Egyptian private businesses and industries in 1961, the era of cosmopolitan Alexandria finally came to an end.

Running off Midan el Tahrir towards the Corniche is **Midan Orabi**, named after the nationalist officer whose uprising led to the 1882 British occupation. Formerly known as the French Gardens, the square like that of Mohammed Ali was once landscaped and planted with flowers and trees. At the far end, overlooking the Eastern Harbour, is the **Monument to the Unknown Soldier**. Originally it honoured the Khedive Ismail; it was built with funds raised by the Italian community and inaugurated in 1938. Its designer was Ernesto Verrucci, architect to King Fuad, Ismail's son, who accompanied his father to Italy at his deposition in 1879 and was educated there. Fuad spoke Italian, French and Turkish (but not Arabic) and had Italian tastes in opera, architecture and mistresses, Verrucci supplying both the second and the third. In the mid-'twenties Verrucci enlarged and refurbished Ras el Tin palace and also gave an exotically Italianate cast to his principal palace at Montazah.

Indeed for the most part the architects and engineers of cosmopolitan Alexandria were Italians. 'The streets between the harbour and the railway station might have been imported from Naples,' wrote an English visitor in 1910, while the beautiful circular bay round which the city was growing up, its Corniche constructed by Italians a few years earlier, seemed 'another Bay of Naples'. For all the commercial and cultural dominance of the Greeks, this visitor could say that 'Alexandria is an Italian city: its vegetation is almost Italian; it has wild flowers. Its climate is almost Italian; it has wind and rain as well as fierce blue skies. Its streets are almost entirely Italian'. If it were not for a few minarets in the old Turkish town built on the Heptastadion, 'you would not believe that you were in a city of Islam'.

The Turkish Town

Walking north out of Midan el Tahrir, you are following the course of the Heptastadion. Silting over the centuries made it a permanent broad neck of land, and during Ottoman times Alexandria's few thousand inhabitants clustered here. With its close-packed houses, some of them overhanging the narrow streets in Turkish style, and its old souks and mosques, it is a very different place to European Alexandria.

In fact two streets head northwards out of the square, Sharia el Nokrashi on the left, Sharia Faransa (the old Rue de France) on the right. If first you follow Sharia el Nokrashi you arrive after a couple of blocks at an open market square in front of the **Shorbagi Mosque**; indeed it is built over stalls which provide it with rent. Dating from 1757, it is unusual in not having a minaret, which in these loudspeaker days hardly matters, but in the past the muezzin would have made the call to prayer from the first-floor arcade. The interior is decorated with fine tiles. Most fascinating is the courtyard behind, reached through a passageway off the street running along the right (south) side of the mosque. This is overlooked by the rear gallery of the mosque, but also by an adjoining building which may have been an old *khan*.

From here you can wriggle through the narrow and sometimes covered lanes to Sharia Faransa, along the right-hand (east) side of which you can identify the **Terbana Mosque**, dating from 1684, by its high doorway of brick, painted red and black in Delta style (there is much more of this at Rosetta), with occasional courses of wood and a Kufic inscription: 'There is no God but God' and 'Mohammed is the Prophet of God'.

Before going in, have a look at the entrance to the cellars round the left-hand side of the building. The columns are ancient. Now go up the steps of the main entrance, arriving at an open-air terrace with two great Corinthian columns of granite, while other columns, some of them placed upside-down, support the gallery along the back. The entire building seems to have been made out of Alexandria's antique past; there are yet more ancient columns propping up the interior and painted gloss white. You will probably be shown round, the gloss paint and similar refurbishments pointed out with pride. Tiles decorate this upstairs entrance to the mosque, but they are in a bad state, the enamel dropping off, but fine where they survive. There are excellent tiles too in the mihrab inside, predominantly blue, though some green; the larger tiles with white daisies are inferior modern work.

As you continue north along **Sharia Faransa** from the Terbana and cross a main intersection, the street becomes narrower and winding with several overhanging balconies in the Turkish style. This is landfall for the island of Pharos. Soon you enter the back of a square, Midan Massagued, dominated by the gleaming white **mosque of Sidi Abu al-Abbas al-Moursi**, whose ornate façade, elegant domes and towering 73m minaret lend a rare note of oriental fantasia to the Corniche skyline. Yet this too was built by an Italian, the architect Mario Rossi, who in the course of his long career at the Ministry of Waqfs (endowed Islamic properties) converted to Islam and built several mosques, including the Ibrahim Mosque with its soaring minaret to the east of Ramleh tram station.

Though the mosque of Abu al-Abbas al-Moursi was constructed in 1943, it stands on the site of a 1775 mosque built by Algerians over the tomb of the 13th-century Andalusian saint. Its vast interior space is created by an arcade of elongated arches resting upon eight monolithic columns of Italian granite. The exterior surfacing, however, is of artifical stone which has required recent repair in places after falling away from its internal steel supporting rods. This was the main square of the Turkish town, the centre of Alexandria, such as it was, before the city was refounded by Mohammed Ali. Between the Abu al-Abbas Mosque and the harbour is the **Bouseiri Mosque**, its own square illuminated with white lights visible from anywhere along the Corniche at night. From this mosque there is a view of Fort Qaytbey and fishing boats, their nets stretched along the harbour wall.

On the Headland

What was the island of Pharos is now an anvil-shaped headland, its points marked by the palace of Ras el Tin (Cape of Figs) to the west and Fort Qaytbey to the east. **Ras el Tin Palace** was built by Mohammed Ali, who made Alexandria his virtual capital. From here he could oversee his harbour and his fleet which, together with his army under the command of his brilliant son Ibrahim, earned him the conquest of Arabia and Syria and the defeat of the forces of the Ottoman sultan on the soil of Asia Minor itself. For a time, Alexandria stood at the centre of an empire as great as that of the Ptolemies. But the British, fearing they would be cut off from India, intervened. In 1840 Admiral Napier, at Ras el Tin Palace, warned Mohammed Ali: 'If Your Highness will not listen to my unofficial appeal to you against the folly of further resistance, it only remains for me to bombard you, and by God I will bombard you and plant my bombs in the middle of this room where you are sitting.' In exchange for dynastic recognition, Mohammed Ali thereafter confined his ambitions to Egypt. Until Nasser's coup, the palace served as the seat of government during the summer months. Here on 26 July 1952 King Farouk abdicated and sailed away to Italy aboard his yacht. It is now the Admiralty headquarters. You cannot get in.

Anfushi Necropolis
adm LE25, includes also the Mustafa Kamel Necropolis, p. 522

Across the square from the palace compound is the **Anfushi Necropolis**, along with that at Chatby the oldest in the city. Its tombs date from the first half of the 3rd century BC (though embellishments were added during Roman times), and were cut out of the limestone ridge that formed what was still then the island of Pharos. There are four of them, arranged in pairs, and in both cases a stairway descends to a court open to the sky off which are several chambers. The occupants were Greek, but they had gone some way to accommodating themselves to Egyptian beliefs and style. The walls are painted to simulate marble, or alabaster blocks, or tiles; the impression is superficially Greek, but notice the lotus capitals, the sun discs, and on the wall of the tunnelled stairway leading to the northern tomb group the traces of scenes showing Osiris, Isis and Horus greeting the deceased. The northern group is reached by a stairway leading down a planted terrace; in the right-hand tomb there is a drawing of a felucca and another of a warship of the sort Cleopatra may have sailed in to Actium. Also in this tomb are Greek scribblings left by a workman of the period named Diodoros, who immortalizes his friend Antiphiles. How innocent these ancients were in their graffiti; we know by what signs our present period would instantly be recognized by archaeologists of the future.

Now walk eastwards along Sharia Ras el Tin towards Fort Qaytbey. There is a boat-building yard along the shore and a fish market farther on. Then on the Eastern Harbour there is the Yacht Club and the Greek Club, and beyond these along the breakwater is **Fort Qaytbey**, damaged during the British bombardment of 1882 but restored in the 1940s. More European than Arab in appearance, it was built in 1480 during the reign of Sultan Qaytbey by a German adventurer from Oppenheim, in the diocese of Mainz, on the site and partly from fragments of the Pharos lighthouse, the wonder of the ancient world.

Fort Qaytbey
open daily 9–4, closed Fri 12–2; adm LE25

The Pharos Lighthouse

It beaconed to the imagination, not only to ships at sea,
and long after its light was extinguished
memories of it glowed in the minds of men.

E.M. Forster

The **Pharos** was built during the reign of Ptolemy Philadelphos, its architect Sostratos, an Asiatic Greek. The sensation it caused was tremendous. Its appeal to both the sense of beauty and to the taste for science was typical of the age, and in the imagination of contemporaries the Pharos became Alexandria and Alexandria became the Pharos. The Pharos exceeded 125m in height and might possibly have touched 150m. Its square bottom storey was pierced with many windows and contained perhaps three hundred rooms where the mechanics and attendants were housed. A double spiral ascent ran through the centre and hydraulic machinery was used for raising fuel to the top. At its cornice were tritons and an inscription by which Sostratos dedicated the Pharos 'to the Saviour Gods; for sailors', the gods being Castor and Pollux who protected mariners, but an allusion to Ptolemy Soter and Berenice, whose worship their son Philadelphos was promoting. Above this was an octagonal second storey, then a circular third storey and finally the lantern.

The workings of the lantern were mysterious. Visitors spoke of a mirror, perhaps of polished steel for reflecting the sun by day, the fire by night; though others described it as made of glass or transparent stone and declared that a man sitting under it could see ships at sea that were invisible to the naked eye. It might have been a lens, and it is not impossible that Alexandrian mathematicians did discover the lens and that their discovery was lost and forgotten when the Pharos fell.

The Pharos retained its form and functions up to the Arab conquest in AD 641. About AD 700 the lantern fell, and perhaps at the same time, but certainly soon after, the two top storeys also fell – the tale is that the Byzantine emperor, frustrated in his ambitions against Egypt because of the early detection of his ships, put it about that the Pharos stood upon Alexander's treasure, whereupon the caliph commenced demolition. The first storey survived intact and Ibn Tulun restored the octagonal storey around AD 880, but an earthquake around 1100 destroyed his work and its place was taken by a mosque. The bottom storey was ruined by a final earthquake in the 14th century. Interestingly, the four stages of the Pharos – square, octagon, round and summit – are exactly reproduced in the minaret of Qaytbey's Mausoleum in Cairo's City of the Dead.

Here on this promontory, Qaytbey built in part at least from the debris of the Pharos and you can see where bits of it have been incorporated into his structure. The enclosure walls describe an irregular pentagon and as you approach, with the open sea to your left, you can make out some granite and marble columns in the northwest section. The sea wall of the Pharos probably diverged slightly from the present walls and where these meet the sea it laps over what might have been ancient foundations. There are numerous column sections in the façade of the keep, and within its entrance are five great monolithic pillars of red Aswan granite. Inside is the Naval Museum.

While approaching the fort along the breakwater you passed the Hydrobiological Museum and the Marine Life Institute (aquarium) – and missed nothing.

Southwest Alexandria

What Alexander flattened he in this case immortalized. Who would know of this obscure Egyptian settlement had his town planners not built upon it the capital of the Hellenistic world? To reach what was once the citadel of Rhakotis, later the acropolis of the Ptolemies, you must today travel about 1.5km southwest from the Corniche, perhaps along Sharias Salah al-Din and Amud el Sawari, in any case through less salubrious parts of the city where impressions in paint, in mud, of children's hands against the walls of squalid streets avert the evil eye.

Pompey's Pillar
adm LE20

The landmark attraction on the mound is **Pompey's Pillar**. After his defeat by Julius Caesar in the civil war, Pompey fled to Egypt where he was murdered in 48 BC; medieval travellers later believed he must be buried here, even that the capital atop the column served as a container for his head. In fact the pillar was raised in honour of Diocletian at the very end of the 4th century AD; he had come to Egypt to defeat a rival, and averted a famine by revictualing Alexandria after it had been under siege. The Arabs called it El Amud el Sawari, Column of the Horseman, and an equestrian statue of the emperor may have pranced on top when Amr entered the city. Within a few years of the column's erection, Diocletian was making a less favourable impression, torturing and slaughtering Christians in their thousands. The column with its base and Corinthian capital rises 27m; the shaft has a circumference of 9m and is of pink Aswan granite. The assemblage is entirely uninteresting, but being the tallest ancient thing in Alexandria it attracts attention. Immediately south of Pompey's Pillar are two pink granite **sphinxes** of the Ptolemaic period; they were not original to this exact spot but were found near by. Here too is a **statue of Isis** found in 1961 in the sea near Fort Qaytbey; her temple had once stood on the island of Pharos and perhaps this comes from it.

Following the gaze of the sphinxes several metres farther south and off the height of the mound is the partly excavated site, marked by a few broken columns and a sign, where the foundation plaques of the **Serapeum**, the Temple of Serapis, were found (*see* Rooms 23 and 3 in the Graeco-Roman Museum). Presumably the temple spread over the entire mound; now a few broken columns and some tunnels cut into the rock to the northwest of Pompey's Pillar are all that remain. Yet in Ptolemaic times this was a place of wonders. Worshippers climbed 100 steps to the sanctuary of the god, where the latest scientific tricks were used to amaze them. The expansion of hot air fuelled by burnt offerings threw open the temple doors and propelled the statue of the god forward, while hydraulic bellows caused spectral trumpet fanfares.

The Serapeum incorporated a library established by Cleopatra, and the tunnels are identified by some as part of it because of the shelf-like niches in their walls. More likely the niches would have held funerary urns containing sacred animals and birds. The destruction of the complex was wrought in AD 391 when the patriarch Theophilos led a mob against it in the final triumph of Christianity. Paganism was overthrown, as was learning. The belief that the older 'mother' Library, part of the Mouseion, was burnt when Julius Caesar fought to maintain himself in the city is now discredited.

4 Catacombs of Kom el Shogafa
adm LE30

A short distance east on Sharia el Nasseriya are the **catacombs of Kom el Shogafa**, the largest funerary complex of the Graeco-Roman period in Egypt. Discovered in 1900 when the ground gave way and a donkey fell down an unsuspected shaft, the catacombs date from the 2nd century AD and are decorated in a curious blend of classical and Egyptian styles. They are a sort of underground Forest Lawn.

The catacombs are on three levels, the lowest flooded and inaccessible. A winding staircase leads down to a rotunda encircled by chambers with sarcophagi and niches for funerary urns. The large room to the left was the banqueting hall where relatives of the deceased saw them out with a feast. The table in the middle, probably of wood, has disappeared, but cut out of the limestone are the three couches where they reclined on mattresses. The broken remains of their pots and dishes gave Kom el Shogafa, the Mound of Shards, its name.

From the rotunda a stairway goes down to the second level. You are now at the central tomb. The decorations are composite, not to say weird. Serpents bearded like pharaohs adorn the vestibule wall at the entrance to the inner chamber. Each holds the suggestive pine cone of Dionysos, who promised resurrection, and the serpent wand of Hermes, who in Greek mythology guided the dead through the underworld. The serpents also wear the double crown of Upper and Lower Egypt, while above them are Medusas in round shields, probably meant to ward off evil and perhaps particularly tomb robbers. In the tomb chamber proper are three large sarcophagi, cut out from the rock. Their lids do not open, for the bodies would have been introduced from the passage which runs right round the chamber with accommodation for 300 mummies. In the niche over each sarcophagus is a relief in Egyptian style. Turning round and facing the entrance, on either side of the door are two extraordinary figures. On the right is Anubis, with a dog's head, but dressed up as a Roman soldier, with sword, lance and shield; on the left is Sobek who, despite being a crocodile, is also shoved into a military costume, with cloak and spear. 'Perhaps the queer couple were meant to guard the tomb, but one must not read too much into them or into anything here – the workmen employed were only concerned to turn out a room that should look suitable for death, and judged by this standard they have succeeded,' wrote Forster.

Cheerful by comparison is the contemporaneous **Tigrane Tomb** which stands in the grounds, removed here from the eastern suburb of Cleopatra. Its scenes of the Egyptian-classical way of death are colourfully painted on white backgrounds with decorative trimmings reminiscent of Laura Ashley wallpaper.

Southeast Alexandria

Museum of Fine Arts
open daily 8–2, closed Fri; adm free

South across the railway tracks from Sharia Horreya, or east from Misr Station along Sharia Mahmoud Bey Salama, is the **Museum of Fine Arts** at 18 Sharia Ahmed Ismail (otherwise known as Sharia Menasce after the prominent Jewish family whose palatial home, which they gave to the Municipality in the 1930s, the Museum of Fine Arts once was). Outside is a sculpture of 'the eternal Egyptian woman' by Mahmoud Mokhtar; inside, Egyptian artists cover the ground from rural simplicities to urban sophistication in styles ranging from flamenco-deco and socialist realism to surrealism.

Between the museum and Sharia Moharrem Bey is Sharia el Maamoun; **Lawrence Durrell** lived on the top floor at No.19 during the latter part of the Second World War and used the tower at its corner as a place to write. Revisiting the place in 1977, he said, 'It's certainly the weirdest feeling to find myself after nearly 40 years in this strange garden belonging to an old Italian architect; and in this garden and in the little tower that I fixed up on the roof of the house I wrote *Prospero's Cell* and some rather good poems for *Personal Landscape* and lived out two and one half years of great, extravagant and colourful life in wartime Alexandria.' The house was sold to developers who to get round a law against tearing down old villas are tearing out supporting walls to ensure that it falls down, which it may have done by the time you get there.

Nouzha Gardens, Zoo and Antoniadis Gardens
open daily 8–4; small fee

About 3km southeast of the Shallalat Gardens are the **Nouzha Gardens**, originally planted for the Khedive Ismail with specimen trees, and **Zoo**. Adjacent, to the south, on the disused Mahmoudieh Canal and opposite Nouzha Airport, are the **Antoniadis Villa and Gardens**, owned originally by a wealthy Greek family (important benefactors of the Graeco-Roman Museum). The villa is used for state affairs, but the gardens are open to the public. They are rather formal, and planted with statues: one of Nelson missing an eye, both arms and his nose; others of Aphrodite, Artemis and the like missing only their clothes. In the area of these gardens Amr and his cavalry camped before entering the city. Here too, in what was the Ptolemaic suburb of Eleusis, lived Callimachos, the 3rd-century BC epigrammatic poet:

Someone told me, Heracleitos, of your end;
and I wept, and thought how often you and I

sunk the sun with talking. Well! and now you lie antiquated
ashes somewhere, Carian friend.
But your nightingales, your songs, are living still;
them the death that clutches all things cannot kill.

The Bibliotheca Alexandrina

Bibliotheca Alexandrina
open Sat–Thurs 11–7, Fri 3–7; adm LE15

The **Library** of ancient Alexandria, together with the Museion of which it formed a part, were founded by Ptolemy I Soter early in the 3rd century BC and quickly became the greatest intellectual and cultural institutions of their age. The Museion was a vast complex of lecture halls, laboratories, observatories, a park and a zoo. Euclid worked out his principles of geometry at the Museion, and Eratosthenes determined that the earth was round and had a diameter of 12,560 kilometres – an error of only 80 kilometres. The Library contained 500,000 scrolls, representing everything written in Greek at that time and many works in other languages too. We owe to its librarians the survival of numerous ancient texts, including Homer.

The **Bibliotheca Alexandrina**, on the Corniche at Chatby, near the Silsileh promontory is an attempt to revive something of that former glory. Its Norwegian and Austrian architects, and its British, Italian and Egyptian builders, have created an enormous disc representing the rising sun emerging from the shore of the Mediterranean within the royal quarter where the ancient Library and the Museion once stood. The new Alexandria Library, whose interior is a dramatic cascade of descending levels, has a capacity for eight million books, and the complex includes a planetarium, conference and exhibition halls, and an arts centre for films, concerts and other cultural activities. The *Impressions of Alexandria* exhibition, depicting the city during its recent cosmopolitan period, is particularly worthwhile. Funded by UNESCO and the Egyptian government, the Bibliotheca Alexandrina has set for itself the goals of becoming an international centre of excellence in chosen fields, first of all in the subjects of Alexandria and Egypt, secondly in the areas of Mediterranean, Middle Eastern and African studies. Using state of the art digital technology, it aims to be Egypt's window on the world and the world's window on to Egypt.

Chatby Necropolis
adm LE10

Less than 500m east from the Bibliotheca Alexandrina are the underground tombs at Chatby. Like the tombs at Anfushi, these at the **Chatby Necropolis**, on Sharia Bur Said (Port Said), date from the 3rd century BC and so share the distinction of being the oldest in the city. They are also similar in plan. But there the resemblance stops. In Ptolemaic times the eastern districts of Alexandria were Greek or Hellenized Jewish, in part explaining the Greek character of the tombs at Chatby and Mustafa Kamel. In contrast, Egyptian burial customs and decorations are most evident on the western side of the city, at Anfushi and Kom el Shogafa, close to the native quarter. Greeks who had gone some way towards accepting Egyptian beliefs were more likely to be buried there. Here, in the use of Doric and Ionic columns, the style is Greek, not Egyptian. From Chatby came the delicate Tanagra terracotta figures seen in the Graeco-Roman Museum.

The Corniche to Montazah

There are numerous public **beaches** along the city's seafront between the Eastern Harbour and Montazah, among them Chatby, Ibrahimiya, Sporting, Cleopatra, Stanley Bay, Glymenopoulo, San Stefano, Sidi Bishr, Miami, Asafra and Mandarah; the public beaches are free but usually crowded and often dirty. There are 47 sewage discharge pipes between Qaytbey's Fort and Montazah, emptying only 40m out to sea, making for some strange encounters. At Montazah itself, and beyond, the pollution becomes negligible.

Mustafa Kamel Necropolis
adm LE25, includes Anfushi Necropolis

The **Mustafa Kamel Necropolis** is on a rise just west of Stanley Bay and a bit back from the Corniche on Sharia el Moasker el Romani (Roman Camp Street), for it was here that Octavian pitched his tents before his final battle with Antony outside the walls, and here too that he afterwards founded his town of Nicopolis (Victory City). The subterranean necropolis cut into the limestone was discovered when the British, who had a barracks here, levelled the ground for a football field in 1933. As at Chatby, the burial chambers are off a central sunken court, but once more Egyptian influence is lacking. Instead the columns, capitals and friezes are purely Doric.

Contrary to popular (including Egyptian) belief, **Gamal Abdel Nasser** did not come from a rural village. You can visit his birthplace at 12 Sharia Kannawaty, south off Sharia Mustafa Kamel, in the quiet lower middle-class area of Bacos. Nasser continued to live in Alexandria until he was 15, attending schools in the Attarine and Ras el Tin areas, before moving to Cairo. The house is supposedly a museum, though there is nothing to see inside, hardly anyone knows it is there, and you will probably have to search for the keeper.

Below the headland just east of the beach at Sidi Bishr are the **Spouting Rocks of Bir Masud**, where the sea has undercut the limestone and spouts up through cracks and blow holes. Many of these holes were modified in Ptolemaic times, giving rise to speculation that the ancient Alexandrians, who enjoyed scientific toys, fitted them with trumpets and mechanical devices.

Royal Jewellery Museum
open daily 9–4, closed Fri 11.30–1.30; adm LE40

The collection at the **Royal Jewellery Museum**, 27 Sharia Ahmed Yehia, Glymenopoulo, gives the impression that someone has made off with the crown jewels. There are some exquisite minor pieces, but the collection hardly represents the accumulated

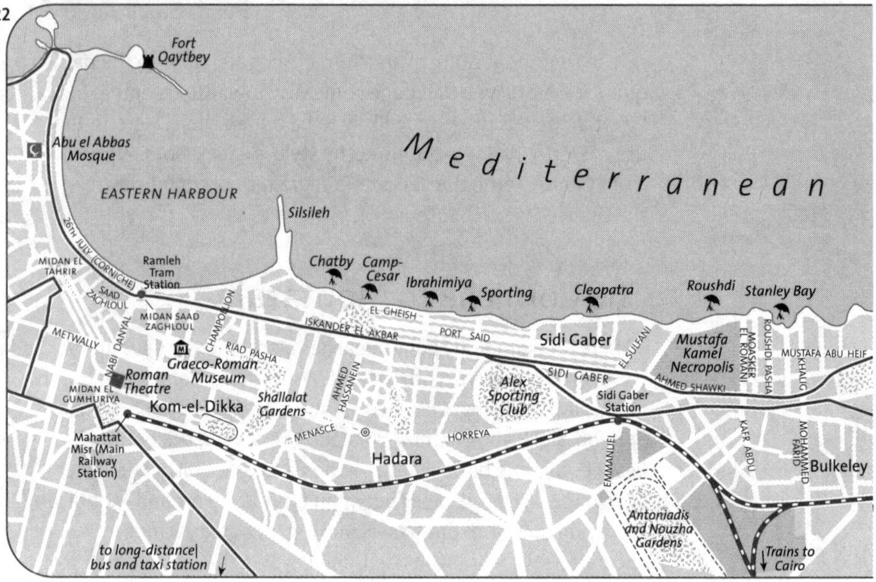

treasure of the dynasty that ruled Egypt from Mohammed Ali to King Farouk, much of which was pocketed by Nasser's Free Officers. From the 1920s the villa was the home of Princess Fatma el Zahraa and was decorated to her taste, which seems to have run the gamut from the Arts and Crafts Movement to ripe cupids dropping off the ceilings, and this is what really makes the visit worth while.

Palace grounds
open 24 hours; adm LE10

At **Montazah** (12km from the Eastern Harbour) is the royal family's former summer residence. Though the palace is closed to the public, its **grounds**, planted with pines from Europe and palms, are open 24 hours. Farouk was here when the 1952 coup occurred in Cairo – he fled to Ras el Tin. He was not in fact the last king of Egypt; his son reigned under the control of a regency council as Fuad II until 1953 when the country was declared a republic.

Montazah Palace, that is the main living quarters, the *haramlik*, was built by Khedive Abbas II in 1893 and during the First World War was converted by the British to a hospital. Here E.M. Forster did some of his Red Cross work, gave lectures on ancient Alexandria, and himself convalesced from jaundice, coming to love the place and often returning to it for weekends. King Fuad I began refurbishing the *haramlik* in 1925, his architect Verrucci making it over in the style of the Florentine *quattrocentesco* except for its high corner tower, an exact copy of that at the Palazzo Pubblico in Siena. Notice the letter F which appears as a motif on the outside. A fortune-teller had told King Fuad that the letter F would bring his family luck, so he named his daughters Fawzia, Faiza, Faika and Fathia, and his only son Farouk who in turn renamed Safinaz, his first wife, Farida, by whom he had three daughters, Ferial, Fawzia and Fadia. In 1951 Farouk married Narriman, neglecting to change her name, and in

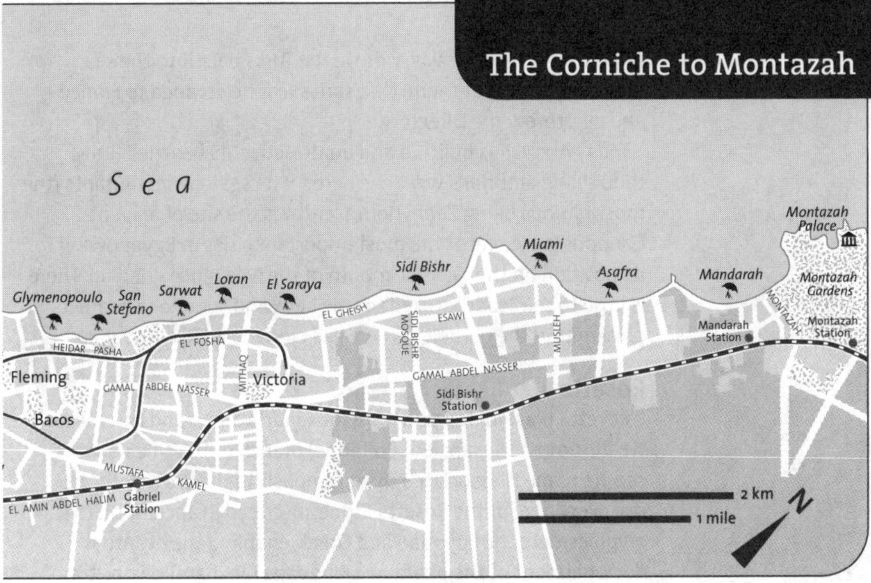

The Corniche to Montazah

January 1952 she bore him his only son, the letter F relegated to second place in Ahmed Fuad. Six months later, Farouk was out of a job. The infant Ahmed reigned briefly as Fuad II, but it was too late.

Abbas II also built the *Salamlik* (men's or reception quarters) near by, but this did not get the Chianti treatment, and it remains merely modestly grandiose. It is now a handsomely renovated deluxe hotel and overlooks a lovely cove with swimming and watersports. The cove is sheltered to the east by the small Tea Island which is reached by a footbridge. A few scattered remains of an ancient settlement, Taposiris Parva, lie about the island. The blot on the west arm of the cove is the Palestine Hotel.

Maamoura beach
adm LE10

The long bay to the east of Montazah is Maamoura with a good sandy **beach**. In the distance you can see the long limestone spur running out to Aboukir.

East of Alexandria

Aboukir (or Abu Qir), 24km east of central Alexandria, is most famous for the two battles fought here in 1798 and 1799. The first was the Battle of the Nile at which Nelson surprised Napoleon's anchored fleet and over the course of two days (1 and 2 August) annihilated it. Though still in control of the country, Napoleon was cut off from France by sea and eventually had to abandon his army and his dreams of Eastern dominion. The circumstances were similar to Antony's at Actium, except that Napoleon's star was still rising. A year later, in July, he personally commanded a battle here against a Turkish force of 15,000 landed by British ships. Napoleon had raced down from Cairo with Kléber and Murat, and with

10,000 men, mostly cavalry, drove the Turks back into the sea, drowning a third of them. That same year he escaped to France and overthrew the Directory.

Today Aboukir is built-up and unattractive, its beaches filthy, though Alexandrians will drive here for its seafood restaurants (the most famous being Zephyrion). Nearby is the site of ancient Canopus, once one of the most important cities in Egypt owing to its position on the Canopic mouth of the Nile, since dried up. There is little to see. Hadrian liked to stay here, and tried to recreate its pleasures in the garden of the Villa Hadriana at Tivoli, near Rome.

Rosetta

Rosetta (Rashid) is 63km from Alexandria and stands on the now westernmost (the ancient Bolbitine) branch of the Nile near the sea. Its name is associated most famously in the West with the discovery here of the **Rosetta Stone**, inscribed in ancient hieroglyphics, demotic Egyptian and Greek, enabling the eventual decipherment of the pharaonic language by Champollion. It is testimony to Napoleon's expedition, which included numerous savants and a well-informed soldiery, that when a Captain Bourchard was shown the stone, turned up by one of his men while restoring Fort Rashid, he immediately recognized its significance.

The town is visited, however, for other reasons: since 1985 it has been the subject of a major restoration project by the Egyptian Antiquities Organization and possesses some of the finest examples in Egypt of Islamic domestic architecture outside Cairo. Founded in the 9th century AD, it flourished while Alexandria faded and declined again as modern Alexandria prospered. It reached its apogee in the 17th and 18th centuries, when it was the most important port in Egypt, and there are still some fine houses dating from this period, built in red and black brick, their façades decorated in the Delta style illustrated, though not nearly so well, by the Terbana Mosque in Alexandria. Many, too, incorporate ancient stones and columns, and have delicately carved *mashrabiyyas*. The oldest and finest of these is the house of **Ali el Fatairi**, 17th-century, just off the main street which runs south, parallel with the Nile, from the train station. This street is fascinating in itself, a market for much of the way, covered by awnings. Other houses are the **Arab Keli**, 18th-century, now a museum; and **El Amaciali**, early 19th-century.

At the bottom of the main street is the most important building in town, the **mosque of Zaghloul**. This is really two mosques, the eastern one smartly painted white, arcades with handsome arches running round a glaring courtyard. The western one, founded in 1600, is more interesting however, partly because it is under a few feet of water and crumbling but mostly for its wonderful forest of columns, as though rising out of a swamp.

Rosetta makes an interesting footnote to Alexandria's history. Its fortunes were built on the default of the greater city. The coast of Egypt here is delta, the shifting sediment of a senseless river. Rosetta can have no sea harbour, the limestone ridges that created the two great harbours of Alexandria do not continue eastward of Aboukir. Alexander saw this potential, that his city could hold its own against land and sea. When the vision is there, Alexandria is willing. Meanwhile it is waiting.

Leaving Rosetta by the north, numerous high chimneys mark **brickworks** along the Nile; here even at the very end of the river's 5,440km journey from its source at Lake Victoria its mud was pressed into service – until 1988 when building with mud brick was banned. Since the building of the High Dam at Aswan, the Nile hardly lays down silt: mud has become a finite commodity in Egypt.

A few kilometres along there is a spit of land, the river washing up on one side, the sea washing up on the other. At the very point there is a small yellow **mosque**. Even as men still pray within it, the sea and the river are rising up through its foundations, curling the paint off its walls, the whole thing disintegrating and tipping towards that line where the blue steady Nile is pounded by the light green waves of the Mediterranean. The lack of mud means that the Nile no longer pushes the Delta out into the Mediterranean. The waves lapping at the mosque are nibbling away at Egypt at the rate of a metre or so each year. The mosque will soon tumble and be drowned. The soldier stands on lonely station, guarding in vain against his country's retreat. You can stand here with him, watching the Mediterranean grow imperceptibly larger.

Tourist Information in Alexandria

ⓘ **Alexandria >**
Midan Saad Zaghloul, **t** *(03) 485 1556; also tourist offices at the Western Harbour's Maritime Station, the main railway station and the airports*

The **Tourist Police, t** (03) 485 0507, are in Midan Saad Zaghloul, near Sharia Nebi Danyal. There are branches at the Maritime Station, the Graeco-Roman Museum and at the entrance to the Montazah gardens.

The **Tourist Friends Association**, **t** (03) 550 1581 or 012 346 0667, has multi-lingual guides to show you the city sites and also introduces visitors and resident foreigners to local customs, habits and colloquial Arabic.

Books and Maps

The American University in Cairo Press publishes three books about Alexandria by Michael Haag. One is *Alexandria Illustrated*, an illustrated guide with maps. Another is *Vintage Alexandria*, a collection of old photographs showing the city and its inhabitants during its cosmopolitan era. The third is *Alexandria: City of Memory* (published in America and Britain by Yale University Press), a literary, social and political portrait of the city during its cosmopolitan heyday in the first half of the 20th century. All three can be obtained at El Maaraf Bookshop, 44 Sharia Saad Zaghloul, at the bookshops of the Graeco-Roman Museum and the Bibliotheca Alexandrina, and at shops in such hotels as the Cecil, Montazah Sheraton and Marriott Renaissance.

Consulates

The **British Consulate** is at 3 Sharia Mena, Roushdi, **t** (03) 546 7001; **Irish Consulate**, 9 Sharia Batalsa (Rue des Ptolemées), **t** (03) 485 2672. There are no American, Canadian, Australian, New Zealand or South African consulates in Alexandria.

Emergencies

For urgent help of any sort, dial **t** 123.

Medical Care

Ask at your hotel. Your consulate or the Tourist Police can also advise.

Money

You can change money at the major hotels and at Thomas Cook, 15 Midan Saad Zaghloul, and at any bank. There are ATMs throughout the city.

Renewing Your Visa

Go to the **Passport Office** at 25 Sharia Talaat Harb, **t** (03) 484 7873, opposite the Leroy Hotel. You will need a photograph and photocopies of the relevant pages of your passport (open daily 8–3, closed Fri; no applications accepted after noon).

Telephones

There is a 24-hour telephone office for domestic and international calls (much cheaper than from the hotels) by the Ramleh tram station in Midan Saad Zaghloul.

Where to Stay in Alexandria

Luxury ($$$$$)

*****El Salamlek Palace Hotel**, Montazah Gardens, **t** (03) 547 7999, *www.sangiovanni.com*. Built in the late 19th century by Khedive Abbas II as a private residence and recently refurbished, this is the most luxurious and exclusive hotel (only 24 rooms) in Alexandria. There is a bar, café, tea lounge and restaurant, but best of all is the agreeable situation (*see* p.522). That being said, it is a long way from town (12km), and the service is not what it should be at this price; the hotel appeals mostly to Gulf Arabs.

Expensive ($$$$)

(★) Hotel Cecil >

****Hotel Cecil**, Midan Saad Zaghloul, **t** (03) 487 7173, *www.sofitel.com*. In the centre of town. Make sure you have a room commanding the magnificent view over the Eastern Harbour. From your balcony you watch the Mediterranean splash against the Corniche; you see the site of the Pharos on the breakwater in the distance; and off to the right on the Silsileh headland you can imagine the palace of the Ptolemies. A Moorish pile built in 1929, the Cecil figures often in Lawrence Durrell's *Alexandria Quartet* and he himself stayed here when he first came to the city. A generation later and it is there in Naguib Mahfouz's *Miramar*. The cavernous rooms, all with balconies, have been refurbished and fully equipped; there is an Art Deco restaurant, Monty's bar, a charming tea lounge, nightclub, bank and Avis desk.

****Windsor Palace**, 17 Sharia el Shohada, **t** (03) 480 8123, **f** (03) 486 6411. Further west along the Corniche from Midan Saad Zaghloul and overlooking the Eastern Harbour. The Windsor was built in 1906, at the same time as the Corniche itself, and is monumentally Edwardian, with enormous rooms and charming décor, though the staff are somewhat lacking in experience and can be fairly hapless, but they are never less than eager and friendly. Newly refurbished.

****Metropole**, 52 Sharia Saad Zaghloul, **t** (03) 482 1467, **f** (03) 482 2040. Recently refurbished, this is another of Alexandria's period hotels. Most rooms have bathrooms. Restaurant (this and the salon outside it with marvellous Art Deco friezes), bar, coffee shop. Rooms on the harbour side have a good view over Midan Saad Zaghloul and the Corniche beyond, but can be noisy at night owing to passing trams. The building once housed the offices of the Third Circle of Irrigation where Constantine Cavafy worked as a government clerk.

*****Montazah Sheraton**, Sharia el Geish at Montazah, **t** (03) 548 0550, *www.sheraton.com*. All rooms with balconies and sea views, colour TV and air conditioning. Restaurant, café, nightclub. Private beach, heated pool; tennis and watersports by arrangement. A well-run and friendly hotel. The great disadvantage for those who want to get the feel of Alexandria is its distance (12km) from the centre.

*****Renaissance**, 544 Sharia el Geish, Sidi Bishr, **t** (03) 549 0935, *www.marriott.com*. Fully equipped rooms, many with sea views, wired for Internet. Gym, sauna, outdoor pool, private beach, several restaurants and bars. 9km east along the Corniche from the heart of Alexandria.

***San Giovanni, 205 Sharia el Geish, **t** (03) 546 7775, **f** (03) 546 4408, *www.sangiovannicleopatra.com/hotel*. At Stanley Bay, with a good seafood restaurant and 24-hour café overlooking the bay. Some of the hotel rooms overlook the street, others overlook the bay; rooms 109, 110 and 111 have access to a sea view terrace.

Moderate ($$$)

Egypt Hotel >

Egypt Hotel, 1 Sharia Degla, on the north side of the Ramleh tram terminus, on the same block as the Egyptair office, **t** (03) 481 4483. This friendly and newly opened hotel is located within a delightful late 1920s Venetian-style building, the work of Alessandro Loria who was also the architect of the Hotel Cecil and several other notable buildings in the city. The rooms are very comfortable with period furnishings and en suite bathrooms; the best have views over the Eastern Harbour. This is a very welcome place in a city suffering from a dearth of moderately priced hotels.

Inexpensive ($$)

Sea Star Hotel >

Sea Star Hotel, 24 Sharia Amin Fakhry, **t** (03) 480 5343, **f** (03) 487 2388. Well located just south of (but not noisily near) the Ramleh tram station, with restaurant, bar, café, nightclub. Rooms are air-conditioned, clean and have private baths; go for the higher floors for more light.

***Ailema**, 21 Sharia Amin Fakhry, **t** (03) 482 7011, **f** (03) 482 2040, on the same street. Though tending towards the shabby, this quiet Greek-run hotel with restaurant and private lift is on the 7th floor where its clean and spacious rooms, some with bath, have views to the sea or over gardens behind.

****Union**, 164 Sharia 26 July, **t** (03) 480 7771, **f** (03) 480 7350. On the top three floors of a building overlooking the Corniche of the Eastern Harbour. Clean rooms and comfortable beds. Reception is on the 5th floor; ask to stay on the 4th to escape the noise from the disco on the 6th.

Cheap ($)

Marhaba >

****Marhaba**, 10 Midan Orabi, **t** (03) 480 0957, **f** (03) 480 9510. A well preserved Edwardian hotel on the west side of the square and not far from the Corniche, with bar, restaurant and café – you can sit on the pavement outside if you like. The rooms are large, comfortable and clean, with fans, baths and balconies, though the trams and buses outside can make for some noise. As good a hotel as those in the inexpensive category.

The pension described in Naguib Mahfouz's *Miramar* was in the vicinity of Silsileh, but the Acropole or the Normandie, each a block west of Midan Saad Zaghloul, could stand in for it:

***Acropole**, 1 Sharia Gamal al Din Yassin, **t** (03) 480 5980. Round the other side of the same block as the Cecil. Do not let the grotty entrance put you off; the pension is on the 4th floor. The place is rather run down, and passing trams mean that the rooms can be noisy, but they are clean, most have balconies and some offer glimpses of the harbour. All rooms have cold water wash basins; the shared bath? rooms have hot water and are clean.

***Normandie**, **t** (03) 480 6830, on the opposite side of the street and closer to the Corniche. On the 5th floor and unchanged since 1950, as you can tell from the photograph hanging in the entrance of a happy European soirée in the pension at the time. In their midst is a beaming Madame Melasse, the former French proprietress; a few years later the plug was pulled on Alexandria's Europeans, but already old and with nowhere to go, Madame Melasse remained. She died in the 1970s aged 90, her memory revered, her pension now run, indeed by some process of osmosis owned, by her former Nubian servant, Abdul Rahim.

Eating Out in Alexandria

Alexandria's restaurants are rarely expensive (if you take Cairo as the comparison), and the range includes French, Italian, Greek, Middle Eastern, Indian and Chinese, with an emphasis on seafood. Most are open for lunch (usually noon–4pm) and dinner (7 or 8pm until at least 11pm).

A number of places that can loosely be described as cafés are included. Here, over coffee, beer or wine and a bite to eat, it can be pleasant to let time pass. *See also* 'Entertainment and Nightlife', below.

Expensive ($$$$)

The Tikka Grill ›

The Tikka Grill, t (03) 480 5114, on the seaward side of the Corniche about halfway along from the Cecil to Fort Qaytbey. Offers the best restaurant setting in Alexandria, with a view along the full sweep of the Eastern Harbour. The menu is varied (Indian, Middle Eastern and Western, grills, seafood and salads) and the food good.

The Fish Market ›

The Fish Market, t (03) 480 5119. Upstairs from the Tikka Grill. Where you can choose your own fish or seafood and have it cooked to your taste.

Moderate ($$$)

Greek Yacht Club, upstairs restaurant, on the spine of land leading out to Fort Qaytbey. Many say this is the best place for fish; you do not need to be a member. The rooms are cool and spacious and there is a large terrace overlooking the Eastern Harbour.

Adora, 33 Sharia Bairam el Tunsi. An Alexandrian institution. An utterly unpretentious place frequented by everyone from locals, invariably men, to upper class couples, Adora (though pronounced Adoura), is located in the fish market area on a back street a block in from the coast road between Fort Qaytbey and Ras el Tin and next to the track where yellow trams occasionally pass, ringing their bells. You eat outside on the sawdust-covered pavement where an assortment of salads and side dishes is brought to your table, though no menu – for your main fish course you must go inside and choose from a selection of fresh sea bass, grey and red mullet, sole, squid and shrimp. *Open 24 hours.*

Restaurant Denis, 1 Sharia Ibn Bassam, a short street between the Ramleh tram station at Midan Saad Zaghloul (Olympic Airways on the corner) and the Corniche, **t** (03) 487 0457. Founded by Greeks; serves wine, beer and does salads and fresh seafood by weight.

Santa Lucia, 40 Sharia Safiya Zaghloul, towards Sharia Horreya, **t** (03) 482 4240. One of Alexandria's older restaurants, founded by a Jew and a Greek but Egyptian-owned now. Its menu is European, its speciality is seafood, and it has live music; Lawrence Durrell kept an account here.

San Giovanni Hotel, at Stanley Bay, 205 Sharia El Geish. This hotel has a good restaurant serving seafood, oriental and Western dishes, and its La Sirène Coffee Shop is open 24 hours. Both have fine sea views.

The Trianon ››

The Trianon, Midan Saad Zaghloul, where Sharia Safiya Zaghloul runs off southwards. One of the old cafés and a favourite of Cavafy's; you can get beer, coffee and light meals until late; the patisserie and restaurant are beautifully decorated in orientalist Art Deco.

Athineos ››

Athineos, diagonally opposite the Trianon, on the north side of the Ramleh tram station. This formerly Greek café and patisserie has an ornate restaurant on the Corniche side.

Pastroudis ››

Pastroudis, 39 Sharia Horreya. After the Hotel Cecil, this is the Alexandrian institution most mentioned in Durrell's *Alexandria Quartet*. Founded by Greeks in 1923, but now Egyptian-run, the style of its restaurant, patisserie and indoor/outdoor café is Art Deco.

Cap d'Or ››

Cap d'Or, Sharia Adib, north off Sharia Salah-Salem. For Art Nouveau, seafood and a bottle of wine.

Cheap ($)

Mohammed Ahmed Foul (no sign in English on the fascia). Numerous English-language advertising signs along Sharia Abd al-Ftah al-Hadari, between and parallel to sharias Nebi Danyal and Safiya Zaghloul, will lead you to it – recognized by its orange awning and the crowds. The *foul* here is the best in town, but older residents, who remember when this was Jewish-run, say the *foul* was even better then.

Baudrot, 14 Sharia Saad Zaghloul. Stark indoors and boring in winter, but a delightful place in summer, when you can have a coffee and pastry, or a beer with a light meal, in the garden at the rear. This, however, is not the original and stylish Baudrot famous during Alexandria's cosmopolitan heyday, which stood at the corner of the Rue Fuad (Horreya) and Rue Cherif Pasha (Salah-Salem) and was described by Durrell as 'twinkling with music and lights'.

The Elite >

The Elite, 43 Sharia Safiya Zaghloul. The closest thing to the easy atmosphere of a Greek taverna in town. It is a measure of how dull Alexandria has become with the passing of its cosmopolitan population that this is the only really bohemian place to relax and drink a Stella and watch the world parade by. The fare is simple but good, a selection of Greek, Egyptian and French. Contrary to commonly held belief, neither its late owner Madame Christina nor the Elite itself have any connection with Cavafy. The Elite dates only from the 1950s, and Madame Christina could not have been more than ten when Cavafy died in 1933. Nevertheless her imaginative 'memory' and the homage she paid to the poet by sticking his portrait and poetry on the walls has kept the misconception going.

Entertainment and Nightlife in Alexandria

You would expect Alexandria to have a lively **nightlife**. It does not. All the old Greek bazouki joints have gone the way of the old Greeks. Belly dancing never much featured in Alexandria and has now been killed off by Gulf Arabs who come to Alexandria to keep cool in the summer and unfortunately bring their kill-joy fundamentalism with them. There are seedy **discos** atop some of the cheaper hotels, such as the Belvedere above the Union, 164 Sharia 26 July. For sheer vulgarity drop in at the **Spitfire Bar** (with a big jet plane stuck above the entrance), Sharia Goufra el Togariya, at the western end of Sharia Saad Zaghloul.

Otherwise, you have to rely on the major hotels. The **Monty Bar** at the Cecil, the **Aquarius Discotheque** at the Montazah Sheraton and the **Jazz Club** at the Renaissance at Sidi Bishr are dining places with live entertainment.

There are several venues for cultural events. The former Mohammed Ali Club, once the resort of cotton brokers, bankers and even the literati (it was here that Forster was introduced to Cavafy), recently refurbished and called now the **Horreya Cultural Palace**, 1 Sharia Horreya, is home to drama, music, painting, poetry and short story clubs. The **Conservatoire de Musique d'Alexandrie**, 90 Sharia Horreya, holds music classes and sponsors concerts and recitals. Concerts, operas, ballets and plays are put on at the **Mohammed Ali Opera House**, 22 Sharia Horreya, built in the 1920s and just recently beautifully refurbished. Worth visiting if only to see how wealthy Alexandrians once lived, **L'Atelier**, 8 Sharia Victor Bassili, three streets east of the Graeco-Roman Museum in what was called the Quartier Grec, was the residence of a Syro-Lebanese family. Now it presents films, lectures and exhibitions of painting and sculpture. Also the **foreign cultural institutes** present programmes of films, concerts and other entertainments.

American Cultural Center, 3 Rue des Pharaons (Sharia Pharana), north and parallel to Sharia Horreya, just behind the Graeco-Roman Museum, **t** (03) 486 1009. This was originally the home of the financier Baron Alfred de Menasce, who belonged to one of city's great Jewish families; when it was built here in the Quartier Grec in the early 1920s it was considered the most beautiful house in the city.

Goethe Institute, 10 Rue des Ptolemées (Sharia Batalsa), **t** (03) 483 9870. This is also in the Quartier Grec and was once the home of the Rolo family, Jews of British nationality, who were major cotton brokers.

Russian Cultural Centre, 5 Rue des Ptolemées (Sharia Batalsa), **t** (03) 486 5645. Though they discourage visitors, it is worth getting in to see the magnficient stairway with its stained glass window rising up from the ground floor.

French Cultural Centre, 30 Sharia Nebi Danyal, **t** (03) 391 8952. Notice the ancient columns which now serve as a gate.

Foreign films are often shown at the Amir Cinema on Sharia Horreya or round the corner in Sharia Safiya Zaghloul at the Rialto or Metro cinemas.

Language

The language of the country is Arabic, but English is taught to every schoolchild and is the foreign language most spoken by Egyptians, with French a close second.

In particular, most staff at hotels, restaurants and travel companies catering to foreigners will speak English, probably French, and perhaps also German and Italian. So along the well-beaten tourist paths, language is unlikely to prove a problem. Even so, the purchase of a traveller's phrase book at home or in Egypt can prove useful, and knowledge of a few words and phrases is always appreciated.

Note that there are several methods of **transliterating Arabic** into the Latin alphabet. For example, the town of Minya can also be written as Minia or Minieh. Sultan (or Fort) Qaytbay can be written as Kait Bay, Qaitbai, Qait Bey, and so on. So in consulting the index or looking for places on maps, bear in mind possible variant spellings.

Used throughout this guide are the words ***sharia*** (street), and ***midan*** (square).

Here are some courtesies and simple questions and remarks to set you off on the right track. Note that the ' (*ain*) is a guttural vowel sound, achieved by constricting the throat as far back as possible.

Hello *ahlan*

Hello/goodbye *Salaam aleikum* (meaning 'peace be upon you', to which the reply is *wa aleikum el salaam*, meaning 'and peace be upon you').

Please *minfadlak* (if addressing a man)
minfadlik (if addressing a woman)

Thank you *shukran*

No thank you *la shukran*

Yes *aywa* or sometimes *naam*

No *la*

I want *'aayiz* (if addressing a man)
'ayza (if addressing a woman)

How much? *bekaam?*

Good *kuwayyis*

Bad *mish kuwayyis*

As well as learning to speak (if not read) a few words in Arabic, it would be useful to be able to recognize the **Arabic numerals**.
Note that, as in the West, units are at the right, preceded by tens, hundreds, etc, as you move left. Recognition will prove a great
help when shopping, examining bills, catching numbered buses, boarding numbered train carriages and looking for your numbered seat.

١	٢	٣	٤	٥	٦	٧	٨	٩	١٠
1	2	3	4	5	6	7	8	9	10

Arab numerals

Glossary

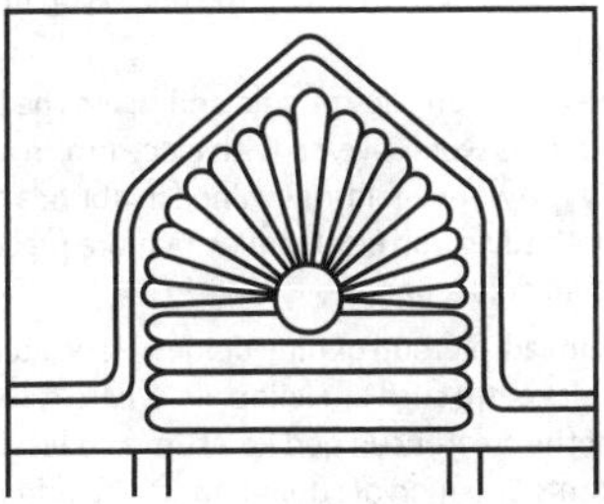

Keel-arch doorway

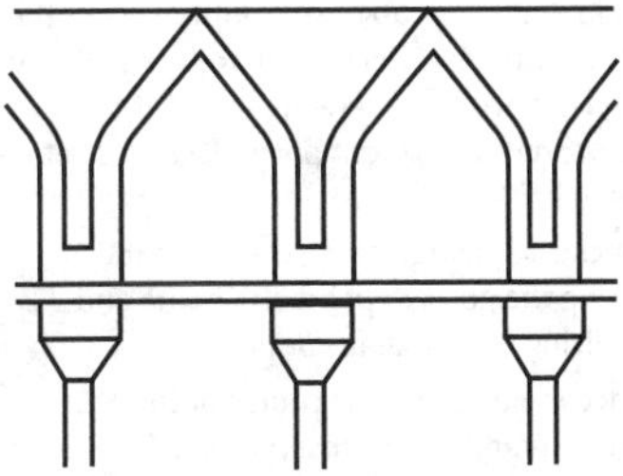

Fatimid keel-arches with wooden tie-beams

ablaq in Arab architecture, the alternating use of red and white or black and white stone.

abu the Arabic for holy man or saint, whether Muslim or Christian.

Amun God of Thebes; as Amun-Re he was associated with the sun god and became the national god during the New Kingdom. His sacred animal was the ram. Along with his wife, Mut, and their son, Khonsu, Amun was one of the Theban triad.

ankh the hieroglyphic sign for life, resembling a cross with a loop in place of the upper arm.

Anubis God of the dead, associated with interment. His sacred animal was the dog or jackal.

Apis the sacred bull of Memphis, buried in the Serapeum at Saqqara (*see* Ptah).

apse a semi-circular domed recess, most frequently at the east end of a church (*see* heikal).

Archimedes' screw an irrigation device introduced during the Ptolemaic period for raising water by means of an inclined screw.

Aten the sun's disc; the life force. Worshipped by Akhenaten, who attacked the priesthood of Amun.

Atum a sun god of Heliopolis, creator of the universe, often combined with Re and represented as a man.

azan the Muslim call to prayer (*see* muezzin).

ba a spirit that inhabits the body during life but is not attached to it; at death it leaves the body and joins the divine spirit (*see* ka).

bab a gate, as Bab Zuwayla.

basilica a building, for example a church, in the form of a long colonnaded hall, usually with one or more apses at the east end, and a narthex at the west end.

Bastet the goddess of Bubastis, a goddess of joy. Her sacred animal was the lioness or cat.

bayt a house, or the self-contained apartments into which Ummayad mansions and Abbasid palaces were divided.

Benben the primeval hill which first arose from the waters.

Bes a protective dwarf-god, averter of evil, helper in childbirth.

Birth house a temple annexe where the annual rites associated with the birth of the god-king were performed. On its interior walls are scenes of the divine marriage and the king's birth.

Book of the Dead the generic name given to a variable collection of spells (including for example the Amduat and the Book of the Gates) which from New Kingdom to Ptolemaic times were written on papyrus and buried with the mummy. They continue the tradition of the Pyramid Texts such as at the Pyramid of Unas and the funerary texts on tomb walls in the Valley of the Kings.

cadi a judge knowledgeable in Islamic law.

caliph literally 'successor' to Mohammed, the title taken by those claiming the spiritual and temporal leadership of Islam.

canopic jars containers placed within ancient tombs to preserve those organs and viscera thought essential for the dead man's continued existence in the afterlife.

capitals Pharaonic and Ptolemaic temples employed capitals decorated either with plant forms (palmiform, papyriform, lotiform) or other motifs (Hathoric, with the human face and cow's ears of Hathor; forms deriving from timber construction such as tent poles). (*See* illustration opposite.)

cartouche in hieroglyphics, the oval band enclosing the god's or pharaoh's name and symbolizing unchanging continuity.

cataract rapids along the course of the Nile, caused by granite outcrops. The First Cataract is at Aswan and there are five more upriver to Khartoum, the Second Cataract near Wadi Halfa being the most formidable. Historically, all have been hazards to navigation.

cavetto cornice one of the most characteristic decorative features in ancient Egyptian architecture, a concave moulding decorated with palmettes. It was used along the tops of walls and pylons, projecting at front and sides. Below it would be a torus moulding.

cenotaph a symbolic rather than actual tomb.

colossus a greater than life-size statue, usually of a king.

colours primary colours usually had particular applications and significance in ancient Egyptian painting. Black represented death: mummies, also Osiris as king of the dead, were commonly depicted in black. Blue was for sky and water, the sky gods painted this colour. Green was the colour of rebirth: Osiris, who overcame death and was reborn, often had his face and limbs painted green; also the solar disc was commonly painted light green on sarcophagi, instead of its usual red. Red was for blood and fire; men's bodies were depicted as reddish brown or brown; it also had a maleficent connotation: Seth was painted reddish brown. White represented silver and was the colour of the moon; it was also the colour of the garments of the gods and the crown of Upper Egypt. Yellow represented gold and was also used as the colour for women's bodies until the mid-XVIII Dynasty; thereafter the only women painted this colour were goddesses.

columns like capitals, ancient columns followed certain decorative motifs, for example papyrus columns modelled after either a single stem and therefore smooth, or after a bundle of stems and therefore ribbed.

crowns the red crown of Lower Egypt was joined with the white crown of Upper Egypt to represent unification of the country (*see* colours). The blue crown or headdress was worn when riding a chariot; it appears after the introduction of the horse into Egypt by the Hyksos *c.* 1600 BC. No matter what headdress the pharaoh wore, he was always shown with the uraeus on his forehead.

electrum an alloy of gold and silver. The tips of obelisks were covered with electrum. In ancient Egypt, where gold was mined in abundance, both silver and electrum were more precious than gold alone.

Ennead a group of nine deities associated with a cult centre such as Heliopolis, where it consisted of the creator sun god Re-Atum and his descendants Shu (god of sunlight and air), Tefnut (goddess of moisture), Geb (earth god), Nut (sky goddess), Osiris (god of the underworld), Isis (goddess of magical powers), Seth (god of chaotic forces) and Nephthys (a funerary goddess).

evil eye the superstition that the envious glance of any passer-by, attracted by an immodest show of wealth, achievement or beauty, can harm or bewitch. Reciting certain verses of the Koran is one way of warding it off. Uzait Horun, the Eye of Horus, is meant to ensure safety and happiness and wards off the evil eye; it may be painted on cars, trucks and fishing boats, or worn as an amulet, particularly by children, who are especially vulnerable. Children also leave their handprints on walls to avert the evil eye. The probable value of the belief is as a social control, minimizing at least the appearance of disparity in people's fortunes and so promoting solidarity.

exonarthex the outer vestibule of a church.

faïence glazed earthenware, often decorated, formed as pottery or in blocks or tiles as a wall facing.

fellahin Egyptian peasants. The singular is fellah.

flagellum a flail or rattle to drive away evil spirits, it could be used only by a pharaoh and so represented the royal authority in carvings and statues. In the other hand was the crook, another royal symbol.

Geb personification of the earth.

hajj the pilgrimage to Mecca that all Muslims should make at least once in their lifetime.

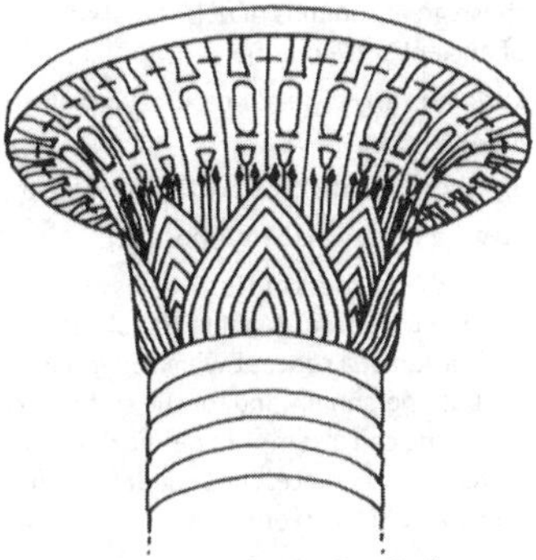

Open Papyrus Capital

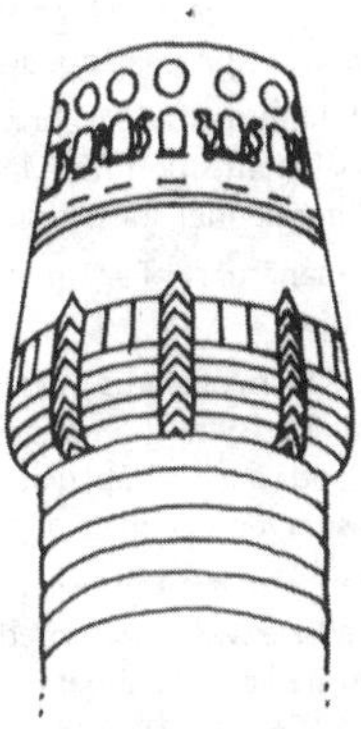

Closed Papyrus Capital

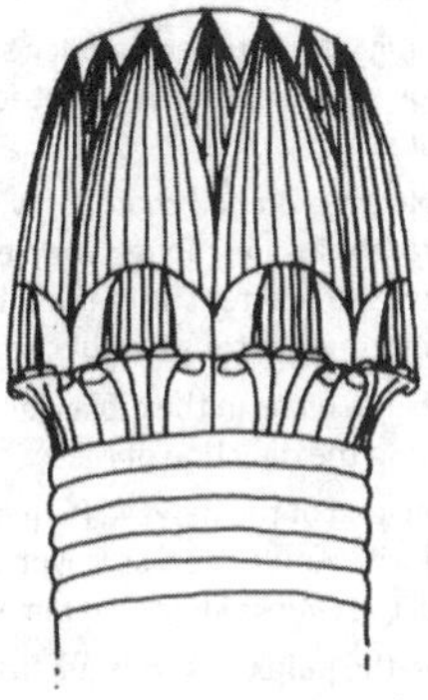

Closed Lotus Capital

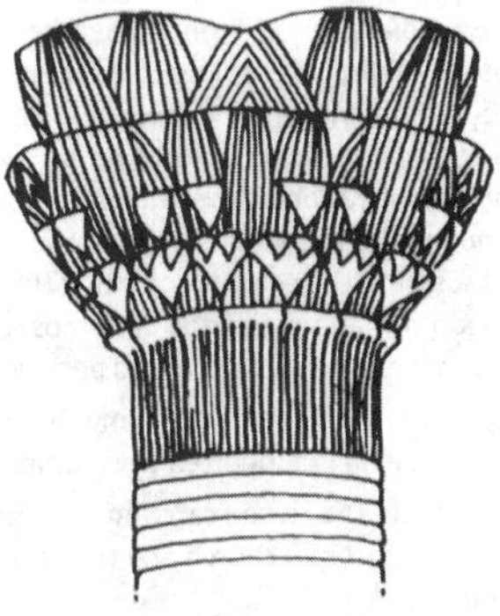

Open Lotus Capital

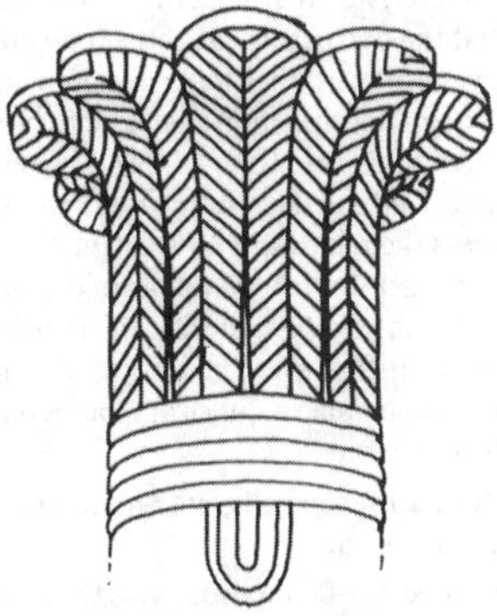

Palm Capital

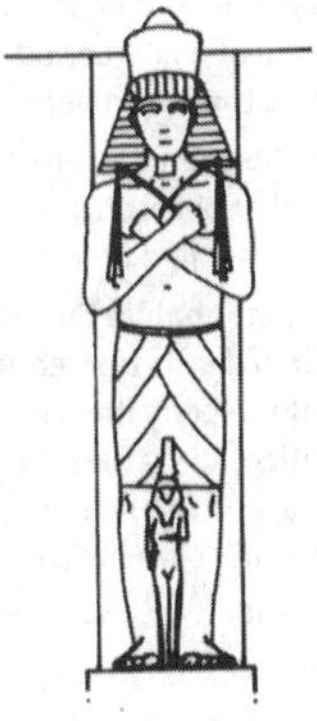

Osirid Pillar

When they have done so, they will often paint a scene of the event on their houses.

hammam a bath, public or private.

Hapy God of the abundant Nile, represented as a man with pendulous breasts.

harem the private family (or specifically the women's) quarter in a house.

Haroeris the elder Horus.

Harpocrates Horus as child.

Hathor the goddess of heaven, joy and love; the Greeks identified her with Aphrodite. She was the deity of Dendera and protector of the Theban necropolis. Her sacred animal was the cow.

Heb-Sed the jubilee marking the thirtieth year of a pharoah's reign (*see* 'Saqqara', p.206).

Hegira Mohammed's flight, or more properly his 'withdrawal of affection' from Mecca in AD 622. The Muslim calender starts from this date.

heikal the sanctuary of a Coptic church; usually there are three.

Herakhte a form of Horus, 'Horus of the horizon', often combined with the sun god as Re-Herakhte and so worshipped at Heliopolis. The falcon was sacred to him.

Horus the son of Isis and Osiris, and revered as the sun god. He was represented as the sun disc or a falcon, his sacred animal.

Hyksos a foreign people who ruled Egypt from Avaris in the Delta during the Second Intermediate Period. Probably Semites and possibly a displaced ruling caste from Palestine, they did not introduce a new culture but rather respected and encouraged Egyptian civilization and its institutions. Nevertheless, the propaganda of the Theban princes who ejected the Hyksos from the country, initiating the New Kingdom, made the period of Hyksos rule synonymous with anarchy and destruction.

hypostyle a hypostyle hall is any chamber whose ceiling is supported by columns or pillars.

iconostasis the screen carrying icons between the main part of a church and the sanctuary or choir.

Isis sister and wife to Osiris, mother of Horus, the patron goddess of Philae. She was most highly revered at a late period. She is often shown with a throne on her head.

ithyphallic: Denoting the erect phallus of a depicted god or pharaoh, most commonly the god Min. It was a sign of fertility.

ka a spirit that inhabits the body during life and may leave it in death, but requires the continued existence of the body (hence mummification or, by substitution, ka statues) for its survival. The ka was personal and individual, in a sense the ideal image of a man's own life (*see* ba).

khan *see* wikala.

khedive viceroy. Mohammed Ali was recognized in 1805 as viceroy of the Ottoman sultan in Istanbul, and his successors retained the title until the outbreak of the First World War in 1914. Egypt's nominal allegiance to the sultan thereupon ceased and its rulers assumed the title of king.

Khnum the patron god of Elephantine Island and the Cataracts. He fashioned man on his potter's wheel. His sacred animal was the ram.

Khonsu son of Amun and Mut; god of the moon. The falcon was sacred to him.

kom the particularly Egyptian word for a tell, those great mounds of debris marking the site of ancient settlements.

kufic an early style of Arabic calligraphy with angular letters.

lily the plant identified with Upper Egypt.

liwan a vaulted hall (*see* mosque).

Maat the goddess of truth, whose symbol was the ostrich feather. Maat is actually the deification of a concept which Egyptians strove for, both personally and for the state. As well as truth, one can attempt to define it as justice, correctness, balance. The best definition is the now rare English word 'meet'.

madrasa *see* mosque.

maristan a hospital.

mashrabiyya interlaced wooden screenwork, used for example to cover street-facing windows in a house.

mausoleum a domed chamber with one or more tombs inside; though simple in form, these structures, characteristic of the City of the Dead, are sometimes of considerable beauty.

mihrab the niche in the qibla wall of a mosque, indicating the direction of Mecca.

Min the god of the harvest, frequently amalgamated with Amun. He was ithyphallically represented. The Greeks identified him with Pan.

minbar the pulpit in a mosque from which the Friday prayer is spoken.

monophysitism strictly, the Christian doctrine that the two natures of Christ (human and divine) are absorbed into one nature (the divine). Though this has often been said to be Coptic belief, that is not true: the Copts do not deny the continued existence of the two natures but stress their unity after the Incarnation. The Latin and Greek Churches emphasise the two natures of Christ, holding that they are unmixed and unchangeable even though indistinguishable and inseparable (Council of Chalcedon, 451); they are diophysite.

Mont a Theban god of war, represented with a falcon's head.

mosque the first mosque was the courtyard of Mohammed's house at Medina, with no architectural refinements except a shaded area at one end. Indeed, the only requirement for a mosque is that it should demarcate a space in which people may gather for saying prayers, such as an open quadrangle marked off by a ditch. From this notion developed the congregational mosque, of which the Ibn Tulun is the most outstanding example. Among non-congregational mosques are two special types which

Minarets

are of Cairene inspiration and development, the cruciform madrasa and the *sabil kuttab*. The madrasa served as a theological college, introduced by Saladin to combat Fatimid Shi'ism. Later it became more complex, a tomb appended and the madrasa formed of four *liwans*, each opening into a central court, hence cruciform. The outstanding example of this type is the Hassan. This pattern was subsequently modified, the court covered over, the east and west *liwans* reduced to vestigial proportions, a Koranic school for boys (*kuttab*) added as a floor above, a public fountain (*sabil*) below.

moulid the birthday of a saint or holy man, Coptic or Muslim; it is often celebrated at the level of folk religion, a pharaonic deity transformed into a Christian saint who in turn resurfaces as a Muslim sheikh.

muezzin a crier who, as from a minaret, calls the faithful to prayer (*see* azan).

Mut the wife of Amun and mother of Khonsu. Her sacred animal was the vulture.

naos the enclosed inner 'house of the god' (also cella), the central room of a temple, though sometimes referring to the entire temple. The sanctuary.

narthex the entrance vestibule at the west end of a church.

nashki a cursive form of Arabic writing, subsequent to kufic.

necropolis Greek for cemetery, literally city (*polis*) of the dead (*necros*).

Neith Goddess of Sais, shown wearing the red crown of Lower Egypt. She was one of the goddesses who protected the dead and the Canopic jars.

Nephthys sister of Isis and Osiris, married to Seth; with outstretched wings, one of the protector goddesses of the dead, guardian of the Canopic jars.

nome an administrative province of ancient Egypt. The chief official of a nome was the nomarch.

Nut Goddess of the sky, often shown supported by Shu.

Opening of the Mouth funerary ceremony by which the mouth of the mummy was symbolically opened to ensure it could partake of nourishment in the afterlife.

Osiris originally a vegetation god, later the god of the underworld. Murdered and dismembered by Seth, he was the husband and brother of Isis and father of Horus.

Ostracon (plural ostraca) potsherds bearing inscriptions.

papyrus a plant identified with Lower Egypt; it served as a writing material from I Dyn to Islamic times.

pronaos a columned porch, leading to the naos.

Ptah the patron god of Memphis and father of the gods. His sacred animal was the Apis bull.

pylon arranged in pairs, forming a monumental gateway to a temple. Where there are several sets of pylons, each preceding a court, they descend in size as the sanctuary of the god is approached, while the floor level rises, creating a focussing or tunnelling effect.

pyramidion the capstone of a pyramid.

qibla wall the wall of a mosque facing Mecca.

Re the sun god, usually combined with another god, such as Atum-Re, Amun-Re or Re-Herakhte. His priesthood was at Heliopolis.

riwaq the arcade around a *sahn*, or a student apartment within the arcade.

Sabbakhin Arabic for diggers of *sabbakh*, a highly fertile earth. The mud brick and organic refuse of ancient sites is a major source of *sebbakh*, so that such sites are often destroyed by *sebbakhin*.

sabil kuttab *see* mosque.

sahn an interior court, usually in a mosque.

sakiya an irrigation device introduced during the Ptolemaic period consisting of buckets attached to a wheel which lifts water to the fields and is driven by circling oxen.

Sebakh, sebakhin: *koms*, those mounds of debris that cover ancient sites, contain *sebakh*, an earth made up of as much as 12% potassium nitrate, sodium carbonate and ammonium chloride, which is used as fertilizer. Those who work the mounds are *sebakhin*.

Sekhmet the lion goddess of war.

Selket scorpion goddess, often shown with a scorpion on her head; she was a guardian of the dead.

Serapis a god invented by the Ptolemies, looking like Zeus but identified with Osiris-Apis.

Seth god of chaos, brother and slayer of Osiris, adversary of Horus, he became a god of war, though after the XXII Dynasty he was reduced to the god of the impure. His sacred animal was possibly the aardvark.

shaduf a simple lever device for lifting water to irrigate the fields. It is operated by hand.

Shia or **Shi'ites** literally partisans, that is those who believe Ali, son in law of the Mohammed, should by divine right have succeeded to the caliphate, and that certain of his descendants have inherited that right. In their view, therefore, the first three caliphs were usurpers. Few Egyptians are Shi'a; nevertheless, the head of Hussein, son of Ali, is supposedly at the Mosque of Sayyidna al-Hussein in Cairo (q.v. for an account of the Shia-Sunni split). *See* Sunni.

Shu the god of the air. He is often shown supporting Nut.

Sobek god of the waters, patron of the Fayyum, the crocodile was sacred to him.

squinches small arches or supports across the corners of a square, enabling the carriage of a dome.

stele an upright stone slab or pillar with an inscription or design, used as a monument or grave marker.

Sunni Orthodox Muslims, who attribute no special religious or political function to the descendants of Mohammed's son-in-law Ali. Virtually all Egyptian Muslims and close to 90% of Muslims worldwide are Sunni. *See* Shia.

tell *see* kom.

Theban triad Amun, his wife Mut and their son Khonsu.

Thoth a moon deity and the god of science. The ibis and baboon were sacred to him.

Torus a convex moulding (*see* cavetto cornice).

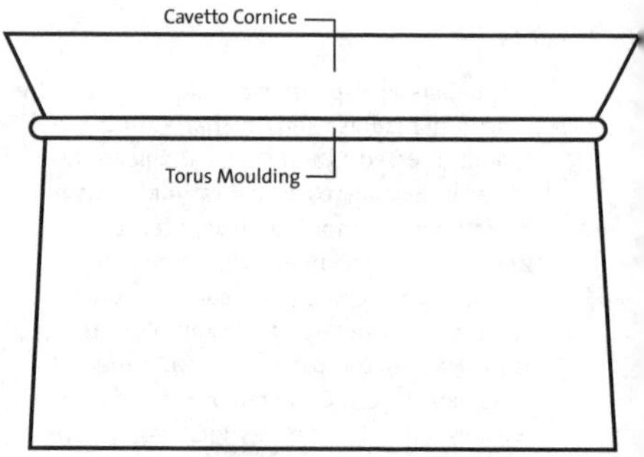

Pharaonic architectural features

uraeus the cobra worn on the forehead of a pharoah as both an emblem and an instrument of protection, breathing flames and destroying enemies.

Ushabti a mummiform figurine, serving in the tomb as deputy for the dead man, carrying out his labour obligations.

wikala an inn for travelling merchants built around a courtyard, with stables and warehouses at ground level and living accommodation above. Other names are *khan* and *okel*.

waqf an endowment for the upkeep of a mosque, for example a nearby apartment house, or shops built into the street level of the mosque, earning rents.

ziyadah the outer court of a mosque.

Further Reading

The literature on Egypt is vast, and apart from pursuing your interest in libraries and bookshops at home there are several bookshops in Cairo worth visiting. The American University in Cairo Press publishes a growing list of books on many aspects of Egypt past and present, including fiction, non-fiction and guides; their titles are widely available in Egypt, and they have their own bookshop in Cairo.

A number of authors are quoted throughout the text of this guide, and you might like to pursue their books according to your interest. The following titles will provide introductions to periods or aspects of Egyptian history. Any of these books can be ordered through *www.abebooks.com* or *www.abebooks.co.uk*

Baines, John and Malek, Jaromir, *Atlas of Ancient Egypt* (NY, 2000; Cairo, 2002). Originally published in 1980, this revised edition of the most comprehensive introduction to the civilization of ancient Egypt includes a complete atlas, descriptions of 90 sites, and chapters on geography, archaeology, history, art and architecture.

Bowman, Alan K., *Egypt After the Pharaohs* (London, 1986). An excellent account of the Graeco-Roman period.

Carter, Howard, *The Tomb of Tutankhamen* (London, in three volumes, 1923, 1927, 1933). Subsequently reprinted in various forms, e.g. abridged, or the first volume only (the most immediate and exciting) as *The Discovery of the Tomb of Tutankhamen*, this is the first-hand account of the greatest Egyptological find of all.

Edwards, I.E.S., *The Pyramids of Egypt* (Harmondsworth, 1991). An expert and orthodox study by the late Keeper of Egyptian Antiquities at the British Museum.

Haag, Michael, *Alexandria: City of Memory* (London, New Haven, Cairo 2004). A literary, social and political portrait of Alexandria during its cosmopolitan heyday in the first half of the 20th century, including in particular the experiences of Constantine Cavafy, E.M. Forster and Lawrence Durrell in the city.

Hassanein, Ahmed, *Lost Oases* (Cairo, 2006). Originally published in London and New York in 1925, this is a classic work of desert exploration by the first man to traverse the Sahara from the Mediterranean to the Sudan and who, along the way, discovered the 'lost' oases of Uweinat and Arkenu, which provided evidence that the deserts of Egypt were once grasslands.

Kamil, Jill, *Christianity in the Land of the Pharaohs: The Coptic Orthodox Church* (London, Cairo, 2002). A full and lavishly illustrated history of Egyptian Christianity.

Kitchen, K.A., *Pharaoh Triumphant* (Warminster, 1982; Cairo, 1990). The life and times of Ramses II by the leading expert on the XIX Dynasty.

Lane, E.W., *Manners and Customs of the Modern Egyptians* (Cairo, 2003). Never out of print since it was first published in 1836, this is the classic survey of Egyptian life in the early 19th century.

Meinardus, Otto F. A., *Monks and Monasteries of the Egyptian Deserts* (Cairo, 1989). The standard work on Egyptian monasticism from its flowering in the deserts during the fourth century AD, and its subsequent influence throughout the Christian world, to the renaissance of the Coptic faith today.

Moorhead, Alan, *The White Nile* (London, 1960) and *The Blue Nile* (London, 1962). Splendidly readable accounts of the early explorations of the upper reaches of the Nile, and of the Ottomans, Napoleon and the British in Egypt.

Rodenbeck, Max, *Cairo: The City Victorious* (London, 1998). An interweaving of history and anecdote from pyramids to traffic jams.

Shaw, Ian, ed., *The Oxford History of Ancient Egypt* (Oxford, 2000). This is the latest attempt to bring the whole of ancient Egyptian history up to the end of the Roman period into a single volume. The predynastic and dynastic periods are handled very well, but the Graeco-Roman period is rather frothy.

Index

Main page references are in **bold**. Page references to maps are in *italics*.

Abbassids 24–5, 37, 82
Aboudi, Mohammed 304
Aboukir 523–4
Abousir 433–4
Abu Bakr 127
Abu Ghurab 20, 199, 200
Abu Rudeis 462
Abu Simbel 383, **392–400**, *395*
temples 396–9
rescue 394
Abusir 199, 200
Abydos 256–9, *258*
accommodation 62
Grand Hotels 48–50
Aga Khan 114, **369**
Aghurmi 405, 410, 411
Agiiba Beach 436
Agouza 91
agriculture 42, 43
Ahmed Hamdi Tunnel 445, 462
Ain Musa 462
Ain Sukhna 446
airlines 58, 59, 80, 488
Akhenaten (Amenophis IV) 22, 47, 148–9, **242**, 256, 282
Hymn to the Sun 246
tomb 245
Akhetaten 241–7, **243**
cliff tombs 245–7
Akhti Hotep 209–10, 211
Alamein 28, 38, **434–5**, 436
alcohol 69–70, 444
Alexander the Great 23, 408, 410–11, 460, 487–9
temple 417
tomb 509, 510
Alexandria 24, 431, **485–529**, *486*, *501*
Alabaster Tomb 509–10
Bibliotheca 40, 520
Chatby Necropolis 520–1
Cleopatra's Needles 495–6
Cleopatra's Palace 495, **496**
corniche 495, **521–3**, *522–3*
Eastern Harbour 495
Fort Qaytbey 515
headland 514–19
Khartoum Column 508
Kom el Dikka 500–1
Kom el Shogafa 495, 518
Montazah 495, **522–3**
museums
Alexandria National 495, **507**
Cavafy 498–9
Fine Arts 519
Graeco-Roman 495, **502–6**, *503*
Royal Jewellery 521–2
Nasser's birthplace 521
orientation 495
Pharos lighthouse 23, 495, **515–16**
Pompey's Pillar 495, **517**
Quartier Grec 508
Ramleh 495, 496, 497
Ras el Tin Palace 514
Roman baths 501
Roman theatre 495, **500**
Serapeum 517–18
Shallalat Gardens 495, **507–10**
tourist information 525
Turkish Town 495, 512–14
Villa of the Birds 501
where to stay 526–7
Ali 36, 127
Amada, temple 390
Amarna 22, **240–7**
cliff tombs 245–7
museum 47
Amarna Letters 148, 244
Amenemhat, tomb 237
Amenophis I 280
Amenophis II 390
tomb 313–14, *315*
Amenophis III 21–2, 269–70, 280
Luxor temple 275–7
palace (Thebes) 343
Amenophis IV *see* Akhenaten (Amenophis IV)
Ammenemes I 21, 222
Ammenemes III 222
colossal seated figures 224–5
mortuary temple 229
Ammon, temple 410–11
Amosis I 21
Amr 24–5, 36, 82, 460, 491, 492
Amun 22, 256, 280, 282–3, 481
Amun herkhopshef, tomb 336
Anglo-Egyptian Treaty 38
animal cults 213, 215–16, 260
Ankhesenamun 318
Antinopolis 238
antiquities 56, 74, 160
Antony, Mark 494, 508–9
Antony, Saint 36, 234, 419, **446–7**, 450
monastery 446–9
Apis bulls 199, 212–15
Arabi, Colonel Ahmed 28
Arabian Desert 91
Arabs 24–7, 36–7, 46, 82–4
see also Islam
Arafat, Yasser 40
Aristarchos of Samos 489
Arius 490
Assiut 248–50
Assyrians 22
Aswan **357–82**, *358*, *365*
Botanical Island 360, 361–2, **367**
Elephantine Island 360, 361, 364–7
High Dam 29, 42, 359, 370, **372–3**
museums
Elephantine Island 366
Nubian 363–4
open air sculpture 371
Nilometer 364–5
Nobles tombs 360, **367–9**
Old Dam 28, 370, **371–2**
Philae 360, 370–1, **375–80**
St Simeon's monastery 360, **369–70**
Sharia el Souk 360
where to stay 380–2
Athanasius 490, 510
ATMs 57–8, 160
Avaris 480
Ay 317, **318**
Amarna tomb 245, **246–7**
Western Valley tomb 318–19
Ayyubids 25–6, 37
al-Aziz, Abu Mansur 25, 37

Babylon 25
Badawi, Said Ahmed el 482–3
Badr 417
Baghdad 25, 26
Bahariya Oases 405, 413, 414, **417**, 418
Bahnasa 234–5
Bahri Mamelukes 26, 37, 83–4
Baket, tomb 237
baksheesh 67, 101
banks 72, 405
al Baqawat 415
Baramous monastery 420, **427–9**

Barquq 26, 37
  mausoleum 140–1
Bawit 247
Bawiti 417, 418
Baybars (1260–77) 26, 37
Baybars (1422–38) 26, 37
  mausoleum 141–3
Beni Hasan 235–8
Beni Suef 233–4
Bent Pyramid 180–1, **217**
Berenice 455
Biban el Muluk 306
bicycles 164
Bigah island 380
Bin Laden, Osama 39
Bir Sitta 417
Birket Siwa 409
Botanical Island 360, 361–2, **367**
British occupation 28, 38, 492
Bubastis 479–80
bull cults 213
Burg el Arab 433–4
Burgi Mamelukes 26, 37, 83–4
Burning Bush 466, 467
buses and coaches 58–9, 60, 81
Buto 483
Byblos 21
Byzantines 23–4, 35–6

Cairo 25, 37, **77–174**, *78*
  Al-Azhar Park 112–13
  Bab al-Azab 110–11
  Bab al-Futuh 129, **139**
  Bab al-Nasr 129, **139**
  Bab Zuwayla 85, 114, **118**, **122–3**
  bazaars 87
    Khan el Khalili 83, 85, **128–9**, *130–1*
    Muski 128
  Cairo Tower 90, 91, 93
  churches
    Abu Sarga 94, 97–8
    al Adra 97
    Hanging Church 94, **96–7**
    Mari Girgis 97
    el Muallaqa 96–7
    St George 97
    St Sergius 97–8
    Sitt Barbara 98
  Citadel 83, 85, 87, 91, **110–12**
  City of the Dead 140–3
  Dokki 91, 92
  downtown 86–7
  eating out 129, 169–72
  Fustat **99–100**, 101
  Garden City 85, 91–2
  Gayer-Anderson House 106
  getting around 88–9
    metro 85, 88, *89*
  Gezira island 84, 87, 90
  Khan el Khalili 83, 85, **128–9**, *130–1*
  madrasas 113
    Qalaun 135
    al-Salih Ayyub 132–3
    Sultan al-Ghurri 124–6
    Sultan Hassan 107–10, **109**
  Manyal Palace 91, **92**
  mausoleums
    Barquq 140–1
    Baybars 141–3
    Imam al-Shaf'i 113–14
    al-Nasr Mohammed 135
    Qalaun 133–5
    Qaytbey 84, 143
    al-Salih Ayyub 132–3
    Shagarat al-Durr 107
    Sultan al-Ghurri 124–6
  Medieval Quarter 87, **101–40**, *102*
  mosques
    Amr 99
    al-Aqmar 137
    Aqsunqur 115
    al-Azhar 126–8
    Barquq 136
    Blue Mosque 115
    al-Hakim 138–9
    Ibn Tulun 82, 85, 87, **103–6**, *104*
    Maridani 115–16
    Mohammed Ali 91, **111**
    Muayyad 123
    al-Nasr Mohammed 112
    Qijmas al-Ishaqi 116–17
    Rifa'i 107
    Sakih Talai 114, **118**
    Sayyidna al-Hussein 128
    Silahdar 138
    Sultan Hassan 84, 85, 87, **107–10**, *109*
  museums 47–8
    Agriculture and Cotton 92–3
    Carriages 112
    Coptic 85, 91, **94–6**
    Egyptian Antiquities 85, **144–57**, *146*
    Egyptian Civilization 100, 145
    Historical 92
    Islamic 85, 87, **119–22**
    Military 112
    Modern Egyptian Art 93
    Oum Kalsoum 93–4
  Muski 128
  Nile 91–4
  Northern Walls 129–40
  Old Cairo 90, 91, **94–9**
  orientation 85–7, 90–1
  Papyrus Institute 92
  Southern Cemetery 113–14
  tourist information 158
  where to stay 86, 164–9
  Zamalek 90
calendars
  Coptic 53
  holidays 52
  Islamic 53–4
  Western 53
Callimachos 519–20
Cambyses, king 411
camel market (Daraw) 356
camel riding 195, 197, 199, 302
Carnarvon, Lord 316
cars 60
Carter, Howard 306, 315–16, 317
cartouches 33
cash machines 57–8, 160
Catherine, Saint 470
Cavafy, Constantine 498–9, 508–9
Cheops Great Pyramid 20, 181, 186, **187–91**, *188*
Chephren's Pyramid 20, 186, **192–4**
children 44, 67
Children of Israel 463
Christianity 24, 35, 423, 489–90
  see also Copts
Churchill, Winston 49
City of St Menas 429–31
Cleopatra 23, 35, 489, 494, 504
  Palace 495, **496**
Cleopatra's Needles 495–6
climate 52–3
clothes
  dress code 76
  packing 72–3
  shopping 162–3
  sizes 66
coaches and buses 58–9, 60, 81
colossi of Memnon 344–5
Constantine, Emperor 24, 36, 423
consulates 54–5, 525
Coptic Nile 247–54
Copts 24, 26–7, **45–6**, 96–9, 491–2
  calendar 53
  festivals 54
  museum (Cairo) 85, 91, **94–6**
  see also monasteries
Council of Chalcedon 24, 36, 459, 490
credit cards 57–8
crime 67–8
Crocodile Grotto 248
Crocodilopolis 226
Cromer, Lord 28
cruises 61–2, 63–4, 81, 347–8, 373
Crusades 25–6, 37, 134, 481–2
Curzon, Lord 426–7
customs formalities 56

Dahab 459, 471, **472**, 473–4
Dahshur 216–17
Dakhla Oasis 405, 413, 414, **415–16**, 418
Dakka, temple 387–8
Damanhur 483
Damietta **481–2**, 483
Daraw 356
debit cards 57–8
Decius, Emperor 24, 36
Deir Abu Maqar 420, **421–4**
Deir el Abyad 250, **251–3**
Deir el Adra 235
Deir el Ahmar 250, **253–4**
Deir Anba Abulu 247
Deir Anba Antunius 446–9

Deir Anba Bishoi 420, **424**
Deir Anba Bula 449–52
Deir el Bahri 319–27
Deir el Baramous 420, **427–9**
Deir al-Hagar 416
Deir el Medina 319–20, 334
Deir el Muharraq 247–8
Deir Sant Katerin 461–2, **464–8**
Deir el Suriani 420, **424–7**
Deirut 247
Dendera 259–64, **262**
Derr, temple 390
Dervishes 126, 174
dialling codes 66, 75
Dimeh el Siba 224
Diocletian, Emperor 24, 36, 490
Dionysias 227
disabled travellers 56–7
diving 74, 471
Dokki 91, 92
dress code 76
Druze 139
Dumyat 481–2
Durrell, Lawrence 497–8, 501–2, 519

Early Dynastic Period 20, 30
Earth's measurement 161
Eastern Desert 353
Edfu **350–3**, 356
Edict of Milan 24, 36
Edict of Tolerance 423
An Egyptian Childhood 234
El Arish 459, **460–1**
El Kab 349, **350**
El Lahun 229–30
El Tor 459
electricity 68
  plug adaptors 73
Elephantine Island 360, 361, **364–7**
embassies 54–5, 66, 68
emergencies 66, 159, 526
Era of Martyrs 24
Erasistratos 489
Eratosthenes 161, 489
Esna 348–50
Euclid 489
exchange rates 57
Exodus 22

Farafra Oasis 405, 413, 414, **416–17**, 418
Farouk, King 29, 38, 49, 522
Fathy, Hassan 303
Fatimids 25, 37, 83
Fatnas island 409
Fayed brothers 510–11
Fayyum 24, **219–30**
Feast of the Assumption 235
Feiran Oasis 462, 463–4
felucca journeys 61, 362, 373
festivals 54
  Bubastis 479–80
  Feast of the Assumption 235
  Luxor 294
  Siyaha 406–7
  Tanta 482–3
First Intermediate Period 20, 31
First World War 28
Flaubert in Egypt 349
food and drink 68–70
Forster, E.M. 499
Forty Days Road 414
Francis of Assisi, Saint 25–6, 482
French occupation 27–8, 38, 84
Fustat 25, 82

Gamassa **482**, 483
Gebel Katerin 461, **470**
Gebel Musa 461, 463, **468–9**
Gebel Serbal 463, 464
Gebel el Teir 235
Geese of Meidum 147
Gezeira Sporting Club 75, 87
Geziret el Faraun 472
al-Ghad Party 40
Ghali, Boutros 46
al-Ghuri 26, 37
  mausoleum 124–6
Giza 91, 176, 179, **184–96**, *187*
  Cheops Great Pyramid 186, **187–91**, *188*
  Chephren's Pyramid 186, **192–4**
  Grand Egyptian Museum 184
  Mycerinus' Pyramid 186, **194**
  Sphinx 186, 191–2
Grand Egyptian Museum 184
Grand Hotels 48–50
Great Pyramid 20, 181, 186, **187–91**, *188*
Great Sand Sea 409
Greeks 23
Gulf of Aqaba 471–4
Gurna **303–5**, 327

Hadrian, Emperor 36, 238
al-Hakim 25, 37, 97, **139**
  mosque 138–9
Hamas 39
al-Hassan 26, 37
  mosque 84, 85, 87, **107–10**, *109*
Hathor 260, 353, 457, 462–3
  Abu Simbel temple 396, **398–9**
  Dendera temple 261–4, *262*
  Philae temple 379–80
Hatshepsut 21, 238, 264, 288, **320–1**
  mortuary temple 321–7, *323*
Hawara 229
Hawaret el Maqta 229
al Hayz 417
health 70–1, 159
Heliopolis 79, 90
Helwan 90
Heracleopolis Magna 234
Herihor 302
Hermopolis Magna 239–40
Herodotus 229
Hibis 415
High Dam 29, 42, 359, 370, **372–3**
Hittites 22
homosexuality 406, 407
Horemheb 283, 292–3
  tomb 314
horse riding 195, 197, 199, 302
Horus 350–3, 351, 379
Horus Road 460
hotels 62
  Grand Hotels 48–50
Hurghada 264, **452–6**
Hussein, Taha 234
Huya, tomb 245
Hyksos 21, 477

Ibn Tulun 25, 82, 103
  mosque 82, 85, 87, **103–6**, *104*
Ikhshidids 24–5, 37
Imhotep 178
  museum 47, **202**
Imperial-Metric tables 66
insurance 71
Internet 54, 158
Ipy, tomb 334
Iron Age 22, 301–2
Isis
  cult 380
  temple (Philae) 375–80, *377*
Islam 44–5
  calendar 53–4
  festivals 54
  prayer time 101, **117**
  Shia Muslims 83, 127
  Sunni Muslims 127
  see also Arabs
Ismail 28
Ismailia 441–3
Israel 29, 38–9, 442
  Children of Israel 463
  Six Day War 29, 39, 441

Jebel Dakrur 406, **411**
Jebel el Mawta 410
Jesus of Nazareth 35

ka 178, 210–11
Kadesh, battle of 397
Kalabsha, temple 374–5
Kalsoum, Oum 93–4
Karanis 223–4
Karnak 22, 265, *266–7*, **279–94**, *284–5*
Khaemhat, tomb 330–1
Khaemweset, tomb 336
Kharga Oasis 405, 413, **414–15**, 418
Kheti, tomb 236–7
Khnum
  Aswan temple 366
  Esna temple 348
Khnumhotep, tomb 237
Kom Aushim 223
Kom Obo 353–6
Koran 45
Korosko 388
Kyrillos VI, Pope 428

Labyrinth 229
Lahun pyramid 230
Lake Manzala 482
Lake Mariut 24, **431–2**, 495
Lake Moeris 222–3
Lake Nasser 383, 386–92
  Abu Simbel 383, **392–400**, 395
  cruises 61–2, 386
Lake Qarun **221–2**, 224
Lampson, Sir Miles 224
Lane, Edward William 106
Late Dynastic Period 22–3, 32–4
Lateran obelisk 290–1
Layer Pyramid 199
Lesseps, Ferdinand de 439, 442
looting of tombs 300–1, 308
Loria, Alessandro 496–7
Luxor 22, 265, *266–7*, **268–79**, *273*
  Court of Ramses II 274–5
  museums
    Ancient Egyptian Art 278–9
    mummification 278
  orientation 268, 272
  temples
    Amenophis III 275–7
    Amun, Mut and Khonsu 274–5
  tourist information 294
  where to stay 295–8

Maadi 90
Maamoura 523
Macarius the Great, Saint 419
Maharraqa, temple 388–9
Mahdi 388
Mahfouz, Naguib 39, 40, 493
Mahmoudiya Canal 28, 492, 495
Mahu, tomb 245, **246**
Mamelukes 26–7, 28, 37, 83–4, 134
  massacre (1811) 110–11
  punishments 124
Manzala, lake 482
maps 71, 159–60
Maraqi 409
Mariut, lake 24, **431–2**, 495
Mark, Saint 35, 45
Marsa Alam 455
mastabas 177
  Akhti Hotep and Ptah Hotep 209–10
  Mereruka 209
  Ti 211–12
Mecca 45
  pilgrims 142
Medinet el Fayyum 225–6
Medinet Habu 337–42, *341*
Medinet Madi 227–8
Medinet Ramadan 441
Meidum 179, 179–80, 181, **217–18**
Mekhu, tomb 368
Memnon 344–5
Memphis 20, 79, 90, 176, **196–9**
Mena House 48–9, 195–6
Menas, Saint 429–31
Menes 20, 177
Menna, tomb 328
Mentuhotep II 20, 322
Mereruka mastaba 209
Merire, tomb 245
Merneptah 22
  tomb 309, 311
Mersa Matruh 405, **435–6**
Mesu Isis, tomb 410
Metric Imperial tables 66
Middle Kingdom 21, 31, 147, 152, 385
Milan, Edict of 24, 36
Minya **235**, 238
Misr 83
Mithras 504–5
al-Mitwalli, el Kutb 123
Moeris, lake 222–3
Mohammed Ali 28, 38, 84, 110–11, 124, 514
  statue 512
  tomb 111
Mohammed, Prophet 24, 36, 44, **45**, 127
Mohandiseen 91
monarchy 29, 38, 49, 522–3
monasteries
  Baramous 420, **427–9**
  Deir el Adra 235
  Deir Anba Abulu 247
  Deir el Muharraq 247–8
  evolution of monasticism 419–20, 446–8
  Red Monastery 250, **253–4**
  St Antony 446–9
  St Bishoi 420, **424**
  St Catherine 461–2, **464–8**
  St Jeremias 208
  St Macarius 420, **421–4**
  St Menas 429–31
  St Paul 449–52
  St Simeon 360, **369–70**
  Suriani (Syrians) 420, **424–7**
  Three Thousand Six Hundred Martyrs 348
  Wadi Natrun 419–29, *421*
  White Monastery 250, **251–3**
money 56, 57–8, 160, 526
Mongols 26
Mons Claudianus 455
Mons Porphyrites 452
Mont 280
Montazah 495, **522–3**
Moqattam Hills 91
Moses 22, 457, 462, 466, 468, **469**
Moulid el Nabi 54
Mubarak, Hosni 29, 39, 40
Muharraq 247–8
mummies 155–6, 504, 506
  museum (Luxor) 278
Muslim Brotherhood 40
Muslims see Arabs; Islam
Mut 415, 417
Mut Talata 416
Mycerinus' Pyramid 20, 186, **194**

Na'ama Bay 471
Nabataean depictions 463
Nag Hammadi 259
Nakht, tomb 328–9
Napoleon Bonaparte 27–8, 38, 84, 492, 523–4
Naqada 264
Narmouthis 227–8
al Nasr 26, 37
  mausoleum 135
Nasser, Gamal Abdel 29, 38–9, 43, 440–1
  birthplace 521
Nasser, Lake *see* Lake Nasser
national holidays 52
Naucratis 483
Neferefre Pyramid 199
Neferikare Pyramid 199
Nefertari 337
  colossi (Abu Simbel) 396
  statues 399
  tomb 336–7
Nefertiti 22, 47, 242, 245
Nekhbet, Temple 350
Neuserre Pyramid 199, 200
New Anada 389–91
New Gurna 304–5
New Kalabsha 371, **374–5**, 383, 386
New Kingdom 21–2, 32, 147–8, 152–3, 301–2, 385
New Sebua 386, **387–9**
New Valley scheme 39, 392, **415**
Nile 42, 231–54
  Abydos 256–9, *258*
  Amarna 22, **240–7**
  Antinopolis 238
  Assiut 248–50
  Beni Hasan 235–8
  Coptic Nile 247–54
  cruises 61, 63–4, 81, 347–8, 373
  Dendera 259–64, 262
  Edfu **350–3**, 356
  Esna 348–50
  Kom Obo 353–6
  Nag Hammadi 259
  Sohag 250–4
  source 374
  swimming 70
Nile, battle of 27, 38, 523
Nile Delta *476*, **477–84**
Niperpathot, tomb 410
Nour, Ayman 40
Nubia 21, **383–400**, *384*
Nubians 385–6
  villages 366–7, 373
Nuweiba 459, 471, **472**, 474

obelisks 182–3
  Cleopatra's Needles 495–6
  Karnak 287–8, 291
  Lateran 290–1
  Luxor 274
  Sesostris I 90, 225
Octavian (Augustus), Emperor 23, 35
Old Gurna 305

Old Kingdom 20, 31, 145, 147, 152, 177
Omar 127
Orabi, Ahmed 479, 492
Osiris 21, 208, 256–7, 260, **379**
temple (Abousir) 433
Oslo Accords 39
Othman 127
Ottomans 27, 37, 84
Oxyrhynchus 234

Pachom 250
packing 72–3
Palestine Mandate 28, 38
Panehsi, tomb 245
Pashas 27
passports 55–6, 526
Paul, Saint 449–52
Pennut, tomb 390–1
permits 76
Peshedu, tomb 334
Petosiris, tomb 240
Pharan 464
Pharaonic dynasties 20–3, 30–4
Pharos lighthouse 23, 495, **515–16**
Philae 360, 370–1, **375–80**
photography 73
Pi-Ramses 480, 481
police 67, 67–8, 158
population 40, 42, 43, 79
Port Fuad 444
Port Safaga 264, **455**
Port Said 443–4
postal services 73, 87, 158–9
Predynastic Period 20, 30
Psusennes I, tomb 481
Ptah-Hotep 209–11
Ptolemy I Soter 23, 34, 489
Ptolemy II Philadelphos 23, 34
Ptolemy III Euergetes 23, 34
Ptolemy IV Philopater 34
Ptolemy IX Soter II 35
Ptolemy V Epiphanes 34
Ptolemy VI Philometor 34
Ptolemy VII Euergetes II 35
Ptolemy VII Neos Philopator 35
Ptolemy X Alexander I 35
Ptolemy XI Alexander II 35
Ptolemy XII Neos Dionysos 35
public holidays 52
Punt 21
Pyramid Texts 208
pyramids 20–1, **175–218**, *176*
Abusir 199, 200
Bent Pyramid 180–1, **217**
Cheops Great Pyramid 181, 186, **187–91**, *188*
Chephren 186, **192–4**
Dahshur 216–17
Hawara 229
history 177–82
Lahun 230
Layer Pyramid 199
Meidum 179, 179–80, 181, **217–18**
Mycerinus 186, **194**
Neferefre 199
Neferikare 199
Neuserre 199, 200
Red Pyramid 180, **216–17**
Sahure 199
Sesostris II 230
Snofru 180–1, 216–17
Step Pyramid 20, 178, 182, 200, **202–7**, *203*, *204*
symbolism 182–3
Unas 20, **207–8**
Unfinished Pyramid 199
Zawiyat el Aryan 199

Qalaun 26, 37
mausoleum 133–5
Qantara 460
Qarat al-Farargi 417
Qarun, lake **221–2**, 224
al-Qasr 416
Qasr el Farafra 416
Qasr Ibrim 391–2
Qasr Qarun 227
Qattara Depression 403–4
Qaytbey 26, 37, **143**, 516
mausoleum 84, **143**
Qena **259–60**, 264
Qift 264
Qurban Bairam 54
Qus 264
Quseir 264, **455**

Raha 463, 464
railways 59–60, 80–1
Ramadan 45, 54, 72, 294
Ramleh 495, 496, 497
Ramose, tomb 329, 329–30
Ramses I 22, 256, 283
tomb 311
Ramses II 22, 282, 283, 305–6, 387
battle of Kadesh 397
colossi
Abu Simbel 396–7
Memphis 198–9
Hittite treaty 287
Pi-Ramses 480, 481
sons 319
statues 399
temples
Abydos 259
Luxor 270–5
Thebes 331–3
Ramses III 22
Karnak temple 283
mortuary temple (Thebes) 337–42, *341*
Sea People battles 339–40
tomb 311
Ramses IV 282
tomb 308–9
Ramses IX, tomb 309
Ramses VI, tomb 310, 311
Ras el Bahr **482**, 483
Ras Mohammed National Park 471–2
Ras el Sana el Hegira 54
Ras Umm Sid 471
Re 20, 200
re-entry visas 76
Re-Harakhte, temple 396–8
Red Monastery 250, **253–4**
Red Pyramid 180, 216–17
Red Sea *438*, 445–56
Hurghada 452–6
monasteries 446–52
Rekhmire, tomb 327–8
restaurants 68–70
Romans 23–4, 35–6
Rosetta 524–5
Rosetta Stone 28, **524**

Sabni, tomb 368
sacred bull cults 213
Sadat, Anwar 29, 39, 424
Sadd al-Ali 386
Sahure Pyramid 199
St Antony's monastery 446–9
St Bishoi monastery 420, **424**
St Catherine's monastery 461–2, 464–8
St Catherine's Mount 461, **470**
St Jeremias' monastery 208
St Macarius' monastery 420, **421–4**
St Menas' monastery 429–31
St Paul's monastery 449–52
St Simeon's monastery 360, **369–70**
Sais 483
Saite Dynasty 22–3
Saladin 25–6, 111
al Salih Ayyub 132–3
Saqqara *176*, 196, **199–216**, *201*
Satet, temple 366
Sawiris, Naguib 46
Sea Peoples 339–40, 477
Second Intermediate Period 21, 31–2
Second World War 28, 38, 434–5
Sehel 373
Selim 27
Seljuq Turks 37
Senmut 321
Sennedjem, tomb 334
Sennufer, tomb 328
Serabit el Khadim 462–3
Serapeum (Saqqara) 213–15
Serapis, temple 455
service taxis 60–1
Sesostris I 222
obelisks 90, 225
Sesostris II, pyramid 230
Seth 379
Seti I 22, 256–7, 282
mortuary temple (Abydos) 257–9, *258*
temple (Thebes) 305–6
tomb *310*, 312–13
Seti II, temple 283

Seven Waterwheels 226
al Shaf'i, Imam 113–14
Shagarat al-Durr 26, 133, **134**, 481
mausoleum 107
Shali 406, 409
Shark Observatory 472
Sharm el Sheikh 55, 459, **471–2**, 473
Sheikh Abada 238
Shenouda III, Pope 421, 424
Shenute 251
Shia Muslims 83, 127
shipping services 58
shopping 73–4
Aswan 380
bargaining 74
Cairo 160–4
conversion tables 66
Giza 195
Luxor 295
opening hours 72
Si-Amun, tomb 410
Silsileh 353
Simeon, Saint 369–70
Sinai 29, 38, 55, **457–74**, *458*
Sinai, Mount 463, 468–9
Sirenput I, tomb 368
Sirenput II, tomb 368
Siwa 403–13
Siwans 404–9
Six Day War 29, 39, 441
Siyaha festival 406–7
Snofru 180–1, 216–17
Sobel and Haroeris, temple 353–6, *355*
Sohag 250–4
solar boat pits 186, **191**
Speos Artemidos 238
Sphinx 186, **191–2**
alabaster 199
spring of Cleopatra 411–12
Step Pyramid 20, 178, 182, 200, **202–7**, *203*, *204*
students 75
Suez 444–5
Suez Canal 28, 29, 38, *438*, **439–41**
sun temples 199, **200**
Sunni Muslims 127
Suriani (Syrians) monastery 420, **424–7**

Taba **472**, 474
Taharka 22
Tanis 480–1
Tanta **482–3**, 483–4
tap water 70
Taposiris Magna 433
taxis 60, 81, 88
Tebtynis 228
telephones 75–6, 158, 526
dialling codes 66, 75
Tell el Amarna 241
Tell Basta 479
Tell el Faramah 460
Ten Commandments 463, 469
Thebes 265, *266–7*, 268–9, **299–346**
Theodosius I 36
Thoth, Temple 350
Three Thousand Six Hundred Martyrs monastery 348
Ti mastaba 211–12
Timur 26
tipping 67, 101
Titi, tomb 336
Tiy 280, 282
toilets 76
tombs
Amarna 245–7
Aswan 360, **367–9**
Beni Hasan 235–8
construction and decoration 309
looting 300–1, 308
Siwa 410
Tanis 481
Thebes
noble tombs 327–31
Valley of the Kings 306–19, *307*
Valley of the Queens 334–7
Topazos 455
Toshka 392
tour operators 63–4, 488
tourist information 54
Tourist Police 67, 158
trains 59–60, 80–1
Trajan, Emperor 36
Tropic of Cancer 161
Tulunids 24–5, 37
Tumanbay 27, 37, 125–6
Tuna el Gebel 240
Tunis 227
Turks 24–7, 37
turquoise mines 462
Tutankhamun 22, **314–18**
cause of death 316–17
curse 315–16
exhibition 156–7
tomb 314–17, *316*
widow 318
Tuthmosis I 21, 280, 288, 320
Tuthmosis II 288, 320
Tuthmosis III 21, 238, 280, 288, **289**, 320–1
tomb 313, *314*
Tuthmosis IV 280
Twain, Mark 185

Ubayyad Beach 436
Umayyads 24–5, 36, 127
Umm Ubaydah 411
Unas' Pyramid 20, **207–8**
Unfinished Pyramid 199
Userhat, tomb 330
Userkaf 200

Valley of the Kings 21, **306–19**, *307*
Amenophis II 313–14, *315*
Ay 318–19
Horemheb 314
Merneptah 309, 311
Ramses II 311
sons 319
Ramses III 311
Ramses IV 308–9
Ramses IX 309
Ramses VI *310*, 311
Seti I *310*, 312–13
Tutankhamun 314–18, *316*
Tuthmosis III 313, *314*
Valley of the Queens 334–7
visas 55–6, 76, 526

Wadi el Deir 463
Wadi Feiran 463–4
Wadi Magara 462
Wadi Moqattab 463
Wadi Natrun 419–29, *421*
Wadi el Sebua, temple 387
Wadi Sidri 462–3
Wahhabis 124
Western Desert 91, **401–36**, *402*
Whirling Dervishes 126, 174
White Monastery 250, **251–3**
women 76

Yacoubian Building 87
Yebu 365–6

Zafarana 446
Zagazig 479
Zaghloul, Saad 493
Zahrat el Medina 356
Zawiyat el Aryan 199
Zoser 20, 177
Step Pyramid 20, 178, 182, 200, **202–7**, *203*, *204*

4th edition published 2009

Cadogan Guides is an imprint of
New Holland Publishers (UK) Ltd
London • Cape Town • Sydney • Auckland

New Holland Publishers (UK) Ltd
Garfield House
86–88 Edgware Road
London W2 2EA

80 McKenzie Street
Cape Town 8001
South Africa

Unit 1, 66 Gibbes Street
Chatswood, NSW 2067
Australia

218 Lake Road
Northcote
Auckland
New Zealand

Cadogan@nhpub.co.uk
t 44 (0)20 7724 7773

Distributed in the United States by Interlink

Cover photographs: © Danita Delimont/Alamy (front), Frédéric Soltan/Sygma/Corbis (back)
Photo essay photographs: © Kicca Tommasi, except pp. 8, 9, 12, 13, 15 (top) © Michael Haag
Maps © Cadogan Guides, drawn by Maidenhead Cartographic Services Ltd
Cover design: Jason Hopper
Photo essay design: Sarah Gardner
Editor: Dominique Shead
Proofreading: Elspeth Anderson
Indexing: Isobel McLean

Printed in Italy by Legoprint
A catalogue record for this book is available from the British Library

ISBN: 978-1-86011-4229

Please help us to keep this guide up to date. Although we have done our best to ensure that the information in this guide is correct at the time of going to press, laws and regulations are constantly changing and standards and prices fluctuate. We would be delighted to receive any comments concerning existing entries or omissions.